PROBABILITY AND STATISTICS

in psychological research and theory

HOLDEN-DAY SERIES IN PSYCHOLOGY
Robert R. Bush, Editor

PROBABILITY AND STATISTICS

in psychological research and theory

Donald W. Stilson
University of Colorado School of Medicine

Holden-Day, Inc.
San Francisco, London, Amsterdam

Library of Congress Catalog Card Number: 66–11141

Printed in the United States of America

PREFACE

THIS book is intended for students of psychology who have had a brief introduction to statistical methods. It is most likely to prove useful to undergraduate students who have a fair amount of psychological sophistication and to beginning graduate students with serious research commitments.

The book is elementary in its approach. Specific statistical knowledge is not presumed, though familiarity with the general nature of statistical thinking will prove helpful. Similarly, no mathematical training beyond algebra is required, though a willingness to think in mathematical terms will facilitate matters for the reader. In short, the book is for students who expect to follow a career in psychological research, who have had little previous training in probability or statistics and little or no mathematics beyond college algebra, and who will acquire more statistical knowledge in the course of their training.

During the past few years, the level of statistical competence required of psychology students has increased steadily, and for many, acquisition of these statistical skills proves to be the highest hurdle on the tortuous path to the Ph.D. There are at least two reasons for this. First, many of these students lack the mathematical training that professional statisticians consider essential for a firm grasp of statistical theory. Second, graduate programs in psychological statistics often proceed rapidly to complex statistical procedures without systematic training in the fundamental concepts on which these procedures are based. Consequently, the student sometimes finds himself in a difficult position. He is expected to understand statistical techniques that often prove challenging to the Ph.D. candidate in mathematical statistics, but he must do so without either the mathematical sophistication or the basic concepts which the statistician considers essential. It is not surprising that otherwise competent students sometimes founder at this point.

PREFACE

One purpose of this book is to provide teaching material that will help students and instructors to cover thoroughly the fundamentals of probability and statistics. The author has tried to do this without either losing sight of the task of psychological research, or presuming knowledge of mathematics beyond college algebra. It is hoped that this will make the more advanced topics in psychological statistics easier for both students and instructors.

During recent years, there has been a rapid and steady increase in the use of probability and statistics in psychological theory, but there have been only occasional hints of this in our statistical text books. Some of this work is important psychology and should not be left beyond the student's ken simply because he lacks a few necessary and often simple ideas. This is the second purpose of the book: to present some of the ideas of elementary probability and statistics which will enable the student to understand the recent theoretical psychology that makes use of these ideas.

Many psychologists have sought the assistance of mathematical statisticians in dealing with problems of research design, data analysis, and theory construction. Such meeting are often entirely fruitless. In spite of the fact that both psychologist and statistician are reasonable, they often seem quite unable to communicate. Indeed, they may be using very different statistical language. The statistician is usually willing to listen to the psychologist's discussion of the psychological problems of the work, but he is sometimes horrified to find that the psychologist's statistical language is archaic and ambiguous. At the same time, the psychologist is likely to be mystified by the statistician's jargon and suspect that his mathematically sophisticated colleague is bent on impressing him with a display of esoteric erudition. The truth of the matter is that they lack a common language. Consequently, a third purpose of this book is to provide the student with some of the language of the statistician and help develop his skill in its use. The intent is to facilitate communication between psychologists and statisticians in the future.

Most chapters contain sections devoted to applications of probability and statistics to psychological *theory*. Although the author considers these sections pertinent and appropriate, some will view them as unnecessary intrusions. Consequently, these sections are noted by an asterisk and can be omitted without disrupting the sequence of the material. On the other hand, if these sections are included, it is the author's feeling that they require lecture support. This is not due to the difficulty of the material so much as to the strangeness of the approach itself. Initially, some students are simply unable to conceive of mathematical formulation as a serious approach to psychological problems. Thus, they sometimes reach an advanced level of training without realizing that, in some areas of their discipline, the mathematical approach has a tradition as old as clear statements of the psychological problems themselves (e.g., Fechner's psychophysics, Ebbinghaus' work on forgetting).

Though free use is made of mathematical notation and algebraic arguments, it has been the author's policy to avoid the substitution of algebraic proofs for intuitive clarification. The preferred procedure has been to include both, and when one or the other had to be omitted, the algebraic argument was discarded. In addition, many of the longer or less important algebraic arguments have been placed in chapter appendices. These also can be omitted without affecting the sequence of the text.

In addition to the sections devoted to applications of probability and statistics to psychological theory, a few special statistical topics appear in starred sections. Whether or not these are included will depend on the predilections of the instructor and the subsequent statistical training anticipated for the students. In any case, these sections can be omitted without disrupting the sequence of the material.

One such section is a brief description of the neo-Bayesian approach to inferential statistics. Although there is no attempt to deal with Bayesian methods systematically, some of the problems of the Bayesian statistician have a decidedly psychological flavor, and it seems unfair to allow the student of psychology to study probability and statistics without at least mentioning this close and perhaps important tie between disciplines.

Throughout the book, statements of important definitions and principles are italicized, and significant formulas are numbered. The intent of this procedure is to alert the student to key points that require his special attention.

Answers to the odd-numbered problems appear in Appendix X. When the solution of a problem depends on material that appears in one of the starred sections, then the problem itself is starred.

Many have contributed to the writing of this book. Jacqueline Miller and Lula Zobec are to be thanked for their patience, care, and skill in typing large portions of the manuscript. Marianne Stilson uncovered countless errors in format, which would otherwise have plagued the reader with confusion and frustration. Z. Joseph Ulehla was kind enough to make a number of helpful suggestions regarding the chapter on hypothesis testing, and Wilson P. Tanner, Jr., read the section on signal detection theory. Leon H. Rappoport, Benjamin J. Winer, M. Frank Norman, Daniel E. Bailey, Raymond W. Frankmann, Frederick J. Todd, and Robert J. Schneider have all read the manuscript at some point in its development. Robert R. Bush, N. John Castellan, Jr., and John Van Laer each labored over two or more versions. The skill and care of these readers led to the elimination of many errors, and their thoughtful and helpful suggestions have usually been incorporated. The author owes special thanks to all of them.

I am indebted to the Literary Executor of the late Sir Ronald A. Fisher, F.R.S., Cambridge, to Dr. Frank Yates, F.R.S., Rothamsted, and to Mssrs Oliver & Boyd Ltd, Edinburgh, for permission to reprint Table III from their book, *Statistical Tables for Biological, Agricultural and Medical Research*.

D.W.S.

TABLE OF CONTENTS

I

INTRODUCTION

THERE seem to be two distinguishable ways in which men think. In the first, a person reasons from given information (usually facts) to conclusions that were not explicit at the outset. Thus, if "only freshmen wear green caps" and "my roommate wears a green cap" are known to be correct, then you can safely conclude that "my roommate is a freshman." The method used to arrive at such a conclusion is called deductive reasoning, and the essential rules for correct deductive conclusions have been known since the ancient Greeks.

The second way of thinking, inductive reasoning, has developed more slowly. Man has been less facile in learning rules that permit him to draw correct inferences from what he sees and hears than he has been in learning to draw conclusions from information that is given to him in linguistic or symbolic form. If five of the ten graduate students you know are married, then assuming there are more than ten graduate students at your university, can you conclude that exactly half of the entire group are married? Obviously not. But on the other hand, must you resign yourself to total ignorance of the marital status of graduate students at your university? In short, just what can you conclude beyond the obvious fact that some graduate students are married and some are not? Perhaps more important, what confidence can you place in your conclusion?

The situation is one of partial ignorance, since you don't know the marital status of *all* graduate students. The problem is how to make an enlightened guess when information is incomplete and, furthermore, to say something about how much confidence you have in your guess. The prescription of systematic and reasonable procedures for doing this forms the core of modern statistics.

Sometimes we act as if "the facts speak for themselves," but a little reflection leads one to reject such a statement. Casual observations of fact rarely point to unequivocal conclusions. For example, of three persons observing a stranger hit "21" three times in succession at a black jack table, the floor manager infers collusion with the dealer, a gambler reduced to the role of onlooker by massive losses marvels at the winner's system, and an aloof mathematician calculates the probability of this occurrence and concludes that it is "unlikely." There is no disagreement on the facts; they are evident to all. But conclusions differ markedly.

Usually, if correct inferences are to be drawn from empirical observations, the procedures for making the observations must be carefully planned. How this is to be done is a question of research planning or experimental design.

The following two sections elaborate on the role of drawing inferences from incomplete information and of experimental design in the scientific enterprise.

I.1
STATISTICS AND DECISION-MAKING WITH INCOMPLETE INFORMATION

How one makes inductive inferences is of paramount importance to all empirical sciences. The scientist makes observations of a particular portion of the world and from these he draws conclusions about the entire domain from which the observations were taken. It is almost never of scientific interest to draw conclusions pertaining only to the observations in hand. The scientist wishes to generalize his results. Put differently, the scientist wants to predict the outcome of observations that he has never made. Modern statistics is a system that provides a rational basis for making such inductive generalizations and for evaluating the confidence that the scientist can place in them. Of course, drawing inferences in this way amounts to selecting from a set of alternatives the one hypothesis that is most compatible with the available information. In other words, statistics provides methods for making decisions on the basis of incomplete information.

Phrased in this way, it becomes clear that the scientist is not the only person who will find statistical methods useful. In business and industry, in the military, and, in fact, in any enterprise in which decisions must be based on only part of the pertinent information, statistical methods often play an important role.

I.2
EXPERIMENTAL DESIGN

The research scientist begins with a conception of the area he is investigating, a theory. This theory may be a detailed description of the pertinent variables and a rigorous formulation of the relationships among them, or it may be a relatively crude and unformalized hunch about what-goes-with-what. A theory may be an extremely abstract logical system that penetrates far beyond observable phenomena, or it may be restricted to a description of properties that are relatively accessible to direct observation. In any case, the scientific theory must yield deductions or expectations that are amenable to empirical investigation. However, the variables involved in such deductions are given in theoretical terms, and in order to permit empirical investigation, they must be given operational meaning. These operationalized variables are then "put together" in an experimental design, which provides a guide to gathering data that either supports the theoretical deduction or detracts from its validity. Thus, the experimental design is a plan that translates a theoretical deduction or hypothesis into a data-gathering procedure. The data themselves are reflections of the real world. They are expected to have certain properties if the theoretical deduction is correct and other properties if it is false. In short, an experimental design is an explicit procedure for asking nature a question. The resulting data constitute nature's reply.

I.3
STATISTICS AS DATA REDUCTION AND DESCRIPTION

Of course these two aspects of statistics do not fit the layman's conception at all. To many people, a statistician is a glorified number juggler, a person whose head is utterly cluttered with numerical information. Although this conception is incomplete, it stems from the role that statistical methods do play in the condensation, summarization, and description of data. In nearly every area of human endeavor within our complex civilization, large collections of information—frequently in numerical form—play an important role. However, in its raw form, such information is mentally indigestible for human beings. To render it comprehensible, there must be some way of abstracting the characteristics that are relevant to the uses to which the information is to be put. Statistics also concerns itself with the development of such descriptive procedures and with the determination of their properties.

Adequate research planning takes into account both the form of the descriptive summary of the data and the way in which inferences are to be drawn, as well as the relevance of the data-gathering procedure to the questions the data are intended to answer. Planning, descriptive summary, and drawing inferences are not independent steps in the research; rather, they are inextricably bound aspects of a single process. This is straightforward enough. It says that one must know what is to be done with the data in order to know how to gather it.

I.4

ERROR

The induction problem arises when we wish to draw general conclusions on the basis of partial information. But incompleteness is not the only difficulty that may be dealt with by using statistical methods. The scientist's data are always contaminated to some extent by "error." That is, observations are influenced by events that are unknown, not understood, or at least not of primary interest to the investigator. The researcher seeks to eliminate or reduce such influences. In fact, a substantial part of his effort is devoted to a relentless campaign against error.

Although error may arise from many sources, there are two general classes to be considered: systematic error and variable error. Systematic error affects observations so that they are consistently too high or too low. Such error is likely to lead the investigator to wrong conclusions, to draw him into the trap of mistaking unknown influences for the effects he set out to learn about.

The effects of variable error are different. Though the observations may be neither too high nor too low "on the average," they fluctuate irregularly when substantial variable error is operating. When the fluctuations due to variable error are large, it may be difficult or impossible to see through the haze of error to the systematic influences that affect the data. The scientist's picture of the domain he is investigating becomes fuzzy and unclear when variable error is operating.

When systematic error operates, the scientist is likely to make a wrong conclusion. When variable error holds sway, his vision is blurred and he may be unable to draw any conclusion at all.

Care must be taken to eliminate, or at least to take account of, influences that consistently elevate or depress observations. For example, it has been found that tachistoscopic thresholds are generally higher for "nasty," four-letter words than for "clean," four-letter words. This has been attributed to the capacity of the human to protect himself from threatening stimuli or to exercise perceptual defense. However, words that appear infrequently in print are known to have higher thresholds than similar but more frequent words. Since nasty, four-letter words rarely appear in print, perhaps the elevated thresholds for such words can be attributed to uncommonness rather than to their threatening aspect. And how to interpret the higher threshold will, of course, depend on which of these alternatives is correct.

In addition to systematic error, observations may be affected by the instability of the measuring process itself or by the instability of the conditions under which observations are made. If you measure the length of a city block using a yardstick, you are unlikely to get the same length on successive attempts. If you measure with a 100-foot steel tape, your measurements will vary less from one attempt to another, but it remains unlikely that exactly the same length will be obtained every time. If an expert judge rates "introversion," he is unlikely to assign to every subject he assesses the same rating as that given by a second judge. Here, the judges are serving as the measuring instrument, and the rating obtained depends in part on which instrument (i.e., which judge) is used to obtain it. Furthermore, a single judge's ratings of one subject usually will vary from time to time (given sufficient time for forgetting to occur between ratings). This variance may be due in part to changes in the subject, but changes in the judge undoubtedly affect the ratings, too.

A second way variable errors may creep into the data is through instability of the conditions under which observations are made. For example, if auditory threshold is the dependent variable, and if the room in which thresholds are determined is quiet at one moment and bombarded with small, irrelevant noises at the next, thresholds will vary with the level of background noise. Similarly, if subjects are greeted by one of two experimenters, the first of whom is a bearish oaf while the other is a warm, gentle soul, the subjects may be angry or anxious in the first case but complacent and relaxed in the second. Such effects are almost certain to produce unwanted variations in the data that will be relegated to the "error" category.

This may seem straightforward so far, but the notion of "error" is subtle and evasive. What is to be called error depends on what one wishes to achieve. Differences between individuals are only error for the psychophysicist attempting to determine the absolute threshold of loudness in the young, human adult. Nothing would please him more than to discover that all his subjects exhibit exactly the same absolute threshold. Instead, he finds that some subjects must be more certain than others that they hear a tone before they affirm its presence, so that the thresholds he measures reflect more than just auditory sensitivity: they are contaminated by the degree of caution exercised by the subject. However, the clinical psychologist investigating "cautiousness" as a personality characteristic may focus his attention on individual differences in the propensity to commit oneself in the presence of ambiguous stimuli. What is unwanted error for the psychophysicist is the meat of the clinician's research.

In summing up, there are three things that can be said of the scientist's data: First, they are always incomplete. The researcher does not include all of the observations to which he hopes to apply his conclusions. Second, variables he knows nothing about or chooses to ignore may influence the data systematically. Finally, the observations will vary due to the instability of the process of measurement or of the conditions of observation.

It is the business of statistics to help the researcher cope with all three of these difficulties.

I.5
ERROR REDUCTION

Clearly, the researcher wants to obtain unequivocal answers to his research hypotheses. One step toward accomplishing this is to reduce error to a minimum. This can generally be done in three ways: by careful experimental design; by designing measurement procedures that are relatively free of measurement error; and, finally, by establishing stable conditions of observation.

I.5.1. By experimental design

In the case of determining tachistoscopic thresholds for neutral and emotionally loaded words, it might be possible to find words in both classes that have equal frequencies of usage. This would undoubtedly be difficult, but it is one method of controlling frequency of usage and thereby eliminating a source of systematic error. Or perhaps certain words could be given an artificial negative connotation by making them the conditional stimuli for painful shocks. Then, the tachistoscopic thresholds for "shock" words would be compared with those for neutral words.

Each of these two approaches is an attempt to eliminate the systematic error due to the infrequency with which "nasty" words appear in print. However, one suspects that the second design asks a different question from the first—a pitfall that must be avoided. In one's zeal for planning convincing research, it is quite possible to design an investigation which will provide an adequate answer to the *wrong question.* In order to be sure that the data-gathering process is relevant to the investigator's hypotheses, careful logical analysis must link tightly the theoretical deductions and the procedure for making observations.

To reduce the variability resulting from individual differences, thresholds for both neutral and threatening words might be obtained from the same subjects. However, practice might lower, or fatigue might elevate, the thresholds of words presented late in an experimental session, regardless of the characteristics of the words themselves. Therefore, the order of presentation of the words might be "counterbalanced." One way to do this is to arrange the words so that each word occupies each ordinal position for the same number of subjects. This sort of attempt to neutralize the effects of unwanted variables (i.e., individual differences, practice, and fatigue in this example) is an important part of experimental design, too.

I.5.2. By the design of measuring instruments

Errors of measurements can be reduced by a wise choice of measuring instrument or by careful design and evaluation of the measurement procedure.

Careful planning of the rating procedure would undoubtedly help reduce measurement errors in the introversion ratings mentioned above. Delineation of what is meant by the term "introversion" and specification of those cues considered relevant would be the first step. Thorough training of the judges in the use of these cues would then help ensure similar ratings by different judges on one occasion and consistent ratings by one judge on different occasions. This kind of procedure is exemplified by the manuals for standard intelligence tests and by the training procedures for the use of these instruments.

I.5.3. By stabilizing the conditions of observation

A stable, clearly specified procedure for obtaining data is another aspect of research planning that will reduce errors. Many research psychologists use sound-insulated rooms, tape-recorded instructions, automatically controlled stimulus presentation, and automatic response-recording devices in an attempt to maintain greater consistency in the data-gathering procedure.

I.6
MANAGEMENT OF RESIDUAL ERROR

Even with careful and ingenious experimental design, well-developed measuring instruments, and stable data-gathering procedures, data are never error-free. What is needed, then, is some procedure for separating the systematic, relevant characteristics of the data from the shrouds of whatever error remains. Solomon Diamond has drawn a delightful literary parallel between the problem of separating systematic effects from error by statistical analysis and the detection of a meaningful sound heard against a background of noise. Diamond's book, *Information and Error*,[1] introduces this as the central problem of statistical methods. According to Diamond, the researcher attempts to separate his data into two parts: that which is due to the influences he intends to investigate, and that which is due to influences irrelevant to the purposes of his investigation (error). Having made such a separation, the researcher can appraise the relative magnitude of the two kinds of influences. Thus, statistical analysis can be conceived of as a filtering process that separates the effects of error from those the researcher intends to appraise.

[1] New York, Basic Books, 1960, Chap. 1.

Before leaving this topic, perhaps a word of caution is in order. In his zeal for eliminating or neutralizing error, the scientist must not blind himself to the possibility that error contains something good. What is thought of as meaningless error in today's data may be the clue to an important discovery tomorrow. One will not be too far from the truth if he equates error and ignorance and tries to exercise a little serendipity in scrutinizing the aspects of his data that he does not understand.

I.7
APPRAISING RESEARCH

Research is done in order to obtain information. If the data provide the information sought, then it is good research. Research that does not provide *important* information can be criticized on grounds of triviality, but it may be properly done research, nonetheless. The distinction between the importance and the quality of research can be characterized by two possible responses to research conclusions. The response, "So what?" expresses doubt about the importance of the work. On the other hand, the response, "I don't believe it," indicates doubt about the adequacy of the execution of the research. It is the latter problem that concerns us here.

Sometimes, research is exploratory. Particular questions are not asked; rather, an area is surveyed empirically in an effort to get an idea what is going on. Such research is considered good if it provides the information with efficiency and small error. Obviously, data that are so contaminated with variable error that it is impossible to extract anything systematic are of little use in any context. If one begins with garbage, no amount of elaboration will transmute it into the gold of scientific discovery.

If a particular question is to be answered by the data, then the research is good if it provides an unequivocal answer to that question. Again, error may make it impossible to answer the question at all, or a wrong answer may be inferred from the systematic effect of variables that have been overlooked or incorrectly deemed unimportant.

I.8
PROBABILITY AND STATISTICS IN THEORETICAL PSYCHOLOGY

The psychological investigator needs the methods of statistics in order to choose appropriate descriptions of his data, to design data-gathering procedures that are relevant to his research hypotheses and relatively free of error, and to deal effectively with the induction problem in drawing conclusions from his observations. Since statistics depends heavily on probability theory, intelligent application of statistical methods requires an understanding of the fundamentals of probability. But these certainly are not the only uses of probability and statistics in psychology, and they may not even be the most important ones. One of the purposes of this book is to sketch some of the ways in which probability and statistics have entered into the formulation of *psychological theory*. Probabilistic and statistical thinking has entered the theoretical conceptualization of virtually every area of psychology. Learning, thinking, problem-solving, intrapsychic conflict, small-group interaction, attitude change, pattern recognition and discrimination, behavior pathology, and many other areas have been dealt with by theoretical psychologists using probability and statistics as prime theoretical tools.

Sometimes one hears that formulations of psychological theory in probabilistic and statistical terms are no more than exercises whose sole function is to amuse their inventors. However, perusal of the major journals of theoretical psychology should promptly dispel any such notions. In almost every area of psychology, there is at least one serious contender for theoretical pre-eminence who depends heavily on probability and statistics in his thinking. Consequently, this book will use material from psychological theory to illustrate some of the ideas of probability and statistics.

There are other reasons why probability and statistics are of interest to psychologists, but these require greater elaboration. The last sections of the next chapter are devoted to them.

SUGGESTED READING

1. Wallis, W. A., and H. V. Roberts, *Statistics: A New Approach*. New York, The Free Press of Glencoe, Inc., 1957, Chaps. 1, 2, and 3.
Chapter 1 discusses statistics from the point of view of decision-making in the face of uncertainty. The second chapter provides two detailed illustrations of "good" research. One example is a study of the change in incidence of serious mental illness over a 150-year period. The third chapter discusses misuses of statistics. It provides a multitude of interesting and often amusing examples.
2. Diamond, S., *Information and Error*. New York, Basic Books, 1960, Chap. 1.
A delightful literary interpretation of statistical analysis as the separation of information from error.
3. Huff, D., *How to Lie with Statistics*. New York, Norton, 1954.
This clever little book deals primarily with descriptive statistics and the ways in which statistical reporting can distort and mislead the unsophisticated. Replete with examples.

II

PROBABILITY, STATISTICS, AND PSYCHOLOGY
Some common roots and converging interests

HISTORICALLY, points of contact between probability, statistics, and psychology are numerous. Some of these points are described briefly in this chapter; towards the end of the chapter, some problems of mutual interest to contemporary psychologists and statisticians are introduced.

II.1
EARLY CONNECTIONS WITH PROBABILITY THEORY

Early in the eighteenth century, Jacob Bernoulli summarized the scattered work on probability and added important results of his own in *Ars Conjectandi* ("The Art of Conjecture"). One of the interesting things in his volume was the suggestion that probability would provide the key to rationalizing social science and the law. Bernoulli thought he foresaw in the social sciences far-reaching and important developments in which probability would become the essential instrument for placing these sciences on a systematic, rational basis. Some of the current theoretical developments in economics, sociology, and psychology suggest that Bernoulli's forecast was correct. Though Bernoulli himself did not attempt such applications, an anonymous essay that appeared some 10 years before *Ars Conjectandi* dealt with the credibility of legal testimony using probabilities. This is a remarkable step when one recalls that probabilities were then thought to have almost no application outside the gambling casino.

During the remainder of the eighteenth century, the number of applications of probability outside the casino increased rapidly. By the early nineteenth century, Laplace was able to include in his *Théorie Analytique des Probabilités* a great variety of scientific and practical applications as well as a thorough-going treatment of games of chance. His initial interest in probability grew from his concern for the occurrence of errors in astronomical observations, and he and Karl F. Gauss independently developed the "theory of errors." The Gaussian curve (or normal probability curve) played a central role in the development of the theory.

It is important to note that this was the first instance in which error was recognized as an integral part of scientific observation and an attempt made to deal with it systematically. More pertinent, the errors dealt with were human errors of observation, so that Laplace and Gauss were dealing with problems of psychological significance in these early probabilistic formulations. It is not surprising that their ideas were extended by later investigators in an attempt to encompass a greater diversity of psychological phenomena.

Half a century later, Fechner utilized the results of Gauss and Laplace[1] when he devised the conceptual and methodological bases of modern psychophysics. Here, at the very beginning of scientific psychology, probabilistic thinking made lasting impressions. Furthermore, the roots of contemporary mental test theory also can be traced directly to the early attempts to deal with observation errors. Measurement error in mental testing is still dealt with much as Gauss and Laplace handled astronomical observation errors.

II.2
SOCIAL SCIENCE AND THE BEGINNINGS OF ACTUARIAL STATISTICS

A prosperous English haberdasher, John Graunt, was the first to note the value of tabulating percentages when trying to make sense of large volumes of data. One of the observations he gleaned from this was that there are more births of males than of females, and he used this to argue that due to the greater hazards of the masculine role (e.g., fighting wars), the natural state of man is monogamy. But a contemporary, William Petty, inferred from Graunt's actuarial methods that the social sciences could and must become quantitative, and he called these early methods of descriptive statistics "political arithmetic."

[1] Fechner also borrowed heavily from Daniel Bernoulli, nephew of Jacob Bernoulli, though it was not his work in probability that interested Fechner as much as his work on the psychological value of money.

By the middle of the eighteenth century, Süssmilch had refined and extended the methods of Graunt and Petty substantially. He asserted that social phenomena, no less than physical events, have causes, and that the regularities found in statistical results reveal the rules of the existing social order. Furthermore, he concluded that stable and meaningful results can be obtained only by examining great numbers. "If I have a hundred cases in support of my conclusion, then can nothing to the contrary be drawn from one case." This seems trivial to us today, but one must remember that anecdote and armchair philosophizing were the only methods of demonstration in the social science of the early 1800's.

Through the middle decades of the nineteenth century, one of the most important contributors to applied statistics was the Belgian mathematician-scientist, Adolphe Quetelet. He made the first serious attempt to combine probability and actuarial methods in the study of man. In the 1830's, he conducted extensive investigations of the distribution of human traits, and it is not particularly surprising to us now to learn that he found many of them to follow the normal curve.[2] Furthermore, he did not miss the analogy between the normal curve of errors of observation and its application to human characteristics. He concluded that the men of a nation grouped around their average "as if they were the results of measurements made on *one and the same person*, but with instruments clumsy enough to justify the size of the variations." Quetelet asserted that nature strives to produce "the average man," but due to the interference of a multitude of tiny accidents, is rarely successful in all respects. Thus, though all men are the same by design, the distribution of a particular characteristic follows the normal curve.

Quetelet also must be credited with one of the first serious efforts to establish a quantitative sociology or what he termed "social physics." Although his contemporary, Auguste Comte, also advocated a quantitative sociology, Quetelet made concrete steps toward its realization. In his *Recherches sur le Penchant au Crime*, he asserted that "we shall determine effects for society as we determine effects by causes in the physical sciences," whereupon he proceeded to cite statistical evidence relating the incidence of crime to age, sex, education, climate, season, and so on. Quetelet made it clear that the method of "social physics" was statistical. Furthermore, the approach to such problems employed by contemporary social scientists is essentially that of Quetelet.

[2] However, Quetelet discovered distributions that were not at all normal (e.g., body weight). These results apparently did not please him, and he made little effort to integrate them in his account of human trait distribution.

II.3

DARWIN'S THEORY OF EVOLUTION AND THE BIOMETRIC MOVEMENT

Quetelet viewed the differences among men as the result of accidental influences intruding on nature's handiwork. These accidental variations were unfortunate from Quetelet's view, since he considered "the average man" to be the most beautiful of the human species. Charles Darwin also observed the variation among the members of a single species, but his interpretation differed vastly from Quetelet's. He built upon it a theory which may emerge as the most significant intellectual accomplishment of the nineteenth century. In retrospect, the fact of individual differences may appear trivial, but Darwin's genius saw its far-reaching implications.

II.3.1. Biological variability and its implications for the evolution of species

Darwin observed that differences among the members of a species left some better equipped than others to survive in their particular environment. Some of these favorable characteristics are inheritable, so that some of the offspring of the well-equipped organism are similarly well-suited to cope effectively and produce progeny. On the other hand, some individuals reflect characteristics that decrease the likelihood of survival and reproduction, and these die and their kind disappear. Over many generations, this process leads to modification of the species, i.e., to the evolution of new species.

Notice that an essential feature of the argument lies in the existence of differences among the members of a species, and that these differences, through the process of natural selection ("survival of the fittest"), lead to new species.

A fundamental tenet of American functional psychology was a straightforward translation of Darwinian principles into the language of behavior. The unsophisticated animal is propelled haphazardly through its environment by its needs. Those behaviors which occur and which contribute to its well-being are repeated, whereas others which are detrimental disappear. Thus, behavioral selection is parallel to Darwin's natural selection. Just as Darwin capitalized on intraspecies variability, the functionalists introduced behavioral variability as a key concept in their psychology of adaptation. What had been viewed as annoying heterogeneity or "error" by earlier biologists and psychologists became the key concepts of the theory of biological evolution and functional psychology.

II.3.2. Biometrika and its founders: Weldon, Pearson, and Galton

In 1901, in the first issue of *Biometrika,* Galton tells us that this journal is to be devoted to "the application to biology of the modern methods of statistics." An editorial in the same issue by Karl Pearson tells why statistics is important in biology. He begins by noting the importance of intraspecies variability, and continues with the assertion that the fundamental process of biological evolution is in essence statistical.

> Evolution must depend upon substantial changes in considerable numbers and its theory therefore belongs to that class of phenomena which statisticians have grown accustomed to refer to as *mass phenomena.* A single individual may have a variation which fits it to survive, but unless that variation appears in many individuals, or unless that individual increases and multiplies without loss of the useful variation up to comparatively great numbers—shortly, until the fit type of life becomes a mass-phenomenon, it cannot be an effective factor in evolution. The moment this point is grasped, . . . we recognize that the problem of evolution is a problem of statistics, in the vital statistics of populations.

Pearson went on to try to show that, in spite of a confessed lack of skill in mathematics, Darwin himself recognized the importance of quantitative and statistical methods in furthering his conception of evolution.

II.3.3. Galton and correlation

Galton observed that in addition to offspring being similar to their parents with respect to inherited characteristics, there was a tendency for offspring to be less extreme than their parents. This phenomenon, which Galton called "reversion," has become known as "regression," and its investigation led to a precise mathematical interpretation of the concept of correlation.

Galton observed, for example, the "reversion" of sons' heights relative to their fathers'. He noted that although tall fathers tend to have tall sons, the sons are not generally as extreme in height as the fathers. He took his notions about this to the Cambridge mathematician, J. D. H. Dickson, and asked that he investigate mathematically the properties of such a relationship (which Galton had formulated in geometric terms). The result of these efforts was a greatly sharpened mathematical method of describing "co-relation."

Galton's first discussion of "reversion" occurred in 1877, but the idea of "co-relation" itself caught his fancy and in 1888 he published "Co-relations and Their Measurement." In 1892, F. Y. Edgeworth introduced the term "coefficient of correlation" and extended the idea of correlation to three and more variables.

Why did the correlation coefficient become important to the biologists?

Initially, because of the widespread belief that "co-relation" among parts was important in biological adaptation. The French naturalist Cuvier had emphasized that the relationship among parts is a critical determiner of an organism's capacity to adapt. Thus, the successful carnivore must have not only sharp teeth but also locomotor speed permitting rapid attack. Cuvier's idea took firm root, and as early as 1888 Galton was aware of the implications of his measure of correlation for describing the relationship among organismic parts. Thus, the first recognized need for the idea of correlation grew from the problems of the biologists.

Out of a concern for biological adaptation and evolution grew an enormous market for statistical application, and during the years following the turn of the twentieth century, the biological statisticians applied themselves diligently in an attempt to keep up with the demand for new and more powerful methods for dealing with biological data and for conceptualizing the problems of biological theory.

II.3.4. Biological statistics and psychology

Some of the men at the heart of the biometric movement are also regarded as important figures in psychology. Galton is especially noteworthy in this respect. He has been credited with the first psychological tests, and he was one of the most important contributors to psychological knowledge during the late nineteenth century. With the growth of mental testing and concern for individual differences, statistical methods spread rapidly among psychologists.

The theory of biological evolution touched upon the psychology of individual differences in at least two ways. First, evolutionary theory had direct implications for trait variability within the human species, and second, the biometrician's methods were found useful for handling the data of individual differences. During the early 1900's, the expert in the psychology of individual differences was usually a more sophisticated statistician than his colleagues in other areas of psychology.

Charles E. Spearman observed that most tests of presumably distinct abilities were correlated with one another, and he concluded that there must be some general intellectual ability at the basis of all special abilities. He labeled this general intellectual factor *g*, and in 1904 he described a statistical method for measuring the extent to which each of several tests depends upon *g*. This was the beginning of factor analysis, a statistical method that has been closely associated with psychology through the work of Spearman, Sir Cyril Burt, and Geoffry H. Thomson in England and that of Louis L. Thurstone in the United States. Though factor analysis had its beginnings in psychology, it has since found its way into genetics, meteorology, and other scientific disciplines as well as remaining a method frequently called upon by psychological investigators.

II.3.5. Fisher

Today, the psychologist who makes regular use of statistical methods for data analysis is likely to be applying techniques that were put in their present form by either Karl Pearson or Sir Ronald A. Fisher. Most of the methods described in current elementary texts on psychological statistics were shaped by the hand of one of these men.

Fisher, though trained as a mathematician, became interested in Mendelian genetics while still a student at Cambridge. This interest led to the conviction that the fine structure of the evolutionary process could be described by application of the Mendelian principles of inheritance. For 20 years he published nothing on his efforts in this direction; finally, a book, *The Genetical Theory of Natural Selection*, was published in 1930. Thus, Fisher had serious biological interests as well as producing some of the most important statistical results of this century.

FISHER'S CLARIFICATION OF THE INDUCTION PROBLEM. Fisher's major statistical contributions can be divided into two parts. First, there was his work developing a systematic theoretical basis for the statistics of induction. This work is best summarized in a paper entitled "On the Mathematical Foundations of the Theory of Statistics" which appeared in the *Transactions of the Royal Society* in 1922 and was extended in "Theory of Statistical Estimation" (*Proceedings of the Cambridge Philosophical Society*) in 1925. In these papers, Fisher defined properties of statistical estimates which made it possible to determine the sense in which an estimate can be considered "good." For example, if one has a set of data (e.g., the marital status of ten randomly selected graduate students) from which it is desired to estimate some characteristic of a larger group from which the observations were drawn (e.g., the proportion of married graduate students in a large department), what makes the estimate a "good" one? The question may sound trivial; it is obvious that one wants the estimate that is closest to the true value. However, complications arise if one tries to specify the precise meaning of "closest." Some of the ways in which this has been handled will be described later; most of them stem from Fisher's work.

Fisher's most fundamental contribution to estimation was his careful and consistent distinction between the observations one has in hand (a sample) and the larger set of unseen observations about which he wishes to draw conclusions (a population). This early work described systematically how one moves from a sample to conclusions about the population from which the sample was drawn. This is in essence the problem of induction.

FISHER'S CONTRIBUTIONS TO EXPERIMENTAL DESIGN. At the close of World War I, Fisher had the choice of becoming chief statistician under

Karl Pearson at the Galton Biometric Laboratory of the University of London, or of going to the Rothamsted Agricultural Station and developing a statistical laboratory there. He chose the latter on the grounds that it would provide greater opportunity for independent research. It is quite possible that this choice had a substantial influence on the course of development of statistics due to the unique character of agricultural experimentation.

In much agricultural field research, one is concerned with comparing the yield of different plant varieties, comparing yields as a function of soil treatment, and so on. However, plants must be set in the earth to grow, and it is quite obvious that the richness of the natural soil varies substantially from one place to another, even within a single field. One is immediately faced with deciding how to distribute plant varieties or soil treatments over an experimental field in such a way that different yields reflect the effects of varieties, or of soil treatments, and not simply the natural soil differences. Faced with this concrete problem, Fisher not only saw the solution but managed to gain additional dividends as well.

First, he showed how varieties or soil treatments could be distributed over the experimental field in random fashion or following methods of systematic counterbalancing, and, furthermore, how to deal statistically with the induction problem in drawing conclusions from the results. In this way, he not only provided procedures for reasonable experimental design, but he also showed how conclusions could be extracted from the data once the design had been executed.

The additional dividends grew from this approach. Fisher was able to devise ways of designing experiments and of analyzing the results when the effects of more than one independent variable were operating. For example, one could include several varieties and several soil treatments in a *single* experiment, and appraise the effects of varieties and of treatments *independently*. In other words, he showed how two or more distinct experimental questions could be answered with a single set of data.

This is all very well for agricultural research, but what of statistics in general? It is remarkable, but if one substitutes the independent variables of psychology for "plots," "varieties," "soil treatments," and so on, many of the experimental designs of agriculture become well-suited to psychological research. In fact, there is scarcely a single scientific discipline that has not made use of Fisher's "agricultural research" procedures. Interestingly enough, in a nontechnical discussion, Fisher chose to illustrate the ideas of experimental design with "The Mathematics of a Lady Tasting Tea." (See the Suggested Reading at the end of this chapter.)

Out of this part of Fisher's work grows an extremely important lesson for the person using statistics: research planning must be undertaken with full anticipation of the method of statistical analysis to be employed. Designing research and coping with the induction problem are not separate, distinct aspects of research. They are intimately related. The investigator must plan the statistical analysis of his data *before* it is gathered or risk placing himself in the hopeless position of being unable to draw valid inferences from his observations.

During the 1930's, Jerzy Neyman and Egon Pearson (Karl Pearson's son) codified in rigorous form the logic of statistical induction as it is most often used today. Their work depended substantially on Fisher's, but there are points on which they disagreed sharply with Fisher's ideas.

II.4
STATISTICAL DECISION THEORY

Although most of the methods now used in the analysis of psychological data were developed by the end of the first third of this century, there is a vanguard of theoretical statistics that has had a substantial impact on psychological thinking.

In the statistical treatments of the induction problem prior to 1950, the relative "cost" of making a wrong decision (i.e., believing an incorrect hypothesis to be true) or the "value" of deciding correctly was not included explicitly. In *Statistical Decision Functions* (1950), Abraham Wald systematically incorporated *value* in the structure of the theory of decision-making. In addition to its influence on statistical theory, this work provided the starting point for many psychological studies of choice-making behavior.

II.4.1. Wald's minimax criterion

Abraham Wald's system provides a rationale for choosing among a set of alternative courses of action when the consequences of each course of action depend upon an unknown "state of nature." In scientific inquiry, a course of action usually consists of concluding that a particular hypothesis is true or that it is false and steering subsequent research and theoretical developments accordingly. The state of nature involved is the actual truth or falsity of the hypothesis in question. However, a nonscientific example will be given in order to illustrate the Wald method.

Consider a vendor of limited capital who must decide whether to sell peanuts or pop at Saturday's football game. (His resources do not permit him to handle both pop and peanuts at the same game.) Our friend's concern is focused on the weather: the wisest action for him to take depends on whether the game is accompanied by rain, sunshine, or freezing weather. In Table II.1, the net profit which the vendor can anticipate for each combination of weather and choice of merchandise is shown. If it rains

Table II.1. Net profits for vendor depending on weather

		State of nature		
		Rain	Shine	Freeze
Course of action	Sell peanuts	\$100	\$90	\$75
	Sell pop	\$50	\$150	\$30

and the vendor has chosen to sell peanuts, he knows from his records that his net profit will be about \$100. However, if he decides to sell pop and freezing weather moves in, profits drop to about \$30, and so on. With this information and no hint as to the weather on Saturday, what is the best course of action to follow?

Being something of a statistician, our vendor applies a decision-making criterion that was introduced by Wald. He first calculates a table of "regrets" for his problem. For example, suppose it rains on Saturday. Then it would clearly be best to sell peanuts, and if this were the vendor's decision, he would experience no regret. Therefore, the amount of regret associated with selling peanuts if it rains is zero in Table II.2. On the other hand, if the vendor decides to sell pop and it rains, then he will regret his decision. The amount of regret equals the net profit for selling peanuts (the best course of action if it rains) less the net profit for selling pop on a rainy Saturday. In an exactly analogous fashion, regrets have been calculated for each of the other two weather conditions in Table II.2.

Table II.2. Regrets for vendor depending on weather

		State of nature			Maximum regret
		Rain	Shine	Freeze	
Course of action	Sell peanuts	0	\$60	0	\$60
	Sell pop	\$50	0	\$45	\$50

The Wald procedure instructs the vendor to look at the regrets *for each course of action* and to note the maximum regret. In the case of peanuts, the maximum regret is \$60, for pop the maximum is \$50. Since the best decision according to the Wald criterion is to pick the course of action for which the maximum regret is a minimum, the vendor's decision is to sell pop. This is the *minimax criterion: choose the course of action for which the maximum regret is a minimum.*

Looking back at Table II.1, you may notice that the *sum* of profits for selling peanuts is \$265 whereas the *sum* for pop is only \$230. Has the Wald procedure taken this kind of information into account? Clearly not, and there are many other criteria which might be used as the basis for selecting a course of action. In the example, the vendor virtually ignored the largest profits and centered his attention on the largest regrets. He was behaving cautiously or conservatively when he applied the minimax criterion, and it would have been possible for him to use other less conservative criteria as a basis for his choice. One of these is discussed below.

II.4.2. The maximum-expected-gain criterion

If our vendor were a more daring businessman, he might reject the minimax procedure as too conservative. Instead, he might try to maximize his average gain or expected gain. Examining the table of net profits (Table II.1), we see that the average profit to be expected if peanuts are sold is

$$\frac{100 + 90 + 75}{3} = \$88.33,$$

whereas the average gain expected if pop is sold is

$$\frac{50 + 150 + 30}{3} = \$76.67.$$

Using this criterion the vendor would choose to sell peanuts rather than pop, since a larger average profit (or expected gain) is associated with the sale of peanuts. This conclusion is not the same as that reached following the minimax criterion.

This last solution may arouse the reader's doubt immediately. Note that net profits have been averaged weighting each of the three weather conditions *equally*. In the vendor's locale rain, sunshine, and freezing weather may be equally likely on a given Saturday during the football season, but in some parts of the country such an assumption would be folly. Furthermore, it would probably be possible to get good data on the *likelihood* of any particular weather in a given area, and such information should be included where it is available. However, if we are really ignorant of the relative likelihood of rain, frost, or sunshine, then perhaps it is justifiable to invoke the principle of equal ignorance and weight each of the three weather conditions equally. If nothing else, this assumption is honored by time. It was introduced first by the English clergyman Thomas Bayes over 200 years ago.

Perhaps it is a little less obvious, but the same assumption was used in obtaining the minimax solution to the vendor's problem. If the probability was known for each of the three weather conditions, this information could be used to enhance the reasonableness of either the minimax or the maximum-expected-gain procedure. However, such refinements are not necessary to give a general idea of the workings of statistical decision theory, and they will not be elaborated here.

The two criteria for decision-making which have been described must not be viewed as an exhaustive list. Many others have been proposed, and a choice among them has to be based on nonstatistical considerations. For example, the extent to which one wishes to be conservative, i.e., to guard against losses as opposed to emphasizing potential gains, is important in choosing a criterion. The circumstances in which a particular decision-making problem arises and the predilections of the decision-maker remain beyond the scope of statistics. Knowledge, wisdom, and foresight are the essential ingredients of a suitable choice of decision-making rationale.

Our vendor had a simple time of it applying decision theory. He can measure net profit quite nicely. But what of the scientist? How does he assess the consequences of each combination of scientific conclusion (course of action) and actual situation (state of nature)? At the present time, suitable methods for measuring the scientific value of being right or the cost of being wrong are not available, and this probably accounts for the infrequency with which scientists make use of statistical decision theory. However, it is well to keep in mind that scientific decisions *are* made and that criteria, whether implicit or explicit, are employed in their making. The statistician's effort to make this process rational and well-understood cannot, therefore, be objected to on the grounds that some of the necessary quantities are not yet measurable. It is paradoxical that the values and criteria which enter into scientific conclusions are so poorly understood when such vagueness is so foreign to the scientific enterprise, but perhaps decision theory will ultimately develop to the point where it can help the scientist understand and clarify his own procedures for reaching decisions.

Within psychology, one might expect that the use of tests for selection of personnel and for placement in educational, military, and industrial settings would profit from the use of statistical decision theory. In such situations, the consequences of decisions sometimes can be evaluated in dollars, and the cost of using tests can be weighed against the gain accruing from their use by means of decision theory. Cronbach and Gleser were sufficiently impressed with this possibility to write a systematic monograph[3]

[3] Cronbach, L. J., and G. C. Gleser, *Psychological Tests and Personnel Decisions*. Urbana, University of Illinois Press, 1957.

outlining the ways in which decision theory might be used to appraise the usefulness of psychological testing programs. Their work depends heavily on Wald's formulation of statistical decision theory.

II.4.3. Statistical decision theory and the psychology of choice

During the past few years, statistical decision theory has been applied to the detection of auditory and visual signals by human subjects.[4] This work has met with considerable success, and it has led to important clarification of the idea of a sensory threshold. If a subject is reluctant to respond "signal present" unless he is very certain he is correct, then, using traditional methods, his "threshold" will appear higher than that of a less cautious but equally sensitive subject. However, the difference is not attributable to a real difference in sensitivity, but rather to a difference in the propensity to respond "signal present." Thus, sensory capacity and a personality characteristic, cautiousness, may be confounded. However, if the detection process is conceptualized using statistical decision theory, then sensitivity and cautiousness are unequivocally distinct in the theoretical formulation,[5] and they can be separated accordingly in the data analysis.

Later we shall discuss this application of statistical theory to human perception in some detail.

Irwin and his collaborators[6] have conducted a series of studies of the way in which statistically naive subjects deal with the induction problem. Their experiments have been designed to find whether the general features of the formal theory of statistical decision-making characterize the decision-making of statistically unsophisticated subjects. The gist of their findings is that they do.

A number of psychologists have been developing psychological theories of choice that are intended to apply to ordinary behavior.[7] These theories did not begin as prescriptions of how one should proceed in making wise decisions; rather, they start from scratch and attempt to describe decision-making as it naturally occurs. Not only do these theories depend heavily on the methods of probability and statistics, but many of the ideas that led to these formulations are outgrowths of statistical decision theory.

[4] See Swets, J. A., W. P. Tanner, Jr., and T. G. Birdsall, "Decision processes in perception." *Psychol. Rev.* **68**, 301–340, 1961.

[5] *Ibid.*

[6] Irwin, F. W., W. A. S. Smith, and J. F. Mayfield, "Tests of two theories of decision in an 'expanded judgment' situation." *J. Exp. Psychol.* **51**, 261–268, 1956; Irwin, F. W., and W. A. S. Smith, "Further tests of theories of decision in an 'expanded judgment' situation." *J. Exp. Psychol.* **52**, 345–348, 1956; "Value, cost, and information as determiners of decision." *J. Exp. Psychol.* **54**, 229–232, 1957.

[7] For example, see Luce, R. D., *Individual Choice Behavior.* New York, John Wiley, 1959; Restle, F., *The Psychology of Judgment and Choice.* New York, John Wiley, 1961.

In this area, there has been extensive cross-fertilization between statistics and psychology.

SUGGESTED READING

Probability

1. Todhunter, I., *A History of the Mathematical Theory of Probability.* Cambridge, Macmillan, 1865.
   This is the standard treatment of the early history of probability.
2. Cramér, H., *The Elements of Probability Theory.* New York, John Wiley, 1955, Chap. 1.
   This is a brief survey of the history of probability which emphasizes the difficulties accompanying the definition of objective probability.

Early statistics

1. Graunt, J., "Foundations of Vital Statistics," in J. R. Newman (ed.), *The World of Mathematics*, III. New York, Simon and Schuster, 1956, pp. 1421–1435.
   Taken from Graunt's pamphlet, *Natural and Political Observations*, on the basis of which Graunt was admitted to the Royal Society.
2. Hawkins, F. H., *Adolphe Quetelet as Statistician.* New York, Columbia University, 1908.
   This gives a glimpse of the whole range of activities of the energetic Belgian scientist as well as detailed discussion of his statistics.

The biometric movement

1. Pearson, K., Editorial in *Biometrika* **1**, 1–6, 1901.
   Describes the *raison d'être* of *Biometrika* and the function it was expected to serve in biology in general and in the development of the theory of biological evolution in particular. Francis Galton also has a few comments on the meaning of biometry and its significance on the four pages following Pearson's editorial.
2. Boring, E. G., *A History of Experimental Psychology.* New York, Appleton-Century-Crofts, 1950.
   The passages on Darwin, Galton, and Karl Pearson, and on correlation, lend psychological perspective to the biometric movement. These also provide an inkling of the way in which statistical methods have become important in psychology. Chapter 8 provides a discussion of the astronomer's attempts to deal with observational errors, one of the first applications of the normal curve. The section on Fechner shows the important role of statistics in the very beginning of experimental psychology (Chapter 14).
3. Fisher, R. A., *Contributions to Mathematical Statistics.* New York, John Wiley, 1950.
   This is a collection of some of Fisher's more important papers. It includes a biography of Fisher written by P. C. Mahalanobis which has been reprinted from *Sankhya.* The remaining papers are quite technical.

4. Fisher, R. A., "Mathematics of a Lady Testing Tea," in J. R. Newman (ed.) *The World of Mathematics*, III. New York, Simon and Schuster, 1956, pp. 1512–1521.
This is an elementary discussion of experimental design which is exemplified by a question of the gustatory sensitivity claimed by a hypothetical lady. Many of the problems of experimental design and some of their solutions are described clearly in nonmathematical language.

Decision theory

1. Bross, I. D. J., *Design for Decision.* New York, Macmillan, 1953.
A clever introduction to decision theory. Numerous ingenious illustrations and a clear indication of the nature of some of the solutions which have been proposed.
2. Chernoff, H., and L. E. Moses, *Elementary Decision Theory.* New York, John Wiley, 1959.
This is a textbook which gives a systematic introduction to decision theory. Although mathematical, it is clearly and interestingly written and far less technical than other treatments.

Psychological decision theory

1. Edwards, W., "Behavioral decision theory." *Annual Rev. Psychol.* **12**, 473–498, 1961.
A brief survey of some recent theoretical and empirical work on the psychology of choice.

III

FUNDAMENTAL CONCEPTS

THE results of any scientific investigation are expected to apply to some range of phenomena that extends beyond the actual data. For example, atomic theory is not limited to the minute proportion of atoms that have been examined in the laboratory; rather, it is intended to encompass the behavior of atoms throughout the universe. Generalization or prediction —the process of applying the results of previous investigations to observations that have not been made—is a most important return for the efforts of the scientist. In fact, the ability to generalize or predict successfully is often cited as the most important criterion for judging the stature of a scientific discipline.

If the scientist finds himself in the embarrassing position of not knowing the range of phenomena to which his results apply, then in a given instance he may be unable to decide whether his predictions should be expected to hold or not. The primitive physicist who postulates that unsupported objects fall toward the center of the *earth* would be in for some disillusionment in the space age. However, within certain spatial limitations (i.e., near the surface of the earth), his principle would work quite well. Our physicist based his principle on a set of terrestrially bound observations, and their validity does not extend beyond the realm in which the observations were made. This can be summarized by the single maxim: One can generalize the conclusions of empirical research only to the range of phenomena that is adequately represented in one's observations. If our physicist has observed events near the surface of the earth only, then he cannot expect his conclusions to apply in other domains such as outer space.

Although they are logically equivalent, the ideas of generalization and prediction are customarily distinguished on the basis of time. If conclusions are extended beyond the observed data, but at a fixed point in time, this is usually referred to as *generalization.* If the conclusions are projected to observations that are to be made in the future, this is *prediction.* The common feature is that both involve going beyond the data in hand to observations which have not been made.

It is not difficult to see that both generalization and prediction are forms of induction. It is the purpose of this chapter to develop a vocabulary for dealing with induction. In Chapter IV we will discover that some of this vocabulary is essential to the fundamental ideas of probability. Thus, the nomenclature introduced here will serve two purposes.

III.1

SETS

Before proceeding to a definition of population and sample, we must have a few concepts clearly in mind. Strictly speaking, these ideas are mathematical, but some of them are so fundamental to ordinary thinking that they are easily grasped. The first idea is that of a set.

Any aggregate or collection of objects, symbols, or persons—in fact any imaginable collection—is a *set.* The items which make up a set are called *elements,* and the elements of a given set may all be similar in some respect or they may have nothing whatever in common. The set consisting of "my house," "cyclotron," and "a herd of elephants" is quite acceptable, though it has no obvious use. The set consisting of 1, 2, and 3 is also acceptable. The set of IQ's for all sixth-graders in a particular school system might prove useful. Similarly, the set of all four-year grade-point averages for seniors in your university might be of interest.

Notice that a set may be defined by *describing* the essential properties of its elements or by simply *listing* the elements one by one. Thus, "the set of all positive integers" is as well defined as the set containing only the elements 1, 2, and 3.

The number of elements in a set may be finite or infinite. In the latter case, it is impossible to list all elements, so that an infinite set must be defined by describing the characteristics of its elements.

Next, the concept of a subset must be introduced. A *subset* is a part of a given set. Thus, since 1, 2, and 3 are all positive integers, the set consisting of 1, 2, and 3 is a subset of the set of all positive integers. *If one set is labeled A and another B, then A is a subset of B if every element in A is also in B.* Thus, the sixth-graders in a particular class is a subset of all school children in a school system.

Notice that according to this definition, a set is a subset of itself. This may seem strained, but it is certainly true since every element of a set is in that set.

III.1.1. Two types of sets

Two types of sets must be distinguished in probability and statistics. The best way to clarify the distinction between them is to compare the conditions under which sets within each type are equal.

UNORDERED SETS. *Two unordered sets are equal if they contain the same elements.* Thus, the unordered set {1, 3, 7} equals the unordered set {3, 1, 7}, since both contain a 1, a 3, and a 7, and neither set contains any other elements. Notice that the elements of an *unordered* set are included in braces.

If a set contains the names of all the sixth-graders in a particular class, and the purpose of this set is simply to show who is a member of the class, then changing the order of the names would not alter class-membership. This is a use of an unordered set.

ORDERED SETS. On the other hand, if pupils' names are listed in order of arithmetical skill, this constitutes an ordered set, and the ordinal position of a name has a significance that does not permit modification of the order without altering the meaning of the set. From this it is reasonable to say that *two ordered sets are equal if they contain the same elements and these elements appear in the same order.* If (1, 3, 7) and (7, 1, 3) are ordered sets, they are *not* equal, but the ordered set (1, 3, 7) does equal (1, 3, 7). The elements of an unordered set are enclosed in braces, but those of an ordered set will be enclosed in parentheses.

III.1.2. Cardinality of sets

The number of elements in a set is sometimes referred to as its cardinality. Two sets are said to have the same cardinality if there exists a one-to-one correspondence between them. That is, if it is possible to pair off the elements of the sets A and B so that each pair contains exactly one element from A and one from B, and so that every element in each set appears in exactly one pair, then A and B are said to have the same cardinality. The existence of a one-to-one correspondence may be established by an actual listing of the pairs or by defining a rule that clearly ensures an exhaustive pairing.

FINITE SETS. It is easy to apply the ideas discussed so far to finite sets. For example, the set {my house, cyclotron, herd of elephants} has the same cardinality as the set (A, B, C), since each of the following pairs contains an element from each set and every element from each set appears in exactly one pair:

"my house" corresponds to A,
"cyclotron" corresponds to B,
"herd of elephants" corresponds to C.

Notice that although the meaning of equality of sets differs for ordered and unordered sets, the interpretation of cardinality is the same for both.

The preceding paragraphs may seem unnecessarily elaborate, but that is because only finite sets have been discussed. The same ideas will now be extended to infinite sets.

COUNTABLY INFINITE SETS. When an ordered set is not finite, it is sometimes convenient to designate it by writing the first few of its elements in order, followed by three dots. The terminal dots indicate that the set is not finite. Thus, $C = (1, 2, 3, \ldots)$ represents the ordered set of *all* counting numbers (i.e., all positive integers). Now, what is the cardinality of C? In considering this question, it will be helpful to examine several other sets that have the same cardinality as C. For example, it is easy to establish a one-to-one correspondence between C and the set of all positive even numbers. It is only necessary to point out that every counting number becomes an even number when doubled. Thus,

twice	the counting	number	1	corresponds	to the even	number	2,
”	”	”	2	”	”	”	4,
”	”	”	3	”	”	”	6,
”	”	”	4	”	”	”	8,

and so on. Since this establishes a one-to-one correspondence between the set of positive even numbers and C, these sets have the same cardinality.

In similar fashion, a one-to-one correspondence can be established between the set of positive odd integers and the positive even integers. (The correspondence can be based on adding 1 to each odd integer.) Therefore, these two infinite sets have the same cardinality. In addition, each of them has the same cardinality as C.

In a similar manner, it is easy to show that the set of all nonzero integers, both positive and negative, has the same cardinality as C. The one-to-one correspondence can be established as follows:

1	corresponds to	1,
2	”	-1,
3	”	2,
4	”	-2,
5	”	3,
6	”	-3,

and so on. This one-to-one correspondence is based on the assignment of positive integers to the odd counting numbers and negative integers to even counting numbers. It demonstrates that the set of all nonzero integers has the same cardinality as C.

Although the ideas of cardinality used with finite sets have simply been extended to infinite sets, statements like "the set of all positive even numbers has the same cardinality as *C*" may seem little short of bizarre. The set of positive even numbers is a subset of *C*, and *C* contains all the odd counting numbers, as well! How can it be said that these sets have the same cardinality? The answer lies in the nature of the reasoning employed. A reasonable interpretation of cardinality was found for finite sets, and this was then applied to infinite sets without change. When dealing with finite sets, the idea of cardinality seemed quite natural and agreed well with intuition. Therefore, the same ideas were used for infinite sets. The fact that intuition may be offended by some of the results does not indicate that this approach is senseless. Rather, the wide acceptance that it has achieved suggests that raw intuition is of little use in dealing with infinite sets.

From the few examples given, it appears that many infinite sets have the same cardinality as the set of counting numbers, *C*. When a set has the same cardinality as the set of all counting numbers, it is said to be *countably infinite* or denumerably infinite.

This leads to an interesting question: Are all infinite sets countably infinite? That is, can every set that is not finite be put in one-to-one correspondence with the set of all counting numbers? Although it may be surprising, the answer is "no." Furthermore, this fact is important in probability and statistics.

UNCOUNTABLY INFINITE SETS. The focus of attention here will be the set of all real numbers. This includes all integers, all numbers that can be written as a ratio of two integers (rational numbers or fractions), plus all numbers that can only be expressed as infinite decimals (irrational numbers). In short, the real numbers consist of all of the positive and negative numbers of ordinary arithmetic and zero.

Any real number can be expressed as an integer plus an infinite decimal. For example, $1\frac{1}{2}$ can be written as 1.5000.... The dots simply indicate that the zeros continue *ad infinitum*. Similarly, 2/3 can be written as 0.6666..., and $\pi = 3.1415926536\ldots$ is an infinite, nonrepeating decimal.

The next step is to show that the set of all real numbers is *not* countably infinite. If it can be shown that the set of real numbers between 0 and 1 has a cardinality greater than the set of counting numbers *C*, then it will be clear that the cardinality of the set of all real numbers also exceeds that of *C*.

To begin with, suppose someone claimed that he had established a one-to-one correspondence between the real numbers between 0 and 1 and *C*, and suppose that the pairings looked something like the following:

1	corresponds to	0.5976. . .,
2	,,	0.6831. . .,
3	,,	0.9812. . .,
4	,,	0.2367. . .,

and so on. Then, it is easy to show that at least one real number has been omitted, so that the claim of a one-to-one correspondence must be false. (Remember that a one-to-one correspondence must include *every* element of each set in exactly one pair.) A real number that has been omitted has a first digit that differs from the first digit of the real number corresponding to 1 (say 6), its second digit differs from the second digit of the real number corresponding to 2 (say 9), its third digit differs from the third digit of the real number corresponding to 3 (say 2), and so on. Since the resulting real number differs from every real number included in the pairs in at least one of its digits, it must have been overlooked. Therefore, a one-to-one correspondence has not been established, and the cardinality of the set of real numbers between 0 and 1 is *not* equal to the cardinality of C.

Notice that this argument does not depend on the basis of the correspondence that has been claimed. No matter how counting numbers and real numbers are paired, it is always possible to find at least one real number that has been overlooked. Therefore, there can be no one-to-one correspondence.

Since the cardinality of the real numbers between 0 and 1 exceeds that of C, it is clear that the cardinality of the set of all real numbers (positive, negative, and 0) also exceeds that of C.

Sets of points constituting straight-line segments are often used to represent sets of real numbers. For example, the points of a straight-line segment one unit long provide a representation of the set of real numbers between 0 and 1. Each point of this line represents one real number. With this sort of geometric interpretation, it is possible to show that the set of real numbers represented by any line segment has the same cardinality as the set of real numbers between 0 and 1. For example, the cardinality of the set between 2 and 5 is the same as that of the set between 0 and 1.

To demonstrate this, first draw a line segment representing each of these sets, as shown in Figure III.1. Next, draw one line through the left end-

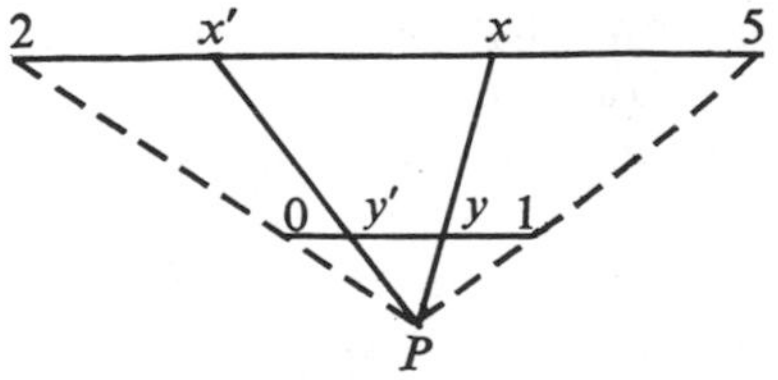

Figure III.1

points of these two lines and another through the right end-points, and label their intersection P (see Figure III.1). Now, for any point x on the 2-to-5 line, a straight line through x and P cuts the 0-to-1 line at a point y. Similarly, a line through P and any point y' on the 0-to-1 line intersects the 2-to-5 line at a point x'. Furthermore, the line through P and x and the line through P and x', where x and x' are distinct, must intersect the 0-to-1 line at distinct points, y and y'. In the same manner, lines drawn through P and distinct points y and y' on the 0-to-1 line must intersect the 2-to-5 line at distinct points x and x'. This means that the set of all such lines defines a one-to-one correspondence between the sets of points defined by the two line segments. Therefore, the two sets of real numbers represented by these line segments have the same cardinality.

Such a demonstration can be constructed for any pair of line segments, provided their length is finite, and, though the reasoning will not be given here, it is possible to show that the cardinality of the set of *all* real numbers is the same as that of the set of real numbers between 0 and 1. Furthermore, if a set can be placed in one-to-one correspondence with the set of all real numbers (or with the set of real numbers between 0 and 1, for that matter), then it is said to be *uncountably* infinite or nondenumerably infinite.[1]

The distinction between countably and uncountably infinite sets may seem like unnecessary detail at this point, but we will discover later that it is an essential distinction in the interpretation of probability.

III.2
POPULATION AND SAMPLE

In general terms, a population is the set of individuals or items or events to which an investigator wishes to apply the conclusions of his research. A sample is a set obtained from a population; it consists of the individuals, items, or events which are examined in the research.

A population is the statistical analogue of the universe of discourse in deductive logic. The universe of discourse is the domain under discussion in a logical analysis; it sets the boundaries within which propositions are to be judged true or false. In statistics, specifying a population (or universe, as it is sometimes called) determines the limits within which one expects an inductive generalization to hold.

The students of a sixth-grade class may be viewed as a sample taken from a population consisting of all of the students in a school system. This

[1] It should not be concluded that this exhausts the "orders of infinity." Infinite sets that cannot be placed in a one-to-one correspondence with either the set of all counting numbers or of all real numbers can be designated. For further discussion, see Reference 3 in the Suggested Reading at the end of this chapter.

sample is not likely to be typical or representative, but it is a sample, nonetheless.

Although the terms "population" and "sample" are most often linked with dependent variables, they are also relevant to independent variables. For example, behavioral response as a function of drug dosage is often studied in psychopharmacological research. In such investigations, the effects on behavior of each of a sample of drug dosages is examined. On the basis of such a study, it might be reported that as dosage of Drug X increases, ability to focus attention decreases and reaction time increases. If these conclusions were based on a sample of moderate dosages only, one might overlook the fact that small quantities of the drug increase the ability to focus attention and decrease reaction time. The difficulty is that the full range of the dosage population has not been representatively sampled.

This is fairly obvious in psychopharmacology; it is also generally true that conclusions can be drawn about the effects of an independent variable only to the extent that a representative sample of its values has been studied. Thus, one might jump to the general conclusion that as magnitude of reward increases, maze running times for rats decrease. Though probably true for relatively small reward magnitudes, it is obvious that the rat's speed of locomotion is physiologically limited. When the magnitude of reward becomes very large, additional increases will not lower running times. In short, general conclusions are likely to be faulty unless the sample of values of the independent variable is representative of the population.

III.2.1. Definition of population

A population is an unordered set that contains all of the persons, objects, or events having specified properties. A member of a population (i.e., person, object, or event) *will be called an element. A population is said to be of size N if it contains N elements.*

The term *specified properties* in the definition refers to the characteristics that distinguish members of the population from nonmembers. The population of adult, male citizens of the U.S. is distinguished by three properties. Of course, to define this population unequivocally, the conditions determining each of the three properties must be made clear. For example, an adult might be defined as one who has reached the age of 21 prior to a given date.

As far as probability and statistics are concerned, a population can often be thought of as a set of symbols. If an observation consists of determining the sex of a person, then a collection of the symbols M and F constitutes the population. If an IQ estimate is an observation, then the population can be thought of as a set of numbers.

III.2.2. Definition of sample

A sample is an ordered set of elements from a population. A sample is said to be of size n if it contains n elements.

This definition offers no surprises with the possible exception of the inclusion of the word "ordered." The best way to understand this is to think of a sample as having a first element, a second element, and so on. Sometimes there is no basis for assigning an order to the elements of a sample, and there are occasions when order can safely be ignored, but it will become apparent in Chapter IV that order is often of paramount importance.

One basis for determining the ordinal position of a sample element is the time at which it is observed. For example, a sample of tosses of a single coin might be taken. The result of the first toss is the first sample element, the second toss determines the second element, etc.

Perhaps the most obvious reason for resorting to a sample instead of examining an entire population is that most populations worthy of serious interest are much too large to permit complete inspection or measurement. A second reason for using samples is that the entire population may be unavailable. For example, if historical records provide the observations, they may be incomplete. If a test has been designed to predict "success" in college, we cannot now assess its efficacy for predicting the performance of future students. Finally, the process of obtaining an observation may destroy it (e.g., testing fuses or matches).

SAMPLING WITH REPLACEMENT. There are two ways in which a sample can be selected. In the first, *sampling with replacement, each element drawn from the population is replaced prior to drawing the next element.*

When sampling with replacement, more than one observation on a single element may be included in one sample. If a population consisted of the elements 1, 2, and 3, then a sample of size 2 might include two 1's, two 2's, or two 3's. If IQ's are being observed, the IQ of a single person may be included more than once in a single sample.

There are many circumstances in which this method of sampling is impossible or unwise. For instance, if making an observation destroys the element, then sampling with replacement is impossible. Administering a psychological test to the same person on successive occasions may mean that the later test result is contaminated by memory or practice effects from a previous test, so that the two observations are not comparable. Similarly, if the physiological aspects of emotional response to an unexpected stimulus were to be investigated, it would not do to expose the same subject to the stimulus situation more than once. Consequently, psychological research frequently requires sampling *without* replacement.

SAMPLING WITHOUT REPLACEMENT. *When sampling without replacement, no element drawn from the population is replaced.*

In sampling with replacement, a single individual could determine every observation in a sample; without replacement, the same element is never observed more than once. Nonetheless, the same numerical value may appear more than once when sampling without replacement, since the population may contain several distinct elements for which the value of an observation is the same (e.g., a few pupils in one class may have the same IQ).

When sampling without replacement, the sample size cannot exceed the population size. However, when sampling with replacement, the sample may contain more elements than the population, since some elements may occur more than once in the sample.

RANDOM SAMPLING. So far, nothing has been said about samples being random, nonrandom, representative, etc. A sample is simply an ordered set of elements from a population. However, if a sample is to be useful in statistical analysis, it is absolutely essential to know the way in which it was obtained.

The most fundamental and important sampling method is random sampling. *A sample of size n is said to be random if it is selected in such a way that every ordered set of n elements from the population has an equal chance of being the sample selected.*

This definition says nothing about the characteristics of the random sample itself. Only the characteristics of the sampling *process* are specified. A random sample can never be identified as such except by examining the procedure by which it was obtained. Thus, it is most correct to speak of "random sampling" rather than "a random sample," although the latter term is usually more convenient.

A random sample may be obtained with replacement or without; the definition is not restricted to either method.

Sometimes a random sample is defined as one "drawn in such a way that every *element* of the population has an equal chance of being chosen." Such a definition is quite adequate when sampling *with* replacement. However, when sampling without replacement from a finite population, after one element has been drawn, the chance that any one of those remaining will be chosen on the second draw is 1 in $N - 1$, not 1 in N, and after the second draw, the chance is 1 in $N - 2$, and so on. Thus, sampling without replacement, a definition requiring that "every *element* have an equal chance of being drawn" becomes difficult to formulate.

To illustrate the definition of random sampling, suppose a random sample of size 2 is to be drawn *with* replacement from a population containing the elements 1, 2, 3, and 4. The 16 possible samples are as listed:

$$\begin{array}{cccc} (1, 1) & (2, 1) & (3, 1) & (4, 1) \\ (1, 2) & (2, 2) & (3, 2) & (4, 2) \\ (1, 3) & (2, 3) & (3, 3) & (4, 3) \\ (1, 4) & (2, 4) & (3, 4) & (4, 4). \end{array}$$

The sampling procedure is random if each of these has the same likelihood of being chosen. Similarly, if sampling *without* replacement, the list of possible samples is as follows:

$$\begin{array}{cccc} (1, 2) & (2, 1) & (3, 1) & (4, 1) \\ (1, 3) & (2, 3) & (3, 2) & (4, 2) \\ (1, 4) & (2, 4) & (3, 4) & (4, 3). \end{array}$$

Since 12 samples are possible, the sampling procedure is random if each of the 12 has the same likelihood of being selected.

Notice that in both of these examples order is distinguished, so that the sample (2, 4) is not equal to (4, 2).

It is important to understand that random sampling does *not* guarantee that a particular sample will be representative of the population from which it is drawn. A random sample *may* be as unrepresentative as a sample selected by any other procedure, since all possible samples have the same likelihood of being selected. In the example involving sampling with replacement, the sample (1, 1) can hardly be considered representative of the population containing 1, 2, 3, and 4, but it is just as likely as the sample (2, 3) when sampling is random. However, in using random samples we are banking on the fact that the observations that typify the population are those that are most frequent and consequently most likely to appear in a particular random sample. But even so, a random sample is not likely to be a precise reflection of the population. In drawing numerous random samples from the same population, it is almost certain that these samples will differ from one another. The important thing is that the differences among samples—the *sampling variability*—follows a pattern when sampling is random, and it is often possible to specify the form of this pattern *before* any samples have been drawn. For example, if we are tossing 10 fair coins, the pattern of sampling variability (and our intuition) tells us that one is more likely to observe 4, 5, or 6 heads on a single toss than 9 or 10 heads, provided the method of tossing the coins is random. However, if the mechanism for tossing the coins were systematic in some unknown way, the pattern of sampling variability could not be specified and nothing could be said a priori about the relative likelihood of tossing any particular number of heads.

It may seem paradoxical to assert that if a sampling process is *random*, then it has *orderly* features which one may be able to describe a priori. But this is the case, and it is probability theory that provides the methods for extracting such orderliness from randomness. In fact, probability theory might well be called "the theory of the orderly characteristics of random processes." In Chapter IV, we shall study some of the laws of probability theory which permit us to describe such orderliness.

Representativeness is sometimes stressed as the important characteristic of random sampling but, as we have seen, a random sample may be quite as nonrepresentative as any other kind of sample. It is the applicability of probability theory to the description of the pattern of sampling variability that makes random sampling important for statistics.

PROBABILITY SAMPLING. Sometimes a population can be divided into segments, and a part of a sample can be taken from each segment. For example, in a six-grade elementary school, a random sample could be drawn from each grade, so that the total sample consists of six random subsamples. This is a form of probability sampling.

Another form of probability sample could be employed in sampling students from a large city school system. First, a random sample of *schools* could be selected, and then a random sample of pupils could be chosen from each of these schools.

Notice that both of these procedures involve randomness at some point in the sampling procedure, but that they require more than just random sampling. One might describe these procedures as "structured" random sampling.

In probability sampling, the goal is to ensure that each of several segments of the population are represented in the sample. However, this must be done in such a way that probability theory can be applied to specify the pattern of sampling variability. Thus, randomness must be incorporated into the sampling scheme.

Random sampling requires that every possible sample has the same chance of being chosen. Probability sampling requires only that the probability of each possible sample can be calculated. *A sample of size n is a probability sample if it is chosen in such a way that every ordered set of n elements of the population has a known probability of being the sample chosen.* The word "known" in this definition means "can be calculated." Oftentimes, the number of possible samples is so large that it is practically impossible to perform all the arithmetic, but it may be possible in principle, nonetheless.

Probability sampling simply requires that probability be applicable to the sampling process, and this means that simple random sampling is a special kind of probability sampling.

PROBLEMS ON SAMPLING

1. Suppose that a population consists of the elements 1, 2, and 3, so that the population size is $N = 3$.

a. How many different samples of size 2 can be obtained from this population sampling with replacement? List all of the possible samples.
b. How many different samples of size 2 can be obtained sampling without replacement? List all possible samples.
c. How many different samples of size 3 can be obtained sampling with replacement? List all such samples.
d. How many different samples of size 3 can be obtained sampling without replacement? List all such samples.

2. Suppose a population consists of three 1's, three 2's, and three 3's, so that $N = 9$. Solve a through d in Problem 1 for this population.
3. A population contains a countably infinite set of 1's, a countably infinite set of 2's, and a countably infinite set of 3's. First, show that the population as a whole is countably infinite. Then solve a through d in Problem 1 for this population.
4. Three draws are made from an opaque urn containing one black ball and one white ball. Each ball is replaced prior to the next draw. How many different samples of size 3 can be obtained? List all of these samples. How many samples of size 3 can be drawn from the urn if sampling without replacement?

*III.2.3. Application to statistical learning theory

William K. Estes and C. J. Burke[2] have proposed a theory of learning that makes extensive use of the ideas of sampling. Their account is similar to that of Edwin Guthrie,[3] but they make more explicit use of the methods of probability and statistics.

According to Estes and Burke, the learning situation constitutes a set of "stimulus elements." These elements are not objectively discernible. It is impossible to point to them one by one in a particular learning situation, but they are assumed to exist, nonetheless.[4]

It is assumed that on a training trial, a certain proportion of these stimulus elements are "registered" by the organism. That is, a sample of stimulus elements is drawn. Furthermore, the sample is assumed to be random. Then, a response is made, and if it is reinforced, each of the stimulus elements sampled on that trial become conditioned to that response. As the proportion of stimulus elements conditioned to a

[2] Estes, W. K., "Toward a statistical theory of learning." *Psychol. Rev.* **57**, 94–107, 1950; Estes, W. K., and C. J. Burke, "A theory of stimulus variability in learning." *Psychol. Rev.* **60**, 276–286, 1953.

[3] Guthrie, E. R., *The Psychology of Learning*. New York, Harper, 1935.

[4] The reader may find it strange that these stimulus elements are "undefined," in the theory. However, it is true that all theories begin with undefined elements or variables at some point. One cannot define everything, since that would leave nothing in terms of which a definition could be made. The real question is whether the theory describes and predicts adequately the phenomena it is intended to encompass.

response increases, the likelihood of that response increases. Thus, from this point of view, an essential feature of learning is a process of psychological random sampling.

Though this approach may seem excessively simple, it has produced a number of precisely defined hypotheses, many of which have found empirical support. In addition, elaborations of the basic conception have generated theories of extinction, spontaneous recovery (in conditioning), passive forgetting, decision-making, competitive game behavior, etc. Later, we will return to this approach to illustrate some of the ideas of probability and statistics that will be introduced.

III.3
CHARACTERISTICS OF POPULATIONS AND SAMPLES

In most research, interest centers on some characteristic of a population or on the differences among populations with respect to a particular characteristic. For example, men and women might differ in their opinion of the deferment of military service for college students. The proportion of college men favoring deferment might be expected to exceed the proportion of college women. Such a proportion defines a characteristic of a population; in one case the college male population and in the other the college female population.

An empirical investigation of opinions about deferment would be unlikely to include the opinion of every college student. Such data-gathering would be much too tedious and expensive. But a sample of males and a sample of females might be obtained which would give a fairly accurate estimate of the proportion favoring educational deferment within each sex. This is the usual form of the statistical induction problem: samples are used in an attempt to draw conclusions about the characteristics of populations.

III.3.1. Parameters

A numerical characteristic of a population is called a parameter. A parameter might be a proportion, an average, a measure of a correlation between variables, or any other numerical characteristic of a population. In the example of the preceding section, the proportion of all college males favoring deferment would constitute a parameter.

III.3.2. Statistics

Usually, samples are used to obtain information about parameters. A sample of male college students could be used to estimate the proportion of all male college students favoring educational deferment.

Thus, an estimate of a parameter can be determined for a sample.

A numerical characteristic of a sample is called a statistic.

III.4
CLASSIFICATION OF STATISTICAL INDUCTION PROBLEMS

The remainder of this chapter is devoted to classifying statistical induction problems. Specific methods are discussed later.

III.4.1. Estimation

When a sample provides an estimate of the value of a parameter, the procedure is called estimation.

POINT ESTIMATION. When a single value is given as an estimate, this is called a point estimate. Thus, a statistic may provide a point estimate. The term *point* simply indicates that the estimate consists of a single number.

A rule for calculating a point estimate of a parameter from a sample is called an estimator.

If a statistic based on a random sample is used as a point estimate, it is unlikely that the estimate will exactly equal the parameter. In fact, if several random samples are taken from a single population, the values assigned by an estimator can be expected to vary from one sample to another. If the pattern of sampling variability is known, the amount of variability from sample to sample of the values generated by an estimator can be described so that some idea of the accuracy of an estimate can be obtained.

INTERVAL ESTIMATION. One way of describing the accuracy of an estimate is to give a range of values which has a certain likelihood of including the unknown parameter. For example, a random sample could be used to estimate the proportion of college males favoring educational deferment. On the basis of the sample, it might be possible to state that the interval from 0.78 to 0.92 has a 95 percent likelihood of including the proportion in this population.

The induction problem beomes a matter of estimation when one is ignorant of the parameters of a population. If no information is available and there is no theoretical basis for hypothesizing the value of a parameter, then a sample can be used to make an enlightened guess at the value of the parameter in question.

III.4.2. Hypothesis testing

The induction problem may take the form of hypothesis testing as well as of estimation. For example, the hypothesis that the proportion of college men favoring educational deferment exceeds the proportion of college women might be investigated using one sample of men and one of women.

In estimation, one attempts to get a reasonable idea of the value of a parameter. In hypothesis testing, it is decided whether a statement about a single parameter or about the relationship among two or more parameters is true. In estimation, the result is a number. In hypothesis testing, a simple *yes* or *no* answer is often obtained, along with statements about the likelihood that this answer is wrong.

In scientific research, the hypotheses are stated in terms of the parameters of certain populations. For example, it might be hypothesized that the average algebraic skill of ninth-graders will be greater following 20 hours of instruction on a teaching machine than following 20 hours of conventional classroom instruction. In statistical terms, this amounts to distinguishing two populations; ninth-grade algebra students who have received teaching machine instruction and ninth-grade students who have received conventional classroom instruction. The average achievement test performance of the former is expected to exceed that of the latter. The two averages are parameters. Finally, the average test performance of a random sample from each population might be compared in order to evaluate the hypothesis. Thus, each sample would be used to estimate the corresponding population average, and hypothesis testing methods would be employed to decide whether the hypothesis is tenable and to appraise the confidence one can place in the decision.

SUGGESTED READING

1. Wallis, W. A., and H. V. Roberts, *Statistics: A New Approach.* New York, Free Press of Glencoe, 1955, Chap. 3.
This chapter provides an excellent discussion of most of the statistical ideas found here. It is especially useful in clarifying the notion of sampling variability or of the pattern of sampling variability.
2. Kemeny, J. G., J. L. Snell, and G. L. Thompson, *Introduction to Finite Mathematics.* Englewood Cliffs, N.J., Prentice-Hall, 1957, Chap. 2.
This is an introduction to sets and their manipulation. This entire book is oriented toward the behavioral sciences, and a number of the illustrations are psychological.
3. Hahn, H., "Infinity," in J. R. Newman (ed.), *The World of Mathematics,* III. New York, Simon and Schuster, 1956, pp. 1593–1611.
The first half of this piece is an unusually lucid introduction to the ideas of Section III.1.2. It was first presented as a public lecture.
4. Halmos, P. R., *Naive Set Theory.* New York, Van Nostrand, 1960.
A readable general introduction to set theory.

IV

PROBABILITY: BASIC CONCEPTS

THERE are two primary reasons why psychologists should become familiar with the principles of probability theory. First, a considerable portion of psychological theory is being formulated in probabilistic terms, and an intelligent reading of this work requires an understanding of the rudiments of probability. Second, statistical estimation and hypothesis testing are often used by the psychologist to appraise the implications of his data, and these methods depend ultimately upon the use of probability. Furthermore, the demands for sophistication in probability seem to be increasing rapidly in both of these areas.

Probability theory is usually referred to as a branch of mathematics, but it need not be abstract mathematics without connection to the real world. It owes its birth as much to the very practical concerns of the gambler as to the investigations of the pure mathematician. Furthermore, the main stream of probability theory has never been entirely free of gamblers, physicists, economists, psychologists, and military men seeking solutions to *their* problems. Whereas some branches of mathematics have developed quite independently of any immediate usefulness, this certainly is not true of probability theory.

If events occurring in the real world can be described in certain ways (which will be discussed below), then the theory of probability becomes applicable. There is no essential reason why we could not *test* the adequacy of probability theory as a description of observable events, just as the empirical adequacy of psychological theory is tested, but most scientists apply probability theory without apparent hesitation. They seem to accept its empirical validity without question. One might wonder if such confidence is defensible, and perhaps it is not, but the success of probability theory is striking. It is doubtful that any other product of the scientific tradition can claim greater scope in its validation. Probability theory has been used to deal with phenomena as disparate as games of chance and quantum mechanics without producing serious doubts about its validity. This is not to imply that doubts will not arise or that probability theory is complete and static. It is growing apace, largely due to the increasing variety of problems scientists are attacking with its aid. As a result, reformulations almost certainly will occur, and there is now disagreement about the proper interpretation of probability itself. However, everyone has a pretty good intuitive idea how probability is to be interpreted, and this enables us to postpone examining these differences until we have a little more common vocabulary and background.

IV.1
GENERAL MEANING OF PROBABILITY

The idea of probability has to do with such intuitive notions as likelihood, possibility—impossibility, and certainty—uncertainty. In fact, our language is full of terms that are intuitive relatives of the mathematical idea of probability. Probability theory provides a systematic way to deal with events whose occurrence is uncertain. It is useful when one wishes to speak as precisely as possible about processes that are influenced by randomness.

IV.2
NOMENCLATURE FOR PROBABILITY CALCULATIONS

In computing probabilities, it is absolutely essential to have a standard nomenclature. Even with such a nomenclature, it is sometimes difficult to avoid ambiguity; with no standard at all, it is impossible.

IV.2.1. Random experiments

When some dynamic, event-generating process is initiated and the results are observed, this is, in a general sense, an experiment. When the outcome of such an experiment is uncertain, then it is called a *random experiment*. Tossing a coin, a die, or depositing a coin in a slot machine and observing the results can be viewed as random experiments.

When a scientific investigator makes a single observation, this may be considered a random experiment. This is because the result of the experiment is uncertain; otherwise there would be no need for it. Consequently, in principle at least, scientific data are amenable to probabilistic analysis.

A single performance of a random experiment will be called a *trial*.

OUTCOMES. On a single trial, one of two or more possible results will occur. These results are called *outcomes*. If a coin is tossed, one outcome is "heads," or simply H, the other is "tails," or T. If a die is rolled, one outcome is "3," and there are five others.

Outcomes must be atomistic in the sense that every relevant distinction among the results must be represented by a distinct outcome. The meaning of the term "relevant" is tricky, but we will try to make it clear in subsequent illustrations.

In designating the outcomes of a random experiment, it is important that they be chosen so that no more than one outcome can occur on a single trial. In other words, outcomes must be *mutually exclusive.*

SAMPLE SPACE. In computing probabilities, it is important to know *all* of the outcomes that are possible. In examining the possible results of a random experiment, one must be sure that the list of outcomes is *exhaustive.* Otherwise, errors are certain to occur when probabilities are calculated.

The set of all possible outcomes of a random experiment is called the sample space of that random experiment.

The outcomes of a sample space are also called *points.* This is simply because it is sometimes convenient to represent a sample space geometrically, designating each outcome as a point.

If a coin is tossed, the sample space contains two points, H and T. Since a sample space is a set, it will be denoted by enclosing the symbols representing its points in braces. This indicates that the outcomes of a sample space form an unordered set. Thus, the sample space for the random experiment "toss one coin" is represented equally well by {H, T} and by {T, H}, since the two sets are identical.

However, if two coins are tossed, each outcome must include the result for both coins. If a penny and a nickel are tossed, then (H, T) might be employed to denote one outcome. The first element of this outcome might refer to the penny, the second to the nickel. The parentheses indicate that an outcome that contains more than one element is an ordered set. Thus (H, T) is distinguished from (T, H), since in the first case H represents the result for the penny, whereas in the second H represents the result for the nickel. From this it can be seen that the entire sample space for the random experiment "toss a nickel and a penny" can be represented as follows: {(H, H), (H, T), (T, H), (T, T)}.

Even if the coins were both pennies, the outcome (H, T) must be distinguished from (T, H). This is true since it is always possible to distinguish the two coins (e.g., by putting a spot of nail polish on one), so that the structure of the random experiment "toss two pennies" is exactly the same as that for "toss a nickel and a penny." Furthermore, the random experiment "toss one penny twice" has the same structure (and, therefore, the same sample space) as each of the two experiments just mentioned. When a single coin is tossed twice, the first element of each outcome represents the result of the first toss, and the second element represents the second toss.

The seventeenth-century French mathematician-scientist d'Alembert overlooked the importance of order within outcomes and argued that in tossing two coins there are only three possibilities, two heads, one head, or no heads. As a consequence, his calculation of the probabilities was incorrect; he believed the probability of each of these outcomes to be 1/3. Apparently he was more mathematician than empirical scientist. Otherwise, a few hundred tosses of two coins almost certainly would have revealed his error.

D'Alembert's difficulty was that he failed to make a relevant distinction among outcomes. Not all of his outcomes were "atomistic," since he treated the distinguishable results (H, T) and (T, H) as the same.

Clearly, it is not necessary to limit the number of elements in an outcome to two. In tossing three coins, the sample space is {(H, H, H), (H, H, T), (H, T, H), (T, H, H,), (T, T, H), (T, H, T), (H, T, T), (T, T, T)}, in which each outcome contains a position for each coin. The sample space for the random experiment "toss one coin three times" is exactly the same.

If one answers a multiple-choice test item for which there are four alternatives, the sample space is {a, b, c, d}. If a test of two such items is given, the sample space is {(a, a), (a, b), (a, c), (a, d), (b, a), (b, b), (b, c), (b, d), (c, a), (c, b), (c, c), (c, d), (d, a), (d, b), (d, c), (d, d)}. For each outcome, the first position represents the response to Item 1, and the second represents the response to Item 2. Under these circumstances, it is clear that (a, d) $\neq$ (d, a), since Alternative a for Item 1 is certainly not the same as Alternative a for Item 2.

EVENTS. *A subset of a sample space is called an event.* That is, any collection of outcomes taken from a single sample space constitutes an event. For the experiment "toss two coins," the event "toss at least one head" is represented by {(H, H), (H, T), (T, H)}, since each of these outcomes and no other contains one or more heads. For the three-coin experiment, the event "toss exactly two heads" is represented by {(H, H, T), (H, T, H), (T, H, H)}, since each of these outcomes and no other satisfies the "exactly two heads" condition. For the two-item test experiment, the event "choose Alternative a for the first item" is {(a, a), (a, b), (a, c), (a, d)}, and {(a, a), (b, b), (c, c), (d, d)} represents the event "choose the same alternative for both items." Thus, from any clear verbal description of an event, one can construct the event symbolically if the sample space is known.

An event is an *unordered* set. Consequently, when the outcomes contained in an event are listed, they are enclosed in braces.

Occurrence of an event. *An event is said to have occurred if one of its outcomes has been observed.* If the outcome (H, H) is observed, then the event "toss at least one head" has been observed, since (H, H) is contained in {(H, H), (H, T), (T, H)}. In the case of the two-item test, observing the outcome (c, c) means that the event "choose the same alternative for both items" has occurred.

The number of ways an event can occur equals the number of outcomes it contains. Thus, in the examples of the preceding paragraph, "toss at least one head" can occur in three ways, and "choose the same alternative for both items" of the multiple choice test can occur in four ways.

IV.3
PROBABILITY DEFINED IN TERMS OF THE SAMPLE SPACE

This section is devoted to introducing probability in terms of the sample space. The approach employed here is not the only one, but it is a systematic procedure that includes built-in safeguards for many of the pitfalls of probability calculations. We shall begin with a few examples.

If two coins are tossed, each of the four possible outcomes will have the same probability if the coins are fair and if they are tossed without favoritism. The assumption that the four outcomes are equiprobable is defended by considering the nature of the coins and the way they are tossed. If there are exactly four equiprobable outcomes, the probability that any one of them will occur is 1/4, and the sum of these four probabilities is 1.

Suppose that a random sample of size 2 is drawn from a population containing the elements 1, 2, and 3, sampling with replacement. A sample of size 2 is an outcome for this experiment, and the sample space is {(1, 1), (1, 2), (1, 3), (2, 1), (2, 2), (2, 3), (3, 1), (3, 2), (3, 3)}. Since the experiment involves drawing a *random* sample, the sample must be taken in such a way that each of the 9 samples has the same probability of being selected. Therefore, the probability that a given sample will be drawn is 1/9. Here, no argument about the structure of the experiment has been given to support the assertion of equiprobability. It has simply been asserted that sampling is random. The experiment might have consisted of drawing two slips of paper from a hat (replacing the first prior to drawing the second), taking pairs of digits between 1 and 3, inclusive, from a table of random numbers, or by rolling a die until exactly two numbers between 1 and 3 inclusive were observed. With a little care, any one of these procedures (and many others) could be expected to generate samples in such a way that the 9 possible samples each had probability 1/9.

Clearly, it is not always possible to assume that the outcomes have equal probabilities. The two-item, multiple-choice test mentioned earlier would have a sample space of equiprobable outcomes only if the alternatives for each item were thoroughly ambiguous or irrelevant, or if the individuals taking the test were utterly ignorant of the subject matter. Generally, one would have to get empirical estimates of the outcome probabilities for a sample space of this kind. Such estimates could be obtained by administering the test to a sample of persons and noting the proportion of individuals who chose each pair of alternatives (i.e., each outcome). These proportions could be treated as estimates of the outcome probabilities.

The essential point is that by a priori logical analysis, by empirical estimation, or by assumption, the probability of each outcome in the sample space must be designated. This may seem an odd statement to *precede* a definition of probability. However, as mentioned earlier and elaborated later in this chapter, one encounters serious disagreements as to the precise interpretation of *applications* of probability. There is no difficulty with the mathematics; that is well understood. The difficulty centers on the exact meaning of stating that the probability of a particular event *in the real world* is 0.5, 0.7, or some other value. The essential fact seems to be that the correct interpretation of applied probabilities depends ultimately upon intuition, and the only real safeguard against idiosyncratic intuition is consensus among those experienced in its use. And how does one acquire experience in its use prior to assimilating its meaning? By (1) calling upon everyday knowledge of the meaning of linguistic expressions of uncertainty (probable, likely) and ordinary experience with uncertain events and by (2) learning and applying the rules for combining and manipulating probabilities. In short, one gets a feeling for it. This may sound like raising oneself by one's boot straps—and there is no denying that it is—but the remarkable power and usefulness of probability seem to justify this approach, especially since there appears to be no real alternative.

In spite of the lack of definition of outcome probabilities, they do have two specific properties. First, *an outcome probability is a non-negative number.* Second, *the sum of all outcome probabilities in a given sample space must be unity.* From these two properties it can be seen that an outcome probability always lies between 0 and +1, inclusive.

Saying that the sum of the outcome probabilities must equal unity amounts to ensuring that some outcome occurs every time the random experiment is performed. Of course, this will be true only if no outcome has been overlooked. Furthermore, the requirement that outcome probabilities sum to 1 provides a rough check on whether or not a sample space and its outcome probabilities have been chosen correctly. However, this check is not foolproof.

IV.3. PROBABILITY IN TERMS OF SAMPLE SPACE

Now, suppose that the sample space for a random experiment has been defined and that a probability has been assigned to each of its outcomes. This done, it is usually the probability of an event that is of interest. *The sum of the probabilities of the outcomes contained in an event equals the probability of that event.*

In the two-coin experiment, the event "no heads" contains just one outcome (T, T). Since the sample space contains four equiprobable outcomes, the probability of "no heads" is 1/4. The event "at least one head" contains the three outcomes (H, H), (H, T), and (T, H), so that its probability is $1/4 + 1/4 + 1/4 = 3/4$. If a six-sided die is tossed, the sample space can be represented by $\{1, 2, 3, 4, 5, 6\}$. The probability of an even number, the event $\{2, 4, 6\}$, is $1/6 + 1/6 + 1/6 = 1/2$.

From these illustrations, it is clear that when the outcomes are equiprobable, the probability of an event is simply the number of outcomes in the event divided by the number of outcomes in the sample space. However, when outcome probabilities are unequal, this simple rule does not apply.

Table IV.1. Proportion of students giving each answer combination

Answer combination (outcome)	Proportion of students (probability)
(a, a)	.03
(a, b)	.02
(a, c)	.01
(a, d)	.05
(b, a)	.05
(b, b)	0
(b, c)	.10
(b, d)	.50
(c, a)	.03
(c, b)	0
(c, c)	0
(c, d)	.10
(d, a)	.03
(d, b)	.01
(d, c)	.02
(d, d)	.05
	1.00

The sample space for a two-item, multiple-choice test was described under "Sample Space" in Section IV.2.1. Suppose that this test has been given to 100 students and that the proportion giving each answer combination (outcome) has been determined. These results are shown in Table IV.1.

Notice first that the sum of the outcome probabilities is 1. This suggests that nothing is drastically amiss. Next, assume that according to the instructor's key the correct answers are "b" for the first item and "d" for the second. (Remember, the left-hand symbol in each outcome represents the response to the first item.) The data show that 50 percent of the students answered both items correctly, so that the event "perfect paper" is {(b, d)}, and its probability is 0.50. The probability that the first item is correct is 0.05 + 0 + 0.10 + 0.50 = 0.65, the sum of the probabilities of the outcomes contained in {(b, a), (b, b), (b, c), (b, d)}. The event "none correct" is {(a, a), (a, b), (a, c), (c, a), (c, b), (c, c), (d, a), (d, b), (d, c)}, and the sum of its outcome probabilities is 0.03 + 0.02 + 0.01 + 0.03 + 0 + 0 + 0.03 + 0.01 + 0.02 = 0.15. The event "at least one item correct" is {(b, a), (b, b), (b, c), (b, d), (a, d), (c, d), (d, d)}, and its probability is 0.05 + 0 + 0.10 + 0.50 + 0.05 + 0.10 + 0.05 = 0.85.

Before continuing, it is necessary to mention two special events that are contained in every sample space. These are the *impossible* or *null* event and the *certain* event. The impossible event contains no outcomes, and since an outcome must occur each time a random experiment is performed, its probability is 0. The certain event contains every outcome in the sample space, and its probability is 1.

In subsequent applications, it will often be convenient to have a brief notation for probability. Consequently, the symbol $\mathbf{P}(A)$ will be used to denote "the probability of the event A."

The approach taken in this introduction to probability may seem unnecessarily cumbersome, but a little facility in its use will go a long way toward solving some moderately difficult probability problems. As a rule of thumb, if you cannot write out the relevant sample space for a probability calculation, or at least visualize its structure, then it is unlikely that you understand the problem well enough to solve it. And if the sample space does not contain too many outcomes, it is nearly always a good investment of time to write it down completely.

IV.4

PROBLEMS ON SAMPLE SPACES, EVENTS, AND ELEMENTARY PROBABILITY CALCULATIONS

1. The random experiment is "toss four coins."
   a. Write out the sample space.
   b. How many outcomes does this sample space contain?

c. Write out the event "exactly two heads." What is its probability?
d. Write out the event "no more than two tails." What is its probability?
e. What is the probability of the impossible event for this experiment? Of the certain event?

2. The random experiment is "toss one coin and one six-sided die simultaneously."
   a. Write out the sample space.
   b. How many outcomes does this sample space contain?
   c. Write out the event "head." What is its probability?
   d. Write out the event "3." What is its probability?
   e. Write out the event "odd number (on the die)." What is its probability?
   f. Write out the event "heads and 3." What is its probability?
   g. Write out the event "tails or an even number (or both)." What is its probability?

3. Recall the two-item, multiple-choice test example and examine Table IV.1.
   a. Write out the event "second item correct." What is its probability?
   b. Write out the event "not a perfect paper." What is its probability?
   c. Write out the event "perfect paper *or* none correct." What is its probability?
   d. Write out the event "first item wrong *and* perfect paper." What is its probability?
   e. What is the random experiment referred to by the probabilities in a–d above?
   f. Comment on the implications of the method used to obtain the outcome probabilities for the sample space listed in Table IV.1.

4. A red, a blue, and a white marble are tossed randomly and simultaneously into a V-shaped trough.
   a. What is the probability that the white marble will be between the red and blue marbles when they come to rest?
   b. What is the probability that the red and white marbles will both come to rest to the left of the blue one?
   c. What is the probability that the red and blue marbles will be side by side, with no marble between them?
   d. Write out the appropriate sample space using r, w, and b for red, white, and blue, respectively.

5. Children sometimes play the following game: they hammer their right fist twice, and on the third time each of the two players forms a fist ("rock"), extends two fingers ("scissors"), or extends all fingers with the hand palm-down ("paper"). If paper and rock occur, then paper wins, since "paper covers rock." Similarly "rock breaks scissors" and "scissors cut paper." If both players make the same play, neither wins.
   a. Write out the sample space for this game.
   b. If you play "rock" and your opponent's choice is random, what is the probability that you will win?
   c. If your plays and those of your opponent are random, what is the probability that you will win on a given trial?

d. If the choice of plays is random for both players, what is the probability that neither will win on a given trial?
e. Suppose your opponent always plays "rock." What strategy should you adopt in order to maximize the number of times you win?
f. If you know that your opponent never plays "rock" and that he tosses a fair coin to choose between "scissors" and "paper," what is the probability that you will win if you never play "paper" and toss your own coin to choose between the other two?
g. With the opponent described in 5f, would it be better for you never to play "scissors" and to choose between "rock" and "paper" by tossing a coin? What is the probability that you will win if you adopt this strategy against this opponent?

IV.5

COMPOUND EVENTS

A fundamental and important part of probability theory is the specification of rules for finding the probability associated with two or more events when only the single-event probabilities are known. For instance, if the probability of the event A and the probability of the event B are known for a given random experiment, what is the probability that *A or B* will occur? This problem asks for the probability that an outcome in A, or in B, or in both will be observed. Similarly, one might want to know the probability that A but not B will occur, i.e., the probability that an outcome that is in A but not in B will occur. This section is devoted to discussing such compound events. In Section IV.8, rules will be described for determining compound-event probabilities from the probabilities of single events.

There are four fundamental ways of combining events. They correspond to the verbal relations *or*, *and*, *but not*, and *implies*. Each of these is defined, discussed, and illustrated in the following subsections.

IV.5.1. Union of events

If A and B are both events in a given sample space, then the union of A and B, $A \cup B$, is the event containing every outcome that is in A or in B or in both. The verbal equivalent of $A \cup B$ is "A or B."

First, notice that the union of two events is itself an event. For example, in the "roll-a-die" experiment, let the event $A = \{1, 3, 5\}$ and $B = \{2, 4, 6\}$. Then their union, $A \cup B$, is $\{1, 2, 3, 4, 5, 6\}$, the certain event. Since the union of two events is itself an event, the probability of the event $A \cup B$ is simply $1/6 + 1/6 + 1/6 + 1/6 + 1/6 + 1/6 = 1$, the sum of the probabilities of its six outcomes.

For the three-coin experiment, let $A = \{(\text{H, H, H})\}$ and $B = \{(\text{H, H, T}),$

(H, T, H), (T, H, H)}. Here A is the event "three heads" and B is "exactly two heads." The union of A and B is $A \cup B$ = {(H, H, H)} ∪ {(H, H, T), (H, T, H), (T, H, H)} = {(H, H, H), (H, H, T), (H, T, H), (T, H, H)}. Descriptively, $A \cup B$ is the event "two or more heads." Since the sample space for this experiment contains eight equiprobable outcomes, four of which are in $A \cup B$, the probability of $A \cup B$ is 4/8. If C = {(T, T, T)}, then $A \cup C$ = {(H, H, H)} ∪ {(T, T, T)} = {(H, H, H), (T, T, T)}, and the probability of $A \cup C$ is 2/8.

The idea of a union can be extended to any number of events. *The union of several events from the same sample space contains every outcome that appears in one or more of them.*

The union of A, B, and C is an event denoted by $A \cup B \cup C$, and it contains every outcome that is in A or in B or in C (or in any two or more of them). If A = {(H, H, H)}, B = {(H, H, T), (H, T, H), (T, H, H)}, and C = {(T, T, H), (T, H, T), (H, T, T)}, then $A \cup B \cup C$ = {(H, H, H), (H, H, T), (H, T, H), (T, H, H), (T, T, H), (T, H, T), (H, T, T)}, which can be described as "one or more heads." The probability of $A \cup B \cup C$ equals 7/8.

IV.5.2. Intersection of events

If an outcome that is common to two events occurs, then the two events are said to have occurred jointly or their intersection is said to have occurred. *If A and B are both events in a given sample space, then the intersection of A and B, $A \cap B$, is the event that contains every outcome that is in both A and B.* The probability that $A \cap B$ will occur is identical to the probability that A *and* B will occur simultaneously.

If A is the event "two or more heads" and B is the event "one or more tails" in the three-coin experiment, then the intersection of A and B is the event "exactly one tail." Symbolically, $A \cap B$ = {(H, H, H), (H, H, T), (H, T, H), (T, H, H)} ∩ {(T, H, H), (H, T, H), (H, H, T), (T, T, H), (T, H, T), (H, T, T), (T, T, T)} = {(T, H, H), (H, T, H), (H, H, T)}, and $\mathbf{P}(A \cap B) = 3/8$.

If two events have no outcomes in common, then their intersection is the impossible event. For instance, if C = {(H, H, H)} and D = {(T, T, T)}, then $C \cap D$ contains no outcomes. In the future, the impossible event will be designated by the Greek letter Φ, so that $C \cap D = \Phi$ in this example.

If $A_1, A_2, \ldots, A_i, \ldots, A_j, \ldots, A_r$ is a collection of r events in a single sample space, and if $A_i \cap A_j = \Phi$ for every pair of events A_i and A_j, then the r events are said to be disjoint or mutually exclusive. Thus, the r events are mutually exclusive if no two of them have a common outcome, and not more than one of them can be observed on a single trial of a random experiment.

Just as the union concept can be extended to more than two events, the intersection of three or more events is a useful idea, too. *The intersection of several events from the same sample space contains every outcome common to all of the events.*

The intersection of A, B, and C is denoted by $A \cap B \cap C$, and it contains every outcome that is in all three events. The intersection of the events "at least two heads," "at least one head," and "at least one tail" is the event "exactly one tail." Symbolically, if $A = \{(H, H, H), (H, H, T), (H, T, H), (T, H, H)\}$, $B = \{(H, H, H), (H, H, T), (H, T, H), (T, H, H), (H, T, T), (T, H, T), (T, T, H)\}$, and $C = \{(T, H, H), (H, T, H), (H, H, T), (T, T, H), (T, H, T), (H, T, T), (T, T, T)\}$, then $A \cap B \cap C = \{(H, H, T), (H, T, H), (T, H, H)\}$. Then, $\mathbf{P}(A \cap B \cap C)$ is 3/8, since it contains three of the eight equiprobable outcomes in the sample space.

IV.5.3. Difference between two events

If A and B are both events in the same sample space, then the difference between A and B, denoted $A \sim B$, is the event containing every outcome that is in A but not in B. When A has occurred but B has not, we know that $A \sim B$ has been observed.

In the three-coin experiment, if A is "two or more heads" and B is "three heads," then $A \sim B$ is "exactly two heads," i.e., $A \sim B = \{(H, H, H), (H, H, T), (H, T, H), (T, H, H)\} \sim \{(H, H, H)\} = \{(H, H, T), (H, T, H), (T, H, H)\}$, and $\mathbf{P}(A \sim B) = 3/8$.

Notice that $A \sim B$ is not generally the same as $B \sim A$. For the immediately preceding example, $B \sim A = \Phi$; there is no outcome in B that is not in A. This is an important property of the difference relation that distinguishes it from union and intersection: although $A \cup B = B \cup A$ and $A \cap B = B \cap A$, $A \sim B$ need not equal $B \sim A$.

A special form of the difference between events is of considerable importance in probability. This is the difference between the certain event, S, and a given event, A. *If A is an event in the sample space S, then the event $S \sim A$ is called the complement of the event A.* Verbally, the event $S \sim A$ means "not A," and it is sometimes written simply as $\sim A$.

In the three-coin experiment, the complement of $A =$ "at least one head" is the event "three tails," so that $S \sim A = \{(T, T, T)\}$. The probability of $S \sim A$ is 1/8.

IV.5.4. Implication of one event by another

Sometimes the occurrence of one event guarantees that another has also occurred. For instance, if "three heads" has occurred, then it is certain that "at least one head" has occurred. *If A and B are events in a single sample space, and if A is a subset of B, denoted $A \subset B$, then the event A is said to imply B.*

Since {(H, H, H)} ⊂ {(H, H, H), (H, H, T), (H, T, H), (T, H, H), (T, T, H), (T, H, T), (H, T, T)}, if "three heads" is observed, then "at least one head" must have occurred, as well.

Notice that according to the definition of $A \subset B$, an event implies itself. In other words, $A \subset A$. Furthermore, if $A \subset B$ *and* $B \subset A$, then A must be identical to B.

Like the difference relation, the implication relation is asymmetrical. The fact that A is contained in B does not mean that B is necessarily contained in A.

IV.5.5. Using diagrams in conceptualizing compound events

As an aid to conceptualizing compound events and computing their probabilities, it is frequently helpful to use a type of diagram devised by the mathematician John Venn and called a Venn diagram. This is done by representing the sample space and each event by a bounded area, as indicated in Figure IV.1. Here, the sample space is shown along with the two events, A and B. The intersection of A and B is represented by the single crosshatched areas of overlap. The union of A and B is the area bounded by the broken line. The doubly crosshatched portion of A is

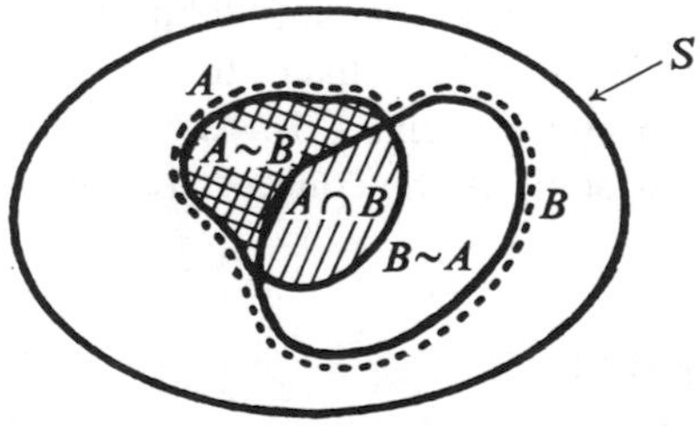

Figure IV.1

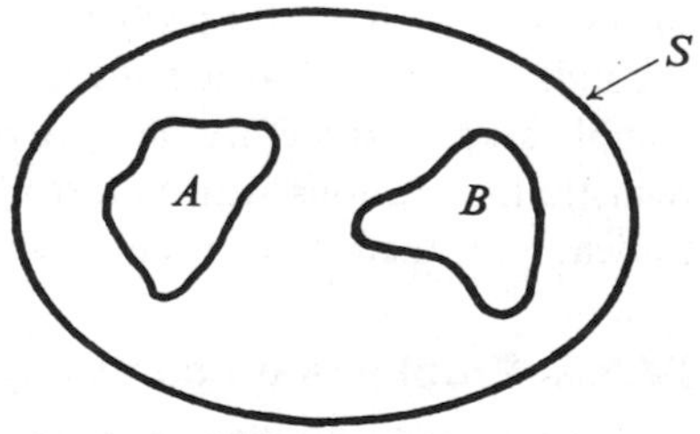

Figure IV.2

$A \sim B$. The portion of B that is not crosshatched is $B \sim A$. The complement of A, $S \sim A$, is the area of S that is not crosshatched at all. It can be seen from this diagram that A and B are *not* mutually exclusive.

In Figure IV.2, A and B are shown as mutually exclusive, i.e., $A \cap B = \Phi$. In this case, $A \sim B = A$ and $B \sim A = B$. The union of A and B is represented by the total area of A and B.

Another special case is conveniently illustrated by the use of Venn diagrams. This is the situation in which one event is a subset of another. In Figure IV.3, all of the outcomes in A are also in B, so that the event A implies B. Under this condition, notice that $A \cap B = A$ and $A \cup B = B$.

Venn diagrams are useful in conceptualizing the relations among

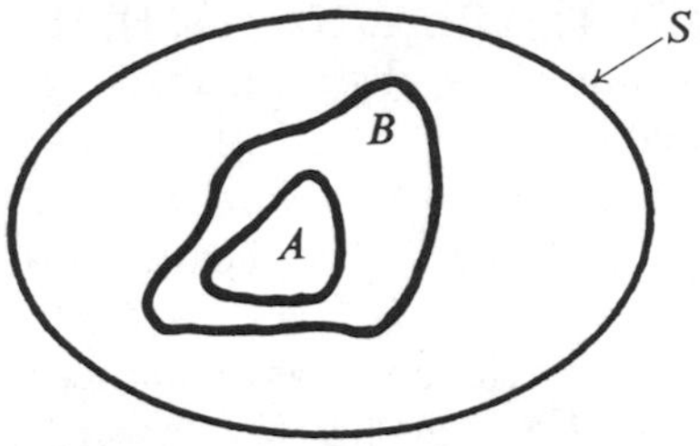

Figure IV.3

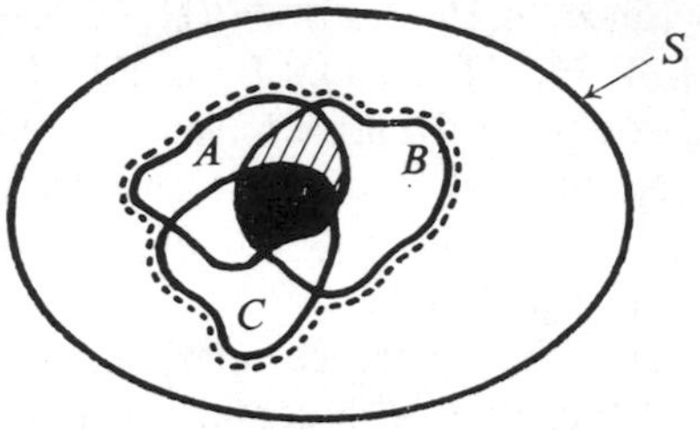

Figure IV.4

three or more events, too. In Figure IV.4, three overlapping events are illustrated. Here, the blacked-out area represents $A \cap B \cap C$. The blacked-out area plus the crosshatched area is $A \cap B$. The area contained by the broken line represents $A \cup B \cup C$, and the portion of A that is neither blacked-out nor crosshatched represents $A \sim B$.

Many other relations among events can be illustrated by using diagrams of this sort, and they are extremely helpful in understanding many problems in probability.

So far, most of the illustrations and problems have come from simple games of chance. There are two reasons for this. First, the gambling casino was the first and probably remains the best probability laboratory. Second, examples that are more realistic or useful are likely to be more complicated, and we are not yet ready to attack them. However, more realistic illustrations will be introduced as soon as the concepts required to deal with them have been presented.

IV.5.6. Problems on compound events

1. The following questions refer to any sample space.
   a. If $A = B$, then what does each of the following equal?
      i. $A \sim B$
      ii. $A \cap B$
      iii. $A \cup B$
   b. If S is a sample space, what does each of the following equal?
      i. $S \sim \Phi$
      ii. $S \cap \Phi$
      iii. $S \cup \Phi$
      iv. $S \cup A$ for any A
      v. $S \cap A$ for any A
   c. If $A \subset B$, is $A = B$?
   d. If $A = B$, does $A \subset B$?
   e. If $A \cup B = A$, does $B \subset A$?
   f. Does $S \subset S$?
   g. If $A \subset B$, what does each of the following equal?
      i. $A \sim B$
      ii. $A \cap B$
      iii. $A \cup B$

h. If $A \subset B$ and $B \subset C$, what does each of the following equal?

i. $A \cap B$	v. $B \cup C$
ii. $A \cap B \cap C$	vi. $B \sim C$
iii. $A \cap C$	vii. $C \sim (A \cap B \cap C)$
iv. $A \cup B \cup C$	viii. $B \sim (B \cap C)$

i. Using *one* Venn diagram, illustrate A, B, and C so that all three of the following conditions are satisfied: (1) $A \cap B \neq \Phi$, (2) $B \cap C = C$, and (3) $A \cap C = \Phi$.

j. Using one Venn diagram, illustrate A, B, C, and D so that all six of the following conditions are satisfied: (1) $A \cap B \neq \Phi$, (2) $B \cap C \neq \Phi$, (3) $A \cap C \neq \Phi$, (4) $A \cap D = \Phi$, (5) $B \cap D \neq \Phi$, and (6) $D \subset C$.

k. Show with Venn diagrams that $A \sim B$ is equal to $A \cap (S \sim B)$.

2. For the following questions, the probability experiment is "roll two dice." Unless otherwise specified, when an event is designated by a number, it refers to the sum of the spots on both dice.
   a. What is the sample space? How many outcomes does it contain?
   b. Write out the event "7." What is its probability?
   c. Write out the union of "7" and "11." Write out the intersection of "7" and "11." What is the probability of this intersection? What is the probability of the union?
   d. Write out the difference between "7" and "a 3 on either die." What is the probability of this difference?
   e. Write out the intersection of "7" and "a 3 on either die." What is the probability of this intersection?
   f. What is the complement of "a number less than 11?" What is the probability of this complement?
   g. What is the intersection of "snake eyes" and "box cars?" What is the probability of this intersection?
   h. What is the probability of the union of "snake eyes" and "box cars?"
   i. Write out the intersection of "7," "a 3 on either die," and "a 4 on either die." What is the probability of this intersection?
   j. Write out the union of the three events given in i and give its probability.
   k. What is the difference between the three events given in i?
3. For the following questions, the probability experiment is "toss one die and one coin simultaneously."
   a. Write out the event "6." What is its probability?
   b. Write out the event "head." What is its probability?
   c. Write out the event "value less than 3 on the die." What is its probability?
   d. Write out the union of items b and c (above). What is its probability?
   e. Write out the intersection of b and c. What is its probability?
   f. Write out the difference between b and c. What is its probability?
   g. Write out the union of b, c, and the event "obtain a 1 on the die." What is its probability?
   h. What is the event "value on the die less than 3 or greater than 2?"
   i. Write out the event "a head and a 6." What is its probability?
   j. If a head is assigned the value 1 and a tail is 0, write out the event "coin and die have equal values." What is its probability?

IV.6

CONDITIONAL PROBABILITY

Of the many fruitful ideas in probability theory, few are as widely useful as conditional probability. Furthermore, it is a simple concept that can be understood easily with the tools now at our disposal. However, its simplicity should not lead one to the conclusion that it is unworthy of careful attention. It occupies a prominent position in the logic of statistical induction, and conditional probability is a crucial idea in many formulations of psychological theory.

IV.6.1. Introduction of conditional probability

Suppose you know that an event, B, has occurred, and you are asked to determine the probability of a second event, A. This amounts to reducing the sample space to B, since if an outcome in B has been observed, an outcome in $S \sim B$ is impossible. For example, in the three-coin experiment, if you know that "two or more heads" has occurred and you are asked to determine the probability of "three heads," the sample space has been reduced to {(H, H, H), (H, H, T), (H, T, H), (T, H, H)}, which contains only four outcomes instead of eight. Given this reduced sample space, the probability of "three heads" is simply 1/4. This is the conditional probability of "three heads" given the occurrence of the event "two or more heads."

If a single die is cast and "some number greater than 3" results, what is the probability that "6" will occur? The reduced sample space is {4, 5, 6}, so that the conditional probability of a 6 given a number greater than 3 is 1/3.

The computation of conditional probability can be illustrated further by use of the Venn diagram in Figure IV.5. If it is known that B has occurred, then the only outcomes in A that are possible are those in $A \cap B$. Thus, the conditional probability of A given B reduces to the probability of $A \cap B$ given the reduced sample space, B. If A and B are events in a sample space of equiprobable outcomes, and if $A \cap B$ contains c out-

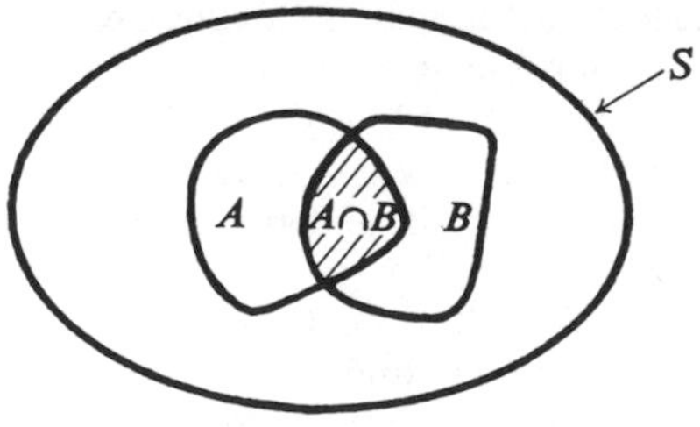

Figure IV.5

comes and B contains b, then the conditional probability of A given B is

$$\mathbf{P}(A \mid B) = \frac{c}{b}.$$

This states that the conditional probability of A given B equals the ratio of the number of equiprobable outcomes that are in both A and B to the number in B. The notation $\mathbf{P}(A \mid B)$ is read "the conditional probability of A given B" or simply "the probability of A given B."

If the numerator and denominator of the right-hand side of this formula are divided by the number of equiprobable outcomes in the entire sample space (call that number s), the result is

$$\mathbf{P}(A \mid B) = \frac{c/s}{b/s}.$$

Since $c/s = \mathbf{P}(A \cap B)$ and $b/s = \mathbf{P}(B)$, the conditional probability of A given B is

$$\mathbf{P}(A \mid B) = \frac{\mathbf{P}(A \cap B)}{\mathbf{P}(B)}.$$

Examination of Figure IV.5 should provide some intuitive justification for this conclusion.

Now, what about the case of unequal outcome probabilities? The idea is the same. If B has occurred, the sample space has been narrowed to the outcomes in B, and the only outcomes in A that are possible are those in $A \cap B$. Thus,

$$\mathbf{P}(A \mid B) = \frac{\text{sum of the probabilities of outcomes in } A \cap B}{\text{sum of the probabilities of outcomes in } B}.$$

The numerator of this formula for conditional probability is equivalent to $\mathbf{P}(A \cap B)$ and the denominator to $\mathbf{P}(B)$, so that

$$\mathbf{P}(A \mid B) = \frac{\mathbf{P}(A \cap B)}{\mathbf{P}(B)}.$$

All of this is summed up in the following statement. *If A and B are events in a given sample space and* $\mathbf{P}(B) \neq 0$, *then the conditional probability of A given the occurrence of B is*

$$\mathbf{P}(A \mid B) = \frac{\mathbf{P}(A \cap B)}{\mathbf{P}(B)}. \qquad [\text{IV.1}]$$

Since this definition makes no sense at all if B cannot occur, the conditional probability of A given B is undefined when $\mathbf{P}(B) = 0$.

Referring to the two-alternative, multiple-choice test data of Table IV.1, what is the conditional probability of "a perfect paper" given "the first item is correct"? If the first of these events is designated A and the second B, the question asks for

$$\mathbf{P}(A \mid B) = \frac{\mathbf{P}(A \cap B)}{\mathbf{P}(B)}.$$

Since $\mathbf{P}(A \cap B) = 0.50$ and $\mathbf{P}(B) = 0.05 + 0 + 0.10 + 0.50 = 0.65$,

$$\mathbf{P}(A \mid B) = \frac{\mathbf{P}(A \cap B)}{\mathbf{P}(B)} = \frac{0.50}{0.65} = 0.77.$$

In short, if a person is selected randomly from among those who got Item 1 correct, the probability is 0.77 that he got a perfect paper. But if nothing is known about a person's test performance, the probability of a perfect paper is only 0.50. These results can be interpreted as showing some connection between the two items of the test, i.e., getting Item 1 right increases the probability that both items are correct.

Conditional probabilities are *not* symmetrical. In general $\mathbf{P}(A \mid B)$ will not equal $\mathbf{P}(B \mid A)$. This is easily seen by inspecting the two formulas,

$$\mathbf{P}(A \mid B) = \frac{\mathbf{P}(A \cap B)}{\mathbf{P}(B)} \quad \text{and} \quad \mathbf{P}(B \mid A) = \frac{\mathbf{P}(A \cap B)}{\mathbf{P}(A)}.$$

Notice the difference between the denominators.

Before proceeding, it will be helpful to examine conditional probability in two special cases.

Suppose that A and B are mutually exclusive events. What is the conditional probability of A given B? From Figure IV.2 and Formula [IV.1], it is clear that if B has occurred, A cannot occur at all, so that the conditional probability of A given B is 0. Thus, if $A \cap B = \Phi$, then $\mathbf{P}(B \mid A) = 0$ and $\mathbf{P}(A \mid B) = 0$.

Another special case occurs when $A \subset B$. If $A \subset B$, then $A \cap B = A$, so that the conditional probability of B given A is

$$\mathbf{P}(B \mid A) = \frac{\mathbf{P}(A \cap B)}{\mathbf{P}(A)} = \frac{\mathbf{P}(A)}{\mathbf{P}(A)} = 1.$$

Of course, this is what is meant when we say that $A \subset B$ means "A implies B."

IV.6.2. Problems on conditional probability

1. The random experiment for the following problems is "toss a coin and a six-sided die simultaneously."
   a. What is the probability of a 6 on the die given heads on the coin?
   b. If heads is assigned the value 1 and tails the value 0, what is the probability of a sum (coin + die) of 5 given the die shows 5 spots?
   c. Given 1 on the die, what is the probability the coin falls tails?

2. The random experiment for the following problems is "roll two six-sided dice." Unless otherwise specified, events designated by a number refer to the sum of the spots on the two dice.
   a. Given that the faces of the two dice are identical, what is the probability of the event "6"?
   b. If the event "7" occurs, what is the probability that at least one die (either one) shows two spots?
   c. Given that the sum of the two dice exceeds 7, what is the probability of "11 or 12"?
   d. If A = "sum of two dice greater than 7" and B = "sum of two dice less than 11," what is the conditional probability of A and B (i.e., $A \cap B$) given that at least one die (either one) shows four spots?
3. A couple has two children. At least one of them is a boy. What is the probability that both are boys? (Assume that **P**(boy) = **P**(girl) = 1/2.)
4. A couple has two children. The first-born is a boy. What is the probability that both of their children are boys? Is this different from Problem 3?

IV.6.3. A problem in psychodiagnosis, Part I

In order to illustrate further the use of conditional probability, a problem in differential psychodiagnosis will be introduced. Later, this analysis will be extended to highlight some very real problems associated with the use of diagnostic tests, as well as to illustrate a number of probability calculations. It should be added that this kind of analysis is applicable to classification problems other than clinical diagnosis.

Suppose that you work in a clinical organization dealing with a relatively stable patient population, and that the Archimedes spiral aftereffect illusion is to be used to differentiate the functionally ill (F) from the brain-damaged (B). Page et al[1] found for their samples that 85 percent of the functionally ill reported the spiral aftereffect illusion (A) whereas 60 percent of the brain-damaged failed to report it ($\sim A$). For their data, then,

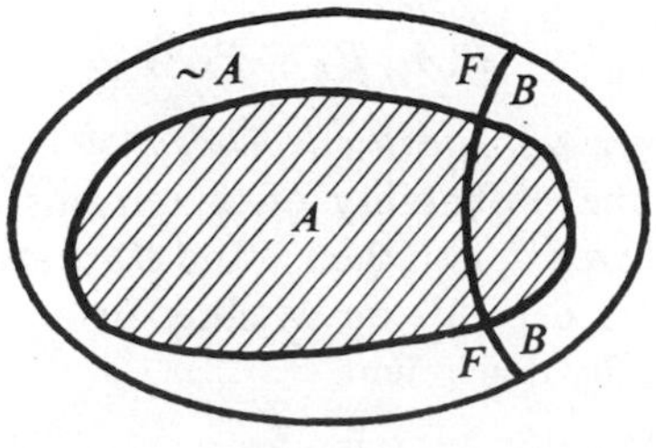

Figure IV.6

[1] Page, H. A., G. Rakita, H. K. Kaplan, and N. B. Smith, "Another application of the spiral aftereffect in the determination of brain damage." *J. Consult. Psychol.* **21**, 89–91, 1957.

the probability that the illusion would be reported by a functionally ill patient was $\mathbf{P}(A \mid F) = 0.85$, and the probability that it would not be reported by a brain-damaged patient was $\mathbf{P}(\sim A \mid B) = 0.60$. The Venn diagram in Figure IV.6 illustrates these probabilities.

These two conditional probabilities, $\mathbf{P}(A \mid F)$ and $\mathbf{P}(\sim A \mid B)$ will be referred to as the *detection rates* for functional illness and brain damage, respectively. Notice that the majority of brain-damaged patients do *not* report the aftereffect, whereas most of the functionally ill *do*.

These two figures certainly tell us something about the usefulness of the test, but $\mathbf{P}(F \mid A)$ and $\mathbf{P}(B \mid \sim A)$ are even more pertinent. In clinical practice, the results of the aftereffect are given, and it is the probability of the diagnostic category that is of interest. How can $\mathbf{P}(B \mid \sim A)$ and $\mathbf{P}(F \mid A)$ be calculated from the information given? Furthermore, how can we estimate the proportion of correct diagnoses obtainable using this test? With a little more sophistication in the use of probability, we will be able to answer such questions.

IV.7
STATISTICAL INDEPENDENCE OF EVENTS

The idea of "independent events" is very widely used. However, there are many different meanings for this term. The general idea, of course, is that when two events are independent, the occurrence of one has no influence on the other. Here, the term "independence" will be given precise meaning.

IV.7.1. Definition of statistical independence of events

In probability theory, statistical independence of events is said to hold when the occurrence of one event has no influence on the *probability* that the other will occur. *If A and B are events in a given sample space and* $\mathbf{P}(B) \neq 0$, *then A and B are statistically independent if*

$$\mathbf{P}(A \mid B) = \mathbf{P}(A). \qquad \text{[IV.2]}$$

Otherwise, A and B are statistically dependent.

This says that if the probability of A remains unchanged regardless of whether B has occurred or not, then A and B are statistically independent. If the probability of A depends on whether or not B has occurred, then A and B are statistically dependent.

IV.7.2. Illustrations of statistical independence of events

When a pair of dice are rolled, are the event "either die is a 6" and the event "7" statistically independent? To answer this question, let A = "either die is a 6" and B = "7". Then, if $\mathbf{P}(A \mid B) = \mathbf{P}(A)$, statistical independence will have been affirmed. Otherwise, these two events are statistically dependent.

Since $A = \{(1, 6), (2, 6), (3, 6), (4, 6), (5, 6), (6, 6), (6, 1), (6, 2), (6, 3), (6, 4), (6, 5)\}$ contains 11 outcomes and $B = \{(1, 6), (2, 5), (3, 4), (4, 3), (5, 2), (6, 1)\}$ contains 6 outcomes, $\mathbf{P}(A) = 11/36$ and $\mathbf{P}(B) = 6/36$. $A \cap B$ contains only the outcomes (1, 6) and (6, 1), so $\mathbf{P}(A \cap B) = 2/36$. Then

$$\mathbf{P}(A \mid B) = \frac{\mathbf{P}(A \cap B)}{\mathbf{P}(B)} = \frac{2/36}{6/36} = \frac{1}{3},$$

which is *not* equal to 11/36, the probability of A. Therefore, the events A and B are statistically *dependent*, i.e., the probability of obtaining a 6 on either die is altered by the knowledge that a 7 has occurred.

On the other hand, the event A = "first die is a 1" and B = "7" are statistically independent. Since $A = \{(1, 1), (1, 2), (1, 3), (1, 4), (1,5), (1, 6)\}$ contains 6 outcomes, $B = \{(1, 6), (2, 5), (3, 4), (4, 3), (5, 2), (6, 1)\}$ contains 6 outcomes, and $A \cap B = \{(1, 6)\}$ contains one outcome, $\mathbf{P}(A) = 6/36$, $\mathbf{P}(B) = 6/36$, and $\mathbf{P}(A \cap B) = 1/36$. Then,

$$\mathbf{P}(A \mid B) = \frac{\mathbf{P}(A \cap B)}{\mathbf{P}(B)} = \frac{1/36}{6/36} = \frac{1}{6},$$

which equals the probability of A. This demonstrates the statistical independence of A and B.

Statistical independence is a form of proportionality. This is quite easy to see in the case of equiprobable outcomes. If the proportion of outcomes in B that are also in A equals the proportion in the sample space that are in A, then A and B are statistically independent. In the highly schematized Venn diagram of Figure IV.7, if each square of the grid represents one outcome, then A and B are statistically independent, since

$$\mathbf{P}(A \mid B) = \frac{\mathbf{P}(A \cap B)}{\mathbf{P}(B)} = \frac{4/160}{16/160} = \frac{1}{4},$$

which equals $\mathbf{P}(A) = 40/160$.

If two events, A and B, are statistically independent, then in addition to the relation $\mathbf{P}(A) = \mathbf{P}(A \mid B)$, it is also true that $\mathbf{P}(B) = \mathbf{P}(B \mid A)$. This can be verified for the example of Figure IV.7, and it is easily demonstrated algebraically. If

$$\mathbf{P}(A) = \mathbf{P}(A \mid B),$$

then

$$\mathbf{P}(A) = \frac{\mathbf{P}(A \cap B)}{\mathbf{P}(B)}.$$

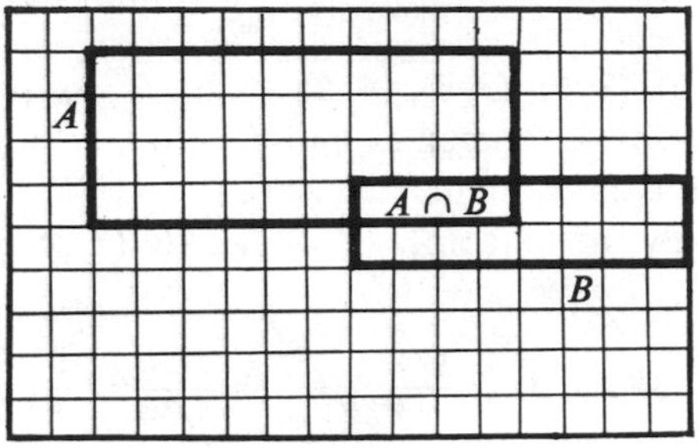

Figure IV.7

and multiplying both sides by $\mathbf{P}(B)/\mathbf{P}(A)$, we obtain

$$\mathbf{P}(B) = \frac{\mathbf{P}(A \cap B)}{\mathbf{P}(A)} = \mathbf{P}(B \mid A).$$

The last line is what we set out to show, i.e., that if A and B are statistically independent, then $\mathbf{P}(A) = \mathbf{P}(A \mid B)$ *and* $\mathbf{P}(B) = \mathbf{P}(B \mid A)$.

Thus, in the example of Figure IV.7, the statistical independence of A and B can be demonstrated by showing that $\mathbf{P}(B \mid A) = \mathbf{P}(B)$, i.e.,

$$\mathbf{P}(B \mid A) = \frac{\mathbf{P}(A \cap B)}{\mathbf{P}(A)} = \frac{4/160}{40/160} = \frac{1}{10},$$

which equals 16/160, the probability of B.

Table IV.2. College attendance, by sex—first data set

Sex	Attended college? Yes	No	Total
Male	50	50	100
Female	50	50	100
Total	100	100	200

Statistical independence will be illustrated further for the artificial data on college attendance by sex that appears in Table IV.2. This table is simply a compact description of the sample space for the experiment "select a person at random from a particular group of 200, determine his sex and whether he attended college." Each outcome consists of two items of information: the sex of the person and his answer to the question. The table tells us that the sample space contains 50 outcomes of the form (male, yes), 50 of (male, no), 50 of (female, yes), and 50 of (female, no). The random experiment is "draw one person randomly," so that the 200 outcomes are equiprobable.

Now, are the events "attended college" and "male" statistically independent? If the first of these events is labeled A and the second B, then $\mathbf{P}(A) = 100/200$, $\mathbf{P}(B) = 100/200$, and $\mathbf{P}(A \cap B) = 50/200$. The conditional probability of A given B is

$$\mathbf{P}(A \mid B) = \frac{\mathbf{P}(A \cap B)}{\mathbf{P}(B)} = \frac{50/200}{100/200} = \frac{1}{2},$$

and $\mathbf{P}(A) = 100/200 = 1/2$. Since $\mathbf{P}(A) = \mathbf{P}(A \mid B)$, the events "male" and "attended college" are statistically independent.

One way of interpreting this result is to say that college attendance is not predictable from knowledge of sex. That is, it makes no difference whether an individual's sex is known or not, the probability that he attended college is 1/2. For these data, then, it can be said that college attendance and sex are uncorrelated.

Table IV.3 provides another set of artificial data for which sex and college attendance are again uncorrelated or statistically independent.

Table IV.3. College attendance, by sex—second data set

	Attended college?		
Sex	Yes	No	Total
Male	60	40	100
Female	30	20	50
Total	90	60	150

If A = "yes" and B = "male," then $\mathbf{P}(A) = 90/150$, $\mathbf{P}(B) = 100/150$, $\mathbf{P}(A \cap B) = 60/150$, and

$$\mathbf{P}(A \mid B) = \frac{60/150}{100/150} = \frac{3}{5}.$$

Since this equals $\mathbf{P}(A) = 90/150$, statistical independence has been demonstrated.

The artificial data of Table IV.4 are somewhat more realistic in that sex and college attendance are correlated or statistically *dependent*. The conditional probability of college attendance given that an individual is a male is 60/100; for a female, the probability of college attendance is 20/100. If one were to predict whether or not a person selected randomly

Table IV.4. College attendance, by sex—third data set

Sex	Attended college? Yes	No	Total
Male	60	40	100
Female	20	80	100
Total	80	120	200

from among the males had attended college, the best bet would be that he had. For a randomly selected female, however, the best prediction is that she has not attended college, since 80 percent of the females have not. Of course, predictions made on the basis of sex alone would not always be correct, but following this procedure would lead to a higher average number of correct predictions than could be expected if sex were ignored. If predictions are made without knowledge of the individual's sex, then the best procedure is always to predict that an individual has *not* attended college since the majority (120 out of the 200) have not.

From the preceding discussion, it can be seen that statistical independence and predictability are closely related ideas.

Before leaving statistical independence, its relationship to the idea of mutually exclusive events should be mentioned. Intuition suggests that two events are "independent" if they are mutually exclusive, but they are *not* statistically independent. Suppose that $A \cap B = \Phi$, that $\mathbf{P}(A) \neq 0$, and that $\mathbf{P}(B) \neq 0$. Then

$$\mathbf{P}(A \mid B) = \frac{\mathbf{P}(A \cap B)}{\mathbf{P}(B)} = 0,$$

and $\mathbf{P}(A \mid B) \neq \mathbf{P}(A)$. Therefore, *if A and B are mutually exclusive, $\mathbf{P}(A) \neq 0$, and $\mathbf{P}(B) \neq 0$, then A and B are statistically dependent.* In other words, mutually exclusive events having nonzero probability are always statistically dependent.

Knowing that $A \subset B$, $B \subset A$, or $A \cap B \neq \Phi$ is insufficient for deciding whether A and B are statistically independent or not. When any one of these three conditions is known to hold, then it is necessary to find whether $\mathbf{P}(A \mid B) = \mathbf{P}(A)$ (or whether $\mathbf{P}(B \mid A) = \mathbf{P}(B)$) in order to choose between statistical independence and statistical dependence.

IV.7.3. Problems on statistical independence of events

The first three questions refer to the probability experiments described in Section IV.6.2.

IV.7. STATISTICAL INDEPENDENCE OF EVENTS

1. For a–c in Problem 1, determine whether the two events mentioned are statistically independent.
2. Follow the same instructions for a–c in Problem 2.
3. Follow the same instructions for 3.
4. The random experiment is to draw a random sample from a finite population consisting of the elements 1, 2, and 3.
   a. When sampling with replacement, is the event "first sample element is a 1" statistically independent of "second sample element is a 1"?
   b. When sampling without replacement, is the event "first sample element is a 1" statistically independent of "second sample element is a 1"?
   c. Summarize your conclusions from a and b.
5. Dr. Nancy Wertheimer[2] has reported data on the incidence of a history of rheumatic disease in schizophrenic patients. In a sample of 1942 patients, she found 6 percent with a known history of rheumatic disease, 21.8 percent with grimacing included in the psychiatric description, and 1.8 percent for whom both grimacing and a history of rheumatic fever were reported.
   a. From these data, enter the appropriate frequencies (to the nearest integer) in the following two-by-two table:

	Grimacing	No grimacing
History of rheumatic disease		
No history of rheumatic disease		

   b. What is the probability of grimacing in this schizophrenic group?
   c. What is the probability of a history of rheumatic fever in this schizophrenic group?
   d. What is the probability experiment to which the probabilities of b and c refer?
   e. What is the conditional probability of grimacing given a history of rheumatic disease?
   f. Are grimacing and a history of rheumatic disease statistically independent events in this schizophrenic group? Demonstrate the correctness of your answer.
   g. Are no grimacing and no history of rheumatic disease statistically independent for this schizophrenic group? Demonstrate the correctness of your answer.
   h. What do the results of f and g mean?

[2] "Rheumatic Schizophrenia: An Epidemiological Study," *Archives of General Psychiatry* **4**, 579–596, 1961.

IV.8

COMPOUND-EVENT PROBABILITIES

Methods for computing the probability of compound events by summing outcome probabilities have already been introduced. However, the following methods often provide helpful shortcuts in calculation, and, further, they make it possible to compute probabilities of compound events in cases where the complete sample space is unknown or very tedious to tabulate. In fact, these methods are applicable when the probabilities associated with single outcomes are not known at all.

IV.8.1. Probability of a union of events

If A and B are mutually exclusive events in a given sample space, then the probability that A or B will occur is

$$\mathbf{P}(A \cup B) = \mathbf{P}(A) + \mathbf{P}(B). \qquad [IV.3]$$

Notice that this rule applies only when $A \cap B = \Phi$.

In the three-coin experiment, if $A = \{(H, H, H)\}$ and $B = \{(T, T, T)\}$, then the probability that "all three coins are alike" is

$$\mathbf{P}(A \cup B) = \mathbf{P}(A) + \mathbf{P}(B) = 1/8 + 1/8 = 1/4.$$

This formula can be extended to the union of three or more events. *If $A_1, A_2, \ldots, A_r$ are all mutually exclusive events in a given sample space, then the probability that at least one of them will occur is*

$$\mathbf{P}(A_1 \cup A_2 \cup \cdots \cup A_r) = \mathbf{P}(A_1) + \mathbf{P}(A_2) + \cdots + \mathbf{P}(A_r). \qquad [IV.4]$$

For example, the probability of rolling 7, 11, or 12 with two dice is

$$\begin{aligned}\mathbf{P}(7 \cup 11 \cup 12) &= \mathbf{P}(7) + \mathbf{P}(11) + \mathbf{P}(12)\\ &= 1/6 + 1/18 + 1/36 = 1/4,\end{aligned}$$

since these three events are mutually exclusive.

But what about the case of overlapping events? What is the rule when the events have outcomes in common? In order to develop this formula, the Venn diagram of Figure IV.8 will prove helpful. From this diagram it can be seen that if $\mathbf{P}(A) + \mathbf{P}(B)$ is computed, the probabilities of outcomes common to A and B will have been included *twice*, since they are included in $\mathbf{P}(A)$ as well as in $\mathbf{P}(B)$. However, if the sum of the outcome probabilities common to A and B is subtracted from $\mathbf{P}(A) + \mathbf{P}(B)$, then the probability of each outcome enters only once. *If A and B are events in a given sample space, then the probability that A or B* (or both) *will occur is*

$$\mathbf{P}(A \cup B) = \mathbf{P}(A) + \mathbf{P}(B) - \mathbf{P}(A \cap B). \qquad [IV.5]$$

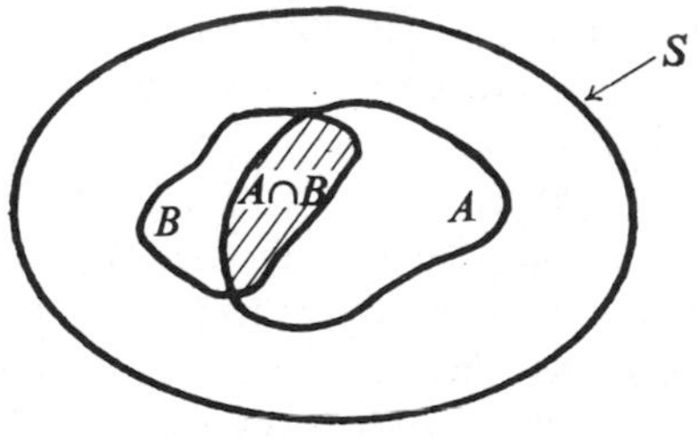

Figure IV.8

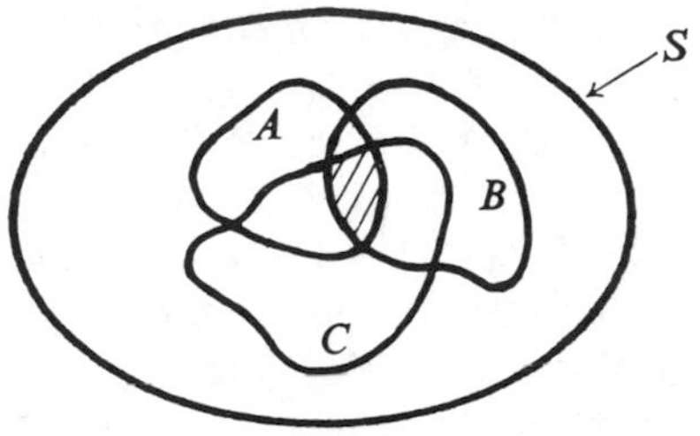

Figure IV.9

If A and B are mutually exclusive, this formula reduces to Formula [IV.3], since $\mathbf{P}(A \cap B)$ will be zero.

If a coin is tossed three times, the probability of "at least two heads" or "at least one tail" can be computed using this rule. Let

A = at least two heads = {(H, H ,H), (H, H, T), (H, T, H), (T, H, H)}
B = at least one tail = {(T, H, H), (H, T, H), (H, H, T), (T, T, H), (T, H, T), (H, T, T), (T, T, T)},

and $A \cap B$ = two heads and one tail = {(H, H, T), (H, T, H), (T, H, H)}, Then, $\mathbf{P}(A) = 1/2$, $\mathbf{P}(B) = 7/8$, and $\mathbf{P}(A \cap B) = 3/8$, so that

$$\mathbf{P}(A \cup B) = \mathbf{P}(A) + \mathbf{P}(B) - \mathbf{P}(A \cap B) = 1/2 + 7/8 - 3/8 = 1.$$

By simply counting the number of outcomes in "at least two heads or at least one tail" and dividing by the number of outcomes in the sample space, this result can be verified.

The Venn diagram in Figure IV.9 will be used to develop a formula for $\mathbf{P}(A \cup B \cup C)$. First, note that A, B, and C overlap and that if $\mathbf{P}(A) + \mathbf{P}(B) + \mathbf{P}(C)$ is computed, the probabilities of the intersections $A \cap B$, $A \cap C$, and $B \cap C$ have each been entered twice. Consequently, it is necessary to subtract each of these probabilities. This gives $\mathbf{P}(A) + \mathbf{P}(B) + \mathbf{P}(C) - \mathbf{P}(A \cap B) - \mathbf{P}(A \cap C) - \mathbf{P}(B \cap C)$. But in subtracting the probabilities of the three intersections, the probability associated with $A \cap B \cap C$ has been reduced to 0. (This probability was added in once for each of the values $\mathbf{P}(A)$, $\mathbf{P}(B)$, and $\mathbf{P}(C)$, and then it was subtracted once for each of the probabilities $\mathbf{P}(A \cap B)$, $\mathbf{P}(A \cap C)$, and $\mathbf{P}(B \cap C)$.) In order to compensate for this overcorrection, $\mathbf{P}(A \cap B \cap C)$ must be added. *If A, B, and C are events in a single sample space, then the probability that at least one of them will occur is*

$$\mathbf{P}(A \cup B \cup C) = \mathbf{P}(A) + \mathbf{P}(B) + \mathbf{P}(C) - \mathbf{P}(A \cap B) - \mathbf{P}(A \cap C) - \mathbf{P}(B \cap C) + \mathbf{P}(A \cap B \cap C). \qquad [IV.6]$$

This is interpreted as the probability of A or B or C.

To illustrate the use of this formula, the probability of rolling a 7, or obtaining a 2 on either die, or obtaining a 5 on either die, will be computed. If A = "7", B = "2 on either die," and C = "5 on either die," then $\mathbf{P}(A) = 6/36$, $\mathbf{P}(B) = 11/36$, and $\mathbf{P}(A \cap B) = 2/36$. Since $C = \{(5, 1), (5, 2), (5, 3), (5, 4), (5, 5), (5, 6), (1, 5), (2, 5), (3, 5), (4, 5), (6, 5)\}$ $\mathbf{P}(C) = 11/36$. The intersection $A \cap C$ contains two outcomes, so that $\mathbf{P}(A \cap C) = 2/36$. $B \cap C$ also contains two outcomes, so that $\mathbf{P}(B \cap C) = 2/36$, and $A \cap B \cap C$ contains the outcomes (2, 5) and (5, 2), so that $\mathbf{P}(A \cap B \cap C)$ is 2/36. Applying Formula [IV.6],

$$\begin{aligned}\mathbf{P}(A \cup B \cup C) &= \mathbf{P}(A) + \mathbf{P}(B) + \mathbf{P}(C) - \mathbf{P}(A \cap B) - \mathbf{P}(A \cap C) \\ &\qquad - \mathbf{P}(B \cap C) + \mathbf{P}(A \cap B \cap C) \\ &= 6/36 + 11/36 + 11/36 - 2/36 - 2/36 - 2/36 + 2/36 \\ &= 24/36 = 2/3.\end{aligned}$$

This is the probability that at least one of the events "7", "2 on either die," or "5 on either die" will occur.

By similar methods, formulas can be developed for the probability of the union of four or more events. The general rule follows.

If S_1 designates the sum of the probabilities of the single events, S_2 designates the sum of the probabilities of the intersections of the events taken two at a time, S_3 the sum of the probabilities of the intersections of the events taken three at a time, and so on, then the probability of the union of the r events $A_1, A_2, \ldots, A_r$ is

$$\mathbf{P}(A_1 \cup A_2 \cup \cdots \cup A_r) = S_1 - S_2 + S_3 - + \cdots \pm S_r. \qquad \text{[IV.7]}$$

Notice that the signs of the terms on the right-hand side of the equation simply alternate.

For two events ($r = 2$),

$$\mathbf{P}(A_1 \cup A_2) = S_1 - S_2 = \mathbf{P}(A_1) + \mathbf{P}(A_2) - \mathbf{P}(A_1 \cap A_2);$$

for three events ($r = 3$),

$$\begin{aligned}\mathbf{P}(A_1 \cup A_2 \cup A_3) &= S_1 - S_2 + S_3 \\ &= \mathbf{P}(A_1) + \mathbf{P}(A_2) + \mathbf{P}(A_3) - [\mathbf{P}(A_1 \cap A_2) \\ &\qquad + \mathbf{P}(A_1 \cap A_3) + \mathbf{P}(A_2 \cap A_3)] + \mathbf{P}(A_1 \cap A_2 \cap A_3);\end{aligned}$$

for four events,

$$\begin{aligned}\mathbf{P}(A_1 \cup A_2 \cup A_3 \cup A_4) &= S_1 - S_2 + S_3 - S_4 \\ &= \mathbf{P}(A_1) + \mathbf{P}(A_2) + \mathbf{P}(A_3) + \mathbf{P}(A_4) \\ &\quad - [\mathbf{P}(A_1 \cap A_2) + \mathbf{P}(A_1 \cap A_3) + \mathbf{P}(A_1 \cap A_4) \\ &\quad + \mathbf{P}(A_2 \cap A_3) + \mathbf{P}(A_2 \cap A_4) + \mathbf{P}(A_3 \cap A_4)] \\ &\quad + [\mathbf{P}(A_1 \cap A_2 \cap A_3) + \mathbf{P}(A_1 \cap A_2 \cap A_4) \\ &\quad + \mathbf{P}(A_1 \cap A_3 \cap A_4) + \mathbf{P}(A_2 \cap A_3 \cap A_4)] \\ &\quad - \mathbf{P}(A_1 \cap A_2 \cap A_3 \cap A_4);\end{aligned}$$

and so on. Later, we will have occasion to use Formula [IV.7].

IV.8.2. Probability of the difference between two events

If A and B are events in a given sample space, then the probability that A but not B will occur is

$$\mathbf{P}(A \sim B) = \mathbf{P}(A) - \mathbf{P}(A \cap B). \qquad \text{[IV.8]}$$

Since the probability associated with the entire sample space, S, is 1, and since the intersection of any event with S equals the event, *the probability of the complement of B is*

$$\mathbf{P}(S \sim B) = 1 - \mathbf{P}(B). \qquad \text{[IV.9]}$$

$\mathbf{P}(S \sim B)$ is sometimes simplified to $\mathbf{P}(\sim B)$, the probability that B will not occur.

For the artificial data of Table IV.4, the probability that a randomly selected person will be a male who has not attended college can be found using Formula [IV.8]. Since $\mathbf{P}(A) = \mathbf{P}(\text{male}) = 100/200$ and $\mathbf{P}(A \cap B) = \mathbf{P}(\text{male who attended college}) = 60/200$, the probability of a male who has not attended college is

$$\begin{aligned} \mathbf{P}(A \sim B) &= \mathbf{P}(A) - \mathbf{P}(A \cap B) \\ &= 100/200 - 60/200 = 40/200 \\ &= 0.2. \end{aligned}$$

The probability of no college attendance is one minus the probability of college attendance. Thus, for Table IV.4,

$$\begin{aligned} \mathbf{P}(\text{no college attendance}) &= 1 - \mathbf{P}(\text{attended college}) \\ &= 1 - 80/200 \\ &= 0.6. \end{aligned}$$

IV.8.3. Probability of an intersection of events

Just as in the case of a union of events, there are shortcuts for computing the probability that the intersection of two or more events will occur.

Suppose that A and B are statistically independent. Then, the conditional probability of A given B equals the probability of A. That is

$$\frac{\mathbf{P}(A \cap B)}{\mathbf{P}(B)} = \mathbf{P}(A).$$

If both sides of this equation are multiplied by $\mathbf{P}(B)$, the result is

$$\mathbf{P}(A \cap B) = \mathbf{P}(A)\mathbf{P}(B).$$

Thus, *if A and B are statistically independent events in a given sample space, then the probability that both A and B will occur is*

$$\mathbf{P}(A \cap B) = \mathbf{P}(A)\mathbf{P}(B). \qquad \text{[IV.10]}$$

For the data of Table IV.2, it was shown that the events "male" and "attended college" are statistically independent. Consequently, the probability that a randomly selected member of this group is a male who has attended college can be computed using Formula [IV.10]. Since **P**(male) = 100/200 and **P**(attended college) = 100/200, the probability of the intersection of these two events is

$$\begin{aligned}\mathbf{P}(\text{male who attended college}) &= \mathbf{P}(\text{male})\mathbf{P}(\text{attended college}) \\ &= (100/200)(100/200) \\ &= 1/4.\end{aligned}$$

By inspection of Table IV.2, it is found that 50 of 200 or 1/4 of the individuals are males who attended college. This provides a check of the calculation.

In Table IV.3, **P**(female) = 50/150 and **P**(attended college) = 90/150. Since these two events were shown to be statistically independent, **P**(female who attended college) = **P**(female)**P**(attended college) = (50/150)(90/150) = 1/5. This is verified by noting that 1/5 of the responses represented in Table IV.3 were for females who attended college.

In Table IV.4, 60 out of 200 individuals are identified as males who attended college. The probability of a male is 100/200 and the probability of college attendance is 80/200, but the product of these two probabilities does not equal the probability of a male who attended college. That is, **P**(male)**P**(attended college) = (100/200)(80/200) = 1/5 is not equal to **P**(male who attended college) = 60/200 = 3/10. The reason, of course, is that for Table IV.4 the events "male" and "attended college" are statistically *dependent*.

In order to develop a formula for computing the probability of the intersection of two statistically dependent events, we will examine again the definition of conditional probability,

$$\mathbf{P}(B \mid A) = \frac{\mathbf{P}(A \cap B)}{\mathbf{P}(A)}.$$

If both sides of this equality are multiplied by $\mathbf{P}(A)$, the result is:

$$\mathbf{P}(A)\mathbf{P}(B \mid A) = \mathbf{P}(A \cap B).$$

From this we conclude that *if A and B are events in a given sample space, then the probability that both A and B will occur is*

$$\mathbf{P}(A \cap B) = \mathbf{P}(A)\mathbf{P}(B \mid A). \qquad \text{[IV.11]}$$

If one begins with the definition of the probability of A given B (rather than the probability of B given A), then

$$\mathbf{P}(B)\mathbf{P}(A \mid B) = \mathbf{P}(A \cap B).$$

Consequently, $\mathbf{P}(A \cap B)$ is equal to $\mathbf{P}(B)\mathbf{P}(A \mid B)$ as well as $\mathbf{P}(A)\mathbf{P}(B \mid A)$.

In Section IV.7.2, it was shown that the events "male" and "attended college" were statistically dependent for the data of Table IV.4. If A = male, B = attended college, and $A \cap B$ = male who attended college, then $\mathbf{P}(A) = 100/200$, and $\mathbf{P}(B \mid A) = 60/100$. Utilizing Formula [IV.11],

$$\mathbf{P}(A \cap B) = \mathbf{P}(A)\mathbf{P}(B \mid A) = (100/200)(60/100) = 60/200,$$

which is the probability that a randomly selected member of this group will be a male who attended college.

Formula [IV.11] can be generalized to the probability of the intersection of three or more events. To illustrate this, suppose that the probability of the joint occurrence of A, B, and C (i.e., $\mathbf{P}(A \cap B \cap C)$) is sought. $A \cap B \cap C$ can be thought of as the intersection of the event $A \cap B$ and the event C. If $A \cap B$ is labeled X, then $A \cap B \cap C = X \cap C$, and according to the formula for the conjunction of two events,

$$\mathbf{P}(A \cap B \cap C) = \mathbf{P}(X \cap C) = \mathbf{P}(X)\mathbf{P}(C \mid X).$$

Since $X = A \cap B$, a second application of the two-event formula gives $\mathbf{P}(X) = \mathbf{P}(A \cap B) = \mathbf{P}(A)\mathbf{P}(B \mid A)$. This result can be substituted for $\mathbf{P}(X)$, so that

$$\begin{aligned}\mathbf{P}(A \cap B \cap C) = \mathbf{P}(X \cap C) &= \mathbf{P}(X)\mathbf{P}(C \mid X)\\ &= \mathbf{P}(A)\mathbf{P}(B \mid A)\mathbf{P}(C \mid X)\end{aligned}$$

and since $\mathbf{P}(C \mid X) = \mathbf{P}(C \mid (A \cap B))$,

$$\mathbf{P}(A \cap B \cap C) = \mathbf{P}(A)\mathbf{P}(B \mid A)\mathbf{P}(C \mid (A \cap B)).$$

To sum up, *if A, B, and C are events in a given sample space, then the probability that A, B, and C will be observed simultaneously is*

$$\mathbf{P}(A \cap B \cap C) = \mathbf{P}(A)\mathbf{P}(B \mid A)\mathbf{P}(C \mid (A \cap B)). \qquad \text{[IV.12]}$$

Intuitively, the probability of $A \cap B \cap C$ was found by multiplying the probability of A by the probability of the part of B that is also in A, and, in turn, multiplying this result by the probability of the part of C that

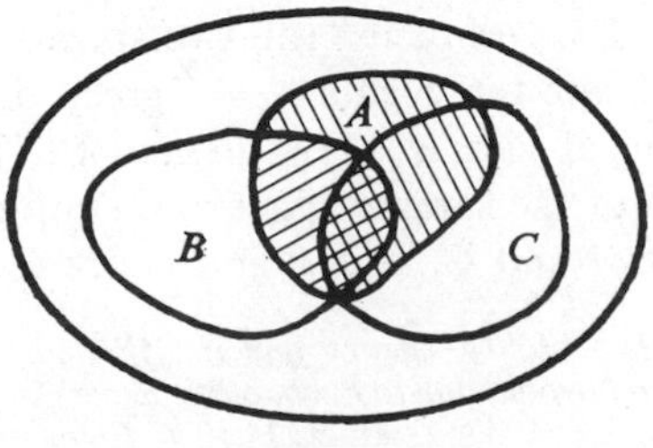

Figure IV.10

is in both A and B. This can be seen by examining the formula for $\mathbf{P}(A \cap B \cap C)$ in light of the Venn diagram of Figure IV.10.

The general formula for the intersection of several events follows. *If $A_1, A_2, \ldots, A_r$ are all events in a given sample space, then the probability of their joint occurrence is*

$$\mathbf{P}(A_1 \cap A_2 \cap \cdots \cap A_r) = \mathbf{P}(A_1)\mathbf{P}(A_2 \mid A_1)\mathbf{P}(A_3 \mid (A_1 \cap A_2)) \cdots \mathbf{P}(A_r \mid (A_1 \cap A_2 \cap \cdots \cap A_{r-1})). \quad [\text{IV.13}]$$

For a more thorough discussion of this formula, the reader should consult one of the standard texts on probability.[3]

IV.9

PAIRWISE AND MUTUAL STATISTICAL INDEPENDENCE OF EVENTS

If every pair among three or more events is found to be statistically independent, one might conclude that the entire set of events is "completely independent." However, *this may not be the case.* When three or more events are involved, the fact that they are statistically independent when considered two at a time does not ensure that they are completely independent (or "mutually independent," as we shall call it).

The formula for the probability of the intersection of three events that was introduced in Section IV.8 is

$$\mathbf{P}(A \cap B \cap C) = \mathbf{P}(A)\mathbf{P}(B \mid A)\mathbf{P}(C \mid (A \cap B)).$$

If $\mathbf{P}(B \mid A) = \mathbf{P}(B)$ and if $\mathbf{P}(C \mid (A \cap B)) = \mathbf{P}(C)$, then this reduces to

$$\mathbf{P}(A \cap B \cap C) = \mathbf{P}(A)\mathbf{P}(B)\mathbf{P}(C),$$

just as one would expect for the case of completely independent events. The important thing to consider here is the second "if." This tells us that even though $\mathbf{P}(B \mid A) = \mathbf{P}(B)$, $\mathbf{P}(A \mid C) = \mathbf{P}(A)$, and $\mathbf{P}(B \mid C) = \mathbf{P}(B)$, the probability of the intersection of A, B, and C is not necessarily equal to the product of their probabilities. It is necessary that $\mathbf{P}(C \mid (A \cap B)) = \mathbf{P}(C)$, too, in order for the simple product rule to hold. To see this, consider the experiment "roll two six-sided dice," a green one and a red one. Designate the events A = "green die is a 2," B = "red die is a 5," C = "sum of dice is a 7." Then, $\mathbf{P}(A) = \mathbf{P}(B) = \mathbf{P}(C) = 1/6$. By enumeration of the sample space and simple counting, it can be verified that A and B, A and C, and B and C are each statistically inde-

[3] Parzen, E., *Modern Probability Theory and its Applications.* New York, John Wiley, 1960; Feller, W., *An Introduction to Probability Theory and its Applications,* I (2nd ed.). New York, John Wiley, 1957; Cramér, H., *The Elements of Probability Theory.* New York, John Wiley, 1955.

pendent pairs of events. This is demonstrated by the following three equalities:

$$\mathbf{P}(B \mid A) = \frac{\mathbf{P}(B \cap A)}{\mathbf{P}(A)} = \frac{1/36}{1/6} = \frac{1}{6} = \mathbf{P}(B),$$

$$\mathbf{P}(A \mid C) = \frac{\mathbf{P}(A \cap C)}{P(C)} = \frac{1/36}{1/6} = \frac{1}{6} = \mathbf{P}(A),$$

$$\mathbf{P}(B \mid C) = \frac{\mathbf{P}(B \cap C)}{\mathbf{P}(C)} = \frac{1/36}{1/6} = \frac{1}{6} = \mathbf{P}(B).$$

Since these events are statistically independent when considered in pairs, it may seem reasonable to conclude that the probability of their joint occurrence is simply the product of their separate probabilities, so that

$$\begin{aligned}\mathbf{P}(A \cap B \cap C) &= \mathbf{P}(A)\mathbf{P}(B)\mathbf{P}(C)\\ &= \frac{1}{6}\cdot\frac{1}{6}\cdot\frac{1}{6} = \frac{1}{216}.\end{aligned}$$

However, inspection of the sample space reveals that $\mathbf{P}(A \cap B \cap C) = 1/36$ not 1/216. What we have failed to consider is whether $\mathbf{P}(C \mid (A \cap B)) = \mathbf{P}(C)$, that is, whether the probability of obtaining a 7 given "2 on the green die" *and* "5 on the red die" is 1/6, the unconditional probability of a 7. Obviously, $\mathbf{P}(C \mid (A \cap B)) = 1$, not 1/6, and that is the difficulty.

What we have done is to show that, although A, B, and C are pairwise independent, they are not mutually independent. To make the distinction explicit, pairwise statistical independence and mutual statistical independence will be defined more precisely.

IV.9.1. Definition of pairwise statistical independence

If $A_1, A_2, \ldots, A_r$ are all events in a given sample space, and if every pair of these events is statistically independent, then the entire set of r events is said to be pairwise statistically independent. The events "7," "2 on the green die," and "5 on the red die" have been shown to be pairwise independent; however, they are not mutually independent.

IV.9.2. Definition of mutual statistical independence

If $A_1, A_2, \ldots, A_r$ are all events in a given sample space, then they are mutually statistically independent if the probability of the intersection of every subset of events equals the product of the probabilities of the single events contained in the intersection.

To demonstrate mutual independence for the three events A_1, A_2, and A_3, it must be shown that

$$\begin{aligned}\mathbf{P}(A_1 \cap A_2) &= \mathbf{P}(A_1)\mathbf{P}(A_2),\\ \mathbf{P}(A_1 \cap A_3) &= \mathbf{P}(A_1)\mathbf{P}(A_3),\\ \mathbf{P}(A_2 \cap A_3) &= \mathbf{P}(A_2)\mathbf{P}(A_3),\end{aligned}$$

and that

$$\mathbf{P}(A_1 \cap A_2 \cap A_3) = \mathbf{P}(A_1)\mathbf{P}(A_2)\mathbf{P}(A_3).$$

If any of these four equalities does not hold, then A_1, A_2, and A_3 are not mutually independent. If only the last equality fails, they are pairwise independent but not mutually independent.

If four events, A_1, A_2, A_3, A_4, are considered, all of the following eleven equations must be shown to hold before we can be sure that the events are mutually independent:

$$\begin{aligned}
\mathbf{P}(A_1 \cap A_2) &= \mathbf{P}(A_1)\mathbf{P}(A_2)\\
\mathbf{P}(A_1 \cap A_3) &= \mathbf{P}(A_1)\mathbf{P}(A_3)\\
\mathbf{P}(A_1 \cap A_4) &= \mathbf{P}(A_1)\mathbf{P}(A_4)\\
\mathbf{P}(A_2 \cap A_3) &= \mathbf{P}(A_2)\mathbf{P}(A_3)\\
\mathbf{P}(A_2 \cap A_4) &= \mathbf{P}(A_2)\mathbf{P}(A_4)\\
\mathbf{P}(A_3 \cap A_4) &= \mathbf{P}(A_3)\mathbf{P}(A_4)\\
\mathbf{P}(A_1 \cap A_2 \cap A_3) &= \mathbf{P}(A_1)\mathbf{P}(A_2)\mathbf{P}(A_3)\\
\mathbf{P}(A_1 \cap A_2 \cap A_4) &= \mathbf{P}(A_1)\mathbf{P}(A_2)\mathbf{P}(A_4)\\
\mathbf{P}(A_1 \cap A_3 \cap A_4) &= \mathbf{P}(A_1)\mathbf{P}(A_3)\mathbf{P}(A_4)\\
\mathbf{P}(A_2 \cap A_3 \cap A_4) &= \mathbf{P}(A_2)\mathbf{P}(A_3)\mathbf{P}(A_4)\\
\mathbf{P}(A_1 \cap A_2 \cap A_3 \cap A_4) &= \mathbf{P}(A_1)\mathbf{P}(A_2)\mathbf{P}(A_3)\mathbf{P}(A_4).
\end{aligned}$$

Only the first six of these equalities need be true in order to establish pairwise independence.

The difference between pairwise and mutual independence may become extremely important in appraising the value of information for predictive purposes. This will be shown below for an example involving dice. Later, the same methods will be used to appraise the diagnostic usefulness of two psychological tests.

Returning to the events $A =$ "green die is a 2," $B =$ "red die is a 5," and $C =$ "7," the probability of each event is 1/6, and as shown above, they are *pairwise* independent. One might suspect, then, that none of these events would help predict any other. Indeed, this is the case if we consider the events only two at a time. Knowledge of whether A has occurred tells us nothing about the likelihood that C will occur. This is because the probability of C is 1/6 regardless of whether A is known to have occurred. Similarly, knowledge of B does not help predict whether C will occur. But if it is known that both A and B have occurred, then the probability of C is 1. Symbolically, this is summarized as follows:

$$\mathbf{P}(C \mid A) = \mathbf{P}(C \mid B) = \mathbf{P}(C) = 1/6,$$

but

$$\mathbf{P}(C \mid (A \cap B)) = \frac{\mathbf{P}(A \cap B \cap C)}{\mathbf{P}(A \cap B)} = \frac{1/36}{1/36} = 1.$$

This example is summarized in Table IV.5. Obviously, conclusions about predictability are not reached by considering the dependence of the variable to be predicted on each of the predictors considered separately. It is necessary to examine the dependence of the criterion on each subset of predictor variables, as well.

Table IV.5. Pairwise independence with mutual dependence

Information given	Probability of a 7
None	1/6
Green die a 2	1/6
Red die a 5	1/6
Green die a 2 and red die a 5	1

An immediate corollary of the definition of mutual statistical independence is that *if* $A_1, A_2, \ldots, A_r$ *are mutually independent events in a given sample space, then the probability of their simultaneous occurrence is*

$$\mathbf{P}(A_1 \cap A_2 \cap \cdots \cap A_r) = \mathbf{P}(A_1)\mathbf{P}(A_2)\cdots\mathbf{P}(A_r). \qquad [\text{IV.14}]$$

Notice again that pairwise independence alone does not assure the applicability of Formula [IV.14].

Later, we shall examine the distinction between pairwise and mutual independence in the context of clinical diagnosis.

IV.10

PROBLEMS ON COMPOUND EVENTS AND STATISTICAL INDEPENDENCE

1. In a follow-up study of VA trainees in clinical psychology who entered training during 1947 and 1948, Kelly and Goldberg[4] attempted to appraise the "job satisfaction" 10 years later of 166 trainees who had completed the Ph.D. in clinical psychology. Table IV.6 summarizes one aspect of the data. Since the trainees included in the VA Selection Research Project were from universities throughout the U.S., perhaps this sample can be used to estimate "job satisfaction" for all of the VA-trained Ph.D.'s who began training during the 1947–48 period.

[4] Kelly, E. L., and L. R. Goldberg, "Correlates of later performance and specialization in psychology: a follow-up study of the trainees assessed in the VA Selection Research Project." *Psychological Monographs* 73, 1–32, 1959. The frequencies given above are based on the percentages of Table 6 of the monograph, where a small error was found in the first row.

Table IV.6. Job satisfaction of psychologists 10 years after training

At the present time, I consider myself *primarily* a:	If I had my life to live over again (knowing what I now know), I would try to end up in:				
	Clinical psychology	Some other field in psychology	Medicine: psychiatry	All other fields	Total
Therapist	31	2	12	6	51
Teacher	18	6	0	1	25
Researcher	10	5	1	6	22
Diagnostician	13	1	7	1	22
Administrator-supervisor	30	5	3	8	46
Total	102	19	23	22	166

a. If you were required to predict the answer to the question (see the table above) for a randomly selected clinician from this population, what would you predict? Why?

b. Would you change your prediction if you knew the area of specialization of the clinician? Why?

c. Describe the sample space represented by the above table. How many elements does each of its outcomes contain?

d. From these data, estimate the probability that a randomly selected member of the population would give "clinical psychology" as his answer to this question.

e. Are the events "therapist" and "try to end up in clinical psychology" statistically independent? Show that your answer is correct.

f. Are the events "diagnostician" and "try to end up in medicine: psychiatry" statistically independent? Show that your answer is correct and comment on the effects of sampling variability on your answer.

g. Identify five mutually exclusive events in the table.

h. Are the events "teacher" and "researcher" statistically independent? Show that your answer is correct.

i. What is the probability that a randomly selected clinician "would try to end up in clinical practice" (i.e., either in clinical psychology or medicine: psychiatry)?

2. The following questions refer to the probability experiment "roll three dice, a white one, a red one, and a green one."

   a. What is the probability that the face of the green die plus the face of the white die ("green plus white") will equal 7?

   b. What is the probability that "green plus white will equal 7" or "red plus white will equal 7"?

   c. What is the probability that "green plus white equals 7" and "red plus white equals 7"?

d. Are the events of c mutually independent? Prove the correctness of your answer.
e. What is the probability that the red die and the green die will show the same number of spots?
f. What is the probability that "red plus white equals 7" but "green plus white does not equal 7"?
g. Are the events "green die and red die show the same number of spots" and "red plus white equals 7" statistically independent? Prove that your answer is correct.
h. Are the events "red plus white equals 7," "green plus white equals 7," and "red die and green die show the same number of spots" mutually independent? Prove that your answer to both questions is correct.
i. Write down symbolically the set of equalities that must be demonstrated in order to answer h affirmatively.

3. Assume that 5 percent of the males and 1 percent of the females in a given population are color-blind. Assume that 60 percent of the population is male and 40 percent is female.
   a. What is the probability that a person drawn randomly from this population is a color-blind male?
   b. Are the events "color-blind" and "male" statistically independent?
   c. Given a male, what is the probability that he is color-blind?

4. In a given department, the probability that a randomly chosen entering graduate student will complete the Ph.D. is 0.40, the probability that he will write the comprehensive examinations is 0.60, and the probability that he will pass them is 0.55. Departmental policy holds that no one completes the Ph.D. without passing comprehensives.
   a. Draw a Venn diagram illustrating this situation.
   b. What is the probability that a randomly selected entering graduate student will pass the comprehensives, given that he takes them?
   c. What is the probability that a randomly selected student who writes the comprehensives will complete the Ph.D.?
   d. What is the probability that a randomly selected entering graduate student will take the comprehensives and will *not* complete the Ph.D.?
   e. Given that a randomly selected entering graduate student takes comprehensives, what is the probability that he will *not* complete the Ph.D.?

5. The four Russian novels *War and Peace*, *Anna Karenina*, *Crime and Punishment*, and *The Brothers Karamazov* are arranged on a shelf in random order.
   a. In how many different orders can the books be arranged?
   b. What is the probability that *War and Peace* is to the left of *Anna Karenina*?
   c. What is the probability that *Crime and Punishment* is to the left of *The Brothers Karamazov*?
   d. Is the event referred to in b statistically independent of that of c?
   e. Demonstrate that your answer to d is correct.

IV.11
THE MEANING OF PROBABILITY

In Section IV.3, it was mentioned that although the abstract, mathematical definition of probability is perfectly clear, there is considerable ambiguity as to the proper interpretation of probability applied to events in the real world. In this section, the mathematical definition of probability is introduced, and three of the most important interpretations of probability are discussed.

IV.11.1. Mathematical definition of probability

If X is any subset (e.g., event) of the set S and if $\mathbf{P}(X)$ is a rule that assigns a number to every X in accord with the following three properties, then $\mathbf{P}(X)$ is said to assign probabilities to the subsets X:

(1) $0 \leq \mathbf{P}(X)$ for every X in S.

(2) $\mathbf{P}(S) = 1$.

(3) If X and Y are subsets of S, then

$$\mathbf{P}(X \cup Y) = \mathbf{P}(X) + \mathbf{P}(Y)$$

if and only if X and Y have no common elements.

This says that if a rule assigns a nonnegative number to every subset of a given set, then these numbers are probabilities if 1 is assigned to the entire set, and if the sum of the numbers assigned to the members of any pair of subsets equals the number assigned to their union only when they are disjoint.

Of course, this mathematical definition says nothing about how one is to interpret the subsets or the numbers assigned to them. As is always the case with pure mathematics, the definition is completely abstract. What is needed is some way of interpreting probability statements about events in the real world.

IV.11.2. Interpretations of probability

Although Savage[5] acknowledges that there is excellent agreement on the mathematical properties of probability, he sums up the difficulties associated with its interpretation in statistics as follows:

> It is unanimously agreed that statistics depends somehow on probability. But, as to what probability is and how it is connected with statistics, there has seldom been such complete disagreement and breakdown of communication since the tower of Babel.

Similar statements hold for nonstatistical applications of probability, as well. In general, the problem reduces to a question of the precise meaning

[5] *The Foundations of Statistics.* New York, John Wiley, 1954, p. 2.

of such statements as "The probability that A will occur is 0.6," when A refers to an event in the real world. Like a number of psychological concepts, "probability" is a difficult idea to capture in a phrase or two, or to define in terms of other clearly understood concepts.

One might well ask how probability theory could have achieved such remarkable success when there is so little agreement on the interpretation of its central concept. The answer seems to be that everyone has a pretty good *intuitive* idea of what probability means, even though it seems to defy clear linguistic formulation. Apparently it is this core of agreement on the intuitive meaning that prevents disastrous distortions in the application of probability, and perhaps it is only the nuances and peripheral characteristics of the idea that make codification so difficult. On the other hand, there may be more than one interpretation of probability, each of which obeys the same laws. The approach taken here is to introduce three interpretations and to make use of each in appropriate contexts.

SUBJECTIVE PROBABILITY. A *subjective probability* is a weight attached to an event by an individual that indicates the strength of his expectation that the event will occur. For example, a person may assign a subjective probability to "receiving a phone call from a friend during an hour's time," to "rain tomorrow," or to "obtaining a Ph.D."

It seems clear that much of our behavior is influenced by the subjective probabilities we attach to future happenings. When we assign a low subjective probability to an event, we often proceed as if it were impossible. When a high subjective probability (though less than complete certainty) has been assigned, we often make all suitable preparations for the event's occurrence.

One of the difficulties entailed in the use of subjective probabilities is that equally well-informed individuals often disagree on the probability that should be assigned to a given event. Because of this, a subjective probability can never be considered independent of the person who generates it. On the other hand, though they may disagree on the exact subjective probability of an event, reasonable individuals of similar knowledge and experience often assign similar subjective probabilities.

A second difficulty is that the subjective probabilities of some persons may follow the rules of probability theory closely, whereas those of others may not. If this is true, then statements about the characteristics of subjective probabilities have to be coordinated with statements about individual differences.

The question of how to measure subjective probabilities constitutes still another problem. It is quite likely that the applicability of the mathematical theory of probability depends on the method of measurement. Although the general problem of measuring subjective magnitudes has a long history in psychology, it is the economists who have been most concerned with measuring subjective probability in the past. Much of this interest has grown from investigations of "consumer behavior," and even though the resulting theories have been formulated in psychological terms, psychologists have shown little interest in them until recently.[6]

If subjective probabilities are used in the formulation of any psychological theory, then it is important to know how closely they conform to the rules of the mathematical theory of probability. Later, we will examine some psychological data that shed light on this question.

PROBABILITY AS A CONSEQUENCE OF LOGICAL STRUCTURE. If asked the probability of rolling a 3 with a single fair die, it is unlikely that you would answer on the basis of a subjective probability. Instead, a logical analysis of the properties of the die and of the process of dice-rolling would be used, In terms of the distribution of mass, as well as geometrically, a fair die is symmetrical, and if tossed without bias, there is no reason to expect the die to come to rest in any particular position. This implies that the six faces are equally likely, so that the probability of rolling a 3 is 1/6. When such a procedure is employed, *probability is a result of a logical analysis* of some dynamic, event-generating process. Many of the examples of probability calculations that appeared earlier in this chapter were based on analyses of this kind.

When probabilities are assigned by a logical analysis of a dynamic system, they need have no meaning other than that implied by the process of analysis itself. The probability is considered correct if the assumptions and logic on which it is based are correct. However, we usually require some *empirical* procedure for demonstrating the correctness of a logically derived probability.

PROBABILITY AS THE LIMIT OF A RELATIVE FREQUENCY. If an uncertain, event-generating process can be repeated many times without changing its characteristics, the idea of probability as the limit of a relative frequency is sometimes used. If a coin is biased, but the extent of bias is unknown, the probability of tossing a head can be estimated by making a number of tosses of the coin. This amounts to taking a sample from the countably infinite population of possible tosses. For example, if heads were obtained 15 times in 20 tosses, then the best guess is that the probability of heads is 3/4. If heads were obtained on 750 of a thousand tosses, confidence that

[6] Edwards, Ward, "The theory of decision making," *Psychol. Bull.* **51**, 380–417, 1954. Includes a 209-item bibliography. Subjective probability per se is discussed on pp. 396–398, though it enters at other points throughout most of the paper. Also, Stefan Vail has written a discussion of some of the alternative formulations of subjective probability in R. M. Thrall, C. H. Coombs, and R. L. Davis (eds.), *Decision Processes*. New York, John Wiley, 1954, 87–98.

the probability of heads is 3/4 would be substantially increased. It is this kind of thinking that has led to the relative-frequency interpretation of probability. In fact, this approach has been followed in an unsuccessful attempt to *define* probability. Nonetheless, the idea on which it is based remains an important interpretation of probability.

Suppose that n is the number of times a random experiment is observed and f is the number of occurrences of the event A. Then, the probability of A is sometimes "defined" as the number approached by f/n as n approaches infinity. In limit notation,

$$\mathbf{P}(A) = \lim_{n \to \infty} \frac{f}{n}.$$

The implication of this statement is that the ratio f/n is supposed to move closer and closer to the "true probability" of A as n approaches infinity.

An immediate consequence of this "definition" is that the absolute value of the difference between f/n and $\mathbf{P}(A)$ should approach 0 as n becomes infinite. In limit notation, this means that[7]

$$\lim_{n \to \infty} |f/n - \mathbf{P}(A)| = 0.$$

Here we must become a little more precise. Exactly what is meant by this last statement? The answer is that for any positive number, δ, no matter how small, there exists a value of n that is sufficiently large to ensure that $|f/n - \mathbf{P}(A)| < \delta$. In other words,[8] by selecting a large enough value of n, we can guarantee that f/n will not differ from $\mathbf{P}(A)$ by more than δ, no matter how small δ might be.

The difficulty with this "definition" is that *it does not work*. As n increases, there is a *chance* that $|f/n - \mathbf{P}(A)|$ will increase, even if $\mathbf{P}(A)$ is the "true probability." For example, a 3 may occur on 36 out of 216 tosses of a fair die. In this case, $|f/n - \mathbf{P}(A)| = 36/216 - 1/6 = 0$. But after 600 tosses, the 3 may have occurred 105 times, so that $|f/n - \mathbf{P}(A)| = 105/600 - 1/6 = 0.0083$. No matter how large n becomes, such increases in the discrepancy between f/n and $\mathbf{P}(A)$ are *possible*, even if 1/6 is the "true probability."

However, the *probability* that $|f/n - \mathbf{P}(A)|$ will be larger than any

[7] The two vertical bars indicate that it is the *absolute value* of the expression $(f/n - \mathbf{P}(A))$ that is to be considered. If a is any algebraic expression or any number, then the absolute value of a (denoted $|a|$) is defined as follows: If $a < 0$, then $|a| = -a$, and if $a \geq 0$, then $|a| = a$. Thus, if $a = 7 - 3$, then $|a| = |7 - 3| = 7 - 3 = 4$. On the other hand, if $a = 3 - 7$, then $|a| = |3 - 7| = -(3 - 7) = 4$.

[8] This can be formulated as a game. The game begins when you select some positive number, δ, that is very small. But the definition says that no matter how small your choice of δ, I can find a value of n that is large enough to ensure that $|f/n - \mathbf{P}(A)| < \delta$.

(small) positive number, δ, does decrease as n increases. This suggests that if the probability that $|f/n - \mathbf{P}(A)| < \delta$ approaches one as n approaches infinity, then $\mathbf{P}(A)$ is the probability of the event A. Indeed, this seems to work quite well. But notice what we have done: we have used the concept we intended to define to construct the definition. Of course, that takes us right back to our starting point. And no matter how one goes about it, such difficulties seem unavoidable in the relative-frequency approach.

Although the limit-of-a-relative-frequency approach does not yield a satisfactory *definition* of probability, it does provide an important interpretation. Often, probabilities obtained from an analysis of logical structure are expected to be compatible with this interpretation. Thus, if the probability of a 3 is considered to be 1/6 on the basis of a logical analysis of die-tossing, then we expect about 1/6 of a large number of tosses of a fair die to result in 3's.

In addition to being unsatisfactory as a definition, the relative-frequency interpretation sometimes leads to difficulties. For example, it seems intuitively sensible to speak of "the probability of rain tomorrow," but strictly speaking there is only one tomorrow, and the idea of "a limit as the number of tomorrows approaches infinity" is not very convincing. Questions like "the probability that one will get a Ph.D." make the limit-of-a-relative-frequency approach even less attractive.

SUGGESTED READING

1. Nagel, E., "The Meaning of Probability" in J. R. Newman (ed.), *The World of Mathematics*, II. New York, Simon and Schuster, 1956.
   A concise philosophical discussion of some of the definitions of probability which have been proposed and some of the difficulties generated by each of them.
2. Poincaré, H., "Chance," in J. R. Newman (ed.), *The World of Mathematics*, II. New York, Simon and Schuster, 1956, pp. 1380–1394.
   A relatively informal exposition of the meaning of probability and of the ways it has been used to make sense of chaos. Filled with a wide variety of illustrations. Written with the characteristic lucidity of Poincaré.
3. Mosteller, F., R. E. K. Rourke, and G. B. Thomas, Jr., *Probability and Statistics*. Reading, Mass., Addison-Wesley, 1961, Chaps. 1–3.
   This is an excellent introduction requiring no special mathematics beyond algebra. It includes many well-chosen examples.
4. Kemeny, J. G., J. L. Snell, and G. L. Thompson, *Introduction to Finite Mathematics*. Englewood Cliffs, N.J., Prentice-Hall, 1957, Chap. IV.
   This chapter introduces probability in a relatively formal but elementary fashion.
5. Cramér, H., *The Elements of Probability Theory*. New York, John Wiley, 1955.

A presentation of probability that is nicely meshed with statistics. In fact, the last third of the book is devoted to statistics. The first four chapters roughly parallel the material of this chapter, and require little beyond algebra; the remaining chapters make frequent use of calculus.

6. Feller, W. *Introduction to Probability Theory and Its Applications*, I (2nd ed.). New York, John Wiley, 1957.
A thorough introduction to probability. The first 130 pages cover virtually everything included in this chapter and the next (aside from particular applications) and much more. Written in a lucid but concise and mathematically sophisticated style. The first 20 pages or so develop probability in terms of the outcome-event, sample-space ideas employed here.
7. Parzen, E., *Modern Probability Theory and Its Application.* New York, John Wiley, 1960.
This volume requires somewhat less mathematical sophistication than Feller, but, at the same time, it makes more extensive use of calculus.

V

PROBABILITY: CALCULATIONS AND SPECIAL APPLICATIONS

WHEN calculating probabilities, it is rarely efficient and often impossible to enumerate all of the outcomes in the relevant sample space. However, it is often possible to compute the probability of an event using shortcut formulas that will be developed in this chapter. After these calculating aids have been described, some applications of probability that are of special interest to psychologists will be introduced.

V.1
PROBABILITY CALCULATIONS

In Sections V.1.1 through V.1.7, computing formulas are introduced and illustrated. Section V.1.8 introduces a general strategy for dealing with probability calculations.

V.1.1. The number of ways of selecting one object from each of several populations

If a random experiment can be conceptualized as a choice of one element from each of several distinguishable sets, in how many ways can this be done? For example, in the experiment "toss a die and a coin simultaneously," how many outcomes are possible? Tossing the die amounts to a random choice of one of its six faces, and tossing the coin is a random selection from the population containing one head and one tail. Another example of this sort of probability experiment is the construction of three-letter nonsense syllables in which the first and last letters are randomly chosen from among the population of consonants and the middle letter is chosen randomly from the population of vowels.

The question is "how many distinct nonsense syllables can be formed in this way?"

Suppose that there are n populations and that a random experiment consists of a random selection of one element from each population. If there are N_1 elements in the first population, N_2 in the second, . . ., N_n in the nth, then the number of ways in which a sample of size n can be obtained is

$$N_1 \cdot N_2 \cdots N_n. \qquad [V.1]$$

It is not difficult to see how this formula is derived. One of N_1 elements is taken from the first population, and for each of these there are N_2 possible choices from the second. Thus, there are $N_1 \cdot N_2$ ways in which the first two elements can be taken. For each pair of elements taken from the first two populations, there are N_3 possibilities for the third element, so that there are $N_1 \cdot N_2 \cdot N_3$ ways of choosing the first three elements of the sample, and so on.

In the case of tossing a coin and a die, $N_1 = 2$, the number of faces on the coin, and $N_2 = 6$, the number of faces on the die, so that there are $N_1 \cdot N_2 = 2 \cdot 6 = 12$ possible results of the experiment.

In the construction of three-letter nonsense syllables, the first letter is a consonant, so $N_1 = 21$. The second letter must be a vowel, so $N_2 = 5$, and since the last letter must be a consonant, $N_3 = 21$. Thus, it is possible to form $N_1 \cdot N_2 \cdot N_3 = 21 \cdot 5 \cdot 21 = 2205$ nonsense syllables following this procedure. (Of course, not all of these will be nonsense. Words like "bat," "cat," and "dog" are included among the 2205 possibilities.)

In sampling consonants without replacement (i.e., if the first and last letters must differ), then $N_1 = 21$, $N_2 = 5$, and $N_3 = 20$, so that there are $N_1 \cdot N_2 \cdot N_3 = 21 \cdot 5 \cdot 20 = 2100$ possible syllables.

If a sample space contains $N_1 \cdot N_2 \cdots N_n$ equiprobable outcomes, then the probability that a specified outcome will occur is $1/(N_1 \cdot N_2 \cdots N_n)$.

V.1.2. The number of ways of ordering several objects

Before proceeding to the ordering problem, it will be necessary to introduce factorial notation. Since it is frequently helpful in probability calculations, it will be useful on many occasions in the future.

FACTORIAL NOTATION. The number "n factorial" is denoted $n!$, and $n! = n \cdot (n-1) \cdot (n-2) \cdots 3 \cdot 2 \cdot 1$. Thus, $5! = 5 \cdot 4 \cdot 3 \cdot 2 \cdot 1 = 120$, and $8! = 8 \cdot 7 \cdot 6 \cdot 5 \cdot 4 \cdot 3 \cdot 2 \cdot 1 = 40{,}320$. In using factorials, $0!$ is defined as equal to 1. This may seem strange, but unless this definition is introduced, the solution of otherwise meaningful problems becomes nonsensical. The justification for defining $0!$ as equal to 1 is that it works, whereas other definitions lead to nonsense.

Factorials of large numbers can be approximated using what is known as Stirling's formula. This formula is

$$n! \cong \left(\frac{n}{e}\right)^n \sqrt{(2\pi n)}, \qquad \text{[V.2]}$$

where π is approximately 3.1416, and e is the base of the natural logarithms, about 2.7183. For $n \geq 9$, the error in this approximation is less than 1 percent. A table of factorials and log factorials for integers up to 75 is given in Appendix I.

ORDERING.

A set of n distinct objects can be arranged in n! orders [V.3]

To illustrate this, the letters a, b, and c can be arranged in the following 6 orders: abc, acb, bac, bca, cab, and cba. Since there are 3 letters, $n! = 3! = 6$ orders. Thus, application of Formula [V.3] and the results of direct enumeration agree.

Five books can be arranged in $5! = 120$ orders on a bookshelf. To see this, suppose that each space on the bookshelf is distinguished as shown in Figure V.1. The first space can be filled by any one of the five books.

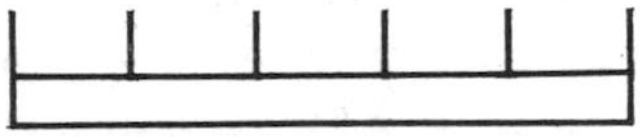

Figure V.1

Once a book has been assigned to the first space, any of the four remaining books can be assigned to the second space, so that there are $5 \cdot 4 = 20$ ways in which the first two spaces can be filled. For each of these 20 assignments, there are three books remaining, so that there are $5 \cdot 4 \cdot 3 = 60$ ways in which the first three spaces may be filled. The fourth space may be occupied by either of the two remaining books, and this leaves one book for the last space. In all, then, there are $5 \cdot 4 \cdot 3 \cdot 2 \cdot 1 = 5! = 120$ ways of ordering the five books on the shelf.

If the ordering of the books is determined randomly, then the probability of a particular order is $1/n! = 1/5! = 1/120$.

V.1.3. The number of ways of obtaining a sample when sampling with replacement

When sampling with replacement, the number of samples of size n that can be taken from a population of size N is

$$N^n. \qquad \text{[V.4]}$$

In examining this formula, it must be remembered that a sample is an *ordered* set.

If a population contains N elements, the first position in a sample may be filled by any one of N elements. Sampling is *with* replacement, so that for each choice of the first element, there remain N possible choices of the second. Consequently, the first two positions of the sample can be filled in any of $N \cdot N = N^2$ ways. For each of the N^2 possible choices of the first two elements of the sample, there are N choices for the third, so that the first three positions can be filled in N^3 ways. Continuing this process, there are N^n ways of taking a sample of size n from a population of size N when sampling with replacement.

To illustrate this formula, suppose that a sample of size $n = 2$ is taken from a population consisting of 1, 2, and 3, sampling with replacement. The sample space for this experiment is {(1, 1), (1, 2), (1, 3), (2, 2), (2, 1), (2, 3), (3, 3), (3, 1), (3, 2)}, and it contains 9 outcomes. Using the formula, $N = 3$ and $n = 2$, so that the number of possible samples is calculated to be $3^2 = 9$. This is the result obtained by counting outcomes in the sample space listed above.

Notice that, when sampling with replacement, the sample size may exceed the population size. For example, if 20 persons each answer a true-false test item, this amounts to taking a sample of size 20 from a population containing the two elements "true" and "false," and there will be 2^{20} possible results of the random experiment "administer a single true-false item to 20 persons." Similarly, for a 20-item true-false test, a single person may give any one of 2^{20} response patterns.

V.1.4. The number of ways of obtaining a sample when sampling without replacement

The formula given in Section V.1.3 is not suitable for sampling without replacement. In this case, the first element of the sample may be any one of the N population elements. However, only $N - 1$ elements

Table V.1. Relationship of element position to number of choices when sampling without replacement

Position of element in the sample	Number of choices possible
first	N
second	$N - 1$
third	$N - 2$
⋮	⋮
$(n - 1)$st	$N - n + 2$
nth	$N - n + 1$

remain for the choice of the second element, since the first was not replaced. For any of the $N(N-1)$ choices of the first two elements of the sample, one of the $N-2$ elements remaining in the population will be chosen as the third element of the sample, and so on, until all n elements have been selected. Table V.1 shows the relation between the position of an element in a sample and the number of ways in which each position can be filled.

When sampling without replacement, a sample of size n may be taken from a population of size N in

$$(N)_n = N(N-1)(N-2)\cdots(N-n+1) = N!/(N-n)! \quad [V.5]$$

different ways.

If three cards are drawn without replacement from a well-shuffled deck, $(N)_n = (52)_3 = 52 \cdot 51 \cdot 50$ different samples may be drawn. The probability of drawing the ace of hearts, ace of clubs, and ace of spades in that order is $1/(N)_n = 1/(52)_3 = 1/(52 \cdot 51 \cdot 50)$.

Notice that in sampling *with* replacement, the probability that a population element will be the ith element of the sample is the same regardless of what elements have been drawn previously. Thus, in sampling *with* replacement every draw is statistically independent of every other. However, the draws are statistically dependent in the case of sampling *without* replacement. Thus, the probability of getting the ace of spades on the first draw is 1/52, but if the ace of spades has been obtained on the first draw, the probability of getting it on the second draw is 0 when sampling without replacement. Similarly, the probability of an ace on the first draw is 4/52, but if an ace is obtained on the first draw, the probability of an ace on the second draw is 3/51. If an ace is not obtained on the first draw, then the probability of an ace on the second is 4/51. In either case, the first and second draws are statistically dependent.

When the population contains a large number of elements and the sample size is small, formulas for sampling with and without replacement yield very similar results. For example, a sample of size 2 may be taken from a population of size 1000 in $N^n = 1000^2 = 1{,}000{,}000$ ways when sampling with replacement and in $(N)_n = (1000)_2 = 1{,}000 \cdot 999 = 999{,}000$ ways when sampling without replacement. The latter figure is only 0.1 percent less than the former.

V.1.5. The number of ways of obtaining a group of objects when sampling without replacement

So far, all formulas have distinguished the order in which elements are drawn. However, it is frequently useful to have formulas in which order is ignored, i.e., formulas for unordered sets or *groups* rather than for ordered sets or samples. The term *group* will be used subsequently to refer to an unordered set. (Groups are often called *combinations* to distinguish them from ordered sets or *permutations*.)

Sampling without replacement from a population of size N, $(N)_n = N!/(N-n)!$ distinct samples of size n can be taken. However, $N!/(N-n)!$ is too large for the number of *groups* of size n. In fact, it is too large by a factor of $n!$, since $n!$ distinct *samples* can be formed from each group of n objects. To adjust $N!/(N-n)!$ to give the number of groups of size n, simply divide by $n!$. This gives

$$\frac{(N)_n}{n!} = \frac{N!/(N-n)!}{n!} = \frac{N!}{n!(N-n)!}.$$

When sampling without replacement, the number of groups of size n which can be taken from a population of size N is

$$\binom{N}{n} = \frac{N!}{n!(N-n)!}, \qquad [V.6]$$

provided that $n \leq N$. *If* $n > N$, *then* $\binom{N}{n} = 0$. $\binom{N}{n}$ *is called a binomial coefficient.*

If a department head is to appoint a committee of 5 from among a 15-member department, he must choose among

$$\binom{N}{n} = \binom{15}{5} = \frac{15!}{5!(15-5)!} = 3003$$

possible committees. In forming committees, the question of the order of appointment is irrelevant. The important thing is who is on the committee.

*V.1.6. The number of ways of obtaining a group of objects when sampling with replacement

Section V.1.5 gives the number of groups that can be obtained when sampling *without* replacement. Next, a formula will be given for the number of *groups* that can be obtained when sampling *with* replacement. Before the formula is presented, an example will be given and the number of possible groups determined by enumeration.

Suppose that a group of $n = 3$ is to be taken from the population {a, b, c, d} sampling with replacement. Sampling with replacement makes it possible to obtain the same element more than once in a single group, so that the possible groups are {a, a, a}, {b, b, b}, {c, c, c}, {d, d, d}, {a, a, b}, {a, a, c}, {a, a, d}, {a, b, b}, {b, b, c}, {b, b, d}, {a, c, c}, {b, c, c}, {c, c, d}, {a, d, d}, {b, d, d}, {c, d, d}, {a, b, c}, {a, b, d}, {a, c, d}, {b, c, d}. Notice that no two groups are identical, so that there are 20 of them.

When sampling with replacement, the number of groups of size n that can be taken from a population of size N is

$$\binom{N+n-1}{n} = \frac{(N+n-1)!}{n!(N-1)!}. \qquad [V.7]$$

V.1.7. The number of ways of dividing several objects into mutually exclusive subgroups

The next formula is that for the *multinomial* coefficient, which gives the number of ways a set of N elements can be divided into r mutually exclusive *groups*, the first of which contains n_1 elements, the second n_2 elements, . . ., and the rth n_r elements, where $n_1 + n_2 + \cdots + n_r = N$.

A set of N elements can be arranged in $N!$ different orders. Each of these $N!$ orders can be used to generate r *samples*, the first n_1 elements of the ordering constituting the first sample, the next n_2 elements the second sample, . . ., and the last n_r elements constituting the rth sample. Thus, the number of ways of dividing N elements into r *samples* with n_1 elements in the first sample, n_2 in the second, . . ., and n_r in the rth is $N!$. But $N!$ is too large for the number of groups, since it distinguishes orders within groups. However, since there are $n_1!$ orders within the first group, $n_2!$ within the second, . . ., $n_r!$ within the rth, $N!$ is too large by a factor of $n_1!\, n_2! \cdots n_r!$. Consequently,

$$\frac{N!}{n_1!\, n_2! \cdots n_r!}$$

is the desired result.

The number of ways a set of N objects can be divided into r mutually exclusive groups, the first group containing n_1 objects, the second containing n_2, . . ., and the rth containing n_r is

$$\frac{N!}{n_1!\, n_2! \cdots n_r!}, \qquad [V.8]$$

where $n_1 + n_2 + \cdots + n_r = N$. This is called the multinomial coefficient.

Note that for $r = 2$ this formula reduces to the binomial coefficient, $\binom{N}{n} = \frac{N!}{n!(N-n)!}$. To show this, all that need be done is to set $n_1 = n$ and $n_2 = N - n$. Since $n + (N - n) = N$, $n_1 + n_2 = N$, and the binomial coefficient can be written as $N!/(n_1!\, n_2!)$. Thus, the binomial coefficient can be interpreted in either of two ways: (1) as the number of ways a group of size n can be formed from a population of size N sampling without replacement, or (2) as the number of ways a set of N objects can be divided into two groups, one containing n_1 objects and the other containing $N - n_1 = n_2$ objects.

Suppose that an experimenter is studying the effect of an experimental treatment, and that two control groups are required. If 25 subjects are available, and if 5 are to be assigned to each control group and 15 to the experimental group, then there are

$$\frac{N!}{n_1!\,n_2!\,n_3!} = \frac{25!}{5!\,5!\,15!}$$

ways in which the assignments can be made.

V.1.8. General procedures and illustrations of probability calculations

The calculation of probabilities by complete enumeration of the sample space and counting equiprobable outcomes was illustrated several times in Chapter IV. However, this method is hopeless when the number of outcomes is large. In this section, a few examples will be computed using some of the formulas of the preceding sections. The general approach followed in these calculations may prove helpful in subsequent applications.

In arriving at the probability of the occurrence of an event, A, the probability has the form

$$\mathbf{P}(A) = \frac{\text{number of outcomes in } A}{\text{number of outcomes in the sample space}},$$

provided that the sample space has equiprobable outcomes. If the sample space does not have equiprobable outcomes, $\mathbf{P}(A)$ equals the sum of the probabilities of the outcomes contained in A.

Suppose that two playing cards are drawn from a deck of 52, and that the first card is replaced and the deck is shuffled before drawing the second. What is the probability that two hearts will be obtained? In order to formulate this problem, let H represent the hearts and $\sim H$ represent the other suits. With this notation, the pertinent characteristics of the sample space can be represented as shown in Table V.2. The first card drawn may be a heart or not, and the same is true for the second card.

Table V.2. Summary of sample space for drawing two hearts

		First card		
		H	$\sim H$	
Second	H	$13^2 = 169$	$39 \cdot 13 = 507$	676
card	$\sim H$	$13 \cdot 39 = 507$	$39^2 = 1521$	2028
		676	2028	2704

Now, in how many ways can two hearts be taken in two draws sampling with replacement? Since the population of hearts contains 13 elements, $N = 13$, and since two cards are drawn, $n = 2$. Thus, there are $13^2 = 169$ ways of obtaining two hearts. This figure is entered in the upper left cell of the table. Since there are 13 hearts and 39 non-hearts, there are $13 \cdot 39 = 507$ ways of obtaining a heart on the first draw and a non-heart on the second. Similarly, there are $39 \cdot 13 = 507$ ways of obtaining a non-heart first and a heart second. These results are entered in the lower left and upper right cells of Table V.2. Finally, two non-hearts are obtainable in $39^2 = 1521$ ways, since this amounts to taking a sample of size 2 from a population of size 39. The sum of the entries in the table, 2704, gives the total number of outcomes in the sample space for the experiment "draw two cards with replacement." The probability of two hearts is

$$\mathbf{P}(H, H) = \frac{169}{2704}.$$

This problem could have been solved more directly in the following way. First, the general form of the probability is

$$\mathbf{P}(H, H) = \frac{\text{number of ways of drawing 2 hearts}}{\text{number of ways of drawing any 2 cards}}.$$

Since sampling is with replacement,

$$\mathbf{P}(H, H) = \frac{13^2}{52^2} = \frac{169}{2704},$$

the result obtained above. However, a formulation like that of Table V.2 has real advantages for more difficult problems.

From Table V.2, it is an easy matter to compute several other probabilities. For example, the probability that the first card is a heart is

$$\mathbf{P}[(H, H) \cup (H, \sim H)] = \frac{169}{2704} + \frac{507}{2704} = 0.25.$$

The probability of drawing at least one heart is

$$\mathbf{P}[(H, H) \cup (H, \sim H) \cup (\sim H, H)] = \frac{169}{2704} + \frac{507}{2704} + \frac{507}{2704} = 0.44,$$

since the three outcomes are mutually exclusive. The conditional probability that the second card is a heart given that the first card is a heart is

$$\mathbf{P}[(H, H) \cup (\sim H, H) \mid (H, H) \cup (H, \sim H)]$$
$$= \frac{\mathbf{P}\{[(H, H) \cup (\sim H, H)] \cap [(H, H) \cup (H, \sim H)]\}}{\mathbf{P}[(H, H) \cup (H, \sim H)]}$$
$$= \frac{\mathbf{P}(H, H)}{\mathbf{P}[(H, H) \cup (H, \sim H)]} = \frac{169/2704}{676/2704} = 0.25.$$

Since this probability is equal to the unconditional probability of obtaining a heart on the second draw, the events "heart on the first draw" and "heart on the second draw" are statistically independent. Of course, they must be independent in sampling with replacement, since the population is completely restored prior to each draw.

Now for a somewhat different kind of example. Suppose that a group of 4 persons is to be selected randomly from among 7 men and 5 women. What is the probability that the group will be equally split between men and women?

If the group is equally split, there will be 2 men and 2 women. The 2 men could be selected from among 7 men in $\binom{7}{2} = 21$ ways. For each way of selecting 2 men, there are $\binom{5}{2} = 10$ ways of selecting 2 women, so that the number of ways of obtaining 2 men and 2 women is $\binom{7}{2}\binom{5}{2} = 21(10) = 210$. The experiment consists of drawing a group of size 4 from a population of $7 + 5 = 12$, and this can be done in $\binom{12}{4} = 495$ ways. Finally

$$\mathbf{P}(\text{2 men and 2 women}) = \frac{\text{number of ways of obtaining a group of 2 men and 2 women}}{\text{number of ways of obtaining a group of 4}} = \frac{\binom{7}{2}\binom{5}{2}}{\binom{12}{4}} = \frac{210}{495}.$$

Suppose that you are one of the 12 persons. What is the probability that you will be one of the 4 chosen? There is only one way of choosing you, and there are $\binom{11}{3}$ ways of choosing the remaining 3 members of the group; therefore,

$$\mathbf{P}(\text{you will be a member of the group}) = \frac{\binom{1}{1}\binom{11}{3}}{\binom{12}{4}} = \frac{1(165)}{495} = \frac{1}{3}.$$

The probability that all 4 members of the group will be women is

$$\mathbf{P}(\text{4 women}) = \frac{\binom{7}{0}\binom{5}{4}}{\binom{12}{4}} = \frac{1(5)}{495} = \frac{1}{99}.$$

Suppose that I offer to play the following game with you.[1] A well-shuffled deck of 52 playing cards is dealt so that you get half the cards. If you have a royal flush among the 26 cards that you receive, I pay you \$5. Otherwise, you pay me \$1. Will you play the game?

You can expect to come out even or increase your wealth only if the probability that you will win is greater than, or equal to, 1/6 (i.e., if the odds are 5 to 1). Your decision, then, should be based on comparing the probability that you will win with 1/6.

First, order makes no difference; a royal flush is the same regardless of the order in which the cards are received. Second, a royal flush can occur in any one of the four suits, and for each suit there is exactly one royal flush. (A royal flush consists of ace, king, queen, jack, and ten all in the same suit.) In order to simplify discussion, the following notation will be used:

$$\mathscr{H} = \text{the event "royal flush in hearts,"}$$
$$\mathscr{D} = \text{the event "royal flush in diamonds,"}$$
$$\mathscr{S} = \text{the event "royal flush in spades,"}$$
and
$$\mathscr{C} = \text{the event "royal flush in clubs."}$$

Since the probability of *at least one* royal flush is required, it is the probability of the union of these four events that must be calculated. Since 26 cards are being dealt, more than one royal flush could be obtained in a single deal, so that the four events are not mutually exclusive.

Recalling Formula [IV.7] for the probability of the union of several overlapping events,

$$\begin{aligned}\mathbf{P}(\mathscr{H} \cup \mathscr{D} \cup \mathscr{S} \cup \mathscr{C}) &= S_1 - S_2 + S_3 - S_4 \\ &= \mathbf{P}(\mathscr{H}) + \mathbf{P}(\mathscr{D}) + \mathbf{P}(\mathscr{S}) + \mathbf{P}(\mathscr{C}) - [\mathbf{P}(\mathscr{H} \cap \mathscr{D}) \\ &\quad + \mathbf{P}(\mathscr{H} \cap \mathscr{S}) + \mathbf{P}(\mathscr{H} \cap \mathscr{C}) + \mathbf{P}(\mathscr{D} \cap \mathscr{S}) \\ &\quad + \mathbf{P}(\mathscr{D} \cap \mathscr{C}) + \mathbf{P}(\mathscr{S} \cap \mathscr{C})] + [\mathbf{P}(\mathscr{H} \cap \mathscr{D} \cap \mathscr{S}) \\ &\quad + \mathbf{P}(\mathscr{H} \cap \mathscr{D} \cap \mathscr{C}) + \mathbf{P}(\mathscr{H} \cap \mathscr{S} \cap \mathscr{C}) \\ &\quad + \mathbf{P}(\mathscr{D} \cap \mathscr{S} \cap \mathscr{C})] - \mathbf{P}(\mathscr{H} \cap \mathscr{D} \cap \mathscr{S} \cap \mathscr{C}).\end{aligned}$$

Now, each of the probabilities in this expression must be found.

Your 26 cards can be dealt in $\binom{52}{26}$ ways. Consequently, there are $\binom{52}{26}$ outcomes in the relevant sample space.

Consider the probability of obtaining a royal flush in hearts. For this event to occur, ace, king, queen, jack, and ten of hearts must be included among the 26 cards dealt. The number of ways in which all 5 of these cards can be obtained is $\binom{5}{5} = 1$. In addition to the 5 cards

[1] This problem was suggested to the writer by Donald Van Ostrand.

included in the royal flush, 21 other cards are obtained from among the remaining 47 cards. These 21 cards can be received in $\binom{47}{21}$ ways, so that

$$\mathbf{P}(\mathscr{H}) = \frac{\binom{5}{5}\binom{47}{21}}{\binom{52}{26}}.$$

Since $\mathbf{P}(\mathscr{D})$, $\mathbf{P}(\mathscr{S})$, and $\mathbf{P}(\mathscr{C})$ are each computed by identical arguments, $\mathbf{P}(\mathscr{H}) = \mathbf{P}(\mathscr{D}) = \mathbf{P}(\mathscr{S}) = \mathbf{P}(\mathscr{C})$, and

$$\begin{aligned} S_1 &= \mathbf{P}(\mathscr{H}) + \mathbf{P}(\mathscr{D}) + \mathbf{P}(\mathscr{S}) + \mathbf{P}(\mathscr{C}) = 4 \cdot \mathbf{P}(\mathscr{H}) \\ &= \frac{4 \cdot \binom{5}{5}\binom{47}{21}}{\binom{52}{26}}. \end{aligned}$$

The next step is to calculate the probability of obtaining any two royal flushes. For example, one could calculate $\mathbf{P}(\mathscr{H} \cap \mathscr{D})$, and since the probability will be the same for each pair of royal flushes, it need be calculated only once. Then, 6 times this value is

$$\begin{aligned} S_2 = \mathbf{P}(\mathscr{H} \cap \mathscr{D}) + \mathbf{P}(\mathscr{H} \cap \mathscr{S}) + \mathbf{P}(\mathscr{H} \cap \mathscr{C}) + \mathbf{P}(\mathscr{D} \cap \mathscr{S}) \\ + \mathbf{P}(\mathscr{D} \cap \mathscr{C}) + \mathbf{P}(\mathscr{S} \cap \mathscr{C}), \end{aligned}$$

since this sum contains $\binom{4}{2} = 6$ equal probabilities.

The event $\mathscr{H} \cap \mathscr{D}$ will occur only if all of the 10 cards in these two royal flushes are obtained. This can occur in $\binom{10}{10} = 1$ way. In addition to these 10 cards, 16 others are received, and these can be obtained in $\binom{42}{16}$ ways, so that

$$\mathbf{P}(\mathscr{H} \cap \mathscr{D}) = \frac{\binom{10}{10}\binom{42}{16}}{\binom{52}{26}}.$$

Consequently,

$$\begin{aligned} S_2 &= \mathbf{P}(\mathscr{H} \cap \mathscr{D}) + \mathbf{P}(\mathscr{H} \cap \mathscr{S}) + \mathbf{P}(\mathscr{H} \cap \mathscr{C}) + \mathbf{P}(\mathscr{D} \cap \mathscr{S}) \\ &\qquad + \mathbf{P}(\mathscr{D} \cap \mathscr{C}) + \mathbf{P}(\mathscr{S} \cap \mathscr{C}) \\ &= \frac{6 \cdot \binom{10}{10}\binom{42}{16}}{\binom{52}{26}}. \end{aligned}$$

By a similar argument, the probability that royal flushes in hearts, diamonds, and spades will occur on a single deal is

$$\mathbf{P}(\mathscr{H} \cap \mathscr{D} \cap \mathscr{S}) = \frac{\binom{15}{15}\binom{37}{11}}{\binom{52}{26}}.$$

Since this is equal to the probability of royal flushes in any other three suits,

$$S_3 = \mathbf{P}(\mathscr{H} \cap \mathscr{D} \cap \mathscr{S}) + \mathbf{P}(\mathscr{H} \cap \mathscr{D} \cap \mathscr{C}) + \mathbf{P}(\mathscr{H} \cap \mathscr{S} \cap \mathscr{C}) + \mathbf{P}(\mathscr{S} \cap \mathscr{D} \cap \mathscr{C})$$

$$= \frac{4 \cdot \binom{15}{15}\binom{37}{11}}{\binom{52}{26}}.$$

Finally, the probability of obtaining four royal flushes on a single deal of 26 cards is

$$S_4 = \mathbf{P}(\mathscr{H} \cap \mathscr{D} \cap \mathscr{S} \cap \mathscr{C}) = \frac{\binom{20}{20}\binom{32}{6}}{\binom{52}{26}}.$$

Now, these results must be substituted in the formula for $\mathbf{P}(\mathscr{H} \cup \mathscr{D} \cup \mathscr{S} \cup \mathscr{C})$ given earlier. This gives

$$\begin{aligned}\mathbf{P}(\mathscr{H} \cup \mathscr{D} \cup \mathscr{S} \cup \mathscr{C}) &= S_1 - S_2 + S_3 - S_4 \\ &= 4\frac{\binom{5}{5}\binom{47}{21}}{\binom{52}{26}} - 6\frac{\binom{10}{10}\binom{42}{16}}{\binom{52}{26}} + 4\frac{\binom{15}{15}\binom{37}{11}}{\binom{52}{26}} - \frac{\binom{20}{20}\binom{32}{6}}{\binom{52}{26}} \\ &\cong 0.1.\end{aligned}$$

(It should be noted that this probability has been computed using logarithms of factorials and is only approximate.)

Since the probability that you will win is considerably less than 1/6, the minimum probability required in order that you can expect to come out even, you would be unwise to play the game at 5 to 1 odds. However, the game would be "fair" if you were invited to play at odds of 9 to 1.

Before leaving the topic, a few procedural rules for calculating probabilities seem in order: (1) If it is feasible, write out the entire sample space. (2) If this is not possible, try to determine the nature of an outcome—how many elements it has, for example. (3) Next, examine the role of ordering in the problem. Can ordering be ignored or not? (4) If enumeration of outcomes is impossible, specify the event for which the probability is to be calculated as precisely as possible. (5) Then decide whether the event is to be treated as a single event or as a compound of two or more events. (6) If the latter, find the appropriate rule for computing the probability of the compound event. (7) Now, for each event in the compound, find the relevant calculational formulas and apply them. (8) Assemble the results following the rule for compound probabilities. The general approach is diagramed in Figure V.2.

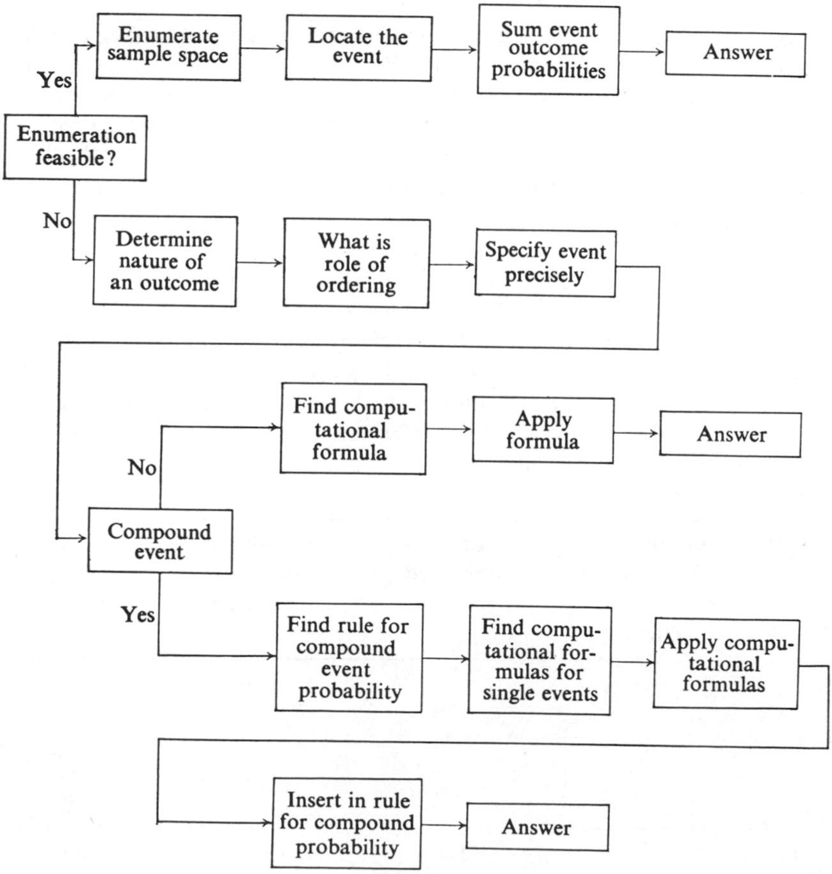

Figure V.2

V.2
PROBLEMS ON COMPUTING PROBABILITIES

1. You are traveling from Jonesville to Smithburg via Middleborough. Since the journey is unfamiliar to you, your route is determined by a

random selection at every choice-point. There are 4 routes from Jonesville to Middleborough and 5 from Middleborough to Smithburg. What is the probability that you will follow the route I always follow?

2. If an organization has 3 presidential candidates, 2 vice-presidential candidates, and 4 persons running for secretary-treasurer, in how many ways can the three leaders of the organization be elected?

3. If the letters q and x are omitted, how many three-letter syllables can be formed with the format "consonant, vowel, consonant" if a letter can be used only once in each syllable? What is the probability that a randomly formed syllable will be the word "dog"?

4. Each of two clinical psychologists independently rank-order six patients according to aggressiveness. Both judges are trained to use exactly the same criteria for assessing aggressiveness and tied ranks are forbidden. However, the six patients are indistinguishable with respect to aggressiveness. What is the probability that the two rankings will agree perfectly?

5. Consider the word Mississippi. Draw a random sample of three letters from this word without replacement.
   a. What is the probability that all three letters are i's?
   b. What is the probability that all three letters are identical?
   c. What is the probability that the number of i's is 0?

6. Price and Deabler[2] have used the Archimedes spiral aftereffect illusion to diagnose brain damage. The spiral was presented four times so that the patient could report the illusion 0, 1, 2, 3, or 4 times. The table below summarizes their data for 120 brain-damaged patients and 40 non-brain-damaged patients.

	Number of reports of the spiral after-effect	Brain-damaged patients	Non-brain-damaged patients	Totals
	0	72	0	72
	1	13	0	13
	2	24	1	25
	3	9	1	10
	4	2	38	40
Totals		120	40	160

Suppose that you draw a patient at random from among the 160 included in the data.

a. What is the probability that he obtained a score of exactly 3?

[2] "Diagnosis of organicity by means of spiral aftereffect." *J. Consult. Psychol.* **19**, 299–302, 1955.

b. What is the probability that he scored less than 2?
c. Given that his score is greater than 3, what is the probability that he has no brain damage?
d. Given a score of 2, what is the probability that he is brain-damaged?
e. Are the events "brain damage" and "score of 3" statistically independent?
f. If the patient had obtained a score of 1, would you bet that he was a brain-damaged patient?

7. The "odd man" among three imbibers is to pay for the next round of drinks. Each tosses a coin, and if the coin of one differs from that of the other two (i.e., one head and two tails or one tail and two heads), the "odd man" must pay. If all are alike, they toss again.
   a. What is the probability that man A will have to pay after only one toss?
   b. What is the probability that A will have to pay after exactly three tosses? (This means that no one pays on the first two tosses.)
   c. What is the probability that no more than two tosses will be required to determine who pays for the next round?
   d. What is the probability that more than three tosses will be required before the next round can be paid for?

8. Two cards are drawn without replacement from a well-shuffled deck.
   a. The first card is an ace. What is the probability that the second is an ace?
   b. At least one of the two cards drawn is an ace. What is the probability that both are aces?
   c. What is the probability that neither card will be an ace?

9. What is the probability of being dealt four aces in a game of five-card stud poker? What is the probability of being dealt a royal flush?

10. The student's knowledge of the course is nil. What is the probability that he will make no errors on a five-item, true-false quiz? What is the probability that he will get none correct?

11. Fifteen subjects are to be randomly divided into an experimental group of ten and a control group of five subjects. How many ways can the division be made? If one experimental group and two control groups of five each are to be formed, in how many ways can the assignment to the three groups be made?

12. In a given department, there are three full professors, five associate professors, and nine assistant professors. A committee is to be formed with two representatives from each rank.
    a. How many ways can this be done?
    b. If there are three members of the department, one from each rank, who are utterly incompatible, what is the probability that all three will be on the committee if the department chairman chooses the two committee members randomly from within each rank?
    c. What is the probability that at least one of the three mutually incompatible persons will be on the committee?

13. How many terms are there in the formula for computing the probability of the union of 10 events that are not mutually exclusive?
14. How many factors are there in the formula for computing the probability of the intersection of 10 statistically dependent events?
15. How many equalities must be shown to hold in order to demonstrate the pairwise independence of 10 events?
16. How many equalities must be shown to hold in order to demonstrate the mutual independence of 10 events?

V.3
SPECIAL APPLICATIONS OF PROBABILITY

In this section, several applications of probability that are of special interest to psychologists are discussed. Many of the principles developed in this and the preceding chapters will be applied.

V.3.1. Probability of matches

The probability formula introduced in this section is applicable to a procedure that has found frequent use in clinical research. The problem is this: a clinician is given N test protocols and N personality descriptions, and he is asked to determine which person produced each protocol, i.e., he is asked to match protocols with personality descriptions.[3] If the clinician is unable to make any valid use of test-protocol information, his matching will be random. If matching is random, what is the probability that he will match correctly M or more protocols to the N personality descriptions? Formulas for dealing with this and similar problems are developed in this section.

Suppose that each of the N personality descriptions is labeled with an integer between 1 and N, and that the test protocol corresponding to each personality description is given the same label (all of this unknown to the clinician, of course). Then a "match" occurs if the clinician assigns Protocol i to Personality Description i. There is exactly one way in which the protocol label i can be matched with the personality description labeled i, but there are $(N - 1)!$ ways in which the remaining $N - 1$ protocols can be assigned. Furthermore, there is a total of $N!$ ways to assign the N test protocols to the N personality descriptions. Consequently, the probability that the ith protocol is correctly matched with the ith personality description is $(N - 1)!/N!$. If we let A_i represent the

[3] Of course, he might be asked to match test protocols with individuals on the basis of interviews, other test protocols, or any other kind of information. Furthermore, the same sorts of probability considerations apply to some methods for determining recognition thresholds, to studies in which a subject attempts to determine the symbol on the face of a card by ESP, and to other procedures where guessing may be involved.

event "i^{th} protocol correctly matched with i^{th} personality description," then

$$\mathbf{P}(A_i) = \frac{(N-1)!}{N!} = \frac{1}{N}.$$

Notice that $\mathbf{P}(A_i)$ is not the probability that *only* the ith protocol is correctly matched. Some of the outcomes in A_i include matches of protocols other than i as well. Furthermore, $\mathbf{P}(A_i)$ is not the probability of at least one match. The probability of at least one match is $\mathbf{P}(A_1 \cup A_2 \cup \cdots \cup A_N)$. $\mathbf{P}(A_i)$ is the probability that at least Protocol i (and perhaps some others) is correctly matched.

Now note that the probability of the union of $A_1, A_2, \ldots, A_N$ is *not* simply $\mathbf{P}(A_1) + \mathbf{P}(A_2) + \cdots + \mathbf{P}(A_N)$, since $A_1, A_2, \ldots, A_N$ are not mutually exclusive. This becomes quite clear when it is observed that

$$S_1 = \mathbf{P}(A_1) + \mathbf{P}(A_2) + \cdots + \mathbf{P}(A_N) = N \cdot \frac{1}{N} = 1.$$

Since it is possible to have no matches at all, 1 is too high for the probability of at least one match.

These results and those that follow will be clearer if we keep a particular example in mind. Table V.3 represents the sample space for matching 4 protocols to 4 personality descriptions (so that $N = 4$). If the clinician is behaving randomly, there are $N! = 4! = 24$ equiprobable assignments of protocols to personality descriptions. For convenience, these outcomes have been labeled 1 through 24.

Table V.3. Sample space for matching protocols with personality descriptions

Personality descriptions	Protocol assignments (outcomes)																							
	1	2	3	4	5	6	7	8	9	10	11	12	13	14	15	16	17	18	19	20	21	22	23	24
1	1	1	1	1	1	1	2	2	2	2	2	2	3	3	3	3	3	3	4	4	4	4	4	4
2	2	2	3	3	4	4	1	1	3	3	4	4	1	1	2	2	4	4	1	1	2	2	3	3
3	3	4	2	4	2	3	3	4	1	4	1	3	2	4	1	4	1	2	2	3	1	3	1	2
4	4	3	4	2	3	2	4	3	4	1	3	1	4	2	4	1	2	1	3	2	3	1	2	1
No. of matches	4	2	2	1	1	2	2	0	1	0	0	1	1	0	2	1	0	0	0	1	1	2	0	0

From Table V.3 it can be seen that $\mathbf{P}$(protocol 1 is correctly assigned) = $\mathbf{P}(A_1) = \mathbf{P}$(outcomes 1, 2, 3, 4, 5, or 6) = 6/24 = 1/4. This is equal to $\mathbf{P}(A_1) = 1/N = 1/4$, as indicated above.

By a similar argument, the probability can be computed that Protocols i and j will be correctly matched with Personality Descriptions i and j, respectively. This is the probability of the intersection of A_i and A_j,

$$\mathbf{P}(A_i \cap A_j) = \frac{1 \cdot (N-2)!}{N!} = \frac{(N-2)!}{N!}.$$

This follows from the fact that the particular pair, i and j, can be matched in only one way, whereas the remaining $N - 2$ protocols can be assigned in any of $(N - 2)!$ orders. Of course, all N protocols can be assigned in $N!$ orders.

From Table V.3, it can be seen that

$$\mathbf{P}(A_1 \cap A_2) = \mathbf{P}(\text{outcomes 1 or 2}) = \frac{2}{24} = \frac{1}{12}.$$

This is identical to the result obtained by the formula

$$\mathbf{P}(A_1 \cap A_2) = \frac{(N-2)!}{N!} = \frac{2!}{4!} = \frac{1}{12}.$$

Since there are $\binom{N}{2}$ ways of choosing the particular pair of protocols, i and j, the sum of the probabilities for all $\binom{N}{2}$ pairs is

$$S_2 = \binom{N}{2}\frac{(N-2)!}{N!} = \frac{N!}{(N-2)!\,2!}\,\frac{(N-2)!}{N!} = \frac{1}{2!}.$$

By a similar argument, the probability that a particular triplet of protocols, i, j, and k, will be correctly matched is

$$\mathbf{P}(A_i \cap A_j \cap A_k) = \frac{(N-3)!}{N!},$$

and since there are $\binom{N}{3}$ triplets, the sum of these probabilities over all triplets is

$$S_3 = \binom{N}{3}\frac{(N-3)!}{N!} = \frac{N!}{(N-3)!\,3!}\,\frac{(N-3)!}{N!} = \frac{1}{3!}.$$

Similarly, $S_4 = 1/4!$, $S_5 = 1/5!$, and so on. Since the clinician can make any of $N!$ assignments of protocols to personality descriptions, the probability that all N will be correctly matched is

$$\mathbf{P}(N \text{ matches}) = \frac{1}{N!}.$$

However, the probability of $N - 1$ matches is zero. If all but one protocol have been correctly matched, then the one remaining has only one place to go and that one place is a match. Therefore, exactly $N - 1$ matches is impossible.

Now we are ready to calculate the probability of at least one match. In other words, we can find the union of the events $A_1, A_2, \ldots, A_N$. Applying Formula [IV.7], the probability of at least one match is

$$\begin{aligned}\mathbf{P}(\text{at least 1 match}) &= \mathbf{P}(A_1 \cup A_2 \cup \cdots \cup A_N) \\ &= S_1 - S_2 + S_3 - + \cdots \pm S_N,\end{aligned}$$

and substituting $S_1 = 1$, $S_2 = 1/2!$, $S_3 = 1/3!, \ldots, S_{N-2} = 1/(N-2)!$, $S_{N-1} = 0$, $S_N = 1/N!$,

$$\begin{aligned}\mathbf{P}(\text{at least 1 match}) = 1 - 1/2! + 1/3! - 1/4! \\ + - \cdots \pm 1/(N-2)! \mp 0 \pm 1/N!.\end{aligned}$$

(Notice that the signs simply alternate.) If N is large, this may be burdensome to calculate, and the approximation

$$\mathbf{P}(\text{at least 1 match}) \cong 1 - \frac{1}{e} = 0.6321$$

can be used, where e is the base of the Naperian logarithms.[4] This approximation is fairly good when N is 6 or more. Of course, 1 − **P**(at least 1 match) is the probability of zero matches, so that

$$\mathbf{P}(0 \text{ matches}) \cong 1 - \left[1 - \frac{1}{e}\right] = \frac{1}{e} = 0.3679.$$

Notice that this approximate formula does not depend on N, so that, to a rather good approximation, the probability of at least one match is a little less than 2/3 for *any N* greater than or equal to 6.

In Table V.3, 15 outcomes yield at least one match. Consequently,

$$\mathbf{P}(\text{at least 1 match}) = \frac{15}{24} = 0.6250.$$

Using the exact computational formula for $N = 4$,

$$\begin{aligned}\mathbf{P}(\text{at least 1 match}) &= 1 - \frac{1}{2!} + \frac{1}{3!} - \cdots \pm \frac{1}{N!} \\ &= 1 - \frac{1}{2!} + \frac{1}{3!} - \frac{1}{4!} \\ &= \frac{15}{24} = 0.6250.\end{aligned}$$

The approximation yields

$$\mathbf{P}(\text{at least 1 match}) \cong 1 - \frac{1}{e} = 0.6321,$$

which is quite close to the exact probability.

[4] The relation $1/e = 1 - 1 + 1/2! - 1/3! + - \cdots$ was employed here. The basis of this equality is described in most introductory texts on calculus.

In order to derive the probability of exactly M matches for all values of M, it would be necessary to introduce a rather elaborate theorem[5] for which we will have little use. Consequently, having shown how the probability of zero, at least one, exactly $N - 1$, and N matches are derived, the general statement follows without further elaboration. *The probability of exactly M matches among N is approximated by*

$$\mathbf{P}(\text{exactly } M \text{ matches}) \cong \frac{1}{M!}\cdot\frac{1}{e} = \frac{0.3679}{M!}. \qquad [\text{V.9}]$$

This approximation is reasonably accurate for N greater than 10. For the exact probability formula, see Feller.[5] The approximation, Formula [V.9], will be used here for all such calculations.

If a clinician has 10 protocols, then the probability that he will match correctly exactly 2 personality descriptions is

$$\mathbf{P}(\text{exactly 2 matches}) \cong \frac{0.3679}{M!} = \frac{0.3679}{2!} = 0.184,$$

and the probability of two or more matches is

$$\begin{aligned}\mathbf{P}(\text{at least 2 matches}) &= \mathbf{P}(2 \text{ matches}) + \mathbf{P}(3 \text{ matches}) + \cdots \\ &\qquad + \mathbf{P}(10 \text{ matches}) \\ &\cong \frac{0.3679}{2!} + \frac{0.3679}{3!} + \frac{0.3679}{4!} + \cdots + \frac{0.3679}{10!} \\ &\cong 0.184 + 0.061 + 0.015 + 0.003 + 0.0005 \\ &\qquad + 0.00007 + 0.000009 + 0.000001 + 0.000000^{+} \\ &\cong 0.264.\end{aligned}$$

In other words, if the clinician has no valid basis for assigning protocols to personality descriptions (i.e., if his assignments are random), the probability that he would be able to get two or more correct is 0.264.

Suppose that a subject is given a card on which six geometric figures are displayed. These figures are then projected one at a time on a screen at a very low level of illumination, and on each of six presentations the subject tries to determine which figure was presented. He is not allowed to give a particular response more than once.[6] He gets three correct (i.e., his response "matches" the stimulus on three presentations). What is the probability that he could do this well if he sees nothing and simply

[5] Feller, W., *An Introduction to Probability Theory and its Applications*, I (2nd ed.). New York, John Wiley, 1957, pp. 90–99.

[6] Actually, the formula given provides a reasonably good approximation even when the subject is permitted to give the same response more than once (i.e., when he "samples with replacement") if N is large enough (say, $N \geq 10$). For details, see Feller, *op. cit.*, pp. 98–99.

guesses on each trial? The question is, what is the probability that $M \geq 3$? The answer is found as follows:

$$\begin{aligned}\mathbf{P}(\text{at least 3 matches}) &= \mathbf{P}(\text{3 matches}) + \mathbf{P}(\text{4 matches}) \\ &\qquad + \mathbf{P}(\text{5 matches}) + \mathbf{P}(\text{6 matches}) \\ &\cong \frac{0.3679}{3!} + \frac{0.3679}{4!} + \frac{0.3679}{5!} + \frac{0.3679}{6!} \\ &\cong 0.061 + 0.015 + 0.003 + 0.0005 \\ &\cong 0.080.\end{aligned}$$

It appears rather unlikely that he would be able to do this well if all of his responses were guesses.

V.3.2. Problems on the probability of matches

1. Consider the sample space in Table V.3.
   a. What is the probability of exactly 3 matches?
   b. What is the probability of exactly 4 matches?
   c. What is the probability of at least 3 matches?
   d. What is the probability of no more than 2 matches?
   e. Compute your answers to a through d using enumeration methods and using the approximation provided by Formula [V.9]. Tabulate the two sets of probabilities and comment on their agreement.
2. Five married couples attend a dinner party. After dinner they dance. Not one of the 5 men dances with his wife on the first dance.
   a. Was the choice of partners random?
   b. Provide evidence in support of your answer to a.
   c. Suppose the only rule observed by the male dancers is "I must not dance with my wife." What is the probability that Mr. Smith will dance with Mrs. Jones on the first dance?
   d. Suppose the only rule observed by the dancers is "I must not dance with the same partner on two successive dances." Mr. Smith and Mrs. Jones did not dance together on the first dance. What is the probability that they will on the second?
3. A subject in an ESP experiment attempts to determine the symbol on each of 6 distinct cards. He is allowed to use each symbol only once. All 6 of his responses are correct. A hard-headed experimental psychologist observes that the probability of that many "hits" is only $1/6^6 = 1/45{,}656$ if the subject has no ESP. The ESP investigator considers this for a moment and asserts that the probability is closer to $1/6! = 1/720$. Take sides and point out explicitly the error in the other calculation.

V.3.3. The law of large numbers

In this section, we shift our attention from probability per se to an application of probability to statistics. This application, the law of large numbers, is an extremely important statistical principle.

It may seem intuitively obvious that a large sample provides a more precise estimate of a parameter than a small one, but here one must be careful. The average salary of 1000 senior industrial executives probably would *not* give a more accurate estimate of the national average income than the average salary of only 100 randomly selected adult citizens. The precision of an estimator can be appraised statistically only when probability sampling is used.

The law of large numbers states that, as the sample size becomes large, the probability that an estimate will differ much from the parameter it estimates becomes small. However, there are two things to keep in mind when applying the law of large numbers.

First, it applies only when some form of probability sampling, such as random sampling, is being used. Second, the statistic in question must be a "sensible" estimate.[7] If the smallest observation in a random sample is used to estimate the population average, then the law of large numbers does not apply. The sample minimum is not a sensible estimate of the population average.

If π *is a parameter,* $\mathscr{E}$ *is a sensible estimator for* π *obtained from a probability sample of size n, and* δ *is any positive number, then the law of large numbers states that* $\mathbf{P}(|\mathscr{E} - \pi| > \delta)$ *decreases towards zero as n increases towards infinity.*[8]

The quantity $|\mathscr{E} - \pi|$ measures the discrepancy between the parameter, π, and the estimator, $\mathscr{E}$. The δ is a small number that is used to make a general statement about the size of the difference between $\mathscr{E}$ and π. The law of large numbers ensures that as n becomes indefinitely large, the probability that $|\mathscr{E} - \pi|$ will exceed δ moves closer and closer to zero, no matter how small δ might be. This is simply a precise and general way of saying that estimates based on large probability samples are less likely to be in error by a given amount than those based on small probability samples.

Notice that the law has to do with *probabilities.* It does not say that discrepancies are never large with large samples, only that this is unlikely.

In the discussion of random sampling in Section III.2.2, it was stated that the main reason for probability sampling is that it permits the application of probability theory. In addition, it was noted that probability samples *may* be as biased or nonrepresentative of a population as any other kind of sample. On the other hand, good estimates of a parameter and reasonable conclusions regarding parameters require that samples be representative. The law of large numbers assures us that estimates obtained from probability samples are unlikely to be much in error when the sample size is large.

[7] In Chap. XII, the meaning of sensible will be clarified.

[8] Remember, the vertical lines in the expression $|\mathscr{E} - \pi|$ refer to the absolute value of the difference between $\mathscr{E}$ and π.

This aspect of the law of large numbers is obviously important in estimation. If estimates are to be made with a small probability of large error, then large samples should be employed. In hypothesis testing, samples must be used to obtain estimates of the parameters to which the hypothesis refers, and confidence as to the correctness of a decision depends in part on the accuracy with which the parameters have been estimated. Thus, the law of large numbers is important for hypothesis testing as well as for estimation.

V.3.4. Problems on the law of large numbers

1. Consider each of the following statements. Which of them are correct statements of the law of large numbers? For each statement, $\mathscr{E}$ is a sensible estimator of the parameter π, and n is the size of the random sample for which $\mathscr{E}$ is computed.
   a. As n becomes large without limit, the difference between $\mathscr{E}$ and π approaches 0.
   b. For sufficiently large n, $|\pi - \mathscr{E}|$ is always less than any arbitrarily small number, δ.
   c. As n goes to infinity, $\pi - \mathscr{E}$ becomes smaller than δ, where δ is a positive number.
   d. As n goes to infinity, $\mathbf{P}(|\mathscr{E} - \pi| > \delta)$ goes to 0 provided that $\delta > 0$.
   e. As n becomes large without limit, the probability that the absolute value of the difference between $\mathscr{E}$ and π will exceed any arbitrary positive number approaches 0.
2. Consider the sample space for each of the following three random experiments: "toss 3 fair coins," "toss 4 fair coins," and "toss 5 fair coins." For each outcome in each of these sample spaces, find the proportion of heads.
   a. In each random experiment, compute the probability that the proportion of heads differs from 1/2 by more than $\delta = 1/6$. What are these 3 probabilities?
   b. Interpret the results of a in terms of the law of large numbers.
   c. What is the status of the 1/2 in a?

V.3.5. Bayes's theorem

In a paper published posthumously in 1763, the Reverend Thomas Bayes provided the earliest systematic approach to the induction problem. The essential ingredient, Bayes's theorem or the principle of inverse probability, is described in this section. Actually, there are no new principles to discuss. In spite of the impressive title, Bayes's theorem is simply an application of conditional probability, but it is an especially interesting and important application.

INTRODUCTION OF BAYES'S THEOREM. In Section IV.6.3, figures reported by Page et al. were mentioned, which estimate the probability that a functionally ill patient (F) will report the Archimedes spiral aftereffect (A) as 0.85, or $\mathbf{P}(A \mid F) = 0.85$. The probability that a brain-damaged patient (B) would *not* report the aftereffect ($\sim A$) was estimated as $\mathbf{P}(\sim A \mid B) = 0.60$. These figures are of interest in appraising the diagnostic merits of the spiral aftereffect illusion. More relevant than detection rates to the diagnostic task of the clinician is the probability that the patient is a member of a particular diagnostic group, given a particular test result (as was pointed out in Section IV.6.3).

The test results can be thought of as data and the diagnoses as hypotheses entertained by the clinician. Then, $\mathbf{P}(F \mid A)$ is the probability that the hypothesis "functional illness" will be correct given the datum that the patient reported the aftereffect illusion. Similarly, $\mathbf{P}(B \mid \sim A)$ is the probability that the hypothesis "brain-damaged" is correct given failure to report the aftereffect. If the proportion of functionally ill, $\mathbf{P}(F)$, and the proportion of brain-damaged, $\mathbf{P}(B)$, are known for the patient population, then $\mathbf{P}(F \mid A)$ and $\mathbf{P}(B \mid \sim A)$ can be estimated. It is Bayes's theorem that provides the machinery for making such calculations. After introducing the theorem in general form, we will return to the psychodiagnostic problem.

Suppose that a set of r mutually exclusive and exhaustive hypotheses is under consideration. Label these hypotheses $H_1, H_2, \ldots, H_r$. These hypotheses are mutually exclusive if, for every pair of hypotheses H_i and H_j, $H_i \cap H_j = \Phi$. They are exhaustive if one of them *must* be true. Thus, the hypotheses F and B are mutually exclusive and exhaustive if every patient in the population must be either functionally ill or brain-damaged, but cannot be both.

Next, assume that the data must fall in one of k mutually exclusive and exhaustive categories, $D_1, D_2, \ldots, D_k$. For example, the spiral aftereffect must be reported or not reported by every patient, and no patient can both report it and fail to report it.

Now, suppose that data D_q are observed. The conditional probability of the correctness of a particular hypothesis, H_m, given the observed data is

$$\mathbf{P}(H_m \mid D_q) = \frac{\mathbf{P}(H_m \cap D_q)}{\mathbf{P}(D_q)}.$$

However, from Formula [IV.11], $\mathbf{P}(H_m \cap D_q)$ can be replaced with $\mathbf{P}(H_m)\mathbf{P}(D_q \mid H_m)$. This gives

$$\mathbf{P}(H_m \mid D_q) = \frac{\mathbf{P}(H_m)\mathbf{P}(D_q \mid H_m)}{\mathbf{P}(D_q)}.$$

The next step is to examine the Venn diagram in Figure V.3. Notice that the crosshatched area, $\mathbf{P}(D_2)$, is equal to $\mathbf{P}(H_1 \cap D_2) + \mathbf{P}(H_2 \cap D_2)$.

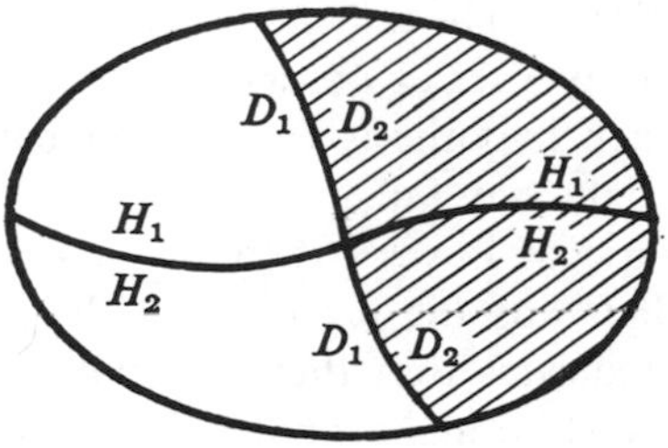

Figure V.3

Similarly, $\mathbf{P}(D_1) = \mathbf{P}(H_1 \cap D_1) + \mathbf{P}(H_2 \cap D_1)$. By examining this and other similar diagrams, one can see that in general,

$$\mathbf{P}(D_q) = \mathbf{P}(H_1 \cap D_q) + \mathbf{P}(H_2 \cap D_q) + \cdots + \mathbf{P}(H_r \cap D_q).$$

Substituting this for $\mathbf{P}(D_q)$, we have

$$\mathbf{P}(H_m \mid D_q) = \frac{\mathbf{P}(H_m)\mathbf{P}(D_q \mid H_m)}{\mathbf{P}(H_1 \cap D_q) + \mathbf{P}(H_2 \cap D_q) + \cdots + \mathbf{P}(H_r \cap D_q)}.$$

The next step is to apply Formula [IV.11] again. Then, $\mathbf{P}(H_1 \cap D_q) = \mathbf{P}(H_1)\mathbf{P}(D_q \mid H_1)$, $\mathbf{P}(H_2 \cap D_q) = \mathbf{P}(H_2)\mathbf{P}(D_q \mid H_2)$, $\ldots$, $\mathbf{P}(H_r \cap D_q) = \mathbf{P}(H_r)\mathbf{P}(D_q \mid H_r)$. Substituting these results leads to

$$\mathbf{P}(H_m \mid D_q) = \frac{\mathbf{P}(H_m)\mathbf{P}(D_q \mid H_m)}{\mathbf{P}(H_1)\mathbf{P}(D_q \mid H_1) + \mathbf{P}(H_2)\mathbf{P}(D_q \mid H_2) + \cdots + \mathbf{P}(H_r)\mathbf{P}(D_q \mid H_r)}.$$

This is Bayes's theorem.

Now the preceding developments will be recapitulated with a full statement of *Bayes's theorem*. *Let $H_1, H_2, \ldots, H_r$ be r mutually exclusive and exhaustive hypotheses, and let $D_1, D_2, \ldots, D_k$ be a mutually exclusive and exhaustive classification of the data. If H_m is one of the r hypotheses and if D_q is the observed data, then the probability that hypothesis H_m is true given the observed data, D_q, is*

$$\mathbf{P}(H_m \mid D_q) = \frac{\mathbf{P}(H_m)\mathbf{P}(D_q \mid H_m)}{\mathbf{P}(D_q)}, \qquad \text{[V.10a]}$$

or identically,

$$\mathbf{P}(H_m \mid D_q) = \frac{\mathbf{P}(H_m)\mathbf{P}(D_q \mid H_m)}{\mathbf{P}(H_1)\mathbf{P}(D_q \mid H_1) + \mathbf{P}(H_2)\mathbf{P}(D_q \mid H_2) + \cdots + \mathbf{P}(H_r)\mathbf{P}(D_q \mid H_r)} \qquad \text{[V.10b]}$$

provided that $\mathbf{P}(D_q) \neq 0$.

Formulas [V.10a] and [V.10b] are equal, but particular applications sometimes make one easier to use than the other.

Notice that $\mathbf{P}(H_m \mid D_q)$ can be calculated for each of the $r \cdot k$ combinations of one hypothesis and one set of observations. Thus, the probability of the correctness of each hypothesis can be calculated for each of the k classes in which the data may fall.

In discussing the use of Bayes's theorem, it is convenient to refer to $\mathbf{P}(H_1)$, $\mathbf{P}(H_2), \ldots, \mathbf{P}(H_r)$ as the *prior* probabilities of the r hypotheses. The word "prior" indicates that they are known before the data have been gathered. The conditional probabilities $\mathbf{P}(H_1 \mid D_q)$, $\mathbf{P}(H_2 \mid D_q), \ldots,$ $\mathbf{P}(H_r \mid D_q)$ are called *posterior* probabilities. They can be calculated only after the data, D_q, have been obtained.

One kind of application of Bayes's theorem can be illustrated by applying it to the psychodiagnosis problem. Some rather surprising and enlightening results are obtained.

A PROBLEM IN PSYCHODIAGNOSIS, PART II. Imagine that 90 percent of a hypothetical patient population are functionally ill and that the remaining 10 percent suffer from brain damage. Then $\mathbf{P}(F) = 0.90$ and $\mathbf{P}(B) = 0.10$. Furthermore, suppose that the detection rates reported by Page et al.[9] for the spiral aftereffect apply, so that $\mathbf{P}(A \mid F) = 0.85$ and $\mathbf{P}(\sim A \mid B) = 0.60$. Now $\mathbf{P}(F \mid A)$ and $\mathbf{P}(B \mid \sim A)$ are to be calculated using Bayes's theorem.

There are two hypotheses, $H_1 = F$ and $H_2 = B$, and the classification of the data is simply $D_1 = A$, $D_2 = \sim A$. Then, by Bayes's theorem (Formula [V.10b]), the probability that a patient is functionally ill given that he has reported the aftereffect is

$$\mathbf{P}(H_1 \mid D_1) = \frac{\mathbf{P}(H_1)\mathbf{P}(D_1 \mid H_1)}{\mathbf{P}(H_1)\mathbf{P}(D_1 \mid H_1) + \mathbf{P}(H_2)\mathbf{P}(D_1 \mid H_2)}$$

or

$$\mathbf{P}(F \mid A) = \frac{\mathbf{P}(F)\mathbf{P}(A \mid F)}{\mathbf{P}(F)\mathbf{P}(A \mid F) + \mathbf{P}(B)\mathbf{P}(A \mid B)}.$$

All of the quantities on the right are known except $\mathbf{P}(A \mid B)$. However, a brain-damaged patient must either report the aftereffect or not, so that $\mathbf{P}(A \mid B) + \mathbf{P}(\sim A \mid B) = 1$. Consequently, $\mathbf{P}(A \mid B) = 1 - \mathbf{P}(\sim A \mid B) = 1 - 0.60 = 0.40$. Then,

$$\begin{aligned}\mathbf{P}(F \mid A) &= \frac{\mathbf{P}(F)\mathbf{P}(A \mid F)}{\mathbf{P}(F)\mathbf{P}(A \mid F) + \mathbf{P}(B)\mathbf{P}(A \mid B)} \\ &= \frac{0.90(0.85)}{0.90(0.85) + 0.10(0.40)} \\ &= 0.950.\end{aligned}$$

[9] *Op. cit.*

A similar calculation can now be made to find the probability that a patient is brain-damaged given that he fails to report the aftereffect. This is accomplished as follows:

$$\mathbf{P}(H_2 \mid D_2) = \frac{\mathbf{P}(H_2)\mathbf{P}(D_2 \mid H_2)}{\mathbf{P}(H_1)\mathbf{P}(D_2 \mid H_1) + \mathbf{P}(H_2)\mathbf{P}(D_2 \mid H_2)}$$

or

$$\mathbf{P}(B \mid \sim A) = \frac{\mathbf{P}(B)\mathbf{P}(\sim A \mid B)}{\mathbf{P}(F)\mathbf{P}(\sim A \mid F) + \mathbf{P}(B)\mathbf{P}(\sim A \mid B)}.$$

Since $\mathbf{P}(\sim A \mid F) + \mathbf{P}(A \mid F) = 1$, $\mathbf{P}(\sim A \mid F) = 1 - \mathbf{P}(A \mid F) = 1 - 0.85 = 0.15$. Then,

$$\mathbf{P}(B \mid \sim A) = \frac{0.10(0.60)}{0.90(0.15) + 0.10(0.60)}$$
$$= 0.308.$$

Following the same procedures, $\mathbf{P}(B \mid A)$ and $\mathbf{P}(F \mid \sim A)$ can be calculated. All of these probabilities are tabulated in Table V.4. Here, it is

Table V.4. Probabilities for psychodiagnosis using spiral aftereffect

Conditional probability	Value of conditional probability
$\mathbf{P}(F \mid A)$	.950
$\mathbf{P}(B \mid \sim A)$	.308
$\mathbf{P}(F \mid \sim A)$	.692
$\mathbf{P}(B \mid A)$	.050

clear that the best diagnostic procedure is to diagnose "functionally ill" whenever the aftereffect is reported, since $\mathbf{P}(F \mid A) = 0.950$ is greater than $\mathbf{P}(B \mid A) = 0.050$. This is simply because patients who report the aftereffect are more likely to be functionally ill than brain-damaged.

But suppose that the aftereffect is not reported. Since $\mathbf{P}(F \mid \sim A) = 0.692$ is greater than $\mathbf{P}(B \mid \sim A) = 0.308$, Bayes's theorem seems to show that the clinician should diagnose "functionally ill" even if the patient fails to report the aftereffect. In other words, *no matter what the results of the aftereffect, he should always diagnose "functionally ill."* This seems strange since the detection rates ($\mathbf{P}(A \mid F) = 0.85$ and $\mathbf{P}(\sim A \mid B) = 0.60$) clearly indicate that failure to report the aftereffect is more likely among brain-damaged patients. What can be amiss?

In order to find out, suppose that we tentatively adopt the following diagnostic procedure: "whenever the aftereffect is reported, diagnose functional illness, and whenever the aftereffect is not reported, diagnose brain damage." In view of the detection rates, at least, this seems quite sensible. Now, using this diagnostic rule, what is the probability that a correct diagnosis will be made?

First, notice that there are two ways of being correct. Either functional illness is correctly diagnosed or brain damage is correctly diagnosed. If a patient is functionally ill, he will be correctly diagnosed if he gives result A, and the probability of this is $\mathbf{P}(A \cap F) = \mathbf{P}(F)\mathbf{P}(A \mid F) = 0.90(0.85) = 0.765$. This is the probability that a patient is functionally ill *and* correctly diagnosed as such. The probability of correctly diagnosing a brain-damaged patient is $\mathbf{P}(\sim A \cap B) = \mathbf{P}(B)\mathbf{P}(\sim A \mid B) = 0.10(0.60) = 0.060$. The union of $(A \cap F)$ and $(\sim A \cap B)$ consists of all correctly diagnosed patients. Therefore, the probability of a correct diagnosis is $\mathbf{P}[(A \cap F) \cup (\sim A \cap B)]$. This is simply the sum of $\mathbf{P}(A \cap F)$ and $\mathbf{P}(\sim A \cap B)$, since $(A \cap F)$ and $(\sim A \cap B)$ are nonoverlapping events; i.e.,

$$\begin{aligned} \mathbf{P}[(A \cap F) \cup (\sim A \cap B)] &= \mathbf{P}(A \cap F) + \mathbf{P}(\sim A \cap B) \\ &= 0.765 + 0.060 = 0.825. \end{aligned}$$

Thus, using the test only and following the tentative diagnostic rule, we can anticipate that 82.5 percent of patients will be diagnosed correctly. However, *if the test results are ignored and every patient is simply diagnosed "functionally ill," we can expect 90 percent of our diagnoses to be correct.* This follows from the fact that 90 percent of the population are functionally ill. In other words, the clinician can do better with no test at all, even though the detection rates for the test are 0.85 for functional illness and 0.60 for brain damage. This, of course, is what the application of Bayes's theorem (summarized in Table V.4) indicated.

On the other hand, if $\mathbf{P}(F) = \mathbf{P}(B) = 0.5$, then ignoring the test and diagnosing every patient as functionally ill would lead to only 50 percent correct. Since it can be shown that 72.5 percent correct can be achieved using the spiral aftereffect and the diagnostic rule given earlier, when $\mathbf{P}(F) = \mathbf{P}(B) = 0.5$, the spiral aftereffect test would be preferable.

The implication of this example is simple enough. The value of a diagnostic test is not to be judged solely on the basis of detection rates. Rather, it is necessary to consider *the incidence of each diagnosis in the particular population in which the test is to be used* and to make an analysis of the sort illustrated here before conclusions are drawn about the diagnostic usefulness of the test.[10]

Of course, this discussion is not intended to imply that the total proportion of correct diagnoses is the only important consideration in

[10] This problem has been discussed thoroughly by Meehl and Rosen in "Antecedent probability and the efficiency of psychometric signs, patterns, and cutting scores." *Psychol. Bull.* **52**, 194–216, 1955.

evaluating the usefulness of a diagnostic test. For example, diagnosing one brain-damaged patient correctly might be worth more than diagnosing one functionally ill patient correctly. "Worth more" might mean that more effective therapy could be instituted in the case of the correctly recognized brain-damaged patient than in the case of the functionally ill. Stated in this way, the problem of differential diagnosis is similar to the problem faced by the peanut vendor described in Chapter II. Like the vendor, the clinician wants to follow the course of action (i.e., adopt the therapeutic procedure) that has the greatest payoff or the least cost.

However, it is difficult to put a dollar and cents value on the outcome of therapy. If some measure could be devised for the value of a therapeutic procedure chosen on the basis of a correct diagnosis, or the cost of a therapy based on an incorrect diagnosis, then the full power of decision theory could be brought to bear on the diagnostic problem. The use of Wald's decision theory in dealing with similar problems has been thoughtfully discussed by Cronbach and Gleser.[11]

There are many situations in which the individual is required to choose among several alternatives (diagnoses, hypotheses, states of nature, etc.) on the basis of incomplete information. For example, the scientist must decide whether or not a given hypothesis is true on the basis of his data, and the structure of this situation is essentially the same as that of the clinical psychologist attempting to make a differential diagnosis. And, like the clinician, the scientist needs to know what it is worth to be right or what it costs to be wrong in order to make decisions on a rational basis.

It is easy to say that the clinician and the scientist and others in similar circumstances do not know the "value" of being right or the "cost" of being wrong, and therefore, that they can safely ignore decision theory. But make no mistake about it, the fact that decisions are made clearly implies that *they do assign values and costs to the consequences of their decisions*, even though this is done in such a way that the unit of value or of cost is unspecifiable. If the basis for such decisions is to be understood, then the measure of value and cost that is being employed must be ferreted out and made explicit. At present, perhaps the best we can do is to keep the problem in view and be prepared to utilize adequate solutions should they appear.

Before leaving the psychodiagnosis problem, a comment must be made on the prior probabilities used in this example. Without any spiral aftereffect data, the prior probability of the hypothesis "functional illness" was known to be 0.90, and the prior probability of the hypothesis "brain damage" was 0.10. In this kind of application, estimates of $\mathbf{P}(F)$ and $\mathbf{P}(B)$ probably could be obtained. For example, one could survey the

[11] *Psychological Tests and Personnel Decisions.* Urbana, University of Illinois Press, 1957.

recent medical records of a given hospital to find the proportions of functionally ill and brain-damaged patients who had been admitted. However, in many statistical applications, there are no data that provide direct estimates of the prior probabilities. Many of the scientists' hypotheses fall in this category. For instance, how can one estimate the probability that drive reduction is the basis for reinforcement?

In such situations the modern Bayesian statistician advocates the use of subjective prior probabilities. With the help of Bayes's theorem, these are combined with the results of observation to obtain the posterior probabilities. The general flavor of the neo-Bayesian's argument in favor of the scientist's use of subjective prior probabilities in hypothesis testing is given in the following section.

BAYES'S THEOREM AND STATISTICAL INDUCTION. In Bayes's formulation of hypothesis testing, the scientist begins with a set of mutually exclusive and exhaustive hypotheses. Furthermore, Bayes assumed that the scientist can assign a probability of correctness to each of these hypotheses *prior* to experimentation. Then, relevant data are gathered and the prior (to the data) probabilities are modified according to Bayes's theorem. The resulting posterior (to the data) probability of correctness of each hypothesis reflects both the influence of the scientist's prior knowledge *and* the import of his data.

It may be surprising that Bayes's approach to hypothesis testing, first published in 1763, has rarely been used. Statisticians and scientists alike usually rejected Bayes's approach because they saw no way to assign prior probabilities to their hypotheses. How can one determine the probability of a scientific hypothesis before gathering data?

Within the past decade, however, the Bayesian approach has been reappraised, and a few statisticians and psychologists now advocate its use in preference to the more conventional methods of statistical inference. When asked where the research scientist can get prior probabilities, their answer is that he should use his knowledge, experience, and intuition to assign *subjective* prior probabilities. In other words, before executing a research plan, he should be able to assign a probability to each of the hypotheses under consideration. These probabilities are chosen to reflect the strength of the investigator's confidence or belief in each of the hypotheses prior to gathering the data.

The neo-Bayesians argue that the scientist is not entirely ignorant before experimentation. He reads the journals; usually he has done research in the area before; and he can bring an enlightened intuition to bear on the hypotheses he is considering. From this background, he must assign a subjective prior probability to each of the hypotheses under consideration. After gathering relevant data, he uses Bayes's theorem to modify the prior subjective probabilities so that the resulting posterior probabilities reflect both the expectations of the investigator and the import of the data. These posterior probabilities then represent the relative strengths of the hypotheses.

One characteristic of this approach that is of special significance for psychologists is the use of subjective probabilities. This raises an important question for psychological research. If one combines subjective and objective probabilities in one mathematical formula (as the neo-Bayesian statistician does when he applies Bayes's theorem), one must ask whether subjective probabilities combine according to the same rules of mathematical probability theory as the objective probabilities do. If subjective probabilities obey different rules, then such a combination has little meaning. In Section *IX.8.5 we shall describe data that are relevant to the question of whether certain rules of probability theory do apply to subjective probabilities.

A related question is how one measures subjective probabilities. It is likely that the method of measurement will affect the extent to which subjective probabilities obey the rules of probability theory, and clearly, the determination of subjective probabilities is a problem in psychological measurement.

Still another reason for interest in the Bayesian approach to the induction problem is that in terms of their subjective probabilities, statistically naive decision-makers may make decisions in a manner consistent with Bayes's theorem. Although not in perfect agreement with Bayes's theorem, data have been reported[12] which suggest that the system recommended by Bayes provides a good first-order approximation to the intuitive decision-making of college students.

It is evident from this section and Section II.4 that modern statistical theory is raising questions requiring serious psychological attention. If it were possible to appraise the costs of wrong decisions and the value of correct decisions in subjective, psychological terms, then the range of applicability of the more sophisticated forms of statistical decision theory would be increased tremendously. In addition, suitable methods for measurement may show that subjective probabilities do follow the rules of probability theory, so that Bayesian methods of statistical induction can be applied. But notice that the questions raised here are psychological, not statistical. Much of the statistical theory already exists. The most serious questions have to do with the properties of subjective costs, values, and probabilities.

[12] Edwards, W., and L. D. Phillips, "Man as transducer for probabilities in Bayesian command and control systems." Paper read at meeting of the American Association for the Advancement of Science, Philadelphia, 1962; Peterson, C. R., Z. J. Ulehla, A. J. Miller, L. E. Bourne, Jr., and D. W. Stilson, "Internal consistency of subjective probabilities." *J. Exp. Psychol.*, in press. The third experiment reported in this paper is relevant.

Problems on Bayes's Theorem

1. In Section V.3.5 it was stated that if the prior probabilities of functional illness and brain damage were both equal to 0.50, then the probability of a correct diagnosis would be 0.725 if the following diagnostic rule were used:

   Diagnose brain damage whenever $\sim A$ is observed.

   Diagnose functional illness whenever A is observed.

   a. What are the four posterior probabilities for functional illness and brain damage when $\mathbf{P}(F) = \mathbf{P}(B) = 0.50$, $\mathbf{P}(A \mid F) = 0.85$, and $\mathbf{P}(\sim A \mid B) = 0.60$?

   b. Discuss the merits of the spiral aftereffect as a diagnostic test for a population in which $\mathbf{P}(F) = \mathbf{P}(B) = 0.50$.

2. You are presented with a mental hospital that admits 100 paranoids (P), 300 schizophrenics (S), and 200 malingerers (M) each year. These numbers remain stable from year to year. You also have a test for which only three mutually exclusive responses are distinguished. They are labeled A, B, and C. The following information on the test is available:

$$\mathbf{P}(A \mid P) = 0.70 \qquad \mathbf{P}(B \mid P) = 0.20$$
$$\mathbf{P}(B \mid S) = 0.80 \qquad \mathbf{P}(A \mid S) = 0.10$$
$$\mathbf{P}(C \mid M) = 0.70 \qquad \mathbf{P}(A \mid M) = 0.10.$$

   a. If this test is to provide the sole basis for diagnosis, what diagnostic decision rule would you adopt?

   b. Find the nine posterior probabilities for the three diagnoses. Do these probabilities seem consistent with your decision rule?

   c. Find the expected proportion of correct diagnoses using the decision rule that maximizes the proportion of correct diagnoses.

   d. Are the events A and P statistically independent? Demonstrate the correctness of your answer.

   e. If test result B is observed, what is the probability that the patient is paranoid or a malingerer?

3. Urn I contains 50 black balls and 50 white balls. In Urn II there are 100 black balls and 50 white ones. I toss a fair coin. If it falls heads, I draw a ball at random from Urn I. If it falls tails, I draw a ball at random from Urn II. You do not see which way the coin falls and you do not know which Urn I take a ball from.

   a. I inform you that I obtained a white ball. What is the probability that it came from Urn I?

   b. What is the best decision rule for you to employ if you wish to maximize the probability that you will guess correctly?

   c. Show that your answer to b is correct.

   d. What is the probability that you will guess correctly using the decision rule you chose for b?

   e. Instead of tossing a coin to choose the urn, suppose I toss a die. If the event {1, 2} occurs, I choose Urn II. If {3, 4, 5, 6} occurs, I choose Urn I. Answer a, b, c, and d for this new procedure.

*V.3.6. Statistical learning theory and simple conditioning

In Section *III.2.3, the general idea of Estes and Burke's statistical learning theory[13] was outlined. In this section, this theory will be applied to simple conditioning.

Suppose that a given conditioning situation consists of N stimulus elements. On each trial, the animal samples randomly from among these N stimulus elements. The probability that a given element will be included in the sample taken on a particular trial is θ. Thus, θ is the proportion of stimulus elements that the animal is expected to respond to on each trial.

On every reinforced trial, all stimulus elements that are responded to become linked to the conditioned response (R). Let X_t represent the number of stimulus elements linked to R immediately following trial t. Now, assume that the probability of the conditioned response following trial t equals the proportion of stimulus elements that have been linked with R up to and including trial t. In other words,

$$\mathbf{P}_t(R) = \frac{X_t}{N},$$

or more simply

$$p_t = \frac{X_t}{N}.$$

Put somewhat differently, the probability of the conditioned response following t reinforced training trials equals the probability that a randomly selected stimulus element has been linked with R on or before trial t.

Now, how does one reinforced trial change the probability of R? In other words, how can p_t be predicted from p_{t-1} if trial t is reinforced? The answer is that the change in the probability of the conditioned response equals the probability that on trial t a stimulus element will be sampled from among those *not* linked with R prior to trial t. If a previously unconnected element is sampled on a reinforced trial, then it becomes linked to R, and this increases the total number of stimulus elements so connected.

The probability that a randomly selected stimulus element is not connected to R at the beginning of trial t is $1 - p_{t-1}$, and since the sample drawn on each trial is random, the probability that a stimulus element will be sampled *and* will be among those not previously conditioned is $\theta(1 - p_{t-1})$. Therefore, the change from trial $t - 1$ to trial t is

$$p_t - p_{t-1} = \theta(1 - p_{t-1}). \qquad \text{[V.11]}$$

[13] Estes, W. K., and C. J. Burke, "A theory of stimulus variability in learning." *Psychol. Rev.* **60**, 276–286, 1953.

Formula [V.11] is useful for describing the course of conditioning, but it would be more convenient to be able to predict p_t directly for any t. Then, a curve representing the course of conditioning as a function of trials (assuming that reinforcement occurs on every trial) could be plotted easily. However, in order to arrive at the equation for this curve, it is most convenient to use the relation $p_t = 1 - (1 - p_{t-1})(1 - \theta)$ rather than Formula [V.11]. The algebraic connection between these expressions is shown in Appendix V.1 at the end of this chapter.

On the first training trial, $\mathbf{P}_0(R)$ equals some probability, p_0. (The probability p_0 may equal zero, but that is not necessary.) Then, the probability of R after one training trial is

$$p_t = 1 - (1 - p_{t-1})(1 - \theta)$$
$$p_1 = 1 - (1 - p_0)(1 - \theta).$$

After two training trials,

$$p_2 = 1 - (1 - p_1)(1 - \theta).$$

But since $p_1 = 1 - (1 - p_0)(1 - \theta)$, this can be substituted in the equation for p_2. Then,

$$\begin{aligned} p_2 &= 1 - (1 - p_1)(1 - \theta) \\ &= 1 - (1 - [1 - (1 - p_0)(1 - \theta)])(1 - \theta) \\ &= 1 - (1 - p_0)(1 - \theta)^2. \end{aligned}$$

Following the third training trial,

$$p_3 = 1 - (1 - p_2)(1 - \theta),$$

and since $p_2 = 1 - (1 - p_0)(1 - \theta)^2$,

$$\begin{aligned} p_3 &= 1 - (1 - [1 - (1 - p_0)(1 - \theta)^2])(1 - \theta) \\ &= 1 - (1 - p_0)(1 - \theta)^3. \end{aligned}$$

It begins to look as though $p_t = 1 - (1 - p_0)(1 - \theta)^t$ for any t, and this is correct.[14] The process begun above can be continued up to any trial, t, and the relation

$$p_t = 1 - (1 - p_0)(1 - \theta)^t \qquad \text{[V.12]}$$

will be found to hold. Consequently, Formula [V.12] is the expression for p_t as a direct function of t that we set out to find.

In order to see whether Formula [V.12] has the characteristics generally ascribed to conditioning curves, it has been plotted in Figure V.4 for $p_0 = 0$ and for $\theta = 0.5$ and $\theta = 0.2$. Although both curves begin at

[14] A general proof can be given by the method of mathematical induction.

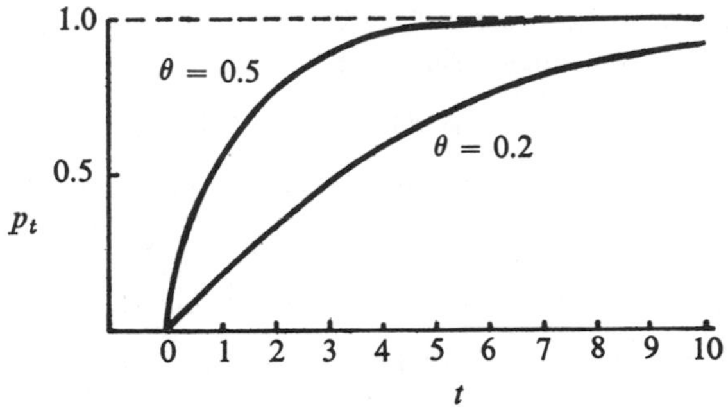

Figure V.4

$p_0 = 0$ and approach 1, the curve for $\theta = 0.5$ rises more rapidly than that for $\theta = 0.2$. This suggests that θ can be interpreted as a rate-of-learning constant. Thus, in the Estes-Burke theory, rate of learning depends on the proportion of stimulus elements sampled on each trial. If the proportion of elements is large, then many of them will become linked with the conditioned response after few trials, and the growth rate of p_t will be large.

Later, we will have occasion to develop the Estes-Burke theory further. It will provide material for the illustration of some of the ideas developed in later chapters.

*V.3.7. Problems on statistical learning theory

For all of the following, assume that every trial is reinforced.

*1. Suppose that $p_{t-1} = 0.66$. What is p_t if $\theta = 0.3$? What is p_{t+1}? What is p_{t+2}?

*2. Assume that $\theta = 0.3$ and $p_0 = 0$. For what value of t is $p_t = 0.66$?

*3. Plot p_t as a function of t for $p_0 = 0$ and $\theta = 0.3$.

*4. Plot $q_t = 1 - p_t$ as a function of t for $p_0 = 0$ and $\theta = 0.3$. Write an expression that permits one to calculate q_t directly for any trial, t. Interpret q_t in conditioning terms.

APPENDIX V.1

In Section *V.3.6, it was stated that the relation $p_t = 1 - (1 - p_{t-1})(1 - \theta)$ follows from $p_t - p_{t-1} = \theta(1 - p_{t-1})$. A proof of this follows.

First, add p_{t-1} to both sides of

$$p_t - p_{t-1} = \theta(1 - p_{t-1}).$$

This yields

$$p_t = p_{t-1} + \theta(1 - p_{t-1}).$$

Nothing essential will be changed if we add $1 - 1 = 0$ to the right-hand side, but it will make things easier. Then,

$$p_t = p_{t-1} + \theta(1 - p_{t-1}) + 1 - 1.$$

Expanding $\theta(1 - p_{t-1})$ and substituting the expanded form leads to

$$p_t = p_{t-1} + \theta - \theta p_{t-1} + 1 - 1,$$
$$p_t = 1 - (1 - p_{t-1} - \theta + \theta p_{t-1}).$$

Since $(1 - p_{t-1} - \theta + \theta p_{t-1})$ equals $(1 - p_{t-1})(1 - \theta)$, p_t can be written as

$$p_t = 1 - (1 - p_{t-1})(1 - \theta).$$

This is the form used in Section *V.3.6 to find p_t as a function of t.

SUGGESTED READING

1. The references to Mosteller, Rourke, and Thomas; Kemeny, Snell, and Thompson; Cramér; Feller; and Parzen appearing at the end of Chapter IV provide extensive information on probability calculations.
2. Bernoulli, J., "The Law of Large Numbers," in J. R. Newman (ed.), *The World of Mathematics*, III. New York, Simon and Schuster, 1956, pp. 1452–1455.
   This selection is from Bernoulli's *Ars Conjectandi.* It is the first attempt at a clear, probabilistic formulation of the law of large numbers.
3. Schlaifer, R., *Introduction to Statistics for Business Decisions.* New York, McGraw-Hill, 1961.
   A clear, simple presentation of the application of Bayesian methods to the induction problem. Although it is an introduction, it contains new material not published elsewhere. Schlaifer has also written a similar but more detailed account, *Probability and Statistics for Business Decisions.* New York, McGraw-Hill, 1959.
4. Edwards, W., H. Lindman, and L. J. Savage, "Bayesian statistical inference for psychological research," *Psychol. Rev.* **70**, 193–242, 1963. Reprinted in R. D. Luce, R. R. Bush, and E. Galanter (eds.), *Readings in Mathematical Psychology*, II. New York, John Wiley, 1965.
   This is perhaps the best brief introduction to Bayesian statistics that is available. Most of the fundamental ideas of the Bayesian approach are described, and some of them are illustrated. It includes comparisons with the Neyman-Pearson theory of hypothesis testing.
5. Non-technical articles pro and con Bayesian statistics have been appearing regularly in the *American Statistician* since 1960.

VI

RANDOM VARIABLES AND MEASUREMENT

THE primary purpose of this chapter is to develop an efficient language for talking about probability in connection with variables. The discussion then turns to measurement and some characteristics of systems of measurement that are important to the research scientist.

VI.1

RANDOM VARIABLES

In empirical research, making an observation can be viewed as performing a random experiment. This is true simply because the results of an observation are uncertain. For example, since a questionnaire item will have been chosen so that **P**(yes) is neither 0 nor 1, administering the item can be thought of as executing a random experiment.

Administration of the WISC (Wechsler Intelligence Scale for Children) to a 10-year-old child provides a little more elaborate example. To the response to each item on the test, a certain "credit" is assigned, such as 0, 1, or 2. The test result consists of a pattern of "credits." This pattern can be viewed as an outcome in the sample space for the random experiment "administer the WISC to a randomly selected 10-year-old child." Now, for each pattern of credits, the test manual specifies a full-scale IQ that is to be assigned to the child. This IQ constitutes a value on a variable.

If the examiner has no information concerning the child he is testing, it is possible to view the administration of the test as a random selection from among the WISC IQ's that are possible for 10-year-old children. Thus, the rule for assigning an IQ to a pattern of WISC item credits is called a *random variable*, and the process of making a random selection of a pattern (giving the test) and applying this rule is called observing a value of a random variable.

VI.1.1. Definition of random variable

If a rule assigns exactly one numerical value to each outcome in a single sample space, then that rule is called a random variable. In short, *a random variable is a function defined on a sample space.* The set of distinct values that are assigned by the random variable is called the *range of the random variable.* The range will be represented as an ordered set, the smallest value assigned by the random variable being the first element. A random variable is sometimes referred to as an *observation variable* or simply as a *variable.*

When a random experiment is performed, an outcome will be observed, and the random variable assigns a value to this outcome. Consequently, the random experiment generates a value from the range of the random variable. This is described as *observing a value of a random variable.*

In the intelligence-test example, the item-response patterns constitute the outcomes. The test manual provides the rule that defines the random variable. The set of possible IQ's listed in the manual is the range of the random variable, and administering the test and determining a full-scale IQ can be described as observing a value of the random variable.

A more complete example of a random variable can be given for the random experiment "toss 3 coins." This variable is defined by the rule "assign the number of heads to each outcome," as shown in Table VI.1. The range of this random variable is (0, 1, 2, 3).

Table VI.1. Number of heads per toss of three coins

Outcome	H,H,H	H,H,T	H,T,H	T,H,H	T,T,H	T,H,T	H,T,T	T,T,T
Value of the random variable	3	2	2	2	1	1	1	0

Random variables usually will be referred to by capital letters. Thus, in the preceding example, the letter X might be used to refer to the number of heads. Furthermore, once an observation has been made, X takes on a particular value. If two heads are observed, then $X = 2$.

Suppose that a rat is running a three-unit T-maze, and that the sequence of initial choices right, left, right (R, L, R) constitutes an errorless trial. Then there are $2^3 = 8$ possible sequences that can occur, and for each of these the number of incorrect initial choices can be determined (see Table VI.2). Here, each sequence of choices is an outcome for the random

Table VI.2. Errors for maze with three choice points

Sample space	R,R,R	L,R,R	R,L,R	R,R,L	L,L,R	L,R,L	R,L,L	L,L,L
Number of errors	1	2	0	2	1	3	1	2

experiment "run a rat in the maze," and the number of errors constitutes a random variable defined on this sample space. The range of this random variable is (0, 1, 2, 3).

If a student takes a 10-item multiple-choice test in which each item has four alternatives, then the sample space will contain 4^{10} outcomes. However, the instructor is not ordinarily interested in the exact pattern of responses, but rather in the number of answers that agree with his scoring key. Thus, if X is a random variable representing the number of correct answers, then the range of X is (0, 1, 2, 3, 4, 5, 6, 7, 8, 9, 10).

From the preceding examples, it can be seen that defining a random variable is simply a way of attaching meaningful labels to events. Numbers are assigned to outcomes in such a way that they describe some characteristic of the outcomes.

Suppose that a random experiment consists of drawing a random sample of size 2 from the population consisting of the elements 1, 2, and 3. If sampling is with replacement, then the first row of Table VI.3 represents the sample space for this experiment. If the mean is computed for each

Table VI.3. Sample space and sample means for random samples of size 2

Sample space	1, 1	1, 2	1, 3	2, 1	2, 2	2, 3	3, 1	3, 2	3, 3
Sample means	1.0	1.5	2.0	1.5	2.0	2.5	2.0	2.5	3.0

of these samples, then the set of possible values of the mean constitutes the range of a random variable defined on this sample space. If the mean is labeled $\bar{X}$, then (1.0, 1.5, 2.0, 2.5, 3.0) is the range of $\bar{X}$.

It is important to understand this example. When a random sample is selected and a statistic is calculated for that sample, the result is a value of a random variable.

Notice that the mean of the population is 2 and that the means of some samples are close to this parameter. The samples (1, 3), (2, 2), and (3, 1) each have a mean exactly equal to the population mean. On the other hand, the samples (1, 1) and (3, 3) each have means that differ considerably from the population mean of 2. Thus, if the mean of a random sample is used to estimate a population mean, the estimate may be close to the population mean or it may be quite different from the population value. The differences among the values of the sample mean reflect the effects of sampling variability.

VI.1.2 Discrete and continuous random variables

Every random variable in the preceding illustrations is *discrete*. For example, the number of heads appearing when three coins are tossed is a discrete random variable. One head might occur, or two heads, but 1.5 heads is impossible. As far as this random variable is concerned, 2 is the smallest number greater than 1. Similarly, if random samples of size 2 are taken with replacement from the population {1, 2, 3}, a sample mean of 1.5 or 2.0 may be observed, but a mean between these values is impossible. In this example, the sample mean is also a discrete random variable.

Theoretically, a discrete random variable can have a countably infinite range. For instance, the range of a random variable may consist of the integers 0, 1, 2, 3, ... Number of training trials is a discrete and countably infinite random variable that is frequently used in theoretical discussions of learning. Learning theorists talk about the "asymptotic level of performance," which is approached as the number of training trials becomes countably infinite. Similarly, in statistics it is sometimes useful to conceptualize a discrete random variable as if its range were countably infinite.

Random variables also may be conceptualized as *continuous*, even though limitations of our measuring instruments always restrict us to discrete observations. Intelligence can be treated theoretically as a continuous variable, but an intelligence test does not measure IQ in fractional values. A measured IQ may be 125 or 126 but not 125.52 or even 125.5. We think about time flowing continuously from one instant to the next, but when reaction times are recorded, the measurements are to the nearest hundredth or perhaps thousandth of a second.

The range of a continuous random variable is always uncountably infinite. One can think of the points on a straight line as representing the values of the range of a continuous random variable, and as we discovered in Section III.1.2, no matter how short the line (provided its length is not zero) it is made up of an uncountably infinite set of points.

In statistical analyses, it is sometimes much easier to proceed as if empirical observations were made on a continuous variable, even though it is perfectly clear that they were not. True, this will introduce some error in the manipulation of the data, but the amount of error is usually sufficiently small to be ignored.

To summarize, a random variable may be conceptualized as discrete or as continuous. If it is continuous, then its range must be uncountably infinite. If it is discrete, it may have either a finite or a countably infinite range. At the same time, empirical-observation variables must be discrete and have a finite range. Continuous and countably infinite discrete variables are employed to simplify our thinking or to reduce the burden of calculation in processing data.

VI.2
MEASUREMENT

Everyone is aware of the importance of measurement in carrying out empirical research, but the exact nature of measurement and its critical role in the scientific enterprise is not always appreciated. In this section, a useful conception of measurement will be introduced, its relation to the idea of a random variable will be described, and some of the properties of measurement procedures that have important bearing on the conclusions drawn from empirical research will be discussed.

VI.2.1. Definition of measurement

Stevens[1] has defined a scale of measurement as a "rule for the assignment of numerals to aspects of objects or events."[2] Thus, the procedure followed in weighing objects with a balance beam constitutes a scale of measurement. Similarly, a substantial part of the manual for a standard intelligence test constitutes a scale of measurement, since it is simply an elaborate rule for assigning IQ's to individuals.

Although Stevens' definition is not universally accepted,[3] it provides a workable starting point for discussing the way in which numbers are used to describe aspects of the real world, and it is this definition that will be referred to subsequently by the terms *scale*, *scale of measurement*, or *system of measurement*.

In psychological research, the rule determining a scale is often deceptively simple. For example, one counts the number of items on a questionnaire that have been answered in a manner consistent with the researcher's key, the frequency with which a particular response follows a given

[1] Stevens, S. S., "Mathematics, measurement, and psychophysics." In S. S. Stevens (ed.), *Handbook of Experimental Psychology*. New York, John Wiley, pp. 1–49 (quote from p. 23).

[2] The term "events" does not refer to subsets of a sample space in this context. Rather, it refers to happenings in the real world.

[3] See Torgerson, W. S., *Theory and Methods of Scaling*. New York, John Wiley, 1958, Chaps. 1–2.

stimulus is recorded, the time separating stimulus presentation and the initiation of a given response is observed, and so on. But such simple measurement procedures require careful scrutiny no less than complex ones. The validity of empirical conclusions always depends upon the nature of the observations on which the conclusions are based.

VI.2.2. Measurement and random variables

When a random variable is defined, a rule is followed to determine the numerical value to be assigned to each outcome in the sample space. According to Stevens, a scale of measurement is a rule for assigning numerals to aspects of objects or events (but here, *events* refers to happenings in the real world). It may appear that the ideas of random variable and scale of measurement are the same, but one must be careful.

A random variable assigns numerical values to *outcomes*, and the outcomes themselves are usually abstractions that are considerably removed from the objects or events of the real world. Consequently, a random variable by itself is not generally the equivalent of a scale of measurement. Nonetheless, it seems reasonable to state that a random variable combined with the procedure for designating the outcomes of the sample space on which it is defined is a scale of measurement.

VI.2.3. Validity of a system of measurement

In evaluating a system of measurement, two important questions can be raised. The first is "What does it measure?" Such a question is obviously important, and though it appears straightforward, it is not easy to see what is required in order to answer it satisfactorily. This question of meaning or of *external validity* is discussed briefly below.

The second question has to do with the internal structure or *internal validity* of a system of measurement. To investigate internal validity, one must examine the kinds of relationships that hold among the values generated by the scale itself. For example, consideration of the internal structure of an intelligence test might lead to questions like the following: "Is there any *psychological sense* in which the difference between an MA of 3 years and one of 6 years is equal to the difference between an MA of 6 years and one of 9 years? If so, what is the nature of this equality and how can it be demonstrated *empirically*?" "What, if any, is the meaning of zero intelligence?" "Is there any *psychological meaning* attributable to the statement that an MA of 6 years represents twice as much intelligence as an MA of 3 years? If so, how is this meaning demonstrable?" In this case, the procedure for assigning MA's is the measure to be scrutinized, and an analysis of the internal validity of MA as measured by a particular test should provide answers to questions like these.

External validity. The fundamental idea in establishing the meaning or external validity of a scale is to find other measures that are related to it and to determine the nature of these relationships. However, differences among the purposes scales are intended to serve lead to different ways of assessing external validity.

Concurrent validity. One form of validation, concurrent validity, is analogous to defining a word by finding a synonym. It also involves the same risk; that is, the meaning of the synonym may be no clearer than the meaning of the word to be defined. Thus, a new test of intelligence might be "validated" by showing that it is correlated with teachers' ratings of intelligence. The obvious difficulty with this approach is that there are no especially convincing reasons for believing that teachers' ratings reflect a useful conception of intelligence. This illustrates a general difficulty of the synonym approach. It is rare that a single criterion is available that is sufficiently well established to serve as the standard for a newer measure. In fact, if such a criterion were available, there would be no logical necessity for a new measure at all. (Of course, a new measure might be sought in order to reduce the time or cost of obtaining information.)

Predictive validity. Another type of validity, predictive validity, may be quite useful in practical situations where the sole purpose of a measure is to predict a particular performance. For example, if a test is developed for the purpose of predicting the amount of insurance sold by men who subsequently become life-insurance salesmen, the test can be appraised solely in terms of its accuracy in making such predictions.

Construct validity. Scales that are intended to represent theoretical constructs are expected to be related to other measures in ways specified by the theory. Under these circumstances, the meaning of a system of measurement is clarified by evolving an *empirically verified* conceptual network of relations between the measure in question and others that are pertinent to the theoretical system. Theoretical predictions involving the scale are made, and if they are borne out by observation, then the validity of the scale is increased. Thus, a scale that is designed to reflect a theoretical construct is not valid or invalid; instead, its meaning is clarified progressively by enriching the empirically verified theoretical context in which it lies. This conception of validity has been termed *construct validity*.[4]

Construct validity has been discussed primarily in connection with psychological *tests*, but there is no reason why it cannot be used to clarify

[4] Cronbach, L. J., and P. E. Meehl, "Construct validity in psychological tests." *Psychol. Bull.* **52**, 281–302, 1955. See also Loevinger, J., "Objective tests as instruments of psychological theory." *Psychol. Rep.* Monograph Suppl. **9**, 636–694, 1957; Campbell, D. T., and D. W. Fiske, "Convergent and discriminant validation by the multi-trait-multimatrix method." *Psychol. Bull.* **56**, 81–105, 1959.

the meaning of other types of measures. For example, one might attempt to validate response latency as a measure of the strength of a learned response. Suppose that rats are to be used as subjects, and that they are to be trained in the acquisition of a running response in a straight-alley maze with a food reward. The following predictions might be made on the basis of some rather general considerations of the nature of learning:

1. Response latency and running time are positively correlated (that is, they increase or decrease together).
2. As the amount of food in the goal box increases, response latencies decrease to a minimum, but with further increases in the amount of food, response latencies remain constant. (The rat could not care less whether he finds one barrel of pellets in the goal box or two barrels.)
3. As food-deprivation time increases, response latencies decrease to a minimum, but with further increases in deprivation time, latencies begin to rise (due to the debilitating effects of starvation).
4. Following training, response latencies will increase during a sequence of unreinforced trials.

Verification of all of these relatively simple predictions would indicate that response latency does have some of the properties that one would wish to attribute to a measure of learning.

Using the ideas of construct validation, one might investigate a measure of verbal intelligence by testing empirically the propositions given below:

1. The correlation between verbal intelligence and the verbal subscale of the WAIS (Wechsler Adult Intelligence Scale) is positive and higher than its correlation with the performance subscale.
2. The correlation between verbal intelligence and the Taylor Manifest Anxiety Scale is zero.
3. The correlation between verbal intelligence and verbal fluency is positive but lower than its correlation with the WAIS verbal subscale.
4. Of the two individuals scoring identically on the WAIS performance subscale, the one scoring higher on a test of reading comprehension will score higher on the measure of verbal intelligence.

Empirical support for all four of these propositions would demonstrate that the test has some of the properties attributed to verbal intelligence by our theory. The verification of additional or more refined propositions concerning the theoretical relations in which this measure enters would add still more to our understanding of it.

From the preceding discussion, it can be seen that construct validity is essentially the amount of integrated knowledge we have of a measure. The more extensive and detailed the empirically verified theoretical context of a scale becomes, the greater is its construct validity.

The theoretical contexts for the predictions in each of the preceding examples are rather vague and crude, but predictions of this kind could be made from some of the current conceptions of the nature of learning and of intelligence. It should not be inferred from these examples, however, that all measures in psychology stem from this kind of theory. In the statistical learning theory of Estes and Burke (see Sections *III.2.3 and *V.3.6), predictions concerning relationships among variables are formulated in explicit, mathematical terms. Verification of these explicit functional relationships amounts to increasing the external validity of the variables in the theory.

One should not proceed to the conclusion that construct validity is a justification for substituting quantity for quality. Verification of a large number of crude theoretical predictions concerning a particular measure adds no more to its validity than establishing a smaller number of precise predictions. The reason for this is clear enough. Data may take many forms and still be consistent with a crude theoretical prediction, but when a prediction is precise, the data must lie within narrow limits if they are to be consistent with it. It is easier to falsify a precise prediction than to falsify a crude one. Thus, if X is being subjected to validation, verifying the theoretical statement "X and Y are related" contributes less to the validation of X than verification of the statement "X is an increasing exponential function of Y."

Finally, construct validation is inextricably linked with the development of theory. In studying the empirical validity of theoretical predictions of relationship among measures, the investigator may concentrate on the nature of the relationships or on the nature of the variables. If he concentrates on relationships, his work would probably be described as theory development, if on variables, as construct validation.

INTERNAL VALIDITY. The internal validity of a scale is determined by the kinds of relations that hold among the values generated by the scale itself. The remainder of this chapter is devoted to elaborating the meaning of internal validity and some of its implications for psychological research. Four types of scale structure can be distinguished,[5] and though further refinements are possible,[6] these four will form the focus of this discussion.

Nominal scales. The most elementary type of measurement is based on the relation "different from." This relation is used when a numeral is assigned to an object or event simply to distinguish it from others. The process is essentially that of naming; neither the absolute magnitude nor the relative magnitude of the numerals has any meaning. For example,

[5] Stevens, *op. cit.*

[6] Coombs, C., H. Raiffa, and R. M. Thrall, "Some views on mathematical models and measurement theory." *Psychol. Rev.* **61**, 132–144, 1954; Stevens, S. S., "Measurement, psychophysics, and utility," in C. W. Churchman and P. Ratoosh (eds.), *Measurement; Definitions and Theories.* New York, John Wiley, 1959, pp. 18–63.

in order to obtain a random sample of students from a given university, a distinct numeral might be assigned to each member of the student body. Selecting a sample of these numerals from a table of random numbers would define a random sample of the student body. In this case, the numeral assigned a student serves as a name or label, and the fact that the numeral assigned one student is larger than that assigned another means nothing more than that the two students are distinct persons.

An extension of this use of numerals is the assignment of one number to all of the individuals sharing a particular property or attribute. This is the use of numerals to designate classes. Thus, in sampling students, each female student might be assigned a 0 and each male a 1.

In assigning football-jersey numbers, a combination of simple labeling and class identification is often used. The first digit of a player's number indicates the position he plays, while the second digit distinguishes him from others playing the same position. If the first digit of a player's number is a 1, he is a quarterback; if the first digit is an 8, he plays end; and so on. The fact that the ends are identified by a larger number than the quarterbacks tells you only that they play different positions. It does not indicate that the end is a bigger or better player than the quarterback. Similarly, the fact that one end is number 88 and another number 84 tells you nothing more than that these are different players who play the same position.

The sort of measurement system described above is called nominal measurement. *When numerals are assigned to events in such a way that any two events bearing the same numeral belong to the same class and any two bearing different numerals belong to distinct classes, then the rule for assigning the numerals constitutes a nominal scale.* A class may contain exactly one individual or it may contain many.

Perhaps simple classification should not be termed *measurement*, but it does seem clear that classification is at the root of all measurement.

In order to establish the internal validity of a nominal scale, it must be shown *empirically* that each pair of events to which the scale assigns distinct numerals differ with respect to the designated characteristic, whereas events bearing the same numeral are identical with respect to the characteristic.

In the case of sex, church preference, or answer to a true-false question, internal validation is perhaps trivial. However, the internal validation of nominal scales for hair color, race, or personality type is likely to prove difficult.

It is useful in discussing types of scale structure to introduce the idea of the *conditions of invariance* of a scale of measurement. This amounts to asking what can be done to *all* of the values generated by a scale without altering the essential relationships among values. Thus, if some operation is performed upon all the values generated by the scale X, the result can be labeled Y and the operation labeled g. Then,

$$Y = g(X)$$

says that there is a function relating X to Y so that exactly one value of Y is assigned to every value of X according to the rule g. The conditions of invariance for a particular scale, X, specify the kinds of functions g that may be applied to X such that the essential relations among values of X are maintained in the relations among *corresponding* values of Y.

In the case of a nominal scale, the essential "different from" relation will be invariant for many kinds of functions. For example, if 100 is added to each of the numerals identifying players on a football team (X), then $Y = 100 + X$ forms the new set of numbers. If one player had number 83 initially and another number 11, their new numbers would be 183 and 111, and 183 is different from 111 just as 83 is different from 11. Similarly, a nominal scale can be transformed by multiplying each of the values it generates by a constant, and by a host of other operations, without destroying the "different from" relation. In short, *the "different from" relation that characterizes a nominal scale is invariant for any one-to-one transformation.*

Ordinal scales. In addition to using numerals to distinguish between classes of objects or events, it may be possible to order the classes with respect to some characteristic. When this is possible, the rule for assigning the numerals is called an ordinal scale, and the relation defining an ordinal scale is "greater than" or "more than." This relation will be symbolized by the greater than sign, $>$.

Suppose that a student is asked to rank his professors according to his judgment of the adequacy of their teaching. If the student was enrolled in five courses, the numeral 5 might be assigned to the best teacher, Professor Smith, a 4 to Professor Jones, and so on. Rank 1 would be assigned to the instructor who was the poorest teacher in the opinion of the student. Of course, the fact that the numerals assigned to Professors Smith and Jones differ by 1 cannot be taken to mean that Smith has one more unit of teaching ability than Jones. The fact that $5 > 4$ can be interpreted to mean only that the student considers Smith's teaching to be superior to Jones's. This same difference in preference could have been represented by assigning the number 67 to Smith and 41 to Jones, since $67 > 41$. An ordinal scale does not give information concerning the *magnitude* of differences in preference; only the direction of differences can be inferred.

If the student was sure that Jones and Smith were both superior to all of his other instructors, but could find no basis for preferring one to the other, he would be compelled to assign the same numeral to both. In this case, it could be said only that Jones and Smith were "equal" in teaching skill. Thus, the assignment of numerals according to an ordinal rule involves two steps: (1) determining whether the members of each pair of objects (or events) are the same as or different from one another, and, (2) if they are different, determining which one has more of the attribute in question.

Even though these two requirements may be met for every pair of objects, an ordinal scale still may *not* have been established. For example, suppose that we ask our student to consider his instructors two at a time and to decide which member of each pair is the better instructor. For the three instructors, Smith, Jones, and Williams, the students might decide the following:

1. Smith is better than Jones.
2. Jones is better than Williams.
3. Williams is better than Smith.

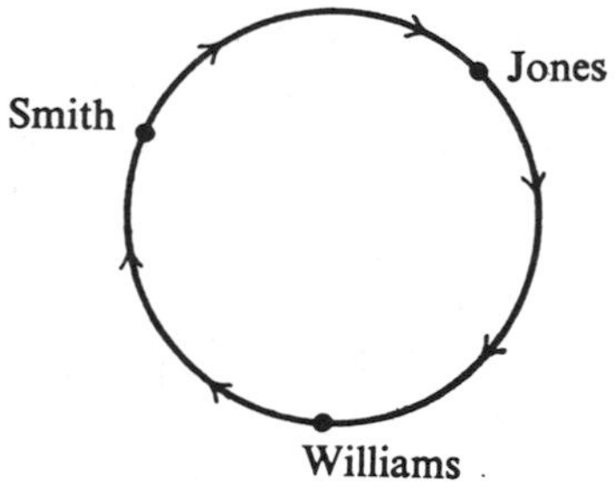

Figure VI.1

The third decision is inconsistent with the two preceding it, since the first two clearly imply that Smith is better than Williams. These pairwise judgments do not permit a straight-line ordering of the three instructors; instead, the circle of Figure VI.1 provides a more suitable diagrammatical representation of this student's pairwise evaluation. The direction of the arrows indicates the direction of the "better than" relation.

Clearly, results such as these are incompatible with one's intuitive idea of "ordering from highest to lowest." In short, an ordering must have a beginning and an end rather than progressing in a circle. In the case of the student's evaluation of his instructors, if Smith is considered a better instructor than Jones, and if Jones is better than Williams, then Smith must be judged better than Williams. In other words, the scale must be *transitive.*

Note that the transitivity property must hold for *all* sets of three individuals to which the scale assigns values.

In order to establish that a rule for measurement constitutes an ordinal scale, two conditions must be shown to hold empirically. If the objects (or events) to which the scale applies are labeled $E_1, E_2, \ldots, E_N$, and the values assigned to these objects by the scale are labeled $S(E_1), S(E_2), \ldots, S(E_N)$, then two conditions must be satisfied in order to demonstrate that the scale is an ordinal scale:

(1) *For every pair of objects,* E_i and E_j, *exactly one of the following statements must be true*:

(a) $S(E_i) = S(E_j)$
(b) $S(E_i) > S(E_j)$
(c) $S(E_j) > S(E_i)$.

It is not sufficient to show that the *numbers* assigned to E_i and E_j are either equal or that one exceeds the other. If $S(E_i) = S(E_j)$, then it must be shown *empirically* that E_i and E_j are *psychologically equivalent* with respect to the attribute that the numbers are intended to reflect. If $S(E_i) > S(E_j)$, then it must be shown *empirically* that E_i has more of the *psychological attribute* in question than does E_j.

(2) *For all triplets of objects to which scale values are to be assigned,* E_i, E_j, *and* E_r, *if* $S(E_i) > S(E_j)$ *and* $S(E_j) > S(E_r)$, *then it must be true that* $S(E_i) > S(E_r)$. The relations that characterize the transitivity property also must be shown to hold *empirically* in order to establish that the numbers are determined by an ordinal scale.

It is important to notice the fundamental procedures involved in validating the internal structure of an ordinal scale. First, empirical procedures must be devised that represent the psychological meaning of the "equal" and "more than" relations. Then, these procedures must be used in a way that yields data permitting tests of Requirements 1 and 2.

In the preceding subsection, we found that the "different from" relation that forms the basis for a nominal scale remains unaltered by any one-to-one transformation. Now, what are the characteristics of transformations that preserve the "more than" relation on which ordinal scales are based? The answer is fairly obvious. Any transformation that preserves order will not alter the internal structure of an ordinal scale. Thus, adding a constant to each of the rankings that our student assigned his five instructors, or multiplying each by a constant, or even taking the log of each, does not alter the *order* of the numerical values assigned. Thus, $5 > 4$ and $\log_{10} 5 > \log_{10} 4$. Table VI.4 summarizes the results of several transformations that do not modify the order of the initial ranking. In brief, *an ordinal scale may be transformed by any monotonic increasing function*[7] *without altering the "greater than" relation.*

Since any monotonic increasing transformation can be applied to the

[7] A function, $g(X)$, is monotonic increasing if for every pair of values X_i and X_j such that $X_i > X_j$, $g(X_i) > g(X_j)$. That is, whenever X increases, $g(X)$ increases as well.

values generated by an ordinal scale without altering the "more than" relation, it is clear that the units of an ordinal scale cannot represent psychological *magnitudes.* To see this, suppose that the student had six instructors instead of five, and that Professor Wilson fell between Smith and Jones. Then the difference between Jones and Wilson would be one

Table VI.4. Transformations for which ordinal scale remains invariant

Transformations (Y)	Orginal ranking (X)				
	1	2	3	4	5
$Y = X + 20$	21	22	23	24	25
$Y = 5X$	5	10	15	20	25
$Y = 5X + 20$	25	30	35	40	45
$Y = \log_{10} X$	0	.301	.477	.602	.699

unit, but it could not represent the same magnitude of difference in teaching skill as the one unit separating Smith and Jones when only five professors were ranked (see Fig. VI.2). Thus, ordinal scale values may depend on the number of items to which the values are assigned, and, obviously, the number of items to which the scale is applied should not affect the *magnitude* of the psychological characteristic of any one of them. Furthermore,

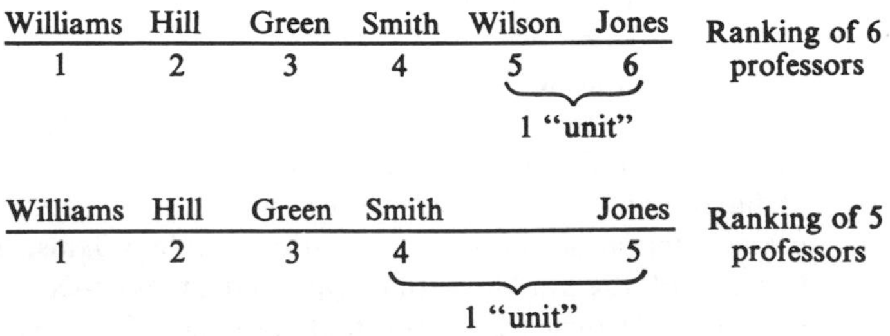

Figure VI.2

suppose the student assigned a 1 to Professor Williams and a 2 to Professor Hill. This provides no evidence to indicate that the difference of 1 separating Smith and Jones represents the same amount of teaching skill as the one unit separating Hill and Williams when five professors are ranked.

Thus, statements about the magnitude of differences require that a standard unit be available and that the unit remains constant over the entire range of the scale.

Interval scales. If a scale does define a constant unit, then it is an interval scale. Temperature Fahrenheit constitutes a familiar interval scale. The increase in average molecular kinetic energy required to raise the temperature of a given body from +1°F to +2°F is the same as the increase required to raise its temperature from +100°F to +101°F.

Mental age does not permit such straightforward interpretation of the unit employed. What can be the operational meaning of adding one year of mental age? And how can one examine empirically the assertion that adding 1 year of MA to an MA of 3 is equivalent to adding 1 year of MA to an MA of 10? Such questions are meaningless within the current framework of intelligence measurement, and it is fair to say that we have no evidence that the measurement of mental age satisfies the equal-unit criterion of an interval scale.

In order to demonstrate that one is dealing with an interval scale, it is necessary to show empirically that the two conditions required for an ordinal scale apply and, in addition, that one other condition is satisfied.[8] If the objects or events to which scale values are to be assigned are denoted $E_1, E_2, \ldots, E_h, \ldots, E_i, \ldots, E_j, \ldots, E_r, \ldots, E_n$, and if the corresponding scale values assigned to these events are $S(E_1)$, $S(E_2), \ldots, S(E_h), \ldots, S(E_i), \ldots, S(E_j), \ldots, S(E_r), \ldots, S(E_n)$, then *the last requirement of an interval scale stipulates that if*

$$S(E_i) - S(E_h) = S(E_r) - S(E_j),$$

then the difference between E_h and E_i must be equal empirically to the difference between E_j and E_r for every set of four scale values that satisfy the equality. In other words, operationally equal differences between the members of pairs of objects must correspond to equal differences between scale values.

Suppose that we have obtained scale values representing the loudness of pure tones E_1, E_2, E_3, and E_4, and suppose that $S(E_2) - S(E_1) = S(E_3) - S(E_2) = S(E_4) - S(E_3)$. That is, according to the scale, the loudness difference between successive tones are psychologically equal. One way to investigate the equality of these intervals is to ask a subject to adjust a tone of variable intensity so that its loudness is midway between

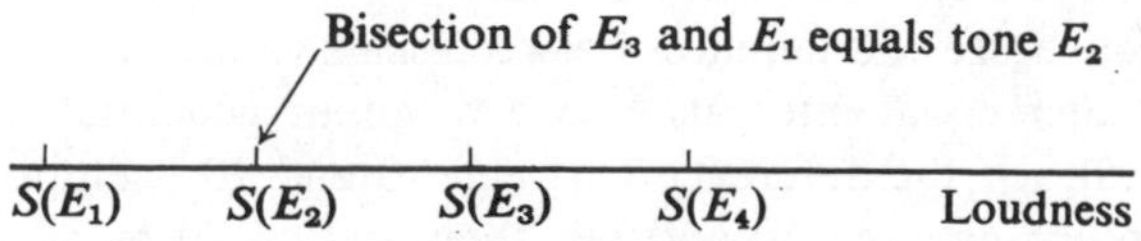

Figure VI.3

[8] This last requirement is stated in the form in which it ordinarily would be investigated empirically. For a formal presentation of the properties of interval scales, see Torgerson, *op. cit.*

E_3 and E_1. If the scale is an interval scale, then the setting of the variable tone should equal the intensity of the tone E_2 (see Fig. VI.3). Similarly, if a subject were asked to bisect the loudness interval between E_4 and E_2, the setting would be expected to equal E_3.

Of course, for a given scale, many tests of the equality of intervals can be devised. In the example, if a subject bisected the interval between E_4 and E_1 and, independently, the interval between E_3 and E_2, the bisection points should be equal if the scale has equal intervals. This is shown diagrammatically in Figure VI.4.

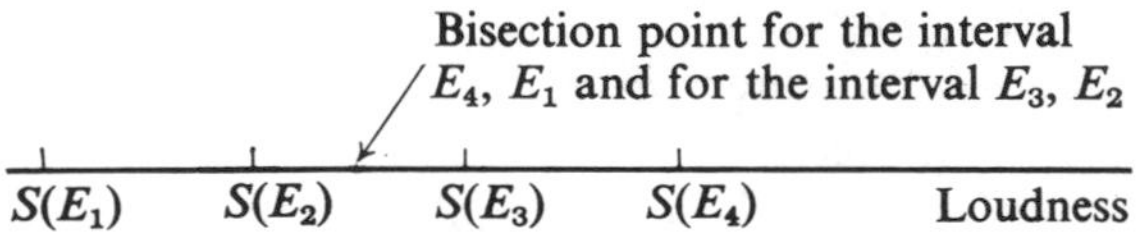

Figure VI.4

Note that the attribution of equal intervals to the measurement of a particular characteristic amounts to a theoretical statement about the nature of the relationships that hold among the values the scale generates. In the example above, the theoretical characteristics of an interval scale led to certain predictions concerning the psychological relationships among tones. These predictions could be evaluated empirically. If the data were consistent with the predictions, this would lend support to the theoretical description of the system of measurement as an interval scale. Otherwise, the theory must be questioned. It is in this sense that study of the internal structure of a scale may be viewed as validation. Internal validation is empirical inquiry into the nature of the relationships among the events to which a scale assigns values.

The equal-interval property of the interval scale remains invariant for any linear transformation[9] of the scale values. If a scale is an interval scale, then multiplying each of the values it generates by a constant and adding a constant to this product yields a set of values that also have the equal-interval property.

Note the effects of such a linear transformation. First, adding a constant shifts the zero point of the scale. This, of course, has no effect upon the relative size of differences between scale values, and consequently, it does not alter equal intervals between values generated by the scale (see Fig. VI.5). If the difference between 10 and 20 is empirically equal to the difference between 50 and 60, then adding 20 to all of the scale

[9] $Y = g(X)$ is a linear transformation (or Y is a linear function of X) if $Y = AX + B$, where A and B are constants. It is called "linear" because the graph of such a function is a straight line. For further discussion of linear functions, see Appendix VIII.1 at the end of Chapter VIII.

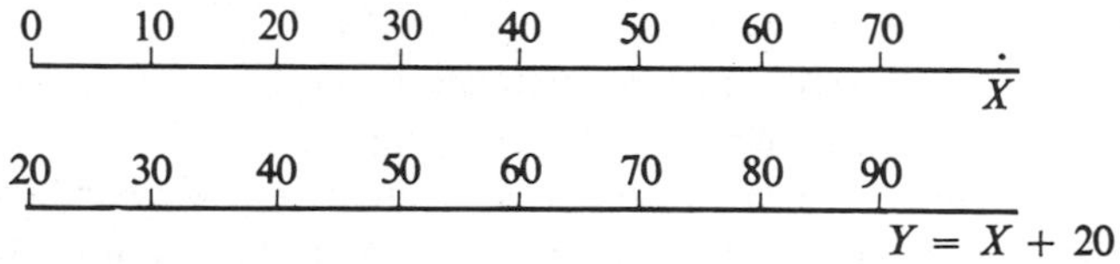

Figure VI.5

values ($Y = X + 20$) generates corresponding differences between 30 and 40 and between 70 and 80 that are equal, too. Second, multiplying by a constant does not alter equal intervals, either. If the transformation $Y = 2X + 20$ is applied to X, then Y retains the equal-interval property. From Figure VI.6, if the difference between 10 and 20 equals empirically the difference between 50 and 60 prior to the transformation, then the corresponding differences are equal after the transformation (i.e., $60 - 40 = 140 - 120$).

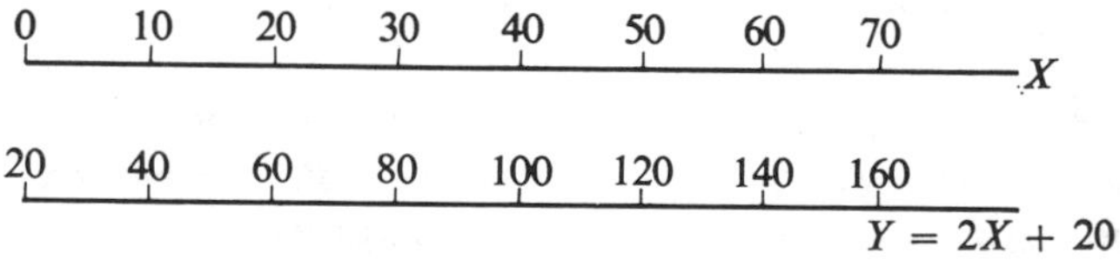

Figure VI.6

It is rare that psychological variables are measured by procedures that satisfy the conditions of an interval scale. However, methods like Thurstone's paired comparisons and successive intervals may yield equal intervals.

Ratio scales. For an interval scale, the choice of a zero point is arbitrary and has no special meaning in terms of the attribute being measured. In the Fahrenheit scale of temperature, for instance, the zero point does not represent the "complete absence" of temperature. The Fahrenheit zero is approximately the lowest temperature that could be produced artificially (at the time the scale was developed) using a mixture of salt, water, and ice. The centigrade zero point is at the freezing point of water, and 100°C is the boiling point of water at sea level. Although the centigrade zero is quite meaningful in terms of water, it does not represent "no temperature at all."

Unlike the Fahrenheit and centigrade scales, the zero point of the Kelvin scale is interpretable as "no temperature at all." At 0°K, the kinetic energy of the molecules of a substance is presumably zero, so that there is no molecular motion. Furthermore, values generated by the Kelvin scale are directly proportional to the average amount of molecular kinetic energy, making it meaningful to talk of temperature ratios. For example, 100°K represents twice the temperature of 50°K, in the sense that 100°K corresponds to twice the average molecular kinetic energy. Thus, if e represents the average molecular kinetic energy and B is a proportionality constant, then temperature Kelvin is directly proportional to kinetic energy, $K = Be$. Suppose that e_{100} is the average kinetic energy corresponding to 100°K and e_{50} is the average kinetic energy corresponding to 50°K. Then,

$$\frac{100}{50} = \frac{Be_{100}}{Be_{50}}$$

$$2 = \frac{e_{100}}{e_{50}},$$

so that the average kinetic energy corresponding to 100°K is twice that corresponding to 50°K.

Neither the Fahrenheit nor the centigrade scales permits such ratio statements. 20°C does not represent twice the kinetic energy of 10°C, nor does this ratio indicate twice the amount of any temperature-related characteristic.

More generally, *if a scale satisfies the requirements for an interval scale and if in addition ratios of the scale values it generates are meaningful, then it is a ratio scale.* Of course, the meaningfulness of ratios must be demonstrated empirically. Thus, for example, suppose that a scale of psychological loudness is constructed, and it is claimed that it is a ratio scale. Consider two tones, to which the scale assigns the values 100 and 200. If the tone assigned the value of 100 is presented as a standard, and subjects are required to adjust the intensity of a second variable tone so that it is twice as loud as the standard, then the settings of the variable tone should be close to the intensity of the tone to which the scale assigns the value 200. Thus, an empirical procedure for generating ratio magnitudes has been constructed, and under the hypothesis that the scale is a ratio scale, a prediction has been made. If the data were consistent with this prediction, then the ratio scale hypothesis would be supported. Of course, it would be necessary to establish the empirical validity of such predictions for a representative sample of loudnesses covering the range of values generated by the scale.

Many other operational procedures might be employed in attempting to verify the ratio predictions generated by such a loudness scale. The variety of such procedures is limited only by the ingenuity of the investigator.

It is easy to see that even though the units of a scale are constant, it will not be an acceptable ratio scale unless its zero point is appropriately located. If a scale of weight read zero only when it was loaded with an actual weight of 100 lbs, then even though its unit was a constant one pound, it would not generate meaningful ratios. For example, a weight that led to a reading of 50 lbs on this scale (actual weight 150 lbs) would not in any sense be twice as heavy as a weight leading to a reading of 25 lbs (actual weight 125 lbs). Thus, a meaningful zero point is a necessary condition for the existence of meaningful ratios, and as with other scale properties, the appropriateness of the zero point must be demonstrated empirically.[10]

For each type of scale discussed so far, we have described the class of transformations for which the properties of the scale remain invariant. *The properties of a ratio scale are invariant for any multiplicative transformation*; that is, ratios of ratio scale values remain meaningful for any transformation that involves simply multiplying each value generated by the scale by a constant.

The most important thing to notice about this transformation is that multiplying the zero point of the scale by a constant yields zero, so that the zero point is unaltered. Furthermore, notice that if $S(E_1)$ and $S(E_2)$ are the ratio scale values assigned events E_1 and E_2, then the ratio of $S(E_1)$ to $S(E_2)$ equals some constant, K. If each of these scale values is multiplied by a constant, then their ratio is unaltered. That is, if

$$\frac{S(E_1)}{S(E_2)} = K,$$

and if C is any constant, then

$$\frac{CS(E_1)}{CS(E_2)} = K,$$

also.

One might expect that psychological variables that can be measured by procedures satisfying the conditions of a ratio scale are rare. However, Stevens and Galanter describe what are presumably ratio scales for several sensory continua.[11] Many of these scales were determined by the method of magnitude estimation.[12] This is an especially simple method of psychological scaling in which a standard tone, for example, might be assigned arbitrarily 10 units of loudness. Then the subject is asked to assign a number to a second tone in such a way that this number represents the ratio of its loudness to that of the standard. The same standard tone is compared with each of several other tones so that the

[10] It should be noted that the zero-molecular-motion interpretation of the Kelvin temperature scale has *not* been shown by *direct* empirical demonstration, though temperatures very close to 0°K have been achieved. However, the theoretical system on which the Kelvin scale is based has been verified empirically in many other respects, so that there is considerable confidence in the theoretical predictions concerning 0°K.

[11] Stevens, S. S., and E. H. Galanter, "Ratio scales and category scales for a dozen perceptual continua." *J. Exp. Psychol.* **54**, 377–411, 1957.

[12] Stevens, S. S. "The direct estimation of sensory magnitudes—loudness." *Amer. J. Psychol.* **69**, 1–25, 1956.

number arbitrarily assigned the standard determines the unit of measurement.

Luce[13] has proposed a theoretical system that specifies certain conditions which ensure the existence of a ratio scale. He also shows how the scale values can be found. It seems unlikely that all psychological characteristics will satisfy the conditions of Luce's system, but if one does, then it can be assigned values generated by a ratio scale. Though further discussion here seems inappropriate, it should be mentioned that this method appears to be suitable for investigating many kinds of variables other than simple sensory continua.

Difficulties resulting from inadequate internal validity. It is important to realize that methods of scaling constitute an important part of psychological theory. Generally, we think of theoretical development as the construction of systems describing the relationships among *distinct* psychological variables. However, the measurement of any characteristic implies certain kinds of relationships among the values generated by the system of measurement itself. If the properties of measuring instruments are ignored, serious errors of interpretation may result. Two examples of this follow.

Suppose that a questionnaire is designed to measure the favorability of student attitudes toward statistics, and that the following four true-false questions are included:

(1) Statistical methods are often used as elaborate procedures to facilitate lying and misrepresentation, so that one must always suspect the motives of those who use statistics.

(2) The ease with which the results of statistical analysis can be used to misrepresent and the subtlety of proper interpretation of statistical results demand that only the highly trained statistician use statistical methods.

(3) So far, it has never been demonstrated that statistical methods are of any use to those concerned with practical affairs.

(4) Although the advanced researcher and the person working on highly specialized problems may have considerable use for statistical methods, the layman certainly has no need for knowledge of statistics in everyday affairs.

Now, suppose students are asked to indicate either agreement or disagreement with each item, and that a one is assigned to each agreement, a zero to each disagreement. The sum of ones and zeros is a student's "score" on the questionnaire. Since this kind of weighting system is not uncommon in psychological research, the example is not entirely unrealistic.

Now, suppose that a particular student agrees with the first item only

[13] Luce, R. D., *Individual Choice Behavior: A Theoretical Analysis.* New York, Wiley, 1959.

and that another student agrees with the third and fourth items only. Using our measuring procedure, the first student has a score of 1 whereas the second obtains a score of 2. Since all of the items are stated in negative form, one might be inclined to conclude that the second student is less favorably disposed toward statistics than the first. However, inspection of the items makes such an interpretation questionable at best. Because of the way the scores are assigned, it is unlikely that even the requirements of an ordinal scale have been satisfied.

With this questionnaire (and with many others used by psychologists), it is quite possible that more than one aspect (of "attitude toward statistics," in this case) is being measured. For the example, the first two questions might be relevant to the equivocality of statistical results. An individual responding to this aspect of statistical methods might reject them on the grounds that statistical results are ambiguous and difficult to interpret. On the other hand, the last two items seem to focus primarily on the practicality of statistical methods. In short, a single score is assigned each person on this test when it is possible that the scale is multidimensional and requires two or more scores. The only way to find out is through empirical investigation of the scale.

Another sort of pitfall may be encountered if insufficient care is exercised in the application of measuring instruments. For illustrative purposes, suppose that a theoretical system leads to the hypothesis that two variables, X and Y, *are related in straight-line fashion* as illustrated in Figure VI.7. Suppose also that, unknown to the investigator, this

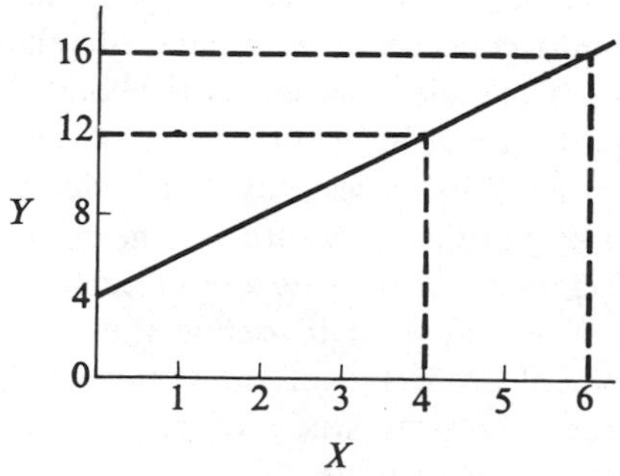

Figure VI.7

hypothesis is correct. However, the researcher is not using a "true" measure of X, but rather an empirical scale that he has developed without investigating its measurement properties. It happens that the scale for X does not satisfy the requirements of an interval scale whereas that for Y does. When the data gathered by our researcher are plotted, the badly bent function of Figure VI.8 results. What is amiss to produce such

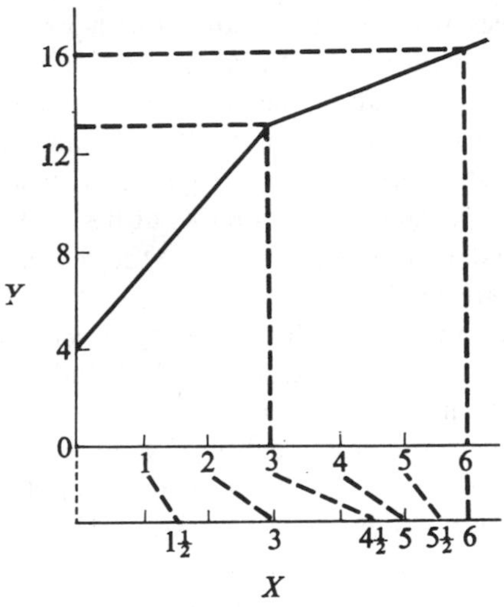

Figure VI.8

a distortion? What the investigator has considered to be equal steps along X for his empirical scale actually correspond to steps that are quite unequal. For example, the interval between 0 and 1 on our researcher's scale is three times the size of the interval between 4 and 5 when measured on a true equal-interval scale. This distortion of the unit of measurement introduces a gross departure of the observed function relating X and Y from the correct, linear function.

Obviously, scales that satisfy only ordinal requirements cannot be used at all to test hypotheses concerning the shape of relationships between conceptual variables. The scale must satisfy the conditions of an interval or ratio scale in order to test such hypotheses. Of course, hypotheses of the form "Y increases as X increases" or "as X decreases Y increases" can be investigated using ordinal measures. The point is that the kind of theory one can investigate confidently depends directly upon the properties of the scales of measurement used to define the observations. Consequently, the measurement properties of empirical variables are important underpinnings for the empirical study of any theoretical system concerning relationships among variables.

VI.3

PROBLEMS ON RANDOM VARIABLES AND MEASUREMENT

1. Toss a coin and a die simultaneously. If the coin shows heads, assign a 1; if tails, a 0. What are possible values of the random variable con-

sisting of the sum of values on the coin and die? Find the probability for each distinct value of this random variable.

2. A probability experiment consists of rolling two dice, a red one and a green one. Subtract the number of spots on the green die from the number on the red. If this difference is used to define a random variable, what are its possible values? What is the probability that the random variable will equal zero?

3. For the sample space of Table VI.2, define the random variable "number correct."

4. Consider the probability experiment "roll a fair 11-sided die." The following table defines a random variable on this sample space:

	Outcomes										
	0	1	2	3	4	5	6	7	8	9	10
Values of the random variable	1	0	0	1	0	0	1	0	0	1	0

Give this random variable a meaningful verbal name. What is the probability that the random variable will take on the value 0?

5. Do a well-functioning spring scale and a balance with standardized weights always measure the same property? Do two interviewers with an identical set of rating instructions always measure the same property? Explain concisely.

6. An investigator reports that he has devised an interval scale for the psychological value of monetary amounts. How would you establish or refute the internal validity of his scale?

7. Does the WAIS IQ satisfy the conditions of an ordinal scale? Discuss this question concisely.

8. Demonstrate that the measurement of length using a yardstick constitutes a ratio scale.

9. Four different theories prescribe the relationship between psychological variables X and Y. The theoretical relationships are given below. In each case, what kind of scale of measurement would be necessary to investigate empirically each of these theoretical proposals? (A and B are constants.)

   a. "X increases with Y"
   b. $Y = AX$
   c. $Y = AX + B$
   d. $Y = X^A$.

10. Suppose that S is a ratio scale. Show that the properties of S do *not* remain invariant when a constant is added to each scale value of S. That is, if S is a ratio scale and C is any constant, show that $T = S + C$ is not a ratio scale. (Use a numerical example if you wish.)

11. If X is an interval scale, show that $\log_{10} X$ is not. (Use a numerical example if you wish.)

SUGGESTED READING

1. Mosteller, F., R. E. K. Rourke, and G. B. Thomas, Jr., *Probability and Statistics*. Reading, Mass., Addison-Wesley, 1961, pp. 155–165.
   A good introduction to discrete random variables. It includes many excellent examples.
2. Feller, W., *Introduction to Probability Theory and its Applications*, I (2nd ed.). New York, John Wiley, 1957, pp. 199–207.
   A brief but more complete introduction to discrete random variables.
3. Hahn, H., "Infinity," in J. R. Newman (ed.), *The World of Mathematics*, III. New York, Simon and Shuster, 1956, pp. 1593–1611.
   If you have difficulty conceptualizing continuous random variables and discrete random variables with infinite ranges, this article may help.
4. Stevens, S. S., "Mathematics, Measurement, and Psychophysics," in S. S. Stevens (ed.), *Handbook of Experimental Pyschology*. New York, John Wiley, 1951, pp. 1–49.
   This is the measurement approach adopted by most psychologists.
5. Suppes, P., and J. L. Zinnes, "Basic Measurement Theory," in R. D. Luce, R. R. Bush, and E. Galanter (eds.), *Handbook of Mathematical Psychology, I.* New York, John Wiley, 1962, pp. 1–76.
   This is a clear but mathematically sophisticated formulation of the process of measurement.

VII

PROBABILITY DISTRIBUTIONS AND STATISTICAL INDEPENDENCE OF RANDOM VARIABLES

BOTH in statistics and in psychological theory, probability is frequently used in connection with variables. Theory and data analyses often have to do with scales like rate of learning, auditory loudness, authoritarianism, introversion, and so on. In this chapter, some of the results of earlier chapters will be applied to random variables, and a convenient nomenclature will be introduced for the purpose. Using this nomenclature, the idea of statistical independence will be extended to random variables.

VII.1
PROBABILITY APPLIED TO RANDOM VARIABLES

In the application of probability to random variables, it is absolutely essential to distinguish sharply between discrete and continuous random variables (see Section VI.1.2). Consequently, they are treated separately in the following sections.

VII.1.1. Probability distributions for discrete random variables

It can be seen from the discussion of discrete random variables that a random variable determines *numerical labels for events* in the sample space of a random experiment. Consequently, if the probabilities associated with the outcomes of a sample space are known, the probabilities associated with the values of any random variable defined on that sample space can be determined.

A convenient illustration of this uses, as the random variable, the number of heads occurring when three coins are tossed. The sample space and the values of this random variable, X, are shown in Table VII.1. It can be seen that three of the eight possible outcomes contain exactly

Table VII.1. Possible outcomes of tossing three coins

Sample space	H,H,H	H,H,T	H,T,H	T,H,H	T,T,H	T,H,T	H,T,T	T,T,T
No. of heads (X)	3	2	2	2	1	1	1	0

two heads, so that the probability of two heads is 3/8. Similarly, the probability of no heads is $\mathbf{P}(X = 0) = 1/8$, and so on. The probabilities associated with each of the four values of X are tabulated at the left in Figure VII.1. This set of pairs, each pair containing a value of X and

$$\begin{aligned} \mathbf{P}(X = 0) &= 1/8 \\ \mathbf{P}(X = 1) &= 3/8 \\ \mathbf{P}(X = 2) &= 3/8 \\ \mathbf{P}(X = 3) &= 1/8 \\ \hline \sum \mathbf{P}(X = x) &= 1 \end{aligned}$$

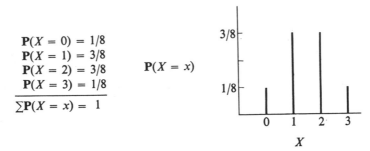

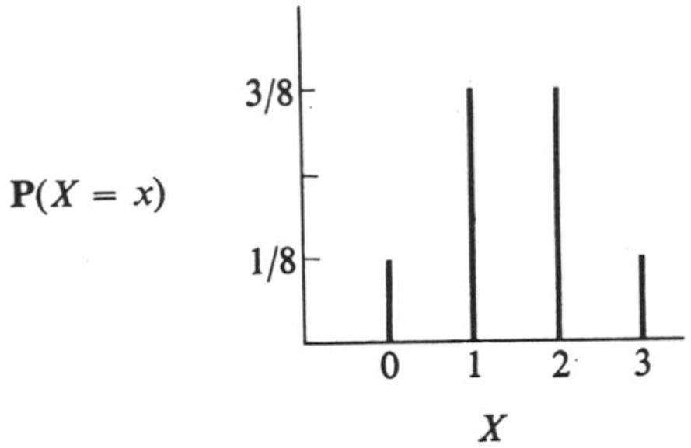

Figure VII.1

its probability, is called the *probability distribution* of X. In its graphic representation, values along the abscissa represent the range of the random variable, and values along the ordinate represent their probabilities.

Notice that one value of the random variable is assigned to every outcome, and that no outcome has more than one value assigned to it. Consequently, the values of the random variable serve as labels for a set of mutually exclusive and exhaustive events, and the sum of the probabilities associated with these events must be unity.

The probability that X will take on any one of a specified set of its possible values can be computed from the probability distribution. For the example, the probability that X will exceed 1 (the probability of tossing more than one head) is

$$\begin{aligned} \mathbf{P}(X > 1) = \mathbf{P}[(X = 2) \cup (X = 3)] &= \mathbf{P}(X = 2) + \mathbf{P}(X = 3) \\ &= 3/8 + 1/8 \\ &= 1/2. \end{aligned}$$

Note that the events $X = 2$ and $X = 3$ are disjoint, since X cannot take on the value 2 and the value 3 at the same time. Similarly, the probability that X exceeds 0 and is less than 3 is

$$\begin{aligned}\mathbf{P}(0 < X < 3) = \mathbf{P}[(X = 1) \cup (X = 2)] &= \mathbf{P}(X = 1) + \mathbf{P}(X = 2)\\ &= 3/8 + 3/8\\ &= 3/4.\end{aligned}$$

If X is a discrete random variable, then the probability distribution of X gives the probability of occurrence of each value in the range of X. A probability distribution will sometimes be referred to as a PD. If X is a random variable having r discrete values, then the probability distribution of X gives

$$\mathbf{P}(X = x_i)$$

for each value of the range of X, $(x_1, x_2, \ldots, x_i, \ldots, x_r)$. Since exactly one value of X is assigned to every outcome in the same space,

$$\sum_{i=1}^{r} \mathbf{P}(X = x_i) = 1.$$

This indicates that one of the values of X must occur whenever an observation is made.

In an example of Section VI.1.1, the random variable was the mean of random samples of size 2, drawn with replacement from the population containing the elements 1, 2, and 3. The sample space and values of the mean appear in Table VII.2. Noting that there are 9 equiprobable outcomes in all, and counting the number of ways each value of the mean can occur, the probability distribution of the mean can be formed as shown in Figure VII.2.

When this example was introduced in Section VI.1.1, the way sample means vary from one random sample to another was discussed. The probability distribution of $\bar{X}$ in Figure VII.2 gives a complete and precise description of this variation for this example.

$$\begin{aligned}\mathbf{P}(\bar{X} = 1.0) &= 1/9\\ \mathbf{P}(\bar{X} = 1.5) &= 2/9\\ \mathbf{P}(\bar{X} = 2.0) &= 3/9\\ \mathbf{P}(\bar{X} = 2.5) &= 2/9\\ \mathbf{P}(\bar{X} = 3.0) &= 1/9\\ \hline \sum_{i=1}^{5} \mathbf{P}(\bar{X} = \bar{x}_i) &= 1\end{aligned}$$

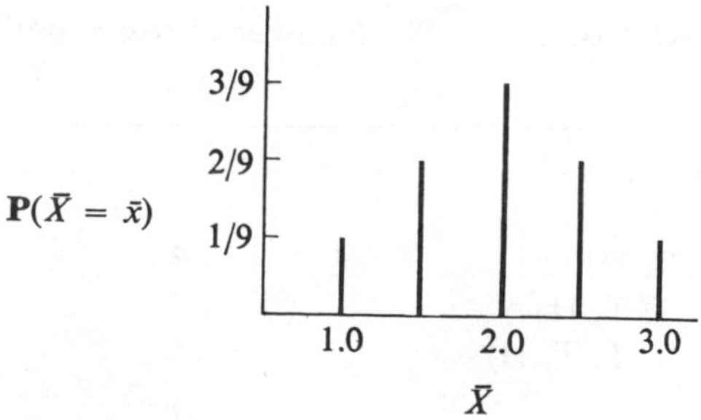

Figure VII.2

It is extremely important to notice that the random variable in this example is an *estimator* (the sample mean), and it is the probability distribution of this estimator that is shown in Figure VII.2. In general, *the probability distribution of an estimator is called a sampling distribution.* (Calling it a sampling distribution should not be allowed to obscure the fact that the sampling distribution of an estimator has all of the properties of any other probability distribution.)

Table VII.2. Random variable for example of Section VI.1.1

Sample space	1, 1	1, 2	1, 3	2, 1	2, 2	2, 3	3, 1	3, 2	3, 3
Sample mean ($\bar{X}$)	1.0	1.5	2.0	1.5	2.0	2.5	2.0	2.5	3.0

As indicated earlier, a discrete random variable may have a countably infinite range. If X is such a variable, and its range is $(x_1, x_2, \ldots, x_i, \ldots)$, then the probability distribution of X gives

$$\mathbf{P}(X = x_i)$$

for each value, x_i. Just as in the case of discrete random variables that have a finite range, the sum of the probabilities of the values of a discrete random variable with an infinite range equals unity. That is,

$$\sum_{i=1}^{\infty} \mathbf{P}(X = x_i) = 1.$$

To illustrate the PD of a discrete random variable with a countably infinite range, consider the number of tosses of a coin until the first head appears. The first few values of this random variable and the outcomes to which they are assigned are shown in Table VII.3. If P is the probability

Table VII.3. Probability distribution of number of tosses until first head

Outcome	Number of tosses until the first head (X)	Probability distribution
(H)	1	$\mathbf{P}(X = 1) = P$
(T, H)	2	$\mathbf{P}(X = 2) = (1 - P)P$
(T, T, H)	3	$\mathbf{P}(X = 3) = (1 - P)^2P$
(T, T, T, H)	4	$\mathbf{P}(X = 4) = (1 - P)^3P$
(T, T, T, T, H)	5	$\mathbf{P}(X = 5) = (1 - P)^4P$
⋮	⋮	⋮

of a head and $(1 - P)$ is the probability of a tail, then the probability that the first head will appear on trial x is $\mathbf{P}(X = x) = (1 - P)^{x-1}P$. This can be seen by examining Table VII.3 and assuming that the tosses of the coin are statistically independent. For example, the probability that the first three tosses are tails and the fourth is a head is $\mathbf{P}(X = 4) = (1 - P)^3P$.

The first thing to notice about this PD is that the range of X, $(1, 2, 3, 4, \ldots)$, is countably infinite. If $0 < P < 1$ and the coin is tossed without bias, no maximum value can be assigned to X, since no matter how large X may be, its probability is always greater than zero. Although $\mathbf{P}(X = 1000) = (1 - P)^{999}P$ will be a very small number, it will always exceed zero if the probability of heads is greater than 0 and less than 1.

This last statement might lead one to suspect intuitively that

$$\sum_{x=1}^{\infty} \mathbf{P}(X = x) = \sum_{x=1}^{\infty} (1 - P)^{x-1}P$$

will exceed unity. To see that this is not the case, suppose that $P = 1/2$. Then,

$$\sum_{x=1}^{\infty} \mathbf{P}(X = x) = \sum_{x=1}^{\infty} (1/2)^{x-1}(1/2) = \sum_{x=1}^{\infty} (1/2)^x.$$

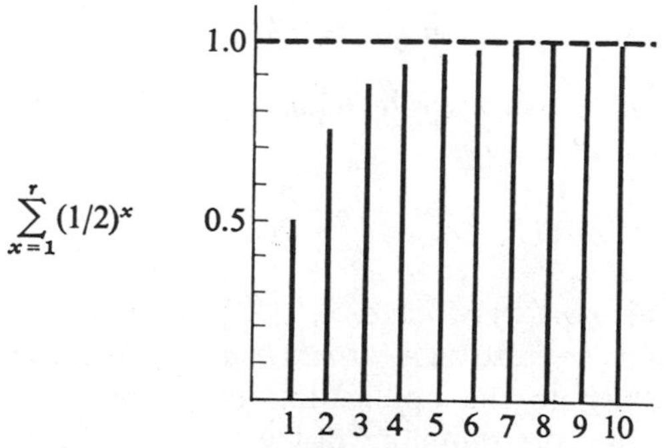

Figure VII.3

In Figure VII.3, $\sum_{x=1}^{r} (1/2)^x$ has been plotted for a few values of r. Notice what happens. For $r = 1$, $\sum_{x=1}^{1} (1/2)^x = 1/2$; for $r = 2$, $\sum_{x=1}^{2} (1/2)^x = 3/4$; for $r = 3$, $\sum_{x=1}^{3} (1/2)^x = 7/8$; and so on. Each term that is added moves the cumulated sum half the distance from its previous value to 1. And no matter how close to 1 the cumulated sum becomes, adding the next term simply increases it by half the remaining distance to 1. Therefore, the sum approaches closer and closer to unity as r increases, but it never exceeds 1. This is illustrated graphically in Figure VII.3.

This example has been limited to $P = 1/2$, but similar demonstrations can be given for other values of P. The important thing to notice is that the sum of a countably infinite set of probabilities is not necessarily greater than 1.

VII.1.2. Cumulative distribution functions for discrete random variables

Many problems are conveniently handled by referring to the probability that a random variable will take on a value less than or equal to some

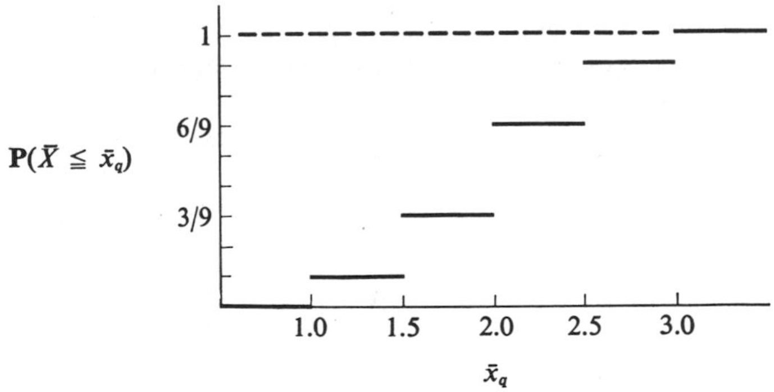

Figure VII.4

specified value. *If X is a discrete random variable, then the cumulative distribution function of X gives*

$$\mathbf{P}(X \leq x_q) = \sum_{i=1}^{q} \mathbf{P}(X = x_i),$$

for each value of the random variable, x_q. A cumulative distribution function is sometimes referred to as a *distribution function* or as a *CDF.*

In order to illustrate the application of a cumulative distribution function, we will use the sampling distribution of Figure VII.2. With

Table VII.4. Values of cumulative distribution function

CDF	Value
$\mathbf{P}(\bar{X} \leq 1.0) = \mathbf{P}(\bar{X} = 1.0)$	$= 1/9$
$\mathbf{P}(\bar{X} \leq 1.5) = \mathbf{P}(\bar{X} = 1.0) + \mathbf{P}(\bar{X} = 1.5)$	$= 3/9$
$\mathbf{P}(\bar{X} \leq 2.0) = \mathbf{P}(\bar{X} = 1.0) + \mathbf{P}(\bar{X} = 1.5) + \mathbf{P}(\bar{X} = 2.0)$	$= 6/9$
$\mathbf{P}(\bar{X} \leq 2.5) = \mathbf{P}(\bar{X} = 1.0) + \mathbf{P}(\bar{X} = 1.5) + \mathbf{P}(\bar{X} = 2.0) + \mathbf{P}(\bar{X} = 2.5)$	$= 8/9$
$\mathbf{P}(\bar{X} \leq 3.0) = \mathbf{P}(\bar{X} = 1.0) + \mathbf{P}(\bar{X} = 1.5) + \mathbf{P}(\bar{X} = 2.0) + \mathbf{P}(\bar{X} = 2.5) + \mathbf{P}(\bar{X} = 3.0)$	$= 1$

these probabilities, the values of the CDF can be found, as shown in Table VII.4. This CDF is plotted in Figure VII.4.

For any CDF, one minus the value of the CDF gives the probability that X will exceed x_q. In other words, $\mathbf{P}(X > x_q) = 1 - \mathbf{P}(X \leq x_q)$, since the event $X > x_q$ is the complement of the event $X \leq x_q$.

VII.1.3. Problems on probability distributions and cumulative distribution functions for discrete random variables

1. Suppose that Y is a random variable equal to the sum of the faces of two dice.
   a. Write out the PD of Y.
   b. Show the PD of Y graphically.
   c. Is $\sum_{y=2}^{12} \mathbf{P}(Y = y) = 1$?
   d. Write out the CDF of Y.
   e. Plot the CDF of Y.
   f. Find the following probabilities:
      i. $\mathbf{P}(Y \leq 12)$
      ii. $\mathbf{P}(Y \leq 7)$
      iii. $\mathbf{P}(Y > 7)$
      iv. $\mathbf{P}(4 < Y < 7)$
      v. $\mathbf{P}[(Y \leq 4) \cup (Y \leq 9)]$
      vi. $\mathbf{P}[(Y \leq 4) \cap (Y \leq 9)]$
      vii. $\mathbf{P}[(Y > 6) \cup (Y > 9)]$
      viii. $\mathbf{P}[(2 \leq Y < 5) \cup (7 \leq Y < 9)]$.
2. A clinician is given 10 test protocols and 10 personality descriptions. He is asked to match these. Assume that his matching is entirely random, and that the random variable X gives the number of correct matches.
   a. Write out the probability distribution and CDF of X and plot each.
   b. Is $\sum_{x=0}^{10} \mathbf{P}(X = x) = 1$? If there is any discrepancy, explain it.
   c. Find the following probabilities:
      i. $\mathbf{P}(X \leq 3)$
      ii. $\mathbf{P}(X \geq 3)$
      iii. $\mathbf{P}(X > 3)$
      iv. $\mathbf{P}[(X \leq 1) \cup (X \geq 7)]$
      v. $\mathbf{P}(3 < X < 6)$
      vi. $\mathbf{P}(3 \leq X \leq 6)$
      vii. $\mathbf{P}[(X \leq 3) \cap (X \leq 6)]$
      viii. $\mathbf{P}[(2 \leq X \leq 4) \cup (5 < X < 8)]$.
3. Let X be the number of tosses of a coin until the first head appears, and let $P = 1/4$ be the probability of a head for this biased coin.
   a. Find $\mathbf{P}(X = 4)$.
   b. Calculate $S_r = \sum_{x=1}^{r} (1 - P)^{x-1}P$ for $r = 1$, $r = 2$, $r = 3$, $r = 4$, and $r = 5$. What is the approximate value of S_r for $r = 100$? For $r = 1000$?
   c. What is $\sum_{x=1}^{\infty} (1 - P)^{x-1}P$?

4. For the example of Table VII.4 and Figure VII.4, the random variable referred to is the mean of random samples of size 2. Explain how a sample mean can be a random variable. What is the meaning of the probability distribution of this random variable? What is this probability distribution called?

VII.1.4. Probability densities for continuous random variables

So far, probability distributions for continuous random variables have not been discussed. The methods for determining probabilities for continuous variables are different from those for discrete variables. Continuous random variables are dealt with in this section.

In the graph of the probability distribution shown in Figure VII.1, the *height* of the vertical line at each value of the range of the random variable represents the probability that the variable will take on that value. Instead of a vertical line, bars might have been used, to form the histogram of Figure VII.5. Since each bar has a width of 1, the *area*

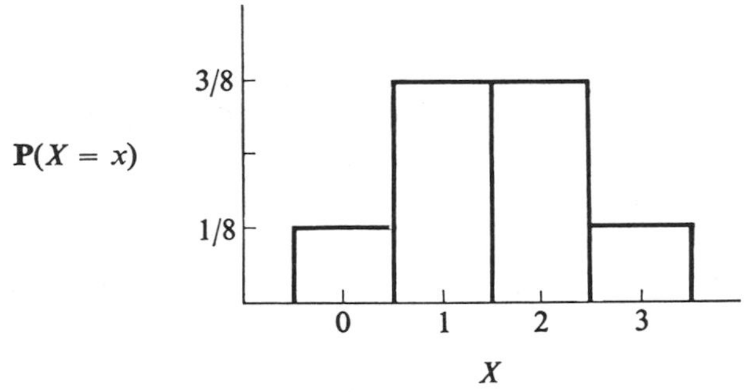

Figure VII.5

of each bar provides a representation of probability. Thus, $\mathbf{P}(X = 2)$ is $1(3/8)$, the area of the bar centered on $X = 2$. The probability that X will be between 1 and 2 inclusive is represented by the total area of the two central bars or $1(3/8) + 1(3/8) = 6/8$. It is essentially this idea of

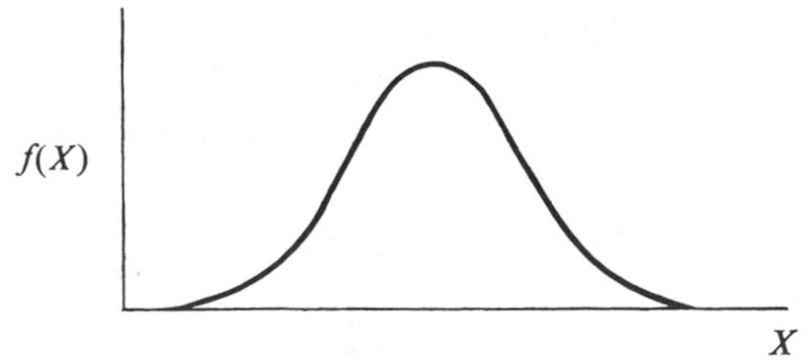

Figure VII.6

using area to represent probability that provides the basis for defining probability for continuous random variables.

Now, suppose that X is a continuous random variable and $f(X)$ is a function used to describe probabilities of the values of X. (For the moment, ignore the question of just *how* these probabilities are to be described. That is the next step.) Then, for every value of X there is a corresponding value of $f(X)$, and if $f(X)$ were plotted graphically, it might look like Figure VII.6. If $f(X)$ were defined appropriately, the probability that a randomly selected value of X would lie between two particular values, a and b, could be represented by the *area* under $f(X)$ between a and b. Such an area is indicated by the crosshatching in

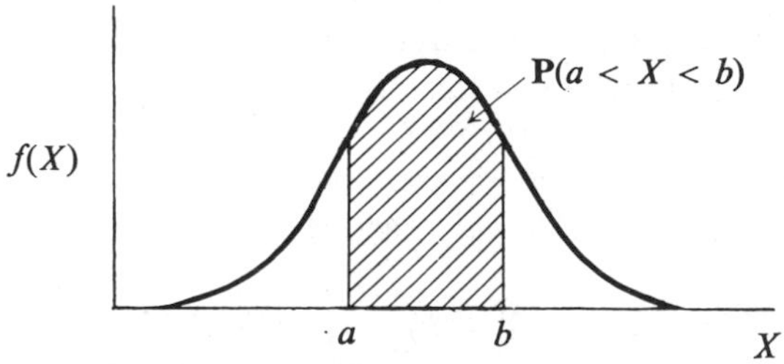

Figure VII.7

Figure VII.7. With this system, the probability that X will take on some value between its minimum and maximum must be 1, so 1 is the total area under $f(X)$, as shown in Fig. VII.8.

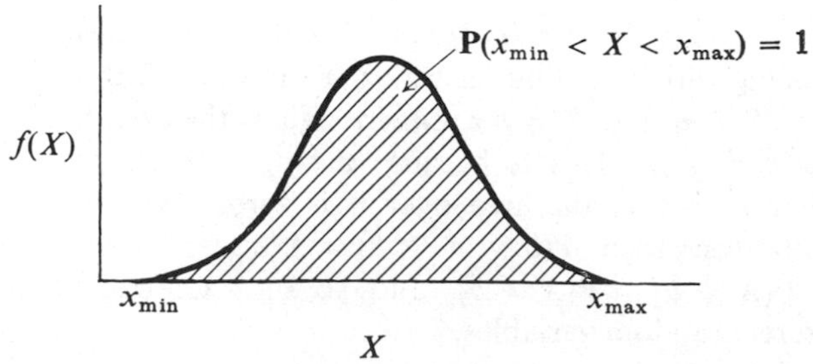

Figure VII.8

This is the approach employed to deal with continuous random variables. Probabilities are obtained by computing areas under an appropriately chosen smooth curve. The expression *appropriately chosen* means a curve selected so that the area under the curve between any two values of the random variable equals the probability that a randomly chosen value of the variable will lie between the two (see Fig. VII.7). If the two values happen to be the maximum and the minimum, then, of course, a randomly selected value *must* lie between them, so that the total area under the curve equals unity (see Fig. VII.8).

At this point, the reader may find himself wondering how one calculates area under smooth curves. Sometimes the definite integral of calculus can be used. *The expression*

$$\int_a^b f(X)dX$$

is called the definite integral of $f(X)$ *between* $X = a$ *and* $X = b$ *(where* $a < b$*). Geometrically, this definite integral*[1] *is simply the area under* $f(X)$ *between* a *and* b*, as illustrated by the crosshatched area in Figure VII.7.* More often, though, it is possible to find the numerical value of the definite integral in standard tables. The use of some of these tables will be discussed later, but right now it seems appropriate to summarize the results of this section.

If X *is a continuous random variable and if* $f(X)$ *is a function of* X *such that for any two values of* X*,* a *and* b *(where* $a < b$*),*

$$\mathbf{P}(a < X < b) = \int_a^b f(X)dX,$$

then $f(X)$ *is the probability density function of* X*. If* $x_{\min}$ *is the smallest value of* X *and* $x_{\max}$ *is the largest, then*

$$\int_{x_{\min}}^{x_{\max}} f(X)dX = 1.$$

Sometimes, a probability density function will be referred to as a DF.

When dealing with a continuous random variable, X, the area under its DF between $X = a$ and $X = b$ *exclusive* equals the area between $X = a$ and $X = b$ *inclusive*. This is because a single point, such as $X = a$, has zero width, so that the area over it is zero. As a consequence, if X is continuous, then $\mathbf{P}(a \leq X \leq b) = \mathbf{P}(a < X < b)$, $\mathbf{P}(X \leq a) = \mathbf{P}(X < a)$, $\mathbf{P}(X \geq b) = \mathbf{P}(X > b)$, and so on. Of course, this is *not* true for discrete random variables.

*CALCULATING AREAS UNDER SMOOTH CURVES. The range of a continuous random variable can be divided into k small and equal steps so that the distance from one step to the next is arbitrarily chosen to be h, where h is a small positive number. Thus, the points $x_1, x_2, \ldots, x_j, \ldots, x_k$ are values of X chosen so that $x_j + h = x_{j+1}$. Next, for each point x_j, a rectangle can be constructed so that its width is h and its height equals

[1] The algebraic meaning of the definite integral is discussed briefly in the following subsection.

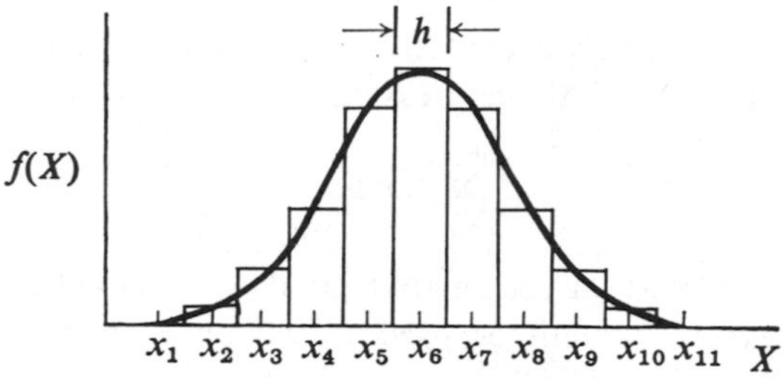

Figure VII.9

$f(x_j)$. Such an arrangement is shown in Figure VII.9 for $k = 11$. Then, the area of the rectangle centered on the point x_j equals the product of its width and its height, so that its area is h times $f(x_j)$. The sum of these rectangular areas approximates the total area under the smooth function, $f(X)$. That is,

$$\sum_{j=1}^{11} f(x_j)h$$

approximates the total area under $f(X)$.

But this is an approximation, and it is not always a good one. For example, in Figure VII.9, the rectangle centered on the point x_5 includes too much area to the left of its center and too little to the right. This would create no difficulty if the "too much" and the "too little" were equal areas, but unfortunately, they are not. Even worse, the rectangle centered on x_6 is simply too big. What can be done to increase the precision of the approximation?

The answer is straightforward. If the number of divisions of X is increased, then h will become smaller, and the amount by which each rectangle includes too much or too little will be reduced. In Figure VII.10,

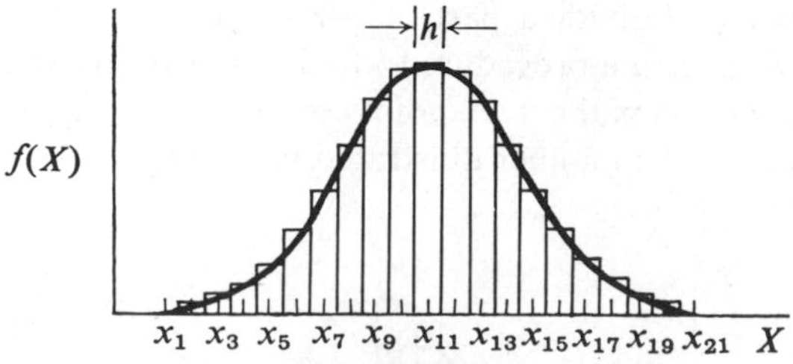

Figure VII.10

the number of divisions has been increased to $k = 21$. The resulting approximation of the area under the smooth curve has clearly improved over that obtained with $k = 11$ (Fig. VII.9). Thus, by choosing k sufficiently large and graphing with care, one could measure the area under a smooth curve fairly accurately. Or, one could choose a value of k and do the arithmetic in the expression

$$\sum_{j=1}^{k} f(x_j)h.$$

This would also provide a reasonably good approximation. Although these approaches are sometimes used to calculate such areas, there is another method that is usually easier to apply. Furthermore, it is an extremely important device in statistics, and it is a clever and basically simple idea.

If letting k become large improves the accuracy of the area approximation

$$\sum_{j=1}^{k} f(x_j)h,$$

why not let it become "indefinitely large"? As k becomes infinite, the error in the approximation should approach zero, since as the number of values, x_j, increases, the width of the rectangles, h, will decrease, and room for error in each rectangle becomes small. In the calculus, this operation is known as finding the definite integral of the function $f(X)$, and it is denoted

$$\int_{x_1}^{x_k} f(X)dX = \lim_{k \to \infty} \left[\sum_{j=1}^{k} f(x_j)h\right].$$

The expression on the left denotes the definite integral of $f(X)$ between x_1 and x_k. But in view of our discussion, this is simply the area under $f(X)$ between x_1 and x_k. The right-hand side of the equation gives the meaning of the definite integral in algebraic terms.

In Figures VII.9 and VII.10, the entire area under $f(X)$ was approximated. That is, we let $x_1 = x_{\min}$ and $x_k = x_{\max}$. However, this is not necessary. We could divide a part of the range of X into k equal steps and then follow the same procedure to find a part of the area under $f(X)$. Thus, the area between the two points, a and b, in Figure VII.7 could be approximated in the manner illustrated in Figure VII.11. The interval

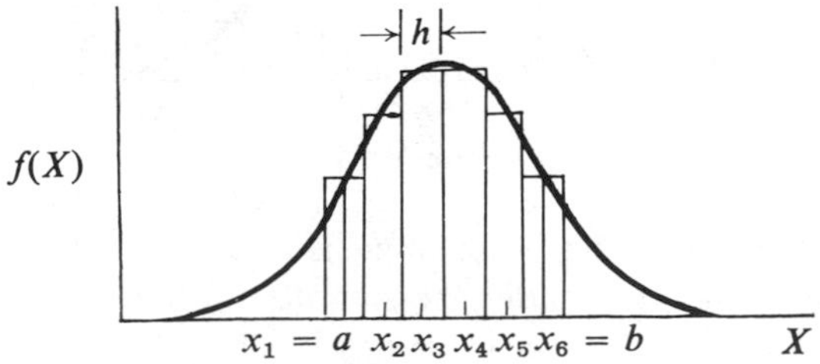

Figure VII.11

separating a and b has been divided into small intervals, each of width h. Then, the probability that X will lie between a and b is approximated by

$$\mathbf{P}(a < X < b) \cong \sum_{j=1}^{6} f(x_j)h.$$

Notice that x_1 must equal a and x_6 must equal b if this is to be a suitable approximation.

To increase precision, the number of intervals can be increased, but it is usually more efficient to compute the definite integral. This is done by letting $a = x_1$ and $b = x_k$ and finding

$$\mathbf{P}(a < X < b) = \int_a^b f(X)dX = \lim_{k \to \infty} \left[\sum_{j=1}^{k} f(x_j)h \right].$$

The numbers a and b are called the *limits of integration.*

If the limits of integration consist of the smallest possible value of the random variable X and the largest possible value, then the value of the integral is 1. Thus,

$$\mathbf{P}(x_{\min} < X < x_{\max}) = \int_{x_{\min}}^{x_{\max}} f(X)dX = 1.$$

VII.1.5. Cumulative distribution functions for continuous random variables

For discrete random variables, the CDF is often most pertinent to statistical calculations, and the same is true for continuous random variables. For a continuous X, the CDF gives the probability that X is less than or equal to some specified value, x_q. This is the same as asking for the probability that a randomly chosen value of X will lie between $-\infty$ and x_q. *If $f(X)$ is the probability density function of the continuous random variable, X, then the cumulative distribution function of X gives*

$$\mathbf{P}(X \leq x_q) = \int_{-\infty}^{x_q} f(X)dX$$

for every value x_q. If X happens to have a finite minimum value, $x_{\min}$, the cumulative distribution function can be written

$$\mathbf{P}(X \leq x_q) = \int_{x_{\min}}^{x_q} f(X)dX.$$

This is true since the area under $f(X)$ below $x_{\min}$ is 0.

The relation between a DF and the corresponding CDF is shown in Figure VII.12 for an example that does not require integration. Notice that the probability density, $f(X)$, equals 1/10 for every value of X and that the total area under $f(X)$ is $(1/10)(10 - 0) = 1$.

Probability is represented by area under a density function, but by the

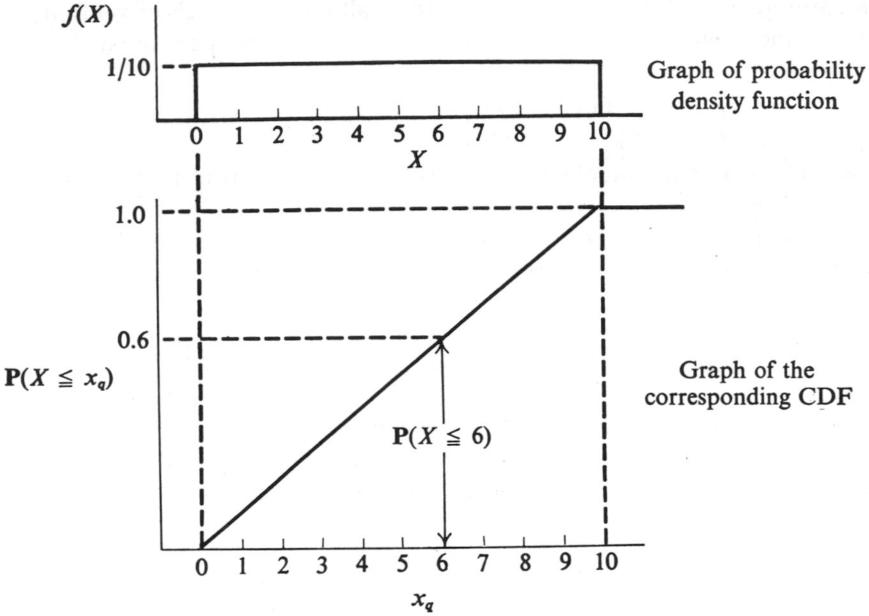

Figure VII.12

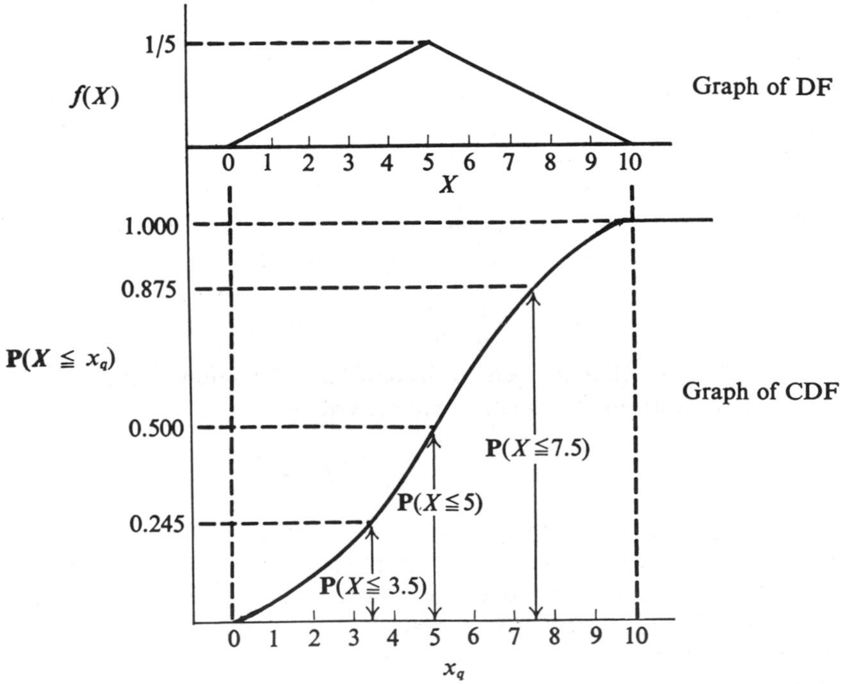

Figure VII.13

height of the CDF. Thus, from the graph of the CDF, $\mathbf{P}(X \leq 6) = 0.6$, and this is equal to the area under $f(X)$ between 0 and 6 (i.e., $(1/10)(6 - 0) = 0.6$). Of course, $\mathbf{P}(X \leq x_{max}) = 1$. This is shown in the graph of the CDF by the fact that its height is 1 at $X = 10$.

Another example of the relation between a DF and the corresponding CDF is presented in Figure VII.13. For this particular DF, the rule for computing the area of a triangle can be applied to find the total area under $f(X)$. This area is (1/2)(base)(altitude) $= (1/2)(10 - 0)(1/5) = 1$. By similar procedures, the height of the CDF can be found for each value of X. For example, $\mathbf{P}(X \leq 5) = 1/2$, $\mathbf{P}(X \leq 3.5) = 0.245$, and $\mathbf{P}(X \leq 7.5) = 0.875$.

Notice that the CDF can be used to compute the probability that the value of a random variable will fall between two points. For instance, from Figure VII.13, $\mathbf{P}(3.5 \leq X \leq 5) = \mathbf{P}(X \leq 5) - \mathbf{P}(X \leq 3.5) = 0.500 - 0.245 = 0.255$. In other words, the probability that a randomly selected value of X will lie between 3.5 and 5 is 0.255. Similarly, the

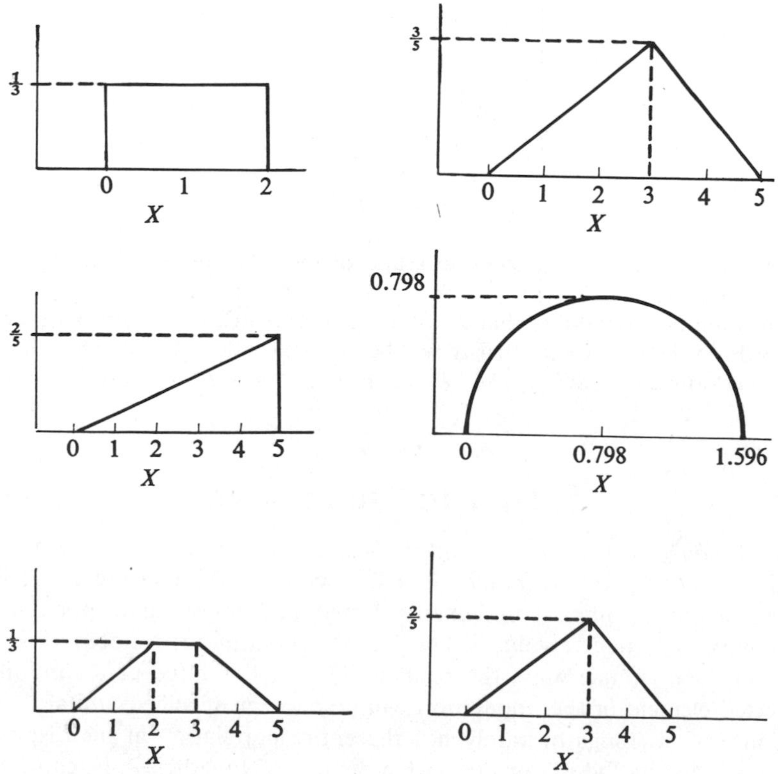

Figure VII.14

probability that a randomly selected value of X will lie between 3.5 and 6.5 is

$$\begin{aligned}\mathbf{P}(3.5 < X < 6.5) &= \mathbf{P}(X \leq 6.5) - \mathbf{P}(X \leq 3.5)\\ &= [1 - \mathbf{P}(X \leq 3.5)] - \mathbf{P}(X \leq 3.5)\\ &= (1 - 0.245) - 0.245 = 0.51.\end{aligned}$$

Note that this calculation depends on the equality of $\mathbf{P}(X \leq 3.5)$ and $\mathbf{P}(X > 6.5)$. These are equal because the DF of X is symmetrical.

VII.1.6. Problems on probability densities and cumulative distribution functions for continuous random variables

1. Examine each of the graphs in Figure VII.14 and decide which of these functions could be probability density functions.
2. The probability density function of a continuous variable, X, is shown graphically in Figure VII.15.

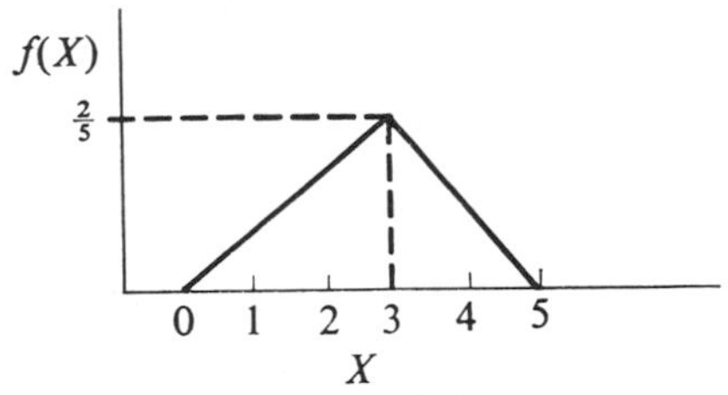

Figure VII.15

a. Draw a reasonably accurate graph of the CDF of X. Give its exact heights for $X = 1$, $X = 3$, $X = 4.5$, and $X = 6$.
b. Find the probability that X will be greater than 2 *and* no greater than 4.
c. Find the probability that X will be no greater than 2 *or* greater than 4.
d. What is $\mathbf{P}(0 \leq X \leq 5)$? What is $\mathbf{P}(0 \leq X \leq 7)$? What is $\mathbf{P}(X > 0)$?

VII.2

FREQUENCY FUNCTIONS

Both probability distributions and probability density functions are always characteristics of a population. For a discrete random variable, the PD gives the probability that an element selected randomly from the population will have a particular value. The DF of a continuous random variable permits one to determine the probability that the value of a randomly selected element of the population will lie between specified limits.

Since an investigator rarely has the entire population at his disposal, he rarely knows the PD or DF with certainty. Nonetheless, he can often determine it with reasonable accuracy by one of two methods: (1) the nature of the process that generates the observations may permit him to determine the PD or DF of the random variable by an analysis of logical structure; or (2) the PD or DF of a random variable may be estimated empirically from a sample.

When observations are tabulated so as to indicate the frequency with which each value of the random variable was observed in the sample, the result is called a *frequency function* or a *frequency distribution.* The frequency may be recorded in either of two forms: (1) the *frequency of* ocurrence of each value of the random variable may be recorded, or (2) the *proportion* or *relative frequency* of the sample occurring at each value of the random variable may be noted. When the latter procedure is followed, the frequency function can be viewed as an estimate of the population PD if the random variable is discrete. The relative frequency of occurrence in the sample of each value of the random variable is an *estimate* of the probability of that value in the population.

In Section VI.1.2 it was mentioned that observations are always discrete in spite of the fact that our theories sometimes involve continuous variables. Nonetheless, the discussion of calculating areas under smooth curves in Section VII.1.4 suggests a way of using a relative frequency function to estimate probabilities associated with a continuous theoretical variable. If x_1 is a value on a discrete observation variable, then the relative frequency of x_1 in a random sample is an estimate of the probability of an observation between $x_1 - (1/2)h$ and $x_1 + (1/2)h$ on the theoretical continuous variable, where h is the difference between adjacent values on the discrete observation variable.

For example, if the random variable, X, represents IQ's, and if $f(X)$ is its DF, then

$$\mathbf{P}(109.5 < X < 110.5) = \int_{109.5}^{110.5} f(X)dX$$

is the theoretical probability corresponding to the proportion of sample IQ's equal to 110. In this example, $x_1 = 110$, $h = 1$, $x_1 - (1/2)h = 109.5$, and $x_1 + (1/2)h = 110.5$.

It must be kept in mind that the frequency function for a random sample has two fundamentally distinct determinants. The first is the nature of the PD or DF (its "shape") in the population. The second is random sampling variability; the exact frequency function obtained will vary from one random sample to another, so that a sample frequency function rarely mirrors the population exactly.

VII.2.1. Presentation of data using a frequency function

Even though the frequency function provides the most complete summary of the information in a sample, its use does not preclude the possibility of distorting the data. This will be illustrated in the following example.

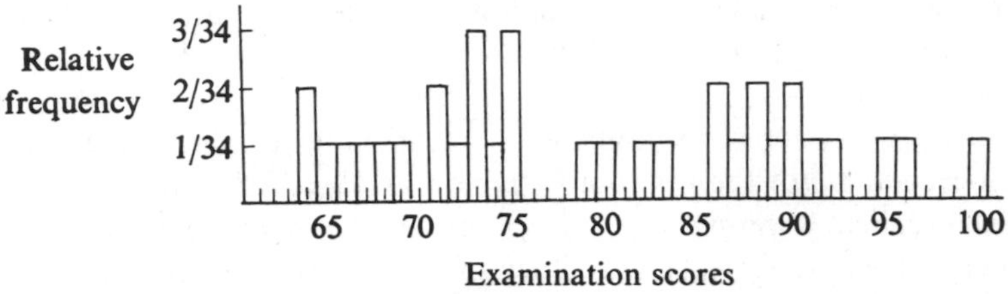

Figure VII.16

In presenting the results of an examination to students, instructors sometimes show the frequency function for the examination scores. Table VII.5 gives the frequency function for an examination in elementary statistics, which is shown graphically in Figure VII.16.

Table VII.5. Frequency function of examination scores

Examination score	Frequency	Relative frequency
100	1	1/34
99	0	0
98	0	0
97	0	0
96	1	1/34
95	1	1/34
94	0	0
93	0	0
92	1	1/34
91	1	1/34
90	2	2/34
89	1	1/34
88	2	2/34
87	1	1/34
86	2	2/34
85	0	0
84	0	0
83	1	1/34
82	1	1/34
81	0	0

Table VII.5. Frequency function of examination scores—continued

Examination score	Frequency	Relative frequency
80	1	1/34
79	1	1/34
78	0	0
77	0	0
76	0	0
75	3	3/34
74	1	1/34
73	3	3/34
72	1	1/34
71	2	2/34
70	0	0
69	1	1/34
68	1	1/34
67	1	1/34
66	1	1/34
65	1	1/34
64	2	2/34
63	0	0
62	0	0
61	0	0
Sum	34	1

From this frequency function, one can get an impression of the range of scores, and perhaps note that scores tend to center on the 70's or 80's. However, the information seems somewhat scattered, and it is difficult to get a clear picture. Perhaps grouping the scores into intervals of 5 units will help. This has been done in Table VII.5 and the corresponding histogram appears in Figure VII.17.

In this form we still get a reasonably clear picture of the range of scores and in addition the impression that the distribution is near-symmetrical and bimodal. The "middle" of the distribution is seen to be somewhere near 75 or 80.

Suppose that the observations had been grouped into intervals of 10 score-units. Would our impressions be clearer? As shown by the histogram of Figure VII.18, they are not. With this grouping,

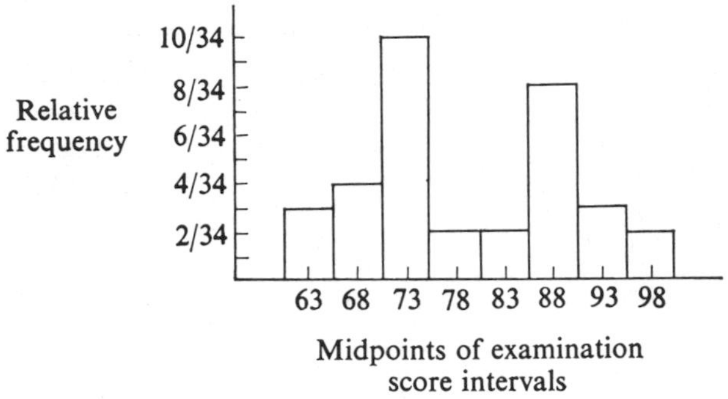

Figure VII.17

things become quite distorted. All indications of bimodality and the fact that the upper and lower tails of the distribution are quite long are not at all clear. Thus, we have moved from the original frequency function of one-unit intervals, in which it was difficult to assimilate the detailed information, to one with intervals of 10 units in which salient features of the data are masked. Of the three frequency functions considered, it appears that the one with 5-unit intervals gives the most enlightening representation of the data, though it is quite possible that some other interval width would have been somewhat better.

The point is that the apparent characteristics of data can be altered by the method of presentation, and any investigator must see to it that his conclusions are not simply artifacts of the way he chooses to present the data. There are no hard and fast rules to follow in this; undistorted presentation of data is dependent on the knowledge, skill, and care of the investigator.

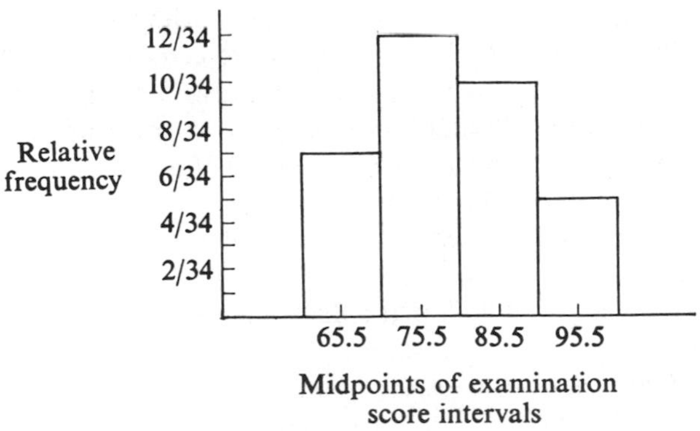

Figure VII.18

VII.3
MULTIVARIATE PROBABILITY DISTRIBUTIONS

So far, probability distributions have been limited to one random variable. However, a moment's reflection will reveal the possibility of calculating the probability that a single probability experiment will generate a value on each of two or more random variables. Thus, if a coin and a six-sided die are tossed simultaneously, the number of spots on the die can be labeled X, and Y can be assigned a value of 1 for heads and 0 for tails on the coin. Then, the probability of, say, $X = 3$ (on the die) *and* $Y = 1$ (on the coin) can be calculated. This probability, $\mathbf{P}[(X = 3) \cap (Y = 1)]$, is a value of the bivariate probability distribution of X and Y.

VII.3.1. Bivariate probability distributions for discrete random variables

If $(x_1, x_2, \ldots, x_i, \ldots, x_r)$ *and* $(y_1, y_2, \ldots, y_j, \ldots, y_m)$ *are the ranges of the discrete random variables X and Y, respectively, then the bivariate probability distribution of X and Y gives*

$$\mathbf{P}[(X = x_i) \cap (Y = y_j)],$$

for every pair of values, x_i *and* y_j. A bivariate probability distribution is sometimes referred to as a *joint probability distribution.*

In constructing the joint PD of two random variables, two values are assigned to each outcome in the sample space, one for each random

Table VII.6. Bivariate probability distribution

Outcome	X	Y	$\mathbf{P}[(X = x_i) \cap (Y = y_j)]$
(1, H)	1	1	1/12
(2, H)	2	1	1/12
(3, H)	3	1	1/12
(4, H)	4	1	1/12
(5, H)	5	1	1/12
(6, H)	6	1	1/12
(1, T)	1	0	1/12
(2, T)	2	0	1/12
(3, T)	3	0	1/12
(4, T)	4	0	1/12
(5, T)	5	0	1/12
(6, T)	6	0	1/12
			Sum = 1

variable. Then, the probability of each distinct pair of values constitutes a value of the bivariate probability distribution of the two variables. This is shown in Table VII.6 for the one-coin, one-die experiment.

It is generally convenient to arrange the joint PD of two random variables in matrix form. This is done by assigning the values of one random variable to rows and the values of the other to columns. The entries in the body of the table are the probabilities assigned the pairs, as shown in Table VII.7 for the preceding example. Looking at the intersection

Table VII.7. Matrix form of joint probability distribution

		X						$\sum_i \mathbf{P}[(X = x_i) \cap (Y = y_j)]$
		1	2	3	4	5	6	
Y	0	1/12	1/12	1/12	1/12	1/12	1/12	1/2
	1	1/12	1/12	1/12	1/12	1/12	1/12	1/2
$\sum_j \mathbf{P}[(X = x_i) \cap (Y = y_j)]$		1/6	1/6	1/6	1/6	1/6	1/6	1

of the second row and second column, we find $\mathbf{P}[(X = 2) \cap (Y = 1)] = 1/12$. The $\mathbf{P}[(X = 6) \cap (Y = 0)]$ is the entry at the intersection of the sixth column ($X = 6$) and the first row ($Y = 0$). Entering such a joint distribution table, we can determine the probability of the simultaneous occurrence of any pair of values, one on X and one on Y.

The sum of all the entries in such a matrix must equal unity, since exactly one pair of values must occur for each performance of the random experiment. That is, $\sum_i \sum_j \mathbf{P}[(X = x_i) \cap (Y = y_j)] = 1$.

Summing the entries in the first row of this table gives the probability that Y will equal 0, $\mathbf{P}(Y = 0) = 1/2$. Thus, the probability distribution of Y alone can be obtained simply by summing the entries in each row. Similarly, the column sums determine the probability distribution of X alone, e.g., $\mathbf{P}(X = 1) = 1/12 + 1/12 = 1/6$.

A probability distribution for a single discrete random variable, obtained by summing the appropriate values in a joint probability distribution, is called a *marginal probability distribution. If* $\mathbf{P}[(X = x_i) \cap (Y = y_j)]$ *is the joint probability distribution of the discrete random variables* X *and* Y, *then*

$$\mathbf{P}(X = x_i) = \sum_j \mathbf{P}[(X = x_i) \cap (Y = y_j)]$$

is the marginal probability distribution of X, and

$$\mathbf{P}(Y = y_j) = \sum_i \mathbf{P}[(X = x_i) \cap (Y = y_j)]$$

is the marginal probability distribution of Y.

A second example of a bivariate probability distribution to be used further is based on the random experiment "roll three six-sided dice." Suppose that one die is red, another white, and the last blue. Then the sample space consists of $6^3 = 216$ three-element outcomes of the form (red, white, blue). Now, two random variables are defined on this sample space. The first of these is the sum of faces on the red and white dice, R; the second is the sum of faces of the blue and white dice, B. The bivariate probability distribution we want is $\mathbf{P}[(R = r) \cap (B = b)]$ for all pairs of values of R and B.

The 11 possible values of R are 2, 3, . . ., 12, and the range of B is identical. One might anticipate $11 \times 11 = 121$ probabilities for the bivariate distribution. However, since some combinations of values of R and B are impossible, they have probability zero. For example, if $R = 12$ (the sum of red and white dice is 12), then the value of B cannot be less than 7, since the white die must contribute 6 to the value of B. Thus, $\mathbf{P}[(R = 12) \cap (B = 5)] = 0$.

In Table VII.8, the number of ways each combination of values of R and B can occur has been tabulated. Dividing each of these numbers by 216 gives the values of the joint PD of R and B. For example, the probability that $R = 7$ and $B = 3$ is 2/216, that is, $\mathbf{P}[(R = 7) \cap (B = 3)] = 2/216$.

Summing across each row and dividing the sum by 216 gives the marginal probability distribution of R. From this marginal distribution, $\mathbf{P}(R = 5) = 24/216$ is the probability of obtaining a sum of 5 on the red and white dice. Of course, summing down each column gives the marginal distribution for B. The operations for obtaining marginal probabilities can be illustrated as follows:

$$\begin{aligned}\mathbf{P}(R = 5) &= \sum_j \mathbf{P}[(R = 5) \cap (B = b_j)] \\ &= 1/216 + 2/216 + 3/216 + 4/216 + 4/216 + 4/216 \\ &\qquad + 3/216 + 2/216 + 1/216 \\ &= 24/216.\end{aligned}$$

To illustrate further, $\mathbf{P}(B = 3) = \sum_i \mathbf{P}[(R = r_i) \cap (B = 3)] = 12/216$.

Probability distributions for two or more random variables are referred to as *multivariate* distributions or simply as joint distributions. Multivariate distributions for three or more discrete random variables are discussed in the references appearing at the end of this chapter.

Table VII.8. Matrix of a bivariate distribution

Note: Entries in the body of the table must be divided by 216 in order to obtain probabilities.

		B											Marginal distribution of *R*
		2	3	4	5	6	7	8	9	10	11	12	
	2	1	1	1	1	1	1	0	0	0	0	0	6/216
	3	1	2	2	2	2	2	1	0	0	0	0	12/216
	4	1	2	3	3	3	3	2	1	0	0	0	18/216
	5	1	2	3	4	4	4	3	2	1	0	0	24/216
	6	1	2	3	4	5	5	4	3	2	1	0	30/216
R	7	1	2	3	4	5	6	5	4	3	2	1	36/216
	8	0	1	2	3	4	5	5	4	3	2	1	30/216
	9	0	0	1	2	3	4	4	4	3	2	1	24/216
	10	0	0	0	1	2	3	3	3	3	2	1	18/216
	11	0	0	0	0	1	2	2	2	2	2	1	12/216
	12	0	0	0	0	0	1	1	1	1	1	1	6/216
Marginal distribution of *B*		$\frac{6}{216}$	$\frac{12}{216}$	$\frac{18}{216}$	$\frac{24}{216}$	$\frac{30}{216}$	$\frac{36}{216}$	$\frac{30}{216}$	$\frac{24}{216}$	$\frac{18}{216}$	$\frac{12}{216}$	$\frac{6}{216}$	$\frac{216}{216}$

VII.3.2. Statistical independence of discrete random variables

In discussing the joint distribution for the experiment "toss one six-sided die and one coin," it was easy to see that any value on the bivariate distribution could be obtained simply by multiplying the values of the marginal probabilities for X and Y alone. Thus,

$$\begin{aligned} \mathbf{P}[(X = 4) \cap (Y = 0)] &= P(X = 4)P(Y = 0) \\ &= (1/6)(1/2) \\ &= 1/12. \end{aligned}$$

However, simple multiplication of the marginal probabilities does *not* give the bivariate probabilities for the variables R and B (in the three-dice experiment). For example, from Table VII.8, $\mathbf{P}(R = 2) = 6/216$ and $\mathbf{P}(B = 4) = 18/216$, but $\mathbf{P}[(R = 2) \cap (B = 4)] = 1/216$, which is *not* equal to $\mathbf{P}(R = 2)\mathbf{P}(B = 4) = (6/216)(18/216) = 1/432$.

What is it that distinguishes these two bivariate distributions? It is that the first two random variables (X and Y in the one-coin, one-die experiment) are statistically independent whereas R and B (in the three-dice experiment) are statistically dependent.

Two discrete random variables X and Y are statistically independent if

$$\mathbf{P}[(X = x_i) \cap (Y = y_j)] = \mathbf{P}(X = x_i)\mathbf{P}(Y = y_j)$$

for every pair of values, x_i and y_j. Otherwise, X and Y are statistically dependent.

Another way of defining statistical independence of random variables is to say that *the discrete random variables X and Y are statistically independent if*

$$\mathbf{P}[(X = x_i) \mid (Y = y_j)] = \mathbf{P}(X = x_i)$$

for every pair of values, x_i and y_j. It is easy to show that this is identical to the first definition. If $\mathbf{P}[(X = x_i) \mid (Y = y_j)] = \mathbf{P}(X = x_i)$, then, by the definition of conditional probability,

$$\frac{\mathbf{P}[(X = x_i) \cap (Y = y_j)]}{\mathbf{P}(Y = y_j)} = \mathbf{P}(X = x_i),$$

and multiplying both sides of the equation by $\mathbf{P}(Y = y_j)$ gives

$$\mathbf{P}[(X = x_i) \cap (Y = y_j)] = \mathbf{P}(X = x_i)\mathbf{P}(Y = y_j).$$

This is the form of the first definition of statistical independence of random variables.

The idea of the statistical independence of discrete random variables is a straightforward extension of the statistical independence of events. Each value of a random variable is an event, and every pair of values (one on X and one on Y) must be statistically independent in order for X and Y to be statistically independent variables. If it is shown that *any* pair of values of two random variables are statistically dependent, then the variables themselves are dependent.

Statistical dependence of random variables provides the conceptual basis for the idea of *correlation.* The connection between these concepts will be examined in greater detail in Chapter IX, but now statistical independence of random variables will be illustrated further.

ILLUSTRATIONS OF STATISTICAL INDEPENDENCE OF DISCRETE RANDOM VARIABLES. To illustrate statistical independence, suppose that X is a true-false question taking on the value 1 for a "yes" response, 0 for "no." In addition, the variable Y is defined as 1 for a schizophrenic patient and 0 for a nonschizophrenic. Then, for any person investigated we assign a pair of values: the value on X indicates his response to the question, and the value on Y his psychiatric status. In Table VII.9, a hypothetical joint PD for X and Y is shown. The marginal probability distributions are also shown.

Table VII.9. Hypothetical joint probability distribution

	Schiz. $(Y = 1)$	Nonschiz. $(Y = 0)$	Marginal distribution of X
Yes $(X = 1)$	.45	.30	.75
No $(X = 0)$	.15	.10	.25
Marginal distribution of Y	.60	.40	1.00

In order to determine whether X and Y are statistically independent, it is necessary to test whether or not the following four equalities hold:

$$\begin{aligned}
\mathbf{P}[(Y = 1) \mid (X = 1)] &= \mathbf{P}(Y = 1),\\
\mathbf{P}[(Y = 1) \mid (X = 0)] &= \mathbf{P}(Y = 1),\\
\mathbf{P}[(Y = 0) \mid (X = 1)] &= \mathbf{P}(Y = 0),\\
\mathbf{P}[(Y = 0) \mid (X = 0)] &= \mathbf{P}(Y = 0).
\end{aligned}$$

The first of these is verified as follows:

$$\begin{aligned}
\mathbf{P}[(Y = 1) \mid (X = 1)] &= \frac{\mathbf{P}[(Y = 1) \cap (X = 1)]}{\mathbf{P}(X = 1)} = \frac{0.45}{0.75} = 0.60\\
&= \mathbf{P}(Y = 1).
\end{aligned}$$

The remaining three equalities can be shown to hold, also, and from this we can conclude that X and Y are statistically independent.

The same conclusion could have been reached by testing these four equalities:

$$\begin{aligned}
\mathbf{P}[(Y = 1) \cap (X = 1)] &= \mathbf{P}(Y = 1)\mathbf{P}(X = 1),\\
\mathbf{P}[(Y = 1) \cap (X = 0)] &= \mathbf{P}(Y = 1)\mathbf{P}(X = 0),\\
\mathbf{P}[(Y = 0) \cap (X = 1)] &= \mathbf{P}(Y = 0)\mathbf{P}(X = 1),\\
\mathbf{P}[(Y = 0) \cap (X = 0)] &= \mathbf{P}(Y = 0)\mathbf{P}(X = 0).
\end{aligned}$$

The fact that these also hold for the example provides a second way of showing that X and Y are statistically independent.

If the bivariate distribution of X and Y were that given in Table VII.10, then we would conclude that X and Y were statistically dependent. Note that the two marginal distributions are the same as before, but that the joint distribution is quite different. Furthermore, of the equalities that

Table VII.10. Joint distribution showing statistical dependence

	Schiz. ($Y = 1$)	Nonschiz. ($Y = 0$)	Marginal distribution of X
Yes ($X = 1$)	.55	.20	.75
No ($X = 0$)	.05	.20	.25
Marginal distribution of Y	.60	.40	1.00

must be tested in order to decide whether X and Y are statistically independent, not one holds for this table. For example,

$$\mathbf{P}[(Y = 0) \cap (X = 1)] = .2 \neq \mathbf{P}(Y = 0)\mathbf{P}(X = 1) = (.4)(.75) = .3.$$

Consequently, X and Y are statistically dependent in Table VII.10.

Note the relation of these calculations to predictability. In Table VII.9, regardless of the value of X, your "best bet" is to predict that $Y = 1$, since 60 percent of those obtaining $X = 1$ are schizophrenic *and* 60 percent of those obtaining $X = 0$ are schizophrenic as well. In other words, it makes no difference how a person responds to the question, the probability that he is schizophrenic is 0.60. In Table VII.10, the probability that $Y = 1$ given $X = 1$ is $0.55/0.75 = 0.73$, whereas the probability that $Y = 1$ given $X = 0$ is only $0.05/0.25 = 0.20$. Consequently, if $X = 1$, the "best bet" is to predict schizophrenia, whereas if $X = 0$, the "best bet" is nonschizophrenia.

Perhaps the most important use of the idea of statistical dependence-independence is in evaluating predictability. If the probability that one variable takes on a particular value depends on the value of a second variable, then the first is to some extent predictable from the second. Of course, this statement leaves something to be desired. The phrase *to some extent predictable* might be elaborated by indicating how *much* predictability exists. This is one function of measures of correlation; they are used to indicate how *much* predictability exists between variables.

PAIRWISE AND MUTUAL STATISTICAL INDEPENDENCE OF DISCRETE RANDOM VARIABLES. In discussing the statistical independence of events, we distinguished between pairwise and mutual statistical independence. This distinction can be extended to random variables.

If X, Y, and Z are discrete random variables with ranges $(x_1, x_2, \ldots, x_i, \ldots, x_r)$, $(y_1, y_2, \ldots, y_j, \ldots, y_m)$, *and* $(z_1, z_2, \ldots, z_q, \ldots, z_v)$, *respectively,* *then X, Y, and Z are pairwise independent if X and Y are statistically independent, X and Z are statistically independent, and Y and Z are statistically independent. If X, Y, and Z are pairwise independent and if, in addition,*

$$\mathbf{P}[(X = x_i) \cap (Y = y_j) \cap (Z = z_q)] = \mathbf{P}(X = x_i)\mathbf{P}(Y = y_j)\mathbf{P}(Z = z_q)$$

for every triplet x_i, y_j, and z_q, then X, Y, and Z are mutually independent.

The ideas of pairwise and mutual independence of discrete random variables are illustrated in the next section.

The Meehl paradox. Meehl[2] has suggested that the lack of relationship between some clinical instruments and some clinical criteria (e.g., diagnostic classifications) may be attributed to the researcher's failure to investigate mutual dependence as well as pairwise dependence (though he does not use these terms). An example given by Meehl will be described in order to make his argument clear.

A two-item, true-false personality inventory is being used in an attempt to distinguish between "schizophrenics" and "normals." A criterion group of 100 known normals and 100 known schizophrenics is used to develop a classification procedure that will permit differential diagnosis on the basis of test performance. The test is administered to the 200 individuals and the hypothetical results are tabulated in Table VII.11.

Table VII.11. Hypothetical results showing pairwise statistical independence

	Item 1			Item 2		
	True ($X_1 = 1$)	False ($X_1 = 0$)	Totals	True ($X_2 = 1$)	False ($X_2 = 0$)	Totals
Schiz. ($Y = 1$)	50	50	100	50	50	100
Normal ($Y = 0$)	50	50	100	50	50	100
Totals	100	100	200	100	100	200

Clearly, each item of the test is statistically independent of diagnostic class membership. Item 1 alone cannot be used to any advantage in making a diagnosis, nor does Item 2 alone contribute useful diagnostic information. In fact, pairwise consideration of either item and diagnosis indicates statistical independence. From these results, one is inclined

[2] Meehl, P. H., "Configural scoring." *J. Consult. Psychol.* **14**, 165–171, 1950. Also, see Meehl's book, *Clinical vs. Statistical Prediction: A Theoretical Analysis and Review of the Evidence.* Minneapolis, University of Minnesota Press, 1954.

to conclude that the test is unrelated to diagnosis. However, as Meehl shows, it is still *possible* that differential diagnosis can be achieved without error. Note that Meehl makes no guarantee of diagnostic *accuracy*; he only shows that *pairwise statistical independence is insufficient to warrant the conclusion that test performance and diagnosis are unrelated.*

To see how this works, suppose the data were tabled for each *group* separately as shown in Table VII.12. Clearly, there is nothing incon-

Table VII.12. Regrouping of data to show mutual statistical dependence

		Normal ($Y = 0$)			Schizophrenic ($Y = 1$)		
		Item 2			Item 2		
		True ($X_2 = 1$)	False ($X_2 = 0$)	Totals	True ($X_2 = 1$)	False ($X_2 = 0$)	Totals
Item 1	True ($X_1 = 1$)	50	0	50	0	50	50
	False ($X_1 = 0$)	0	50	50	50	0	50
Totals		50	50	100	50	50	100

sistent between these two tabulations and those of Table VII.11. But it is clear in Table VII.12 that when the two test items are considered jointly, diagnosis can be determined from the test without error. Anyone who gives the same response to both items is normal and anyone who gives a different response to the two items is schizophrenic. Consequently, the

Table VII.13. Probability of schizophrenia for various response patterns

Test information Item 1	Item 2	Probability of schizophrenic	Probability of normal
T	T	0	1
T	F	1	0
F	T	1	0
F	F	0	1
none		0.5	0.5

two items permit the correct diagnosis of all 200 individuals. This relationship between test information and diagnosis is summarized differently in Table VII.13.

It is easy to show that each of the two test items is statistically independent of diagnosis. However, the three variables are not mutually independent, since

$$\mathbf{P}[(X_1 = 1) \cap (X_2 = 1) \cap (Y = 1)] = 0$$

(that is, a schizophrenic never answers "yes" to both items), whereas

$$\mathbf{P}(X_1 = 1)\mathbf{P}(X_2 = 1)\mathbf{P}(Y = 1) = (1/2)(1/2)(1/2) = 1/8.$$

Thus, by studying mutual statistical independence, we find that the test is an effective diagnostic instrument (for the 200 individuals considered), whereas, if only pairwise statistical dependence is examined, the test appears worthless.

Of course, this procedure need not be restricted to two-item tests or to items having only two alternatives. However, if more than a few items, or items having more than two or three alternatives, are used, the number of response patterns (see Table VII.13) becomes extremely large. If N is the number of items and each item has r alternatives, then there are r^N possible response patterns. If a test contains 10 items each of which has 5 alternatives, then there are $5^{10} = 9{,}765{,}625$ possible patterns, and a table for this test analogous to Table VII.13 would have 9,765,625 rows. In order to get data in each of these 9,765,625 rows *or* to show that some of these patterns never occur, it would be necessary to administer the test to millions of subjects.

Clearly, an analysis of statistical independence involves relating response *patterns* or *configurations* to a criterion, and methods of this kind are often referred to as *configural scoring*, *pattern* analysis, or *configural* analysis. In this section, it has been shown that these methods can be conceived of as analyses of mutual statistical dependence, though there are other quite different ways of formulating the same problem.[3]

Pairwise and mutual statistical independence can be defined for four or more random variables quite easily, but since we will have no occasion to use such general definitions, none is presented here. Feller[4] gives a

[3] Horst, P., "Pattern analysis and configural scoring." *J. Clin. Psychol.* **10**, 3–11, 1954. For a thorough discussion of this problem, see Lubin, A., and H. G. Osburn, "A theory of pattern analysis for the prediction of a quantitative criterion." *Psychometrika* **22**, 63–73, 1957; and Osburn, H. G., and A. Lubin, "The use of configural analysis for the evaluation of test scoring methods." *Psychometrika* **22**, 359–371, 1957.

[4] *Introduction to Probability Theory and its Applications*, I (2nd ed.). New York John Wiley, 1957, pp. 204–205.

succinct, general discussion of the statistical independence of discrete random variables.

VII.3.3. Problems on multivariate distributions for discrete random variables

1. The following questions are to be answered on the basis of the bivariate distribution of Table VII.8.
   a. What is $\mathbf{P}[(4 < R < 10) \cap (B > 8)]$?
   b. What is $\mathbf{P}[(4 < R < 10) \cup (B > 8)]$?
   c. What is $\mathbf{P}[(R \geq 5) \cap (B \geq 10)]$?
   d. What is $\mathbf{P}[(B < 7) \mid (R \geq 5)]$?
   e. What is $\mathbf{P}[(R > 10) \cup (R < 4)]$?
   f. What is $\mathbf{P}[(8 \leq B < 12) \cup (B = 1)]$?
2. Roll two dice, one black and one white. Define D as the face of the black die minus the face of the white and S as their sum.
   a. What is the range of the random variable D?
   b. What is the range of the random variable S?
   c. How does the *shape* of the joint distribution of D and S compare with that of R and B in Problem 1?
   d. What is $\mathbf{P}(D < 0)$?
   e. What is $\mathbf{P}(D = 0)$?
   f. What is $\mathbf{P}[(D < 0) \cup (S > 7)]$?
   g. Given $D = 0$, what is the probability distribution of S? Compare this with the marginal distribution of B in Problem 1.
3. We are interested in the predictability of schizophrenia from knowledge of (1) whether one or more parents died before the person was 6 years of age and (2) whether the person was an only child. The (artificial) data are as follows:

	At least 1 parent died	No parent died	Total	Only child	At least 1 sib.	Total
Schizophrenic	25	75	100	40	60	100
Hospitalized nonschiz.	100	300	400	160	240	400
	125	375	500	200	300	500

   The following questions refer to the 500 individuals included in the study.
   a. Is either historical variable by itself related to diagnosis?
   b. What does your answer to a lead you to conclude?
   c. Could the data be mutually independent? If so, give an example of how they could be mutually independent. If not, give an example of how they might be mutually dependent. Use the following tables:

	Schizophrenics		Hospitalized Nonschizophrenics	
	At least 1 parent died	No parent died	At least 1 parent died	No parent died
Only child				
At least 1 sib.				

d. Suppose that the data for this hypothetical research fell as follows:

At least 1 parent died	Only child	Number of schizophrenics	Number of hospitalized nonschizophrenics
yes	yes	10	60
yes	no	15	40
no	yes	30	100
no	no	45	200
	Totals	100	400

i. Is parental status statistically independent of diagnosis? Demonstrate the correctness of your answer.
ii. Is sibling status statistically independent of diagnosis? Demonstrate the correctness of your answer.
iii. Are the two historical variables and diagnosis mutually independent? Demonstrate that your answer is correct.
iv. What is the marginal distribution for diagnosis?
v. What is the marginal distribution for parental status?

4. Suppose that the random variable X has range $(1, 2, 3, \ldots)$ and that the probability distribution of X is $\mathbf{P}(X = x) = (1/2)^x$. In addition, suppose that Y is a random variable with probability distribution $\mathbf{P}(Y = y) = 0.155(2^y)/y!$ and range $(1, 2, 3, \ldots)$. If the joint distribution of X and Y is

$$\mathbf{P}[(X = x) \cap (Y = y)] = \frac{0.155(2^y)}{y!(2^x)},$$

are X and Y statistically independent? Demonstrate the correctness of your answer.

*VII.3.4. Bivariate probability density functions for continuous random variables

All of the preceding discussion of joint distributions and of statistical independence was limited to discrete random variables. In this section, the same ideas are applied to continuous random variables.

For a single, continuous, random variable, probability was represented graphically by area under the probability density function. For a bivariate density function, it is *volume* that is the graphic analogue of probability. If X and Y have a "rectangular" distribution, as illustrated in Figure VII.19, then the probability that X will take on a value between x_1 and

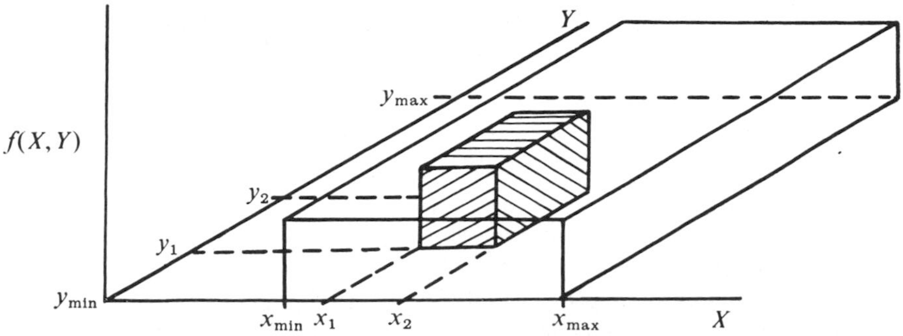

Figure VII.19

x_2 *and* that Y will lie between y_1 and y_2 is represented by the crosshatched volume indicated.

If $f(X, Y)$ is the joint density function of the continuous random variables X and Y, then $f(X, Y)$ gives the height of the curve for each pair of values of X and Y. In the illustration, $f(X, Y)$ has the same height for all X such that $x_{min} \leq X \leq x_{max}$ and Y such that $y_{min} \leq Y \leq y_{max}$; that is, $f(X, Y) = K$, where K is a constant. The probability that $x_1 < X < x_2$ *and* $y_1 < Y < y_2$ is

$$\mathbf{P}[(x_1 < X < x_2) \cap (y_1 < Y < y_2)] = (x_2 - x_1)(y_2 - y_1)K.$$

This amounts to nothing more than computing the appropriate volume.

The random variable X must take on one of its values between x_{min} and x_{max}, and, similarly, Y must take on a value between y_{min} and y_{max}, so that the total volume under the DF must equal 1. In Figure VII.19, the volume is simply the product of the length, width, and height of the bivariate DF. The length is $(x_{max} - x_{min})$, the width is $(y_{max} - y_{min})$, and the height is $f(X, Y) = K$, so that the total volume (or total probability) is

$$(x_{max} - x_{min})(y_{max} - y_{min})K = 1.$$

Of course, $f(X, Y)$ is not always a rectangular solid, so that simple multiplication does not always work. If the surface of the joint density function is curved, then it is necessary to calculate the appropriate volume by integration. (Of course, integration will work in the example of Figure VII.19, too, but it is unnecessary.)

If X and Y are continuous random variables and f(X, Y) is a function such that

$$\mathbf{P}[(x_1 < X < x_2) \cap (y_1 < Y < y_2)] = \int_{y_1}^{y_2} \int_{x_1}^{x_2} f(X, Y)dXdY$$

for any pair of values of X, x_1 and x_2 ($x_1 < x_2$), and for any pair of values of Y, y_1 and y_2 ($y_1 < y_2$), then f(X, Y) is the bivariate density function of X and Y. Furthermore,

$$\int_{y_{\min}}^{y_{\max}} \int_{x_{\min}}^{x_{\max}} f(X, Y)dXdY = 1.$$

Accordingly, the total volume under the surface defined by the bivariate probability density function must be 1.

Definite integration in two variables can be thought of as the calculation of a certain volume under a surface. The limits of integration (at the top and bottom of each integral sign) determine *which* volume. What

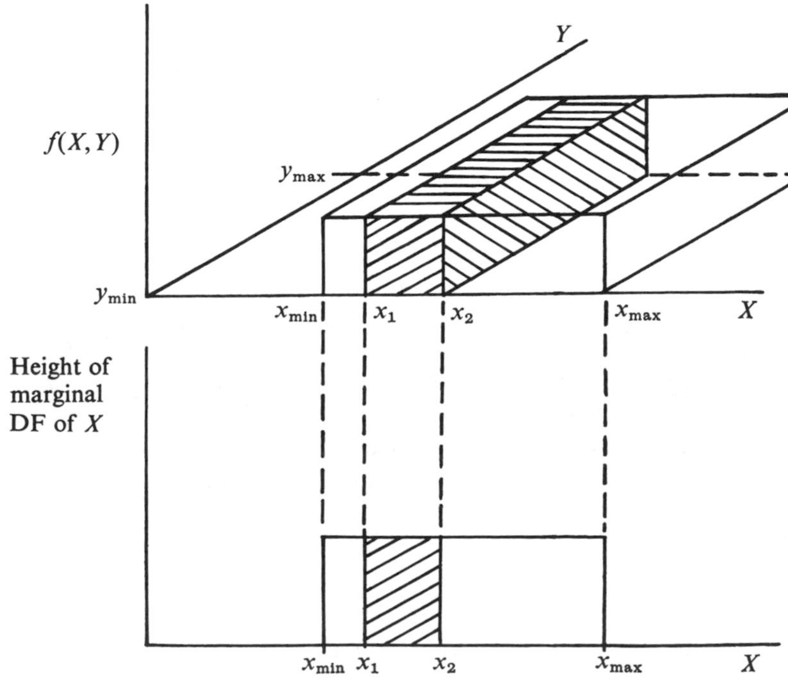

Figure VII.20

necessitates the use of integration is that the surface defined by $f(X, Y)$ may be curved.

Just as for discrete random variables, the marginal distribution of either X or Y can be determined from $f(X, Y)$. However, instead of summing probabilities over all values of Y to find the marginal probability of X, it is necessary to integrate over Y. *If the joint density function of X and Y is $f(X, Y)$, then the marginal probability that X will lie between x_1 and x ($x_1 < x_2$) is*

$$\mathbf{P}(x_1 < X < x_2) = \int_{y_{\min}}^{y_{\max}} \int_{x_1}^{x_2} f(X, Y) dX dY,$$

and the marginal probability that Y will lie between y_1 and y_2 ($y_1 < y_2$) is

$$\mathbf{P}(y_1 < Y < y_2) = \int_{y_1}^{y_2} \int_{x_{\min}}^{x_{\max}} f(X, Y) dX dY.$$

In computing the first integral above, volume is being transformed into area. That is, all the volume (probability) under $f(X, Y)$ between x_1 and x_2 is being recast as area under the DF of one random variable, X. This is illustrated in Figure VII.20 for the bivariate DF of Figure VII.19.

The area between x_1 and x_2 under the marginal DF of X (lower part of Fig. VII.20) corresponds to the crosshatched volume in the upper part of the figure. The effect of integration of Y from $y_{\min}$ to $y_{\max}$ is to eliminate Y as a variable. At the same time, integration over X is between x_1 and x_2, so that the resulting probability is $\mathbf{P}(x_1 < X < x_2)$ with Y ignored.

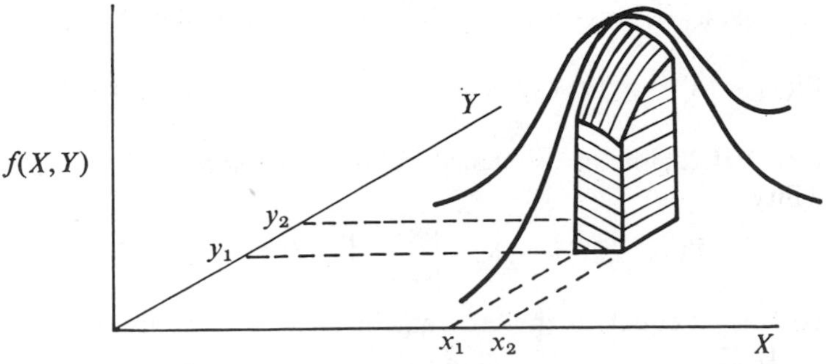

Figure VII.21

In Figures VII.21 and VII.22, these ideas are illustrated for a bivariate DF that does not assign equal height to every pair of values. In Figure VII.21, the crosshatched volume represents

$$\mathbf{P}[(x_1 < X < x_2) \cap (y_1 < Y < y_2)],$$

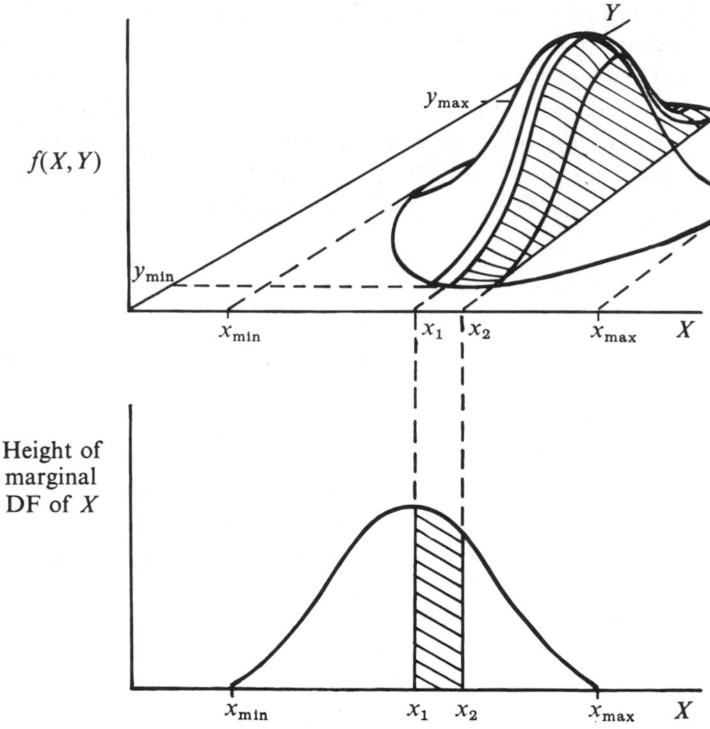

Figure VII.22

the volume under the curved surface between x_1 and x_2 and between y_1 and y_2. Just as before, such a volume would be calculated from

$$\mathbf{P}[(x_1 < X < x_2) \cap (y_1 < Y < y_2)] = \int_{y_1}^{y_2} \int_{x_1}^{x_2} f(X, Y) dX dY.$$

In Figure VII.22, the crosshatched volume corresponds to the marginal probability,

$$\mathbf{P}(x_1 < X < x_2) = \int_{y_{min}}^{y_{max}} \int_{x_1}^{x_2} f(X, Y) dX dY.$$

This volume is equal to the crosshatched area in the lower portion of Figure VII.22.

*STATISTICAL INDEPENDENCE OF CONTINUOUS RANDOM VARIABLES. The application of the idea of statistical independence to continuous random variables is similar to that for discrete random variables. *Two continuous random variables, X and Y, are statistically independent if*

$$\mathbf{P}[(x_1 < X < x_2) \cap (y_1 < Y < y_2)] = \mathbf{P}(x_1 < X < x_2)\mathbf{P}(y_1 < Y < y_2)$$

for all pairs of values on X, x_1 and x_2 ($x_1 < x_2$), and for all pairs of values on Y, y_1 and y_2 ($y_1 < y_2$). For discrete random variables, statistical independence requires that the probability of the joint occurrence of every pair of values equal the product of their marginal probabilities. The statement for continuous variables is analogous, since the probability of the joint occurrence of values in specified intervals must equal the product of the marginal probabilities for those intervals.

Since any continuous random variable has an uncountably infinite set of possible values, it is never possible to calculate all of the probabilities required to establish independence for continuous variables. However, one never has complete data for presumably continuous variables; instead, only finite samples of observations are ever available. From such sample information, shortcut methods are available that permit one to decide whether the two variables are statistically independent in the population. These are called correlation methods.

*PAIRWISE AND MUTUAL STATISTICAL INDEPENDENCE OF CONTINUOUS RANDOM VARIABLES. The distinction between pairwise and mutual statistical independence can be drawn for continuous as well as for discrete random variables. *If X, Y, and Z are continuous random variables, and if each pair among them is statistically independent, then X, Y, and Z are pairwise statistically independent. If in addition,*

$$\mathbf{P}[(x_1 < X < x_2) \cap (y_1 < Y < y_2) \cap (z_1 < Z < z_2)] \\ = \mathbf{P}(x_1 < X < x_2)\mathbf{P}(y_1 < Y < y_2)\mathbf{P}(z_1 < Z < z_2)$$

for every pair of values of X, x_1 and x_2, for every pair of values of Y, y_1 and y_2, and for every pair of values of Z, z_1 and z_2, then X, Y, and Z are mutually statistically independent.

If three continous variables are mutually independent, then there can be no prediction from any one to another, or from any two to the other, just as for discrete random variables. However, pairwise independence among continuous variables does not guarantee that prediction from some pair of variables to a third is impossible. The "Meehl paradox" may arise for continuous variables as well as for discrete variables.

The ideas of joint density functions and of pairwise and mutual statistical independence can be extended to any number of continuous random variables. However, we will have little use for these generalizations.[5]

[5] Multivariate probability distributions for continuous random variables are discussed by Mood, A. M., *Introduction to the Theory of Statistics.* New York, McGraw-Hill, 1950, 74–76; by Cramér, H., *The elements of Probability Theory.* New York, Wiley, 1955, 67–70; and Parzen, E., *Modern Probability Theory and Its Application.* New York, Wiley, 1960.

*VII.3.5. Problems on multivariate density functions for continuous random variables

*1. For each of the bivariate distributions in Figure VII.23, show graphically $\mathbf{P}[(x_1 < X < x_2) \cap (y_1 < Y < y_2)]$, $\mathbf{P}(y_1 < Y < y_2)$, and $\mathbf{P}[(x_1 < X < x_2) \cup (y_1 < Y < y_2)]$.

*2. For each of the two distributions in Problem 1, show graphically the marginal distribution of Y.

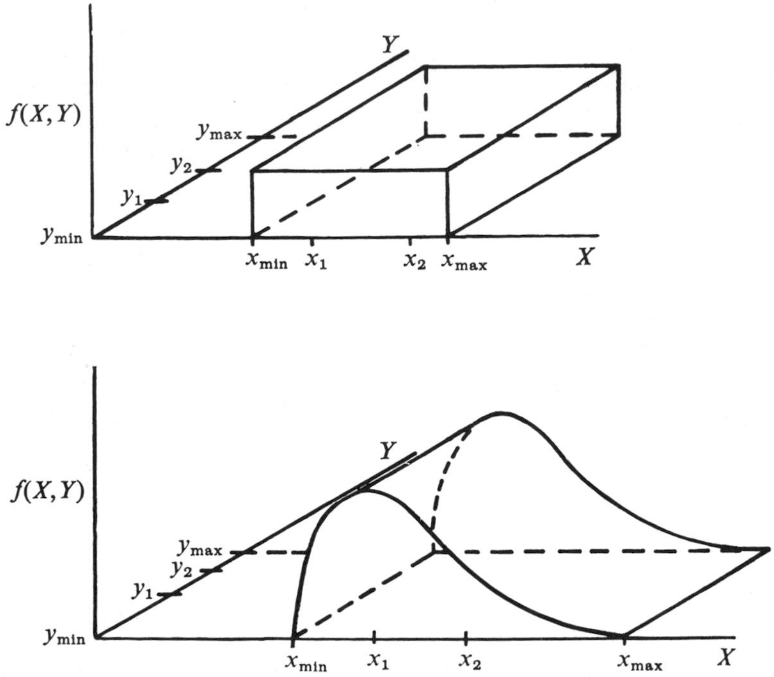

Figure VII.23

*3. Draw a graph of the marginal distribution of X for each of the illustrations in Problem 1.

*4. Illustrate the following probabilities graphically for the bivariate distribution in Fig. VII.24:

a. $\mathbf{P}[(x_1 < X < x_2) \cap (y_1 < Y < y_2)]$

b. $\mathbf{P}[(x_1 < X < x_2) \cup (y_1 < Y < y_2)]$

c. $\mathbf{P}(x_1 < X < x_2)$

d. $\mathbf{P}(y_1 < Y < y_2)$

e. From the graph of $f(X, Y)$, construct a graph of the marginal distribution of X. Locate x_1 and x_2 so that their positions correspond to those in the bivariate distribution.

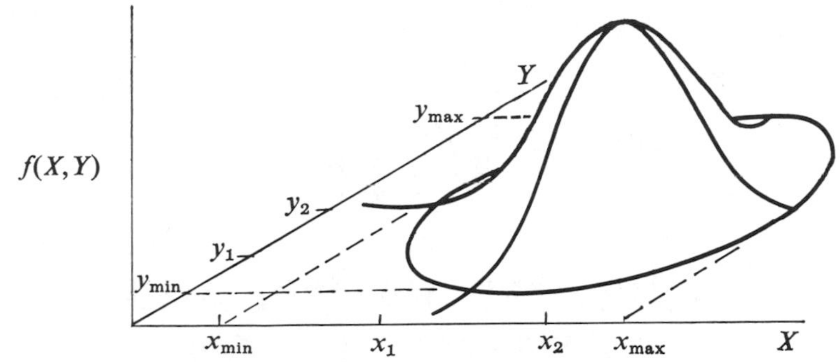

Figure VII.24

SUGGESTED READING

1. Mosteller, F., R. E. K. Rourke, and G. B. Thomas, Jr., *Probability and Statistics.* Reading, Mass., Addison-Wesley, 1961.
Perhaps the best elementary discussion of probability distributions. Includes univariate distributions of discrete variables (pp. 155–167), continuous variables (pp. 221–224), and bivariate distributions for discrete variables (pp. 209–220).
2. Feller, W., *Introduction to Probability Theory and its Applications*, I (2nd ed.). New York, John Wiley, 1957, pp. 199–207.
A concise introduction to discrete random variables and their probability distributions. Includes both univariate and (briefly) multivariate distributions. A discussion of statistical independence is included in these pages, as well. Continuous random variables are not discussed.
3. Cramér, H., *The Elements of Probability Theory.* New York, John Wiley, 1955, pp. 57–70.
Provides an introduction to both PD's and DF's plus a discussion of multivariate distributions. Requires elementary calculus.
4. Mood, A. M., *Introduction to the Theory of Statistics.* New York, McGraw-Hill, 1950, Chaps. 3 and 4.
Chapter 3 is a discussion of discrete probability distributions, Chapter 4 deals with continuous variables. Both univariate and multivariate distributions are included. Parts of Chapter 4 require elementary calculus.
5. Parzen, E., *Modern Probability Theory and Its Application.* New York, Wiley, 1960.
Contains discussions of both discrete and continuous multivariate distributions. The calculus is used freely.

VIII

EXPECTED VALUES AND THEIR ESTIMATION

NOW that the concepts of random variable, probability distribution, and density function are in hand, we are ready to introduce a useful parameter and its estimator. The estimator is the sample arithmetic mean, and the corresponding parameter is the population mean. However, in discussing population means, the more general and more useful idea of an expected value will be used. Roughly speaking, an expected value is a population mean, but it will be defined more precisely later, and its greater breadth and flexibility will be illustrated. First, however, the sample arithmetic mean will be introduced and some of its properties described.

VIII.1

THE ARITHMETIC MEAN OF A SAMPLE

The term "average" is as ambiguous as it is ubiquitous. Newspapers and magazines as well as scientific journals are replete with "averages" having profound implications for the welfare of the community and often of the world. Perhaps the most frequently reported "average" is the arithmetic mean of a sample of observations.

If $X_1, X_2, \ldots, X_k, \ldots, X_n$ *are the observations of a sample of size* n, *then*

$$\bar{X} = \frac{\sum_k X_k}{n} \qquad \text{[VIII.1]}$$

is the arithmetic sample mean of the random variable X.

Notice that the index k refers to the ordinal position of an observation in the sample. X_1 takes on a value when the first observation is made,

X_2 takes on a value when the second is made, and so on. If the sample consists of the 10 Wechsler IQ's 92, 108, 129, 114, 104, 116, 133, 99, 112, and 101, observed in that order, then $X_1 = 92$, $X_2 = 108, \ldots, X_{10} = 101$. The arithmetic mean for this sample is

$$
\begin{aligned}
\overline{X} &= \frac{\sum_k X_k}{n} \\
&= \frac{X_1 + X_2 + \cdots + X_{10}}{10} \\
&= \frac{92 + 108 + 129 + 114 + 104 + 116 + 133 + 99 + 112 + 101}{10} \\
&= 110.8.
\end{aligned}
$$

Drawing a random sample of size n from a population generates an outcome that contains n elements. The set of all such outcomes obtainable from a particular population constitutes a sample space. The formula for the arithmetic sample mean is a rule for assigning a number to each outcome. Consequently, it defines a random variable.

Subsequently, the term "sample mean" is to be understood as "arithmetic sample mean."

VIII.1.1. Problems on the sample mean

1. If a sample consists of the observations 93, 102, 95, 116, and 99, what is the arithmetic mean of this sample?
2. We are interested in the "average sex" of a group of six people. They are as follows: man, woman, woman, woman, man, woman. Assign a 1 to each man, a 0 to each woman. What is the sample mean? What is the meaning of this mean?
3. In light of Problem 2, is it reasonable to say that a proportion is a particular kind of arithmetic mean? Defend your answer concisely.
4. Compute $\sum_k (X_k - \overline{X})$ for the data of Problem 1 and then calculate it for the data of Problem 2.

VIII.2

RULES FOR MANIPULATING SAMPLE MEANS

There are several rules for the algebraic manipulation of sample means. Some of these lead to useful calculational shortcuts, and others describe properties of the sample mean as an estimator. Furthermore, there are analogous rules for manipulating population means (or expected values) which will prove useful later.

VIII.2.1. Sample mean of a constant

If every observation in a sample of size n has the same value, K, then the mean of the sample is K. In other words,

$$\bar{K} = \frac{\sum K}{n} = \frac{\overbrace{K + K + \cdots + K}^{n \text{ terms}}}{n} = \frac{nK}{n} = K.$$

VIII.2.2. Sample mean of a constant times a random variable

If $\bar{X}$ is the mean of the sample $(X_1, X_2, \ldots, X_n)$, and if K is any constant, then the mean of $KX_1, KX_2, \ldots, KX_n$, is $K\bar{X}$.

This is shown by writing the mean of $KX_1, KX_2, \ldots, KX_n$, as

$$\overline{KX} = \frac{KX_1 + KX_2 + \cdots + KX_n}{n}.$$

Since K appears in every term in the numerator, the mean can be rewritten as

$$\overline{KX} = K\frac{(X_1 + X_2 + \cdots + X_n)}{n},$$

which is equal to K times the sample mean of X. This proves the introductory statement.

VIII.2.3. Sample mean of a random variable plus a constant

A similar result is obtained when a constant is added to every value of a sample. *If $\bar{X}$ is the mean of the sample $(X_1, X_2, \ldots, X_n)$, and if K is any constant, then the mean of $X_1 + K, X_2 + K, \ldots., X_n + K$ is $\bar{X} + K$.*

To prove this, begin by writing the mean of $X + K$, which is

$$\overline{X + K} = \frac{(X_1 + K) + (X_2 + K) + \cdots + (X_n + K)}{n}.$$

The K is added n times in the numerator, so that

$$\overline{X + K} = \frac{X_1 + X_2 + \cdots + X_n + nK}{n},$$

or

$$\overline{X + K} = \frac{X_1 + X_2 + \cdots + X_n}{n} + \frac{nK}{n}.$$

The first term, $(X_1 + X_2 + \cdots + X_n)/n$, equals $\bar{X}$, and $(nK)/n = K$, which reduces the preceding expression to $\bar{X} + K$. Thus, the mean of a sample of observations, to each of which is added a constant, is equal to the mean of the observations alone plus the constant.

VIII.2.4. Sample mean of a sum of random variables

If $\overline{X}$ is the mean of the sample $(X_1, X_2, \ldots, X_k, \ldots, X_n)$, and if $\overline{Y}$ is the mean of the sample $(Y_1, Y_2, \ldots, Y_k, \ldots, Y_n)$, then the sum of X and Y is $X_1 + Y_1, X_2 + Y_2, \ldots, X_k + Y_k, \ldots, X_n + Y_n$, and the sample mean of $X + Y$, denoted $\overline{X + Y}$, is

$$\overline{X + Y} = \overline{X} + \overline{Y}.$$

Notice that for each value of X there is a corresponding value of Y, and that the correspondence is indicated by the index, k. Thus, X_1 and Y_1 correspond, X_2 and Y_2 correspond, and so on. This correspondence is determined by some connection between the observations X_k and Y_k. For instance, X_k might be the raw score of individual k on the performance subscale of the Wechsler Adult Intelligence Scale and Y_k the raw score of the *same person* on the verbal subscale. Then the sum $X_k + Y_k$ is the full-scale raw score for person k.

To show that the sample mean of $X + Y$ equals the sum of $\overline{X}$ and $\overline{Y}$, begin by applying the definition of a sample mean to $X + Y$. The sample mean of $X + Y$ is

$$\begin{aligned}
\overline{X + Y} &= \frac{\sum_k (X_k + Y_k)}{n} \\
&= \frac{(X_1 + Y_1) + (X_2 + Y_2) + \cdots + (X_k + Y_k) + \cdots + (X_n + Y_n)}{n} \\
&= \frac{(X_1 + X_2 + \cdots + X_k + \cdots + X_n) + (Y_1 + Y_2 + \cdots + Y_k + \cdots + Y_n)}{n} \\
&= \frac{\sum_k X_k}{n} + \frac{\sum_k Y_k}{n} \\
&= \overline{X} + \overline{Y}.
\end{aligned}$$

Since we began with the mean of $X + Y$ and found it to equal $\overline{X} + \overline{Y}$, the demonstration is complete.

Suppose we had the sample of data shown in Table VIII.1. If the mean of the right-hand column of Table VIII.1 is computed, it is found to equal the sum of the means $\overline{X}$ and $\overline{Y}$. That is,

$$\begin{aligned}
\overline{X + Y} &= \overline{X} + \overline{Y} \\
106.83 &= 50.50 + 56.33 \\
106.83 &= 106.83.
\end{aligned}$$

Table VIII.1. Sample of weighted scores from Wechsler Adult Intelligence Scale

Person (k)	Verbal subscale, weighted score (X_k)	Performance subscale, weighted score (Y_k)	Full-scale weighted score ($X_k + Y_k$)
1	40	48	88
2	64	66	130
3	55	69	124
4	59	56	115
5	35	41	76
6	50	58	108
	$\overline{X} = 50.50$	$\overline{Y} = 56.33$	$\overline{X + Y} = 106.83$

So far, the sample mean of a sum of more than two random variables has not been mentioned. However, the rule for two is easily extended to three or more. *If $X_1, X_2, \ldots, X_m$ are each random variables, and if $\overline{X}_1$ is the sample mean of X_1, $\overline{X}_2$ is the sample mean of X_2, and so on, then the mean of $X_1 + X_2 + \cdots + X_m$ is*

$$\overline{X_1 + X_2 + \cdots + X_m} = \overline{X}_1 + \overline{X}_2 + \cdots + \overline{X}_m.$$

The correctness of this result will be demonstrated for $m = 3$ random variables. To show that

$$\overline{X_1 + X_2 + X_3} = \overline{X}_1 + \overline{X}_2 + \overline{X}_3,$$

begin by letting $Y = X_2 + X_3$. Then, $X_1 + X_2 + X_3 = X_1 + Y$, and applying the rule for the sum of two random variables,

$$\overline{X_1 + X_2 + X_3} = \overline{X_1 + Y} = \overline{X}_1 + \overline{Y}.$$

But since Y was set equal to $X_2 + X_3$, the rule for two variables can be applied to Y, so $\overline{Y} = \overline{X_2 + X_3} = \overline{X}_2 + \overline{X}_3$. Substituting this result for $\overline{Y}$,

$$\begin{aligned}\overline{X_1 + X_2 + X_3} &= \overline{X}_1 + \overline{Y} \\ &= \overline{X}_1 + \overline{X}_2 + \overline{X}_3.\end{aligned}$$

This completes the proof for the case of three random variables. By a straightforward extension of this procedure, the rule can be shown to apply to any number of variables.[1]

[1] By the method of mathematical induction, a general proof can be constructed quite easily.

VIII.2.5. Sample mean of a linear function of random variables

If the reader is unfamiliar with the idea of a linear function of several variables, then before proceeding he should read Appendix VIII.1 at the end of this chapter.

The rule introduced in this section encompasses all of those in the preceding four sections. *If X_1, $X_2, \ldots, X_m$ are each random variables and if $\bar{X}_1$ is the sample mean of X_1, $\bar{X}_2$ is the sample mean of X_2, and so on, and if A, B_1, $B_2, \ldots, B_m$ are all constants, then the mean of $Y = A + B_1X_1 + B_2X_2 + \cdots + B_mX_m$ is*

$$\bar{Y} = A + B_1\bar{X}_1 + B_2\bar{X}_2 + \cdots + B_m\bar{X}_m. \qquad \text{[VIII.2]}$$

First, suppose that $m = 1$ so that $Y = A + B_1X_1$. If we let $B_1X_1 = Z$, then Y can be rewritten as $Y = A + B_1X_1 = A + Z$. By the rule of Section VIII.2.3, $\bar{Y} = A + \bar{Z}$. Further, by the rule of Section VIII.2.2, $\bar{Z} = \overline{B_1X_1} = B_1\bar{X}_1$, and substituting $B_1\bar{X}_1$ for $\bar{Z}$ gives

$$\bar{Y} = \overline{A + B_1X_1} = A + \bar{Z} = A + B_1\bar{X}_1.$$

This shows that the rule is correct for $m = 1$. Following similar procedures, it can be shown that the rule holds for any specific value of m.[2]

Suppose that a short form of the Wechsler Adult Intelligence Scale is being used to obtain efficient estimates of verbal, performance, and full-scale IQ's. We will call the short form CAD since it includes the comprehension (X), arithmetic (Y), and digit symbol (Z) subtests. X and Y are verbal subtests, whereas Z is a performance subtest. Since there are six subtests in the verbal scale and five in the performance scale, the total weighted score for the performance scale is estimated from $5Z$ and the weighted score for the verbal scale is estimated from $(6/2)(X + Y)$ or $(6/2)X + (6/2)Y$. The estimate of the full-scale score is

$$(6/2)X + (6/2)Y + 5Z.$$

This estimate is a linear function of the subtests in which the constant $A = 0$, $B_1 = 6/2$, $B_2 = 6/2$, and $B_3 = 5$.

If for a given 22-year-old subject, $X = 10$, $Y = 8$, and $Z = 12$, then his verbal weighted score would be estimated as

$$\begin{aligned} (6/2)X + (6/2)Y &= (6/2)(10) + (6/2)(8) \\ &= 54; \end{aligned}$$

his performance weighted score as

$$\begin{aligned} 5Z &= 5(12) \\ &= 60; \end{aligned}$$

[2] A proof for any m can be obtained by the method of mathematical induction.

and his full-scale weighted score as

$$(6/2)X + (6/2)Y + 5Z = \frac{6}{2}(10) + \frac{6}{2}(8) + 5(12)$$
$$= 114.$$

These weighted scores correspond to IQ's of 95, 112, and 102, respectively.[3]

If, for a sample of 22-year-olds, $\bar{X} = 10.1$, $\bar{Y} = 9.3$, and $\bar{Z} = 11.0$, then the mean full-scale weighted score would be estimated by

$$\overline{(6/2)X + (6/2)Y + 5Z} = \frac{6}{2}\bar{X} + \frac{6}{2}\bar{Y} + 5\bar{Z}$$
$$= \frac{6}{2}(10.1) + \frac{6}{2}(9.3) + 5(11.0)$$
$$= 113.2.$$

VIII.2.6. Problems on manipulating sample means

1. Each of the following questions refers to the data of Problem 1 in Section VIII.1.1. These data will be referred to as observations on the random variable X.
   a. Find the mean of KX, where $K = 1.5$.
   b. Show that the mean of $1.5(X)$ equals 1.5 times the mean of X for these data.
   c. What is the mean of $X + 2$?
   d. Show that the mean of $X + 2$ equals $\bar{X} + 2$.
   e. Find the mean of $1.5(X) + 2$.
   f. Show that the mean of e equals $1.5(\bar{X}) + 2$.
2. For the variables X and Y of Table VIII.1:
   a. Show that the mean of $2 + 3X + 0.5Y$ equals $2 + 3\bar{X} + 0.5\bar{Y}$.
   b. Suppose that $A = 0$, $B = 1$, and $C = -1$. Find the mean of $W = A + BX + CY$.
   c. What is the interpretation of the random variable W?
   d. Generalize your conclusions from c in a precise statement.
3. Is an arithmetic sample mean a linear function of the observations of a sample? Defend your answer.

VIII.3
EXPECTED VALUES

The definitions and rules introduced so far are applicable to samples only. Now it is necessary to introduce analogous results for population means or expected values.

[3] This was determined by entering the appropriate tables in Wechsler, D., *Wechsler Adult Intelligence Scale*. New York, The Psychological Corporation, 1955.

When dealing with expected values, discrete and continuous random variables must be distinguished. Just as probability distributions and density functions are distinguished, the definition of expected value differs for discrete and continuous random variables.

VIII.3.1. Expected value of a discrete random variable

If X is a discrete random variable with probability distribution $\mathbf{P}(X = x_i)$, *then the expected value of X is*

$$E(X) = \sum_i \mathbf{P}(X = x_i)x_i. \qquad \text{[VIII.3]}$$

The expected value of X is also called μ, the *population mean of X.*

When a population is finite, this definition reduces to simply summing the values of the random variable assigned to the elements of the population and dividing by N, the number of elements. To illustrate this, we will use the number of heads in a toss of three coins. The values of this random variable and its PD are given in Table VIII.2. Since there are

Table VIII.2. Probability distribution of a random variable

	X			
	0	1	2	3
$\mathbf{P}(X = x_i)$	1/8	3/8	3/8	1/8

eight possible outcomes ($X = 0$ for one, $X = 1$ for three, $X = 2$ for three others, and $X = 3$ for one), the arithmetic mean of X is

$$(0 + 1 + 1 + 1 + 2 + 2 + 2 + 3)/8 = 1.5.$$

Replacing addition of like terms by multiplication, a briefer form of this expression is $[1(0) + 3(1) + 3(2) + 1(3)]/8 = 1.5$. Since there is a common denominator, this expression can be rewritten as

$$\frac{1}{8}(0) + \frac{3}{8}(1) + \frac{3}{8}(2) + \frac{1}{8}(3) = 1.5.$$

In this calculation, each value of X is multiplied by its probability and the sum of these products computed. This is exactly what is required in the definition of the expected value of a discrete random variable, so for this example,

$$E(X) = \sum_i P(X = x_i)x_i = \frac{1}{8}(0) + \frac{3}{8}(1) + \frac{3}{8}(2) + \frac{1}{8}(3) = 1.5.$$

Here, we set out to compute the arithmetic mean of X and found that this was equivalent to computing the expected value of X. However, as the next section shows, the idea of an expected value is more general than the sum of the values of a random variable divided by their number.

An expected value is the *arithmetic mean* of a random variable in a particular population; that is, it is a parameter. *An expected value is never a characteristic of a sample.*

VIII.3.2. Expected value of a continuous random variable

The expected value of a discrete random variable is found by multiplying each value of the variable by its probability and summing these products. For a continuous random variable, X, that has density function $f(X)$, we also begin by obtaining $f(x)x$ for each value, x. However, since the range of X is uncountably infinite, it is difficult to see how one obtains the sum of these products. We will rely on diagrams to show how this difficulty is overcome.

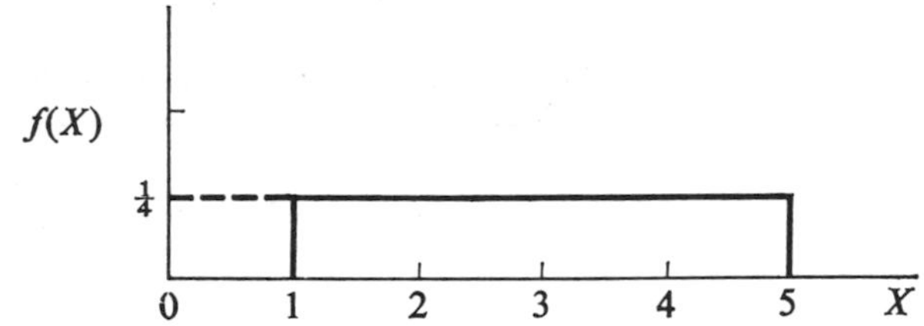

Figure VIII.1

Suppose that Figure VIII.1 represents $f(X)$. To find $E(X)$ we begin by plotting $f(X)X$. The graph of $f(X)X$ is shown in Figure VIII.2. For $X = 1$, $f(X)X$ equals $(1/4)(1) = 1/4$, and for $X = 5$, $f(X)X$ is $(1/4)(5) = 1\frac{1}{4}$.

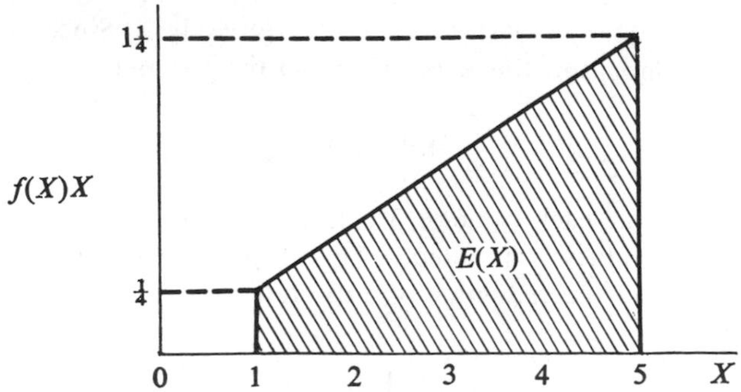

Figure VIII.2

Probabilities associated with continuous random variables are represented by areas under the DF. Similarly, the expected value of a continuous random variable equals the total area under $f(X)X$. Since the area under $f(X)X$ (Figure VIII.2) is 3, $E(X) = 3$.

Though the area under $f(X)X$ was found by simple arithmetical calculation in this example, it would be difficult to get a precise value of this area if $f(X)$ were curvilinear. In Figure VIII.3, a curvilinear DF has been

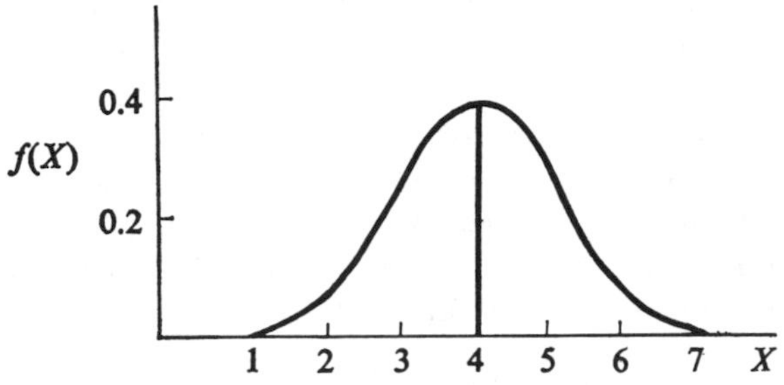

Figure VIII.3

plotted. The first step in finding the expected value of this random variable is to compute $f(X)X$ for each value of X. This is plotted in Figure VIII.4. The expected value of X is the area under this curve, which can

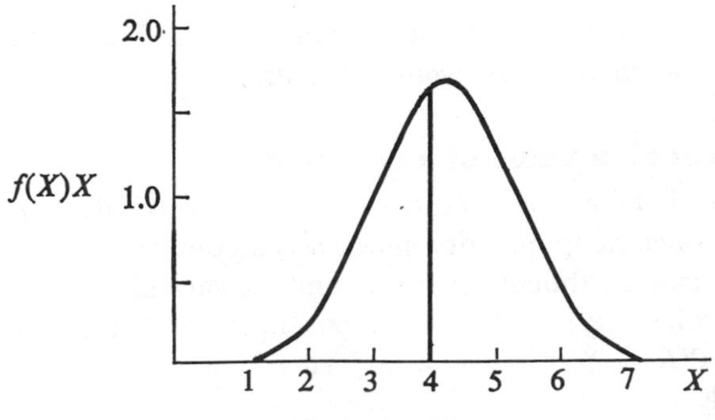

Figure VIII.4

be computed by finding the definite integral of $f(X)X$ over the full range of X.

If $f(X)$ is the density function of the continuous random variable, X, then the expected value of X is

$$E(X) = \int_{-\infty}^{\infty} f(X)XdX. \quad \text{[VIII.4]}$$

The expected value of a continuous variable has the same interpretation as that of a discrete random variable. It is a population mean. Expected values of both continuous and discrete random variables will be referred to by the symbol μ as well as by $E(X)$.

VIII.3.3. Problems on expected values

1. Compute the expected value for each of the following:
   a. The random variable given in Table VII.1.
   b. The random variable, Y, of Problem 1 of Section VII.1.3.
   c. The random variable of Problem 2 of Section VII.1.3.
2. For each of the graphs of Problem 1 of Section VII.1.6 which could be the DF of a continuous random variable, construct a second graph of $f(X)X$.
3. Using graphical methods, approximate $E(X)$ for each of the density functions of Problem 2. Locate $E(X)$ on the graph of the DF in each case.
4. Construct an example of a density function of a continuous variable not included in the text or problems for which

$$E(X) = x_{\min} + \frac{x_{\max} - x_{\min}}{2}.$$

VIII.4

RULES FOR MANIPULATING EXPECTED VALUES

The rules for the algebraic manipulation of expected values are analogous to those for the sample mean. Although the logical bases of these rules will be developed only for discrete random variables, *the same rules apply to both discrete and continuous variables.*

VIII.4.1. Expected value of a constant

The first rule is that *the expected value of a constant is equal to that constant.* For example, since the population mean μ is a constant, $E(\mu) = \mu$.

A constant can be thought of as a random variable that assigns one value with probability 1. If K is a constant so that $\mathbf{P}(K = K) = 1$, then $E(K) = \mathbf{P}(K = K)K = 1K = K$. This demonstrates the correctness of the first rule.

VIII.4.2. Expected value of a function of a random variable

Frequently, we deal with a function of a random variable rather than with the random variable itself. For instance, if X is a random variable and K is a constant, then $Y = KX$ is a new random variable defined on the same sample space as X. KX is also a function of X. If K and B are constants, then $Z = KX + B$ and $W = KX^2 + B$ are both functions of X that define new random variables on the same sample space.

If $h(X)$ is a function of the discrete random variable, X, and if $\mathbf{P}(X = x_i)$ is the probability distribution of X, then the expected value of the random variable $h(X)$ is defined as[4]

$$E[h(X)] = \sum_i \mathbf{P}(X = x_i)h(x_i). \qquad \text{[VIII.5]}$$

This definition will be illustrated for the variable "number of heads" when three coins are tossed using the functions $h(X) = KX$ and $g(X) = KX^2 + B$, where $K = 2$ and $B = 1$. Following Formula [VIII.5] and referring to Table VIII.3,

Table VIII.3. Preliminary calculations for expected values of two functions of a random variable

X	0	1	2	3
$\mathbf{P}(X = x_i)$	1/8	3/8	3/8	1/8
$h(X) = 2X$	0	2	4	6
$g(X) = 2X^2 + 1$	1	3	9	19

$$\begin{aligned} E[h(X)] = E[2X] &= \sum_i \mathbf{P}(X = x_i)2x_i \\ &= \mathbf{P}(X = 0)2(0) + \mathbf{P}(X = 1)2(1) + \mathbf{P}(X = 2)2(2) \\ &\qquad + \mathbf{P}(X = 3)2(3) \\ &= \frac{1}{8}(0) + \frac{3}{8}(2) + \frac{3}{8}(4) + \frac{1}{8}(6) \\ &= 3. \end{aligned}$$

Similarly,

$$\begin{aligned} E[g(X)] = E(2X^2 + 1) &= \sum_i \mathbf{P}(X = x_i)(2x_i^2 + 1) \\ &= \mathbf{P}(X = 0)(2(0)^2 + 1) + \mathbf{P}(X = 1)(2(1)^2 + 1) \\ &\quad + \mathbf{P}(X = 2)(2(2)^2 + 1) + \mathbf{P}(X = 3)(2(3)^2 + 1) \\ &= \frac{1}{8}(1) + \frac{3}{8}(3) + \frac{3}{8}(9) + \frac{1}{8}(19) \\ &= 7. \end{aligned}$$

VIII.4.3. Expected value of a constant times a random variable

In the first of the above calculations, we found that $E(2X) = 3$. Previously $E(X)$ was found to be 1.5. Thus, for this case at least, $E(2X) = 3 = 2(1.5) = 2E(X)$. If K is a constant, is it true in general that $E(KX) = KE(X)$? It is quite easy to show that it is.

[4] If $h(X)$ is a function of the *continuous random variable* X, and if $f(X)$ is the DF of X, then the expected value of the random variable $h(X)$ is defined as $E[h(X)] = \int_{-\infty}^{\infty} f(X)h(X)dX$.

First, since KX is a function of X, we can apply the rule that $E[h(X)] = \sum_i \mathbf{P}(X = x_i)h(x_i)$ by substituting Kx_i for $h(x_i)$. Then, $E(KX) = \sum_i \mathbf{P}(X = x_i)Kx_i$. If there are r possible values of X, then

$$E(KX) = \mathbf{P}(X = x_1)Kx_1 + \mathbf{P}(X = x_2)Kx_2 + \cdots + \mathbf{P}(X = x_r)Kx_r.$$

But since K appears in every term of this sum,

$$E(KX) = K[\mathbf{P}(X = x_1)x_1 + \mathbf{P}(X = x_2)x_2 + \cdots + \mathbf{P}(X = x_r)x_r].$$

The term in brackets is simply $E(X)$, so

$$E(KX) = KE(X).$$

This result is summarized by stating that *if X is a random variable and K is a constant, then $E(KX) = KE(X)$.*

VIII.4.4. Expected value of a random variable plus a constant

If $E(X)$ is the expected value of X and K is any constant, then $E(X + K)$ equals $E(X) + K$.

To prove this, begin by applying the definition of the expected value of a function of a random variable:

$$E[h(X)] = E(X + K) = \sum_i \mathbf{P}(X = x_i)(x_i + K)$$
$$= \sum_i \mathbf{P}(X = x_i)x_i + \sum_i \mathbf{P}(X = x_i)K.$$

The expression $\sum_i \mathbf{P}(X = x_i)x_i$ is simply $E(X)$, so

$$E(X + K) = E(X) + \sum_i \mathbf{P}(X = x_i)K.$$

If r is the number of values in the range of X, then

$$E(X + K) = E(X) + K[\mathbf{P}(X = x_1) + \mathbf{P}(X = x_2) + \cdots + \mathbf{P}(X = x_r)].$$

Now the sum in brackets contains all of the values of the PD of X, so that it must equal 1. Therefore,

$$E(X + K) = E(X) + K(1) = E(X) + K,$$

which is the desired result.

The expected value of the number of heads in a toss of three coins was found to be 1.5. If the number of heads is called X, then the expected value of X plus $K = 2$ is

$$E[h(X)] = E(X + 2) = \sum_i \mathbf{P}(X = x_i)(x_i + 2)$$
$$= \frac{1}{8}(0 + 2) + \frac{3}{8}(1 + 2) + \frac{3}{8}(2 + 2) + \frac{1}{8}(3 + 2)$$
$$= 3.5.$$

Using the rule just derived,

$$E(X + K) = E(X) + K$$
$$E(X + 2) = E(X) + 2 = 1.5 + 2$$
$$= 3.5,$$

which is the result obtained by computing $E(X + 2)$ directly.

VIII.4.5. Expected value of a sum of random variables

The sum of two random variables includes the sum of every possible pair of values. We have already dealt with several such sums. For instance, if the number of spots on one six-sided die is called X and the number on the other is called Y, $X + Y$ is the random variable that is pertinent to the game of craps. In discussing discrete bivariate distributions (Section VII.3.1), the sum of spots on a red and a white die was called R, the sum of white and blue was called B. R and B are each the sum of two random variables.

If $E(X)$ is the expected value of X, and $E(Y)$ is the expected value of Y, then the expected value of the sum of X and Y is

$$E(X + Y) = E(X) + E(Y).$$

If X is the number of spots on one six-sided die, and Y is the number on another, then the expected value of $X + Y$ can be found by direct calculation as follows:

$$E(X + Y) = \sum_i \sum_j \mathbf{P}[(X = x_i) \cap (Y = y_j)](x_i + y_j).$$

Since X and Y are statistically independent in this example,

$$\begin{aligned} E(X + Y) &= \sum_i \sum_j \mathbf{P}(X = x_i)\mathbf{P}(Y = y_j)(x_i + y_j) \\ &= \underbrace{\frac{1}{6}\frac{1}{6}(1 + 1) + \frac{1}{6}\frac{1}{6}(1 + 2) + \frac{1}{6}\frac{1}{6}(1 + 3) + \cdots + \frac{1}{6}\frac{1}{6}(6 + 6)}_{36 \text{ terms}} \\ &= 7. \end{aligned}$$

However, it is much simpler to apply the rule for the sum of two random variables,

$$\begin{aligned} E(X + Y) &= E(X) + E(Y) \\ &= 3.5 + 3.5 \\ &= 7. \end{aligned}$$

Using the marginal distributions of R and B in Table VII.8, $E(R) = 7$ and $E(B) = 7$, so $E(R + B) = E(R) + E(B) = 7 + 7 = 14$. By direct calculation from Table VII.8,

$$E(R + B)$$
$$= \sum_i \sum_j \mathbf{P}[(R = r_i) \cap (B = b_j)](r_i + b_j)$$
$$= \underbrace{\frac{1}{216}(2 + 2) + \frac{1}{216}(2 + 3) + \frac{1}{216}(2 + 4) + \cdots + \frac{1}{216}(12 + 12)}_{\text{91 nonzero terms}}$$
$$= 14.$$

In this example, R and B are statistically dependent, so $\mathbf{P}[(R = r_i) \cap (B = b_j)]$ is not simply the product of $\mathbf{P}(R = r_i)$ and $\mathbf{P}(B = b_j)$. However, notice that *the rule $E(X + Y) = E(X) + E(Y)$ holds regardless of whether X and Y are statistically independent.*

This rule for the sum of two random variables will not be proved here, though a proof is given in Appendix VIII.2 at the end of this chapter. The appendix also describes how this rule can be extended to the sum of any number of random variables. *If $X_1, X_2, \ldots, X_m$ are random variables having expected values $E(X_1), E(X_2), \ldots, E(X_m)$, respectively, then the expected value of their sum is*

$$E(X_1 + X_2 + \cdots + X_m) = E(X_1) + E(X_2) + \cdots + E(X_m).$$

VIII.4.6. Expected value of a linear function of random variables

All of the preceding rules for manipulating expected values can be summarized in a single rule. *If $X_1, X_2, \ldots, X_m$ are random variables having expected values $E(X_1), E(X_2), \ldots, E(X_m)$, respectively, and if $A, B_1, B_2, \ldots, B_m$ are constants, then the expected value of the linear function $A + B_1X_1 + B_2X_2 + \cdots + B_mX_m$ is*

$$E(A + B_1X_1 + B_2X_2 + \cdots + B_mX_m)$$
$$= A + B_1E(X_1) + B_2E(X_2) + \cdots + B_mE(X_m). \quad \text{[VIII.6]}$$

First, consider the simplest case where $m = 1$. Then, the rule states that $E(A + B_1X_1) = A + B_1E(X_1)$. Since A is a constant and B_1X_1 is a random variable, the rule of Section VIII.4.4 tells us that $E(A + B_1X_1) = A + E(B_1X_1)$. Now, B_1X_1 is simply a constant times a random variable, so that $E(B_1X_1) = B_1E(X_1)$. Substituting this result, $E(A + B_1X_1) = A + E(B_1X_1) = A + B_1E(X_1)$, which is the result required for $m = 1$.

By methods similar to those illustrated in the last part of Appendix VIII.2, it can be shown that the statement is true for any specified value of m.

VIII.4.7. Expected value of a product of random variables

The rule for the expected value of the product of two random variables is not applicable unless an important condition is satisfied. *If X and Y are statistically independent random variables, then the expected value of the product of X and Y is*

$$E(X \cdot Y) = E(X)E(Y). \qquad \text{[VIII.7]}$$

The product of two random variables, X and Y, is obtained by multiplying each value of X by each value of Y. The set of all such products forms the range of the random variable $X \cdot Y$.

In Section VII.3.1 (Table VII.7), the joint distribution of the results of tossing a coin (Y) and a die (X) was discussed. In this example, the values of $X \cdot Y$ are 0, 1, 2, . . ., 6 and these were obtained by finding the products $0 \cdot 1$, $0 \cdot 2$, $0 \cdot 3$, $0 \cdot 4$, $0 \cdot 5$, $0 \cdot 6$, $1 \cdot 1$, $1 \cdot 2$, $1 \cdot 3$, $1 \cdot 4$, $1 \cdot 5$, and $1 \cdot 6$. The probability that $X \cdot Y$ will take on the particular value $x_i \cdot y_j$ is

$$\mathbf{P}(X \cdot Y = x_i \cdot y_j) = \mathbf{P}[(X = x_i) \cap (Y = y_j)],$$

the joint probability of x_i and y_j. For example, from Table VII.7 it can be seen that

$$\mathbf{P}(X \cdot Y = 4 \cdot 1) = \mathbf{P}[(X = 4) \cap (Y = 1)] = 1/12.$$

For this example, $E(Y) = 0.5$ and $E(X) = 3.5$, so

$$E(X \cdot Y) = E(X)E(Y) = 3.5(0.5) = 1.75.$$

This can be checked by calculating $E(X \cdot Y)$ directly:

$$\begin{aligned} E(X \cdot Y) &= \sum_i \sum_j \mathbf{P}[(X = x_i) \cap (Y = y_j)]x_i \cdot y_j \\ &= \underbrace{\frac{1}{12}(1 \cdot 0) + \frac{1}{12}(2 \cdot 0) + \cdots + \frac{1}{12}(6 \cdot 1)}_{12 \text{ terms}} \\ &= 1.75, \end{aligned}$$

which agrees with the results obtained using the rule.

It is quite easy to prove that this rule is correct. To begin with, the expected value of $X \cdot Y$ is

$$E(X \cdot Y) = \sum_i \sum_j \mathbf{P}[(X = x_i) \cap (Y = y_j)]x_i \cdot y_j.$$

If X and Y are statistically independent, then

$$\mathbf{P}[(X = x_i) \cap (Y = y_j)] = \mathbf{P}(X = x_i)\mathbf{P}(Y = y_j),$$

so $E(X \cdot Y)$ becomes

$$E(X \cdot Y) = \sum_i \sum_j \mathbf{P}(X = x_i)\mathbf{P}(Y = y_j)x_i \cdot y_j.$$

Since a quantity with the subscript i remains a constant when summing over j, this can be rewritten

$$E(X \cdot Y) = \sum_i \mathbf{P}(X = x_i)x_i \sum_j \mathbf{P}(Y = y_j)y_j.$$

But since $\sum_i \mathbf{P}(X = x_i)x_i = E(X)$ and $\sum_j \mathbf{P}(Y = y_j)y_j = E(Y)$,

$$E(X \cdot Y) = E(X)E(Y).$$

This rule can be extended to any number of *mutually independent* random variables: *If* $X_1, X_2, \ldots, X_m$ *are mutually independent random variables having expected values* $E(X_1), E(X_2), \ldots, E(X_m)$, *then the expected value of their product is*

$$E(X_1 \cdot X_2 \cdots X_m) = E(X_1)E(X_2) \cdots E(X_m).$$

VIII.5

SUMMARY OF RULES FOR MANIPULATING SAMPLE MEANS AND EXPECTED VALUES

None of the rules for expected values was shown to hold for continuous random variables, but *all of them apply to both discrete and continuous variables equally well.*

Table VIII.4 summarizes all of the rules for sample means and expected values.

Table VIII.4. Rules for manipulating sample means and expected values

Expected values	Sample means
$E(K) = K$, K a constant	If each observation is a constant, K, then K equals the sample mean
$E(KX) = KE(X)$	$\overline{KX} = K\overline{X}$
$E(K + X) = K + E(X)$	$\overline{K + X} = K + \overline{X}$
$E(X_1 + X_2 + \cdots + X_m) = E(X_1) + E(X_2) + \cdots + E(X_m)$	$\overline{X_1 + X_2 + \cdots + X_m} = \overline{X}_1 + \overline{X}_2 + \cdots + \overline{X}_m$
$E(A + B_1X_1 + B_2X_2 + \cdots + B_mX_m) = A + B_1E(X_1) + B_2E(X_2) + \cdots + B_mE(X_m)$	$\overline{A + B_1X_1 + B_2X_2 + \cdots + B_mX_m} = A + B_1\overline{X}_1 + B_2\overline{X}_2 + \cdots + B_m\overline{X}_m$
$E(X \cdot Y) = E(X)E(Y)$ if X, Y are statistically independent	Seldom used

VIII.6

PROBLEMS ON MANIPULATING EXPECTED VALUES

1. For the bivariate distribution of Table VII.8, find
   a. $E(3)$
   b. $E(2R)$
   c. $E(1 + 2R + 2.5B)$
   d. $E(R - B)$.
2. Prove that your answer to Problem 1b is correct for this example.
3. Can Formula [VIII.7] be used to calculate $E(R \cdot B)$, where R and B are the random variables of Table VII.8? Why?
4. Consider the following table:

X	1	2	3	4	5	6
$\mathbf{P}(X = x_i)$	1/10	1/10	2/10	3/10	2/10	1/10
$h(x_i) = 2x_i^2 + 1$	3	9	19	33	51	73

   a. Is $h(X) = 2X^2 + 1$ defined on the same sample space as X?
   b. Write out the probability distribution of $h(X)$.
5. Suppose that Z is a function of the random variable X, such that $Z = h(X)$.
   a. Is Z a random variable?

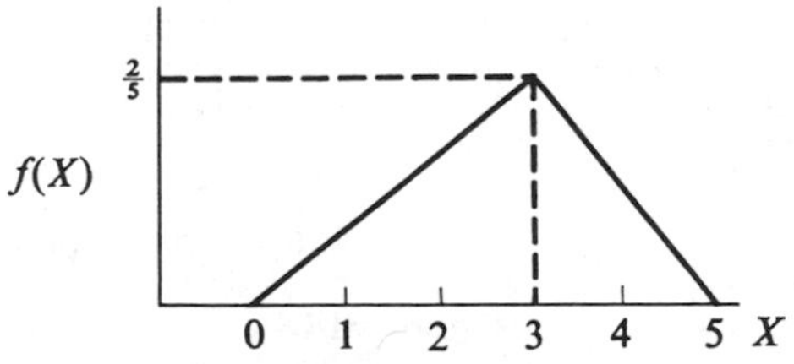

Figure VIII.5

   b. If Figure VIII.5 represents the DF of X, and if $Z = 2X$, plot the CDF of Z.
   c. Plot the CDF of $Z = X^2$.

VIII.7

SPECIAL PROPERTIES OF EXPECTED VALUES AND SAMPLE MEANS

There are two properties of sample means and of expected values that show how they measure the "middle" or "center" of a set of values. In addition to contributing to our understanding of means and expected values, these properties will provide some useful algebraic shortcuts.

VIII.7.1. Sum of deviations from the sample mean

One way of interpreting a sample mean is as the "center of frequency" of a sample. To give this a concrete interpretation, suppose the frequency

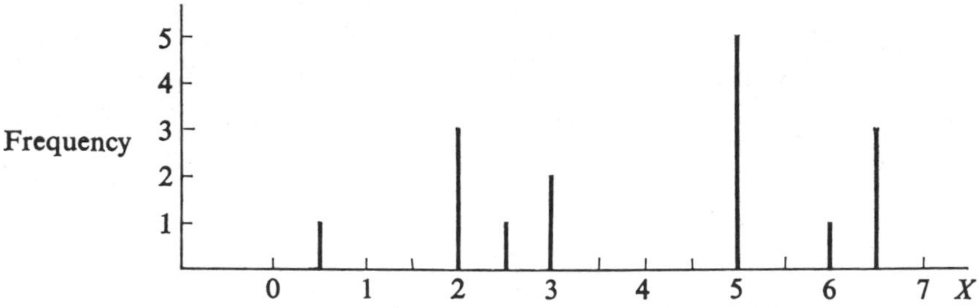

Figure VIII.6

function of Figure VIII.6 were obtained for a sample of $n = 16$ observations. This frequency function can be given a concrete representation by transforming it into piles of bricks on a "weightless" seven-foot

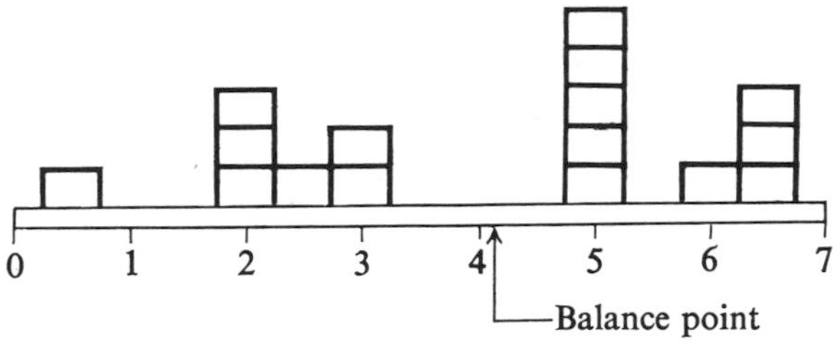

Figure VIII.7

plank, as shown in Figure VIII.7. The numbers along the plank represent distances from its left end, and the mean distance of the 16 bricks determines the balance point of the plank. Thus, at a point

$$\bar{X} = \frac{1(0.5) + 3(2) + 1(2.5) + 2(3) + 5(5) + 1(6) + 3(6.5)}{16} = 4.094.$$

feet from its left end, the plank balances. Similarly, the "center" of the frequency function of Figure VIII.6 is at 4.094 units, the arithmetic mean.

Thus, the distribution of frequency (distribution of weight in the case of the plank) is the same on both sides of the sample mean, so that $\sum_k (X_k - \bar{X}) = 0$. *If $X_1, X_2, \ldots, X_k, \ldots, X_n$ is a sample with mean $\bar{X}$, then*

$$\sum_k (X_k - \bar{X}) = 0. \qquad \text{[VIII.8]}$$

This can be verified for the data of Figure VIII.6, and it is easy to prove that $\sum_k (X_k - \bar{X}) = 0$. To begin with,

$$\begin{aligned}\sum_k (X_k - \bar{X}) &= (X_1 - \bar{X}) + (X_2 - \bar{X}) \\ &\qquad + \cdots + (X_k - \bar{X}) + \ldots + (X_n - \bar{X}) \\ &= X_1 + X_2 + \cdots + X_k + \cdots + X_n \underbrace{- \bar{X} - \bar{X} - \cdots - \bar{X}}_{n \text{ terms}} \\ &= \sum_k X_k - n\bar{X}.\end{aligned}$$

Now, the definition of the sample mean is $\bar{X} = \sum_k X_k/n$, and multiplying both sides by n gives $n\bar{X} = \sum_k X_k$. Therefore,

$$\begin{aligned}\sum_k (X_k - \bar{X}) &= \sum_k X_k - n\bar{X} \\ &= \sum_k X_k - \sum_k X_k \\ &= 0.\end{aligned}$$

This completes the demonstration.

VIII.7.2. Expected value of deviations of a random variable from its expected value

There is an exactly analogous result for the expected value of a random variable. *If $E(X) = \mu$ is the expected value of the random variable X, then*

$$E(X - \mu) = 0. \qquad [\text{VIII.9}]$$

Since $X - \mu$ is a linear function of X in which $m = 1$, $A = -\mu$, and $B = 1$, by the rule of Section VIII.4.6,

$$E(X - \mu) = E(X) - \mu.$$

However, since $E(X) = \mu$,

$$\begin{aligned}E(X - \mu) &= \mu - \mu \\ &= 0.\end{aligned}$$

This completes the proof.

VIII.7.3. Sum of squared deviations from the sample mean

There is a second way in which the arithmetic sample mean can be interpreted as the "center" of a frequency function. Suppose that in the expression $\sum_k (X_k - C)^2$, C can be any number. Then, if C is set equal to $\bar{X}$, the sum of squared deviations from $\bar{X}$ is smaller than the sum of squared deviations from any other number. Thus, the sample mean is the reference point about which the sum of squared deviations of the observations is a minimum.

In the example of Figure VIII.6,

$$\begin{aligned}\sum_k (X_k - \bar{X})^2 &= (0.5 - 4.094)^2 + 3(2 - 4.094)^2 + (2.5 - 4.094)^2 \\ &\quad + 2(3 - 4.094)^2 + 5(5 - 4.094)^2 + (6 - 4.094)^2 \\ &\quad + 3(6.5 - 4.094)^2 \\ &= 56.11.\end{aligned}$$

If any number other than 4.094 is substituted for $\bar{X}$ in this formula, then the sum of squared deviations will exceed 56.11.

If $X_1, X_2, \ldots, X_k, \ldots, X_n$ is a sample with mean $\bar{X}$, then

$$\sum_k (X_k - \bar{X})^2 < \sum_k (X_k - C)^2, \qquad \text{[VIII.10]}$$

where C is any number not equal to $\bar{X}$. A proof of this result is given in Appendix VIII.3, at the end of the chapter.

VIII.7.4. Expected value of squared deviations of a random variable from its expected value

Just as the sum of squared deviations from a sample mean equals a minimum, so the expected value of the squared deviation of a random variable from its expected value is also a minimum. *If μ is the expected value of X, then*

$$E[(X - \mu)^2] < E[(X - C)^2], \qquad \text{[VIII.11]}$$

where C is any number other than μ.

The calculation of $E[(X - \mu)^2]$ will be illustrated for the number of heads obtained when tossing three coins. The first row of Table VIII.5

Table VIII.5. Probability distribution and squared deviations for values of a random variable

X	0	1	2	3
$\mathbf{P}(X = x_i)$	1/8	3/8	3/8	1/8
$(X - \mu)^2$	$(0 - 1.5)^2$	$(1 - 1.5)^2$	$(2 - 1.5)^2$	$(3 - 1.5)^2$

gives the range of this random variable and the second row gives its probability distribution. The third row gives $(X - \mu)^2$. From calculations done earlier, $\mu = E(X) = 1.5$. Since $E[(X - \mu)^2]$ is the expected value of a function of X,

$$\begin{aligned}E[h(X)] = E[(X - \mu)^2] &= \sum_i \mathbf{P}(X = x_i)(x_i - \mu)^2 \\ &= \frac{1}{8}(0 - 1.5)^2 + \frac{3}{8}(1 - 1.5)^2 \\ &\quad + \frac{3}{8}(2 - 1.5)^2 + \frac{1}{8}(3 - 1.5)^2 \\ &= 0.75.\end{aligned}$$

From Formula [VIII.11], we know, for example, that $E[(X - 2)^2] > 0.75$, since $\mu \neq 2$. In fact, $E[(X - 2)^2] = 1$.

Appendix VIII.4 contains a general proof that $E[(X - \mu)^2] < E[(X - C)^2]$ for $C \neq \mu$.

VIII.8
UNBIASED ESTIMATORS

One of the many uses of expected values is in the definition of unbiasedness of an estimator.

VIII.8.1. Definition of unbiasedness

To show how this definition is used, an example from Section VII.1.1 will be reintroduced. Table VIII.6 contains the sampling distribution of the mean for random samples of size 2 drawn with replacement from a population containing the elements 1, 2, and 3. The expected value of

Table VIII.6. A sampling distribution of the mean

$\bar{X}$	1.0	1.5	2.0	2.5	3.0
$\mathbf{P}(\bar{X} = \bar{x}_j)$	1/9	2/9	3/9	2/9	1/9

X for this population is

$$E(X) = \sum_i \mathbf{P}(X = x_i)x_i = (1/3)1 + (1/3)2 + (1/3)3 = 2.$$

In addition, since the sampling distribution of the sample mean is known (Table VIII.6), the expected value of the mean for random samples of size 2 can be calculated. This expected value is

$$E(\bar{X}) = \sum_j \mathbf{P}(\bar{X} = \bar{x}_j)\bar{x}_j = \frac{1}{9}(1.0) + \frac{2}{9}(1.5) + \frac{3}{9}(2.0) + \frac{2}{9}(2.5) + \frac{1}{9}(3.0)$$
$$= 2.$$

Notice that the expected value of the sample mean equals the population mean. This is the explicit meaning of the statement that the sample mean is an unbiased estimator for the population mean.

One way to interpret this result is to imagine taking from this population a *very* large number of random samples of size 2 and calculating the mean for each sample. Following this procedure, one would expect the mean of the sample means to equal the population mean. By a much less tedious theoretical shortcut, we have shown for this example that $E(\bar{X}) = E(X)$.

An estimator is unbiased if its expected value equals the parameter it estimates.

VIII.8.2. Unbiasedness of sample mean

If sampling is random and with replacement or from an infinite population, then each value of the sample is an observation on the *same random variable.* When $X_1, X_2, \ldots, X_k, \ldots, X_n$ are the n observations of a random sample, the subscript distinguishes only the position of each observation in the sample. Then if μ is the expected value of X in the population, each element in the sample is an observation on X and its expected value is μ. Thus, $E(X_k) = \mu$ for each observation, X_k.

With these preliminaries, we are ready to show that *if the population mean of X is μ, then the mean of the random sample $(X_1, X_2, \ldots, X_n)$ is an unbiased estimator for μ, that is, $E(\bar{X}) = \mu$.*

To begin with,

$$\begin{aligned} E(\bar{X}) &= E\left(\frac{\sum_k X_k}{n}\right) \\ &= E\left[\frac{1}{n}(X_1 + X_2 + \cdots + X_n)\right] \\ &= \frac{1}{n} E[X_1 + X_2 + \cdots + X_n]. \end{aligned}$$

Since the expected value of each observation in a random sample is μ, and since $X_1 + X_2 + \cdots + X_n$ is simply a sum of random variables,

$$\begin{aligned} E(\bar{X}) &= \frac{1}{n}[E(X_1) + E(X_2) + \cdots + E(X_n)] \\ &= \frac{1}{n}[\underbrace{\mu + \mu + \cdots + \mu}_{n \text{ terms}}] \\ &= \frac{1}{n}[n\mu] = \mu. \end{aligned}$$

Since we have shown that $E(\bar{X}) = \mu$, the sample mean is an unbiased estimator for the population mean.

Later, the unbiasedness (or biasedness) of other estimators will be discussed.

*VIII.9

MATCHING THEOREM OF THE ESTES-BURKE LEARNING THEORY

In Section *III.2.3 the stimulus sampling learning theory of Estes and Burke[5] was introduced, and in Section *V.3.6 their theory was applied to simple conditioning. In this section, an extremely interesting result of the Estes-Burke theory will be developed. This result has become known as the *matching theorem*. But before examining it, we must deal with the consequences of unreinforced trials.

The approach is to find the expected proportion of previously conditioned stimulus elements that will be sampled on a particular unreinforced trial. It is assumed that p_t, the probability of the "light-on" response, is decreased by this amount on each unreinforced trial.

If a random sample of proportion θ of the stimulus elements in the situation is "registered" by the subject on each trial, then the probability that a given element from among those previously connected to the response will be sampled on trial t is θp_{t-1}. This is because, first, θ is the expected proportion of stimulus elements sampled on each trial; second, p_{t-1} is the proportion connected to the "light-on" response at the end of trial $t - 1$; and, third, the events "sampled on trial t" and "connected to the 'light-on' response at the end of the trial $t - 1$" are statistically independent, since stimulus elements are assumed to be sampled randomly (see Section *V.3.6). Then, it is assumed that proportion θp_{t-1} of the previously conditioned stimulus elements are disconnected from the "light-on" response if trial t is unreinforced. Therefore, when no light appears, the change in the probability of the "light-on" response is

$$p_t - p_{t-1} = -\theta p_{t-1}. \qquad \text{[VIII.12]}$$

The negative sign indicates that the probability of the "light-on" response is decreasing.

By the same method used in Section *V.3.6 to deal with reinforced trials, it can be shown from Formula [VIII.12] that p_t during extinction is given by

$$p_t = p_0(1 - \theta)^t, \qquad \text{[VIII.13]}$$

where p_0 is the "light-on" response probability just prior to beginning extinction. For $t = 0$, p_t equals p_0. As t increases, p_t approaches 0 asymptotically.

[5] Estes, W. K., and C. J. Burke, "A theory of stimulus variability in learning." *Psychol. Rev.* **60**, 276–286, 1953. For a more complete and systematic discussion, see Estes, W. K., "The statistical approach to learning." In Koch, S. (ed.). *Psychology: A Study of Science*, II. New York, McGraw-Hill, 1959.

Extinction curves for $p_0 = 1$ and for $\theta = 0.2$ and $\theta = 0.5$ are shown in Figure VIII.8, from which it can be seen that the rate of extinction depends on the same rate parameter, θ, that governs acquisition (see Fig. V.4).

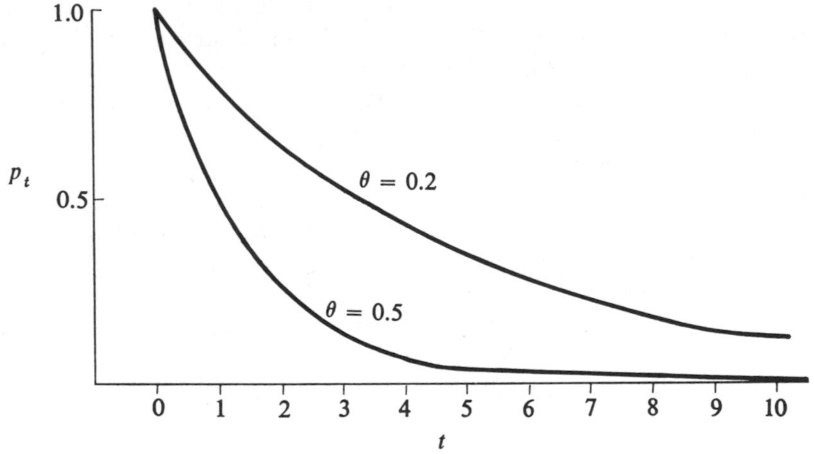

Figure VIII.8

With this preparation, we are ready to deal with the matching theorem. First, it will be described in general terms, and then the probabilistic argument on which it is based will be presented.

Suppose that a subject is asked to guess repeatedly whether or not a light will go on. The experimenter controls the light, and he arranges things so that the light goes on randomly with probability Π. This means that, on any trial, **P**(light on) $= \Pi$ and **P**(light not on) $= 1 - \Pi$. After the subject has made his guess, the light either goes on or not. Thus, the subject has knowledge of results trial by trial.

The occurrence of the light on a given trial is considered reinforcement for the response indicating that the light will occur. Failure of the light can be thought of as an unreinforced extinction trial for the same response. Then, the matching theorem states that, as training proceeds, the probability that the subject will give the "light-on" response approaches the actual probability, Π, that the light will go on.

Now that we have functions for dealing with both reinforced and unreinforced trials (Formulas [V.11] and [VIII.12]), what is the function describing the course of learning when reinforcement is intermittent? That is, how does response probability change if the light goes on with probability Π and if the light does not go on with probability $(1 - \Pi)$ on any given trial? The answer to this question is formulated by finding the expected value of the appropriate random variable. This random variable is the change in the probability of the "light-on" response from trial $t - 1$ to trial t. We shall denote it by $P_t - P_{t-1}$.

Since reinforcement occurs with probability Π,

$$\mathbf{P}[P_t - P_{t-1} = \theta(1 - p_{t-1})] = \Pi$$

and

$$\mathbf{P}[P_t - P_{t-1} = -\theta p_{t-1}] = 1 - \Pi.$$

In other words, the likelihood that the probability of the "light-on" response will be increased is equal to the probability of reinforcement, and the likelihood that it will be decreased equals the probability of no reinforcement. This is summarized in Table VIII.7.

Table VIII.7

	Reinforcement (light goes on)	No reinforcement (light does not go on)
Random variable, $P_t - P_{t-1}$	$\theta(1 - p_{t-1})$	$-\theta p_{t-1}$
Probability distribution	Π	$1 - \Pi$

The expected change in the probability of the "light-on" response (i.e., the expected value of $P_t - P_{t-1}$) is found by applying the definition of an expected value to the information in Table VIII.7. Then,

$$E(P_t - P_{t-1}) = \Pi[\theta(1 - p_{t-1})] + (1 - \Pi)(-\theta p_{t-1}).$$

Expanding the right-hand side of this equation gives

$$\begin{aligned} E(P_t - P_{t-1}) &= \Pi\theta - \Pi\theta p_{t-1} - \theta p_{t-1} + \Pi\theta p_{t-1} \\ &= \Pi\theta - \theta p_{t-1}. \end{aligned}$$

Since $E(P_t - P_{t-1}) = E(P_t) - E(P_{t-1})$,

$$E(P_t) - E(P_{t-1}) = \theta\Pi - \theta p_{t-1}.$$

Now, p_{t-1} and p_t are theoretical "light-on" response probabilities. Therefore, if behavior goes according to theory, $E(P_t) = p_t$, $E(P_{t-1}) = p_{t-1}$, and

$$p_t - p_{t-1} = \theta\Pi - \theta p_{t-1}.$$

Adding $\Pi - \Pi = 0$ to the right-hand side of this equation will not alter the equality, so that

$$\begin{aligned} p_t - p_{t-1} &= \theta\Pi - \theta p_{t-1} + \Pi - \Pi, \\ p_t &= p_{t-1} + \theta\Pi - \theta p_{t-1} + \Pi - \Pi, \end{aligned}$$

and rearranging terms,

$$p_t = \Pi - [\Pi - p_{t-1} - \theta\Pi + \theta p_{t-1}].$$

But since $[\Pi - p_{t-1} - \theta\Pi + \theta p_{t-1}] = [\Pi - p_{t-1}](1 - \theta)$,

$$p_t = \Pi - [\Pi - p_{t-1}](1 - \theta). \qquad \text{[VIII.14]}$$

Formula [VIII.14] permits one to calculate the probability of the "light-on" response on trial t when the probability for trial $t - 1$, Π, and θ are known. Since Π is experimenter-controlled, it is known, and θ is a parameter characterizing the subject that can be estimated (methods for estimating it will not be discussed here).

Using the method employed in Section *V.3.6 for the case of reinforcement on every trial, it can be shown that

$$p_t = \Pi - [\Pi - p_0](1 - \theta)^t, \qquad \text{[VIII.15]}$$

where p_0 is the probability of the "light-on" prediction prior to any training. With this function, the entire course of learning can be predicted when reinforcement is intermittent.

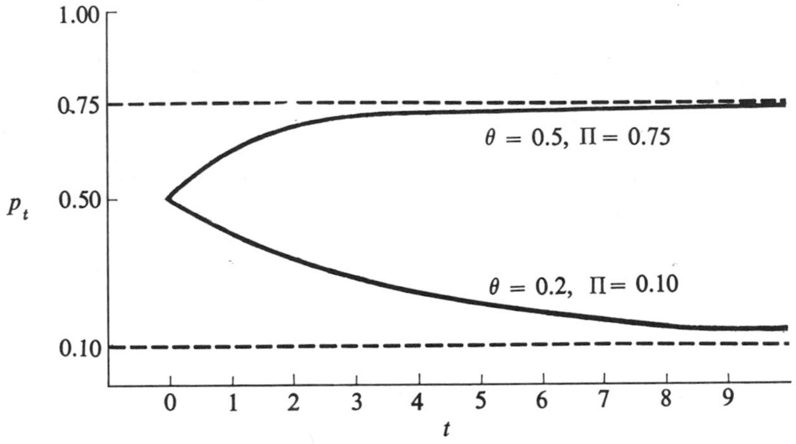

Figure VIII.9

In Figure VIII.9, p_t has been plotted for $\Pi = 0.75$, $p_0 = 0.5$, and $\theta = 0.5$, and for $\Pi = 0.1$, $p_0 = 0.5$, and $\theta = 0.2$. Notice what is happening to both of these curves. As t increases, p_t approaches Π. That this must be true can be seen from $p_t = \Pi - (\Pi - p_0)(1 - \theta)^t$. If θ is chosen so that[6] $0 < \theta < 1$, then $0 < 1 - \theta < 1$. Furthermore, when a number between 0 and 1 is raised to a power, the result is smaller than the original number (e.g., $0.5^2 = 0.25 < 0.5$). Consequently, as t increases, $(1 - \theta)^t$ approaches zero, so that

$$\lim_{t \to \infty} p_t = \lim_{t \to \infty} [\Pi - [\Pi - p_0](1 - \theta)^t]$$
$$= \Pi.$$

[6] Though this eliminates the values 0 and 1, these two values are of little interest. See Problem *4 in Section *VIII.10.

This is the matching theorem: *As t increases*, p_t *approaches* Π *asymptotically*. Thus, as learning progresses, response probability converges on the probability that the response will be reinforced.

If this does characterize the learning process, is it reasonable? In one way it is not. If Π is the probability that the light will go on, and p_∞ is the asymptotic probability that the subject predicts that it will go on, then the asymptotic probability of a correct prediction is $\Pi p_\infty + (1 - \Pi)(1 - p_\infty)$. This is simply the probability that the light will go on *and* be predicted to go on, plus the probability that it will not go on *and* be predicted not to go on. Now, if $\Pi = p_\infty = 0.75$, then the asymptotic probability of a correct response is

$$\Pi p_\infty + (1 - \Pi)(1 - p_\infty) = 0.75(0.75) + (1 - 0.75)(1 - 0.75) = 0.625.$$

However, the subject would be correct with probability 0.75 if he *always* guessed "light-on." This strategy of always predicting the most frequent event has been called the *maximizing* strategy.[7] Unless Π is equal to 0, 0.5, or 1, the maximizing strategy always leads to a higher probability of being correct than the matching strategy predicted by the Estes-Burke theory. Nonetheless, when t is large, curves of the mean of p_t for several subjects are in many situations described quite well by Formula [VIII.15]. This occurs because, "on the average," subjects employ the matching strategy.

*VIII.10

PROBLEMS ON THE ESTES-BURKE THEORY

*1. How would you describe the difference between a subject for whom $\theta = 0.3$ and a subject for whom $\theta = 0.1$? Assume that θ was evaluated in the same learning task for both subjects.

*2. How do changes in θ affect the matching behavior predicted by the Estes-Burke theory?

*3. Suppose that $\Pi = 0.5$ and that a subject has been trained to asymptotic performance in a light-guessing experiment. Now extinction training is begun. Plot the theoretical curve describing the course of extinction for $\theta = 0.3$.

*4. What would happen to the extinction and acquisition curves of the Estes-Burke theory if $\theta = 0$? If $\theta = 1$?

[7] Note the structural similarity of these results and the diagnostic strategies discussed in Section V.3.5. It is interesting that Estes has applied an elaboration of the stimulus sampling theory described here to the intuitive, clinical behavior of the diagnostician. The results are described in a paper entitled "Of models and men." *Amer. Psychol.* **10**, 609–617, 1957.

*5. What role does the difference between Π and p_0 play in acquisition according to the Estes-Burke theory?

*6. Plot p_t as a function of t for $\theta = 0.4$, $p_0 = 0.5$, and $\Pi = 0.9$. Plot p_t as a function of t for $p_0 = 0.5$, $\theta = 0.4$, and $\Pi = 0.25$.

APPENDIX VIII.1

Linear functions

Many applications of probability and statistics and of psychological theory employ the idea of a linear function. This appendix is devoted to a brief description of linear functions and some of their properties.

The function $Y = 2X + 1$ is a linear function; that is, Y is a linear function of X. It is called *linear* because the plot of $Y = 2X + 1$ is a straight line, as shown in Figure VIII.10. More generally, *if B and A are constants, then $Y = BX + A$ is a linear function in one variable.*

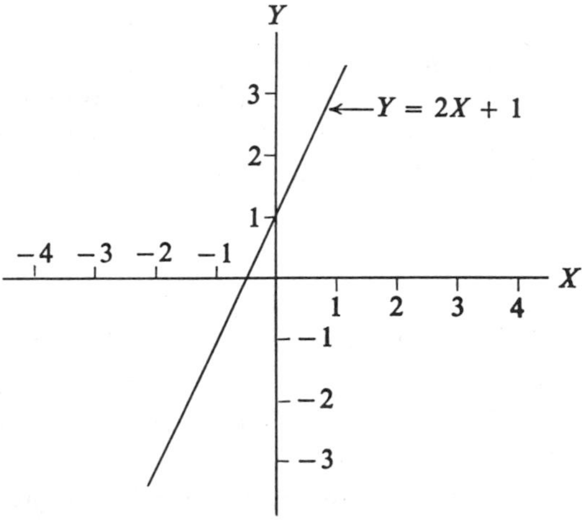

Figure VIII.10

The constant B gives the rate of increase of Y as a function of X. Thus, for the function $Y = 2X + 1$, $B = 2$ means that Y increases 2 units for each unit of increase in X. The constant A determines the vertical position of a particular line having slope B on the graph. Clearly, there are many parallel lines that have slope B, and in order to specify one of them, the constant A must be given, too. In the example, $A = 1$, and this indicates that the function $Y = 2X + 1$ intersects the Y-axis at $Y = 1$. From this it can be seen that specifying the slope and the Y-intercept of a straight line completely determines its graph.

So far, linear functions of only one variable have been discussed. However, the idea of a linear function can be extended to any number of variables. For example, the function $Y = 3 + 2X_1 + 1.5\,X_2$ is a linear function of the two variables X_1 and X_2. Such a function defines a plane in three dimensions (Fig. VIII.11). A point on this three-dimensional graph can be located for each triplet of values, one on X_1, one on X_2, and one on Y. If $X_1 = 1$ and $X_2 = 2$, then $Y = 3 + 2X_1 + 1.5X_2 = 3 + 2(1) + 1.5(2) = 8$, so that the three numbers, $X_1 = 1$, $X_2 = 2$, and $Y = 8$ locate a point on the plane defined by $Y = 3 + 2X_1 + 1.5\,X_2$.

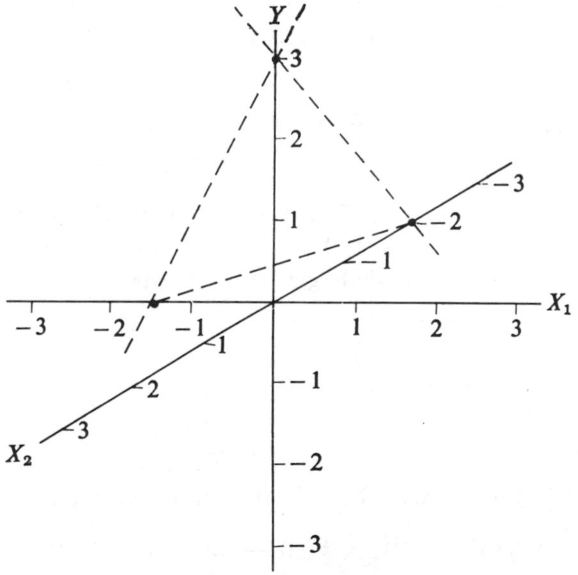

Figure VIII.11

The general formula for a linear function in two variables is $Y = A + B_1X_1 + B_2X_2$ where A, B_1, and B_2 are constants. The constant A gives the Y-intercept, the point on the Y-axis through which the plane passes, and B_1 gives the rate of increase in Y as a function of increases in X_1. In the example, $B_1 = 2$, so that for each unit of increase in X_1, the value of Y increases 2 units. In the same way, B_2 gives the rate of increase in Y with increases in X_2. In the example, this is 1.5.

It is difficult to represent a three-dimensional space graphically, but the broken line that slopes *up* to the right in Figure VIII.11 is intended to show the position of the plane $3 + 2X_1 + 1.5\,X_2$ as a function of X_1 with $X_2 = 0$. In other words, it is a plot of the straight line $3 + 2X_1 + 1.5(0) = 3 + 2X_1$. It shows where the plane defined by the linear function

$3 + 2X_1 + 1X_2$ cuts through the X_1-Y plane. The broken line that slopes *down* to the right represents the position of the same plane with respect to X_2; it is the line $3 + 2(0) + 1.5X_2 = 3 + 1.5X_2$, a line showing where $3 + 2X_1 + 1.5X_2$ cuts through the X_2-Y plane.

The idea of a linear function can be extended to any number of variables. Thus, $Y = 6 + 2X_1 + 3X_2 + 2.5X_3 + 2X_4$ is a perfectly acceptable linear function of the variables X_1, X_2, X_3, and X_4. Of course, graphing such a function is impossible, but the *algebraic idea* of linearity permits such an extension. In general, *if* $X_1, X_2, \ldots, X_m$ *are variables and* A, $B_1, B_2, \ldots, B_m$ *are constants, then*

$$Y = A + B_1X_1 + B_2X_2 + \cdots + B_mX_m$$

is called a linear function of the variables $X_1, X_2, \ldots, X_m$.

APPENDIX VIII.2

Proof that $E(X + Y) = E(X) + E(Y)$

The purpose of this appendix is to prove that if X and Y are discrete random variables, then $E(X + Y) = E(X) + E(Y)$. In order to show that this relation is correct, we begin with the expected value of $X + Y$,

$$\begin{aligned} E(X+Y) &= \sum_i \sum_j \mathbf{P}[(X = x_i) \cap (Y = y_j)](x_i + y_j) \\ &= \sum_i \sum_j \mathbf{P}[(X = x_i) \cap (Y = y_j)]x_i \\ &\qquad + \sum_i \sum_j \mathbf{P}[(X = x_i) \cap (Y = y_j)]y_j. \end{aligned}$$

The term $\sum_i \sum_j \mathbf{P}[(X = x_i) \cap (Y = y_j)]x_i$ can be written as

$$\sum_i \{\mathbf{P}[(X = x_i) \cap (Y = y_1)]x_i + \mathbf{P}[(X = x_i) \cap (Y = y_2)]x_i + \cdots + \mathbf{P}[(X = x_i) \cap (Y = y_r)]x_i\},$$

where r is the number of distinct values on Y. Since x_i appears in each term, it can be removed from the brackets to form

$$\sum_i x_i\{\mathbf{P}[(X = x_i) \cap (Y = y_1)] + \mathbf{P}[(X = x_i) \cap (Y = y_2)] + \cdots + \mathbf{P}[(X = x_i) \cap (Y = y_r)]\},$$

and writing the expression in braces in summation notation gives

$$\sum_i x_i \sum_j \mathbf{P}[(X = x_i) \cap (Y = y_j)].$$

However, $\sum_j \mathbf{P}[(X = x_i) \cap (Y = y_j)]$ is a value from the marginal PD of X; that is, $\sum_j \mathbf{P}[(X = x_i) \cap (Y = y_j)] = \mathbf{P}(X = x_i)$. Consequently,

$$\sum_i x_i \sum_j \mathbf{P}[(X = x_i) \cap (Y = y_j)] = \sum_i x_i\mathbf{P}(X = x_i) = E(X).$$

Returning to $E(X + Y)$ and substituting for $\sum_i \sum_j \mathbf{P}[(X = x_i) \cap (Y = y_j)]x_i$, we have

$$E(X + Y) = E(X) + \sum_i \sum_j \mathbf{P}[(X = x_i) \cap (Y = y_j)]y_j.$$

Now the expression $\sum_i \sum_j \mathbf{P}[(X = x_i) \cap (Y = y_j)]y_j$ can be handled in a manner that is exactly analogous to the treatment of $\sum_i \sum_j \mathbf{P}[(X = x_i) \cap (Y = y_j)]x_i$, so that

$$E(X + Y) = E(X) + E(Y).$$

This completes the proof.

One might guess that the expected value of the sum of three random variables could be treated similarly; that is, $E(X + Y + Z) = E(X) + E(Y) + E(Z)$. This is correct. It is a simple matter to show this by using the result for two random variables. The first step is to let $W = X + Y$. Then $E(X + Y + Z) = E[(X + Y) + Z] = E[W + Z]$. Applying the rule for two random variables, $E(X + Y + Z) = E(W + Z) = E(W) + E(Z)$. Now, substituting $E(X + Y)$ for $E(W)$,

$$\begin{aligned} E(X + Y + Z) = E(W + Z) &= E(W) + E(Z) \\ &= E(X + Y) + E(Z) \\ &= E(X) + E(Y) + E(Z), \end{aligned}$$

and this completes the proof.

This procedure can be extended to any number of random variables, though a general proof involves the use of mathematical induction and will not be included here.

APPENDIX VIII.3

Proof that $\sum_k (X_k - \bar{X})^2 < \sum_k (X_k - C)^2$ for any number $C \neq \bar{X}$

To begin the proof, set $C = \bar{X} + a$ for $a \neq 0$. Then, using the question mark to remind us of the purpose of the proof, and replacing C with $\bar{X} + a$,

$$\begin{aligned} \sum_k (X_k - \bar{X})^2 &\overset{?}{<} \sum_k (X_k - C)^2 \\ &\overset{?}{<} \sum_k [X_k - (\bar{X} + a)]^2 \\ &\overset{?}{<} \sum_k [(X_k - \bar{X}) - a]^2 \\ &\overset{?}{<} \sum_k [(X_k - \bar{X})^2 - 2a(X_k - \bar{X}) + a^2] \\ &\overset{?}{<} \sum_k (X_k - \bar{X})^2 - 2a \sum_k (X_k - \bar{X}) + \sum_k a^2. \end{aligned}$$

Since a^2 is a constant,

$$\sum_k a^2 = \underbrace{a^2 + a^2 + \cdots + a^2}_{n \text{ terms}},$$

so that

$$\sum_k a^2 = na^2.$$

Making this substitution,

$$\sum_k (X_k - \bar{X})^2 \overset{?}{<} \sum_k (X_k - \bar{X})^2 - 2a \sum_k (X_k - \bar{X}) + na^2.$$

But according to Section VIII.7.1, $\sum_k (X_k - \bar{X}) = 0$, so that

$$\sum_k (X_k - \bar{X})^2 \overset{?}{<} \sum_k (X_k - \bar{X})^2 - 0 + na^2.$$

Subtracting $\sum_k (X - \bar{X})^2$ from both sides of the inequality,

$$0 < na^2.$$

The last line must hold, since n and a^2 are always positive. This completes the proof.

APPENDIX VIII.4

Proof that $E[(X - \mu)^2] < E[(X - C)^2]$ *for any number* $C \neq \mu$

To begin with, let $C = \mu + a$ where $a \neq 0$. Then, using the question mark as in Appendix VIII.3,

$$\begin{aligned} E[(X - \mu)^2] &\overset{?}{<} E[(X - C)^2] \\ &\overset{?}{<} E\{[X - (\mu + a)]^2\} \\ &\overset{?}{<} E\{[(X - \mu) - a]^2\} \\ &\overset{?}{<} E[(X - \mu)^2 - 2a(X - \mu) + a^2]. \end{aligned}$$

Then, by the rule for the expected value of a sum of random variables,

$$\begin{aligned} E[(X - \mu)^2] &\overset{?}{<} E[(X - \mu)^2] - E[2a(X - \mu)] + E(a^2) \\ &\overset{?}{<} E[(X - \mu)^2] - 2aE(X - \mu) + E(a^2). \end{aligned}$$

Now, since $E(X - \mu) = 0$ and $E(a^2) = a^2$,

$$E[(X - \mu)^2] \overset{?}{<} E[(X - \mu)^2] - 2a(0) + a^2.$$

Subtracting $E[(X - \mu)^2]$ from both sides of the inequality,

$$0 < a^2,$$

since a^2 is always positive. This completes the proof.

SUGGESTED READING

1. References 1, 2, and 3 of the reading suggested for Chapter VII include discussions of expected values. References 1 and 2 are restricted to discrete random variables and do not presuppose calculus. Some uses of calculus enter the discussion of Reference 3.
2. Kemeny, J. G., J. L. Snell, and G. L. Thompson, *Introduction to Finite Mathematics.* Englewood Cliffs, N.J., Prentice-Hall, 1957, pp. 166–171.
   A brief introduction to expected values. No calculus required, but this section assumes familiarity with other parts of the book.
3. Parzen, E., *Modern Probability Theory and its Applications.* New York, John Wiley, 1960, pp. 343–370.
   This section gives a more sophisticated and complete discussion of expected values than the preceding sources. Calculus is used freely.

IX

SOME DESCRIPTIVE CHARACTERISTICS OF POPULATIONS AND SAMPLES

IN this chapter, several descriptive characteristics of populations and samples will be defined, described, and illustrated. In each case, the nature of the problem faced by most data gatherers should be kept in mind: that is, one ordinarily has a *sample* of observations from which conclusions about a *population* are to be extracted. Consequently, the relationship between an estimator and the parameter it estimates is of the utmost importance, and a considerable portion of this chapter is devoted to the discussion of this relationship. First, however, a few general comments about the use of descriptive statistics are in order.

IX.1
DATA DESCRIPTION AND SUMMARIZATION—GENERAL COMMENTS

Any investigator has a choice among several ways of presenting or summarizing his data, and the reasonableness of his conclusions always depends in part on the wisdom of his choice. This multiplicity of descriptive alternatives is undoubtedly at the root of the suspicion with which many people view statistics. It has led to Disraeli's reference to "lies, damn lies, and statistics" and to the observation that "though figures don't lie, liars figure." It has even led to a clever and enlightening little book entitled *How to Lie with Statistics.*[1]

The problem is straightforward. One can use descriptive statistics to

[1] Huff, D., *How to Lie with Statistics.* New York, Norton and Co., 1954.

summarize certain aspects of the data at the expense of others. This "flexibility" forms the basis for the possibility of misrepresentation, either inadvertently or with the intent to deceive. Obviously, it is the inadvertent distortion of data that we can do something about in this discussion. Such distortion is best avoided by a thorough understanding of the descriptive properties of statistics. As a corollary, you can best guard against being taken in by distortions by developing a statistically sophisticated eye.

In addition, it is extremely important to understand the nature of the substantive problem one is handling statistically. The characteristics of the data and the use to be made of a statistical summary are at the heart of any wise choice of descriptive statistics.

In this chapter, three types of parameters and their corresponding estimators are discussed. First, measures of the average, central tendency or location of a random variable are described. (Two such measures have been described already. The ideas of expected value and sample mean are so important in statistics that they were discussed in detail in a separate chapter.) Next, measures of dispersion, variability, or spread-outness are introduced. Then, one way of measuring relationship, co-variation, or correlation is described. Finally, some useful formulas for computing measures of dispersion are introduced.

IX.2

MEASURES OF CENTRAL TENDENCY

When measures of central tendency are described, they are usually treated as if they referred to a characteristic of a variable. However, it is more nearly correct to view an average as a property of the PD or the DF of a random variable. In fact, an average can be viewed as a kind of "center" of a PD or DF, and it is differences in the meaning of this term that distinguish among measures of central tendency.

IX.2.1. The Mode

POPULATION MODE OF A DISCRETE RANDOM VARIABLE. Perhaps the simplest kind of center is the point of maximum concentration of probability. Thus, *the population mode of the discrete random variable X is the value of X that has the highest probability.* The mode of a discrete variable is illustrated in Figure IX.1.

POPULATION MODE OF A CONTINUOUS RANDOM VARIABLE. *The population mode of the continuous random variable X is the value for which the density function of X has maximum height.* This is illustrated in Figure IX.2.

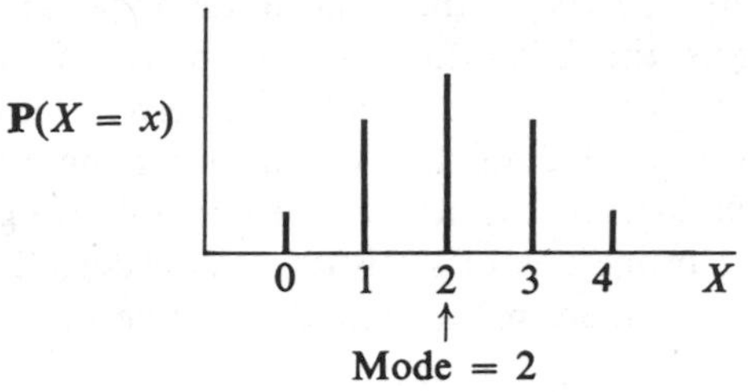

Figure IX.1

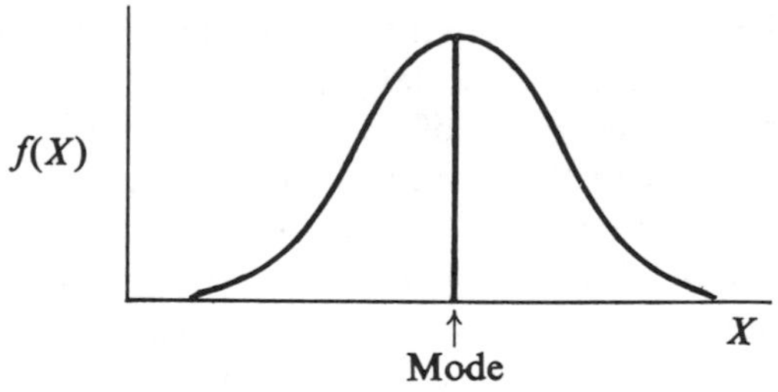

Figure IX.2

SAMPLE MODE. If the mode is estimated from a sample, then *the sample mode is the observed value with the highest frequency*. For the examination data summarized by the frequency function of Figure VII.17, the sample

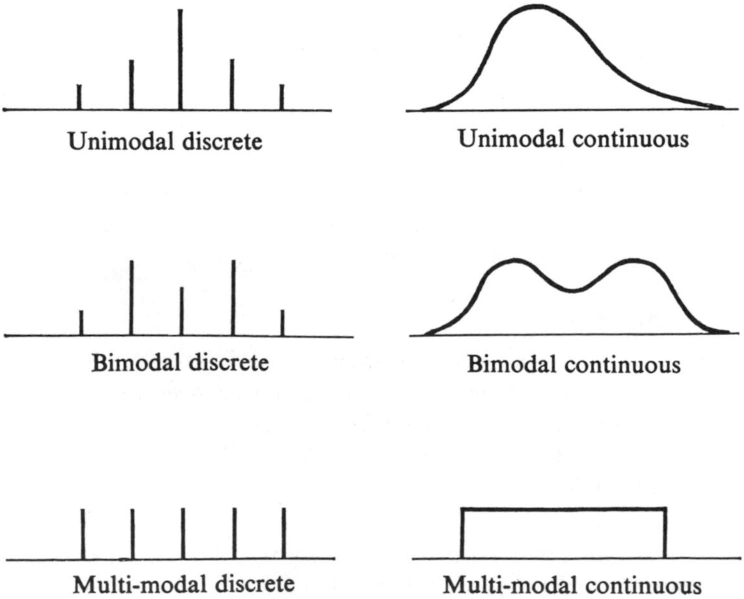

Figure IX.3

mode lies in the interval 70.5 to 75.5. As a matter of convention, the midpoint of this interval, 73.0, would be called the *sample mode.*

CHARACTERISTICS OF THE MODE. Notice that the mode for the ungrouped data (Fig. VII.16) is not uniquely defined. There are 3 individuals who scored 73 on the examination, and 3 others who scored 75. Since no more than 3 persons obtained any single score, either 73 or 75 is the mode. But which? There is no way to decide on the basis of these data.

Usually, we think of a "center" as unique, but random samples having two or more modes are quite common. They may arise as a result of random-sampling variability, or they may be accurate reflections of a multimodal population; there is no practical way to determine which is the case. Furthermore, the fact that a random sample has a single mode provides no guarantee that the population is unimodal.

Similarly, a population may have one mode, several modes, or as many modes as there are values of the random variable (see Fig. IX.3). This fact constitutes a serious shortcoming of the population mode.

Extreme values of a random variable influence the location of the mean even though they are infrequent, but the mode is not at all affected by

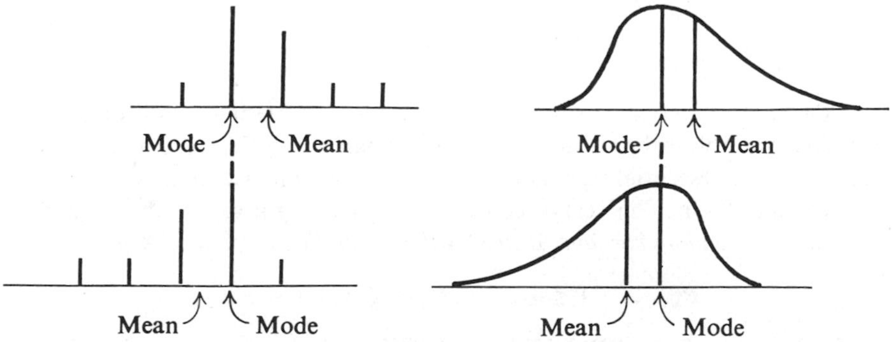

Figure IX.4

improbable extremes. In Figure IX.4, the upper and lower distribution of each pair have the same mode, but their means are quite different.

IX.2.2. The median

The median has less sampling variability than the mode. Also, it is more sensitive to the shape of the PD or DF than the mode, though less so than the mean.

POPULATION MEDIAN OF A CONTINUOUS RANDOM VARIABLE. *The population median V of the continuous random variable X is the value for which*

$$\mathbf{P}(X > V) = \mathbf{P}(X < V) = 1/2.$$

In other words, the median is the value of X that divides its DF into halves. This is illustrated in Figure IX.5.

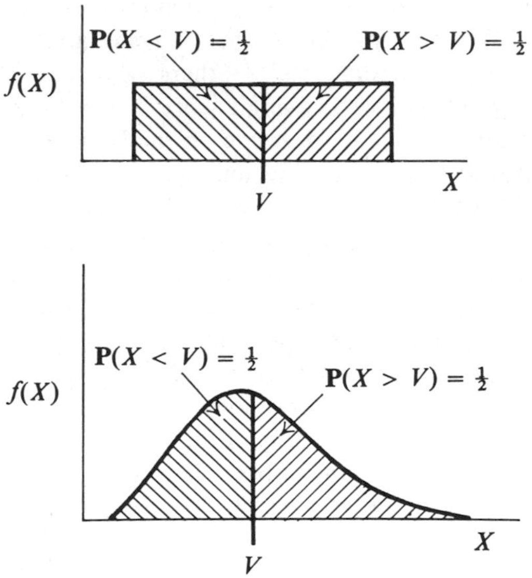

Figure IX.5

POPULATION MEDIAN OF A DISCRETE RANDOM VARIABLE. For discrete random variables, the definition of the median is a little more awkward. However, the essential idea is the same; the median is chosen so that it divides the PD into halves, or comes as near halving it as possible. *If X is a discrete random variable, then V is the population median of X if*

$$\mathbf{P}(X > V) \leq 1/2 \quad \textit{and} \quad \mathbf{P}(X < V) \leq 1/2.$$

In the case of the PD in Figure IX.6, it is easy to find a value that satisfies this definition. Any number greater than 1 and less than 2 can

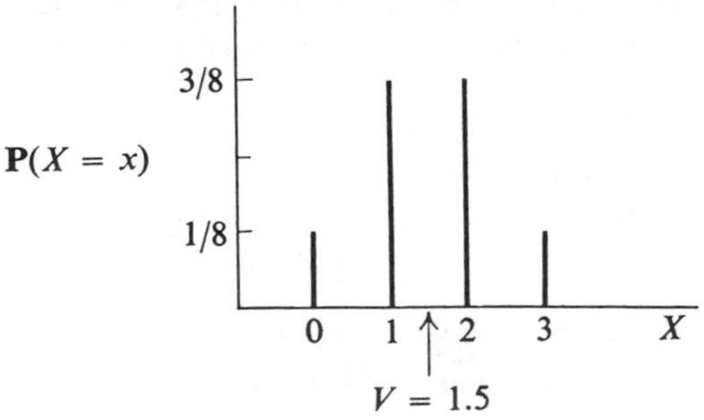

Figure IX.6

be the median. Thus, 1.1, 1.5, and 1.7 all satisfy the definition. As a matter of convention, *when the population median lies between adjacent values of a discrete random variable, the midpoint of the interval is designated the population median.* In the example, $V = 1.5$, the point midway between $X = 1$ and $X = 2$. Since $\mathbf{P}(X > 1.5) = \mathbf{P}(X = 2) + \mathbf{P}(X = 3) = 3/8 + 1/8 = 1/2$, and $\mathbf{P}(X < 1.5) = \mathbf{P}(X = 0) + \mathbf{P}(X = 1) = 1/8 + 3/8 = 1/2$, the conditions of the definition are satisfied.

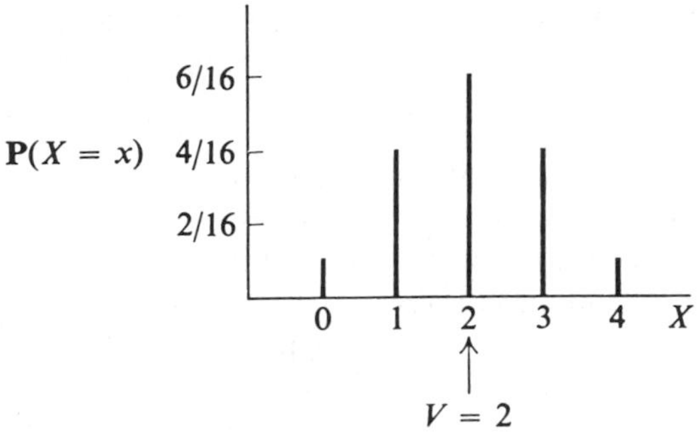

Figure IX.7

For the PD of Figure IX.7 it is unnecessary to split an interval. Since $\mathbf{P}(X < 2) \leq 1/2$ and $\mathbf{P}(X > 2) \leq 1/2$, the median is 2. Furthermore, 2 is the only value that satisfies the definition for this PD.

So far, the population median of a discrete random variable has been discussed in connection with symmetrical PD's only. Now, consider the skewed PD in Figure IX.8. Since $\mathbf{P}(X < 1) = 0.41$ and $\mathbf{P}(X > 1) = 0.15 + 0.03 + 0.002 = 0.182$, the median is 1.

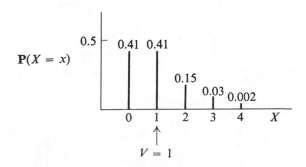

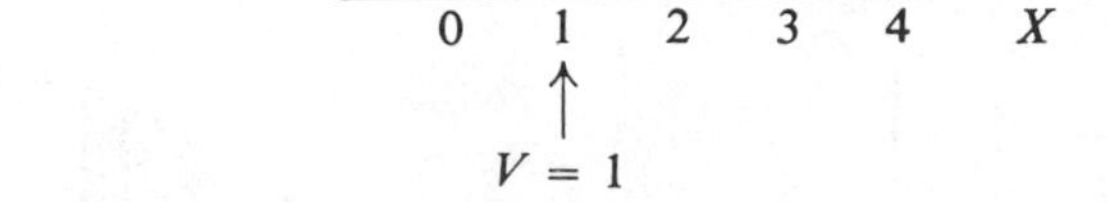

Figure IX.8

SAMPLE MEDIAN. Since observations are always discrete, the definition of the sample median is similar to that of the population median for a discrete random variable. *Suppose that the observations of a sample are ordered so that* $X_{[1]}$ *is the smallest observation,* $X_{[2]}$ *the next smallest, and so on to the largest observation,* $X_{[n]}$. *Then, if n is an odd number, the sample median is* $X_{[(n+1)/2]}$, *and if n is an even number, the median is midway between* $X_{[n/2]}$ *and* $X_{[(n/2)+1]}$. *The sample median will be denoted by the symbol M.*

The following two examples involve random samples from an infinite population in which 1, 2, 3, . . ., 100 are equiprobable. The sample (93, 44, 59, 99, 33, 60, 68, 98, 53, 73, 34) contains 11 observations, so that the sample median is the sixth largest, $M = 60$. The sample (16, 40, 95, 56, 44, 58, 96, 5, 8, 18) contains 10 observations, so that its median is midway between 40 and 44; that is, $M = 42$.

Characteristics of the median

Effects of extreme values. An important characteristic of the median is that it is less sensitive to extreme values than is the mean. To illustrate this, consider the random sample (67, 59, 75). Both the median and the mean of this sample are 67. Now, suppose that a fourth observation is added to this sample and that this observation is a 1. The mean of these 4 observations is 50.5, a shift of 16.5 units. However, the new *median*

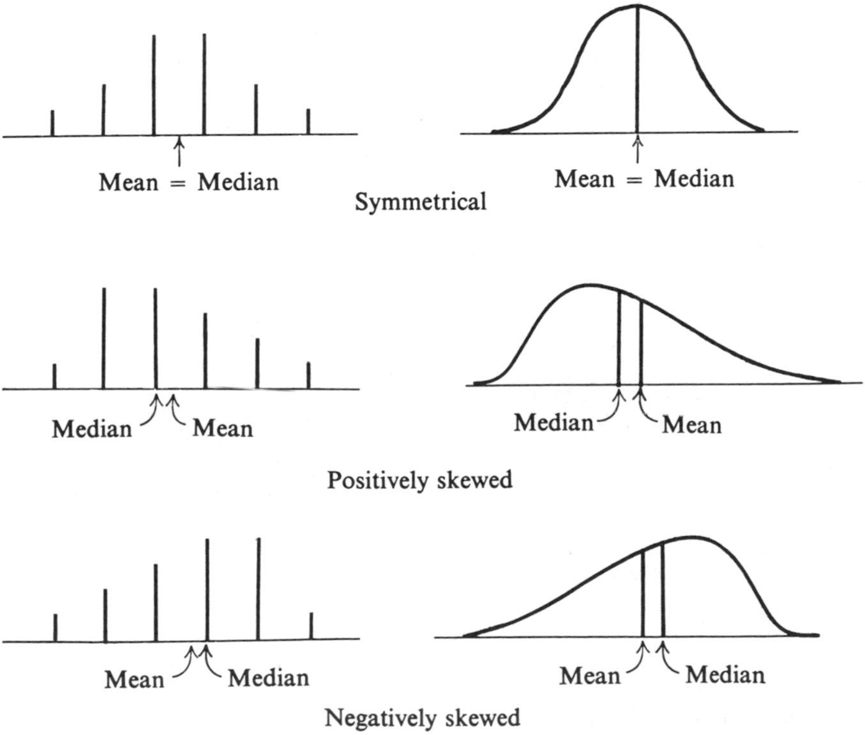

Figure IX.9

is 63, a change of only 4. This illustrates the greater resistance of the median to the effects of extreme values.

An asymmetrical distribution of extreme values contributes to the skewness of a distribution. If a PD or DF is symmetrical, then the mean and median are equal. The mean exceeds the median for positively skewed distributions, and the median exceeds the mean when the distribution is negatively skewed. These three cases are illustrated in Figure IX.9 for several populations. Exactly analogous relations between median and mean hold for samples, too.

Expected value of absolute deviations from the population median. For the population mean, $E(X - \mu) = 0$ and $E[(X - \mu)^2] < E[(X - C)^2]$ for any $C \neq \mu$. Can similar properties be found for the population median? It turns out that *if V is the population median of X, and if C is any constant, then*

$$E(|X - V|) \leq E(|X - C|). \qquad \text{[IX.1]}$$

To illustrate this result, the distribution shown in Figure IX.8 will be used. The median is 1, and C will be set equal to the expected value of this distribution, 0.808. Using these values, it will be shown that for this distribution

$$E(|X - V|) = E(|X - 1|) \leq E(|X - 0.808|) = E(|X - \mu|).$$

Substituting for the expected values,

$$\sum_i \mathbf{P}(X = x_i)|x_i - 1| \leq \sum_i \mathbf{P}(X = x_i)|x_i - 0.808|,$$

or

$$\begin{aligned} 0.41|0 - 1| &+ 0.41|1 - 1| \\ &+ 0.15|2 - 1| + 0.03|3 - 1| \\ &\qquad + 0.002|4 - 1| \leq 0.41|0 - 0.808| + 0.41|1 - 0.808| \\ &\qquad\qquad + 0.15|2 - 0.808| + 0.03|3 - 0.808| \\ &\qquad\qquad + 0.002|4 - 0.808| \\ &\qquad 0.626 \leq 0.661, \end{aligned}$$

and the expected value of the absolute deviations from the median *is* less than or equal to the expected value of the absolute deviations from the mean. Of course, if the PD or DF is symmetrical, then $E(|X - V|)$ equals $E(|X - \mu|)$, since $\mu = V$.

Sum of absolute deviations from the sample median. An exactly analogous characteristic holds for the sample median. *If M is the sample median and C is any constant, then*

$$\sum_k |X_k - M| \leq \sum_k |X_k - C|. \qquad \text{[IX.2]}$$

This can be checked easily for the samples in the discussion of the sample median.

Biasedness of the sample median. When sampling from a population having a symmetrical probability distribution or density function, the sample median is an unbiased estimator for the population median. This will be illustrated for samples of size 3 drawn from a population having the symmetrical PD of Figure IX.10. Each *group* that can be drawn from

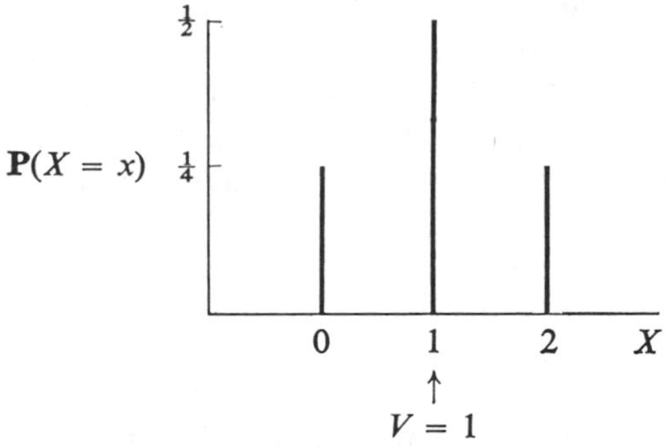

Figure IX.10

this population, the value of the median for each group, and the probability of obtaining each group,[2] are shown in Table IX.1. The table lists groups rather than samples, since the median depends only on the values and not on the order in which they are observed.

The sampling distribution of the median is found by summing the probabilities for each value of the sample median. For example, $\mathbf{P}(M = 0) = 1/64 + 6/64 + 3/64 = 10/64$. Consequently, the sampling distribution of M is

$$\mathbf{P}(M = 0) = 10/64$$
$$\mathbf{P}(M = 1) = 44/64$$
$$\mathbf{P}(M = 2) = 10/64.$$

The expected value of M is

$$E(M) = \frac{10}{64}(0) + \frac{44}{64}(1) + \frac{10}{64}(2) = 1,$$

[2] Note that the outcomes are *not* equiprobable. Thus, the probability of the *group* containing the elements 0, 0, and 1 was computed by observing that a group containing two zeros and a one can be arranged in $3!/(2!\,1!) = 3$ orders. Then the probability that one of these orders will be obtained is $3(1/4)^2(1/2)$. The probability of a 0, a 1, and a 2 is $[3!/(1!\,1!\,1!)](1/4)^2(1/2)$. (The expression $3!/(1!\,1!\,1!)$ is an application of Formula [V.8], the multinomial coefficient.)

Table IX.1. Generation of sampling distribution of the median

Group	Probability of group	Median
000	$1\cdot(1/4)^3 = 1/64$	0
111	$1\cdot(1/2)^3 = 8/64$	1
222	$1\cdot(1/4)^3 = 1/64$	2
001	$3\cdot(1/4)^2 1/2 = 6/64$	0
002	$3\cdot(1/4)^3 = 3/64$	0
011	$3\cdot(1/2)^2 1/4 = 12/64$	1
022	$3\cdot(1/4)^3 = 3/64$	2
112	$3\cdot(1/2)^2 1/4 = 12/64$	1
122	$3\cdot(1/4)^2 1/2 = 6/64$	2
012	$6\cdot(1/4)^2 1/2 = 12/64$	1
	Sum $= 1$	

and since the population median is 1, $E(M) = V$. This shows that for samples of size three the sample median is an unbiased estimator for V for the symmetrical PD of Figure IX.10.

However, *when the probability distribution of the observation variable is asymmetrical, the sample median is a biased estimator for the population median.* This is readily illustrated by computing the expected value of the sample median for random samples of size 3 drawn from a population

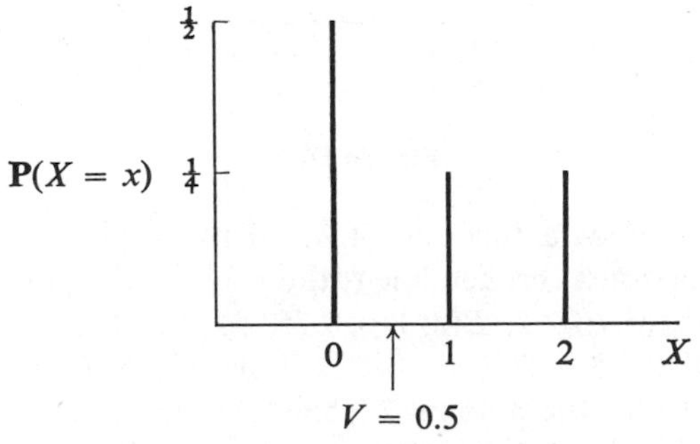

Figure IX.11

having the PD of Figure IX.11. Proceeding in the same way as in the symmetrical example, the sampling distribution of M is

$$\mathbf{P}(M = 0) = 32/64$$
$$\mathbf{P}(M = 1) = 22/64$$
$$\mathbf{P}(M = 2) = 10/64.$$

The expected value of M is

$$E(M) = \frac{32}{64}(0) + \frac{22}{64}(1) + \frac{10}{64}(2) = \frac{42}{64} = 0.656.$$

Since the population median is $V = 0.5$, $E(M) \neq V$ and M is biased. However, even when M is biased, the amount of bias approaches zero as the sample size, n, becomes large. That is,

$$\lim_{n \to \infty} |E(M) - V| = 0,$$

regardless of the shape of the PD or DF of the observation variable. *When the amount of bias of an estimator approaches zero as n becomes infinite, the estimator is said to be asymptotically unbiased. Thus, the sample median is asymptotically unbiased.*

This can be illustrated by computing $E(M)$ for samples of size 1, 2, 3, . . ., 8 drawn from the asymmetrical population shown in Figure IX.11

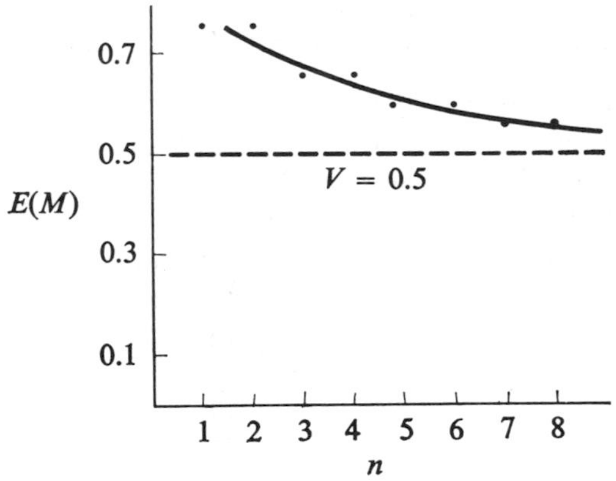

Figure IX.12

and plotting $E(M)$ as a function of n. This graph is shown in Figure IX.12. The horizontal broken line is the value of the population median. For $n = 1$ and for $n = 2$, $E(M) = 0.75$, so that the amount of bias is $|E(M) - V| = |0.75 - 0.50| = 0.25$. For $n = 5$ or $n = 6$, $E(M) = 0.60$, indicating that the amount of bias has decreased to 0.10. Extrapolating from this graph, one infers that for $n = 20$ or so, the amount of bias is negligible. The curved line has been inserted to give a general idea of the way in which the bias decreases.

IX.2.3. Geometric mean

The last measure of location to be discussed is the geometric mean. It is of general interest as a descriptive statistic, but it is particularly important in some areas of psychological theory.

SAMPLE GEOMETRIC MEANS. *The geometric mean of the sample* $(X_1, X_2, \ldots, X_n)$ *is*

$$(X_1 \cdot X_2 \cdots X_n)^{1/n}, \qquad \text{[IX.3]}$$

provided all of the observations are positive. In other words, the geometric mean is the *n*th root of the mutual product of the observations.

Taking the *n*th root is most convenient using logarithms, and the sample geometric mean is usually calculated by finding

$$\text{antilog}\left[\frac{1}{n}(\log X_1 + \log X_2 + \cdots + \log X_n)\right].$$

The random sample (6, 2, 4, 6, 1, 3, 5, 6) was obtained (with replacement) from a population containing the equiprobable values 1, 2, 3, 4, 5, and 6. The geometric mean of this sample is obtained by first calculating the arithmetic mean of the logs of the observations. In Table IX.2 the sum

Table IX.2. Values for calculating geometric mean of a sample

X	Log X	Frequency of X	Frequency times log X
1	0	1	0
2	.3010	1	.3010
3	.4771	1	.4771
4	.6021	1	.6021
5	.6990	1	.6990
6	.7782	3	2.3346
		$n = 8$	$\sum \log X = 4.4138$

of the logs is seen to be 4.4138, so that the arithmetic mean of the logs is 4.4138/8 = 0.5517. The geometric mean is the antilog of 0.5517, approximately 3.562.

Notice that if any observation is less than or equal to zero, the sample geometric mean becomes meaningless.

POPULATION GEOMETRIC MEANS. *The population geometric mean of a random variable X is*

$$\text{antilog}\,[E(\log X)], \qquad \text{[IX.4]}$$

provided that all values of the range of X are positive.

For example, the geometric mean of a random variable having equiprobable values 1, 2, 3, 4, 5, and 6 is

$$\begin{aligned}
\text{antilog}\,[E(\log X)] &= \text{antilog}\left[\sum_i \mathbf{P}(X = x_i)\log x_i\right] \\
&= \text{antilog}\left[\frac{1}{6}\log 1 + \frac{1}{6}\log 2 + \frac{1}{6}\log 3 + \frac{1}{6}\log 4 \right.\\
&\qquad\qquad \left. + \frac{1}{6}\log 5 + \frac{1}{6}\log 6\right] \\
&= \text{antilog}\left[\frac{1}{6}(0 + 0.3010 + 0.4771 + 0.6021 \right.\\
&\qquad\qquad \left. + 0.6990 + 0.7782)\right] \\
&= \text{antilog}\left[\frac{1}{6}(2.8574)\right] = \text{antilog}\,[0.4762] \\
&= 2.994.
\end{aligned}$$

Note that if any value of X is zero or less, then the geometric mean is undefined, because log X is undefined when $X \leq 0$.

CHARACTERISTICS OF THE GEOMETRIC MEAN. When all values are equal, the geometric mean and the arithmetic mean are identical. Otherwise, the geometric mean is the smaller of the two, because the use of logarithms "compresses" large observations. For example, 1000 is ten times as large as 100, but the log of 1000, which is 3, is only half again as large as the log of 100, which is 2. And even though 100 is ten times as large as 10, log 100 = 2 is only twice log 10 = 1.

*GEOMETRIC MEANS IN PSYCHOPHYSICAL THEORY. According to Fechner's law,[3] sensory magnitudes are related to the corresponding physical stimulus magnitudes by a logarithmic function. If ψ represents sensory magnitude and S represents the corresponding physical stimulus magnitude, the relation between ψ and S is as illustrated in Figure IX.13. Notice that at the absolute sensory threshold ($\psi = 0$), the physical stimulus magnitude exceeds zero.

Now suppose that we wish to determine the midpoint between the two sensory magnitudes, ψ_1 and ψ_2, and, further, that we want to determine the physical magnitude that corresponds to this sensory midpoint. To make this concrete, we ask a subject to adjust a variable-intensity 1000-cps tone so that its loudness is midway between a 0.01-microwatt-per-square-centimeter tone (S_1) and one of 0.025 microwatt per square centimeter (S_2). The physical midpoint of these two tones is $(0.01 + 0.025)/2 = 0.0175$ microwatt per square centimeter. However, if loudness is related

[3] Boring, E. G., *A History of Experimental Psychology* (2nd ed.). New York, Appleton-Century-Crofts, 1950, pp. 287–289.

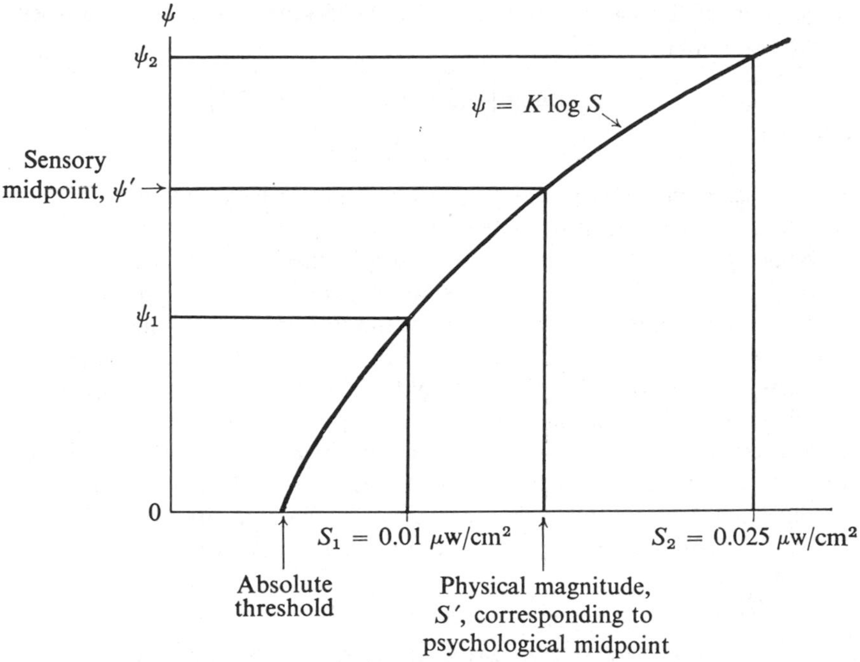

Figure IX.13

to physical intensity by a logarithmic function, then 0.0175 will *not* correspond to the sensory midpoint.

Suppose that $\psi = K \log S$ (where K is a constant) is the log function relating ψ and S. If S' is the intensity that corresponds to the sensory midpoint $\psi' = (\psi_1 + \psi_2)/2$, then, according to Fechner's law, $\psi' = K \log S'$, $\psi_1 = K \log S_1$, and $\psi_2 = K \log S_2$. Therefore, $\psi' = (\psi_1 + \psi_2)/2$ can be rewritten substituting each of these three expressions as follows:

$$\psi' = \frac{\psi_1 + \psi_2}{2}$$

$$K \log S' = \frac{K \log S_1 + K \log S_2}{2}.$$

Solving for S',

$$S' = \text{antilog}\left[\frac{1}{2}(\log S_1 + \log S_2)\right].$$

The right-hand side is simply the geometric mean of S_1 and S_2. Thus, Fechner's law leads to the prediction that the geometric mean of the two physical intensities corresponds to the sensory midpoint. The theoretical prediction of the sensory midpoint of a 0.025- and a 0.01-microwatt-per-square-centimeter tone is

$$S' = \text{antilog}\left[\frac{1}{2}(\log 0.01 + \log 0.025)\right]$$
$$= 0.016 \text{ microwatt/sq cm.}$$

Of course, such a theoretical prediction could be tested by comparing a subject's settings with this prediction.

Notice that, with this formulation, the idea of a psychological "midpoint" of several stimuli becomes well defined. In fact, Helson[4] has defined the adaptation level of a set of stimuli as essentially the geometric mean of their physical magnitudes. In hefting weights, for example, subjects tend to describe those weights exceeding the geometric mean weight as "heavy," those below it as "light." If a heavier weight is added to the sequence so that the geometric mean is increased, the lower limit of weights called "heavy" will be increased. Thus, the geometric mean weight is the "midpoint" separating psychologically "heavy" from "light." Similar applications have been made to other sensory continua.[5]

IX.3
PROBLEMS ON MEASURES OF CENTRAL TENDENCY

1. For the PD of Figure IX.8,
   a. Find the population median, V.
   b. Find $\mu = E(X)$.
   c. Is $E(|X - V|) \leq E(|X - \mu|)$? Demonstrate the correctness of your answer for this example.
   d. Is the mode unique for this population?
   e. What is the value of the geometric mean?
   f. You use M based on samples of size 3 from this population, and I use M based on samples of size 10. Whose estimator is most biased for the population median, yours or mine?

2. You toss a fair, six-sided die 5 times. The result is (5, 3, 6, 1, 1).
   a. What is the median of this sample?
   b. What is the mean of this sample?
   c. Which is greater, $\sum_k (X_k - M)^2$ or $\sum_k (X_k - \bar{X})^2$? Show that your answer is correct for these data.
   d. What is the mode for this sample?
   e. Compare the sample mode, median, and mean of this sample with the corresponding parameters. Account for the discrepancy between each statistic and the corresponding parameter.

[4] Helson, H., "Adaptation-level as a basis for a quantitative theory of frames of reference." *Psychol. Rev.* **55**, 297–313, 1948.
[5] *Ibid.*

f. If GM denotes the geometric mean of the sample, which is larger, $\sum_k |X_k - GM|$ or $\sum_k |X_k - M|$? Defend your answer theoretically, and then show that it is numerically correct for this example.
g. Which statistic is closest to its parameter for this sample, Mode, M, $\bar{X}$, or GM?

3. Suppose that the range of X is (0, 1) and that $\mathbf{P}(X = 0) = 2/3$, $\mathbf{P}(X = 1) = 1/3$. For samples of size 3 drawn from this population with replacement,
   a. Find the PD of the sample median.
   b. Find the PD of the sample mean.
   c. Find $E(\bar{X})$ and $E(M)$ for $n = 3$.
   d. Is either $\bar{X}$ or M biased? If so, what is the magnitude of bias?

IX.4
MEASURES OF VARIABILITY

Measures of central tendency often describe important aspects of research data, but sometimes central tendency is not the focus of attention. It may be the variability, dispersion, or spread-outness of the observations that is of most interest.

What sorts of processes affect variability? Almost any selection process will reduce variability as well as alter the location of a distribution. For instance, the mean weight of university football players is well above the male college mean, but the variability of weights is also smaller for football players. Similarly, the distribution of college IQ's is likely to be narrower and more concentrated about its mean than that of the general population.

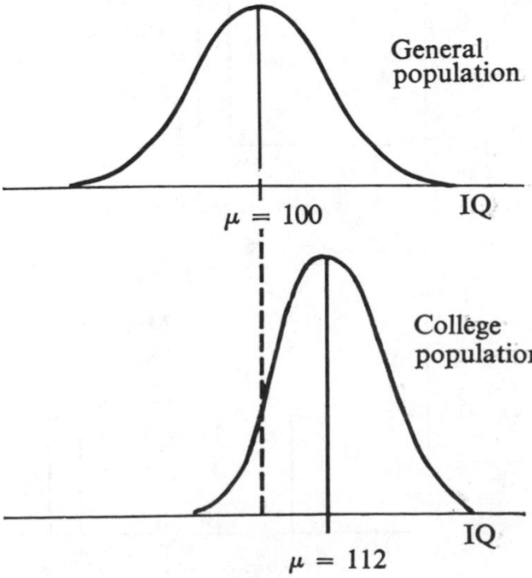

Figure IX.14

A hypothetical illustration of this is shown in Figure IX.14. The process of college student selection has virtually eliminated the lower extreme, and thus reduced the variability.

The preceding illustrations involve differences in both location and variability, but it is quite possible that two distributions differ in variability when they have identical locations. Suppose, for instance, that an attempt is made to increase the favorability of an attitude through group discussion with a trained leader. Discussion may simply strengthen the negative attitudes of some diehards, whereas others who are more malleable exhibit more favorable attitudes as a consequence of the intervention. Such different responses to discussion would increase the dispersion of attitudes without necessarily altering the central tendency. The way this might happen is illustrated in Figure IX.15. The mean is the same for both distributions, but variability is greater following intervention.

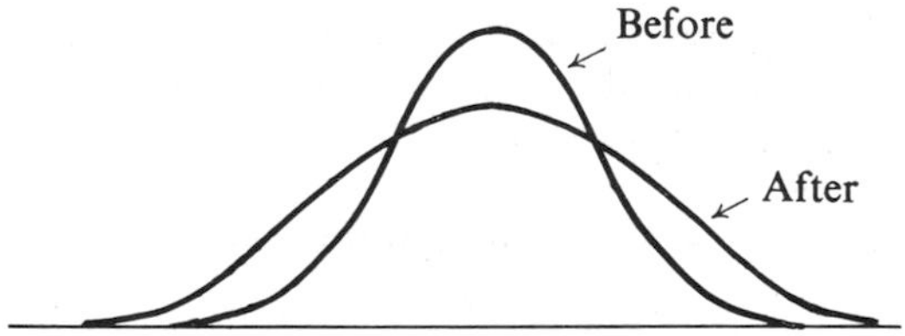

Figure IX.15

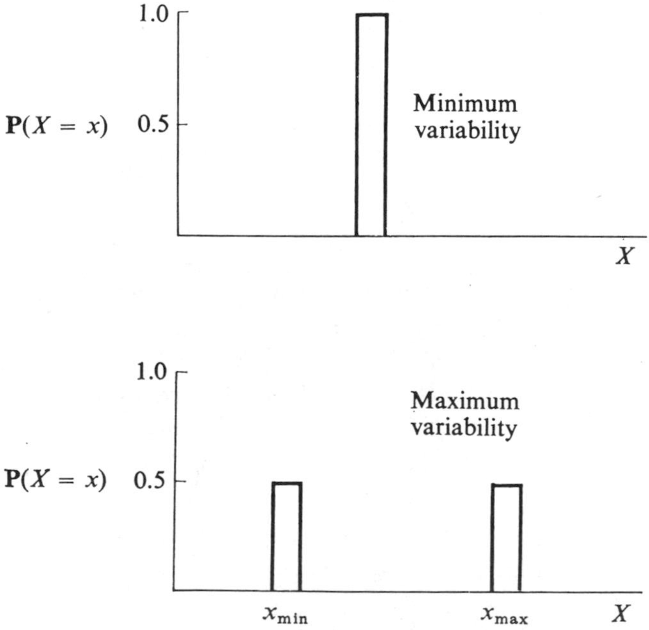

Figure IX.16

If a random variable has only one possible value, then variability is minimal. On the other hand, if half of the values of a variable are at the maximum value and half are at the minimum, then variability is as large as possible (for a random variable having those particular limiting values). These two extremes are illustrated in Figure IX.16.

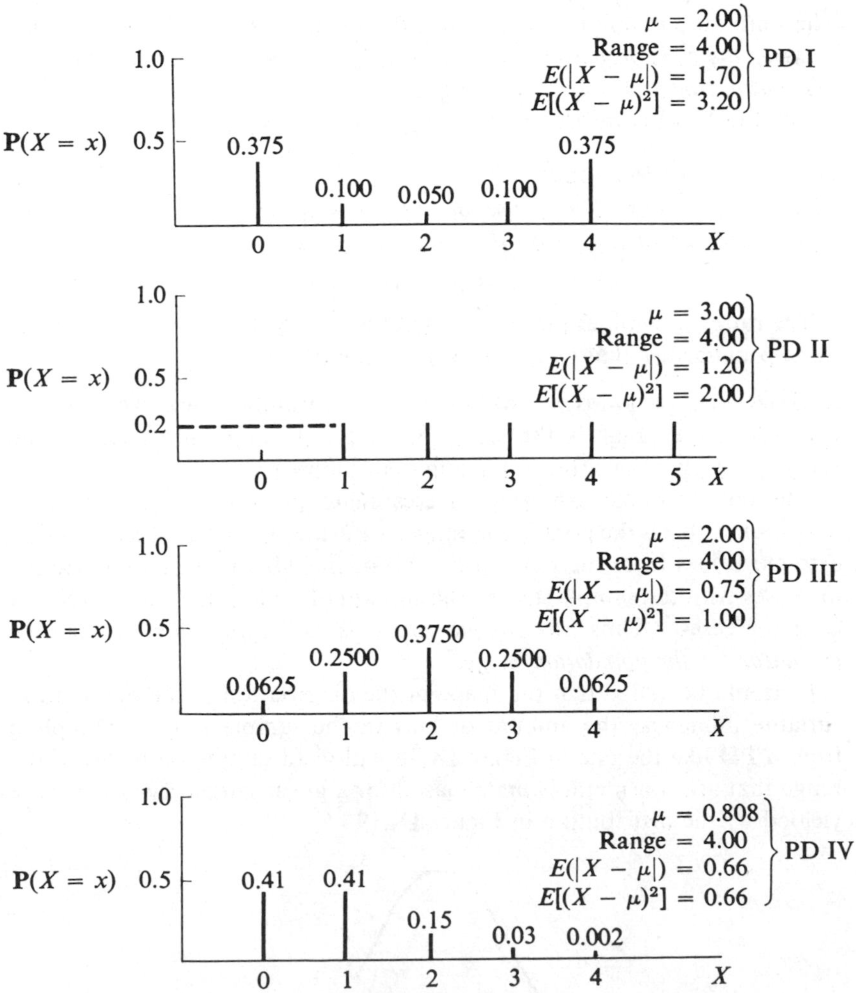

Figure IX.17

Of course, as illustrated in Figure IX.17, there are many degrees of variability between these two extremes. The most frequent values of X are at the extremes of the range of PD I. For PD II, each value of X has the same probability. Most occurrences of X lie near the mean of PD III, whereas PD IV is less variable than III because it has been "squeezed" toward its minimum value. Such compression toward a single extreme reduces variability just as compression toward the middle does.

So far, the discussion of variability has been very general; it is now time to develop some quantitative measures.

IX.4.1. Population range

The simplest measure of dispersion is the range. *If $x_{\max}$ is the maximum value of the random variable X, and if $x_{\min}$ is its minimum value, then the population range of X is $x_{\max} - x_{\min}$.*

For PD I in Figure IX.17, the range is $x_{\max} - x_{\min} = 4 - 0 = 4$.

IX.4.2. Sample range

If the observations of a sample are arranged in order from the smallest, $X_{[1]}$, to the largest, $X_{[n]}$, then the sample range is

$$X_{[n]} - X_{[1]}.$$

The range sometimes provides a useful measure of dispersion, but it has some peculiarities that should be kept in mind.

PROPERTIES OF RANGES. Although they certainly appear to differ in dispersion, the range is the same for every PD in Figure IX.17. The range is simply insensitive to the apparent differences.

The sample range can never overestimate the population range; its maximum value is the population range. Furthermore, the likelihood that extreme values from the population will be included in a random sample increases with the sample size, so the amount of underestimation decreases as n increases. Thus, *the sample range is an asymptotically unbiased estimator for the population range.*[6]

It should be added that the shape of the distribution of the observation variable influences the amount of bias in the sample range. Sampling from a PD like the one in Figure IX.18 will yield sample estimates of the range that are considerably *more* biased for a given sample size than those yielded by the distribution in Figure IX.19.

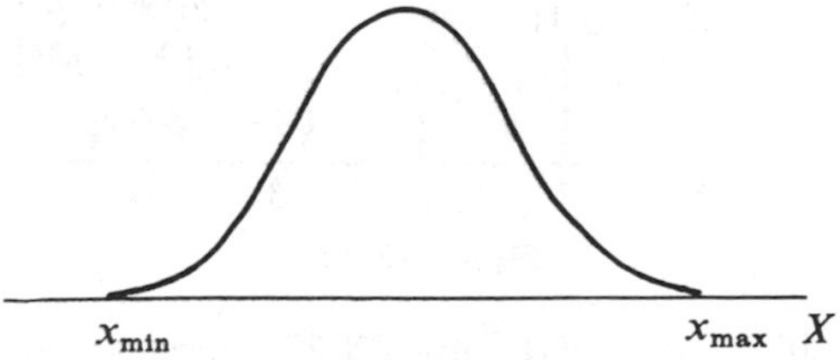

Figure IX.18

[6] This is true if the population range is finite. Otherwise, the sample range makes little sense as an estimator.

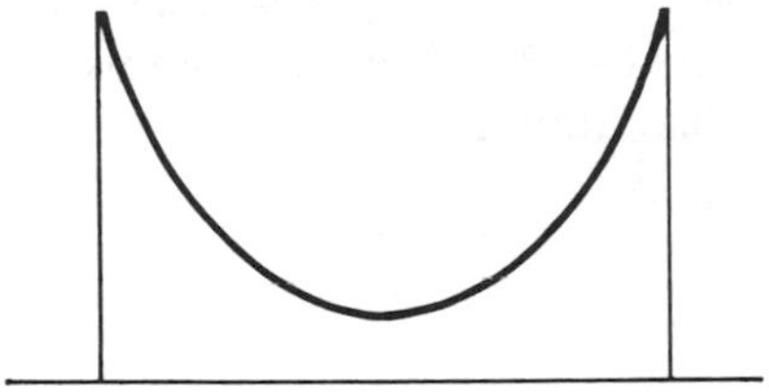

Figure IX.19

IX.4.3. Population mean deviation

Since the range is insensitive to some variations in dispersion and is biased, other measures of variability might be more useful.

One way of conceptualizing dispersion is to think of the mean *distance* of the values of a random variable from the expected value. If the mean of these distances is large, then variability is large. The fact that distance is independent of direction (above or below the mean) suggests that the absolute value of the difference between each value of the variable and its mean would provide a suitable measure of distance. Then, the expected value of the absolute difference provides a measure of the dispersion of a population.

If the expected value of the random variable X is μ, then the population mean deviation of X is

$$E(|X - \mu|). \qquad [IX.5]$$

In order to illustrate the application of the definition, the mean deviation of PD I in Figure IX.17 will be calculated. Applying the definition of the expected value of a function of a discrete random variable,

$$\begin{aligned} E(|X - \mu|) &= \sum_i \mathbf{P}(X = x_i)|x_i - \mu| \\ &= 0.375|0 - 2| + 0.10|1 - 2| + 0.05|2 - 2| \\ &\qquad + 0.10|3 - 2| + 0.375|4 - 2| \\ &= 1.7. \end{aligned}$$

Similar calculations yield the values of $E(|X - \mu|)$ for the remaining three PD's of Figure IX.17.

IX.4.4. Sample mean deviation

The population mean deviation can be estimated from *the sample mean deviation which is defined as*

$$MD = \frac{\sum_k |X_k - \bar{X}|}{n}. \qquad [IX.6]$$

The random sample (4, 0, 1, 0, 3) was drawn from the population defined by PD I in Figure IX.17. The mean of this sample is 1.6, and the resulting sample mean deviation is

$$\begin{aligned} MD &= \frac{\sum_k |X_k - \bar{X}|}{n} \\ &= \frac{|4 - 1.6| + |0 - 1.6| + |1 - 1.6| + |0 - 1.6| + |3 - 1.6|}{5} \\ &= 1.52. \end{aligned}$$

PROPERTIES OF THE SAMPLE MEAN DEVIATION. The definition of the sample mean deviation might suggest that it is an unbiased estimator, but it is biased. A population having equiprobable values 1, 2, and 3 will be used to illustrate this. For random samples of size 4 drawn with replacement from this population, the sampling distribution of the mean deviation is as follows:

$$\begin{aligned} \mathbf{P}(MD = 0) &= 3/81 \\ \mathbf{P}(MD = 0.375) &= 16/81 \\ \mathbf{P}(MD = 0.500) &= 24/81 \\ \mathbf{P}(MD = 0.750) &= 32/81 \\ \mathbf{P}(MD = 1.000) &= 6/81 \\ \hline \sum \mathbf{P}(MD = md) &= 1. \end{aligned}$$

The expected value of the sample mean deviation is

$$\begin{aligned} E(MD) &= \frac{3}{81}(0) + \frac{16}{81}(0.375) + \frac{24}{81}(0.500) + \frac{32}{81}(0.750) + \frac{6}{81}(1.000) \\ &= 0.593, \end{aligned}$$

but the population mean deviation is

$$\begin{aligned} E(|X - \mu|) &= \frac{1}{3}|1 - 2| + \frac{1}{3}|2 - 2| + \frac{1}{3}|3 - 2| \\ &= 0.667. \end{aligned}$$

Therefore, $E(MD) \neq E(|X - \mu|)$, and the bias is $E(MD) - E(|X - \mu|) = 0.593 - 0.667 = -0.074$. "On the average," then, the sample mean deviation will underestimate the corresponding parameter by 0.074 when $n = 4$. Notice that the bias appearing in this example arose even though the observation variable has a symmetrical PD.

As a descriptive measure of dispersion, the mean deviation is very appealing. It is easily interpreted, and the way in which it reflects variability is quite clear. Nonetheless, it is rarely used. In addition to being biased, the mean deviation has at least three other shortcomings. First, since absolute values are awkward to manipulate algebraically, it is difficult to develop mathematical relations involving the mean deviation. Second, the mean deviation has not played an important role in the mathematical results which are important to statistics, though other measures of dispersion have. Third, the mean deviation is not "additive." That is, the mean deviation of a sum of independent random variables is not equal to the sum of their mean deviations. This important relation does hold for the variance, the measure of dispersion that will be introduced next.

IX.4.5. Population variance

The variance is based on averaging the distances of the values of a random variable from its mean in a manner similar to that used for the mean deviation. However, distance from the mean here is measured by the square of the difference between each value of the variable and the mean. The variance equals the expected value of these squared differences.

The population variance of the random variable X is

$$E[(X - \mu)^2], \qquad \text{[IX.7]}$$

where μ is the expected value of X. The population variance is denoted by the symbol σ^2.

Notice that squaring increases the effect of high and low values much more than the absolute value of the difference does. This is due to the rapid acceleration of $(X - \mu)^2$ as a function of $(X - \mu)$, as shown in Figure IX.20. For comparison purposes, $|X - \mu|$ is also plotted in

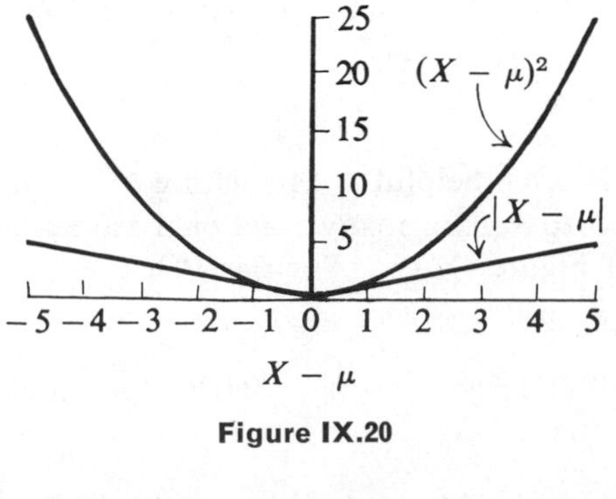

Figure IX.20

Figure IX.20. A value that is 5 units from the mean contributes 5 units to the mean deviation, but $5^2 = 25$ units to the variance. A deviation of 5 units contributes only 5 times as much to the mean deviation as a deviation of 1 unit, but a deviation of 5 contributes 25 times as much to the variance as a deviation of 1.

To see how the variance weights extremes, the variances of PD I and PD III of Figure IX.17 will be compared. For PD I,

$$\begin{aligned} E[(X - \mu)^2] &= \sum_i \mathbf{P}(X = x_i)(x_i - \mu)^2 \\ &= 0.375(0 - 2)^2 + 0.10(1 - 2)^2 + 0.05(2 - 2)^2 \\ &\qquad + 0.10(3 - 2)^2 + 0.375(4 - 2)^2 \\ &= 3.2, \end{aligned}$$

and for PD III,

$$\begin{aligned} E[(X - \mu)^2] &= \sum_i \mathbf{P}(X = x_i)(x_i - \mu)^2 \\ &= 0.0625(0 - 2)^2 + 0.25(1 - 2)^2 + 0.375(2 - 2)^2 \\ &\qquad + 0.25(3 - 2)^2 + 0.0625(4 - 2)^2 \\ &= 1. \end{aligned}$$

The mean deviation of PD I is only a little over twice that of PD III (see Fig. IX.17), but the variance of PD I is more than three times that of PD III.

The population standard deviation, another measure of dispersion, is equal to the square root of the population variance. The symbol σ will be used to denote the population standard deviation.

PROPERTIES OF THE POPULATION VARIANCE. Several relations that evolve from the definition of the population variance will prove useful later. Some of these clarify the meaning of the variance itself, and others provide time-saving calculation shortcuts.

The first of these states that *if X is a random variable and μ is its mean, then*

$$\sigma^2 = E(X^2) - \mu^2. \qquad \text{[IX.8]}$$

This relationship is often helpful in calculating σ^2. For example, it may eliminate the need to square many fractional values of $(X - \mu)$, as is true for PD IV of Figure IX.17. For this PD, $\mu = 0.808$, so that

$$\begin{aligned} \sigma^2 &= E(X^2) - \mu^2 \\ &= 0.41(0)^2 + 0.41(1)^2 + 0.15(2)^2 + 0.03(3)^2 + 0.002(4)^2 - (0.808)^2 \\ &= 0.661. \end{aligned}$$

The same result is obtained by direct application of Formula [IX.7] with which the variance was introduced.

It is quite easy to show that $\sigma^2 = E(X^2) - \mu^2$. To begin with, $\sigma^2 = E[(X - \mu)^2] = E[X^2 - 2\mu X + \mu^2]$. Now, $X^2 - 2\mu X + \mu^2$ is a linear function of the random variables X and X^2 with constants 1, -2μ, and μ^2. Consequently, by the rule for the expected value of a linear function of random variables,

$$\begin{aligned}\sigma^2 &= E[X^2 - 2\mu X + \mu^2] \\ &= E(X^2) - 2\mu E(X) + \mu^2.\end{aligned}$$

Since $E(X) = \mu$, the last line becomes

$$\begin{aligned}\sigma^2 &= E(X^2) - 2\mu(\mu) + \mu^2 \\ &= E(X^2) - 2\mu^2 + \mu^2 \\ &= E(X^2) - \mu^2.\end{aligned}$$

This demonstrates that σ^2 equals $E(X^2) - \mu^2$.

There is another relation that helps clarify certain properties of the population variance. *If the variance of X is σ^2 and the expected value of X is μ, then*

$$E(X^2) = \sigma^2 + \mu^2. \qquad \text{[IX.9]}$$

In other words, the expected value of the square of a random variable equals its variance plus the square of its mean.

In order to show that this is correct, recall Formula [IX.8]:

$$\sigma^2 = E(X^2) - \mu^2.$$

Adding μ^2 to both sides yields

$$\sigma^2 + \mu^2 = E(X^2),$$

and this is the relation specified by Formula [IX.9].

This result is quite plausible when it is recalled that the expected value of the squared deviations from the mean is σ^2, and that $E(X^2)$ is simply the expected value of the square of the variable with the mean *included.*

Two other useful properties of the variance will be introduced next. First, *if X is a random variable with variance σ^2, and if K is any constant, then the variance of the random variable X + K is σ^2.* In short, shifting the *location* of a PD or DF does not alter its dispersion. This is illustrated in Figure IX.21.

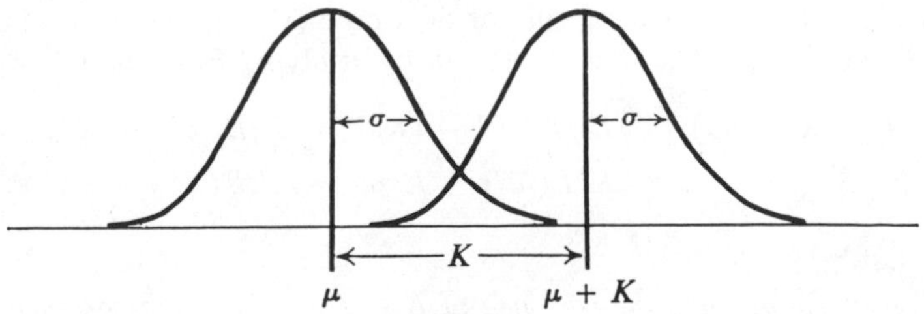

Figure IX.21

The correctness of this rule is easy to demonstrate algebraically. If the mean of X is μ, then the mean of $X + K$ is $\mu + K$ (by the rule of Section VIII.4.4) and the variance of $X + K$ is

$$E\{[(X + K) - (\mu + K)]^2\} = E[(X + K - \mu - K)^2]$$
$$= E[(X - \mu)^2].$$

Thus, the variance of $(X + K)$ equals the variance of X.

On the other hand, a change of scale (increasing or decreasing the *unit* of observation) does alter dispersion. A change of scale involves multiplying each value of a random variable by a constant. This is illustrated in Figure IX.22. In the lower DF, each value of the random variable, X,

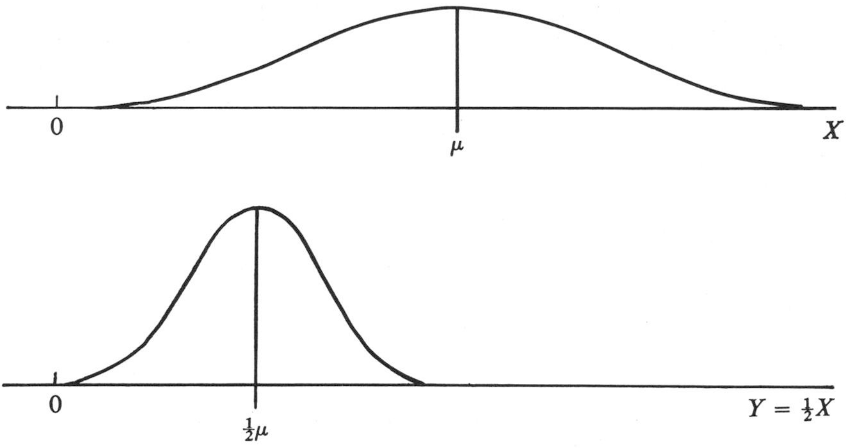

Figure IX.22

has been multiplied by 1/2. By the rule of Section VIII.4.3, the mean of $Y = (1/2)X$ is 1/2 the mean of X. Also, notice how all the values of Y are compressed to the left relative to X. This, of course, reflects a reduction of dispersion.

The general effect of multiplying each value of a variable by a constant can be found algebraically. If the variance of X is σ^2, its mean is μ, and K is a constant, then, by the rule of Section VIII.4.3, the mean of KX is $K\mu$. The variance of KX can be found by applying Formula [IX.8]:

$$E[(KX - K\mu)^2] = E[(KX)^2] - (K\mu)^2 = E[K^2X^2] - K^2\mu^2$$
$$= K^2E(X^2) - K^2\mu^2 = K^2(E(X^2) - \mu^2)$$
$$= K^2\sigma^2.$$

If K is a constant, then the variance of KX is K^2 times the variance of X. The standard deviation of KX is $\sqrt{(K^2\sigma^2)} = K\sigma$.

IX.4.6. Sample variance

So far, nothing has been said about estimating the population variance from a sample. *If* $(X_1, X_2, \ldots, X_k, \ldots, X_n)$ *is a random sample drawn with replacement from any population, or without replacement from an infinite population, and* $\bar{X}$ *is the mean of this sample, then the sample variance is*

$$S^2 = \frac{\sum_k (X_k - \bar{X})^2}{n - 1}. \qquad [IX.10]$$

Under the same conditions, the population standard deviation can be estimated by the sample standard deviation,

$$S = \sqrt{S^2}. \qquad [IX.11]$$

This definition is quite natural and would have been suspected in advance except for the appearance of $n - 1$ rather than n in the denominator. The reason for using $n - 1$ is straightforward: it makes S^2 an unbiased estimator for the population variance. If n were used, the estimator would be biased. But that is not the whole story. We shall have more to say about the use of $n - 1$ later in this chapter.

Properties of the sample variance. To illustrate the unbiasedness of S^2, we will use an example involving random samples of size 2 drawn with replacement from a population containing the values 1, 2, and 3 in equal proportions. The sample variance will be computed for each of the 9 possible samples, and the expected value of S^2 will be determined. Then, $E(S^2)$ can be compared with σ^2 for this population.

The sample space for samples of size 2 is found in the first row of Table IX.3. Below each outcome is its probability, and in the third row the variance of each of the samples is given. For example, the variance of the sample (1, 3) is

$$S^2 = \frac{\sum (X - \bar{X})^2}{n - 1} = \frac{(1 - 2)^2 + (3 - 2)^2}{2 - 1} = 2.$$

Table IX.3. Generation of sampling distribution of variance

	Outcomes								
	1, 1	1, 2	1, 3	2, 1	2, 2	2, 3	3, 1	3, 2	3, 3
Probability	1/9	1/9	1/9	1/9	1/9	1/9	1/9	1/9	1/9
S^2	0	1/2	2	1/2	0	1/2	2	1/2	0

Since $S^2 = 1/2$ for 4 of the 9 samples, $\mathbf{P}(S^2 = 1/2) = 4(1/9) = 4/9$. By similar calculations, the sampling distribution of S^2 is as follows:

$$\begin{aligned} \mathbf{P}(S^2 = 0) &= 3/9 \\ \mathbf{P}(S^2 = 1/2) &= 4/9 \\ \mathbf{P}(S^2 = 2) &= 2/9 \\ \hline \sum \mathbf{P}(S^2 = s^2) &= 1. \end{aligned}$$

The expected value of S^2 is

$$\begin{aligned} E(S^2) &= \sum \mathbf{P}(S^2 = s^2)s^2 \\ &= \frac{3}{9}(0) + \frac{4}{9}\left(\frac{1}{2}\right) + \frac{2}{9}(2) \\ &= \frac{2}{3}, \end{aligned}$$

and the variance of the population is

$$\begin{aligned} \sigma^2 = E[(X - \mu)^2] &= E(X^2) - \mu^2 \\ &= \frac{1}{3}(1)^2 + \frac{1}{3}(2)^2 + \frac{1}{3}(3)^2 - (2)^2 \\ &= \frac{2}{3}. \end{aligned}$$

Since $E(S^2) = \sigma^2$, S^2 is an unbiased estimator for σ^2.

In Chapter XI, an algebraic proof is given showing that S^2 is an unbiased estimator for σ^2. This proof is the best explanation of why $n - 1$ (rather than n) appears in the denominator of Formula [IX.10]. However, a preliminary explanation will be given here.

To begin with, if the population mean were known but σ^2 were not, then replacing $\bar{X}$ by μ and $n - 1$ by n in Formula [IX.10] leads to the estimator

$$Q^2 = \frac{\sum_k (X_k - \mu)^2}{n}.$$

Q^2 turns out to be unbiased, and this suggests that it is the estimation of $\bar{X}$ in Formula [IX.10] that makes it necessary to use $n - 1$ to make S^2 unbiased. As the following discussion indicates, this is correct.

Suppose that a random sample is drawn and used to estimate σ^2. In addition, suppose that $\bar{X}$ differs from μ, as it will for most random samples. This indicates that the sample includes a disproportionate number of values either above or below the population mean. Furthermore, disproportionate representation in the sample means a clustering of observations within the range of values that is over-represented. Since the same values are used to calculate $\sum (X - \bar{X})^2$ and $\bar{X}$, the clustering that shifts $\bar{X}$ away from μ also makes $\sum (X - \bar{X})^2$ too small. But according to the law of large numbers (Section V.3.3), the variability of $\bar{X}$ decreases as n increases. Therefore, the likelihood of disproportionate representation in the sample decreases with large n. This is reflected by the fact that it makes little difference whether $\sum (X - \bar{X})^2$ is divided by n or by $n - 1$ when n is large.

The preceding discussion does not show why it is $n - 1$ rather than $n - 2$ or some other quantity that makes S^2 unbiased; it shows only that some adjustment is necessary and that $n - 1$ has some of the proper characteristics.

CALCULATION SHORTCUTS FOR THE SAMPLE VARIANCE. Two labor-saving shortcut formulas are available. The first of these is

$$S^2 = \frac{\sum X^2 - (\sum X)^2/n}{n - 1}. \qquad \text{[IX.12]}$$

In order to show that this is identical with Formula [IX.10], it is only necessary to show that

$$\sum (X - \bar{X})^2 = \sum X^2 - \frac{(\sum X)^2}{n},$$

since the denominators of formulas [IX.12] and [IX.10] are the same.

Beginning with the numerator of Formula [IX.10],

$$\begin{aligned} \sum (X - \bar{X})^2 &= \sum (X^2 - 2\bar{X}X + \bar{X}^2) \\ &= \sum X^2 - 2\bar{X}\sum X + \sum \bar{X}^2 = \sum X^2 - 2\bar{X}(n\bar{X}) + n\bar{X}^2 \\ &= \sum X^2 - 2n\bar{X}^2 + n\bar{X}^2 = \sum X^2 - n\bar{X}^2 \\ &= \sum X^2 - n\left(\frac{\sum X}{n}\right)^2 = \sum X^2 - n\frac{(\sum X)^2}{n^2} \\ &= \sum X^2 - \frac{(\sum X)^2}{n}. \end{aligned}$$

Since this equals the numerator of Formula [IX.12], it shows that Formulas [IX.12] and [IX.10] are identical.

If both sides of Formula [IX.12] are multiplied by $n/n = 1$, then

$$\frac{n}{n} S^2 = \frac{n}{n}\left[\frac{\sum X^2 - (\sum X)^2/n}{n - 1}\right],$$

$$S^2 = \frac{n \sum X^2 - (\sum X)^2}{n(n - 1)}. \qquad \text{[IX.13]}$$

This is the second shortcut. It is especially convenient when working on a desk calculator.

Both of these formulas will be illustrated by computing S^2 for a random sample of size 5 drawn with replacement from a population consisting of the three equiprobable elements 1, 2, and 3. The sample is (3, 2, 2, 3, 3). Table IX.4 sets forth the preliminary calculations.

Table IX.4. Preliminary calculations for the sample variance

X	X^2
3	9
2	4
2	4
3	9
3	9
$\sum X = 13$	$\sum X^2 = 35$

Applying Formula [IX.12],

$$S^2 = \frac{\sum X^2 - (\sum X)^2/n}{n - 1} = \frac{35 - (13)^2/5}{5 - 1}$$
$$= 0.3.$$

Using Formula [IX.13],

$$S^2 = \frac{n \sum X^2 - (\sum X)^2}{n(n - 1)} = \frac{5(35) - (13)^2}{5(5 - 1)}$$
$$= 0.3,$$

which is identical to the result of the previous calculation.

IX.5
PROBLEMS ON MEASURES OF DISPERSION

1. For the data of Problem 1 in Section VIII.1.1,
   a. Find the range.
   b. Find the mean deviation.
   c. Find the variance.
   d. What is the variance if 7.63 is added to each observation?
   e. What is the variance of 1.6 times each of the original observations?
2. If $\sigma_X{}^2 = 25$ is the variance of X, what is the variance of
   a. $2X$?
   b. $2X + 7$?

3. If $E(X^2) = 75$ and $\mu_X = 8.0$, what is σ_X^2?
4. Find the variance of the random variable $h(X)$ in Problem 4 of Section VIII.6.
5. For the variable of the preceding problem, find the variance and mean deviation.
6. Compute the variance of PD IV of Figure IX.17.
7. Now compute $E[(X - V)^2]$, where V is the median of the distribution referred to in Problem 6.
   a. What is $E[(X - V)^2]$?
   b. Which is larger, $E[(X - V)^2]$ or the population variance, σ^2?
   c. State a principle that should lead you to anticipate the results found for b.
8. For the distribution referred to in Problem 6, show that $E[(X - \mu)^2] = E(X^2) - \mu^2$.
9. Suppose that the range of X is (1, 2, 3, 4) and that each of the values of X has the same probability.
   a. Find the value of S^2 for each of the possible samples of size 2 taken with replacement from this population.
   b. Find the sampling distribution of S^2 for samples of size 2 from this population.
   c. Show that $E(S^2) = \sigma^2$. What does this demonstrate?
   d. For the example, what is the variance of the random variable S^2 for samples of size 2?
10. One might guess that the sample standard deviation is an unbiased estimator for the population standard deviation. However, this is *not* true. For the example introduced in Table IX.3, show that the standard deviation of random samples of size 2 is a biased estimator for the standard deviation of this population.

IX.6
CENTRAL MOMENTS

Several ways of describing the location and dispersion of PD's, DF's, and sample frequency distributions have been described. However, location and dispersion measures indicate little about skewness. Of course, an elongated tail will increase dispersion, but distributions of many forms have the same variance. For example, 1.26 is the variance of both of the PD's in Figure IX.23, though they clearly differ in skewness. Apparently, what is needed is a measure of skewness relative to dispersion. Such a measure will be developed in Section IX.6.2 after a necessary idea has been introduced.

Earlier, $E(X - \mu)$ and $E[(X - \mu)^2]$ were defined. Similarly,

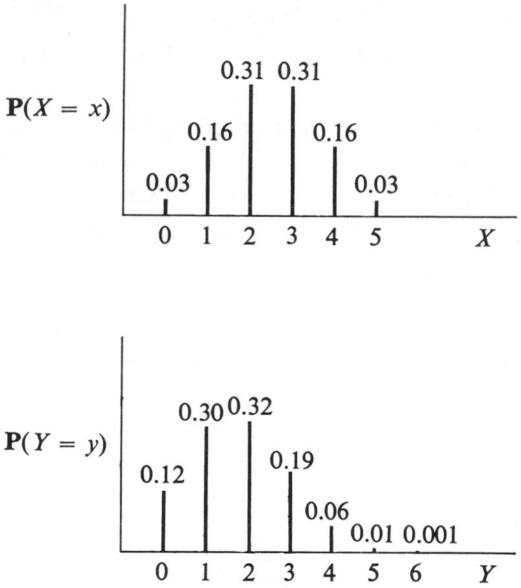

Figure IX.23

$E[(X - \mu)^3]$, $E[(X - \mu)^4]$, and so on, could also be defined if they were thought to be of use. Expected values of this form are called central moments or moments about the mean. *If μ is the expected value of the random variable X, then the rth central moment of X is*

$$E[(X - \mu)^r]. \qquad \text{[IX.14]}$$

From this definition, it is clear that we have already dealt with two central moments, the ones for $r = 1$ and $r = 2$. Now, the third central moment will be used to develop a measure of skewness.

IX.6.1. The third central moment

The third central moment for the upper PD of Figure IX.23 is

$$\begin{aligned} E[(X - \mu_X)^3] &= \sum \mathbf{P}(X = x)(x - \mu_X)^3 \\ &= 0.03(0 - 2.5)^3 + 0.16(1 - 2.5)^3 + 0.31(2 - 2.5)^3 \\ &\quad + 0.31(3 - 2.5)^3 + 0.16(4 - 2.5)^3 + 0.03(5 - 2.5)^3 \\ &= 0. \end{aligned}$$

This reflects *an important characteristic of the third central moment: it is always zero for symmetrical probability distributions and symmetrical density functions.* However, the third central moment of the lower PD of Figure IX.23 is

$$\begin{aligned}E[(Y - \mu_Y)^3] &= \sum \mathbf{P}(Y = y)(y - \mu_Y)^3 \\ &= 0.12(0 - 1.8)^3 + 0.30(1 - 1.8)^3 + 0.32(2 - 1.8)^3 \\ &\quad + 0.19(3 - 1.8)^3 + 0.06(4 - 1.8)^3 + 0.01(5 - 1.8)^3 \\ &\quad + 0.001(6 - 1.8)^3 \\ &= 2.22.\end{aligned}$$

The positive value of this third central moment indicates that the lower PD of Figure IX.23 is elongated to the right, that is, positively skewed. If the elongated tail had extended to the left, then the third central moment would have been negative.[7] This is because the cube of $(Y - \mu_Y)$ retains the sign of the difference, so if the majority of large differences are negative, the third moment will be negative.

If a sample is used to estimate the third central moment, the estimator is

$$\frac{\sum_k (X_k - \bar{X})^3}{n - 2}. \qquad \text{[IX.15]}$$

The use of $n - 2$ in the denominator makes the estimate unbiased in the same way that $n - 1$ makes S^2 an unbiased estimator of the second central moment.

IX.6.2. Measures of skewness

The third central moment does measure skewness, but it makes no allowance for the fact that large dispersion as well as asymmetry affects its value. However, *the ratio of the third central moment to the cube of the standard deviation provides a measure of the skewness of a distribution relative to its dispersion.*

In the case of the upper PD of Figure IX.23, this measure is

$$\frac{E[(X - \mu_X)^3]}{\sigma_X{}^3} = \frac{0}{(\sqrt{1.26})^3} = 0,$$

since the distribution is symmetrical. However, for the lower PD,

$$\frac{E[(Y - \mu_Y)^3]}{\sigma_Y{}^3} = \frac{2.22}{(\sqrt{1.26})^3} = 1.57.$$

Although the positive sign of this ratio is easily interpreted as positive skewness, the exact meaning of its magnitude is not evident, since there

[7] It should be noted that the third central moment can be zero for some asymmetrical probability distributions. However, this can happen only when there are irregular gaps in the PD. Such distributions are rarely encountered.

are no upper limits on either $\sigma_Y{}^3$ or the absolute value of $E[(Y - \mu_Y)^3]$. About the best that can be done is to use this measure to determine the relative skewness of two or more distributions.

If a sample is used to estimate the population value of this measure of skewness, the estimator is

$$\frac{\sum_k (X_k - \bar{X})^3}{(n - 2)S^3}. \qquad [IX.16]$$

In the discussion of sensitivity to extreme values in Section IX.2.2, the way in which the difference between mean and median reflects skewness was described. The ratio of this difference to the dispersion of a PD or DF *provides the simple measure of skewness,*

$$\frac{\mu - V}{\sigma}. \qquad [IX.17]$$

An estimate of this index can be obtained from

$$\frac{\bar{X} - M}{S}, \qquad [IX.18]$$

where M is the sample median.

IX.7

PROBLEMS ON CENTRAL MOMENTS AND MEASURES OF SKEWNESS

1. Find the third central moment of PD IV in Figure IX.17.
2. Apply two measures of skewness to the PD referred to in Problem 1. Comment on the relative success of these two measures for this distribution and discuss the implications of any discrepancies between the two.
3. Consider the measure of skewness, $(\mu - V)/\sigma$. Construct a unimodal PD for which this measure is negative.

IX.8

TWO MEASURES OF RELATIONSHIP

In addition to measures of location, dispersion, and skewness, two important measures of predictability or relationship will be introduced in this chapter. Besides being extremely useful for describing data, these measures will enable us to develop some useful statistical theory at the end of this chapter.

If two variables are related and if the relationship between them is known explicitly, then values of one can be predicted from values of the other. In the case of Fechner's law, if one knows the value of the constant K, then the equation $\psi = K \log S$ permits the prediction of sensory magnitude, ψ, from knowledge of the physical magnitude of the stimulus, S. This is an instance of an explicitly described correlation. However, if empirical estimates of sensory magnitudes are plotted against physical stimulus magnitudes, the plotted points will not all fall on the curve defined by the function $\psi = K \log S$. At best, the data points will scatter in the neighborhood of this curve. This scattering means that Fechner's law does not permit exactly correct predictions, and appraising the amount of error of prediction is an important adjunct of the description of relationship. The mechanics of prediction will not be dealt with here, but two methods for measuring *predictability* will be described.

IX.8.1. Population covariance

The most fundamental concept in this discussion is the idea of covariation. Two variables are said to covary if they rise and fall together. Covariation is large when the behavior of the two variables is closely linked and small when the values of the variables are unrelated. The *covariance* is a measure of covariation.

If the mean of X is μ_X and the mean of Y is μ_Y, then the population covariance of X and Y is

$$\sigma_{XY} = E[(X - \mu_X)(Y - \mu_Y)]. \qquad \text{[IX.19]}$$

In order to calculate the population covariance of two random variables, their joint PD must be known. If X and Y are discrete, then their covariance is

$$\begin{aligned}\sigma_{XY} &= E[(X - \mu_X)(Y - \mu_Y)]\\ &= \sum_i \sum_j \mathbf{P}[(X = x_i) \cap (Y = y_j)](x_i - \mu_X)(y_j - \mu_Y).\end{aligned}$$

Before illustrating the calculation of σ_{XY}, it will be convenient to develop an equivalent formula that simplifies computation. Beginning with Formula [IX.19],

$$\begin{aligned}\sigma_{XY} &= E[(X - \mu_X)(Y - \mu_Y)] = E[XY - \mu_X Y - \mu_Y X + \mu_X\mu_Y]\\ &= E(XY) - \mu_X E(Y) - \mu_Y E(X) + E(\mu_X\mu_Y)\\ &= E(XY) - \mu_X\mu_Y - \mu_Y\mu_X + \mu_X\mu_Y\\ &= E(XY) - \mu_X\mu_Y.\end{aligned}$$

Consequently, the formula

$$\sigma_{XY} = E(XY) - \mu_X\mu_Y \qquad \text{[IX.20]}$$

can be used to calculate the population covariance.

The bivariate distribution for the simultaneous toss of a coin and a six-sided die has been reproduced in Table IX.5. The covariance of X and Y will be computed for this example.

Table IX.5. Bivariate distribution for tosses of coin and die

		X (die)					
		1	2	3	4	5	6
Y (coin)	1	1/12	1/12	1/12	1/12	1/12	1/12
	0	1/12	1/12	1/12	1/12	1/12	1/12

The mean of X is $\mu_X = 3.5$, and the mean of Y is $\mu_Y = 0.5$, so the covariance is

$$\begin{aligned}
\sigma_{XY} &= E(XY) - \mu_X\mu_Y \\
&= \sum_i \sum_j \mathbf{P}[(X = x_i) \cap (Y = y_j)]x_i y_j - \mu_X\mu_Y \\
&= \frac{1}{12}(1)(1) + \frac{1}{12}(1)(2) + \frac{1}{12}(1)(3) + \frac{1}{12}(1)(4) + \frac{1}{12}(1)(5) \\
&\quad + \frac{1}{12}(1)(6) + \frac{1}{12}(0)(1) + \frac{1}{12}(0)(2) + \frac{1}{12}(0)(3) + \frac{1}{12}(0)(4) \\
&\quad + \frac{1}{12}(0)(5) + \frac{1}{12}(0)(6) - (3.5)(0.5) \\
&= 0.
\end{aligned}$$

This says that there is no relationship between X and Y; that is, that X and Y do not covary. Furthermore, these two variables are statistically independent, and *if two random variables are statistically independent, then their covariances must be zero.*

It is easy to prove this statement. First, by the rule of Section VIII.4.7, if X and Y are statistically independent, then $E(XY) = E(X)E(Y)$. Consequently,

$$\begin{aligned}
\sigma_{XY} &= E(XY) - \mu_X\mu_Y = E(X)E(Y) - \mu_X\mu_Y = \mu_X\mu_Y - \mu_X\mu_Y \\
&= 0,
\end{aligned}$$

which is what we set out to show.

Now it must be added that *zero covariance does not imply statistical independence.* To see this, consider Figure IX.24. This plot is a representation of the bivariate distribution of X and Y. Since each of 10 pairs

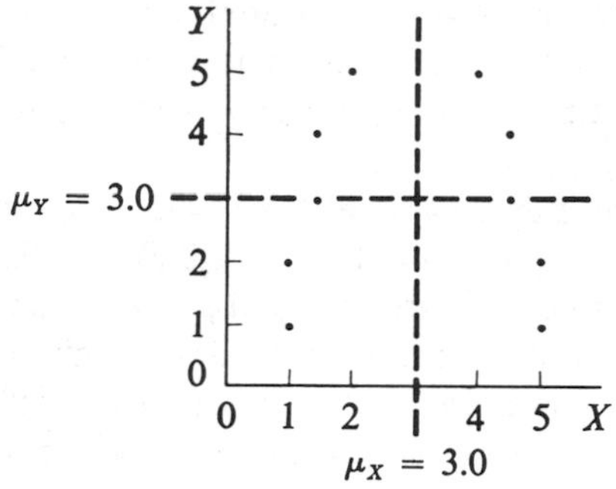

Figure IX.24

of values occurs once, $\mathbf{P}[(X = x) \cap (Y = y)] = 1/10$ for every pair, and the covariance of X and Y is

$$\begin{aligned}\sigma_{XY} &= E(XY) - \mu_X\mu_Y = \sum_i \sum_j \mathbf{P}[(X = x_i) \cap (Y = y_j)]x_i y_j - \mu_X\mu_Y \\ &= \frac{1}{10}(1)(1) + \frac{1}{10}(1)(2) + \frac{1}{10}(1.5)(3) + \cdots + \frac{1}{10}(5)(1) - (3)(3) \\ &= 0.\end{aligned}$$

However, in spite of the fact that the covariance is zero, X and Y are statistically *dependent*. For suppose that Y is to be predicted from X. If $X = 2$, then the prediction of Y would be 5, and it is certain to be correct, since $\mathbf{P}[(Y = 5) \mid (X = 2)] = 1$. But since this is not equal to $\mathbf{P}(Y = 5) = 2/10$, X and Y are statistically dependent.

This shows that statistical independence is a more general description of relationship or predictability than is covariance. Zero covariance does not ensure that two variables are unrelated, but statistical independence does. Even though the covariance of two variables is zero, it is a good idea to plot the bivariate distribution and see whether they are also statistically independent.

In order to illustrate graphically how the covariance reflects association, the joint distribution of the one-coin, one-die problem has been plotted

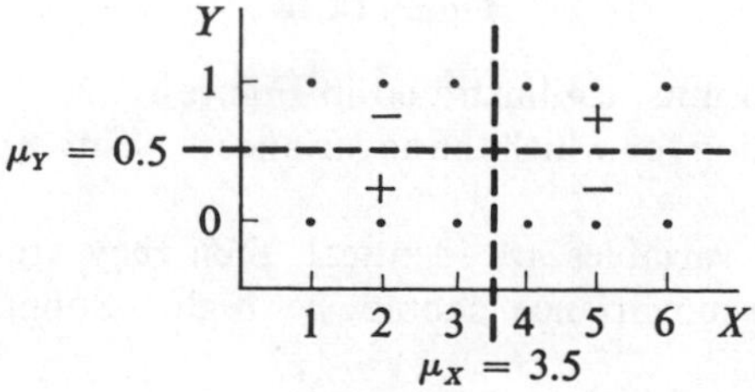

Figure IX.25

in Figure IX.25. The broken lines locate the means of the two variables in the distribution, and each dot represents a pair of values, one on X and one on Y. For example, the upper left-hand dot represents the event $(X = 1) \cap (Y = 1)$.

Now, consider the point $(X = 6) \cap (Y = 1)$. Its contribution to the covariance is $(X - \mu_X)(Y - \mu_Y) = (6 - 3.5)(1 - 0.5) = +1.25$. This product is positive, since 6 is greater than $\mu_X = 3.5$ and 1 is greater than $\mu_Y = 0.5$. In fact, all of the points in the upper right quadrant contribute *positive* products to the covariance. In the lower left quadrant of this plot, every value of X is less than μ_X and every value of Y is less than μ_Y. Consequently, the products $(X - \mu_X)(Y - \mu_Y)$ are always positive in this quadrant, too, so that both the upper right and lower left quadrants are called positive quadrants. On the other hand, products from the upper left and lower right quadrants are always negative, so they are referred to as negative quadrants.

From this it appears that the value of the covariance will be positive when the majority of points are in the two positive quadrants and negative when the majority lie in the two negative quadrants. This is partly true, but it is not the whole story. The magnitude of a product, $(X - \mu_X)\cdot(Y - \mu_Y)$, depends on the distance of X and Y from their respective means. If either distance is small, then their product will be small in absolute value. If both distances are large, then the product will have a large absolute value. The covariance will be negative if the majority of points giving moderate or large (in absolute value) products fall in the

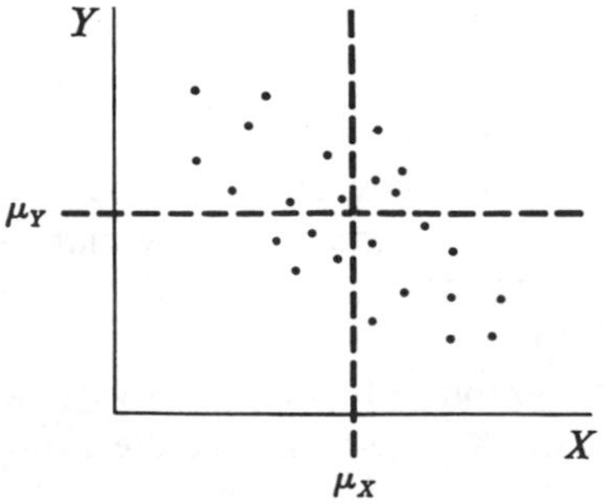

Figure IX.26

two negative quadrants, as illustrated in Figure IX.26. An example of a bivariate distribution for which the covariance is positive appears in Figure IX.27.

If two random variables are identical, then they are certainly closely linked, and their covariance should be high. Suppose that $X = Y$. Then,

$$\sigma_{XY} = \sigma_{XX} = E[(X - \mu_X)(X - \mu_X)] = E[(X - \mu_X)^2] = \sigma_X^2,$$

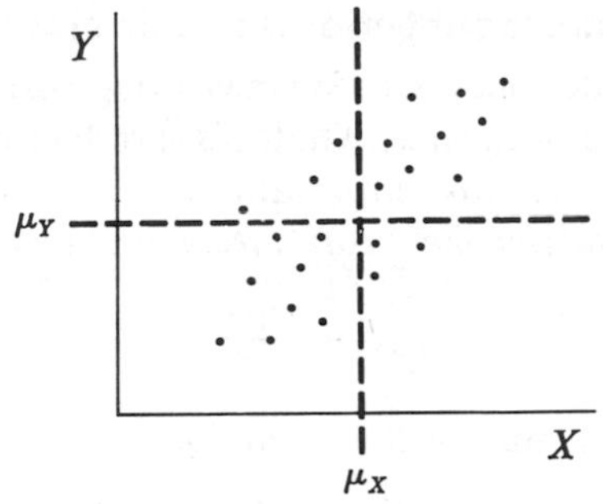

Figure IX.27

so that the covariance reduces to the variance. Thus, a variable covaries with itself to the extent that it varies at all.

The absolute value of σ_{XY} reflects the strength of association between X and Y. But since σ_{XY} depends on the unit of measurement of X and Y as well as on the strength of relationship between them, some standard is needed against which σ_{XY} can be compared. Such a standard is provided by the maximum value of σ_{XY}. *If σ_X is the standard deviation of X, and σ_Y is the standard deviation of Y, then the covariance of X and Y, σ_{XY}, must lie between $-\sigma_X\sigma_Y$ and $+\sigma_X\sigma_Y$, inclusive.*[8]

If σ_{XY} equals $\sigma_X\sigma_Y$, then all of the points of the bivariate plot of X and Y must lie on a straight line that rises from left to right. If $\sigma_{XY} = -\sigma_X\sigma_Y$, then all of the points must lie on a straight line that falls from left to right. These two extremes are illustrated in Figure IX.28. It is important

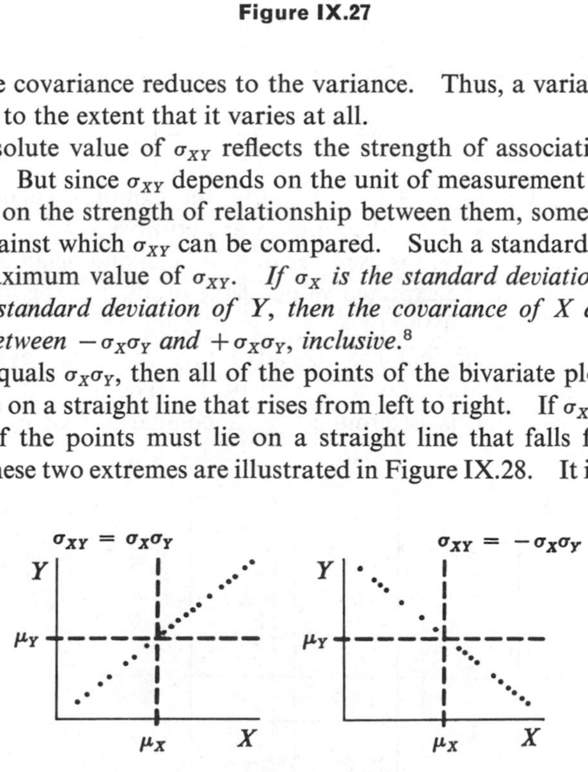

Figure IX.28

to notice that all of the points must lie on a *straight* line in order for the covariance to take on either of its extreme values.[9]

[8] A proof of this statement can be found in most textbooks on mathematical statistics.

[9] The reasons for this will not be elaborated here. A discussion of this aspect of covariation is more straightforward if another approach is taken. Such an approach can be found under the heading of "linear regression" in many textbooks.

IX.8.2. Population product-moment correlation coefficient

The covariance provides one basis for measuring correlation, and though there are many other measures, Galton's product-moment correlation coefficient is certainly the most important.

The population product-moment correlation of X and Y is defined as

$$\rho_{XY} = \frac{\sigma_{XY}}{\sigma_X \sigma_Y}. \qquad \text{[IX.21]}$$

If σ_{XY} takes on its maximum value, then $\sigma_{XY} = \sigma_X\sigma_Y$, and

$$\rho_{XY} = \frac{\sigma_{XY}}{\sigma_X\sigma_Y} = \frac{\sigma_X\sigma_Y}{\sigma_X\sigma_Y} = 1.$$

If σ_{XY} equals its minimum value, then $\sigma_{XY} = -\sigma_X\sigma_Y$, and

$$\rho_{XY} = \frac{\sigma_{XY}}{\sigma_X\sigma_Y} = \frac{-\sigma_X\sigma_Y}{\sigma_X\sigma_Y} = -1.$$

Consequently, $-1 \leq \rho_{XY} \leq +1$. Of course, the sign of ρ_{XY} is determined by the sign of σ_{XY}, since σ_X and σ_Y are always positive.

The term *product moment* is used because the sign and magnitude of the coefficient depend on the expected value of the product of the first central moment terms, $(X - \mu_X)$ and $(Y - \mu_Y)$ (see Section IX.6).

The correlation coefficient has the advantage over the covariance of being independent of the units of X and of Y. The units of ρ_{XY} are σ_X and σ_Y, and its value is determined by a comparison of σ_{XY} with its maximum value, $\sigma_X\sigma_Y$.

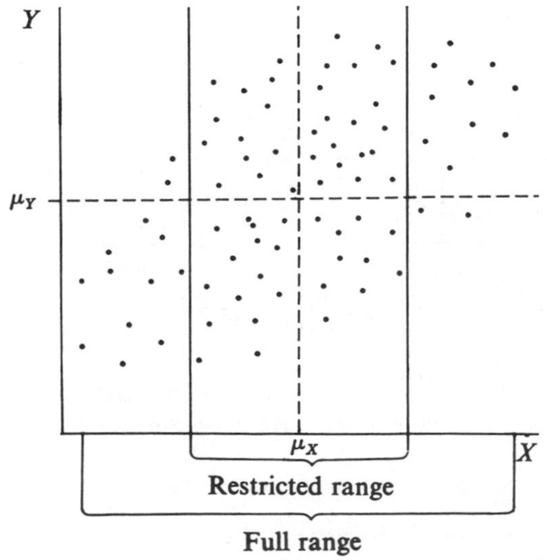

Figure IX.29

This has some important implications for the interpretation of the correlation coefficient. For example, suppose that the standard deviation of X is reduced by some selection process. Inspection of Formula [IX.21] might suggest that this would increase ρ_{XY}. However, restricting the variability of X affects the numerator, σ_{XY}, as well as the denominator of ρ_{XY}. This effect is illustrated in Figure IX.29. If the variance of X is reduced by eliminating its extreme values, then some of the products, $(X - \mu_X)(Y - \mu_Y)$, which contribute most heavily to the covariance of X and Y are lost. In addition, nearly all of the eliminated products lie in the two positive quadrants. As a result, the balance of positive and negative products is shifted toward the negative, and the covariance is decreased. If the range of Y were also restricted, then the distribution and magnitude of points in + and − quadrants would become about equal, and the covariance (and therefore the correlation coefficient) would be near zero. While variance is reduced by restriction of the range of either variable, the effect on the covariance is greater and the correlation coefficient is decreased in absolute magnitude.

In Section VII.3.1, the joint distribution of the random variables B and R was described. As described there, B equals the sum of the faces of a blue die and a white die, and R is the sum of the face of the same white die and that of a red die. The joint distribution for these variables is given in Table VII.8. The covariance of this distribution is

$$\begin{aligned}\sigma_{BR} &= E(BR) - \mu_B\mu_R \\ &= \underbrace{\frac{1}{216}(2)(2) + \frac{1}{216}(2)(3) + \frac{1}{216}(2)(4) + \cdots + \frac{1}{216}(12)(12)}_{\text{91 terms having nonzero probability}} - (7)(7) \\ &= 3.03.\end{aligned}$$

From the marginal distributions of B and R (also given in Table VII.8), the standard deviations can be computed. Then, $\sigma_B = 2.42$ and $\sigma_R = 2.42$, and from this,

$$\rho_{BR} = \frac{\sigma_{BR}}{\sigma_B\sigma_R} = \frac{3.03}{(2.42)(2.42)} = 0.52.$$

One might conclude from this that B and R are "moderately correlated."

The main reason for introducing this example is to give a concrete and clearly interpretable example of one form of mechanism that may produce correlation. Here, B and R have the white die in common. But notice that the common element is random (the white die is tossed along with the other two), just as the aspects that B and R do not share are random. Often, correlations other than +1 or −1 are determined by a random linkage of this kind. Sometimes, one of the two variables is a partial "cause" of the other, but a nonzero correlation in itself does not imply a causal relation.

Nonrandom linkage can be illustrated by tossing a die on a glass table top. The side facing up is read as X and the side facing down as Y. Then, X and Y are statistically dependent, so that knowledge of X permits the prediction of Y without error. Here, the mechanism connecting X and Y is not random in any way, even though observed values of either variable are random. But in spite of their inflexible link, it is inappropriate to say that X causes Y or that Y causes X.

IX.8.3. Sample covariance

In calculating a population covariance, all possible pairs of values of the two random variables must be included in the calculation. When a random sample is used to estimate a covariance, only some of the pairs are available. However, it is important to keep in mind that a sample covariance or correlation cannot be computed unless the sample consists of *paired* observations. For example, in estimating the covariance between chronological age and mental age, a pair of observations is obtained for each person in the sample. The sample consists of n pairs, each pair containing a CA and an MA for one person.

Suppose that a sample consists of the n bivariate observations (X_1, Y_1), (X_2, Y_2), (X_3, Y_3), . . . , (X_n, Y_n). *Then the sample covariance of X and Y is*

$$S_{XY} = \frac{\sum_k (X_k - \bar{X})(Y_k - \bar{Y})}{n - 1}. \qquad \text{[IX.22]}$$

For purposes of calculation, it is usually simpler to work with the equivalent formula,

$$S_{XY} = \frac{\sum_k X_k Y_k - \left[\left(\sum_k X_k\right)\left(\sum_k Y_k\right)\right] / n}{n - 1}. \qquad \text{[IX.23]}$$

To show that Formulas [IX.22] and [IX.23] are equal, it is necessary to show that their numerators are identical. This proof is analogous to the demonstration that Formulas [IX.10] and [IX.12] for the sample variance are equivalent.

Multiplying Formula [IX.23] by n/n leads to a formula that is more efficient on most desk calculators. This is

$$S_{XY} = \frac{n \sum_k X_k Y_k - \left(\sum_k X_k\right)\left(\sum_k Y_k\right)}{n(n - 1)}. \qquad \text{[IX.24]}$$

A random sample of 10 bivariate observations was drawn from the bivariate population defined by the white, red, and blue dice. This sample is (9, 8), (11, 9), (4, 8), (5, 4), (4, 4), (5, 8), (7, 7), (8, 9), (5, 9), (5, 6). The first element in each pair is the value on B (blue plus white dice) and the second is on R (red plus white dice). The preliminary calculations are summarized in Table IX.6.

Table IX.6. Preliminary calculations for determining S_{BR}

B	B^2	R	R^2	BR
9	81	8	64	72
11	121	9	81	99
4	16	8	64	32
5	25	4	16	20
4	16	4	16	16
5	25	8	64	40
7	49	7	49	49
8	64	9	81	72
5	25	9	81	45
5	25	6	36	30
$\sum_k B_k = 63$	$\sum_k B_k^2 = 447$	$\sum_k R_k = 72$	$\sum_k R_k^2 = 552$	$\sum_k B_k R_k = 475$

Applying Formula [IX.23],

$$S_{BR} = \frac{\sum_k B_k R_k - \left[\left(\sum_k B_k\right)\left(\sum_k R_k\right)\right]/n}{n - 1}$$

$$= \frac{475 - [(63)(72)]/10}{10 - 1}$$

$$= 2.38,$$

and using Formula [IX.24],

$$S_{BR} = \frac{n \sum_k B_k R_k - \left(\sum_k B_k\right)\left(\sum_k R_k\right)}{n(n - 1)}$$

$$= \frac{10(475) - (63)(72)}{10(10 - 1)}$$

$$= 2.38.$$

This value is lower than the population covariance, $\sigma_{BR} = 3.03$, but one expects a statistic to vary from one sample to another and to differ on most occasions from the parameter.

As with the variance, $n - 1$ is used instead of n because it makes S_{XY} an unbiased estimator for σ_{XY}. A proof of this is given in Appendix XI.1 at the end of Chapter XI.

IX.8.4. Sample product-moment correlation coefficient

The sample product-moment correlation coefficient is defined by

$$r_{XY} = \frac{S_{XY}}{S_X S_Y}. \qquad \text{[IX.25]}$$

This definition is analogous to the definition of ρ_{XY} for a population. However, calculations can be simplified by applying some of the short-cuts used in calculating S_{XY}, S_X, and S_Y. Two helpful computational formulas for r_{XY} will be developed.

To begin with,

$$r_{XY} = \frac{S_{XY}}{S_X S_Y} = \frac{\dfrac{\sum_k X_k Y_k - \dfrac{\left(\sum_k X_k\right)\left(\sum_k Y_k\right)}{n}}{n-1}}{\sqrt{\dfrac{\sum_k X_k^2 - \dfrac{\left(\sum_k X_k\right)^2}{n}}{n-1}}\sqrt{\dfrac{\sum_k Y_k^2 - \dfrac{\left(\sum_k Y_k\right)^2}{n}}{n-1}}}$$

$$= \frac{\dfrac{1}{n-1}\left[\sum_k X_k Y_k - \dfrac{\left(\sum_k X_k\right)\left(\sum_k Y_k\right)}{n}\right]}{\dfrac{1}{n-1}\sqrt{\sum_k X_k^2 - \dfrac{\left(\sum_k X_k\right)^2}{n}}\sqrt{\sum_k Y_k^2 - \dfrac{\left(\sum_k Y_k\right)^2}{n}}}$$

$$r_{XY} = \frac{\sum_k X_k Y_k - \dfrac{\left(\sum_k X_k\right)\left(\sum_k Y_k\right)}{n}}{\sqrt{\left[\sum_k X_k^2 - \dfrac{\left(\sum_k X_k\right)^2}{n}\right]\left[\sum_k Y_k^2 - \dfrac{\left(\sum_k Y_k\right)^2}{n}\right]}}. \qquad \text{[IX.26]}$$

Although this last formula is quite useful, it is sometimes easier to multiply this by $n/n = 1$ and use

$$r_{XY} = \frac{n\sum_k X_k Y_k - \left(\sum_k X_k\right)\left(\sum_k Y_k\right)}{\sqrt{\left[n\sum_k X_k^2 - \left(\sum_k X_k\right)^2\right]\left[n\sum_k Y_k^2 - \left(\sum_k Y_k\right)^2\right]}} \qquad \text{[IX.27]}$$

The calculation of r_{BR} will be demonstrated using the same sample of 10 bivariate observations used to calculate S_{BR}. Table IX.6 summarizes the preliminary calculations. Using these,

$$r_{BR} = \frac{\sum_k B_k R_k - \frac{\left(\sum_k B_k\right)\left(\sum_k R_k\right)}{n}}{\sqrt{\left[\sum_k B_k^2 - \frac{\left(\sum_k B_k\right)^2}{n}\right]\left[\sum_k R_k - \frac{\left(\sum_k R_k\right)^2}{n}\right]}}$$

$$= \frac{475 - \frac{(63)(72)}{10}}{\sqrt{\left[447 - \frac{(63)^2}{10}\right]\left[552 - \frac{(72)^2}{10}\right]}}$$

$$= 0.52.$$

Since the denominator of r_{XY} in Formula [IX.25] is a product of biased estimators, one might guess that r_{XY} is a biased estimator for ρ_{XY}. Although this is correct, *the sample product-moment correlation coefficient is asymptotically unbiased.*[10]

In order to get a visual impression of the range of variation of the correlation coefficient, the reader should examine the plots in Figures IX.31 and IX.32 of the next section. The sample correlation coefficient for each of these plots appears in the upper left-hand corner.

*IX.8.5. Subjective probability and probability theory: an application of correlation

In Sections IV.11.2 and V.3.5 the question of how well subjective probabilities conform to the rules of mathematical probability theory was raised. Here, data will be described that indicate the extent to which subjects employ certain rules of probability theory in manipulating their subjective probabilities.[11] The sample correlation coefficient proves to be a helpful device for examining these data.

Each of the 12 college students who served as subjects provided two kinds of subjective probability estimates. The first kind required the subject to indicate the number of his acquaintances out of 100 to whom each of 20 one-word trait descriptions would apply. This number divided by 100 provides an unconditional, subjective probability estimate,

[10] The amount of bias is proportional to $1/n$. See Cramér, H., *Mathematical Methods of Statistics*. Princeton, Princeton University Press, 1946, pp. 354–359.

[11] The writer wishes to thank A. Omer Dery for his help in collecting and analyzing these data.

$\mathbf{P}'(A_i)$, for each trait name, A_i. The prime on the **P** is to remind us that this is a subjective probability estimate which may or may not follow the rules of probability theory.

The second task required the subjects to estimate conditional, subjective probabilities. The protocol for obtaining these subjective probability estimates is illustrated in Figure IX.30. The subject was required to place a check at the appropriate point on the scale to the right of each of the 19 listed traits. Then, the subject was instructed as follows: "If knowing a person is WITTY tells you nothing about whether one of the listed traits applies to him, then place an 'X' through the listed trait as well as indicating the number of WITTY persons in 100 you would expect to have the trait." Thus, the subject was asked to indicate each trait that he considered to be independent of "witty." This procedure was repeated for each of the 20 adjectives, so that a total of $20(19) = 380$ conditional, subjective probabilities was estimated by each subject. These will be denoted $\mathbf{P}'(A_i \mid A_j)$.

When a subject places an "X" through a listed trait, A_i, does this mean that he considers it to be *statistically independent* of the given trait? If so, then, for a particular trait, A_q, the mean of the $\mathbf{P}'(A_q \mid A_j)$ for those instances in which an "X" is placed through A_q should equal $\mathbf{P}'(A_q)$. Plotting this mean against $\mathbf{P}'(A_q)$ should yield points falling on a straight, 45-degree line that passes through the origin.

Such plots are shown in Figure IX.31 for 4 subjects who are fairly representative of the 12 studied. The sample correlation coefficient was calculated for each subject, and its value appears in the upper left-hand corner of each plot.

All of the points in the plot for Subject T cling rather closely to the theoretical 45-degree line. It appears that this subject followed the theoretical rule for statistical independence fairly closely. The plots for Subjects F and H suggest that their rule represents a clockwise rotation away from the theoretical, 45-degree line. However, Subject D seems to be operating on quite a different basis. He indicated independence when the conditional probability was low or zero. This implies that he interpreted independence as mutual exclusivity. (If two events, A and B, are mutually exclusive, then $\mathbf{P}(A \mid B) = \mathbf{P}(B \mid A) = 0$.) Note that although Subject D does not follow the rule for statistical independence, he is quite systematic in his application of mutual exclusivity.

One might view these results as nothing more than variations in the subjects' interpretation of the instructions. However, it is interesting that of the 12 subjects, Subject T and one other chose an interpretation that follows the meaning of statistical independence closely, whereas Subject D chose an interpretation that is quite compatible with the idea of mutually exclusive events. Some subjects seem to have adopted a

100 persons are known to be witty. How many of them would you expect to be:

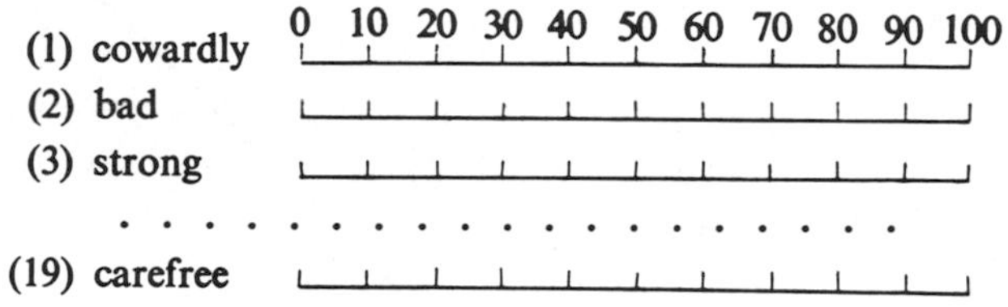

Figure IX.30

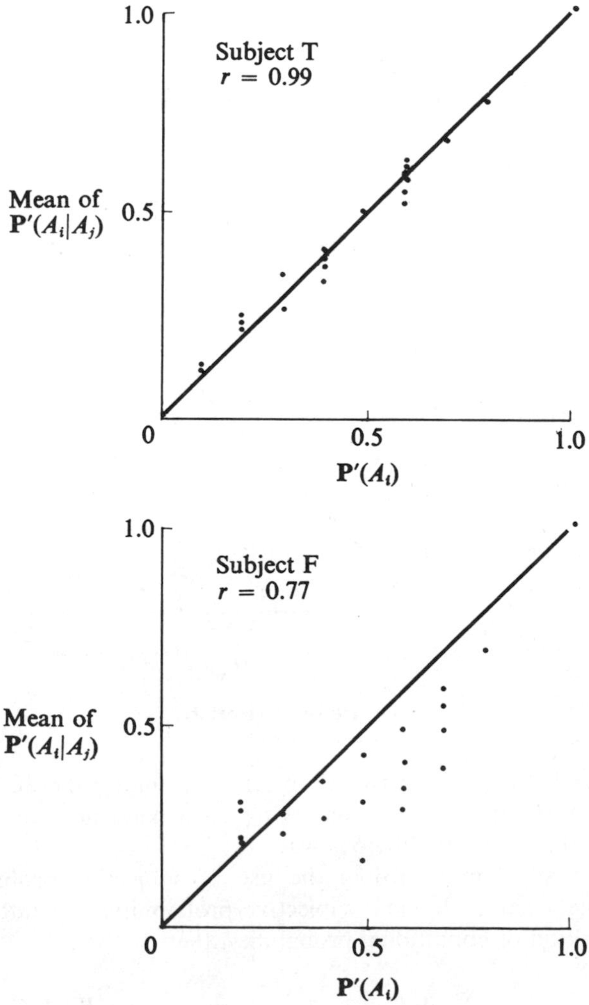

Figure IX.31 (Part 1)

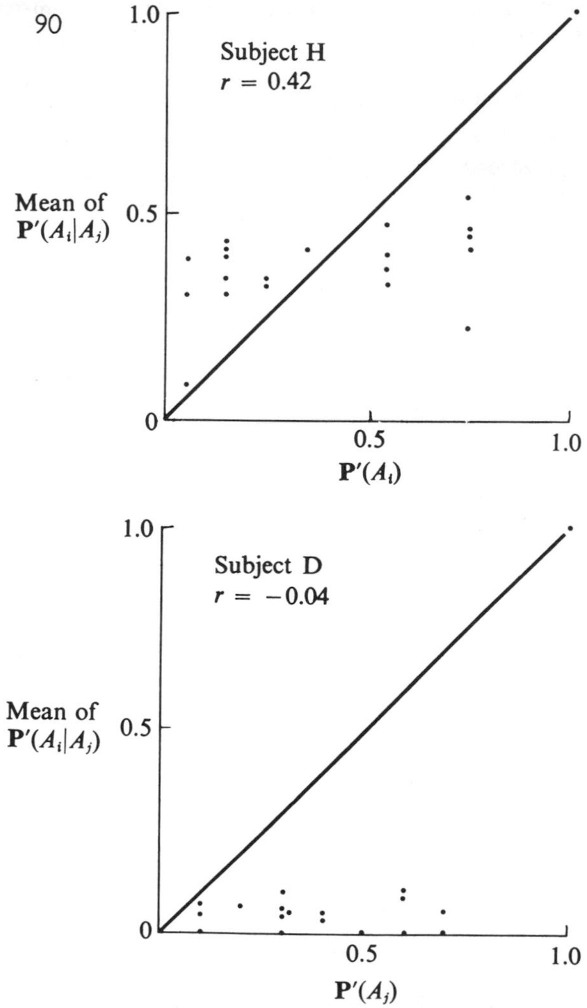

Figure IX.31 (Part 2)

compromise between these two (Subject F is among these), and others (like Subject H) appear to be operating on a basis not connected with probability theory in any obvious way.

A second question regarding the use of subjective probability was asked of these data. If these subjective probabilities operate according to the definition of conditional probability, then

$$\mathbf{P}'(A_i \mid A_j) = \frac{\mathbf{P}'(A_i \cap A_j)}{\mathbf{P}'(A_j)} \quad \text{and} \quad \mathbf{P}'(A_j \mid A_i) = \frac{\mathbf{P}'(A_i \cap A_j)}{\mathbf{P}'(A_i)}.$$

Multiplying both sides of the equation on the left by $\mathbf{P}'(A_j)$ gives

$$\mathbf{P}'(A_j)\mathbf{P}'(A_i \mid A_j) = \mathbf{P}'(A_i \cap A_j),$$

and multiplying both sides of the right-hand equation by $\mathbf{P}'(A_i)$ gives

$$\mathbf{P}'(A_i)\mathbf{P}'(A_j \mid A_i) = \mathbf{P}'(A_i \cap A_j).$$

Then,

$$\mathbf{P}'(A_i)\mathbf{P}'(A_j \mid A_i) = \mathbf{P}'(A_j)\mathbf{P}'(A_i \mid A_j),$$

since both sides of this equation are equal to $\mathbf{P}'(A_i \cap A_j)$. If the subjects' subjective probabilities follow the mathematical definition of conditional probability, then a plot of $\mathbf{P}'(A_i)\mathbf{P}'(A_j \mid A_i)$ against $\mathbf{P}'(A_j)\mathbf{P}'(A_i \mid A_j)$ should yield points lying close to a straight, 45-degree line that rises to the right. Plots of the actual relationship appear in Figure IX.32 for the 4 subjects discussed above. The sample correlation coefficient for each plot appears in the upper left-hand corner.

There is a tendency for the points in these plots to pile up near the origin. If this were not the case, the correlation for Subject H would probably be close to zero instead of 0.31, so that one is inclined to conclude that there is little tendency for Subject H to follow the mathematical definition of conditional probability. On the other hand, the correlation of 0.89 for Subject T indicates a rather strong proclivity for the mathematical rule. The other two subjects seem to be roughly guided by the rule, but they are less precise in its application than Subject T.

These data indicate that there are substantial individual differences in the extent to which subjective probability estimates conform to the mathematical definition of conditional probability. However Peterson et al.[12] found that correlations of the type reported in Figure IX.32 were lower for subjects who showed high variability due to error in their subjective probability estimates. It may be that the apparent inapplicability of probability theory found for some subjects is attributable to the obliteration of a systematic relationship by high variable error (see Section I.4). This seems plausible since more stable methods for assessing subjective probabilities led to higher correlations.[13]

IX.9
PROBLEMS ON COVARIANCE AND CORRELATION

1. Among grade-school children, the population correlation between mental age and weight is positive and quite high. Among adults, the population

[12] Peterson, C. R., Z. J. Ulehla, A. J. Miller, L. E. Bourne, Jr., and D. W. Stilson, "Internal consistency of subjective probabilities." *J. Exp. Psychol.*, in press. The, experiment leading to the data of Figures IX.31 and IX.32 is described and discussed in this paper along with two other experiments.

[13] *Ibid.*

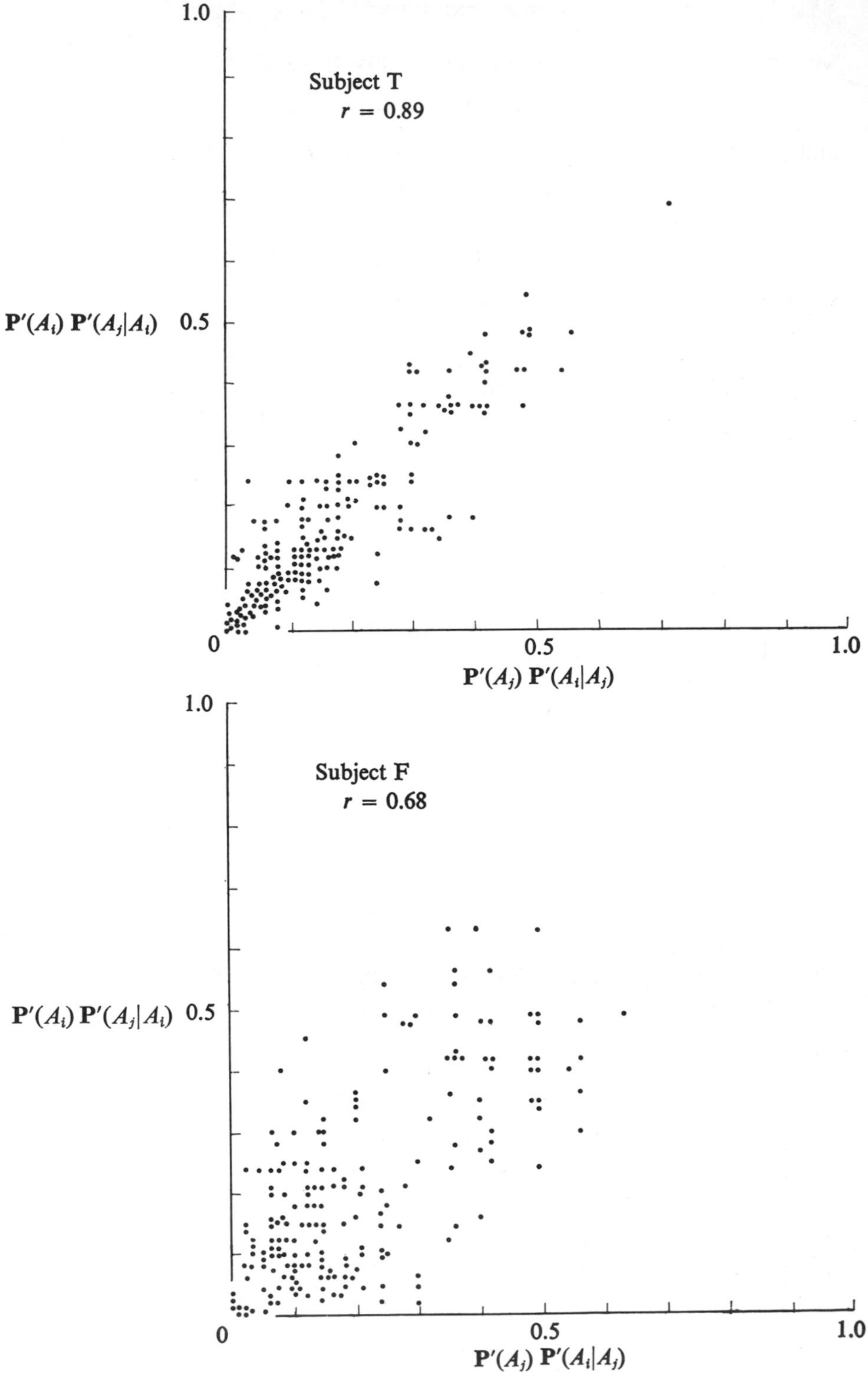

Figure IX.32 (Part 1)

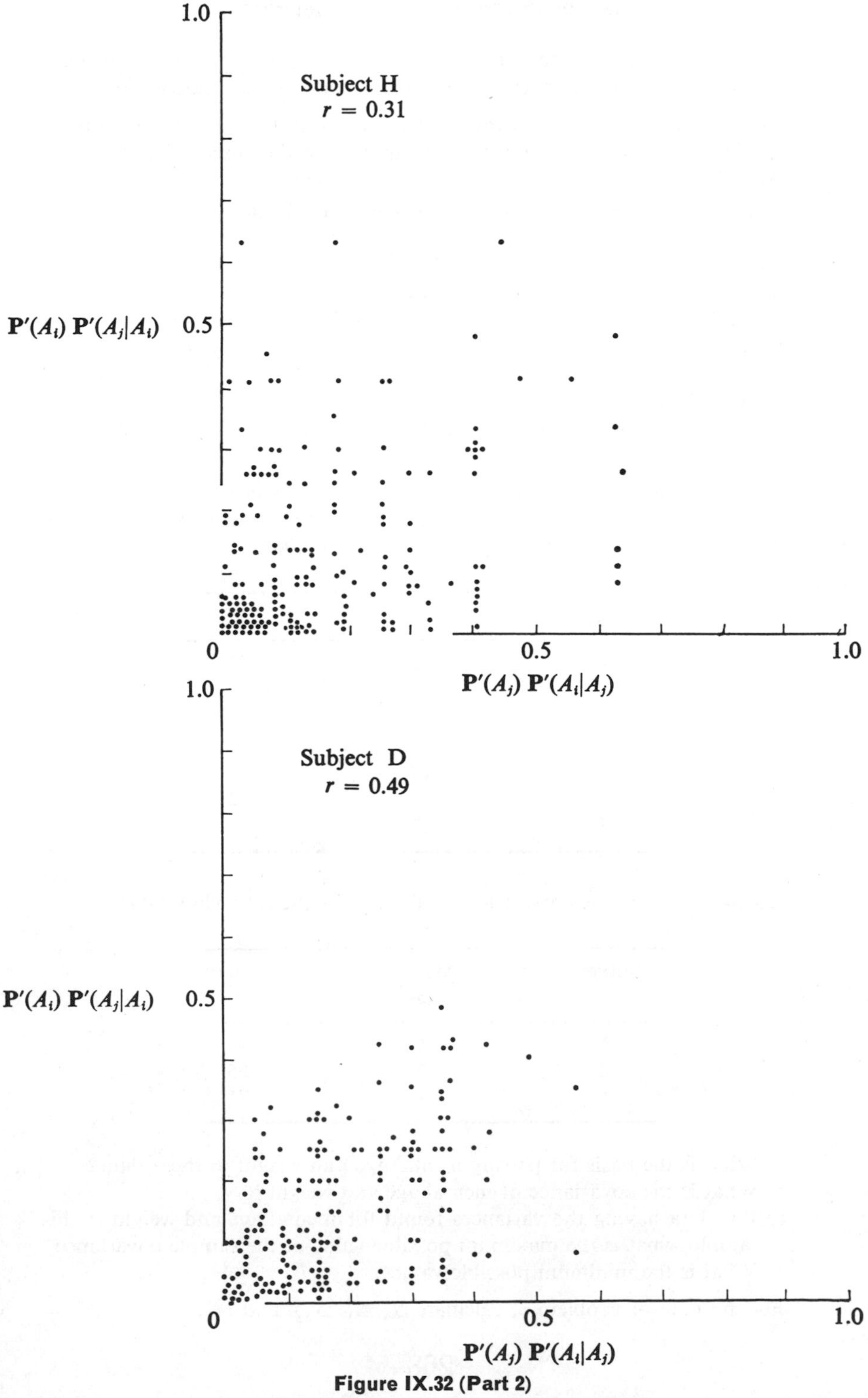

Figure IX.32 (Part 2)

correlation between these two variables is positive but close to zero. Comment on the difference between these two bivariate populations.

2. Roll a four-sided die and a three-sided die. Call the number of spots on the four-sided die X. Subtract the number on the three-sided die from X, and call the result D.
   a. Find the bivariate probability distribution of X and D.
   b. Find σ_X^2 and σ_D^2.
   c. What formula did you use in b?
   d. What other formula could you have used in b?
   e. Find the covariance of X and D.
   f. In e, did you use $E[(X - \mu_X)(D - \mu_D)]$ or $E(XD) - \mu_X\mu_D$?
   g. Which of the formulas in f do you think is simpler for the problem of e?
   h. What is the value of ρ_{XD}?
   i. Briefly analyze the mechanism that produces covariation between X and D.

3. Plot the following bivariate data. By visual inspection of this plot, decide whether the correlation coefficient for these data is closest to 1.00, 0.95, 0.80, 0.50, 0, −0.50, −0.80, −0.95, or −1.00.

Subject	X	Y
1	7	21
2	7	24
3	9	21
4	11	17
5	14	17
6	16	12
7	17	13

4. Calculate the sample correlation coefficient for the following data:

Subject	Mental age	Weight
1	5	45
2	7	55
3	9	71

   a. What is the basis for pairing mental age and weight in these data?
   b. What is the covariance of mental age and weight?
   c. For data having the variances found for mental age and weight in this sample, what is the maximum possible value of the sample covariance? What is the minimum possible value?

5. For the data of Problem 3, calculate S_X, S_Y, S_{XY}, and r_{XY}.

IX.10

DEGREES OF FREEDOM

Many estimators have associated with them a quantity called *degrees of freedom.* For example, the number of degrees of freedom associated with the sample variance is $n - 1$. As we have seen, the use of $n - 1$ in the formula for S^2 makes it an unbiased estimator for σ^2, but its significance extends beyond this. In fact, the concept of degrees of freedom plays an important role in connection with other estimators, including S_{XY}, r_{XY}, and $\bar{X}$, and the purpose of this section is to introduce a geometric interpretation of degrees of freedom.

In general, *the number of degrees of freedom associated with an estimator is defined as the number of independent dimensions with respect to which it is free to vary as a function of random sampling variability in the observations on which it is based.* We shall begin by illustrating the applicability of this concept to the sample mean. It turns out that, for a random sample of any size, $\bar{X}$ has one degree of freedom associated with it.

If X_1 is the observation variable of a random sample of size 1, then its random variability can be represented by a single dimension. Since $\bar{X} = X_1$ for $n = 1$, variation in $\bar{X}$ due to random sampling variability is also unidimensional, so that $\bar{X}$ has one degree of freedom associated with it when $n = 1$.

When $n = 2$, each possible sample can be represented by a point in a two-dimensional space in which the coordinate axes represent the observation variables, X_1 and X_2. By examining the graph of such a space in Figure IX.33, we discover that *every* sample for which $\bar{X} = 1.0$ is represented by a point on the straight line labeled $\bar{X} = 1.0$. This should not be surprising since the sample mean is a linear function of the two observations (i.e., $\bar{X} = (1/n)X_1 + (1/n)X_2$), and, as shown in Appendix VIII.1, a function of this kind is represented graphically by a straight line. Similarly, all samples for which $\bar{X}$ has a particular value are located on a single straight line. For example, the samples (3, 0), (1.5, 1.5), and (1, 2) all have means of 1.5 and all are represented by points on the straight line labeled $\bar{X} = 1.5$ in the figure. If one such line is constructed for each value in the range of $\bar{X}$, then a family of parallel lines is formed. Now notice that there is *no* variability in $\bar{X}$ among samples falling on any single line. $\bar{X}$ only varies from one parallel line to another along the broken line that passes through the origin in Figure IX.33. Since this broken line is unidimensional, $\bar{X}$ is sensitive to random sampling variability in only one dimension, giving it one degree of freedom when $n = 2$.

In Figure IX.34, an analogous graph is shown for $n = 3$. Thus, any sample for which $\bar{X} = 1.0$ is represented by a point that falls on the plane labeled $\bar{X} = 1.0$. (For the sake of clarity, only a portion of each plane

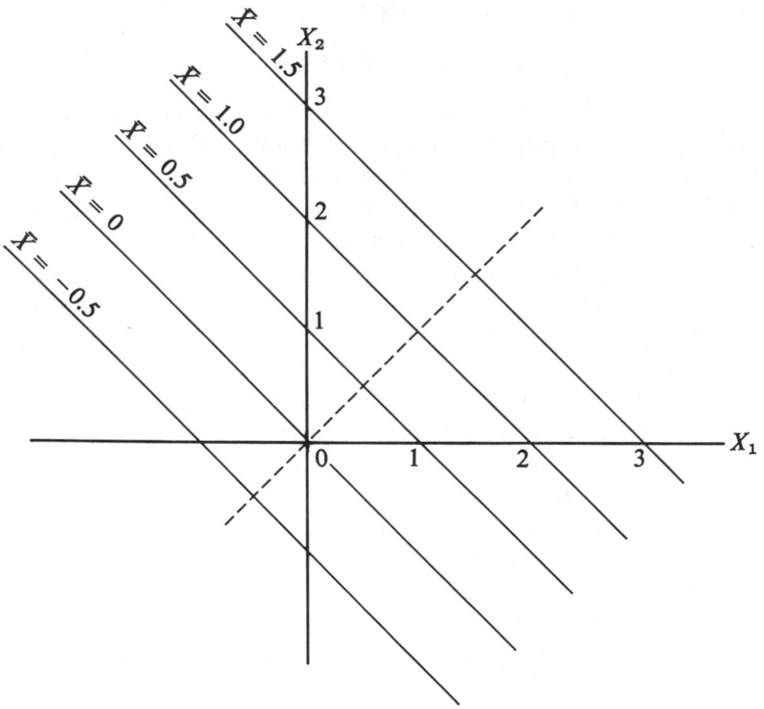

Figure IX.33

is shown.) For example, the samples (3, 0, 0), (2, 1, 0), and (1, 1, 1) are each represented by points in this plane. Furthermore, all samples represented by points in one such plane have the same mean. Therefore, there is no variation in $\bar{X}$ among samples represented by points in a single plane. The only variation in the sample mean that can be attributed to sampling variability is that between planes. This between-plane variability can be represented by points along the single broken line in Figure IX.34. Therefore, $\bar{X}$ varies with respect to one dimension, giving it one degree of freedom when $n = 3$.

Graphic representation becomes impossible for $n > 3$, but one degree of freedom is associated with the mean of a random sample of any size. Perhaps some intuitive grasp of this can be obtained from the preceding illustrations.

Next, the number of degrees of freedom associated with estimators for the population variance will be discussed. To begin with, consider

$$Q^2 = \frac{\sum_k (X_k - \mu)^2}{n}$$

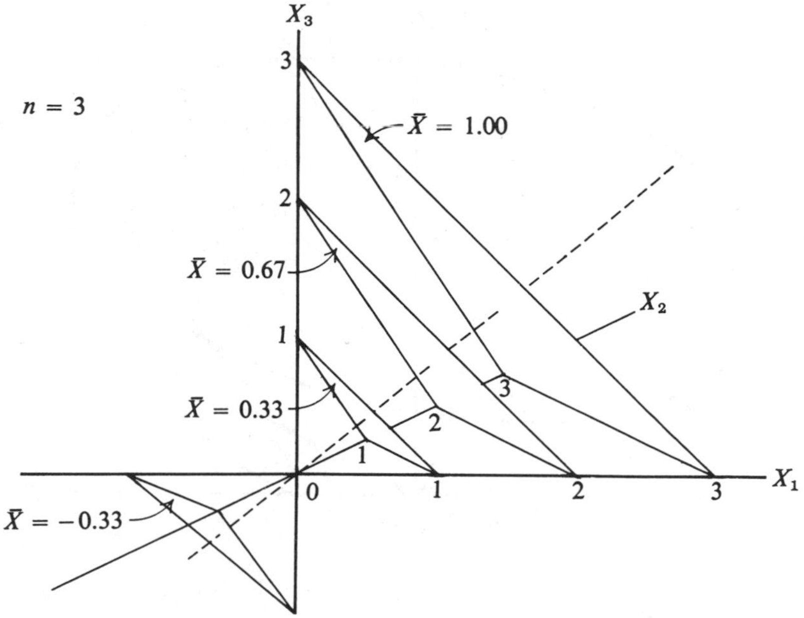

Figure IX.34

for $n = 1$. By plotting Q^2 as a function of $X_1 - \mu$, as shown in Figure IX.35, the value of Q^2 can be seen to vary as a function of random variability in $X_1 - \mu$, which can be represented by one dimension. Therefore, there is one degree of freedom associated with Q^2 when $n = 1$.

Similarly, variability in Q^2 as a function of $X_1 - \mu$ and $X_2 - \mu$ is shown in Figure IX.36 for $n = 2$. Since Q^2 varies as a function of random fluctuation in both $X_1 - \mu$ and $X_2 - \mu$, Q^2 has two degrees of freedom

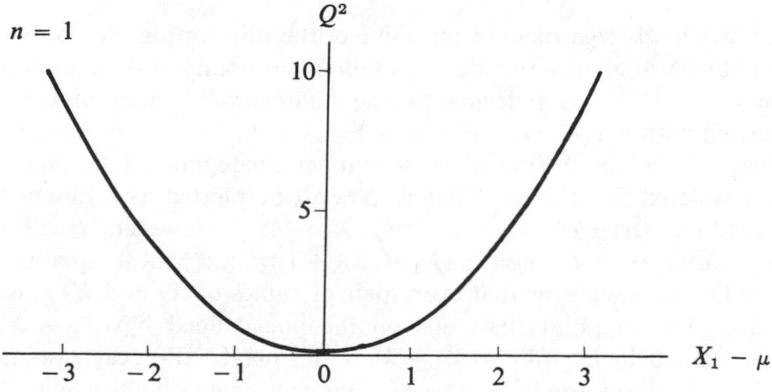

Figure IX.35

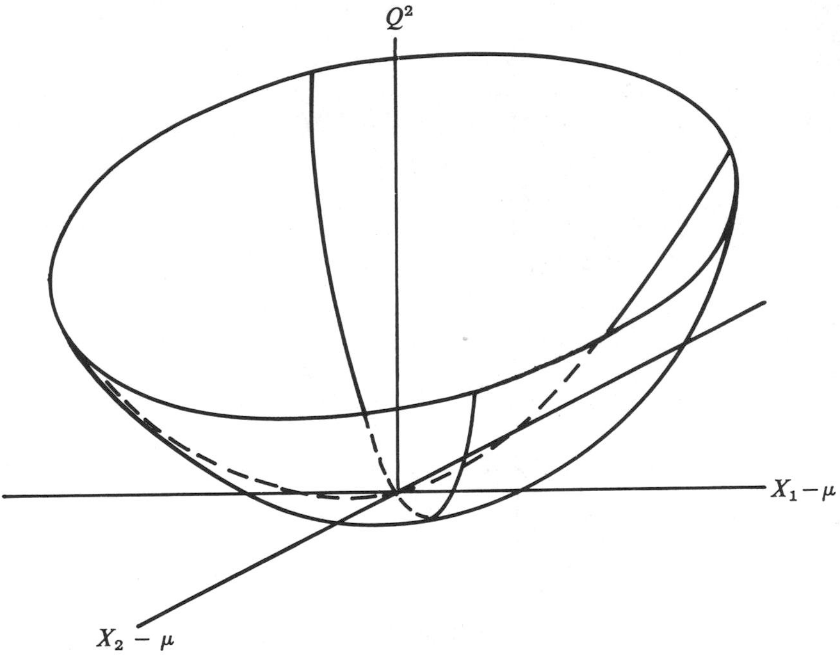

Figure IX.36

associated with it when $n = 2$. Similarly, there are n degrees of freedom associated with Q^2 for a random sample of size n.

From this, one might expect that there are n degrees of freedom associated with the estimator S^2, but, as stated earlier, this is not the case. For example, suppose that $n = 1$. Then,

$$S^2 = \frac{(X_1 - \bar{X})^2}{n - 1} = \frac{(X_1 - X_1)^2}{1 - 1} = \frac{0}{0}.$$

This result holds regardless of the value of the observation X_1, so that S^2 does not vary at all as a function of random variability in the observation when $n = 1$. This is reflected by the number of degrees of freedom associated with S^2, which is $n - 1 = 1 - 1 = 0$.

Now, S^2 will be examined in a manner analogous to the way Q^2 was considered for $n = 2$. That is, S^2 will be plotted as a function of the random variables $X_1 - \bar{X}$ and $X_2 - \bar{X}$. However, recall that $\sum(X - \bar{X}) = 0$, so, for $n = 2$, $(X_1 - \bar{X}) + (X_2 - \bar{X})$ must equal 0. In Figure IX.37, this means that every pair of values of X_1 and X_2 must be represented by a point that falls on the line defined by $(X_1 - \bar{X}) + (X_2 - \bar{X}) = 0$ in the $(X_1 - \bar{X})$—$(X_2 - \bar{X})$ plane. For each point on this line, the corresponding value of S^2 is represented by a height. But since S^2 varies only as a function of random variability along the line

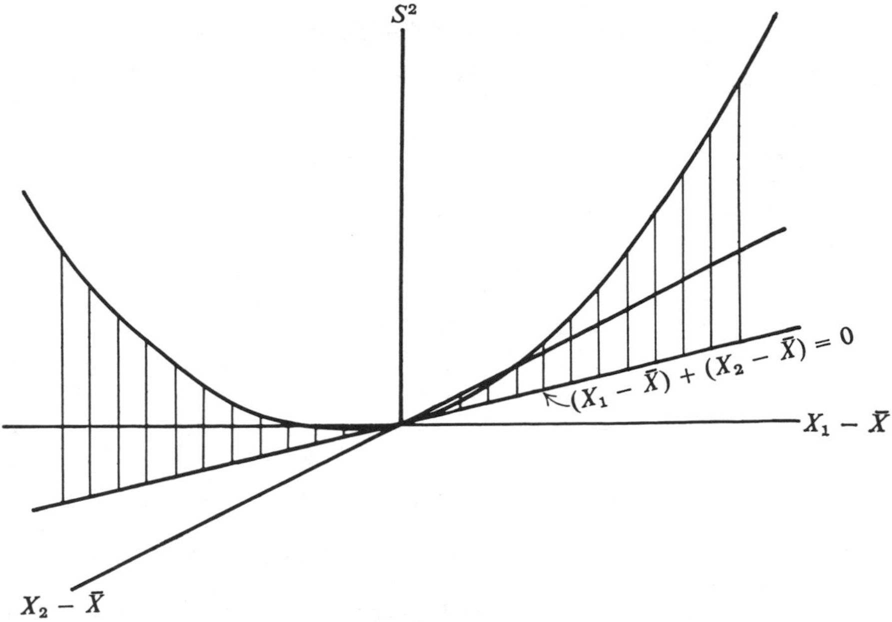

Figure IX.37

$(X_1 - \bar{X}) + (X_2 - \bar{X}) = 0$, it reflects sampling variability along only one dimension. Therefore, S^2 has $n - 1 = 2 - 1 = 1$ degree of freedom associated with it when $n = 2$. Similarly, when $n = 3$, the random variability reflected by S^2 is limited to a plane defined by the restriction $(X_1 - \bar{X}) + (X_2 - \bar{X}) + (X_3 - \bar{X}) = 0$, so that the number of degrees of freedom associated with S^2 equals the number of dimensions of this plane, $n - 1 = 3 - 1 = 2$.

Graphic representation is impossible for $n > 3$, but, again, the number of degrees of freedom associated with S^2 is $n - 1$ for any sample size.[14]

By similar although somewhat more complicated methods, it is possible to illustrate that there are $n - 1$ degrees of freedom associated with the sample covariance and $n - 2$ associated with the sample correlation coefficient. Due to the awkwardness of treating them graphically, these applications of the concept of degrees of freedom will not be elaborated, but it is hoped that the examples given will provide some intuitive grasp of the idea.

[14] It is often said that one degree of freedom is "lost" due to the restriction imposed by estimating $\bar{X}$, on which S^2 depends (i.e., by the restriction $\sum (X - \bar{X}) = 0$). Although this is true for S^2, it is a very narrow interpretation of degrees of freedom. For example, there is one degree of freedom associated with $\bar{X}$ for any sample size, so that, by this interpretation, $n - 1$ have been "lost." But $\bar{X}$ does not depend on restrictions imposed by any other estimator.

IX.10.1. Problems on degrees of freedom

1. For $n = 10$, how many degrees of freedom are associated with the estimators
   a. $\bar{X}$?
   b. S^2?
   c. Q^2?

2. For the random sample of size 2 shown in the table, find S_{XY}, S_X, S_Y, and r_{XY}.

Subject	Mental age (X)	Weight (Y)
1	8	80
2	12	60

   a. What are the values of these estimates?
   b. Can you invent a sample of $n = 2$ bivariate observations for which $r_{XY} \neq 1$?
   c. What does your answer to b have to do with the number of degrees of freedom associated with r_{XY}?
   d. If μ_X and μ_Y were known, would this affect the number of degrees of freedom for estimates of the population correlation coefficient?

3. For a sample of $n = 2$ observations, $\bar{X} = 7$ and $S^2 = 8$. What are the observations?

4. Does the fact that it is possible to find an answer to Problem 3 have anything to do with degrees of freedom? Explain.

5. For the mental age data of Problem 2,
   a. What is the estimate of the third central moment?
   b. Does this result suggest that the population PD is symmetrical?
   c. Does your answer to a have anything to do with the number of degrees of freedom for this estimator? Why?

IX.11
SOME RULES FOR FINDING VARIANCES

We will encounter a number of statistical problems that can be handled with the aid of a few rules regarding the variance of sums and linear functions of random variables. These rules are introduced in the remaining sections of this chapter.

IX.11.1. Variance of a sum of two random variables

If X and Y are random variables having variances ${\sigma_X}^2$ and ${\sigma_Y}^2$, respectively, then the variance of $X + Y$ is

$$\sigma^2_{X+Y} = {\sigma_X}^2 + {\sigma_Y}^2 + 2\sigma_{XY}, \qquad \text{[IX.28]}$$

where σ_{XY} is the covariance of X and Y. This relation can be expressed in terms of the correlation coefficient as well, since

$$\rho_{XY} = \frac{\sigma_{XY}}{\sigma_X \sigma_Y}$$

and

$$\rho_{XY}\sigma_X\sigma_Y = \sigma_{XY}.$$

Substituting $\rho_{XY}\sigma_X\sigma_Y$ for σ_{XY} in Formula [IX.28] gives

$$\sigma^2_{X+Y} = \sigma_X{}^2 + \sigma_Y{}^2 + 2\rho_{XY}\sigma_X\sigma_Y, \qquad \text{[IX.29]}$$

a second form for the same rule.

If the two variables constituting the sum are positively correlated, then a high value on one variable will be more likely to occur in conjunction with a high value on the other. This makes the probability of large values of the sum greater than it would be if the correlation were zero. Also, since low values on one of the variables are more likely to be associated with low values on the other, the probability of very small sums is greater when the correlation is positive. Thus, the formula for σ^2_{X+Y} includes the term $2\sigma_{XY}$ (or $2\rho_{XY}\sigma_X\sigma_Y$) to account for this added dispersion.

If the correlation is negative, the term $2\sigma_{XY}$ becomes negative. This is because a negative correlation reduces the probability of extreme sums, so that the variance of the sum is less when they are negatively correlated than when the correlation is positive or zero.

A derivation of Formula [IX.28] follows. First, let $W = X + Y$. Then,

$$\begin{aligned}\sigma^2_{X+Y} = \sigma_W{}^2 &= E(W^2) - (\mu_W)^2 \\ &= E[(X + Y)^2] - (\mu_X + \mu_Y)^2.\end{aligned}$$

Then,

$$\begin{aligned}\sigma^2_{X+Y} &= E(X^2 + 2XY + Y^2) - (\mu_X{}^2 + 2\mu_X\mu_Y + \mu_Y{}^2) \\ &= E(X^2) + 2E(XY) + E(Y^2) - \mu_X{}^2 - 2\mu_X\mu_Y - \mu_Y{}^2 \\ &= [E(X^2) - \mu_X{}^2] + [E(Y^2) - \mu_Y{}^2] + 2[E(XY) - \mu_X\mu_Y] \\ &= \sigma_X{}^2 + \sigma_Y{}^2 + 2\sigma_{XY}.\end{aligned}$$

If Formula [IX.28] is applied to the sum of B and R in the example using red plus white dice and blue plus white dice,

$$\begin{aligned}\sigma^2_{B+R} &= \sigma_B{}^2 + \sigma_R{}^2 + 2\sigma_{BR} \\ &= 5.83 + 5.83 + 2(3.03) \\ &= 17.72.\end{aligned}$$

Using Formula [IX.29],

$$\begin{aligned}\sigma^2_{B+R} &= \sigma_B{}^2 + \sigma_R{}^2 + 2\rho_{BR}\sigma_B\sigma_R \\ &= 5.83 + 5.83 + 2(0.52)(2.415)(2.415) \\ &= 17.72.\end{aligned}$$

If the calculations for the example of Section IX.8.4 (Table IX.6) are used to estimate σ^2_{B+R}, the estimate is exactly analogous to Formula [IX.28]:

$$\begin{aligned}S^2_{B+R} &= S_B{}^2 + S_R{}^2 + 2S_{BR} \\ &= 5.57 + 3.73 + 2(2.38) \\ &= 14.06.\end{aligned}$$

Notice that if X and Y have zero covariance, then the variance of their sum is

$$\sigma^2_{X+Y} = \sigma_X{}^2 + \sigma_Y{}^2. \qquad \text{[IX.30]}$$

IX.11.2. Variance of a sum of three or more random variables

In order to compute the variance of the sum of three random variables, X, Y, and Z, it is easiest to set $W = X + Y$ and then find the variance of $W + Z$. Thus,

$$\sigma^2_{X+Y+Z} = \sigma^2_{W+Z} = \sigma_W{}^2 + \sigma_Z{}^2 + 2\sigma_{WZ}.$$

But since $W = X + Y$,

$$\sigma_W{}^2 = \sigma_X{}^2 + \sigma_Y{}^2 + 2\sigma_{XY}.$$

Substituting this in the expression for σ^2_{X+Y+Z} gives

$$\begin{aligned}\sigma^2_{X+Y+Z} = \sigma^2_{W+Z} &= \sigma_W{}^2 + \sigma_Z{}^2 + 2\sigma_{WZ} \\ &= \sigma_X{}^2 + \sigma_Y{}^2 + 2\sigma_{XY} + \sigma_Z{}^2 + 2\sigma_{WZ}.\end{aligned}$$

To find σ_{WZ} in terms of X, Y, and Z, find

$$\begin{aligned}\sigma_{WZ} &= E(WZ) - \mu_W\mu_Z \\ &= E[(X + Y)(Z)] - (\mu_X + \mu_Y)(\mu_Z) = E[XZ + YZ] \\ &\qquad - (\mu_X\mu_Z + \mu_Y\mu_Z) \\ &= E(XZ) + E(YZ) - \mu_X\mu_Z - \mu_Y\mu_Z = E(XZ) - \mu_X\mu_Z \\ &\qquad + E(YZ) - \mu_Y\mu_Z \\ &= \sigma_{XZ} + \sigma_{YZ}.\end{aligned}$$

Returning to the last expression for σ^2_{X+Y+Z} and substituting $\sigma_{XZ} + \sigma_{YZ}$ for σ_{WZ},

$$\begin{aligned}\sigma^2_{X+Y+Z} &= \sigma_X{}^2 + \sigma_Y{}^2 + 2\sigma_{XY} + \sigma_Z{}^2 + 2(\sigma_{XZ} + \sigma_{YZ}) \\ &= \sigma_X{}^2 + \sigma_Y{}^2 + \sigma_Z{}^2 + 2\sigma_{XY} + 2\sigma_{XZ} + 2\sigma_{YZ}.\end{aligned}$$

One can show[15] that *the variance of the sum of the random variables* $X_1, X_2, \ldots, X_m$ *is*

$$\sigma^2_{X_1+X_2+\cdots+X_m} = \sigma^2_{X_1} + \sigma^2_{X_2} + \cdots + \sigma^2_{X_m} + \underbrace{2\sigma_{X_1X_2} + 2\sigma_{X_1X_3} + \cdots + 2\sigma_{X_{m-1}X_m}}_{m(m-1)/2 \text{ terms}}. \quad [IX.31]$$

Of course, since $\sigma_{X_iX_j} = \rho_{X_iX_j}\sigma_{X_i}\sigma_{X_j}$, *the* $\rho_{X_iX_j}\sigma_{X_i}\sigma_{X_j}$ *can be substituted for the* $\sigma_{X_iX_j}$ *in Formula* [IX.31].

Notice that the number of covariance terms, $2\sigma_{X_iX_j}$, in Formula [IX.31] equals the number of groups of size 2 that can be selected from among m items. That is, there are $\binom{m}{2} = m(m-1)/2$ such terms.

If the variance of a sum of random variables is to be estimated from sample information, then

$$S^2_{X_1+X_2+\cdots+X_m} = S^2_{X_1} + S^2_{X_2} + \cdots + S^2_{X_m} + \underbrace{2S_{X_1X_2} + 2S_{X_1X_3} + \cdots + 2S_{X_{m-1}X_m}}_{m(m-1)/2 \text{ terms}} \quad [IX.32]$$

provides such an estimate.

IX.11.3. Variance of a linear function of random variables

If $A, B_1, B_2 \ldots, B_m$ *are constants and* $X_1, X_2, \ldots, X_m$ *are random variables, then the variance of the linear function* $A + B_1X_1 + \cdots + B_mX_m$ *is*

$$\sigma^2_{A+B_1X_1+\cdots+B_mX_m} = B_1{}^2\sigma^2_{X_1} + \cdots + B_m{}^2\sigma^2_{X_m} + \underbrace{2B_1B_2\sigma_{X_1X_2} + \cdots + 2B_{m-1}B_m\sigma_{X_{m-1}X_m}}_{m(m-1)/2 \text{ terms}}. \quad [IX.33]$$

One of the most important applications of this rule is to find the variance of a difference, $X_1 - X_2$. In this difference, $A = 0$, $B_1 = 1$, and $B_2 = -1$. Then applying Formula [IX.33],

$$\sigma^2_{X_1-X_2} = B_1{}^2\sigma^2_{X_1} + B_2{}^2\sigma^2_{X_2} + 2B_1B_2\sigma^2_{X_1X}$$
$$= \sigma^2_{X_1} + \sigma^2_{X_2} - 2\sigma^2_{X_2X_1}.$$

For the three-dice example, the variance of $B - R$ is

$$\sigma^2_{B-R} = \sigma_B{}^2 + \sigma_R{}^2 - 2\sigma_{BR}$$
$$= 5.83 + 5.83 - 2(3.03)$$
$$= 5.60.$$

[15] A general proof can be constructed by the method of mathematical induction.

Notice that a positive correlation between X_1 and X_2 decreases the variance of $X_1 - X_2$ and that a negative correlation increases it. This is exactly the opposite of the effect of correlation on the variance of a sum of two random variables. An expression exactly analogous to Formula [IX.33] can be used to estimate the variance of a linear function of random variables from sample information.

IX.12

PROBLEMS ON THE VARIANCE OF LINEAR FUNCTIONS OF RANDOM VARIABLES

1. Refer to the example of the random variables B and R that were introduced in Section VII.3.1 (Table VII.8).
   a. Find the variance of $B + R$.
   b. Find the variance of $6(B + R)$.
   c. Find the variance of $+2 - 6B + 3R$.
   d. Find the variance of $-1000 - 6B + 3R$.
   e. Comment on the difference between σ^2_{B+R} and σ^2_{B-R}.
2. Suppose that a random sample of size n is drawn with replacement from a population in which the variance is σ^2. Label these observations X_1, $X_2, \ldots, X_n$. Since sampling is with replacement, the variance of the first observation is σ^2, the variance of the second is σ^2, and so on.
   a. What is the variance of $X_1 + X_2 + \cdots + X_n$?
   b. What is the variance of

$$\bar{X} = \frac{1}{n} X_1 + \frac{1}{n} X_2 + \cdots + \frac{1}{n} X_n?$$

   c. What is the standard deviation of $\bar{X}$?
3. In the first illustrative example of Section IX.8.1 (Fig. IX.25) the covariance was shown to be zero. What is the variance of $X + Y$ where X is the face of a coin and Y the face of the six-sided die?

SUGGESTED READING

1. Almost any modern text in statistics provides a discussion of the descriptive measures discussed in this chapter.
2. Wallis, W. A., and H. V. Roberts, *Statistics: A New Approach.* New York, Free Press of Glencoe, 1956.
   The chapters in this book on averages, variability, and correlation provide excellent discussions of most of the measures introduced here.
3. Goedicke, V., *Introduction to the Theory of Statistics.* New York, Harpers, 1953, pp. 201–212.
   This provides a discussion of the rule for finding the variance of a sum.

X

USEFUL PROBABILITY DISTRIBUTIONS AND DENSITY FUNCTIONS

THIS chapter is devoted to some probability distributions and density functions that are useful in statistics or in the formulation of psychological theory. Although only a few of the most important are included, others are discussed in the references given at the end of the chapter.

A probability distribution or density function is determined by (1) the characteristics of the population from which observations are made, (2) the method of sampling, and (3) the random variable on which the observations are made. Given sufficient information concerning these three things, it is sometimes possible to deduce the PD or DF of a variable. Examples of this appear in the following sections.

X.1
PROBABILITY DISTRIBUTIONS

X.1.1. Binomial populations and the binomial distribution

If a population, S, is divided into two mutually exclusive and exhaustive subclasses, A and $S \sim A$, *so that the probability that a randomly chosen element will be from A is P and the probability that it will be from* $S \sim A$ *is* $1 - P$, *then the population is a binomial population.*

Many such populations can be found. The male-female dichotomy, right and wrong responses to a single test item, choosing black or white alternatives on a particular trial in a T-maze, and so on. In fact, we have already dealt with several problems involving binomial populations (e.g., tossing a single coin).

In a binomial population, an element from the subclass A can be assigned the value 1 and an element from $S \sim A$ the value 0. This amounts to defining a random variable with range (0, 1). The sample space on which this random variable is defined consists of all of the population elements. The random experiment is a random choice of an element from the population.

If this two-valued random variable is called Y, then for a finite population containing N elements,

$$\mathbf{P}(A) = P = \frac{\sum_j Y_j}{N}.$$

Since $Y = 1$ for each element in A and $Y = 0$ for each element in $S \sim A$, $\sum_j Y_j$ equals the number of elements in A. Dividing this number by N gives $\mathbf{P}(A) = P$. Furthermore, since

$$E(Y) = \sum \mathbf{P}(Y = y)y = P(1) + (1 - P)(0) = P,$$

P is also the expected value of Y.

Suppose that $Y = 1$ for each male in the student body of a particular university and $Y = 0$ for each female. Then, if 6000 of the 10,000 in the student body are males,

$$\begin{aligned} E(Y) &= P(1) + (1 - P)(0) = \frac{6000}{10{,}000}(1) + \left(1 - \frac{6000}{10{,}000}\right)(0) \\ &= 0.6, \end{aligned}$$

the proportion of males.

Later, we will have occasion to use the variance of Y. This can be found easily. First, notice that $(0)^2 = 0$ and $(1)^2 = 1$. Consequently, $E(Y) = E(Y^2) = P$. Then, applying Formula [IX.8] for the population variance,

$$\begin{aligned} \sigma_Y^2 &= E(Y^2) - [E(Y)]^2 = P - P^2 \\ &= P(1 - P). \end{aligned}$$

The standard deviation of Y is $\sqrt{[\mathbf{P}(1 - P)]}$.

For the example involving men and women in a university student body, the variance of Y is $\sigma_Y^2 = P(1 - P) = 0.6(1 - 0.6) = 0.24$.

Sampling from a binomial population: the binomial distribution. When sampling from a binomial population, it is usually the number of elements from the class A that is included in a sample that is important. If a random sample of size n is drawn with replacement from a finite binomial population, and a one is assigned to every element from A, and a zero to every element from $S \sim A$, then an outcome is an ordered set of n elements, each of which is either 0 or 1. For example, the random sample (1, 0, 1, 1, 0, 0, 1, 0, 1, 1) might be the outcome for the random experiment "draw a random sample of size 10 with replacement" from the student body described above. Then,

$$\sum_{k=1}^{10} Y_k = 1 + 0 + 1 + 1 + 0 + 0 + 1 + 0 + 1 + 1 = 6$$

is the number of men in this random sample. In more general terms, if the random variable X is defined by $X = \sum_k Y_k$, then X is the number of elements that are from the subclass A of a binomial population, and the range of X is $(0, 1, \ldots, n)$. *If a random sample of size n is drawn with replacement from any binomial population, or without replacement from an infinite binomial population, then*

$$\mathbf{P}(X = x) = \binom{n}{x} P^x(1 - P)^{n-x} \qquad \text{[X.1]}$$

is the probability that exactly x of the elements of the sample are from subclass A of the population. This probability distribution is called the binomial probability distribution.

In order to show how this formula was obtained, the joint probability of exactly x elements from A and exactly $n - x$ from $S \sim A$ must be found. Since sampling is random, the observations are mutually independent, and $P^x(1 - P)^{n-x}$ is the probability of exactly x elements from A and $n - x$ from $S \sim A$ *in a particular order*. Now, notice that there are $\binom{n}{x}$ distinguishable orders for a group containing x 1's and $(n - x)$ 0's, and that these orders are mutually exclusive.[1] Consequently, $\mathbf{P}(X = x)$ is simply the sum of the probabilities of the $\binom{n}{x}$ outcomes in the event $X = x$. Since each of these outcomes has probability $P^x(1 - P)^{n-x}$, this sum is

$$\mathbf{P}(X = x) = \binom{n}{x} P^x(1 - P)^{n-x}.$$

This is the probability given in Formula [X.1].

In the student-body example,

$$\mathbf{P}(X = x) = \binom{n}{x} P^x(1 - P)^{n-x}$$

$$\mathbf{P}(X = 6) = \binom{10}{6}(0.6)^6(0.4)^{10-6}$$

$$= 0.251;$$

the probability of exactly 6 men in a random sample of size 10. The

[1] For example, if $n = 3$ it is impossible that the outcomes (1, 1, 0) and (1, 0, 1) both occur.

binomial PD for $X =$ "the number of men in a sample of size 10" is shown graphically in Figure X.1. The probability was obtained for each value of X by applying Formula [X.1].

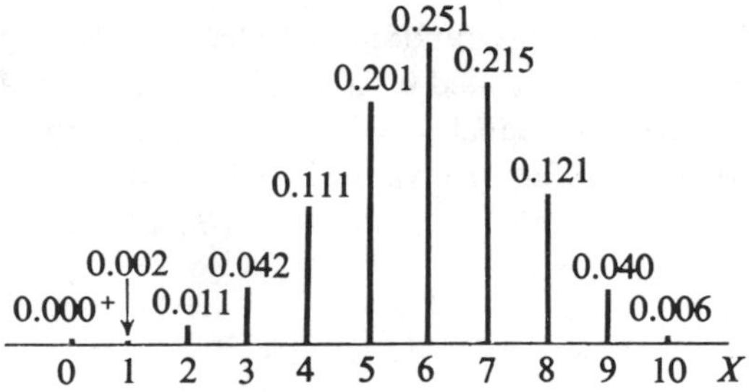

Figure X.1

In many applications, it is not the probabilities associated with the single values of X that are of interest, but rather the probability that X will lie within certain limits. For example, $\mathbf{P}(4 \leq X \leq 7)$ can be calculated from Figure X.1 by

$$\begin{aligned}
\mathbf{P}(4 \leq X \leq 7) &= \mathbf{P}(X = 4) + \mathbf{P}(X = 5) + \mathbf{P}(X = 6) + \mathbf{P}(X = 7) \\
&= \binom{10}{4}(0.6)^4(0.4)^{10-4} + \binom{10}{5}(0.6)^5(0.4)^{10-5} \\
&\quad + \binom{10}{6}(0.6)^6(0.4)^{10-6} + \binom{10}{7}(0.6)^7(0.4)^{10-7} \\
&= 0.111 + 0.201 + 0.251 + 0.215 \\
&= 0.778.
\end{aligned}$$

In computing such probabilities for *discrete* random variables it is necessary to be very careful to interpret $>$, $<$, $\geq$, and $\leq$ correctly.

Another kind of calculation that is frequently useful is of the form $\mathbf{P}[(X < 1) \cup (X > 9)]$. In the example,

$$\begin{aligned}
\mathbf{P}[(X < 1) \cup (X > 9)] &= \mathbf{P}[(X = 0) \cup (X = 10)] \\
&= \mathbf{P}(X = 0) + \mathbf{P}(X = 10) \\
&= \binom{10}{0}(0.6)^0(0.4)^{10-0} + \binom{10}{10}(0.6)^{10}(0.4)^{10-10} \\
&= 0.000 + 0.006 \\
&= 0.006.
\end{aligned}$$

From this, it is easy to find $\mathbf{P}(1 \leq X \leq 9)$. Since $\mathbf{P}[(X < 1) \cup (X > 9)] = 0.006$,

$$\mathbf{P}(1 \leq X \leq 9) = 1 - \mathbf{P}[(X < 1) \cup (X > 9)] = 1 - 0.006 = 0.994.$$

CUMULATIVE BINOMIAL DISTRIBUTION FUNCTION. Cumulative binomial probabilities are frequently used in statistical applications. For the binomial PD, the probability that X is less than or equal to x_q is

$$\mathbf{P}(X \leq x_q) = \sum_{x=0}^{x_q} \mathbf{P}(X = x) = \sum_{x=0}^{x_q} \binom{n}{x} P^x (1 - P)^{n-x}.$$

In the example in Figure X.1, the value of the CDF for $x_q = 5$ is

$$\begin{aligned}\mathbf{P}(X \leq 5) &= \sum_{x=0}^{5} \binom{10}{x} P^x (1 - P)^{10-x} \\ &= \mathbf{P}(X = 0) + \mathbf{P}(X = 1) + \mathbf{P}(X = 2) + \mathbf{P}(X = 3) \\ &\qquad + \mathbf{P}(X = 4) + \mathbf{P}(X = 5) \\ &= 0.000 + 0.002 + 0.011 + 0.042 + 0.111 + 0.201 \\ &= 0.367.\end{aligned}$$

By applying such a calculation to each value of x_q, the CDF is obtained. This is shown graphically in Figure X.2.

CALCULATING BINOMIAL PROBABILITIES. There are several ways to facilitate the calculation of binomial probabilities. First, and most helpful, extensive tables of binomial probabilities have been constructed for many combinations of n and P. A list of such tables and their coverage

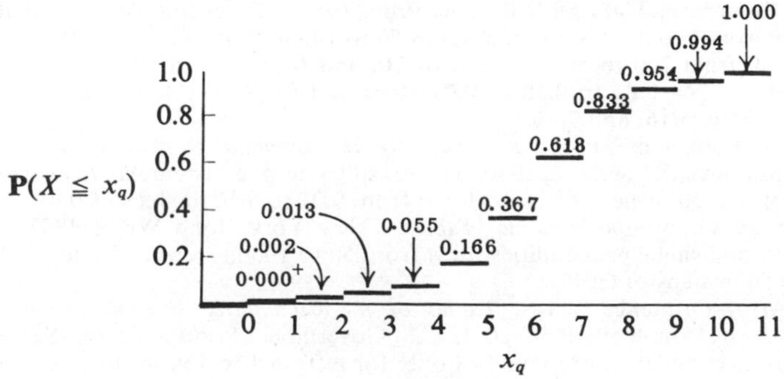

Figure X.2

is given below.[2] In addition, Appendix II of this book contains binomial probabilities for n from 2 to 25 in steps of 1 and for $P = 0.01, 0.05, 0.10, 0.20, 0.30, 0.40, 0.50, 0.60, 0.70, 0.80, 0.90, 0.95$, and 0.99. For example, if $n = 10$ and $P = 0.6$, the table gives $\mathbf{P}(X = 6) = 0.251$.

For combinations of n and P not found in readily available tables, the table of factorials and log factorials in Appendix I may prove useful.

MEAN AND VARIANCE OF A BINOMIAL DISTRIBUTION. For the two-valued variable Y, it has been shown that $E(Y) = P$ and that $\sigma_Y^2 = P(1 - P)$, Next, we shall find the mean and variance of $X = \sum_k Y_k$. By Formula [VIII.6],

$$\begin{aligned} E(X) = E\Big(\sum_k Y_k\Big) &= E(Y_1) + E(Y_2) + \cdots + E(Y_n) \\ &= \underbrace{P + P + \cdots + P}_{n \text{ terms}} \\ &= nP. \end{aligned}$$

Therefore, *if X has a binomial probability distribution, then the expected value of X is*

$$\mu_X = E(X) = nP. \qquad \text{[X.2]}$$

By similar reasoning, it is easy to show that *if X has a binomial probability distribution, then the variance of X is*

$$\sigma_X^2 = nP(1 - P). \qquad \text{[X.3]}$$

Since $X = \sum_k Y_k$, the formula for the variance of a sum of random variables can be applied. Furthermore, since the observations of a random sample are mutually independent, the covariance of any pair of

[2] Harvard Computation Laboratory, *Tables of the Cumulative Binomial Distribution*. Cambridge, Harvard University Press, 1955. Gives cumulative probabilities only for n from 1 to 50 in steps of 1, from 50 to 100 in steps of 2, from 100 to 200 in steps of 10, from 200 to 500 in steps of 20, and from 500 to 1000 in steps of 50. P is given for $P = 0.01$ to 0.50 in 0.01 steps and for $P = 1/3, 1/6, 1/8, 3/8, 1/12, 5/12, 1/16, 3/16, 5/16$, and $7/16$.

National Bureau of Standards, *Tables of the Binomial Probability Distribution*. Applied Mathematics Series 6, 1950. Gives single-term and cumulative probabilities for n from 1 to 50 in steps of 1 and for P from 0.01 to 0.50 in steps of 0.01.

Romig, H. G., *50–100 Binomial Tables*. New York, John Wiley, 1953. Gives cumulative and single probabilities for n from 50 to 100 in steps of 5 and for P from 0.01 to 0.50 in steps of 0.01.

U.S. Army Ordnance Corps, *Tables of the Cumulative Binomial Probabilities*. Ordance Corps Pamphlet ORDP 20–1, U.S. Government Printing Office, (September) 1952. Gives cumulative probabilities only for n from 1 to 150 in steps of 1 and for P from 0.01 to 0.50 in steps of 0.01.

Y values is zero (see Section IX.11.2). Since the variance of each Y is $P(1 - P)$,

$$\begin{aligned}\sigma_X{}^2 &= \sum_k \sigma_{Y_k}{}^2 \\ &= \sigma_{Y_1}{}^2 + \sigma_{Y_2}{}^2 + \cdots + \sigma_{Y_n}{}^2 \\ &= \underbrace{P(1 - P) + P(1 - P) + \cdots + P(1 - P)}_{n \text{ terms}} \\ &= nP(1 - P),\end{aligned}$$

which is, again, Formula [X.3].

SAMPLE PROPORTION. Frequently, the mean of the Y-values in a sample is used to estimate P, the mean of a binomial population. The mean of Y for a sample of size n is

$$\bar{Y} = \frac{\sum_k Y_k}{n} = \frac{X}{n}.$$

Rather than referring to $\bar{Y}$ as a mean, it is customary to call this estimate the sample proportion and designate it with the symbol p. However, one should not lose sight of the fact that p is the sample mean of a random variable having range (0, 1).

Since $p = X/n = (1/n)X$, the rule for finding the expected value of a constant times a random variable can be applied to find

$$E(p) = E\left(\frac{1}{n} X\right) = \frac{1}{n} E(X) = \frac{1}{n}(nP) = P.$$

Therefore, *the sample proportion is an unbiased estimator for the population proportion.*

The variance of p is found by applying the rule for the variance of a constant times a random variable. Since $p = (1/n)X$, multiplying the variance of X by $(1/n)^2$ gives the variance of p,

$$\begin{aligned}\sigma_p{}^2 &= \left(\frac{1}{n}\right)^2 \sigma_X{}^2 = \left(\frac{1}{n}\right)^2 nP(1 - P) \\ &= \frac{P(1 - P)}{n}.\end{aligned}$$

Consequently, *the variance of a random sample proportion is*

$$\sigma_p{}^2 = \frac{P(1 - P)}{n}. \qquad \text{[X.4]}$$

APPLICATIONS OF THE BINOMIAL DISTRIBUTION. There are two types of application for the binomial PD. First, the point of concern may be the number (or the proportion) of elements in a random sample that are from one subclass of a binomial population. The number of heads appearing in a toss of 10 coins or the number of men in a sample of 10 students are illustrations of this type of application. Second, when two mutually exclusive and exhaustive events are possible, the number of occurrences of one of them in a sequence of trials may be of interest. For example, the binomial distribution can be applied to find the probability of X heads in 10 tosses of a single coin.

This second type of application—to a sequence of trials—can be described by the binomial distribution provided that (1) the outcome of any trial can be assigned to one of two mutually exclusive and exhaustive classes, (2) the probabilities P and $(1 - P)$ remain constant for every trial, and (3) the results of the trials are mutually independent. These three conditions make a sequence of trials formally identical to the process of random sampling with replacement, or without replacement from an infinite binomial population. When they are satisfied, then the random process is said to generate *Bernoulli trials.*

In Section VII.1.1, we developed a formula for the PD of the number of the trial on which an event with probability P first occurs. This PD is applicable only when the three conditions of Bernoulli trials are satisfied. For example, suppose that $\mathbf{P}(\text{Heads}) = P = 3/4$ for a bent coin. Then, if X is the trial on which the first head appears, $\mathbf{P}(X = x) = (1 - P)^{x-1}P = (1/4)^{x-1}(3/4)$.

A sequence of training trials in which an animal is learning a dichotomous discrimination does not ordinarily satisfy the conditions of Bernoulli trials. Given that the animal made a correct response with probability 1/2 at the beginning of training, it is unlikely that this probability will remain constant.

Bernoulli trials and the gambler's fallacy. There is a widely held belief that, in a sequence of Bernoulli trials, one of the two events is more likely following a long run of the other. However, if the random process satisfies the conditions of Bernoulli trials, as many games of chance do, then this is clearly incorrect. Nonetheless, this belief forms the basis for the majority of gambling systems, and, for this reason, it is called the "gambler's fallacy."

In roulette, one who believes the gambler's fallacy might assert that zero is especially unlikely to occur during the few trials immediately following its occurrence. In Dostoevski's *The Gambler*, Alexey Ivanovitch gives the following advice: ". . . zero has only just turned up, . . . so now it won't turn up for a long time. You will lose a great deal if you stake on zero; wait a little, anyway." Alexey Ivanovitch has asserted that the trials in roulette are statistically dependent. However, a fair roulette wheel has constant probabilities, and the trials are mutually independent, so that the events $A = \{0\}$, and $S \sim A = \{1, 2, \ldots, 36\}$ should satisfy the conditions of Bernoulli trials.

**Subjective probability estimates by psychology students.* Bilodeau[3] has described an interesting application of the binomial distribution in a study of subjective probability. He invited his subjects to play the old shell game. On each trial, a pea was presumably placed under one of three walnut shells, the choice of shell being random, and the subject's task was to guess which shell hid the pea. This amounts to a sequence of Bernoulli trials in which the probability that the pea is under a given shell is $P = 1/3$. However, in Bilodeau's version, there was no pea. The data consisted of the trial on which the subject first expressed doubt as to the existence of the pea, and after a firm expression of doubt or 50 trials, whichever occurred first, the subject was asked to estimate the probability that there was a pea.

If n is the trial on which a subject first openly questioned the existence of a pea, then, assuming there were a pea, the probability that it would not have been seen on or before the nth trial is

$$\mathbf{P}(X = 0) = \binom{n}{0}(1/3)^0(2/3)^{n-0} = (2/3)^n.$$

Thus, $(2/3)^n$ is the conditional probability that no pea would be seen on or before the nth trial if there actually were a pea.

Table X.1 summarizes the results for three groups of students in terms

Table X.1. Results of Bilodeau's shell-game experiment

Subject groups	Median trial on which doubt first expressed	Median subjective probability of a pea given no pea seen	Objective binomial probability of no pea being seen given one is present
Clinical psychology graduate students ($n = 15$)	6	.05	.088
Experimental psychology graduate students ($n = 13$)	13	.01	.005
Undergraduates ($n = 30$)	10	.04	.017

[3] Bilodeau, E. A., "Statistical versus intuitive confidence." *Amer. J. Psychol.* **65**, 271–277, 1952.

of (1) the median number of trials before the subject first expressed doubt about the existence of the pea, (2) the median of the students' subjective probabilities that there was a pea, and (3) the objective binomial probability of seeing no pea for the indicated median numbers of trials if a pea were present.

For the clinical psychology graduate students, the median trial on which doubt of the existence of a pea was first expressed was the sixth trial. The objective probability that the pea would not be seen for six trials if indeed there were a pea is $(2/3)^n = (2/3)^6 = 0.088$. Similar calculations were made for the other two student groups.[4]

The event "pea present" can be viewed as a hypothesis, and "pea not seen" as data. Furthermore, it seems plausible that the subjective probability of the pea was near 1 during the early trials (the subjects "trusted" the investigator) and well above the objective probabilities that the pea would not be seen given it were present. As the number of trials, n, increased, the objective, binomial probability,

$$\mathbf{P}(\text{data} \mid \text{hypothesis}) = (2/3)^n$$

necessarily decreased, and when no pea appeared the subjective probability, $\mathbf{P}(\text{hypothesis} \mid \text{data})$, must also have declined. Judging from Table X.1, the subjects openly challenged the existence of the pea when subjective and objective probabilities became about equal.

Although it is highly speculative, there may be a connection between these results and some of the widely accepted practices in hypothesis testing. Typically, the scientist calculates the objective probability, $\mathbf{P}(\text{data} \mid \text{hypothesis})$, and if this probability is judged small enough (usually 0.01 to 0.05) the hypothesis is rejected. Notice, however, that it is *not* the probability of the hypothesis given the data that provides the basis for the decision. Rather, when $\mathbf{P}(\text{data} \mid \text{hypothesis})$ is in the neighborhood of 0.01 to 0.05, the scientist apparently assigns a corresponding small subjective probability, $\mathbf{P}(\text{hypothesis} \mid \text{data})$, by some implicit, intuitive process. Since objective probabilities are subjectively judged "small enough" if they are about 0.01 to 0.05, it seems likely that when the subjective probability, $\mathbf{P}(\text{hypothesis} \mid \text{data})$, is small enough to lead one to doubt the hypothesis, then its value is also in the neighborhood of 0.01 to 0.05. Bilodeau's results also suggest that when the subjective $\mathbf{P}(\text{hypothesis} \mid \text{data})$ is small enough to lead one to reject the hypothesis, it is about equal to the objective $\mathbf{P}(\text{data} \mid \text{hypothesis})$.

If this interpretation were correct, it would probably disturb the neo-Bayesian statistician (Section V.3.5). He would point out that $\mathbf{P}(A \mid B)$

[4] It would have been preferable to calculate the binomial probability separately for each subject and to compare this value with the subjective probability estimate, but individual data were not published.

is not usually equal to $\mathbf{P}(B \mid A)$, as discussed in Section IV.6.1, so that if the objective **P**(data | hypothesis) is generally equal to the subjective **P**(hypothesis | data), this is contrary to probability theory. He would undoubtedly suggest that the objective **P**(data | hypothesis) should be transformed to the subjective **P**(hypothesis | data) by the systematic application of Bayes' theorem (Section V.3.5).

X.1.2. Finite binomial populations and the hypergeometric distribution

The binomial distribution is applicable only when sampling without replacement from an infinite binomial population, or with replacement from any binomial population. *When sampling without replacement from a finite binomial population, the probability distribution of* $X = \sum_k Y_k$ (defined in Section X.1.1) *is the hypergeometric distribution,*

$$\mathbf{P}(X = x) = \frac{\binom{R}{x}\binom{N-R}{n-x}}{\binom{N}{n}}, \qquad \text{[X. 5]}$$

where N is the population size, R is the number of elements in the population that fall in the subclass A, and n is the sample size. Note that

$$P = \mathbf{P}(A) = R/N.$$

The number of ways exactly x elements can be obtained from among the R elements in class A is $\binom{R}{x}$. The remaining $n - x$ elements in the sample are from among the $N - R$ elements of $S \sim A$, and they can be obtained in $\binom{N-R}{n-x}$ ways. Consequently, the number of ways of obtaining a group of size n containing exactly x elements from A is $\binom{R}{x}\binom{N-R}{n-x}$. Finally, the number of ways of obtaining a group of size n from a population of size N is $\binom{N}{n}$, so that

$$\mathbf{P}(X = x) = \frac{\binom{R}{x}\binom{N-R}{n-x}}{\binom{N}{n}},$$

which is Formula [X.5].

To illustrate the hypergeometric distribution, consider sampling without replacement from an urn containing 4 black balls and 4 white ones. Here, $N = 8$ and R, the number of black balls, equals 4. If a random sample of size 5 is drawn from the urn, what is the probability that the number of black balls, X, will equal 3? Applying the hypergeometric probability distribution,

$$\mathbf{P}(X = x) = \mathbf{P}(X = 3) = \frac{\binom{R}{x}\binom{N-R}{n-x}}{\binom{N}{n}} = \frac{\binom{4}{3}\binom{8-4}{5-3}}{\binom{8}{5}}$$

$$= \frac{24}{56}.$$

The probability that $X = 5$ is

$$\mathbf{P}(X = 5) = \frac{\binom{4}{5}\binom{8-4}{5-5}}{\binom{8}{5}}.$$

Here we encounter the expression

$$\binom{4}{5} = \frac{4!}{5!\,(4-5)!} = \frac{4!}{5!\,(-1)!},$$

which is equal to 0, as stated in Section V.1.5. Consequently,

$$\mathbf{P}(X = 5) = \frac{\binom{4}{5}\binom{8-4}{5-5}}{\binom{8}{5}} = \frac{0\binom{4}{0}}{\binom{8}{5}} = 0.$$

The hypergeometric PD for this example is shown graphically in Figure X.3.

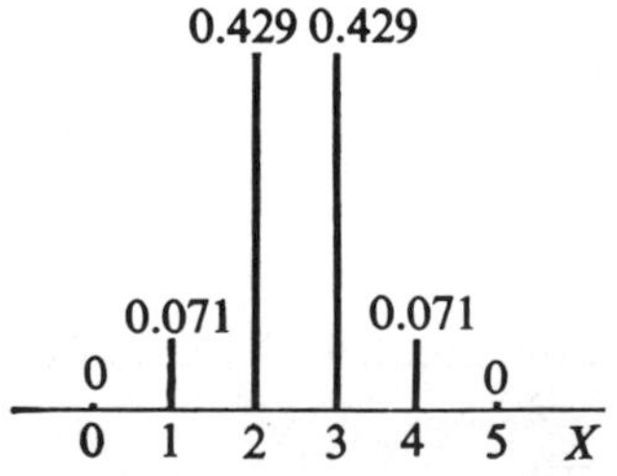

Figure X.3

CUMULATIVE HYPERGEOMETRIC DISTRIBUTION FUNCTION. From the hypergeometric distribution of Figure X.3 it is easy to construct the corresponding CDF by applying

$$\mathbf{P}(X \leq x_q) = \sum_{x=0}^{x_q} \mathbf{P}(X = x) = \sum_{x=0}^{x_q} \frac{\binom{R}{x}\binom{N-R}{n-x}}{\binom{N}{n}}.$$

A graph of this CDF is shown in Figure X.4.

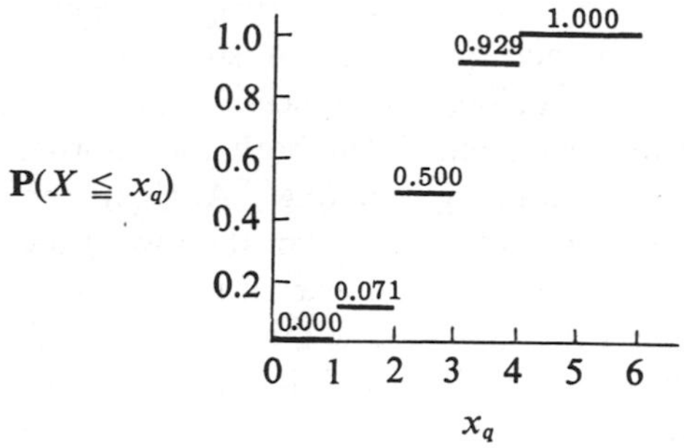

Figure X.4

MEAN AND VARIANCE OF A HYPERGEOMETRIC DISTRIBUTION. *If X has a hypergeometric probability distribution, then*

$$E(X) = n\frac{R}{N} = nP. \qquad [X.6]$$

This is identical to the expected value of a variable that has a binomial distribution. A derivation of this formula is given in Appendix X.1 at the end of this chapter.

Direct calculation of $E(X)$ from the hypergeometric distribution of Figure X.3 gives 2.5, and $E(X) = nP = 5(4/8) = 2.5$, also.

If X has a hypergeometric distribution, then the variance of X is

$$\sigma_X^2 = n\left(\frac{R}{N}\right)\left(1 - \frac{R}{N}\right)\left(\frac{N-n}{N-1}\right) = nP(1-P)\left(\frac{N-n}{N-1}\right). \qquad [X.7]$$

This formula is the same as that for the binomial distribution except for the factor $(N - n)/(N - 1)$, which is sometimes referred to as the *finite population factor*. It adjusts the variance for the fact that sampling is without replacement. Clearly, if n is small relative to N, then $(N - n)/(N - 1)$ will be near 1, and the adjustment will have little effect.

The variance of the hypergeometric distribution of Figure X.3 is

$$n\left(\frac{R}{N}\right)\left(1 - \frac{R}{N}\right)\left(\frac{N-n}{N-1}\right) = 5\left(\frac{4}{8}\right)\left(1 - \frac{4}{8}\right)\left(\frac{8-5}{8-1}\right) = 0.536.$$

This result can be verified by direct calculation from Figure X.3.

AN APPLICATION OF THE HYPERGEOMETRIC DISTRIBUTION. A part of the Tri-Ethnic Research Project[5] has produced data describing the sociometric structure of a high school in the Southwest. In this high school,

[5] The Tri-Ethnic Research Project is supported by NIMH Grant No. 3M–9156. The writer extends his thanks to Dr. Richard Jessor and the project for permission to discuss these data. However, the analysis described is the sole responsibility of the author.

there were 46 Anglos, 41 Spanish-Americans, and 36 Indians.[6] To study ethnic cleavage, a part of the Tri-Ethnic Project, the extent to which ethnic groups interact with each other was investigated. If there is no ethnic cleavage, one expects sociometric choices to be statistically independent of the ethnic group membership of both the chooser and the chosen. Then the chooser's ethnic group (e.g., Anglos) and all others (e.g., Spanish-Americans and Indians) form the two subclasses of a finite binomial population. If this formulation is correct, then the number of choices from within the chooser's ethnic group will follow a hypergeometric probability distribution, and it can be used to determine the expected number of choices from the chooser's own ethnic group, given that choices are independent of group membership. If the actual number of choices from within the chooser's ethnic group is close to this expected value, it suggests that there is no ethnic cleavage.

Many sociometric relations among school children were investigated, but only one will be discussed here. Each student in the high school was asked "Who are the five kids *in this school* you would choose to mess around with?" If we consider the choices made by a particular Anglo student, the school becomes a finite binomial population consisting of $41 + 36 = 77$ non-Anglos and 45 Anglos (assuming that the chooser will not name himself). Then the Anglo student selects a sample of $n = 5$ from among the 122 other pupils. If his choices are independent of the Anglo, non-Anglo dichotomy, the probability that all five of his choices will be Anglos is

$$\mathbf{P}(X = x) = \frac{\binom{R}{x}\binom{N - R}{n - x}}{\binom{N}{n}}$$

$$\mathbf{P}(X = 5) = \frac{\binom{45}{5}\binom{77}{0}}{\binom{122}{5}} = 0.006,$$

where X is the number of Anglos chosen, R is the number of Anglos other than the chooser, and N is the total number of pupils other than the chooser. This says that the probability that an Anglo will make all of his five choices from among Anglos is only 0.006 *if* his choices are independent of ethnic group membership. The entire hypergeometric probability distribution calculated on the basis of this assumption is shown in Figure X.5.

[6] Three other students did not fall in any of these three ethnic groups. For the sake of simplicity, they were ignored in this analysis.

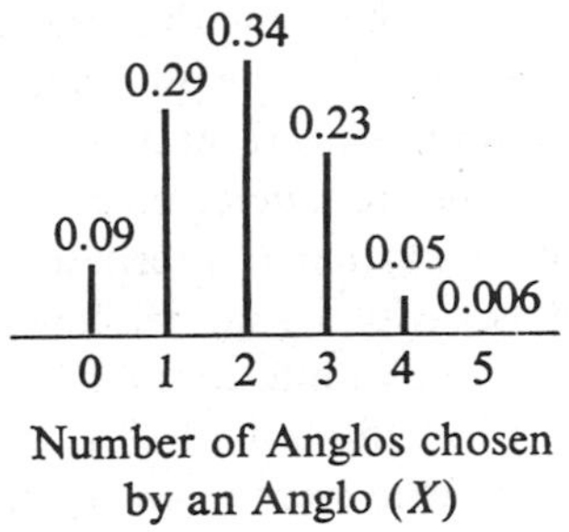

Figure X.5

Perhaps the most important information as far as ethnic cleavage is concerned is the expected value of X, which is $n(R/N) = 5(45/122) = 1.84$. This means that *if there is no ethnic cleavage*, one expects a mean of 1.84 Anglos to be chosen by each Anglo. If the observed mean were more than 1.84, then one would suspect that choices are not independent of ethnic group membership, and that ethnic cleavage does exist. In Chapter XIII, this question will be examined further.

One item of information that will be useful in that analysis is the variance of the number of choices made by an Anglo. Under the assumption that this variable follows a hypergeometric distribution, the variance is

$$\begin{aligned}\sigma^2 &= n\left(\frac{R}{N}\right)\left(1 - \frac{R}{N}\right)\left(\frac{N-n}{N-1}\right)\\ &= 5\left(\frac{45}{122}\right)\left(1 - \frac{45}{122}\right)\left(\frac{122-5}{122-1}\right)\\ &= 1.125.\end{aligned}$$

It should be noted that a similar analysis could be made for Indians or for Spanish-Americans. Also, all three ethnic groups can be distinguished in a single analysis that is a simple extension of the one just illustrated. But the example should indicate the general characteristics of this approach, and it will not be developed further here.

This example illustrates the way a PD such as the hypergeometric can be useful in conceptualizing a particular psychological problem. Further, such thinking may provide clues that contribute to the formulation of psychological theory.

X.1.3. Multinomial populations and the multinomial distribution

If a population can be divided into r mutually exclusive and exhaustive subpopulations, $A_1, A_2, \ldots, A_r$, then the population is called a multinomial population.

From this definition it can be seen that the multinomial population is a straightforward generalization of the binomial population to more than two subclasses. For example, the responses of a group of persons to a single, multiple-choice question determine a multinomial population in which those who choose a particular alternative constitute one subclass. If a college population is divided into freshmen, sophomores, juniors, and seniors, this also constitutes a multinomial population in which $r = 4$. If a sample were drawn from this population, then X might denote the number of sample members who were from A_1 (freshmen), Y the number from A_2 (sophomores), W the number from A_3 (juniors), and Z the number from A_4 (seniors). If the sample size is n, then $X + Y + W + Z = n$. If $P_1 = \mathbf{P}(A_1)$, $P_2 = \mathbf{P}(A_2)$, $P_3 = \mathbf{P}(A_3)$, $P_4 = \mathbf{P}(A_4)$, then $P_1 + P_2 + P_3 + P_4 = 1$, since the A's are mutually exclusive and exhaustive.

If a random sample is drawn from a binomial population, then X is the number of elements from A, and $n - X$ is the number from $S \sim A$. Thus, the binomial is a special case of the multinomial population in which $r = 2$, $P_1 = P$, $P_2 = 1 - P$, $A_1 = A$, $A_2 = S \sim A$, $X = X$, and $Y = n - X$.

In order to keep a concrete reference during the development of the rationale for the multinomial PD, an illustrative example will be used.

It is known that laboratory rats generally show a preference for glucose solutions of higher concentration. But the rat can display such preferences only if he can discriminate among concentrations. That is, a rat will show a clear behavioral preference for a 10 percent glucose solution over an 8 percent solution only if it can distinguish between the two.

Suppose that 12 animals have had extensive experience running to a goal box equipped with three drinking tubes, one containing 5 percent glucose, one 7 percent, and one 9 percent. On the basis of extensive work on palatability,[7] the rats can be expected to prefer the strongest, 9 percent solution if it can be discriminated from the other two. If the rats cannot distinguish among solutions, the the probabilities $\mathbf{P}$(5 percent chosen) $= P_1$, $\mathbf{P}$(7 percent chosen) $= P_2$, and $\mathbf{P}$(9 percent chosen) $= P_3$ will all equal 1/3. If $P_1 = P_2 = P_3 = 1/3$, about 1/3 of the 12 animals are expected to run to each of the three drinking tubes on a test trial.

In Table X.2, the hypothetical data for a test trial are shown. The numbers assigned the rats indicate the order in which they were run in the apparatus. The number of animals choosing the 5 percent solution is $X = 4$, the number choosing the 7 percent is $Y = 2$, and the number choosing the 9 percent solution is $Z = 6$.

Now, what is $\mathbf{P}[(X = 4) \cap (Y = 2) \cap (Z = 6)]$ if the hypothesis of

[7] Work by P. T. Young, for example.

Table X.2. Hypothetical data for discrimination test

Rat number	1	2	3	4	5	6	7	8	9	10	11	12
Choice	9%	5%	7%	9%	7%	9%	9%	5%	5%	9%	9%	5%

indiscriminability is true? First, the probability that four animals chose the 5 percent solution is

$$P_1^X = \left(\frac{1}{3}\right)^4,$$

that two chose 7 percent is

$$P_2^Y = \left(\frac{1}{3}\right)^2,$$

and that six chose 9 percent is

$$P_3^Z = \left(\frac{1}{3}\right)^6.$$

Consequently, the probability of exactly four 5 percent choices, two 7 per cent choices, and six 9 percent choices in a *particular order* is

$$P_1^X P_2^Y P_3^Z = \left(\frac{1}{3}\right)^4 \left(\frac{1}{3}\right)^2 \left(\frac{1}{3}\right)^6.$$

The number of distinguishable orders for which $X = 4$, $Y = 2$, and $Z = 6$ is determined using the multinomial coefficient (Section V.1.7),

$$\frac{n!}{X!\,Y!\,Z!} = \frac{12!}{4!\,2!\,6!}.$$

Consequently, the probability that one of these will occur is

$$\mathbf{P}[(X = x) \cap (Y = y) \cap (Z = z)] = \frac{n!}{x!\,y!\,z!} P_1^x P_2^y P_3^z,$$

$$\mathbf{P}[(X = 4) \cap (Y = 2) \cap (Z = 6)] = \frac{12!}{4!\,2!\,6!} \left(\frac{1}{3}\right)^4 \left(\frac{1}{3}\right)^2 \left(\frac{1}{3}\right)^6$$

$$= 0.026.$$

Using the same argument, probabilities can be calculated for any multinomial population.

Suppose that a random sample is drawn with replacement from any multinomial population, or without replacement from an infinite multinomial population. If X is the number of sample elements from the subclass A_1, Y is the number from $A_2, \ldots,$ and Z is the number from A_r, then

$$\mathbf{P}[(X = x) \cap (Y = y) \cap \cdots \cap (Z = z)] = \frac{n!}{x!\,y!\cdots z!} P_1^x P_2^y \cdots P_r^z, \quad \text{[X.8]}$$

where $n = X + Y + \cdots + Z$ *and* $P_1, P_2, \ldots, P_r$ *are the population proportions in the subclasses* $A_1, A_2, \ldots, A_r$, *respectively, with* $P_1 + P_2 + \cdots + P_r = 1$.

In most statistical applications of the multinomial distribution, the probabilities of all combinations of values of $X, Y, \ldots, Z$ that are equally probable or less probable than an observed combination must be found. Even for rather small n and r, this becomes exceedingly tedious. An approximation for this calculation is described in Section XIII.8.2.

X.1.4. Discrete rectangular distribution

One of the simplest and most useful PD's is the discrete rectangular distribution. It finds numerous applications in statistical methods that depend on the rank order of the observations.

If each of the values of a discrete random variable has the same probability, then the variable is said to have a rectangular probability distribution.

Tossing a fair, six-sided die generates a rectangular PD. This PD has been used in several illustrations. Tables of random digits constitute random samples from a population having a discrete rectangular distribution of the digits 0 through 9, inclusive. Appendix III contains a random sample of 2500 such digits. This table can also be treated as a sample from the population of values 00, 01, 02, . . . , 99. In other words, pairs of digits can be viewed as values of a random variable having range (00, 01, 02, . . . , 99), and each value of this random variable has probability 0.01. This idea can be extended to any number of digits.

The table of Appendix III has many uses. For example, it can be used to assign subjects to experimental and control conditions randomly. To do this, first select a subject. Then, choose a digit from the table of Appendix III by some random procedure (e.g., "close your eyes and point"). If the digit is odd, assign the subject to the experimental condition. Otherwise, he receives the control treatment. Then, select the next subject, and move to the next random digit in the column. Repeat the assignment procedure for this subject. Proceeding down the column, each successive subject is assigned according to whether the next digit is odd or even. The process continues down one column after another until all subjects have been assigned.

MEAN AND VARIANCE OF A SPECIAL DISCRETE RECTANGULAR DISTRIBUTION. Many statistical procedures have been devised for dealing with ranked data. This section is devoted to finding the mean and variance of a set of ranks. However, the formulas for these two parameters are much simpler if we utilize shortcut rules for determining the sum and the sum of squares of the first r ranks. These are given in this section.

The sum of the first r positive integers is

$$\sum_{x=1}^{r} x = \frac{r(r+1)}{2}. \qquad [X.9]$$

To illustrate this formula, suppose that $r = 6$. Then

$$\sum_{x=1}^{r} x = \sum_{x=1}^{6} x = 1 + 2 + 3 + 4 + 5 + 6 = 21 = \frac{6(6+1)}{2} = \frac{r(r+1)}{2}.$$

Further verification of Formula [X.9] can be obtained by checking other values of r.[8]

The second rule is that *the sum of the squares of the first r positive integers is*

$$\sum_{x=1}^{r} x^2 = \frac{r(r+1)(2r+1)}{6}. \qquad [X.10]$$

If $r = 6$, then

$$\begin{aligned}\sum_{x=1}^{r} x^2 = \sum_{x=1}^{6} x^2 &= 1^2 + 2^2 + 3^3 + 4^2 + 5^2 + 6^2 \\ &= 91 \\ &= \frac{6(6+1)[2(6)+1]}{6} = \frac{r(r+1)(2r+1)}{6}.\end{aligned}$$

This rule can be demonstrated to hold for other values of r.[9]

Now we are ready to find formulas for the expected value and variance of a set of ranks. Suppose that X is a random variable with range $(1, 2, \ldots, r)$, and assume that the PD of X is $\mathbf{P}(X = x) = 1/r$. Then, the expected value of X is

$$\begin{aligned}E(X) &= \sum_{x=1}^{r} \mathbf{P}(X = x)x = \frac{1}{r}(1) + \frac{1}{r}(2) + \cdots + \frac{1}{r}(r) \\ &= \frac{1}{r}\sum_{x=1}^{r} x.\end{aligned}$$

Now, Formula [X.9] can be applied as follows:

$$\begin{aligned}E(X) &= \frac{1}{r}\sum_{x=1}^{r} x = \frac{1}{r}\frac{r(r+1)}{2} \\ &= \frac{r+1}{2}.\end{aligned}$$

This is the simplified formula for $E(X)$.

[8] A proof can be constructed using mathematical induction.
[9] A proof can be constructed using mathematical induction.

Similarly, the variance of X is

$$E\{[X - E(X)]^2\} = E(X^2) - [E(X)]^2.$$

Applying the simplified formula for $E(X)$,

$$E\{[X - E(X)]^2\} = \sum_{x=1}^{r} \mathbf{P}(X = x)x^2 - \left(\frac{r+1}{2}\right)^2$$

$$= \frac{1}{r}\sum_{x=1}^{r} x^2 - \frac{(r^2 + 2r + 1)}{4}.$$

Now Formula [X.10] can be applied to the sum in this expression. Then,

$$E\{[X - E(X)]^2\} = \frac{1}{r}\left(\frac{r(r+1)(2r+1)}{6}\right) - \left(\frac{r^2 + 2r + 1}{4}\right)$$

$$= \frac{r^2 - 1}{12}.$$

These results can be summarized as follows: *if the range of the random variable X consists of the first r positive integers, and if $\mathbf{P}(X = x) = 1/r$, then the expected value of X is*

$$E(X) = \frac{r+1}{2} \qquad \text{[X.11]}$$

and the variance of X is

$$E\{[X - E(X)]^2\} = \frac{r^2 - 1}{12}. \qquad \text{[X.12]}$$

If a supervisor ranks the clinical skill of six clinical psychology trainees, and if one of the trainees is chosen randomly, then the expected value of his rank is

$$E(X) = \frac{r+1}{2} = \frac{6+1}{2} = 3.5$$

and its variance is

$$E\{[X - E(X)]^2\} = \frac{r^2 - 1}{12} = \frac{(6)^2 - 1}{12} = \frac{35}{12}.$$

CUMULATIVE RECTANGULAR DISTRIBUTION FUNCTION. The CDF for a variable that has a discrete rectangular distribution is simply a stair with tread height equal to $1/r$, where r is the number of values in the range of the variable. The CDF for digits having a rectangular distribution is shown in Figure X.6.

X.1.5. Poisson distribution

Although the Poisson distribution has found relatively few applications in psychology, it has been widely used in other areas. For example, it has provided an important tool for analyzing the incidence of industrial

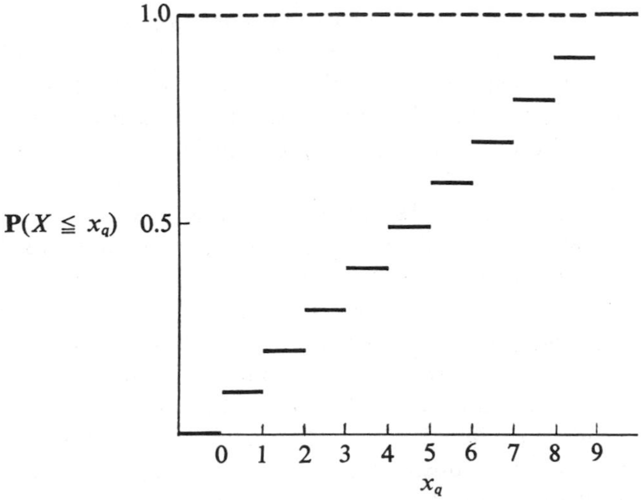

Figure X.6

accidents, and it will be introduced in this context. Then, two psychological applications will be described.

Suppose that the incidence of accidents in a large manufacturing complex is being investigated, and that data are collected on the number of accidents per week. One week, two accidents might occur, another week four, and so on. Assume that the probability that an accident will occur during any single working hour is P. If there are 40 working hours in a week, then a week is a sample of 40 time periods and the probability of an accident during a randomly chosen work hour is P. If P remains constant from hour to hour, and if accident occurrences are mutually independent, then the successive hours of the work week can be considered a sequence of Bernoulli trials (see Section X.1.1). Under these conditions, recording the occurrence or nonoccurrence of an accident during each of the 40 working hours is equivalent to taking a random sample of size 40 from a binomial population in which P is the probability of an accident during a randomly selected hour and $1 - P$ is the probability of no accident. The probability that an accident will occur in exactly X out of the 40 working hours is given by the binomial probability

$$\mathbf{P}(X = x) = \binom{n}{x} P^x (1 - P)^{n-x} = \binom{40}{x} P^x (1 - P)^{40-x}.$$

Even if accidents are mutually independent, it is quite possible that more than one accident will occur during a single hour, and since only occurrence or nonoccurrence is being recorded, this means that our records are really inadequate. One way to minimize this difficulty is to reduce the unit of time. For example, the work week might be divided into 160 quarter-hours with probability $P/4$ that an accident will occur during a randomly chosen quarter-hour. Of course, to be even more certain that no more than one accident occurred per time unit, the work week could be divided into smaller units, but there is a practical limit to such refinements. (It would be virtually impossible to pinpoint accidents to the second, for example.)

It is clear that as the number of time units per week is increased, the probability of an accident during a randomly chosen time unit becomes smaller (as n increases, P decreases). At the same time, the mean number of accidents *per week* remains the same whether accidents are recorded per hour, per quarter-hour, or per minute. If this argument is carried to its logical conclusion, we let n (the number of time units) become countably infinite and let P approach 0 as a limit in such a manner that nP remains constant. What is the effect of this on the binomial probability? As shown in Appendix X.2, the appearance of the binomial changes remarkably under these conditions and becomes

$$\mathbf{P}(X = x) = \frac{(nP)^x e^{-nP}}{x!},$$

where e is the base of the natural logarithms (about 2.7183), and X is the number of accidents per week.

Since nP is the expected number of accidents per week, nP can be referred to as μ, and

$$\mathbf{P}(X = x) = \frac{\mu^x e^{-\mu}}{x!}.$$

This is the Poisson PD.

Initially, X was defined as the number of time units in which an accident occurred, but since two or more accidents have probability 0 of occurring at precisely the same moment, X is now the number of accidents per week. Note also that X can take on only positive, integral values or 0, so that the range of X is $(0, 1, 2, 3, \ldots)$. The initial maximum value of X was n, but when n was permitted to become countably infinite this upper limit was removed.

DEFINITION OF THE POISSON DISTRIBUTION. *If the range of the random variable X is $(0, 1, 2, \ldots)$, if the mean of X is μ, and if the probability distribution of X is*

$$\mathbf{P}(X = x) = \frac{\mu^x e^{-\mu}}{x!}, \qquad \text{[X.13]}$$

then X has a Poisson probability distribution.

If the mean number of accidents per week were 2, then

$$\mathbf{P}(X = 0) = \frac{\mu^x e^{-\mu}}{x!} = \frac{2^0 e^{-2}}{0!} = 0.135,$$

$$\mathbf{P}(X = 1) = \frac{2^1 e^{-2}}{1!} = 0.271,$$

$$\mathbf{P}(X = 2) = \frac{2^2 e^{-2}}{2!} = 0.271,$$

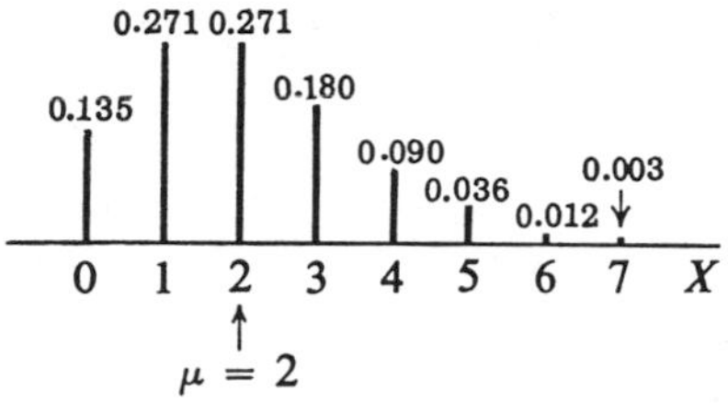

Figure X.7

and so on. This distribution is plotted in Figure X.7. Since

$$\sum_{x=0}^{7} \mathbf{P}(X = x) = \sum_{x=0}^{7} \frac{2^x e^{-2}}{x!} = 0.998,$$

the probabilities are very small for $X > 7$ and they have been omitted from Figure X.7.

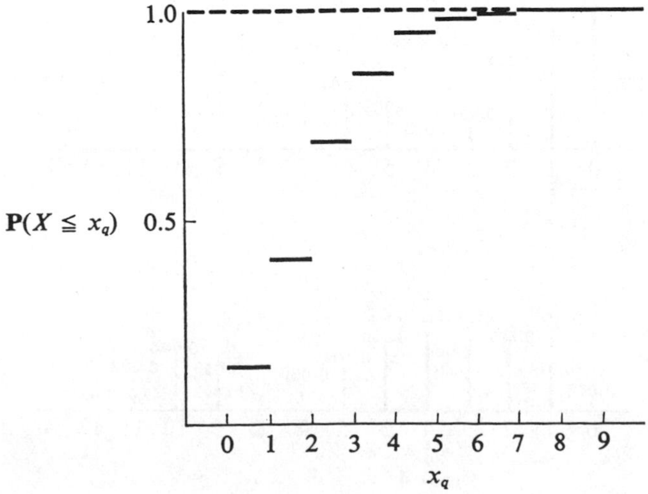

Figure X.8

CUMULATIVE POISSON DISTRIBUTION FUNCTION. The CDF for a Poisson distribution with $\mu = 2$ is illustrated in Figure X.8. The probability that X will be 3 or less is

$$\begin{aligned}\mathbf{P}(X \le x_q) = \mathbf{P}(X \le 3) &= \sum_{x=0}^{3} \mathbf{P}(X = x) \\ &= \mathbf{P}(X = 0) + \mathbf{P}(X = 1) + \mathbf{P}(X = 2) + \mathbf{P}(X = 3) \\ &= 0.135 + 0.271 + 0.271 + 0.180 \\ &= 0.857,\end{aligned}$$

so this is the height of the CDF at $X = 3$.

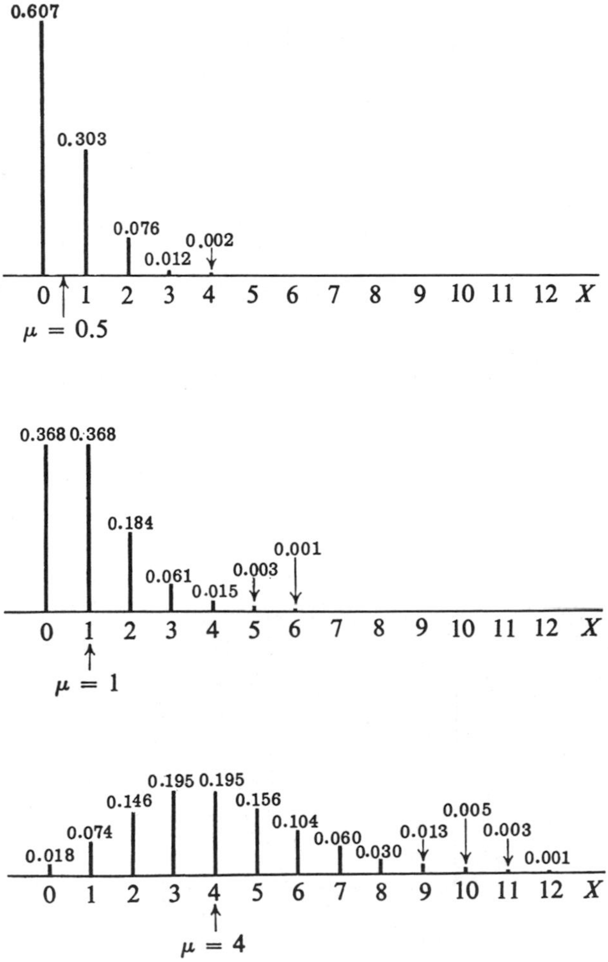

Figure X.9

MODE, MEAN, AND VARIANCE OF THE POISSON DISTRIBUTION. *The mode of a Poisson distribution is the largest integer less than or equal to* μ. This can be seen to hold for the distributions represented in Figures X.7 and X.9.

An important property of the Poisson distribution is that its expected value always equals its variance.[10] Thus, *if X has a Poisson distribution, if the expected value of X is μ, and if its variance is σ^2, then*

$$\mu = \sigma^2.$$

Consequently, when sampling randomly from a population that has a Poisson distribution, the same mean, $\bar{X}$, provides an unbiased estimate of either the mean or the variance of the population.

Extensive tables of Poisson probabilities have been constructed by Molina.[11] The table of Appendix IV gives values of the Poisson CDF for values of μ from 0.05 to 1.0 in steps of 0.05, from 1.1 to 2.0 in steps of 0.1, and from 2.2 to 4.0 in steps of 0.2.

CONDITIONS FOR APPLYING THE POISSON DISTRIBUTION. So far, only one process leading to a Poisson distribution has been discussed. However, many phenomena besides accident rate can be expected to follow this PD. The distribution of the number of yeast cells per unit volume of home brew, of the number of red blood cells per unit volume of blood, or of the number of raisins per loaf of raisin bread, would be approximated by a Poisson distribution. The essential feature is that some event (accident, yeast cell, red blood cell, raisin) is distributed randomly through a continuous medium (time, brew, plasma, dough), and the total amount of the medium occupied or displaced by the events is small relative to the total. If samples of the medium are examined, then the frequency of the event per sample can be approximated by a Poisson distribution.

*AN APPLICATION OF THE POISSON DISTRIBUTION TO PSYCHOLOGICAL THEORY. With the possible exception of accident frequency, none of these illustrations is especially pertinent to psychology. However, Mueller[12] has used the Poisson distribution to find theoretical relationships among several measures of operant conditioning (response latency, response probability, response rate, and number of trials to extinction). Some of Mueller's results are summarized below.

[10] A proof is given by Mood, A. M., *Introduction to the Theory of Statistics*. New York, McGraw-Hill, 1950, pp. 101–102.

[11] Molina, E. C., *Poisson's Exponential Binomial Limit*. New York, Van Nostrand, 1945. Probabilities are given to six decimal places for 300 values of μ between 0.001 and 100.

[12] Mueller, C. G., "Theoretical relationships among some measures of conditioning." *Proc. Nat. Acad. Sci.* **36**, 123–130, 1950.

Suppose that an operant conditioning situation is examined. The bar-pressing rat in a Skinner box provides a concrete basis for discussion. If v is the rate of bar-pressing per unit time, then vt is the mean number of responses expected during time interval t. Furthermore, if bar-pressing is randomly distributed over time, then X will follow a Poisson distribution,[13] and

$$\mathbf{P}(X = x) = \frac{\mu^x e^{-\mu}}{x!} = \frac{(vt)^x e^{-vt}}{x!}$$

gives the probability that exactly x bar-presses will occur during time interval t.

In order to relate this formulation to response latency, consider $\mathbf{P}(X = 0)$. This is the probability that no response occurs during a time interval of length t. Then, notice that

$$\mathbf{P}(X = 0) = \frac{e^{-vt}(vt)^0}{0!} = e^{-vt},$$

so that e^{-vt} is the probability that the time preceding the first reponse is greater than t. If L is response latency, then

$$\mathbf{P}(L > t) = e^{-vt}$$

and

$$\mathbf{P}(L \leq t) = 1 - e^{-vt}. \qquad \text{[X.14]}$$

From this it is clear that $1 - e^{-vt}$ *is the cumulative distribution function for response latency.* A plot of this CDF is shown in Figure X.10 for $v = 0.1$, or a mean response rate of 1 response per 10-second period.

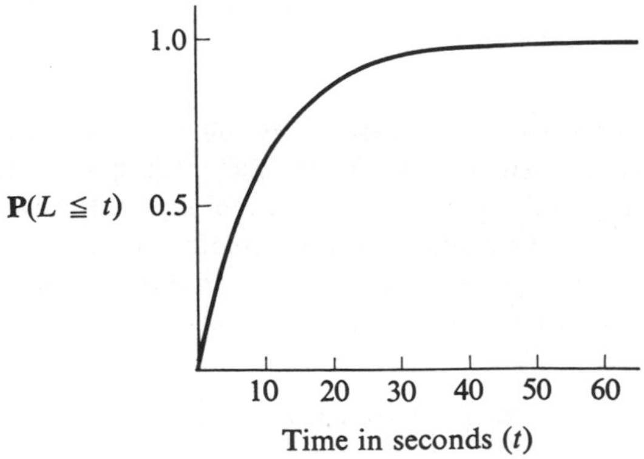

Figure X.10

[13] Notice that the "continuous medium" here is time and that the event dichotomy is response, no-response.

Using this cumulative distribution function, the probability that the latency of a given response will be between $t_1 = 10$ and $t_2 = 20$ seconds when $v = 0.1$ is

$$\begin{aligned}\mathbf{P}(t_1 < L < t_2) &= \mathbf{P}(L \leq t_2) - \mathbf{P}(L \leq t_1)\\ &= 1 - e^{-vt_2} - (1 - e^{-vt_1})\\ &= 1 - e^{-.1(20)} - 1 + e^{-1.(10)}\\ &= -e^{-2} + e^{-1} = -0.135 + 0.368\\ &= 0.233.\end{aligned}$$

Notice that the probabilities 0.135 and 0.368 were obtained from Appendix IV for $\mu = 2$ and $\mu = 1$, respectively, with $X = 0$.

If $v = 0.1$, the probability that the latency of a given response will exceed 30 seconds is

$$\mathbf{P}(L > t) = 1 - \mathbf{P}(L \leq t) = 1 - (1 - e^{-vt}) = e^{-vt} = e^{-.1(30)} = 0.50.$$

Notice that it is easy to apply this formulation to actual operant behavior. By observing response rates for a sample of time intervals, the mean response rate, v, can be estimated. Then, using this estimate of v, Formula [X.14] can be used to describe the probability of a response latency lying between any two specified times. Other applications are discussed below.

It is sometimes assumed that the rate of responding during extinction is proportional to the "response strength" that remains to be extinguished. If M is the total number of responses required to complete extinction (during a single session) and m is the number already elicited, then according to this assumption the rate of response immediately after m extinction responses is

$$v = K(M - m),$$

where K is a constant. Combining this assumption with the application of the Poisson distribution described in the beginning of this section, the probability of exactly x responses during the time interval, t, immediately following the mth extinction response is

$$\mathbf{P}(X = x) = \frac{e^{-vt}(vt)^x}{x!} = \frac{e^{-K(M-m)t}[K(M - m)t]^x}{x!}, \qquad \text{[X.15]}$$

where K is a constant governing rate of response that depends on the unit of time and on the animal. By setting $X = 0$, this formulation also predicts the cumulative distribution function of the latency of the $(m + 1)^{\text{st}}$ extinction trial.[14] Thus, several distinct measures of conditioning

[14] Estes uses some of Mueller's results in dealing with operant conditioning from the point of view of statistical learning theory. See "Toward a statistical theory of learning." *Psychol. Rev.* **57**, 94–107, 1950.

performance can be related explicitly using the Poisson distribution. In his discussion, Mueller introduces conditions and relations other than those described here, and he compares some of his theoretical results with appropriate data. Further discussion of processes that generate a Poisson distribution can be found in Feller.[15]

The important thing to notice here is that a bit of probability theory has been used to develop a theoretical network relating several behavioral measures. Of course, the empirical validity and the tenability of the assumptions of this procedure require the same scrutiny as any psychological theorizing, but the economy of the procedure should be evident. It is sometimes feasible to apply probability theory to other psychological problems without inventing a specialized theoretical system, and the possibility of such economies should not be overlooked.

AN APPLICATION OF THE POISSON DISTRIBUTION TO PSYCHOLOGICAL DATA. Mednick[16] has reported data that appear to be described quite well by the Poisson distribution. He measured generalization in a group of patients known to be suffering from cortical brain damage. (The intent was to compare the stimulus generalization performance of this group with that of schizophrenic and nonpsychiatric patients.) A description of his procedure follows.

The subject was seated facing a horizontal line of 11 lights. During a sequence of 20 training trials, he was required to release a key each time the center light went on. Then, in the course of 40 generalization trials (48 training trials were interspersed among these) on which one of the 10 off-center lights went on, the number of key releases was recorded. This was considered a measure of the subject's propensity for stimulus generalization. The empirical frequency function of the number of responses is shown in Table X.3.

Inserting the sample mean of 1.55 instead of μ, the Poisson probabilities were estimated using the formula

$$\mathbf{P}(X = x) = \frac{\bar{X}^x e^{-\bar{X}}}{x!} = \frac{(1.55)^x e^{-1.55}}{x!},$$

where X is the number of generalization responses. The results of these calculations appear in the third column of Table X.3.

On casual inspection, it appears that the theoretical Poisson probabilities correspond reasonably well to the observed relative frequencies. In Chapter XIII this relationship will be examined more closely.

[15] *An introduction to probability theory and its applications*, I, 2nd ed. New York, John Wiley, 1957, Chaps. 6 and 17.

[16] Mednick, S. A., "Distortions in the gradient of generalization related to cortical brain damage and schizophrenia." *J. Ab. Soc. Psychol.* **51**, 536–542, 1955.

Table X.3. Data from Mednick's generalization experiment

Number of generalization responses (X)	Empirical relative frequency function	Poisson probabilities
0	.25	.212
1	.30	.329
2	.25	.255
3	.12	.132
4	.03	.051
5	.03	.016
6	.02	.004
7 or more	0	.001
	1.00	1.000

X.2
PROBLEMS ON DISCRETE PROBABILITY DISTRIBUTIONS

1. A random sample of $n = 5$ is to be drawn from an infinite binomial population in which $P = 1/3$.
   a. What is $\mathbf{P}(X = 2)$?
   b. What is $\mathbf{P}(2 \leq X \leq 4)$?
   c. What is $\mathbf{P}[(X \leq 1) \cup (X \geq 4)]$?
   d. What is μ_X?
   e. What is σ_X^2?
   f. If $p = X/n$, find $\mathbf{P}(p = 0.4)$, $\mathbf{P}(0.4 \leq p \leq 0.8)$, $\mathbf{P}[(p \leq 0.2) \cup (p \geq 0.8)]$, μ_p, and σ_p^2.
2. If $Q = 1 - P$, then $1 = [P + Q]^4 = [P + (1 - P)]^4$. Show that
$$[P + (1 - P)]^4 = (P + Q)^4 = \sum_{x=0}^{4} \binom{4}{x} P^x Q^{n-x}.$$
3. Suppose that X has a binomial distribution. For n fixed, what value of P makes σ_X^2 maximal? For $n = 10$, plot σ_X^2 as a function of P.
4. Upon running a stop sign, your friend remarks that ticketing for such violations is a matter of chance, and since he got a ticket for running a stop sign yesterday, there's nothing to worry about for a while. Concern for your physical well-being aside, comment on your friend's remark in terms of probability theory.
5. Formulate the situation of Problem 4 as a sequence of Bernoulli trials. What is P, what is n, what is A, etc.?

6. A random sample of size 10 is drawn from an infinite binomial population in which $P = 1$.
   a. What is the probability distribution of X?
   b. What is σ_X^2?
7. An energetic psychologist is attempting to train 20 rats to a difficult visual discrimination. On Trial 100, 15 rats choose the correct alternative. Suppose that by the 100th trial no learning has occurred (so that **P**(correct choice) = **P**(incorrect choice) = 1/2), and that the disproportionate number of rats going to the correct alternative is an accident of random sampling.
   a. What is the probability of results as favorable to, or more favorable to, the hypothesis of correct discrimination as 15 out of 20 if no learning has occurred by Trial 100?
   b. If no learning has occurred, what is the expected number of animals making a correct choice on Trial 100?
   c. Learning might be demonstrated either by consistent choice of the correct alternative or by consistent avoidance of the correct alternative. What is the probability of results as unfavorable to the hypothesis of no learning as 15 out of 20 correct if a consistent preference for either alternative is considered evidence for learning?
8. Under what condition is the binomial distribution symmetrical?
9. Draw a random sample of size 4 (without replacement) from an urn containing 10 black balls and 20 white balls.
   a. What probability distribution is appropriate for finding the probability of a given number of black balls?
   b. If X is the number of black balls in the sample, find
      i. $\mathbf{P}(X = 3)$
      ii. $\mathbf{P}[(X \leq 1) \cup (X \geq 3)]$
      iii. $\mathbf{P}[(X > 1) \cap (X < 3)]$
      iv. $E(X)$
      v. σ_X^2.
10. A psychiatric ward has 6 neurotic patients and 14 non-neurotics. Patients are presumably assigned randomly to physicians, but one physician has 5 neurotics among the 10 patients assigned to him.
    a. If we assume that patients are assigned randomly, what is the probability that this physician would have 5 or more neurotics assigned to him?
    b. Would you be inclined to accept or suspect the randomness of patient-assignment on the basis of this information?
    c. How is your answer to b connected with your answer to a?
11. A senior psychiatrist observes with pride that 8 of the last 10 schizophrenic first admissions he has treated have recovered or shown improvement.
    a. Knowing that about 2/3 of those diagnosed schizophrenic at first admission recover with almost any or no treatment, would you be inclined to congratulate him on his therapeutic effectiveness or refer him to a treatise on probability?

b. If in the long run he is achieving nothing in excess of the 2/3 "recovery" figure, what is the probability that at least 8 of his last 10 schizophrenic patients would recover?
c. If you decided to refer him to some literature on probability, what topic would be most pertinent.
d. In answering b you have made some assumptions. Exactly what are they?

12. Suppose that $P_1 = 1/4$, $P_2 = 1/4$, and $P_3 = 1/2$ for an infinite multinomial population. In a random sample of six observations, $X = 1$, $Y = 2$, and $Z = 3$.
    a. Find $\mathbf{P}[(X = 1) \cap (Y = 2) \cap (Z = 3)]$.
    b. Find a triplet of values, one on X, one on Y, and one on Z, that is less probable than the one obtained.
    c. If we were interested primarily in X, then the marginal PD of X would be a binomial distribution, and $Y + Z = n - X$. With this in mind, what is $E(X)$?

13. The expected value of a set of ranks is 5. How many items have been ranked? What is the variance of this PD?

14. The variance of a set of ranks (X) is 2. What is the range of X? What is $\mathbf{P}(X = 1)$? What is $\mathbf{P}(2 \leq X \leq 7)$?

15. Can you suggest a speculative formulation of how a Poisson process might account for the data reported in Section X.1.5? What is the continuous medium, what is the event occurring in this medium, etc.? (Perhaps considering variations in "attention" or "set" over time will be helpful)

16. A stingy baker has allowed for one raisin per loaf in a batch of raisin bread dough. He has thoroughly mixed dough and raisins and obtains 100 small loaves.
    a. If you are a customer, what is the probability that you will get no raisins in the loaf you purchase?
    b. If you buy four loaves, what is the probability that you will get no raisins?
    c. What is the probability of 5 or more raisins in a single loaf?
    d. What is the expected number of raisins per loaf?
    e. What is the variance of the number of raisins per loaf?

X.3
DENSITY FUNCTIONS

With one exception, all of the distributions introduced so far in this chapter have applied to discrete random variables only. However, some of the most important distributions in statistics are continuous, and three of these are introduced in this section.

X.3.1. Rectangular density function

The discrete rectangular PD is characterized by equal probability for each value of the variable. Analogously, if X is a continuous random variable and the density function, $f(X)$, has the same height for each value in the range of X, then X is said to have a rectangular density function. More precisely, *if the continuous random variable X can take on any value between α and β ($\beta > \alpha$), and if the density function of X is*

$$\left.\begin{aligned} f(X) &= \frac{1}{\beta - \alpha} \quad \text{for } \alpha \leq X \leq \beta \\ f(X) &= 0 \qquad \textit{otherwise,} \end{aligned}\right\} \qquad \text{[X.16]}$$

and (between the two lines above)

then X has a rectangular density function.

If $\beta = 5$ and $\alpha = 1$, then the rectangular DF for X is

$$f(X) = \frac{1}{\beta - \alpha} = \frac{1}{5 - 1} = \frac{1}{4} \quad \text{for } 1 \leq X \leq 5$$

and

$$f(X) = 0 \quad \text{otherwise.}$$

This DF is shown graphically in Figure X.11.

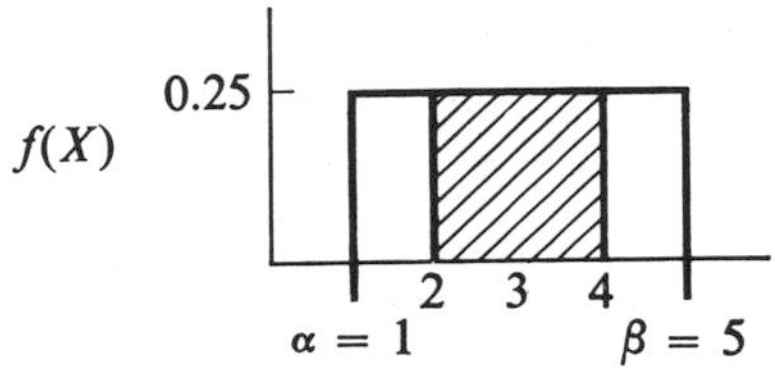

Figure X.11

If $f(X)$ is a DF, then the probability that an observation on X will lie between two specified values must equal the area under $f(X)$ between these values. Thus, $\mathbf{P}(2 < X < 4)$ is represented by the crosshatched area of Figure X.11. Since this area is equal to the product of the height of $f(X)$ and the distance from 2 to 4,

$$\mathbf{P}(2 < X < 4) = \frac{1}{4}(4 - 2) = \frac{1}{2}.$$

MEAN AND VARIANCE OF A RECTANGULAR DENSITY FUNCTION. It is clear that the expected value of X is midway between α and β. Therefore, if the density function of X is given by Formula [X.16], then the expected value of X is

$$E(X) = \frac{\alpha + \beta}{2}. \qquad \text{[X.17]}$$

In the example of Figure X.11,

$$E(X) = \frac{\alpha + \beta}{2} = \frac{1 + 5}{2} = 3.$$

Although we will not derive it, *if X has a rectangular density function, then the variance of X is*

$$\frac{(\beta - \alpha)^2}{12}. \qquad [X.18]$$

The variance of the example of Figure X.11 is

$$E\{[X - E(X)]^2\} = \frac{(\beta - \alpha)^2}{12} = \frac{(5 - 1)^2}{12} = 1.33.$$

X.3.2. Normal density function

Without doubt, the most important DF in statistics is the normal distribution. It is of special interest in itself and, in addition, it is related to many other PD's and DF's.

In the second chapter, the application of the normal distribution to astronomical errors of observation and its use by Quetelet to describe the natural distribution of human characteristics were mentioned. Occasionally, it has even been asserted that the normal distribution is the essential template for the distribution of all natural characteristics. But in addition to its usefulness as a descriptive tool, the normal distribution plays a central role in the statistical theory of hypothesis testing and estimation. Some of this theory will be introduced in the next chapter, but, first, the normal DF must be defined and some of its properties described.

Definition of the normal density function. *If X is a continuous random variable taking on values from $-\infty$ to $+\infty$, if the mean of X is μ and its variance is σ^2, and if the density function of X is*

$$f(X) = \frac{1}{\sigma\sqrt{(2\pi)}} e^{-1/(2\sigma^2)(X-\mu)^2}, \qquad [X.19]$$

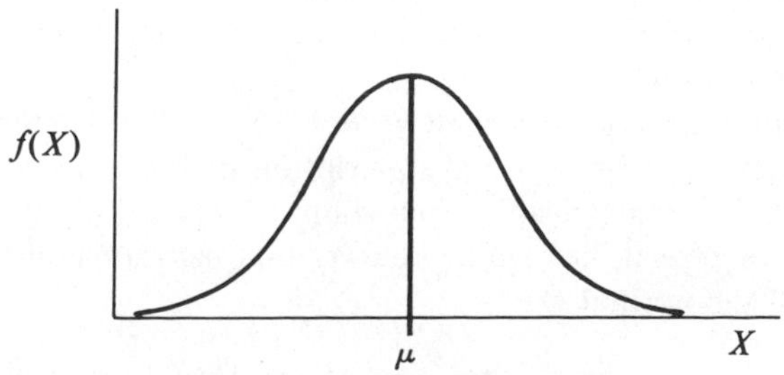

Figure X.12

then X is said to have a normal density function. In this formula, π is approximately 3.1416 and e is the base of the natural logarithms, about 2.7183. Figure X.12 shows graphically the shape of a normal DF.

A psychological variable that frequently shows an approximately normal distribution is IQ. Figure X.13 shows a frequency distribution[17]

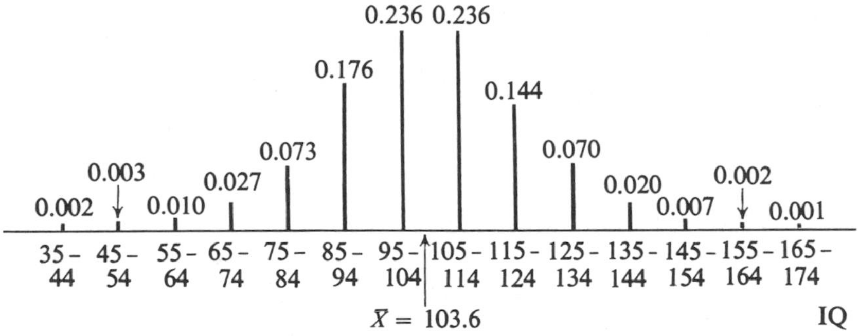

Source: Terman, L. M., and M. A. Merrill, *Measuring Intelligence.* New York, Houghton-Mifflin, 1937.

Figure X.13

of IQ's for 2904 children ranging from age 2 to age 18. This is the standardization group for the 1937 revision of the Stanford-Binet. The standard deviation of this distribution is about 16.4.

It is important to notice that IQ's are only approximately normally distributed. First, intelligence is not measured continuously. One may have a measured IQ of 115 or 116 but not of 115.6 or any other value between them. Second, although the range of a normally distributed variable extends from $-\infty$ to $+\infty$, an intelligence test does not yield IQ's beyond certain finite limits.

In general, then, the normal curve is used as a convenient approximation of some empirical distributions, but no empirically defined variable can have an exactly normal density function. Thus, *the normal distribution is a theoretical density function* which may describe an observation variable more or less accurately.

The specific meaning of *normal probability density function* is given by Formula [X.19], not by a verbal description of the characteristics of the normal curve ("symmetrical," "bell-shaped," etc.). Many other formulas define symmetrical, bell-shaped curves that lack some of the important properties of the normal DF.

[17] Adapted from Terman, L. M., and M. A. Merrill, *Measuring Intelligence.* New York, Houghton-Mifflin, 1937, p. 49.

SOME PROPERTIES OF THE NORMAL DENSITY FUNCTION. The random variable, X, enters the formula for the normal DF in the exponent only. In addition, since the quantity $(X - \mu)$ is squared, the height of a normal DF depends only on the *distance* of X from μ and not on the sign of $(X - \mu)$. This is the feature that makes the normal DF symmetrical about μ.

When $X = \mu$, $X - \mu = 0$, and the entire exponent is zero. Then,

$$f(X) = f(\mu) = \frac{1}{\sigma\sqrt{(2\pi)}} e^0 = \frac{1}{\sigma\sqrt{(2\pi)}}.$$

Since the sign of the exponent is negative, $f(X)$ takes on its maximum value when $X = \mu$ and the exponent is zero. Consequently, *the mode of a normal distribution equals its mean*, and the modal height of a normal DF is $1/[\sigma\sqrt{(2\pi)}]$.

Although no proof is given here,[18] the total area under the normal DF is 1. Since it is symmetrical about the mean, 1/2 of the area under the curve is above the mean and 1/2 is below. Therefore, *the median of a normal distribution equals the mean and the mode.*

QUETELET DEMONSTRATES FRAUD. Quetelet examined the frequency function of height for 100,000 French army conscripts. He discovered, instead of the usual nearly normal distribution of young men's heights, that there was an area of congestion just below the minimum height required by the French army and a regrettable sparsity of observations just above the minimum. He concluded that some of the shorter conscripts had stooped to deceit. In fact, on the basis of the assumption that height is normally distributed, Quetelet estimated that some 2000 conscripts had avoided military service by artificially diminishing their height during measurement.[19]

COMPUTING NORMAL PROBABILITIES. Before describing calculation procedures for normal probabilities, it will be necessary to introduce a rule for normally distributed random variables. This rule is stated without proof.[20]

If X has a normal density function, and if Z is defined by the linear function $Z = BX + A$, where A and B are constants, then Z also has a normal density function. This rule will be applied shortly.

The calculation of areas under a normal DF would be greatly simplified if an appropriate table were available, but a distinct table would be

[18] A proof can be found in Mood, A. M., *Introduction to the Theory of Statistics.* New York, McGraw-Hill, 1950.

[19] Should one conclude from this that moral stature and physical stature are correlated? If not, exactly why not?

[20] Mood, A. M., *op. cit.*, provides a proof.

required for every combination of values of μ and σ. Such a table would be cumbersome indeed. However, it is possible to eliminate μ and σ entirely from the equation for the normal DF by introducing a new variable that is a function of X. This variable is defined by

$$Z = \frac{X - \mu}{\sigma},$$

where μ is the mean and σ is the standard deviation of X. Here, Z is a linear function of X in which the slope constant $B = 1/\sigma$, and the intercept constant is $A = \mu/\sigma$. Consequently, according to the rule introduced above, if X has a normal DF, then Z is normally distributed, too. Furthermore, by the rule of Section VIII.4.6, the expected value of Z is

$$E(Z) = E\left[\frac{X - \mu}{\sigma}\right] = E\left[\frac{1}{\sigma}X - \frac{\mu}{\sigma}\right] = \frac{1}{\sigma}\mu - \frac{\mu}{\sigma} = 0,$$

and, according to the rule of Section IX.11.3, the variance of Z is $(1/\sigma)^2$ times the variance of X,

$$\sigma_Z{}^2 = \left(\frac{1}{\sigma}\right)^2 \sigma^2 = 1.$$

To sum up these results, *if X has a normal DF with mean μ and variance σ^2, then $Z = (X - \mu)/\sigma$ has a normal DF with mean $\mu_Z = 0$ and variance $\sigma_Z{}^2 = 1$.* Then, the DF for Z is

$$f(Z) = \frac{1}{\sigma_Z\sqrt{(2\pi)}}\, e^{-1/(2\sigma_Z{}^2)(Z - \mu_Z)^2}.$$

But substituting 0 for μ_Z and 1 for $\sigma_Z{}^2$ makes this

$$f(Z) = \frac{1}{\sqrt{(2\pi)}}\, e^{-Z^2/2},$$

which is called the standardized normal DF. Values of the random variable Z are referred to as standardized normal deviates.

Tables of areas under the normal DF are entered using Z. Since any random variable, X, can be transformed to Z if its mean and variance are known, these tables are quite general.

Cumulative normal distribution function. The table of Appendix V contains areas under the standardized normal DF corresponding to

$$\mathbf{P}(Z \leq z_q) = \int_{-\infty}^{z_q} \frac{1}{\sqrt{(2\pi)}}\, e^{-Z^2/2}\, dZ,$$

for values of z_q from 0 to 3.49 in steps of 0.01. Cumulative probabilities are not given directly for $z_q < 0$. However, since the normal DF is symmetrical, cumulative probabilities for negative values of z_q can be obtained by noting that

$$\mathbf{P}(Z < -z_q) = 1 - \mathbf{P}(Z \leq +z_q).$$

This is illustrated in Figure X.14. Notice that the areas corresponding to $1 - \mathbf{P}(Z \leq z_q)$ and $\mathbf{P}(Z < -z_q)$ are equal.

In order to find $\mathbf{P}(X \leq x_q)$, x_q must be transformed to a corresponding Z-value, z_q, so that the table of Appendix V can be entered. To illustrate this procedure, it will be assumed that the mean (103.6) and the standard

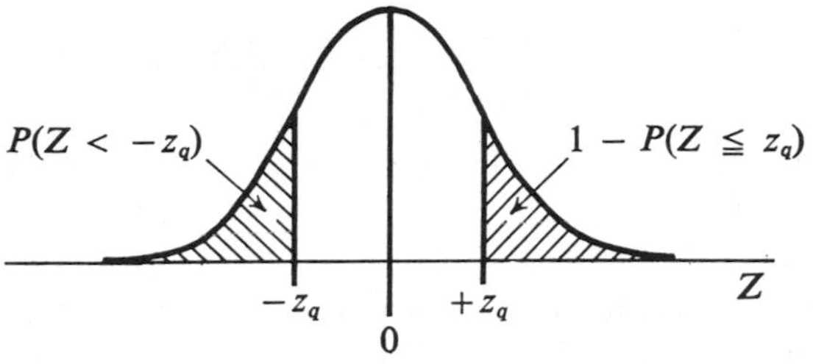

Figure X.14

deviation (16.4) of Figure X.13 are parameters. (They are based on a large sample.) Then, if X is IQ, the probability of an IQ less than or equal to $x_q = 120$ is found from

$$\mathbf{P}(X \leq x_q) = \mathbf{P}\left(\frac{X - \mu}{\sigma} \leq \frac{x_q - \mu}{\sigma}\right) = \mathbf{P}(Z \leq z_q)$$

$$\mathbf{P}(X \leq 120) = \mathbf{P}\left(\frac{X - 103.6}{16.4} \leq \frac{120 - 103.6}{16.4}\right) = \mathbf{P}(Z \leq 1).$$

Entering the table of Appendix V, $\mathbf{P}(Z \leq 1) = 0.8413$. Consequently, $\mathbf{P}(X \leq 120) = 0.8413$.

In Section VII.2, a method was described that permits the use of a relative frequency function to approximate the DF of a continuous random variable. The same general approach can be used to increase the accuracy with which a DF approximates probabilities associated with a discrete random variable. This procedure will be illustrated for the example just presented.

If intelligence is conceptualized as continuous, then an observed IQ of 120 can be thought of as representing the interval from 119.5 to 120.5, since an IQ cannot be measured with greater precision than one unit. Then, $\mathbf{P}(X \leq 120)$ is best interpreted as $\mathbf{P}(X \leq 120.5)$. Following this procedure,

$$\mathbf{P}(X \leq x_q) = \mathbf{P}\left(\frac{X - \mu}{\sigma} \leq \frac{x_q - \mu}{\sigma}\right) = \mathbf{P}(Z \leq z_q)$$

$$\mathbf{P}(X \leq 120.5) = \mathbf{P}\left(\frac{X - 103.6}{16.4} \leq \frac{120.5 - 103.6}{16.4}\right) = \mathbf{P}(Z \leq 1.03).$$

Entering the table in Appendix V, $\mathbf{P}(Z \leq 1.03) = 0.8485$ is the estimate of $\mathbf{P}(X \leq 120)$.

To illustrate further, we will calculate $\mathbf{P}(X \leq 84)$ using the same "correction for continuity." To begin with, $\mathbf{P}(X \leq 84)$ can be interpreted more precisely as $\mathbf{P}(X \leq 84.5)$, since an observation of 84 is represented by the interval 83.5 to 84.5 on the continuous, theoretical variable. Then

$$\mathbf{P}(X \leq 84.5) = \mathbf{P}\left(\frac{X - 103.6}{16.4} \leq \frac{84.5 - 103.6}{16.4}\right) = \mathbf{P}(Z \leq -1.16).$$

Negative values of Z are not listed in Appendix V, but the symmetry of the normal DF assures us that $\mathbf{P}(Z \leq -1.16) = 1 - \mathbf{P}(Z \leq +1.16)$. From Appendix V, $\mathbf{P}(Z \leq -1.16) = 1 - \mathbf{P}(Z \leq +1.16) = 1 - 0.8770 = 0.1330$, and this is our estimate of the empirical probability, $\mathbf{P}(X \leq 84)$. The procedure followed here is illustrated graphically in Figure X.14.

To estimate $\mathbf{P}(X > 132)$, first note that an IQ of 132 is represented theoretically by the interval 131.5 to 132.5. Then, $\mathbf{P}(X > 132)$ is interpreted as $\mathbf{P}(X > 132.5)$, and

$$\begin{aligned}\mathbf{P}(X > 132.5) = 1 - \mathbf{P}(X \leq 132.5) &= 1 - \mathbf{P}\left(Z \leq \frac{132.5 - 103.6}{16.4}\right) \\ &= 1 - \mathbf{P}(Z \leq +1.76) = 1 - 0.9608 \\ &= 0.0392.\end{aligned}$$

Sometimes the probability that X lies between two values must be found. For instance, we could find $\mathbf{P}(z_1 < Z < z_2)$ where $z_1 < z_2$. The area corresponding to such a probability is illustrated in Figure X.15. Notice

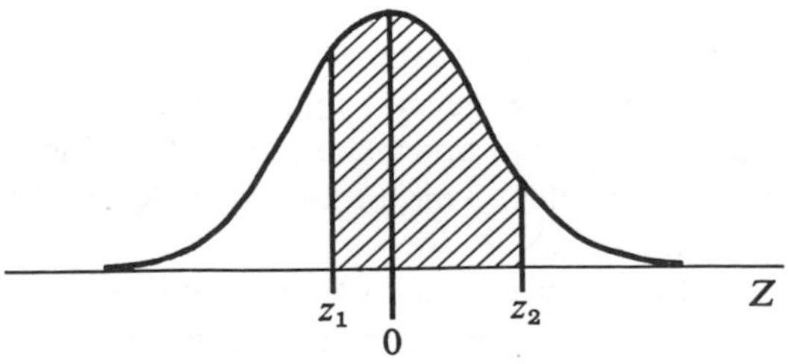

Figure X.15

that $\mathbf{P}(z_1 < Z < z_2)$ is equal to $\mathbf{P}(Z < z_2) - \mathbf{P}(Z \leq z_1)$. This can be seen in the diagram by noting that if the area to the left of z_1 is subtracted from *all* of the area to the left of z_2, then the difference is the area between z_1 and z_2. If $z_1 = (x_1 - \mu)/\sigma$ and $z_2 = (x_2 - \mu)/\sigma$, then

$$\mathbf{P}(x_1 < X < x_2) = \mathbf{P}(z_1 < Z < z_2) = \mathbf{P}(Z < z_2) - \mathbf{P}(Z \leq z_1).$$

To find $\mathbf{P}(92 < X < 130)$ for the IQ example, the correction for continuity is applied, and

$$\begin{aligned}\mathbf{P}(92.5 < X < 129.5) &= \mathbf{P}\left(\frac{92.5 - 103.6}{16.4} < Z < \frac{129.5 - 103.6}{16.4}\right)\\ &= \mathbf{P}(-0.68 < Z < +1.59)\\ &= \mathbf{P}(Z < +1.59) - \mathbf{P}(Z < -0.68)\\ &= 0.9441 - 0.2483\\ &= 0.6958.\end{aligned}$$

This result is described by saying that a randomly selected individual from this population has a probability of 0.6958 of obtaining an IQ greater than 92 and less than 130.

Suppose we wished to know the probability that a randomly selected individual's IQ will deviate from $\mu = 103.6$ by 16.4 IQ points or more. First, we must find the probability that $X - 103.6 > 16.4$ *or* $X - 103.6 < -16.4$, since in either case, X is more than 16.4 points from 103.6. Since the events $X - 103.6 > 16.4$ and $X - 103.6 < -16.4$ are mutually exclusive (both cannot occur), the simple addition rule is applicable.

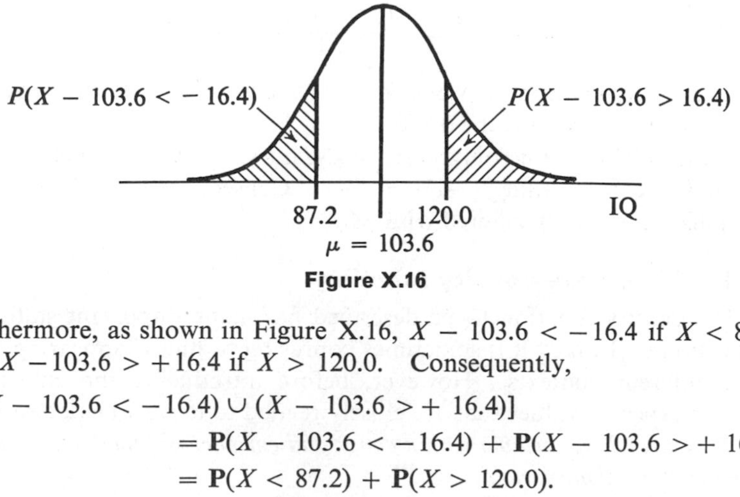

Figure X.16

Furthermore, as shown in Figure X.16, $X - 103.6 < -16.4$ if $X < 87.2$ and $X - 103.6 > +16.4$ if $X > 120.0$. Consequently,

$$\begin{aligned}&\mathbf{P}[(X - 103.6 < -16.4) \cup (X - 103.6 > +16.4)]\\ &\qquad = \mathbf{P}(X - 103.6 < -16.4) + \mathbf{P}(X - 103.6 > +16.4)\\ &\qquad = \mathbf{P}(X < 87.2) + \mathbf{P}(X > 120.0).\end{aligned}$$

The Z-values corresponding to $x_1 = 87.2$ and $x_2 = 120.0$ are $z_1 = (87.2 - 103.6)/16.4 = -1.0$ and $z_2 = (120.0 - 103.6)/16.4 = +1.0$. Then,

$$\begin{aligned}&\mathbf{P}[(X - 103.6 < -16.4) \cup (X - 103.6 > +16.4)]\\ &\qquad = \mathbf{P}(X < 87.2) + \mathbf{P}(X > 120.0)\\ &\qquad = \mathbf{P}(Z < -1.0) + \mathbf{P}(Z > +1.0)\\ &\qquad = 0.1587 + 0.1587\\ &\qquad = 0.3174.\end{aligned}$$

This is the theoretical probability that a person selected randomly from this population will have an IQ that differs by at least 16.4 units from the mean. More succinctly, it is $\mathbf{P}(|X - 103.6| > 16.4)$.

Obviously, many other probabilities can be calculated using a theoretical normal DF, but the principles are the same as those employed in the preceding examples. In computing such probabilities, the helpfulness of diagrams cannot be overestimated. Many false starts and erroneous results can be avoided by the judicious use of diagrams like those of Figures X.15 and X.16.

HEIGHT OF A NORMAL DENSITY FUNCTION. Later, we shall have occasion to use the height of a standardized normal DF. This can be done by direct calculation from Formula [X.19], but the table of Appendix VI facilitates matters considerably. The use of this table will be illustrated for a normal DF used to approximate the frequency function of Figure X.13.

Suppose we wish to estimate the height of this DF at $X = 110$. First it is necessary to find the standardized normal deviation corresponding to $X = 110$. This is

$$Z = \frac{X - \mu}{\sigma} = \frac{110 - 103.6}{16.4} = +0.39.$$

By linear interpolation between $Z = 0.35$ and $Z = 0.40$ in Appendix VI, the height is found to be 0.370.

Appendix VI contains only positive Z-values, but the symmetry of the normal DF ensures that $f(-Z) = f(Z)$. Consequently, if $Z < 0$, then Appendix VI is simply entered with $|Z|$.

X.3.3. Chi-square density function

The last density function to be described has many important statistical applications. In fact, it is sometimes confusing to find it appearing in so many different contexts. However, before introducing the chi-square DF, two expected values that are closely related to it must be determined.

If X is a random variable with mean μ and variance σ^2, then the expected value of the random variable

$$Z^2 = \left(\frac{X - \mu}{\sigma}\right)^2$$

is 1.

It is easy to demonstrate that this is correct. In Section X.3.2, it was shown that the expected value of $Z = (X - \mu)/\sigma$ is 0 and its variance is 1. Then, by Formula [IX.9],

$$\begin{aligned} E(Z^2) &= \sigma_Z^2 + \mu_Z^2 = 1 + 0 \\ &= 1, \end{aligned}$$

which is what we set out to demonstrate.

The next step is to find the variance of Z^2. By Formula [IX.8], this variance is

$$E\{[Z^2 - E(Z^2)]^2\} = E[(Z^2)^2] - [E(Z^2)]^2.$$

Since we have just found that $E(Z^2) = 1$,

$$\begin{aligned} E\{[Z^2 - E(Z^2)]^2\} &= E[(Z^2)^2] - [E(Z^2)]^2 \\ &= E(Z^4) - (1)^2. \end{aligned}$$

Now, if X has a normal DF, it can be shown[21] that $E(Z^4) = 3$. Then,

$$\begin{aligned} E\{[Z^2 - E(Z^2)]^2\} &= E(Z^4) - (1)^2 = 3 - 1 \\ &= 2. \end{aligned}$$

Thus, the variance of $Z^2 = (X - \mu)^2/\sigma^2$ is 2.

A SPECIAL CASE OF THE CHI-SQUARE DENSITY FUNCTION. A summary of these results is included in the following statement. *If X has a normal density function with mean μ and variance σ^2, then the random variable*

$$Z^2 = \left(\frac{X - \mu}{\sigma}\right)^2$$

has expected value 1 *and variance* 2. *Furthermore, Z^2 has a chi-square density function.*[22]

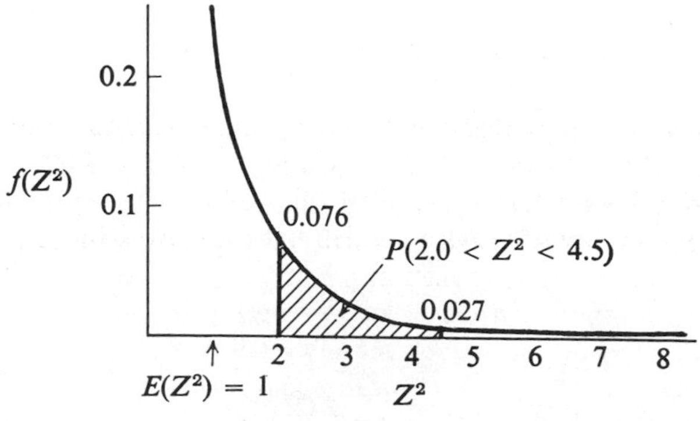

Figure X.17

The chi-square DF of $Z^2 = (X - \mu)^2/\sigma^2$ is shown graphically in Figure X.17, and it is defined by the expression

$$f(Z^2) = \frac{1}{\sqrt{(2\pi)}}(Z^2)^{-1/2}e^{-Z^2/2},$$

[21] The proof of this is beyond the scope of this text.

[22] A proof of this statement requires more mathematical elaboration than is appropriate here. A relatively simple proof can be found in Lewis, D., *Quantitative Methods in Psychology*. New York, McGraw-Hill, 1960, pp. 259–260.

where $\pi \cong 3.1416$ and e is the base of the natural logarithm system, $e \cong 2.7183$. For $Z^2 = 0$, the height of $f(Z^2)$ is infinite.

In order to find the probability that Z^2 will lie between two particular values, one must find the area under $f(Z^2)$ between them. Thus, in Figure X.17, $\mathbf{P}(2.0 < Z^2 < 4.5)$ is represented by the crosshatched area. This area is equal to

$$\mathbf{P}(2.0 < Z^2 < 4.5) = \int_{2.0}^{4.5} \frac{1}{\sqrt{(2\pi)}} (Z^2)^{-1/2} e^{-Z^2/2} \, dZ^2,$$

but, fortunately, it is unnecessary to evaluate this integral. Tables of areas under the chi-square DF are readily available. We will turn to their use after developing the chi-square DF somewhat further.

General form of the chi-square density function. *If*

$$(X_1, X_2, \ldots, X_k, \ldots, X_n)$$

is a random sample from a population that has a normal DF with mean μ *and variance* σ^2, *and if*

$$Z_k = \frac{X_k - \mu}{\sigma}$$

for each value of k, *then the random variable*

$$\chi^2 = \sum_{k=1}^{n} Z_k^2 = \sum_{k=1}^{n} \frac{(X_k - \mu)^2}{\sigma^2}$$

has a chi-square density function with mean n *and variance* $2n$.

In the preceding section it was shown that $E(Z^2) = E[(X - \mu)^2/\sigma^2] = 1$, so that $E(\chi^2)$ is simply the expected value of a sum of mutually independent random variables[23] each of which has expected value 1. Thus,

$$\begin{aligned} E(\chi^2) &= E\left(\sum_{k=1}^{n} Z_k^2\right) \\ &= \sum_{k=1}^{n} E(Z_k^2) \\ &= \underbrace{1 + 1 + \cdots + 1}_{n \text{ terms}} \\ &= n. \end{aligned}$$

The chi-square DF depends on the mean and variance just as the normal DF does. However, the mean and variance of a chi-square DF are

[23] The other parts of this statement will not be derived here. However, References 2, 3, 4, and 5 at the end of this chapter provide more complete discussions of the chi-square DF.

completely dependent (the variance is twice the mean), whereas they are quite independent for an unstandardized normal DF. In effect, then, a particular chi-square DF is determined by only one parameter, $E(\chi^2)$. This parameter will be denoted by the symbol D.

In general, the chi-square distribution is defined by

$$f(\chi^2) = \frac{1}{2^{D/2}\Gamma\left(\frac{D}{2}\right)} (\chi^2)^{D/2-1} e^{-\chi^2/2},$$

where e is the base of the natural logarithm system and $D = E(\chi^2)$. The symbol $\Gamma(D/2)$ refers to the gamma function. For integral values of D (which are the only ones that concern us here), the gamma function becomes

$$\Gamma\left(\frac{D}{2}\right) = \left(\frac{D}{2} - 1\right)! = \left(\frac{D}{2} - 1\right)\left(\frac{D}{2} - 2\right)\cdots 3\cdot 2\cdot 1$$

whenever D is even, and

$$\Gamma\left(\frac{D}{2}\right) = \left(\frac{D}{2} - 1\right)\left(\frac{D}{2} - 2\right)\cdots\frac{3}{2}\cdot\frac{1}{2}\cdot\sqrt{\pi}$$

whenever D is odd.[24]

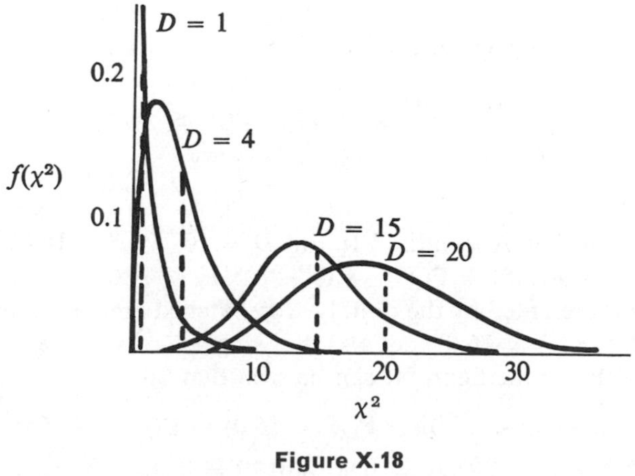

Figure X.18

In Figure X.18, the chi-square DF has been plotted for $D = E(\chi^2) = 1$, 4, 15, and 20. Notice that for $D = 20$ the DF is much more nearly symmetrical. In fact, it looks as if it would approach the shape of a

[24] The gamma function permits a generalization of the idea of the factorial of an integer ($n!$) to fractional numbers. Thus, if one plots $\Gamma(X)$ as a function of X, the plot is a *continuous curve* that passes through 0!, 1!, 2!, 3!, and so on. The gamma function is discussed in most textbooks on advanced calculus.

normal DF for sufficiently large values of D. As we shall see later, this is correct.

CALCULATIONS WITH THE CHI-SQUARE DENSITY FUNCTION. Since a single parameter determines a particular chi-square DF, the table of its CDF in Appendix VII can be entered when only the parameter $D = E(\chi^2)$ is known. For example, suppose $D = 10$. Then,

$$\mathbf{P}\left(\sum_{k=1}^{10} \frac{(X_k - \mu)^2}{\sigma^2} \leq 16.0\right) = \mathbf{P}(\chi^2 \leq 16.0)$$

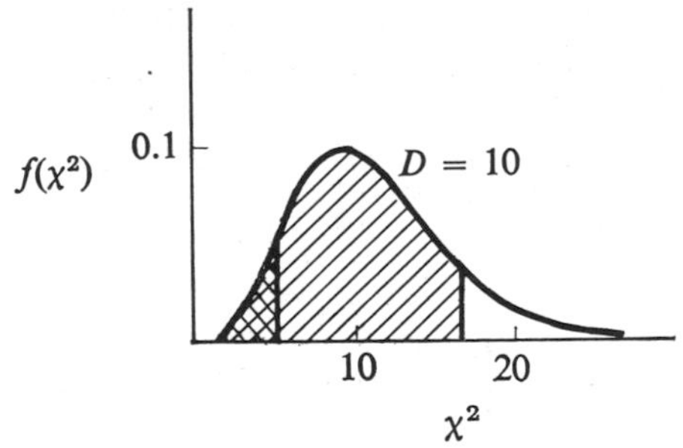

Figure X.19

can be determined by finding the entire crosshatched area of Figure X.19. This is the area under $f(\chi^2)$ to the left of $\chi^2 = 16.0$. That, is

$$\mathbf{P}\left(\sum_{k=1}^{10} \frac{(X_k - \mu)^2}{\sigma^2} \leq 16.0\right) = \mathbf{P}(\chi^2 \leq 16.0)$$
$$= \int_0^{16.0} f(\chi^2)d\chi^2.$$

Entering the table of Appendix VII for $D = 10$, $\mathbf{P}(\chi^2 \leq 16.0)$ is 0.90. Similarly, $\mathbf{P}(\chi^2 \leq 4.865) = \mathbf{P}(\sum_{k=1}^{10} (X_k - \mu)^2/\sigma^2 \leq 4.865) = 0.10$. This probability is represented by the doubly crosshatched area of Figure X.19.

The $\mathbf{P}(4.865 < \chi^2 < 16.0)$ equals the singly crosshatched area of Figure X.19. From the figure, it can be seen that

$$\mathbf{P}(4.865 < \chi^2 < 16.0) = \mathbf{P}(\chi^2 < 16.0) - \mathbf{P}(\chi^2 \leq 4.865)$$
$$= 0.90 - 0.10 = 0.80.$$

Similarly,

$$\mathbf{P}[(\chi^2 \leq 4.865) \cup (\chi^2 > 16.0)] = 1 - \mathbf{P}(4.865 < \chi^2 \leq 16.0)$$
$$= 1 - 0.80 = 0.20.$$

This is represented by the area under $f(\chi^2)$ to the left of 4.865 plus the area under $f(\chi^2)$ to the right of 16.0.

Before leaving this introduction, it should be mentioned that the expected value of a chi-square distribution is often referred to as the number of degrees of freedom associated with chi-square. The reason for this will become clearer in Chapters XI and XIII when particular applications of the chi-square DF are described.

X.4
PROBLEMS ON DENSITY FUNCTIONS

1. If X is a continuous random variable with DF $f(X) = 0.05$ for $20 \leq X \leq 40$ and $f(X) = 0$ otherwise,
   a. What is $E(X)$?
   b. What is the variance of X?
   c. What is $\mathbf{P}(15 < X < 20)$?
   d. What is $\mathbf{P}(25 < X \leq 35)$?
   e. What is $\mathbf{P}[(X < 25) \cup (X > 35)]$?
   f. What is $\mathbf{P}(30 < X < 50)$?

2. X is a continuous random variable that has a rectangular DF. The variance of X is 12. What is the range of X? If $x_{\min} = 1$, what is $E(X)$? What is the DF of X?

3. If X has a normal DF with $\mu = 100$ and $\sigma = 15$,
   a. Find $\mathbf{P}(X > 100)$.
   b. Find $\mathbf{P}(-1 < Z < 1)$.
   c. Find $\mathbf{P}[(Z > 1.96) \cup (Z < -1.96)]$.
   d. Find $\mathbf{P}[(X > 145) \cup (X < 55)]$.
   e. Find the value, x_0, such that $\mathbf{P}(X > x_0) = 0.50$.
   f. Find the value, x_0, such that $\mathbf{P}(X \leq x_0) = 0.01$.
   g. Find the value, x_0, such that $\mathbf{P}(X > x_0) = 0.05$.
   h. Find a positive number, a, such that $\mathbf{P}(X > \mu + a) = 0.50$.
   i. Find a positive number, a, such that $\mathbf{P}(X > \mu + a) = 0.05$.
   j. Find a positive number, a, such that $\mathbf{P}[(X > \mu + a) \cup (X < \mu - a)] = 0.10$.
   k. Find a positive number, a, such that $\mathbf{P}[(X > \mu + a) \cup (X < \mu - a)] = 0.20$.

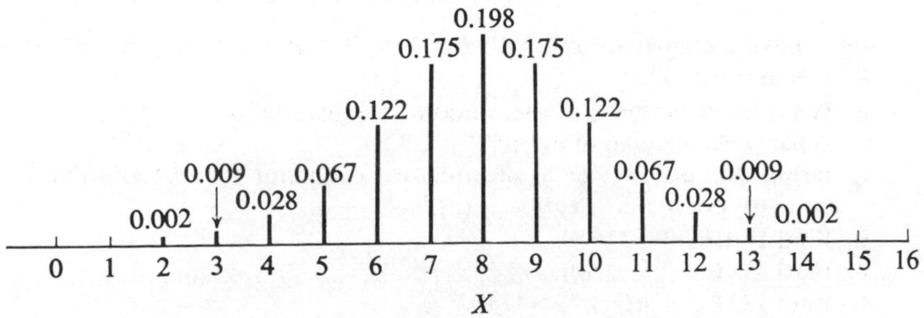

Figure X.20

l. Find a positive number, a, such that $\mathbf{P}(|X - \mu| > a) = 0.10$.
m. Find a positive number, a, such that $\mathbf{P}(|X - \mu| > a) = 0.20$.
n. Find $\mathbf{P}[(X > 120) \cup (X < 70)]$.

4. The probability distribution in Figure X.20 has a mean of 8 and a variance of 4.
   a. Construct the CDF of X and plot it.
   b. Now construct the CDF of Y, where Y is a normally distributed random variable with mean 8 and variance 4. Plot this CDF, too.
   c. Compare the CDF's of a and b on a single graph.

5. W is normally distributed and $E(W) = 5$, $E\{[W - E(W)]^2\} = 3$. A random sample, $(W_1, W_2, \ldots, W_k, \ldots, W_{10})$, is drawn from the population. Let $\chi^2 = \sum_{k=1}^{n} (W_k - 5)^2/3$.
   a. What is $\mathbf{P}(\chi^2 \leq 16.0)$?
   b. What is $\mathbf{P}(7.0 < \chi^2 < 16.0)$?
   c. What is $\mathbf{P}(\chi^2 > 7.0)$?
   d. What is $\mathbf{P}[(\chi^2 > 16.0) \cup (\chi^2 < 3.0)]$?
   e. What is $\mathbf{P}(|\chi^2 - 10.0| > 5.0)$?
   f. What is $E(\chi^2)$?
   g. What is $E\{[\chi^2 - E(\chi^2)]^2\}$?

6. When μ is known,

$$Q^2 = \frac{\sum_{k=1}^{n} (X_k - \mu)^2}{n}$$

is an unbiased estimator for the population variance, σ^2. Multiplying both sides of this definition by n gives

$$nQ^2 = \sum_{k=1}^{n} (X_k - \mu)^2.$$

Now, assume that $(X_1, X_2, \ldots, X_k, \ldots, X_n)$ is a random sample from a normally distributed population having mean μ and variance σ^2. Then, according to the results of Section X.3.3,

$$\chi^2 = \frac{nQ^2}{\sigma^2} = \sum_{k=1}^{n} \frac{(X_k - \mu)^2}{\sigma^2}$$

must have a chi-square DF with $E(\chi^2) = D = n$. Suppose that $\sigma^2 = 10$, $\mu = 6$, and $n = 25$.
   a. What is the variance of the random variable nQ^2/σ^2?
   b. What is the median of nQ^2/σ^2?
   c. Using the fact that Q^2 is an unbiased estimator for σ^2 (note that μ is known), prove that $E(\chi^2) = E(nQ^2/\sigma^2) = n$.
   d. Find $\mathbf{P}(nQ^2/\sigma^2 \leq 15.0)$.
   e. Find $\mathbf{P}(nQ^2/\sigma^2 \leq 37.0)$.
   f. Find $\mathbf{P}(15.0 < nQ^2/\sigma^2 < 37.0)$.
   g. Find $\mathbf{P}[(nQ^2/\sigma^2 > 37.0) \cup (nQ^2/\sigma^2 < 15.0)]$.

X.5
RELATIONS AMONG SOME PROBABILITY DISTRIBUTIONS

An important way of enhancing one's understanding of the probability distributions and density functions that have been introduced is to see how they are related to one another. Furthermore, it is frequently easier to compute probabilities for one and substitute these as approximate probabilities for another. Such approximations may be advantageous either because calculations are less tedious or because more extensive tables are available for one distribution.

X.5.1. Binomial and the normal distributions

Under some conditions, the normal distribution can be used to approximate binomial probabilities. The accuracy of this approximation increases as n becomes large and decreases as P deviates from 1/2.

The normal DF is defined for a continuous variable, whereas the binomial distribution is defined only for a discrete variable. This discrepancy must be considered in finding the most accurate normal approximation of binomial probabilities.

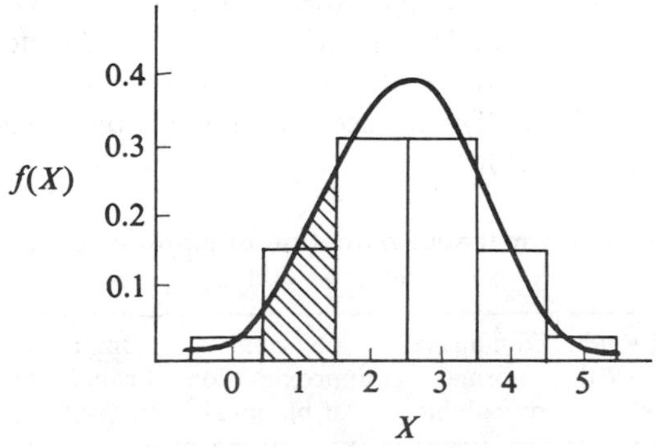

Figure X.21

In Figure X.21, the binomial distribution for $n = 5$ and $P = 1/2$ and a normal distribution with the same mean and variance are shown. How can the two be linked so that areas under the normal DF approximate the binomial probabilities? First, recall that the *area* of the bars of a histogram can be used to represent probability for a discrete random variable. Now, in Figure X.21, the bar over $X = 1$ actually extends from 0.5 to 1.5, so the area under the normal curve between 0.5 and 1.5 could be used to approximate the area of this bar. But how is this area under the normal curve to be computed?

First, the expected value of the binomial variable X is $nP = 5(1/2) = 2.5$ and its variance is $nP(1 - P) = 5(1/2)(1/2) = 1.25$. If we assume that X is approximately normally distributed, then the random variable

$$Z = \frac{X - nP}{\sqrt{[nP(1 - P)]}}$$

must be approximately normally distributed with mean 0 and variance 1. If the Z-values corresponding to $X = 0.5$ and $X = 1.5$ are found, then by entering the table of Appendix V, $\mathbf{P}(X \leq 0.5)$ and $\mathbf{P}(X \leq 1.5)$ can be approximated. For $X = 0.5$,

$$Z = \frac{X - nP}{\sqrt{[nP(1 - P)]}} = \frac{0.5 - 2.5}{\sqrt{1.25}} = \frac{-2.0}{1.12} = -1.79,$$

and for $X = 1.5$,

$$Z = \frac{1.5 - 2.5}{1.12} = -0.89.$$

From the table of Appendix V, $\mathbf{P}(X \leq 1.5) \doteq \mathbf{P}(Z \leq -0.89) = 0.1867$, and $\mathbf{P}(X \leq 0.5) = \mathbf{P}(Z \leq -1.79) = 0.0367$. Then, $\mathbf{P}(0.5 < X < 1.5) = \mathbf{P}(X \leq 1.5) - \mathbf{P}(X \leq 0.5) = 0.1867 - 0.0367 = 0.15$. The crosshatched area in Figure X.21 represents this normal approximation of the binomial probability, $\mathbf{P}(X = 1)$. The approximation yields 0.15 whereas the exact binomial probability is 0.156. In a similar way, the normal approximation has been found for each value of X with $n = 5$ and $P = 1/2$, as shown in Table X.4. The procedure on which these calculations were based is summarized below.

Table X.4. Normal approximation of binomial probabilities
$(n = 5, P = 1/2)$

X	$Z = \frac{X + 0.5 - nP}{\sqrt{[nP(1 - P)]}}$ for $X < n$	Cumulative normal probability	Normal approximation of binomial	Binomial probability	Discrepancy to nearest thousandth
0	−1.79	.0367	.0367	.031	+.006
1	−0.89	.1867	.1500	.156	−.006
2	0	.5000	.3133	.312	+.001
3	+0.89	.8133	.3133	.312	+.001
4	+1.78	.9633	.1500	.156	−.006
5	+∞	1.0000	.0367	.031	+.006

If X has a binomial distribution with expected value nP and variance $nP(1 - P)$, then $\mathbf{P}(X \leq x_q)$ approaches the normal cumulative probability,

$$\mathbf{P}\left(Z \leq \frac{x_q + 0.5 - nP}{\sqrt{[nP(1 - P)]}}\right)$$

as n increases without bound. Consequently, the binomial probabilities $\mathbf{P}(X = x)$ *can be approximated as follows:*

$$\mathbf{P}(X = 0) \cong \mathbf{P}\left(Z \le \frac{+0.5 - nP}{\sqrt{[nP(1 - P)]}}\right),$$

$$\mathbf{P}(X = x) \cong \mathbf{P}\left(Z \le \frac{x + 0.5 - nP}{\sqrt{[nP(1 - P)]}}\right) - \mathbf{P}\left(Z \le \frac{x - 0.5 - nP}{\sqrt{[nP(1 - P)]}}\right)$$

for $1 \le X \le n - 1$, *and*

$$\mathbf{P}(X = n) \cong 1 - \mathbf{P}\left(Z \le \frac{n - 0.5 - nP}{\sqrt{[nP(1 - P)]}}\right).$$

Notice that even for $n = 5$ the approximation is reasonably good when $P = 0.5$. This is reflected by the relatively small discrepancies between binomial probabilities and their normal approximations. However, if $P = 0.2$ and $n = 5$, the approximation is less accurate. This is illustrated in Table X.5.

Table X.5. Normal approximation of binomial probabilities
($n = 5$, $P = 0.2$)

X	$Z = \frac{X + 0.5 - nP}{\sqrt{[nP(1-P)]}}$ for $X < n$	Cumulative normal probability	Normal approximation of binomial	Binomial probability	Discrepancy to nearest thousandth
0	-0.56	.2877	.2877	.328	$-.040$
1	$+0.56$	.7123	.4246	.410	$+.015$
2	$+1.68$	.9535	.2412	.205	$+.036$
3	$+2.79$	.9974	.0439	.051	$-.007$
4	$+3.92$	.9999	.0025	.006	$-.003$
5	$+\infty$	1.0000	$.0001^{+}$	$.000^{+}$	.000

No complete statement can be made about the conditions under which this approximation is sufficiently accurate; however, it is frequently proposed that it be used only if $nP > 5$ *and* $n(1 - P) > 5$. Notice that this condition was *not* satisfied by either of the examples. Whether or not this rule is satisfactory depends on the requirements of the particular problem at hand. However, when P is close to 0 or to 1, the normal approximation of the binomial PD becomes inadequate unless n is very large. Under these circumstances, the Poisson PD provides a more accurate approximation of binomial probabilities.

X.5.2. Binomial and Poisson distributions

When n is large and P is small, the mean and variance of a binomial distribution become approximately equal. This is illustrated for a few selected values of n and P in Table X.6. In addition, the binomial

Table X.6. Mean and variance of binomial distribution
(n large; P small)

P	n	nP	$nP(1 - P)$
.1	5	.50	.45
.1	10	1.00	.90
.1	100	10.00	9.00
.05	5	.25	.2375
.05	10	.50	.4750
.05	100	5.00	4.75

distribution is positively skewed for small values of P. The fact that the Poisson distribution is positively skewed with mean and variance equal suggests that, under some circumstances, Poisson probabilities might be approximated using the binomial distribution. Furthermore, as shown in Appendix X.2, the Poisson distribution can be derived by supposing that, for a binomial distribution, $n \to \infty$ and $P \to 0$ while $nP = \mu$ remains constant. This also indicates a connection between Poisson and binomial distributions when n is large and P is small.

The precision of the Poisson approximation of the binomial distribution will be examined for $n = 5$ and $P = 0.1$. The binomial mean, $nP = 5(0.1) = 0.5$, is used to enter the table of the Poisson PD in Appendix IV. The binomial probabilities and the Poisson approximation are compared in the Table X.7.

Table X.7. Poisson approximation of binomial probabilities
($nP = 0.5$)

X	Binomial probability	Poisson probability	Discrepancy
0	.590	.606	+.016
1	.328	.304	−.024
2	.073	.076	+.003
3	.008	.012	+.004
4	$.000^{+}$	.002	+.002
5	$.000^{+}$	$.000^{+}$	.000

For $n = 20$ and $P = 0.05$, the Poisson approximation never differs more than 0.01 from the exact binomial probability. This comparison is made in Table X.8.

So far, the Poisson distribution has been referred to as an approximation of the binomial distribution, but it is equally possible to approximate

Table X.8. Poisson approximation of binomial probabilities ($nP = 1$)

X	Binomial probability	Poisson probability	Discrepancy
0	.358	.368	+.010
1	.377	.368	−.009
2	.189	.184	−.005
3	.060	.061	+.001
4	.013	.015	+.002
5	.002	.003	+.001
6	$.000^{+}$	.001	+.001
7	$.000^{+}$	$.000^{+}$	.000

the Poisson with the binomial. Suppose that one wished to approximate a Poisson distribution having $\mu = \sigma^2 = 1$ using binomial tables. The best approximation would be obtained by finding the smallest table value of P and the largest table value of n such that $nP = 1$. Using the binomial table of Appendix II, the best that can be done is to use $n = 20$ and $P = 0.05$, so that $nP = 20(0.05) = 1 = \mu$. Then, on the basis of Table X.8, the maximum error would be 0.01. However, if more extensive binomial tables were available, so that larger n and smaller P could be found such that $nP = 1$, then the amount of error in the approximation could be reduced.

X.5.3. Hypergeometric and binomial distributions

When the binomial and hypergeometric distributions were derived, the only difference between the arguments was that sampling *without* replacement from a *finite* population was assumed for the hypergeometric PD.

When sampling randomly from an *infinite*, binomial population, then, regardless of whether sampling is with or without replacement, the probability calculations will be the same. The reason for this is straightforward. If the binomial population is infinite, then drawing a finite number of elements from it does not alter either P or the number of elements remaining in the population. From this it might be expected that the discrepancy between binomial and hypergeometric probabilities would decrease as the size of a finite population increased. To illustrate that this is the case, Table X.9 gives the exact hypergeometric probability that $X = 2$ for a random sample of size 5 drawn from a population in which $P = R/N = 0.4$ and with the population size varying from $N = 10$ to $N = 60$ ($n = 5$, $P = 0.4$, and $X = 2$ are fixed throughout Table X.9). Since the corresponding binomial probabilities must be calculated under the assumption that sampling is with replacement, they do not change as a

Table X.9. Comparison of binomial and hypergeometric probabilities

N	Binomial $\mathbf{P}(X = 2)$	Hypergeometric $\mathbf{P}(X = 2)$	Discrepancy
10	.346	.477	.131
15	.346	.420	.074
30	.346	.378	.032
60	.346	.364	.018

function of N. However, as shown in Table X.9, the effect of taking nonreplacement into account decreases as the population size increases. Thus, when N is large, the binomial PD can be used to approximate hypergeometric probabilities.

There is one other thing to consider in appraising the accuracy of this approximation. Perhaps the easiest way to see this is to recall that, although the expected value of both the hypergeometric and the binomial distributions is nP, their variances differ. The variance of a hypergeometric distribution is

$$nP(1 - P)\left(\frac{N - n}{N - 1}\right),$$

whereas the factor $(N - n)/(N - 1)$ does not appear in the variance of a binomial distribution. However, when sampling without replacement, this finite population factor approaches 1 as $N - n$ becomes large. This suggests that when N is large and n is small in comparison with N, then the binomial approximation of hypergeometric probabilities entails small error.

In Appendix X.3, it is proved that hypergeometric and binomial probabilities become identical when $N \to \infty$.

X.5.4. Chi-square and normal density functions

In Figure X.18, it is clear that as $D = E(\chi^2)$ increases, the chi-square distribution becomes more nearly symmetrical.

For $D = E(\chi^2)$ large, the random variable $\sqrt{(2\chi^2)}$ has an approximately normal distribution with mean $\sqrt{(2D - 1)}$ and variance 1. Consequently, $\sqrt{(2\chi^2)} - \sqrt{(2D - 1)}$ has an approximately normal distribution with mean 0 and variance 1 for large values of D.[25]

For example, with $D = E(\chi^2) = 25$, $\mathbf{P}(\chi^2 \leq 40.647) = 0.975$ using the table of Appendix VII. Using the normal approximation, $\mathbf{P}(\chi^2 \leq 40.647)$ is approximately equal to

$$\begin{aligned}\mathbf{P}[Z \leq \sqrt{(2\chi^2)} - \sqrt{(2D - 1)}] &= \mathbf{P}\{Z \leq \sqrt{[2(40.647)]} - \sqrt{[2(25) - 1]}\} \\ &= \mathbf{P}(Z \leq +2.02) = 0.9783.\end{aligned}$$

[25] Hald, A., *Statistical Theory with Engineering Applications.* New York, John Wiley, 1952, p. 258.

X.6

PROBLEMS ON THE RELATIONS AMONG SOME DISTRIBUTIONS

1. A random sample of 18 observations is drawn from an infinite binomial population. X is the number of observations in a sample that is from subpopulation A, where $\mathbf{P}(A) = 0.7$.
   a. Use the normal DF to approximate the following binomial probabilities.
      i. $\mathbf{P}(X \leq 15)$
      ii. $\mathbf{P}(X < 15)$
      iii. $\mathbf{P}(X > 10)$
      iv. $\mathbf{P}(X \geq 15)$
      v. $\mathbf{P}(10 < X \leq 15)$
      vi. $\mathbf{P}[(X \leq 10) \cup (X > 15)]$
      vii. $\mathbf{P}[(X > 10) \cap (X \leq 15)]$.
   b. If $p = X/n$, find the normal approximation of the following probabilities.
      i. $\mathbf{P}(p \leq 0.833)$
      ii. $\mathbf{P}(p < 0.833)$
      iii. $\mathbf{P}(p > 0.555)$
      iv. $\mathbf{P}(p \geq 0.833)$
      v. $\mathbf{P}(0.555 < p \leq 0.833)$
      vi. $\mathbf{P}[(p \leq 0.555) \cup (p > 0.833)]$
      vii. $\mathbf{P}[(p < 1/3) \cup (p > 2/3)]$.

2. A random sample of size 33 is drawn from a binomial population in which $P = 0.03$. Use the Poisson distribution to approximate each of the following.
   a. $\mathbf{P}(X \leq 1)$
   b. $\mathbf{P}(X = 0)$
   c. $\mathbf{P}(X > 1)$
   d. $\mathbf{P}(X > 0)$
   e. $\mathbf{P}(0 < X < 3)$
   f. $\mathbf{P}(X \geq 3)$
   g. $\mathbf{P}[(X > 1) \cap (X < 3)]$
   h. $\mathbf{P}(X = 5)$.

3. Compare the variance of the binomial population with that of the Poisson PD of Problem 2.

4. A task of vigilance is being studied. Radar operators watch the scope display of a radar simulator and report each blip they see. Blips are introduced randomly at a mean rate of one per minute, so that during an observation period of 1 hour 40 minutes, 100 blips are presented to each operator. If the probability that a given blip will not be detected is 0.02, and if errors are assumed to be statistically independent from blip to blip, answer the following questions for a 1-hour 40-minute observation period.
   a. Using the appropriate Poisson approximation,
      i. What is the probability of at least three misses?

ii. What is the probability of no more than two misses?
iii. What is the expected number of misses?

b. Though P is only 0.02, n is quite large. Use a normal approximation to answer the questions of a. How do these results compare with those of the Poisson approximation?

5. A random sample of size 5 is drawn from a finite binomial population in which $N = 10$ and $R = 4$. X is the number of elements from the subpopulation containing 4 elements.
   a. Find the population mean and standard deviation of X.
   b. Construct the CDF of X.
   c. Using the appropriate mean and standard deviation, plot the normal CDF that could be used to approximate this hypergeometric distribution.
   d. Use the normal approximation to find,
      i. $\mathbf{P}(X = 2)$
      ii. $\mathbf{P}(X \leq 2)$
      iii. $\mathbf{P}(X > 2)$
      iv. $\mathbf{P}(X = 5)$.
   e. How well do the probabilities of d compare with the corresponding exact hypergeometric probabilities?

APPENDIX X.1

If X has a hypergeometric distribution, then $E(X) = nP$

This derivation depends on the definition of an expected value and some algebra. To begin with, note that

$$\sum_{x=0}^{n} \mathbf{P}(X = x) = \sum_{x=0}^{n} \frac{\binom{R}{x}\binom{N-R}{n-x}}{\binom{N}{n}} = 1.$$

Multiplying these equations by $\binom{N}{n}$,

$$\binom{N}{n} \sum_{x=0}^{n} \mathbf{P}(X = x) = \sum_{x=0}^{n} \binom{R}{x}\binom{N-R}{n-x} = 1\binom{N}{n}.$$

Now, adding *and* subtracting R from N and adding *and* subtracting x from n alters nothing. Therefore, $N = N + R - R$ and $n = n + x - x$, and

$$\sum_{x=0}^{n} \binom{R}{x}\binom{N-R}{n-x} = \binom{N}{n} = \binom{N+R-R}{n+x-x}$$

$$= \binom{R+(N-R)}{x+(n-x)}.$$

This result will be used shortly, but first we must examine the definition of the expected value of the hypergeometric PD. This is defined by

$$E(X) = \sum_{x=0}^{n} \frac{x\binom{R}{x}\binom{N-R}{n-x}}{\binom{N}{n}} = 0 + \sum_{x=1}^{n} \frac{x\binom{R}{x}\binom{N-R}{n-x}}{\binom{N}{n}}$$

$$= \frac{1}{\binom{N}{n}} \sum_{x=1}^{n} \frac{xR!}{x!\,(R-x)!} \binom{N-R}{n-x}.$$

Cancelling x in numerator and denominator and separating R from $R!$ gives

$$E(X) = \frac{R}{\binom{N}{n}} \sum_{x=1}^{n} \frac{(R-1)!}{(x-1)!\,(R-x)!} \binom{N-R}{n-x}.$$

The range of summation can be changed from 1 to n to 0 to $n - 1$ if the summation index is changed from x to $x - 1$. This is true since this is only a change in *notation*. Then,

$$E(X) = \frac{R}{\binom{N}{n}} \sum_{x-1=0}^{n-1} \frac{(R-1)!}{(x-1)!\,(R-x)!} \binom{N-R}{n-x}$$

$$= \frac{R}{\binom{N}{n}} \sum_{x-1=0}^{n-1} \binom{R-1}{x-1}\binom{N-R}{n-x}.$$

Now, by direct analogy to the result obtained at the beginning of the proof,

$$\sum_{x-1=0}^{n-1} \binom{R-1}{x-1}\binom{N-R}{n-x} = \binom{(R-1)+(N-R)}{(x-1)+(n-x)},$$

so

$$E(X) = \frac{R}{\binom{N}{n}} \sum_{x-1=0}^{n-1} \binom{R-1}{x-1}\binom{N-R}{n-x} = \frac{R}{\binom{N}{n}} \binom{(R-1)+(N-R)}{(x-1)+(n-x)}$$

$$= \frac{R}{\binom{N}{n}} \binom{N-1}{n-1} = \frac{R}{\dfrac{N!}{n!\,(N-n)!}} \frac{(N-1)!}{(n-1)!\,[N-1-(n-1)]!}$$

$$= n\frac{R}{N} = nP.$$

This is the result we set out to obtain.

APPENDIX X.2

Proof that as $n \to \infty$ and $P \to 0$ with $nP = \mu$ remaining constant, the binomial distribution approaches the Poisson distribution

In this proof, the binomial distribution will be put in an appropriate form by algebraic manipulation. Then, we let $P \to 0$ and $n \to \infty$ with $\mu = nP$ fixed, and see what happens.

To begin with, the binomial probability is

$$\mathbf{P}(X = x) = \binom{n}{x} P^x(1 - P)^{n-x}$$

$$= \frac{n!}{x!(n-x)!} P^x(1 - P)^{n-x}.$$

Now, since $\mu = nP$ for a binomial population, it follows that $P = \mu/n$. In addition,

$$\frac{n!}{x!\,(n-x)!} = \frac{n(n-1)\cdots(n-x+1)}{x!}.$$

These results can be substituted in

$$\mathbf{P}(X = x) = \frac{n!}{x!\,(n-x)!} P^x(1 - P)^{n-x}$$

to give

$$\mathbf{P}(X = x) = \frac{n(n-1)\cdots(n-x+1)}{x!} \left(\frac{\mu}{n}\right)^x \left(1 - \frac{\mu}{n}\right)^{n-x}.$$

Shifting terms about,

$$\mathbf{P}(X = x) = \frac{n(n-1)\cdots(n-x+1)}{n^x} \frac{\mu^x}{x!} \left(1 - \frac{\mu}{n}\right)^{n-x}$$

$$= \frac{n}{n} \frac{(n-1)}{n} \cdots \frac{(n-x+1)}{n} \frac{\mu^x}{x!} \left(1 - \frac{\mu}{n}\right)^n \left(1 - \frac{\mu}{n}\right)^{-x}$$

$$= 1\left(1 - \frac{1}{n}\right) \cdots \left(1 - \frac{x-1}{n}\right) \frac{\mu^x}{x!} \left(1 - \frac{\mu}{n}\right)^n \left(1 - \frac{\mu}{n}\right)^{-x}.$$

Now, let $n \to \infty$. Remembering that $\mu = nP$ must remain constant, all factors except $\mu^x/x!$ and $[1 - (\mu/n)]^n$ go to 1. Furthermore (as shown in introductory calculus texts),

$$\lim_{n \to \infty} \left(1 - \frac{\mu}{n}\right)^n = e^{-\mu}.$$

Making these substitutions,

$$\mathbf{P}(X = x) = 1(1)\cdots(1) \frac{\mu^x}{x!} e^{-\mu}(1)$$

$$= \frac{\mu^x e^{-\mu}}{x!}.$$

This, of course, is the equation for the Poisson PD. Since $\mu = nP$, it can also be written as

$$\mathbf{P}(X = x) = \frac{(nP)^x e^{-nP}}{x!}.$$

APPENDIX X.3

Proof that the hypergeometric probability distribution approaches the binomial distribution as the population size approaches ∞

The proof begins with some algebraic manipulation of the hypergeometric formula:

$$\mathbf{P}(X = x) = \frac{\binom{R}{x}\binom{N-R}{n-x}}{\binom{N}{n}} = \frac{\dfrac{R!}{x!\,(R-x)!}\,\dfrac{(N-R)!}{(n-x)!\,[N-R-(n-x)]!}}{\dfrac{N!}{n!\,(N-n)!}}$$

$$= \frac{n!\,(N-n)!}{N!}\,\frac{R!}{x!\,(R-x)!}\,\frac{(N-R)!}{(n-x)!\,(N-R-n+x)!}$$

$$= \frac{n!}{x!\,(n-x)!}\,\frac{(N-n)!}{N!}\,\frac{R!}{(R-x)!}\,\frac{(N-R)!}{(N-R-n+x)!}$$

$$= \binom{n}{x}\frac{1}{N(N-1)\cdots(N-n+1)}\,\frac{R(R-1)\cdots(R-x+1)}{1}$$
$$\times\,\frac{(N-R)(N-R-1)\cdots(N-R-n+x+1)}{1}.$$

Now, dividing numerator and denominator by N^n,

$$\mathbf{P}(X = x) = \binom{n}{x}\frac{R}{N}\frac{(R-1)}{N}\cdots\frac{(R-x+1)}{N}$$
$$\times\,\frac{\dfrac{(N-R)}{N}\dfrac{(N-R-1)}{N}\cdots\dfrac{(N-R-n+x+1)}{N}}{\dfrac{N}{N}\dfrac{(N-1)}{N}\cdots\dfrac{(N-n+1)}{N}}$$

$$= \binom{n}{x}P\left(P-\frac{1}{N}\right)\cdots\left(P-\frac{(x-1)}{N}\right)$$
$$\times\,\frac{(1-P)\left(1-P-\dfrac{1}{N}\right)\cdots\left(1-P-\dfrac{(n-x-1)}{N}\right)}{1\left(1-\dfrac{1}{N}\right)\cdots\left(1-\dfrac{(n-1)}{N}\right)},$$

since $P = R/N$ and $1 - P = 1 - (R/N) = (N - R)/N$. For any sample size, as $N \rightarrow \infty$, all the ratios with N in the denominator become 0. Then

$$\mathbf{P}(X = x) = \binom{n}{x} \frac{\overbrace{P(P)\cdots(P)}^{x \text{ factors}}\ \overbrace{(1 - P)(1 - P)\cdots(1 - P)}^{n-x \text{ factors}}}{\underbrace{1(1)\cdots(1)}_{n \text{ factors}}}$$

$$= \binom{n}{x} P^x(1 - P)^{n-x}.$$

Since this is a binomial probability, the proof is complete.

SUGGESTED READING

1. Almost any modern text on statistical methods includes a discussion of binomial, normal, and chi-square distributions. In addition to these, most texts in mathematical statistics deal with the hypergeometric, multinomial, Poisson, and rectangular distributions.

2. Hald, A., *Statistical Theory with Engineering Applications.* New York, John Wiley, 1952.
This is a clearly written text which requires an intermediate level of mathematical sophistication including some calculus. It contains thorough chapters on the normal (Chapter 6), binomial (Chapter 21), Poisson (Chapter 22), and chi-square (Chapter 10) distributions. The multinomial distribution is described in Chapter 2. The hypergeometric distribution is introduced on pp. 40–43, and its relation to the binomial distribution is treated on pp. 690–691.

3. Hogg, R. V., and A. T. Craig, *Introduction to Mathematical Statistics.* New York, Macmillan, 1959.
Chapter 2 gives a concise introduction to the binomial, Poisson, normal, and chi-square distributions. The presentation is compact and clear, but calculus is required.

4. Mood, A. M., *Introduction to the Theory of Statistics.* New York, McGraw-Hill, 1950.
Chapter 3 includes binomial, multinomial, Poisson, and hypergeometric distributions. Chapter 6 includes the continuous rectangular distribution, the normal and chi-square distributions, and several others. Calculus is required for most of these sections.

5. Lewis, D., *Quantitative Methods in Psychology.* New York, McGraw-Hill, 1960.
Chapter 7 contains a detailed discussion of the normal DF, including its derivation from a binomial process. Chapter 8 contains introductions to the binomial and Poisson distributions, and the chi-square DF is discussed in Chapter 9. All the calculus necessary to read these chapters can be found in Chapters 5 and 6.

XI

SAMPLING DISTRIBUTIONS

METHODS of applying probability to random variables were described in Chapter VII, and a number of useful PD's and DF's were introduced in Chapter X. Several parameters and their estimators were defined and discussed in Chapter IX. The task of this chapter is to combine these results so that we will have methods of applying probability to estimators. Then the problems of estimation and hypothesis testing can be attacked in Chapters XII and XIII.

When a random sample is drawn from a population, a random experiment is performed. The sample space consists of all samples of a given size that might be observed. A value of an estimator can be assigned to each outcome (each possible sample), and these values form the range of a random variable. Then, *the probability distribution or density function of an estimator is called a sampling distribution.*

In previous discussions, there have been several examples of sampling distributions. These illustrations (for the sample mean, see Section VII.1.1; for the sample median, see Section IX.2.2; for the sample mean deviation, see Section IX.4.4; and for the sample variance, see Section IX.4.6) were presented in order to illustrate certain characteristics of these estimators. In this chapter, attention is focused on the properties of sampling distribution themselves and on some principles that describe the sampling behavior of many estimators.

XI.1

LEVELS OF STATISTICAL ANALYSIS

In working with sampling distributions, it is absolutely necessary to distinguish several descriptive levels. What these levels are and how they are to be distinguished will be elaborated with the aid of an example. This example has to do with the problem of ethnic cleavage introduced in Section X.1.2.

When an Anglo pupil designates the five others he would "choose to mess around with," some of his choices may be Anglo (A) and some not (N). For example, one pupil's choices might be represented by (A, N, N, A, A). An outcome of this sort constitutes the raw data, and the sample space for a single chooser consists of 2^5 such outcomes.

If one is investigating ethnic cleavage, then the number of Anglo choices (number of A's) summarizes an important feature of the set of choices made by each subject. This amounts to defining a random variable, X, on the set of choices available to a single subject. Thus, $X = 3$ for the outcome (A, N, N, A, A). This variable, number of Anglos chosen, might well be the focus of an investigator's attention. If so, it would be called the *observation variable*.

Given the five choices made by each of a sample of nine subjects, the investigator can calculate the mean of X for this sample. This mean is a value on a random variable, too, but it is determined for a sample of subjects, not for an individual.

The important thing to notice about this example is that it forms a parallel hierarchy of descriptive levels. The organization of this hierarchy is shown in Table XI.1. The right-hand column of Table XI.1 refers to

Table XI.1. Descriptive levels of statistical analysis

Level	Outcome or random variable	Probability
I	Sample space of *raw data*, e.g., (A, N, N, A, A)	Probabilities of raw data units, e.g., **P**(A, N, N, A, A)
II	*Observation variable*, X, with range (0, 1, . . ., 5)	PD of observation variable, $\mathbf{P}(X = x)$
III	*Estimator*, $\bar{X}$, with range (0, 0.11, 0.22, . . ., 5.0)	Sampling distribution of estimator, $\mathbf{P}(\bar{X} = \bar{x})$

probabilities, the central column to outcomes and random variables.

In most of the work engaged in from now on, *it is absolutely essential to distinguish among the three levels of this hierarchy, especially between Levels II and III, and to know the level at which one is operating at every point.* In order to facilitate the distinction between Levels II and III, a random variable at Level II will be referred to as an *observation variable* and a random variable at Level III will be referred to as an *estimator*.

The PD or DF of an estimator will be called a *sampling distribution,* whereas an observation variable has a *probability distribution* or *density function.*

It is usually quite evident what is an estimator and what is an observation variable, but *no hard and fast rule can be given for distinguishing the two.* Both are random variables, and it is often only the focus of interest of the investigator that determines the distinction.

XI.2
SAMPLING DISTRIBUTIONS AND THE LAW OF LARGE NUMBERS

Even though the mean is ordinarily obtained for only one random sample, it could be calculated for each of many random samples of the same size from a given population. If the number of samples were very large, the frequency function of these sample means should approximate the theoretical sampling distribution of the mean. The variance of this distribution is central to the discussion of this and the following sections.

XI.2.1. Variance of a random sample mean

If a random sample of size n is drawn from an infinite population or with replacement from a finite population, and if σ^2 is the variance of the observation variable X, then the variance of the sample mean is

$$\sigma_{\bar{X}}^2 = \frac{\sigma^2}{n}. \qquad \text{[XI.1a]}$$

If sampling without replacement from a finite population of size N, then

$$\sigma_{\bar{X}}^2 = \frac{N-n}{N-1}\frac{\sigma^2}{n}. \qquad \text{[XI.1b]}$$

In either case, $\sqrt{\sigma_{\bar{X}}^2} = \sigma_{\bar{X}}$ *is called the standard error of the mean.* The finite population factor, $(N - n)/(N - 1)$, was discussed in Sections X.1.2 and X.5.3.

These formulas for the variance of a random sample mean show clearly that, as n increases, the sampling variability of the mean decreases. This is a more explicit description of the *way* the precision of this estimator increases with n than that given by the law of large numbers. In the case of Formula [XI.1a], the variance of the sample mean is inversely proportional to the sample size. The same inverse relation between $\sigma_{\bar{X}}^2$ and n holds when sampling without replacement from a finite population, but, in addition, increasing n decreases the finite population factor.

When we refer to the variance of a random sample mean, it is the variance of the sampling distribution of the mean that is specified. In Section

VII.1.1, the sampling distribution was found for the mean of random samples of size 2 drawn with replacement from a population having a discrete rectangular distribution.[1] This sampling distribution appears in Table XI.2. The variance of the mean can be computed directly from this table.

Table XI.2. Sampling distribution for mean of random samples of size 2

$\bar{X}$	1.0	1.5	2.0	2.5	3.0
$\mathbf{P}(\bar{X} = \bar{x})$	1/9	2/9	3/9	2/9	1/9

Since the population mean of X is 2, the variance of the mean of random samples of size 2 is

$$\begin{aligned}\sigma_{\bar{X}}^2 = E[(\bar{X} - \mu)^2] &= \sum \mathbf{P}(\bar{X} = \bar{x})(\bar{x} - \mu)^2 \\ &= \frac{1}{9}(1.0 - 2)^2 + \frac{2}{9}(1.5 - 2)^2 + \frac{3}{9}(2.0 - 2)^2 \\ &\qquad + \frac{2}{9}(2.5 - 2)^2 + \frac{1}{9}(3.0 - 2)^2 \\ &= \frac{1}{3}.\end{aligned}$$

However, it is much simpler to apply Formula [XI.1a] to obtain the same result. Since the population variance of the observation variable is 2/3 and the sample size is 2, the variance of the sample mean is

$$\sigma_{\bar{X}}^2 = \frac{\sigma^2}{n} = \frac{2/3}{2} = \frac{1}{3}.$$

DERIVATION OF VARIANCE OF A RANDOM SAMPLE MEAN. The importance of Formula [XI.1a] seems to justify the presentation of its derivation. On the other hand, Formula [XI.1b] is used less often and its derivation will not be given here.

When sampling from an infinite population or with replacement from a finite population, the observations of a random sample are mutually independent. Furthermore, the observations of such a sample can be thought of as n random variables each of which has the same mean μ and variance σ^2. The first step is to find the variance of the sum of the observations, $X_1 + X_2 + \cdots + X_n = \sum X = n\bar{X}$. Since the observa-

[1] This population contained the values 1, 2, and 3 with equal probability. The variance of the observation variable (X) in this population is 2/3, the mean is 2.

tions are mutually independent, the variance of their sum equals the sum of their variances (Section IX.11.2), so that

$$\sigma^2_{n\bar{X}} = \underbrace{\sigma^2 + \sigma^2 + \cdots + \sigma^2}_{n \text{ terms}}$$
$$= n\sigma^2.$$

Now recall that the variance of a random variable multiplied by a constant is equal to the square of the constant times the variance of the original variable. If $n\bar{X}$ is multiplied by $1/n$, then the variance of $1/n(n\bar{X}) = \bar{X}$ is

$$\sigma_{\bar{X}}{}^2 = \left(\frac{1}{n}\right)^2 \sigma^2_{n\bar{X}} = \frac{1}{n^2}\, n\sigma^2 = \frac{\sigma^2}{n}.$$

This completes the proof.

Notice that in this derivation *there is no restriction on the shape of the PD or DF of the observation variable, X.*

A sample proportion is simply the sample mean of a random variable, Y, that has range (0, 1). If $\mathbf{P}(Y = 1) = P$, then, as shown in Section X.1.1, $\sigma_Y{}^2 = P(1 - P)$. If p is the proportion of ones in a sample of size n, then from Formula [XI.1a],

$$\sigma_p{}^2 = \sigma_{\bar{Y}}{}^2 = \frac{\sigma_Y{}^2}{n} = \frac{P(1 - P)}{n}.$$

If sampling from an infinite binomial population, or with replacement from a finite binomial population, then the variance of the random sample proportion is

$$\sigma_p{}^2 = \frac{P(1 - P)}{n}. \qquad \text{[XI.2a]}$$

If sampling without replacement from a finite binomial population of size N, then the variance of the sample proportion is

$$\sigma_p{}^2 = \frac{N - n}{N - 1}\,\frac{P(1 - P)}{n}. \qquad \text{[XI.2b]}$$

In both cases, the standard error of a proportion is $\sigma_p = \sqrt{\sigma_p{}^2}$.

XI.2.3. Changes in sampling distribution as sample size increases

The effect of increasing sample size can be illustrated in detail by comparing the sampling distributions of the mean for random samples of sizes 2, 3, 4, and 5 when sampling with replacement from a population with equiprobable values 1, 2, and 3. These four sampling distributions are shown in Figure XI.1. As the sample size increases, the probabilities become more concentrated about the population mean of 2. This "central compression" is reflected by the decrease in the variance of $\bar{X}$ as n increases. For $n = 2$, $\sigma_{\bar{X}}{}^2 = 0.333$; for $n = 3$, $\sigma_{\bar{X}}{}^2 = 0.222$; for $n = 4$, $\sigma_{\bar{X}}{}^2 = 0.165$; and for $n = 5$, $\sigma_{\bar{X}}{}^2 = 0.133$.

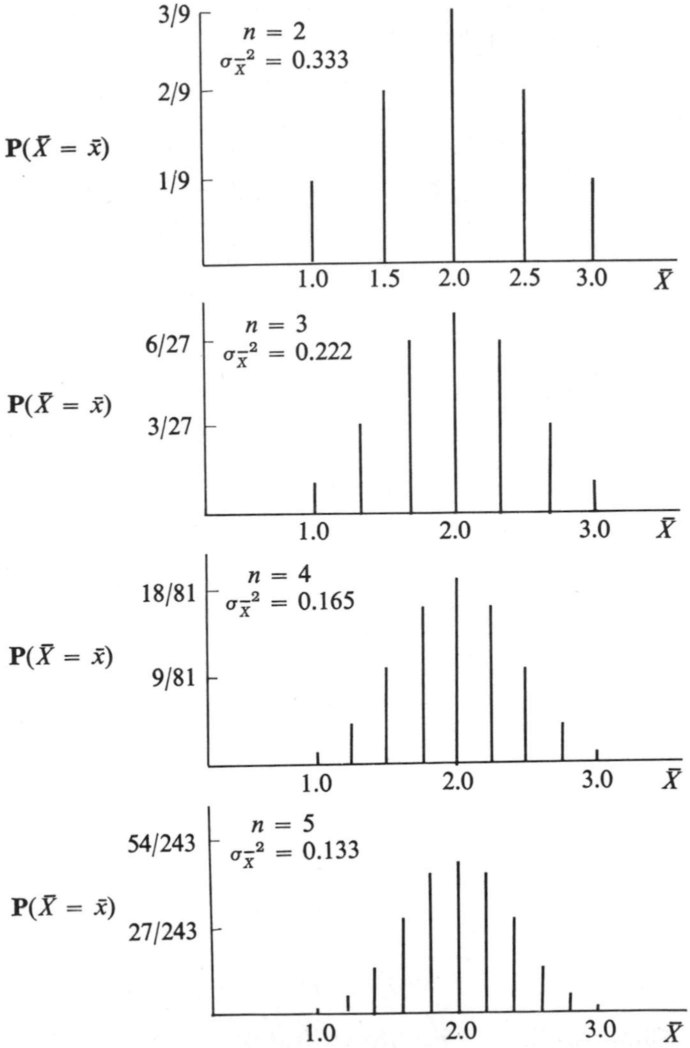

Figure XI.1

A similar decrease in variability with increased sample size can be shown for the sample variance. The sampling distribution of S^2 has been computed for random samples of sizes 2, 3, 4, and 5 drawn with replacement from the same population. These four sampling distributions are plotted in Figure XI.2.

Notice that, as n increases, the probabilities of extreme values of S^2 become smaller and the distributions become more concentrated about $E(S^2) = \sigma^2 = 2/3$. Thus, for both $\bar{X}$ and S^2, increasing sample size

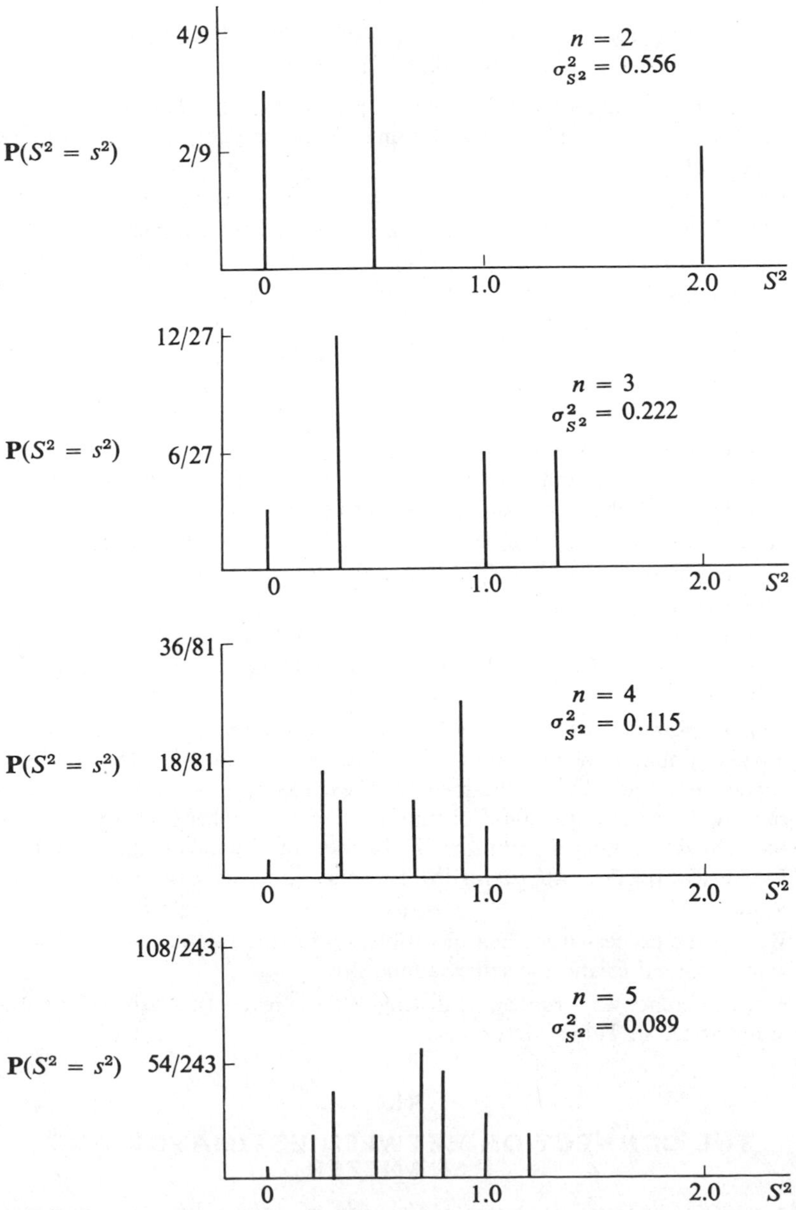

Figure XI.2

decreases the variance of the sampling distribution. A similar conclusion applies to all of the estimators described in Chapter IX.

XI.3

PRELIMINARY PROBLEMS ON SAMPLING DISTRIBUTIONS

1. What are the differences between a probability distribution, a density function, and a sampling distribution? Is a sampling distribution a DF or a PD?
2. Suppose that the variance of an observation variable X is $\sigma^2 = 225$. What is the standard error of the mean for random samples of $n = 100$?
3. Suppose that the sampling distribution of the mean of Problem 2 is a normal distribution. If it is assumed that the population mean of this observation variable is $\mu = 50$, find the following probabilities:
   a. $\mathbf{P}(\bar{X} > 52)$
   b. $\mathbf{P}(\bar{X} \leq 52)$
   c. $\mathbf{P}(47 < \bar{X} \leq 53)$
   d. $\mathbf{P}[(\bar{X} \leq 47) \cup (\bar{X} > 53)]$
   e. $\mathbf{P}[(\bar{X} > 47) \cup (\bar{X} > 50)]$
   f. $\mathbf{P}[(\bar{X} \leq 47) \cup (\bar{X} > 52)]$
   g. $\mathbf{P}(47 < \bar{X} \leq 52)$.
4. Construct a graph that clearly indicates the probability for each item of Problem 3. Label the ordinate and abscissa appropriately.
5. A random sample of size 25 is to be drawn from an infinite binomial population in which $P = 0.7$. Find the following probabilities using a normal approximation.
   a. $\mathbf{P}(p > 0.8)$
   b. $\mathbf{P}[(p < 0.2) \cup (p > 0.8)]$
   c. $\mathbf{P}[|p - P| \geq 0.2]$
   d. $\mathbf{P}(0.5 < p < 0.9)$
   e. $\mathbf{P}[(p \leq 0.5) \cup (p \geq 0.9)]$.
6. Random samples of 3 observations each are drawn from an infinite rectangular population containing the values 5, 6, 7, and 8. One thousand such samples are drawn, the median of each sample is computed, and the relative frequency function of the median is recorded. Construct the *theoretical* sampling distribution of the median that this empirical relative frequency function approximates and then find its expected value and variance.
7. Repeat the process described in Problem 6 for the sample range. Use the same population and the same sample size.
8. With reference to Problem 7, distinguish the levels of statistical analysis summarized in Table XI.1.

XI.4

THE CONNECTION BETWEEN ESTIMATOR AND PARAMETER

The expected value of an estimator depends upon the value of the parameter it is used to estimate. This dependence is summarized in Table XI.3 for several important estimators. The expected value of an unbiased estimator equals the parameter it estimates, and the expected value of an asymptotically unbiased estimator approaches the parameter as the sample

Table XI.3. Relationship of estimators to parameters

Estimator	Relation to parameter	Biased/unbiased
Arithmetic mean	$E(\bar{X}) = \mu$	Unbiased
Variance	$E(S^2) = \sigma^2$	Unbiased
Median	$\lim_{n \to \infty} [E(M) - V] = 0$	Asymptotically unbiased
Range*	$\lim_{n \to \infty} [E(\text{Range}) - \gamma] = 0$	Asymptotically unbiased
Mean deviation*	$\lim_{n \to \infty} [E(MD) - \delta] = 0$	Asymptotically unbiased

* γ represents the population range, δ the population mean deviation. The sample range is asymptotically unbiased only if the population range is finite.

size becomes large. Notice that one or the other of these two characteristics is essential in addition to the decreasing variability property. An estimator whose variability decreased as n increased would be worse than useless if the amount of its bias increased at the same time.

The strictly unbiased estimator is unbiased regardless of the shape of the distribution of the observation variable. However, as n increases, the *rate* with which the asymptotically unbiased estimator approaches zero bias depends upon the shape of the distribution of the observation variable. For example, the median is unbiased if the observation variable has a symmetrical distribution, but, as skewness increases, the amount of bias increases for a given sample size (see Section IX.2.2).

*XI.5

CHEBYSHEV'S INEQUALITY

During the latter half of the nineteenth century, the Russian mathematician P. L. Chebyshev[2] proved a surprising inequality concerning all probability distributions and density functions. Although our primary concern here lies in its implications for sampling distributions, it is applicable to any PD or DF.

Chebyshev's inequality states that if X is a random variable with mean μ and variance σ^2, then for any positive number, δ,

$$\mathbf{P}(|X - \mu| \geq \delta) \leq \frac{\sigma^2}{\delta^2}. \qquad [XI.3]$$

Thus, the probability that a randomly selected value of a variable will deviate δ or more from its mean is not greater than σ^2/δ^2. This is illustrated in Figure XI.3. The inequality asserts that the area to the right of

[2] The English spelling varies considerably, e.g., "Tchebychef."

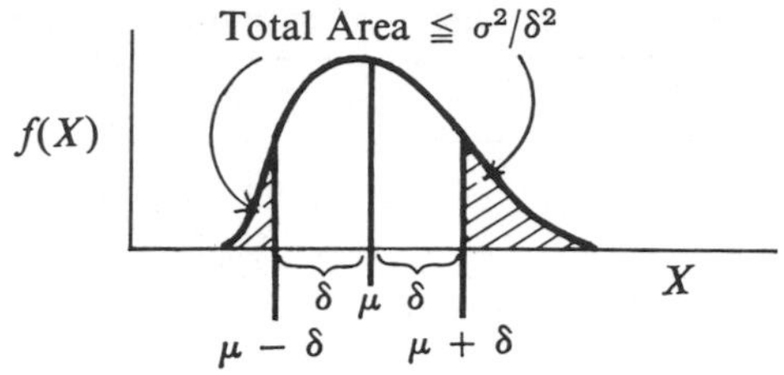

Figure XI.3

$\mu + \delta$ plus the area to the left of $\mu - \delta$ cannot exceed σ^2/δ^2. Of course, as δ increases, the probability that an observation will be more than δ units from the mean becomes less, since σ^2/δ^2 decreases as δ increases.

The surprising thing is that Chebyshev's inequality places no restrictions on the PD (or DF) of the variable in question. In fact, the inequality can be applied when the PD (or DF) is unknown. Only the mean and the variance must be known (since δ is chosen arbitrarily).

Since estimators are random variables, the inequality is applicable to sampling distributions, too. In the case of the sample mean, the inequality becomes

$$\mathbf{P}(|\bar{X} - \mu| \geq \delta) \leq \frac{\sigma_{\bar{X}}^2}{\delta^2} = \frac{\sigma^2/n}{\delta^2} = \frac{\sigma^2}{n\delta^2},$$

where n is the size of the random sample on which $\bar{X}$ is based and σ^2 is the variance of the observation variable, X. In this form, the inequality combines two things that we have discovered by other means. First, it says that large deviations of $\bar{X}$ from μ are unlikely, since $\sigma^2/(n\delta^2)$ is small when δ is large. Second, as n increases, the probability that $\bar{X}$ will deviate from μ by any given amount decreases.

However, the inequality does not tell us the exact probability of a deviation of size δ or greater, it only gives an *upper limit* for that probability. In order to determine the exact probability of a deviation, it *is* necessary to know the PD (or DF) of the random variable.

The inequality will be illustrated for the distribution of mean IQ's for a sample of school children. Suppose that the population has a mean IQ of 103.6 with a standard deviation of 16.4. What is the *maximum* probability that the mean of a random sample of $n = 100$ will be 5 IQ points or more from the population mean? According to the inequality,

$$\mathbf{P}(|\bar{X} - \mu| \geq \delta) \leq \frac{\sigma^2}{n\delta^2}$$

$$\mathbf{P}(|\bar{X} - 103.6| \geq 5) \leq \frac{(16.4)^2}{100(5)^2}$$

$$\mathbf{P}(|\bar{X} - 103.6| \geq 5) \leq 0.108.$$

This says that the probability that the mean of a random sample of 100 observations will be 108.6 or more or 98.6 or less is at most 0.108.

If mean IQ happened to be normally distributed for this population, then the exact probability of a deviation of 5 units or more could be calculated in the following way:

$$\begin{aligned}\mathbf{P}(|\bar{X} - 103.6| \geq 5) &= \mathbf{P}[(\bar{X} \leq 98.6) \cup (\bar{X} \geq 108.6)] \\ &= 0.0022.\end{aligned}$$

In this case, it is clear that the inequality is correct. The exact probability of a deviation of 5 units or more is much less than 0.108, so that the inequality is very conservative. Of course, the discrepancy between the exact probability and the upper limit, $\sigma^2/(n\delta^2)$, is not this great for all distributions (a normal distribution was assumed in the example), but the inequality is always "safe."

A proof of Chebyshev's inequality for discrete random variables is given in Appendix XI.4. It depends only upon the definition of a population variance and is quite simple.

The statement of Chebyshev's inequality for the sample mean provides the basis for a simple proof of the applicability of the law of large numbers to the sample mean. All that is necessary is to note that as $n \to \infty$, the right-hand side of the inequality goes to zero.[3] In other words, the probability that a random sample mean will deviate from the population mean by more than any fixed amount, δ, tends toward zero as the sample size increases without limit. This should make it clear how the law of large numbers and the Chebyshev inequality are related. Essentially, they are different aspects of the same relationship. The law of large numbers emphasizes the "limiting" ($n \to \infty$) characteristics, whereas Chebyshev's inequality applies to any sample size.

XI.6

PROBLEMS ON THE ESTIMATOR-PARAMETER RELATION AND CHEBYSHEV'S INEQUALITY

1. What is the magnitude of bias for the sample median of Problem 6 in Section XI.3? For the sample mean?

2. What is the magnitude of bias for the sample range of Problem 7 in Section XI.3?

[3] James Bernoulli proved a form of the law of large numbers for the binomial distribution some 150 years prior to the appearance of Chebyshev's inequality. In spite of the fact that Bernoulli was an excellent mathematician, he reports that he required 20 years to complete the proof!

3. At what level of analysis (described in Table XI.1) is one operating when the bias of an estimator is dealt with?
4. In one university, the mean grade-point for the student body of 2500 is 2.1. An instructor notes that the mean for his elementary statistics class of 49 students is 2.4. If the variance of grade-points in the student body is 0.5, and the statistics class is considered a random sample from the student body,
   a. What is the variance of the sample mean?
   *b. What is the maximum probability that such a sample mean would deviate by 0.3 or more from the student body mean?
   c. What is the expected value of mean grade-point for the class?
   d. What is the expected value of the variance of grade-point in the class?
   e. If the instructor assumed mean grade-point to be normally distributed, what is the probability that the class mean would deviate as much as 0.3 from the population mean?
   f. Answers to a, *b, c, d, and e all require the assumption that the class is a random sample from the student body. Comment on the reasonableness of such an assumption.

*5. For Problem 2 of Section XI.3, what is the maximum probability that the mean of a random sample of 100 observations will differ from the population mean by 3 units or more? Compare your answer to that of Problem 3d of Section XI.3.

XI.7
TWO IMPORTANT METHODS FOR DETERMINING SAMPLING DISTRIBUTIONS

The value of an estimator will vary from one random sample to another, and one might easily conclude that this variability is capricious. However, *the variability of an estimator is always orderly if the estimator is based on probability sampling* (e.g., random sampling). *Moreover, it is often possible to specify the sampling distribution of an estimator prior to observing any samples at all.* When this is possible, explicit procedures for estimating population parameters or for testing hypotheses about these parameters can be developed. In other words, *the sampling distribution provides the conceptual bridge between descriptive statistics and the procedures for estimation and hypothesis testing.*

The problem of how to determine the sampling distribution of an estimator is one of the most important in theoretical statistics. In this section, two fundamental methods of finding sampling distributions will be described. These methods solve only a few of the problems that are pertinent to psychological research, but both yield results that have a number of practical applications. They will be referred to as the *method of enumeration* and the *central limit theorem.*

XI.7.1. Finding sampling distributions by enumeration

The method of enumeration consists of listing all of the random samples (of a given size) that can be obtained from a specified population, calculating the value of the estimator for each sample, and determining the probability of each such value. In this way, the sampling distribution of the estimator can be determined.

This procedure might be called the method of "brute force" enumeration. It involves nothing ingenious, subtle, or elegant. Furthermore, it is entirely inapplicable to continuous observation variables, and unless calculation shortcuts can be found, it is extremely tedious for large samples and for discrete observation variables that have a large number of possible values. Nonetheless, the method is actually employed; it has been used to construct the sampling distribution tables of several widely used statistics.

This method was used to find the sampling distributions shown in Figures XI.1 and XI.2 and those used in Chapter IX. In these instances, of course, n was very small.

XI.7.2. Finding sampling distributions by applying the central limit theorem

One of the most important landmarks in the history of statistics is the development of the central limit theorem. Since it was first proved in 1733 by De Moivre, its range of applicability has increased steadily, and its implications for statistics are enormous. Numerous applications of the central limit theorem (CLT) occur throughout statistics, and familiarity with it is essential for anyone who expects to make intelligent use of statistical methods.

In spite of its importance, the CLT cannot be proved here. Even in its simpler forms, it makes demands on mathematical sophistication that are beyond the scope of this book. However, many sources do provide proofs.[4]

In general terms, *the CLT provides the basis for the conclusion that the sampling distributions of a number of useful estimators are approximately normal for large random samples.* The crucial and surprising thing about the CLT is that, *for all practical purposes, this conclusion applies regardless of the shape of the PD or DF of the observation variable.* Although the

[4] A. M. Mood gives a proof of the CLT for the mean in *Introduction to the Theory of Statistics.* New York, McGraw-Hill, 1950, pp. 136–139.

A proof of the De Moivre-Laplace theorem (the CLT applied to proportions) can be found in Cramér, H., *The Elements of Probability Theory.* New York, John Wiley, 1955, pp. 96–102.

W. Feller gives a very general statement of the CLT in *An Introduction to Probability Theory and its Applications,* I, 2nd ed. New York, John Wiley, 1957, p. 239, but does not offer a proof. References are given by Feller.

CLT is not true for all estimators (e.g., it is not true of the range), it does apply to many of the most useful ones, such as the mean, proportion, median, and variance.

Actually, we have already used the De Moivre–Laplace version of the CLT in discussing the normal approximation of the binomial distribution.

In Figure XI.1, the sampling distribution of the mean is shown for random samples of sizes 2, 3, 4, and 5. The observation variable has a *rectangular* PD, but notice that the sampling distribution of $\bar{X}$ is symmetrical and unimodal even for samples of size 2. Furthermore, for $n = 5$, the sampling distribution of $\bar{X}$ looks a good deal like a normal distribution. If n were still larger, this similarity would become even more evident.

In Figure XI.2, sampling distributions of the variance are shown for samples drawn from the same *rectangular* population. The sampling distribution of S^2 for $n = 2$ is anything but normal; however, that for $n = 5$ is considerably more like a normal distribution. If the sampling distribution of S^2 were calculated for $n = 25$ or so, its kinship with the normal distribution would be apparent.

In these illustrations, it is important to keep in mind that the observation variable has a *rectangular distribution*, but, in spite of this, the sampling distributions of $\bar{X}$ and of S^2 begin to resemble the normal distribution even for samples of size 5.

Quite reasonably, one might ask what happens if X has a *bimodal* distribution? How can the sampling distribution of $\bar{X}$, for example, be anything like a normal distribution? The answer is that for large n, $\bar{X}$ will have an approximately normal distribution, even though X has a bimodal distribution.

To illustrate, suppose that the observation variable has the bimodal PD shown in Table XI.4. What will happen to the sampling distribution of the mean as the sample size increases? The distributions shown in

Table XI.4. Bimodal probability distribution

X	0	1	2	3	4
$\mathbf{P}(X = x)$	1/11	4/11	1/11	4/11	1/11

Figure XI.4 were determined for random samples of size 2, 3, and 4 drawn from this population. The bimodality of the distribution of X is reflected in the sampling distribution of the mean when $n = 2$ or $n = 3$, but for $n = 4$ the distribution is clearly unimodal, and it is beginning to look like a normal distribution. With further increases in n, this similarity increases steadily.

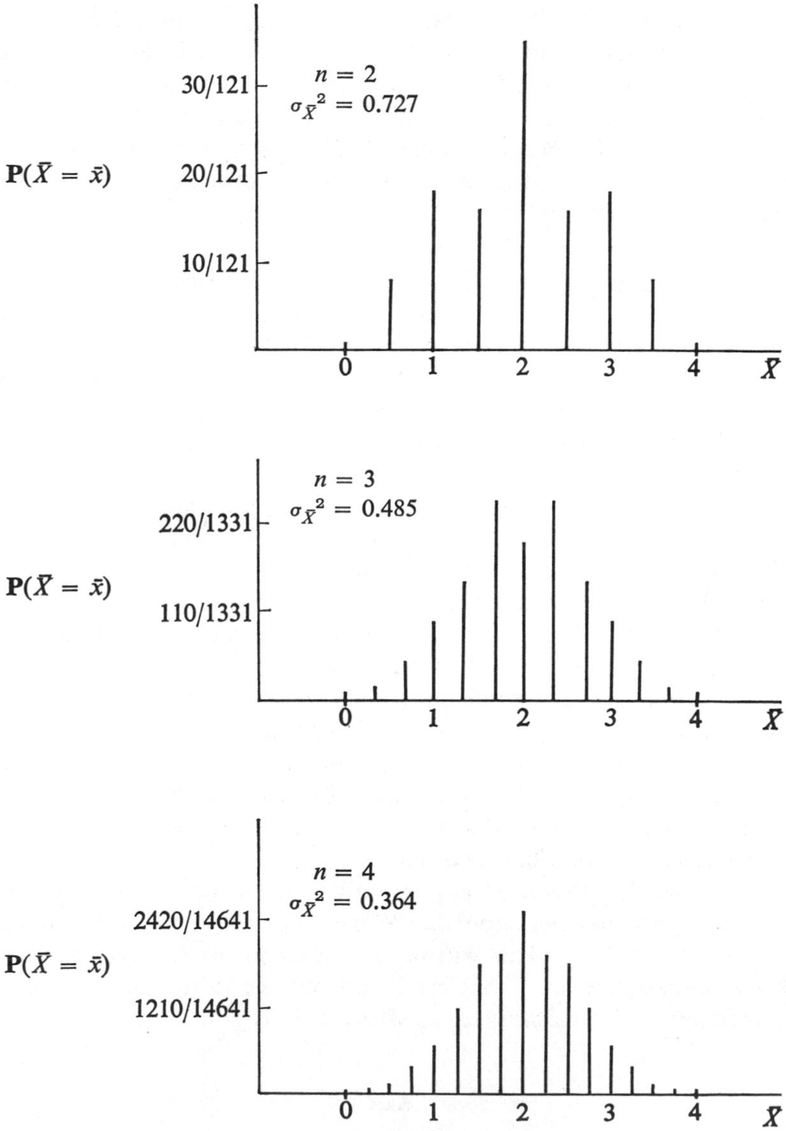

Figure XI.4

There are two main points to be noted in these illustrations. First, as n increases, the rate with which a sampling distribution approaches normality depends on the estimator. For instance, the sampling distribution of $\bar{X}$ approaches normality more rapidly than that of S^2 (compare Figs. XI.1 and XI.2). Second, the shape of the PD (or DF) of the observation variable is important. For example, $\bar{X}$ approaches a normal sampling distribution more closely for a given n when X has a rectangular distribution than when X has a bimodal distribution (compare Figs. XI.1 and XI.4). From this it is clear that the question "How large must n be before the CLT becomes applicable?" has no general answer. All that can be said is that it depends on the shape of the distribution of the observation variable and on the estimator.

CASE OF THE MEAN OF A NORMALLY DISTRIBUTED OBSERVATION VARIABLE. One important special case requires comment. When *the observation variable has a normal distribution*, can the CLT be applied to the sample mean? The answer is that the CLT is unnecessary. The sampling distribution of the mean will be *exactly* normal for *any* sample size. But, before elaborating this, it will be necessary to state an important statistical principle.

In Section X.3.2 it was stated that a linear function of a single normally distributed random variable has a normal distribution. This result is perfectly general. It can be shown[5] that *if* $X_1, X_2, \ldots, X_n$ *are mutually independent random variables each of which has a normal density function, and if* $A, B_1, B_2, \ldots, B_n$ *are constants, then the linear function* $Y = A + B_1X_1 + B_2X_2 + \cdots + B_nX_n$ *has a normal density function, too.*

If $n = 1$ and X_1 is the single normally distributed observation variable, then $\bar{X}$ is identical to X_1 and must also be normally distributed. For $n > 1$, $\bar{X}$ is a linear function of the observations, in which $A = 0$ and $B_1 = B_2 = \cdots = B_n = 1/n$. Consequently, according to the principle just stated, $\bar{X}$ will have a normal sampling distribution if the density function of the observation variable is normal.

Notice that this discussion applies only to the sample mean. The fact that X is normal does *not* imply that S^2 has a normal sampling distribution for any sample size. (This will become clear in the following section.) This difference between $\bar{X}$ and S^2 is attributable to the fact that $\bar{X}$ is a *linear* function of the observations whereas S^2 is not.

XI.8

SAMPLING DISTRIBUTION OF THE SAMPLE VARIANCE

One reason for introducing the chi-square distribution in Section X.3.3 is that the sampling distribution of the sample variance is a close relative of the chi-square distribution.

[5] No proof of this will be given here, but see References 2 and 4 at the end of Chapter X.

If $(X_1, X_2, \ldots, X_k, \ldots, X_n)$ *is a random sample from a normally distributed population that has mean* μ *and variance* σ^2*, then*

$$\chi^2 = \frac{(n-1)S^2}{\sigma^2} = \frac{\sum_k (X_k - \bar{X})^2}{\sigma^2} \qquad \text{[XI.4]}$$

has a chi-square distribution with expected value $n - 1$ *and variance* $2(n - 1)$.

In Appendix XI.3 it is proved that $E[\sum_k (X_k - \bar{X})^2] = (n - 1)\sigma^2$. Then,

$$E\left[\frac{(n-1)S^2}{\sigma^2}\right] = E\left[\frac{\sum_k (X_k - \bar{X})^2}{\sigma^2}\right] = \frac{1}{\sigma^2} E\left[\sum_k (X_k - \bar{X})^2\right]$$

$$= \frac{1}{\sigma^2}(n-1)\sigma^2$$

$$= n - 1.$$

This shows that $E(\chi^2) = E[(n - 1)S^2/\sigma^2] = n - 1$.

Notice that this expected value is equal to the number of degrees of freedom associated with S^2. Thus, the expected value of a chi-square distribution is often referred to as the number of *degrees of freedom* associated with it. However, one should not lose sight of the fact that the number of degrees of freedom is simply an expected value.

In Section X.3.3 it was stated that the variance of a chi-square DF equals twice its expected value. This same conclusion applies here. Since $E(\chi^2) = E[(n - 1)S^2/\sigma^2] = n - 1$, the variance is $2(n - 1)$.

Notice carefully the difference between the results of this section and those of Section X.3.3. Here, it is stated that the random variable $(n - 1)S^2/\sigma^2 = \sum_k (X_k - \bar{X})^2/\sigma^2$ has a chi-square distribution with expected value $n - 1$ and variance $2(n - 1)$. In Section X.3.3 it is $\sum_k Z_k^2 = \sum_k (X_k - \mu)^2/\sigma^2$ that has a chi-square distribution with expected value n and variance $2n$. In one case, the population mean is known, in the other it is not.

Since it is $(n - 1)S^2/\sigma^2$ that has a chi-square distribution and not S^2, how can the chi-square distribution be used to find the sampling distribution of S^2? In order to answer, we shall deal with the cumulative chi-square distribution function.

If $\mathbf{P}(\chi^2 \le \chi_q^2)$ is the chi-square CDF, then

$$\mathbf{P}(\chi^2 \le \chi_q^2) = \mathbf{P}\left(\frac{(n-1)S^2}{\sigma^2} \le \chi_q^2\right).$$

Performing the same algebraic operations on both sides of the inequality

$(n-1)S^2/\sigma^2 \leq \chi_q^2$ will not alter its validity. Multiplying both sides by σ^2 and dividing both sides by $n-1$,

$$\mathbf{P}(\chi^2 \leq \chi_q^2) = \mathbf{P}\left(S^2 \leq \frac{\sigma^2\chi_q^2}{n-1}\right).$$

It can be seen that $\mathbf{P}[S^2 \leq \sigma^2\chi_q^2/(n-1)]$ is a value of the CDF of S^2. Consequently, the relation

$$\mathbf{P}(\chi^2 \leq \chi_q^2) = \mathbf{P}\left(S^2 \leq S_q^2 = \frac{\sigma^2\chi_q^2}{n-1}\right) \qquad \text{[XI.5]}$$

permits one to use the chi-square CDF to determine values of the CDF of S^2. Examples of such applications are given below.

Suppose that a random sample of size 27 is drawn from a normally distributed population in which $\sigma^2 = 25$. What is the value of S_q^2 such that $\mathbf{P}(S^2 \leq S_q^2) = 0.1$? To solve the problem we must find S_q^2 such that

$$\mathbf{P}(\chi^2 \leq \chi_q^2) = \mathbf{P}\left(S^2 \leq S_q^2 = \frac{\sigma^2\chi_q^2}{n-1}\right) = 0.1$$

$$= \mathbf{P}\left(S^2 \leq S_q^2 = \frac{25(\chi_q^2)}{27-1}\right) = 0.1.$$

Since $E(\chi^2) = D = n - 1 = 27 - 1 = 26$, we find from Appendix VII that $\mathbf{P}(\chi^2 \leq 17.292) = 0.1$. Substituting 17.292 for χ_q^2 in the above equation,

$$\mathbf{P}(\chi^2 \leq 17.292) = \mathbf{P}\left(S^2 \leq S_q^2 = \frac{25(17.292)}{26}\right) = 0.1,$$

$$\mathbf{P}(S^2 \leq 16.63) = 0.1.$$

This probability is from the CDF of S^2 itself.

Now, suppose that we are looking for the probability that S^2 will exceed 35 for the same normally distributed population and the same random sample size. Then, applying Formula [XI.5],

$$\mathbf{P}(S^2 > 35) = 1 - \mathbf{P}\left(S^2 \leq 35 = \frac{\sigma^2\chi_q^2}{n-1}\right) = 1 - \mathbf{P}(\chi^2 \leq \chi_q^2)$$

defines the probability we are after. Since $\sigma^2 = 25$ and $n = 27$, the relation $35 = \sigma^2\chi_q^2/(n-1)$ can be used to find χ_q^2. Thus,

$$35 = \frac{\sigma^2\chi_q^2}{n-1}$$

$$35 = \frac{25(\chi_q^2)}{27-1}$$

$$\chi_q^2 = 36.40.$$

Entering the table of Appendix VII, $\mathbf{P}(\chi^2 \leq \chi_q^2) = \mathbf{P}(\chi^2 \leq 36.40) =$ 0.912, and returning to the original probability statement,

$$\mathbf{P}(S^2 > 35) = 1 - \mathbf{P}(S^2 \leq 35) = 1 - \mathbf{P}(\chi^2 \leq 36.40)$$
$$= 1 - 0.912 = 0.088.$$

For values of $D = n - 1$ that are too large for the table of Appendix VII, the normal approximation described in Section X.5.4 can be used.

From the foregoing examples it should be clear how the chi-square DF can be used to find probabilities associated with the sampling distribution of the sample variance when the observation variable has a normal DF. In the next two chapters these procedures will be applied.

*XI.9

DEPENDENCE AMONG ESTIMATORS

The question raised in this section is as follows: If more than one statistic is computed for a single random sample, and if the value of one of them is high, does this increase the probability that the other is high (or low)? In short, are estimators that are based on the same random sample correlated? This question is raised since the rationale for some statistical methods depends on the independence of the mean and variance of random samples from a single population.

To provide a partial answer, the bivariate distribution of $\bar{X}$ and S^2 will be examined for random samples of size 4 drawn with replacement from a rectangular population having the values 1, 2, and 3. The sampling distribution of each of these estimators by itself has been considered already; now their bivariate sampling distribution is to be scrutinized.

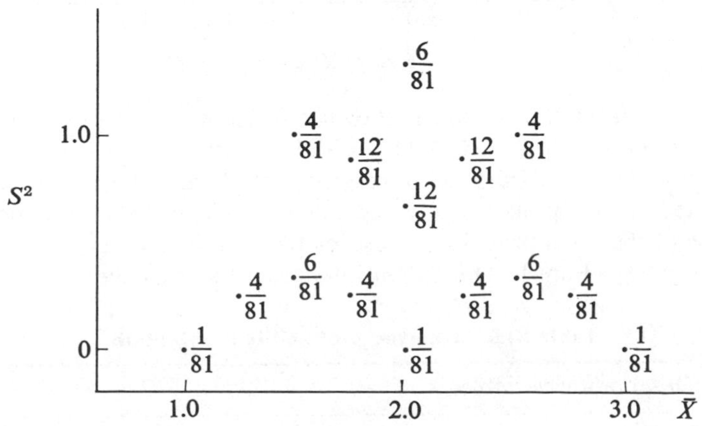

Figure XI.5

For each of the possible samples from the rectangular population, the values of $\bar{X}$ and of S^2 are located on the bivariate PD of Figure XI.5. The number beside each point indicates the probability of each pair of values (one on $\bar{X}$ and one on S^2).

It is quite clear that $\bar{X}$ and S^2 are statistically dependent. For example, $\mathbf{P}(S^2 = 0.25 \mid \bar{X} = 2) = 0$ though $\mathbf{P}(S^2 = 0.25) = (4 + 4 + 4 + 4)/81 = 16/81$. However, the covariance of $\bar{X}$ and S^2 is 0. This means that there is no general tendency for mean and variance to increase or decrease together.

One should not conclude from this example that the sample mean and variance are always uncorrelated. The joint PD of mean and variance has been plotted in Figure XI.6 for random samples of size 3 drawn with

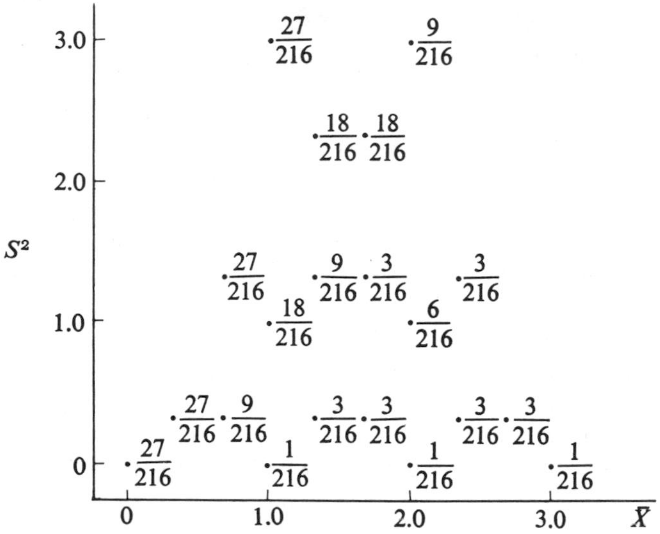

Figure XI.6

replacement from the skewed PD shown in Table XI.5. Beside each point in Figure XI.6 is $\mathbf{P}[(\bar{X} = \bar{x}) \cap (S^2 = s^2)]$.

Examination of Figure XI.6 reveals that $\bar{X}$ and S^2 are positively correlated as well as statistically dependent. (The correlation is positive because of the small probabilities associated with the points falling in the lower right quadrant.) One might infer from this that the sample mean

Table XI.5. Skewed probability distribution

Observation variable, X	0	1	2	3
$\mathbf{P}(X = x)$	1/2	1/6	1/6	1/6

and variance are correlated when the observation variable has a skewed distribution.

In general, the relation between sample mean and variance can be summarized as follows. *First, random sample mean and variance are statistically independent if and only if the observation variable has a normal DF. Second, the product-moment correlation between random sample mean and variance is*[6]

$$\rho_{\bar{X}, S^2} = \frac{n-1}{n^2} E[(X - \mu)^3],$$

where n is the sample size, μ is the population mean of the observation variable X, and $E[(X-\mu)^3]$ is the third central moment of X.

Since the PD of the observation variable is symmetrical for the example of Figure XI.5, the third central moment is zero and

$$\rho_{\bar{X}, S^2} = \frac{n-1}{n^2} E[(X - \mu)^3] = \frac{4-1}{(4)^2}(0) = 0.$$

This means that the sample mean and variance are uncorrelated. On the other hand, since the third central moment of the PD in Table XI.5 is 1,

$$\begin{aligned}\rho_{\bar{X}, S^2} &= \frac{n-1}{n^2} E[(X - \mu)^3] = \frac{3-1}{(3)^2}(1) \\ &= +0.222.\end{aligned}$$

This shows that there is a slight tendency for large values of S^2 to occur in conjunction with large values of $\bar{X}$ in random samples of size 3 from this positively skewed population.

Even when there is marked skewness, so that the third central moment is large in absolute magnitude, the correlation between mean and variance may still be small for large samples. For example, if $n = 20$, then for the PD of Table XI.5

$$\begin{aligned}\rho_{\bar{X}, S^2} &= \frac{n-1}{n^2} E[(X - \mu)^3] = \frac{20-1}{20^2}(1) \\ &= 0.0475.\end{aligned}$$

XI.10
PROBLEMS ON SAMPLING DISTRIBUTIONS

1. A class of 36 school children has a mean IQ of 95. Assume the class is a random sample from the school and that the variance for the entire

[6] No proof of these results can be given here. For a proof and further discussion, see Cramér, H., *Mathematical Methods of Statistics*. Princeton, Princeton University Press, 1946, pp. 348–349.

school is 256. If the mean for the whole school were 100, what is the probability that a randomly selected class of 36 would have a mean of 95 or lower? Assume a student body of 500.

2. With reference to Problem 1, what is the probability that the class mean would differ by as much as 5 IQ points from the population mean of 100?

3. If IQ were not normally distributed, would your answers to Problems 1 and 2 be defensible? On what basis?

4. For the situation described in Problem 1, assume that IQ is normally distributed.

   a. What is the expected value of the sample variance, S^2?
   b. What is the probability that $S^2 \leq 196$?
   c. What is the probability that $S^2 \geq 324$?
   d. What is $\mathbf{P}[(S^2 \leq 196) \cup (S^2 \geq 324)]$?
   e. What is $\mathbf{P}[|S^2 - \sigma^2| < 60]$?

5. Suppose that X is an observation variable that has a Poisson distribution with mean equal to 50.

   a. Is it legitimate to assume that $(n - 1)S^2/\sigma^2$ has a chi-square distribution for random samples of size 20 from this Poisson population?
   b. Defend your answer to a.
   c. Suppose that the chi-square distribution is applicable. Find $\mathbf{P}(|S^2 - \sigma^2| > 4)$.

6. In Chapter X, methods that could be used to approximate the binomial or hypergeometric distributions with a normal DF were described. It was also implied that under certain conditions the Poisson distribution was nearly normal. For each of these connections with the normal distribution, answer the following questions:

   a. What is the random variable that is approximately normally distributed?
   b. Under what conditions is the error of this approximation small?
   c. How is the error related to sample size? What other factors affect the magnitude of errors?
   d. Under what conditions do the binomial, hypergeometric, and Poisson distributions acquire the same shape?
   e. What do your answers to a, b, c, and d tell you about the significance of the normal distribution in statistics?

*7. Random samples are drawn from a population in which $E[(X - \mu)^3] = -1.5$.

   a. If the variance of the population is 1, apply a measure describing the degree of skewness.
   b. Show graphically the general shape the distribution is likely to have.
   c. Calculate the correlation between sample mean and sample variance for $n = 5$; for $n = 10$; for $n = 100$; Comment on the results.

*8. Refer to Problems 6 and 7 of Section XI.3.

   a. Write out in tabular form the joint PD of sample range and sample mean.

b. Display this joint PD graphically.
c. Are sample mean and sample range correlated in this example? What is the value of $\rho_{\bar{X},\ \text{Range}}$?

APPENDIX XI.1

Proof that the sample covariance is an unbiased estimator for the population covariance

In Chapter IX it was asserted that the sample covariance is an unbiased estimator of the population covariance. In order to prove unbiasedness, it must be shown that $E(S_{XY}) = \sigma_{XY}$.

For convenience, Formula [IX.24] for S_{XY} is used to initiate the proof:

$$\begin{aligned} E(S_{XY}) &= E\left[\frac{n \sum XY - (\sum X)(\sum Y)}{n(n-1)}\right] \\ &= \frac{1}{n(n-1)}\{E(n \sum XY) - E[(\sum X)(\sum Y)]\} \\ &= \frac{1}{n(n-1)}\{nE(\sum XY) - E[(X_1 + \cdots + X_n)(Y_1 + \cdots + Y_n)]\}. \end{aligned}$$

The term $E(\sum XY)$ can be written out as $E(X_1Y_1 + \cdots + X_nY_n)$, and the product $(X_1 + \cdots + X_n)(Y_1 + \cdots + Y_n)$ forms a sum of n^2 products, n of which are of the form X_kY_k and $n^2 - n$ are of the form X_kY_r, where $k \neq r$. This is illustrated below for $n = 3$:

$$\begin{array}{c} X_1 + X_2 + X_3 \\ \underline{Y_1 + Y_2 + Y_3} \end{array}$$

$$\underbrace{X_1Y_1 + X_2Y_2 + X_3Y_3}_{n=3 \text{ terms}} + \underbrace{X_1Y_2 + X_1Y_3 + X_2Y_1 + X_2Y_3 + X_3Y_1 + X_3Y_2}_{n^2 - n = 3^2 - 3 = 6 \text{ terms}}.$$

Returning to the last expression for $E(S_{XY})$ and substituting these equivalents,

$$\begin{aligned} E(S_{XY}) &= \frac{1}{n(n-1)}\{nE(\underbrace{X_1Y_1 + \cdots + X_nY_n}_{n \text{ terms}}) - E(\underbrace{X_1Y_1 + \cdots + X_nY_n}_{n \text{ terms}} \\ &\qquad + \underbrace{X_1Y_2 + X_1Y_3 + \cdots + X_{n-1}Y_n}_{n^2 - n \text{ terms}})\} \\ &= \frac{1}{n(n-1)}\{n[\underbrace{E(X_1Y_1) + \cdots + E(X_nY_n)}_{n \text{ terms}}] \\ &\qquad - \underbrace{E(X_1Y_1) - \cdots - E(X_nY_n)}_{n \text{ terms}} \\ &\qquad - \underbrace{E(X_1Y_2) - \cdots - E(X_{n-1}Y_n)}_{n^2 - n \text{ terms}}\} \\ &= \frac{1}{n(n-1)}\{\underbrace{(n-1)E(X_1Y_1) + \cdots + (n-1)E(X_nY_n)}_{n \text{ terms}} \\ &\qquad \underbrace{- E(X_1Y_2) - \cdots - E(X_{n-1}Y_n)}_{n^2 - n \text{ terms}}\}. \end{aligned}$$

In order to continue, we must consider the two types of terms, $E(X_k Y_k)$ and $E(X_k Y_r)$. Recalling that the subscript represents only the ordinal position of a bivariate observation within the sample, and that every observation is a pair of values on the same variables X and Y, $E(X_k Y_k) = E(XY)$ for each k. Then, since

$$\sigma_{XY} = E(XY) - \mu_X\mu_Y,$$
$$E(XY) = \sigma_{XY} + \mu_X\mu_Y,$$

and $\sigma_{XY} + \mu_X\mu_Y$ can be substituted for each $E(X_k Y_k)$.

When $k \neq r$, $E(X_k Y_r)$ is the expected value of a product of statistically independent observations, since X_k and Y_r are not paired. (For example, X_k might be the chronological age of the kth subject and Y_r the mental age of the rth subject. Therefore, X_k and Y_r are statistically independent.) Consequently, by the rule of Section VIII.4.7,

$$E(X_k Y_r) = E(X)E(Y) = \mu_X\mu_Y.$$

Returning to the last expression for $E(S_{XY})$, these results can be substituted as follows:

$$\begin{aligned}
E(S_{XY}) &= \frac{1}{n(n-1)} [\underbrace{(n-1)E(X_1Y_1) + \cdots + (n-1)E(X_nY_n)}_{n \text{ terms}} \\
&\qquad \underbrace{- E(X_1Y_2) - \cdots - E(X_{n-1}Y_n)}_{n^2-n \text{ terms}}] \\
&= \frac{1}{n(n-1)} [\underbrace{(n-1)(\sigma_{XY} + \mu_X\mu_Y) + \cdots + (n-1)(\sigma_{XY} + \mu_X\mu_Y)}_{n \text{ terms}} \\
&\qquad \underbrace{- \mu_X\mu_Y - \cdots - \mu_X\mu_Y}_{n^2-n \text{ terms}}] \\
&= \frac{1}{n(n-1)} [n(n-1)\sigma_{XY} + n(n-1)\mu_X\mu_Y - (n^2-n)\mu_X\mu_Y] \\
&= \frac{1}{n(n-1)} [n(n-1)\sigma_{XY}] \\
&= \sigma_{XY}.
\end{aligned}$$

This completes the proof that $E(S_{XY}) = \sigma_{XY}$.

APPENDIX XI.2

Proof that S^2 is an unbiased estimate of σ^2

If we recall that the variance of X is simply the covariance of X with itself, i.e., $S_{XX} = S_X{}^2$ and $\sigma_{XX} = \sigma_X{}^2$, then X can be substituted for Y throughout the proof of Appendix XI.1. This shows that S^2 is an unbiased estimate of σ^2.

APPENDIX XI.3

Proof that $E[\sum_k (X_k - \bar{X})^2] = (n - 1)\sigma^2$

In Appendix XI.2 it was shown that $E(S^2) = \sigma^2$. Since $\sum_k (X_k - \bar{X})^2 = (n - 1)S^2$,

$$E\left[\sum_k (X_k - \bar{X})^2\right] = E[(n - 1)S^2] = (n - 1)E(S^2)$$
$$= (n - 1)\sigma^2.$$

This completes the proof.

APPENDIX XI.4

Proof of Chebyshev's inequality: if the mean of the discrete random variable X is μ and if its variance is σ^2, then for any positive number, δ,

$$\mathbf{P}(|X - \mu| \geq \delta) \leq \frac{\sigma^2}{\delta^2}$$

The proof begins by writing the definition of the variance,

$$\sigma^2 = \sum \mathbf{P}(X = x)(x - \mu)^2.$$

Now, suppose that the sum is restricted to those differences, $(x - \mu)$, which satisfy the relation $|x - \mu| \geq \delta$. In other words, all terms of the above sum for which $|x - \mu| < \delta$ are deleted from the sum. Call the sum remaining after these deletions $\sum^*$. Then, it is certainly true that

$$\sigma^2 \geq \sum^* \mathbf{P}(X = x)(x - \mu)^2.$$

Since each of the squared differences of this last sum equals or exceeds δ^2, the inequality will continue to hold if each $(x - \mu)^2$ is replaced by δ^2. Thus,

$$\sigma^2 \geq \sum^* \mathbf{P}(X = x)\delta^2$$
$$\sigma^2 \geq \delta^2 \sum^* \mathbf{P}(X = x)$$
$$\frac{\sigma^2}{\delta^2} \geq \sum^* \mathbf{P}(X = x).$$

Since $\sum^*$ includes all x such that $|x - \mu| \geq \delta$,

$$\sum^* \mathbf{P}(X = x) = \mathbf{P}(|X - \mu| \geq \delta).$$

Making this substitution for $\sum^*$,

$$\frac{\sigma^2}{\delta^2} \geq \mathbf{P}(|X - \mu| \geq \delta),$$

or

$$\mathbf{P}(|X - \mu| \geq \delta) \leq \frac{\sigma^2}{\delta^2}.$$

This completes the proof.

SUGGESTED READING

1. Wallis, W. A., and H. V. Roberts, *Statistics: A New Approach.* New York, Free Press of Glencoe, 1957, Chap. 11.
The use of enumeration as a method is discussed and illustrated, and several nonmathematical illustrations of the operation of the central limit theorem are given. An excellent introduction.
2. Any modern statistics text includes a discussion of sampling distributions. See the references at the end of Chapter X.

XII

INTRODUCTION TO ESTIMATION

THE general idea of estimation was introduced in Section III.4.1. An important principle that applies to many estimators, the law of large numbers, was described in Section V.3.3. Unbiasedness and asymptotic unbiasedness were introduced in connection with several estimators in Chapter IX, and in the preceding chapter some of these results were reviewed and a few general principles regarding sampling distributions were described. In this chapter, some of the systematic methods for defining and evaluating point estimators are introduced. Then methods for constructing interval estimates are described.

XII.1

METHODS OF DEFINING POINT ESTIMATORS

Most of the estimators that have been introduced are defined in a way that seems exceedingly "natural." For example, sample means and medians are calculated in exactly the same way as the corresponding parameters are determined for a finite population. However, the most natural definition of an estimator is not always best. For example, the obvious formulas for estimating the population variance and covariance are biased.

What constitutes a good estimator depends not only on the parameter to be estimated but also on the PD or DF of the observation variable. For example, the formula $(X_{\max} + X_{\min})/2$ would provide reasonable estimates of the population mean if the PD or DF of Figure XII.1 characterized the observation variable. However, this estimator would not be so desirable for a variable that followed a normal distribution. Similarly, when sampling from a population having a Poisson distribution,

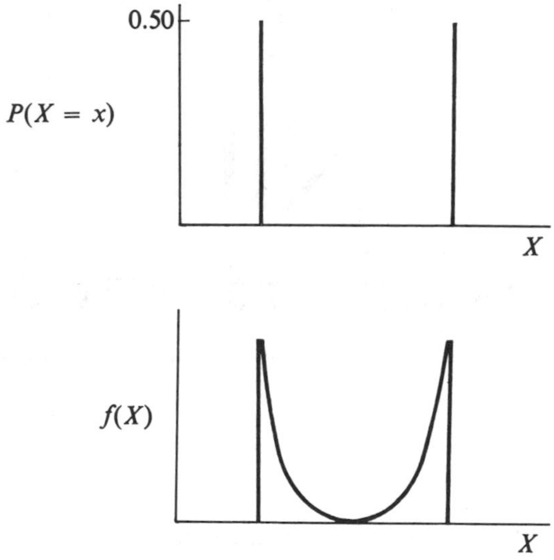

Figure XII.1

which provides the best estimate of μ, $\bar{X}$ or S^2? This is a moot question since the population mean and variance of a Poisson distribution are identical. But notice the difference between the formulas for these two estimators.

XII.1.1. Method of analogy

Perhaps the most obvious way to define an estimator is to determine how the parameter is computed for a finite population, and to apply the same calculational procedure to a sample. This will be referred to as the *method of analogy*.

In spite of its intuitive appeal, following this method may produce difficulties. For one thing, it ignores differences among the probability distributions of observation variables. Thus, when sampling from a finite population, it fails to distinguish between the variance of a hypergeometric and a binomial distribution (see Sections X.1.1 and X.1.2). Nonetheless, estimators that have desirable properties often result from the method of analogy.

XII.1.2. Method of maximum likelihood

The method of *maximum likelihood* was introduced by Fisher as a way of defining a "good" estimator. The conceptual basis for maximum-likelihood estimators is illustrated in the following example.

Suppose that the proportion of college males favoring draft deferment for education were 0.85. Then, if a random sample of 100 college males were surveyed, it is unlikely that the corresponding sample proportion would be near 0.05. It is more likely that it would be in the neighborhood of 0.80 or 0.90. In other words, the value of the parameter influences the sampling distribution of the corresponding estimator.[1] Following the method of maximum likelihood, we choose as the estimate the value of the parameter that would make the observed random sample most likely.

Notice that this is not the method of *maximum probability*. A probability cannot be assigned to a sample estimate on the basis of the sample itself. There is nothing random or probabilistic about a sample once it has been obtained. Thus, Fisher introduced the term *likelihood* to avoid a misuse of *probability*.

Furthermore, notice that the likelihood is assigned to the sample, not to the parameter. The logic is inverted. It says, choose as the estimate the value the parameter must have in order to maximize the likelihood of the obtained observations. This can be stated in a manner analogous to conditional probability. If π is the parameter and $(X_1, X_2, \ldots, X_n)$ is the sample, then the maximum-likelihood estimate is the value of π that maximizes

$$L[(X_1 \cap X_2 \cap \cdots \cap X_n)|\pi],$$

where L indicates that it is likelihood rather than strict probability that is to be maximized.[2]

When the maximum-likelihood procedure is used to obtain an estimator for a particular parameter, the result will depend on the distribution of the observation variable as well as the parameter itself. For example, $(X_{\max} + X_{\min})/2$ provides a maximum-likelihood estimator for the mean of a population that has a rectangular distribution, but if the observation variable has a normal DF, then $\sum X/n$ is the maximum-likelihood estimator for μ.

When sampling from a normal population, $\sum_k (X_k - \bar{X})^2/n$ provides a maximum-likelihood estimator for σ^2 when μ is unknown. Of course, this is a biased estimator. On the other hand, $\sum X/n$, the maximum-likelihood estimator for μ when sampling from the same population, is unbiased. This suggests an important conclusion: the method used to define an estimator does *not* determine all of its properties.

There are other procedures for defining estimators, but they will not be discussed here. Perhaps it is more important to consider the properties of estimators once they are defined. This is the task of the next few sections.

[1] To illustrate this in the extreme, suppose that *all* college males favored deferment for education. Then, *every* random sample would yield 100 percent favoring deferment. Here is an extreme case where the parameter completely determines the corresponding statistic for any sample.

[2] Most texts on mathematical statistics include a complete, mathematical definition of maximum-likelihood estimators. See, for example, Wolf, F., *Elements of Probability and Statistics*. New York, McGraw-Hill, 1961.

XII.2
SOME PROPERTIES OF POINT ESTIMATORS

In Chapters IX and XI there are several references to bias or lack of bias in specific estimators, and it was implied that asymptotic unbiasedness is a desirable property. In Section XI.2.3 it was stated that the random-sampling variability of an estimator should decrease as the sample size increases. In this section, we shall describe properties that provide a more comprehensive basis for assessing an estimator.

XII.2.1. Consistency

The first of these properties combines into one the ideas of asymptotic unbiasedness and decreasing sampling variability with increasing sample size. It is called *consistency*.

If $\mathscr{E}$ is an estimator for the parameter π, then $\mathscr{E}$ is a consistent estimator[3] *for π if*

$$\lim_{n \to \infty} E[(\mathscr{E} - \pi)^2] = 0, \qquad \text{[XII.1]}$$

where n is the size of the random sample that determines $\mathscr{E}$.

First, note that the definition places no restrictions on the sampling distribution of the estimator $\mathscr{E}$. It can be used to appraise any estimator regardless of the shape of the sampling distribution.

Next, the implications of consistency can be seen more clearly if we examine it in somewhat different form. In the expression

$$E[(\mathscr{E} - \pi)^2] = E[\mathscr{E}^2 - 2\pi\mathscr{E} + \pi^2],$$

$[E(\mathscr{E})]^2$ can be *both* added and subtracted inside the brackets on the right without destroying the equality. Therefore,

$$\begin{aligned} E[(\mathscr{E} - \pi)^2] &= E[\mathscr{E}^2 - 2\pi\mathscr{E} + \pi^2 + [E(\mathscr{E})]^2 - [E(\mathscr{E})]^2] \\ &= E(\mathscr{E}^2) - [E(\mathscr{E})]^2 + \pi^2 - 2\pi E(\mathscr{E}) + [E(\mathscr{E})]^2 \\ &= \sigma_{\mathscr{E}}^2 + [\pi - E(\mathscr{E})]^2. \end{aligned}$$

The term $\sigma_{\mathscr{E}}^2$ is the variance of the estimator, and $[\pi - E(\mathscr{E})]^2$ is simply the square of its bias.

If $\mathscr{E}$ is consistent, then

$$\lim_{n \to \infty} E[(\mathscr{E} - \pi)^2] = 0,$$

and since $E[(\mathscr{E} - \pi)^2] = \sigma_{\mathscr{E}}^2 + [\pi - E(\mathscr{E})]^2$, this is equivalent to

$$\lim_{n \to \infty} \{\sigma_{\mathscr{E}}^2 + [\pi - E(\mathscr{E})]^2\} = 0.$$

[3] When Fisher first introduced the idea of consistency, he required that $\lim_{n \to \infty} \mathbf{P}(|\mathscr{E} - \pi| > \delta) = 0$ for any positive number, δ. Since the intent of the definition given here is the same as that of Fisher's, the term *consistency* is retained.

Since $\sigma_{\mathscr{E}}^2$ and $[\pi - E(\mathscr{E})]^2$ both must be positive, the expression $[\sigma_{\mathscr{E}}^2 + [\pi - E(\mathscr{E})]^2]$ can go to zero only if $\sigma_{\mathscr{E}}^2$ and $[\pi - E(\mathscr{E})]^2$ both go to zero. In other words, $\mathscr{E}$ is consistent if it is unbiased or asymptotically unbiased *and* its sampling variability decreases to zero as the sample size increases without limit.

With consistency stated in this form, it is easy to show that $\bar{X} = \sum X/n$ is a consistent estimator for μ. To do this, we must replace π with μ and $\mathscr{E}$ with $\bar{X}$. Then, it must be shown that

$$\lim_{n\to\infty} \sigma_{\mathscr{E}}^2 = \lim_{n\to\infty} \sigma_{\bar{X}}^2 = \lim_{n\to\infty} \frac{\sigma_X^2}{n} = 0$$

and that

$$\lim_{n\to\infty} [\pi - E(\mathscr{E})]^2 = \lim_{n\to\infty} [\mu - E(\bar{X})]^2 = 0.$$

Since $E(\bar{X}) = \mu$, $[\mu - E(\bar{X})]^2 = [\mu - \mu]^2 = 0$ for *any* sample size, so $\lim_{n\to\infty} [\mu - E(\bar{X})]^2$ is certainly zero. As n increases, σ_X^2/n must decrease toward 0. Consequently, we conclude that $\bar{X} = \sum X/n$ is a consistent estimator for μ for random samples from any population.

In a similar way, it can be shown that $S^2 = \sum_k (X_k - \bar{X})^2/(n - 1)$ is a consistent estimator for the population variance. Although S^2 is consistent for random samples from any population, we shall demonstrate it only for sampling from a normally distributed population.

If X has a normal DF with variance σ^2, then, as stated in Section XI.8, $(n - 1)S^2/\sigma^2$ has a chi-square DF with variance $2(n - 1)$. Now, if the variance of

$$\chi^2 = \frac{(n - 1)S^2}{\sigma^2}$$

is $2(n - 1)$, then the variance of

$$\frac{\sigma^2}{n - 1}\chi^2 = \frac{\sigma^2}{n - 1}\,\frac{(n - 1)S^2}{\sigma^2} = S^2$$

is

$$\sigma_{S^2}^2 = \left(\frac{\sigma^2}{n - 1}\right)^2 2(n - 1) = \frac{2\sigma^4(n - 1)}{(n - 1)^2} = \frac{2\sigma^4}{n - 1}.$$

Furthermore, since $E(S^2) = \sigma^2$ for all sample sizes,

$$\lim_{n\to\infty} \{\sigma_{\mathscr{E}}^2 + [\pi - E(\mathscr{E})]^2\} = \lim_{n\to\infty} \{\sigma_{S^2}^2 + [\sigma^2 - E(S^2)]^2\} = \lim_{n\to\infty} \left\{\frac{2\sigma^4}{n - 1} + 0\right\} = 0.$$

However, not all estimators are consistent. For example, if sampling from a badly skewed Poisson population, then $(X_{max} + X_{min})/2$ is not a consistent estimator for the population mean. As n increases,

$$E\{[\pi - E(\mathscr{E})]^2\} = E\{[\mu - E([X_{max} + X_{min}]/2)]^2\}$$

increases also.[4]

A good *estimate* is one that is close to the parameter. Similarly, a good *estimator* is one that yields estimates that are close to the parameter "on the average." In addition, it is intuitively reasonable that the "average closeness" of an estimator should be greater for large random samples than for small ones. It is exactly these ideas that are given precise meaning in the definition of consistency.

XII.2.2. Sufficiency

Another property that contributes to a formulation of the meaning of a good estimator is sufficiency. *An estimator is sufficient when it utilizes all of the sample information that is relevant to the parameter.* The idea here is that the sampling distribution of an estimator should depend on the parameter it estimates, and, furthermore, if it is a sufficient estimator, it will be maximally dependent on the parameter.

Intuitively, it can be seen that $\bar{X} = \sum X/n$ is a sufficient estimator for the population mean, whereas, in general, $(X_{max} + X_{min})/2$ is not. The latter estimator obviously omits relevant information (for $n > 2$), so that its sampling distribution is relatively independent of the population mean.

Sufficiency can be given a precise definition, but it will not be presented here.[5]

*XII.2.3. Efficiency

In Section XI.7.2 it was stated that many estimators have sampling distributions that are well approximated by the normal DF when the sample size is large. The idea of efficiency can be applied only to estimators that have this property.

If $\mathscr{E}'$ is an estimator for π that has an asymptotically normal sampling distribution, and if there is no other asymptotically normal estimator $\mathscr{E}$, for which

$$\lim_{n \to \infty} \left[\frac{E[(\mathscr{E}' - \pi)^2]}{E[(\mathscr{E} - \pi)^2]}\right] > 1, \qquad \text{[XII.2]}$$

[4] As n increases, the probability increases that larger and larger values will be X_{max} for the sample. Since the small values of X have high probabilities, they are likely to be included in a sample of any size. Consequently, the expected value of the squared discrepancy between $(X_{max} + X_{min})/2$ and μ increases with n.

[5] See Reference 2 at the end of this chapter.

then $\mathscr{E}'$ is said to be an efficient estimator of π. In this definition, n refers to the size of the sample on which both $\mathscr{E}'$ and $\mathscr{E}$ are based.

The general idea here is that if, for large n, an estimator comes as close to the parameter "on the average" as any other asymptotically normal estimator, then it is efficient. The definition involves a comparison between two estimators of the function used to define consistency, so that an estimator is efficient if a combination of its bias and its variability is as small for large n as that of any other asymptotically normal estimator.

Why does efficiency apply only to asymptotically normal estimators? For one thing, the definition is based in part on a comparison of variances (see interpretation of consistency in Section XII.2.1), and such a comparison is ambiguous if the shapes differ for the distributions being compared. By restricting the definition to asymptotically normal estimators, comparability is ensured. Furthermore, since many useful estimators *do* have asymptotically normal sampling distributions, this restriction does not seriously limit the range of applicability.

*XII.2.4. Relative efficiency

For each of the properties of estimators that have been introduced so far, an estimator either has the property or it does not. Sometimes one must choose among estimators on the basis of a quantitative comparison. One such basis is relative efficiency.

The expression used to define consistency, $E[(\mathscr{E} - \pi)^2]$, provides a meaningful measure of the waywardness of an estimator. Relative efficiency is defined by a comparison of the waywardness of two estimators. *If $\mathscr{E}'$ is an efficient estimator and $\mathscr{E}$ is any other asymptotically normal estimator, then the relative efficiency of $\mathscr{E}$ as an estimator for π is*

$$\frac{E_n[(\mathscr{E}' - \pi)^2]}{E_n[(\mathscr{E} - \pi)^2]}, \qquad \text{[XII.3a]}$$

where the subscript n indicates that the comparison is for samples of size n only.

In Section XII.2.1 it was shown that

$$E[(\mathscr{E} - \pi)^2] = \sigma_{\mathscr{E}}{}^2 + [\pi - E(\mathscr{E})]^2.$$

Consequently, Formula [XII.3a] is identical to

$$\frac{\sigma^2_{\mathscr{E}'_n} + [\pi - E_n(\mathscr{E}')]^2}{\sigma^2_{\mathscr{E}_n} + [\pi - E_n(\mathscr{E})]^2}. \qquad \text{[XII.3b]}$$

The n in formulas [XII.3a] and [XII.3b] indicates that relative efficiency may vary from one sample size to another and that it can be calculated only for a specified sample size. For example, the relative efficiency of $(X_{\max} + X_{\min})/2$ is 1 (compared to $\bar{X} = \sum X/n$) for samples of size 2 drawn from a normal population. This is true since the two estimators are identical for $n = 2$. However, for $n = 20$, the relative efficiency of $(X_{\text{max}} + X_{\text{min}})/2$ drops to 0.35.

Relative efficiency is a useful measure for appraising short-cut estimators. Its application is illustrated in the following section.

*XII.3
SHORT-CUT ESTIMATORS

Many labor-saving computation procedures are available for estimating the population mean, standard deviation, and other parameters.[6] Although the importance of these methods is lessened by the widespread availability of digital computers, calculational short cuts are sometimes helpful in the preliminary examination of data.

*XII.3.1. Short cut for estimating the population mean

Since the mean and median of a symmetrical population are identical, both the sample mean and the sample median are unbiased estimators for either parameter. Since the sample median is easier to calculate for small samples, it can serve as a short-cut estimator for either the mean or median of a symmetrical population. On the other hand, if time and labor are of no consequence, the sample mean can be used to estimate either parameter.

When the observation variable has a normal DF with known variance, then the table in Appendix VIII can be used to determine the variance of the sampling distribution of the median. The second column of this table gives a constant for each sample size from $n = 2$ to $n = 20$. Multiplying the population variance of the observation variable by this constant gives the variance of the sample median. For example, if $n = 5$, and if $\sigma^2 = (16.4)^2$ is the variance of the observation variable, then the constant is 0.287 and the variance of M is $0.287(16.4)^2 = 77.19$. The standard error of the median is the square root of this figure.

Now, suppose that the *sample median* is to be used to estimate the median or the mean of a normal population. What is the relative efficiency of this procedure compared to the use of $\bar{X} = \sum X/n$? If the population variance of the observation variable were σ^2 and if n were 10, then, from Appendix VIII, the variance of the sample median would be $0.138\sigma^2$. The variance of the sample mean is $\sigma^2/10$. Now, Formula [XII.3b] can be applied to measure the relative efficiency of M. This gives

$$\frac{\sigma^2_{\mathscr{E}'_n} + [\pi - E_n(\mathscr{E}')]^2}{\sigma^2_{\mathscr{E}_n} + [\pi - E_n(\mathscr{E})]^2} = \frac{\sigma^2/10 + [\mu - E_{10}(\bar{X})]^2}{0.138\sigma^2 + [\mu - E_{10}(M)]^2}.$$

[6] Dixon, W. J., and F. J. Massey, Jr., *Introduction to Statistical Analysis.* New York, McGraw-Hill, 1957. Chapter 16 describes many convenient procedures for estimating both location and dispersion parameters.

Since in a symmetrical population $E(M) = V = \mu$ and $E(\bar{X}) = \mu$,

$$\frac{\sigma^2/10 + [\mu - E_{10}(\bar{X})]^2}{0.138\sigma^2 + [\mu - E_{10}(M)]^2} = \frac{\sigma^2/10 + 0}{0.138\sigma^2 + 0}$$
$$= 0.723.$$

Therefore, we can say that the relative efficiency of the sample median is 0.723. This same figure can be found directly by entering the table of Appendix VIII for $n = 10$ and picking up the value in the third column.

As n increases, the efficiency of M relative to $\bar{X}$ declines. However, the decline is not smooth and continuous, as is shown in Figure XII.2.

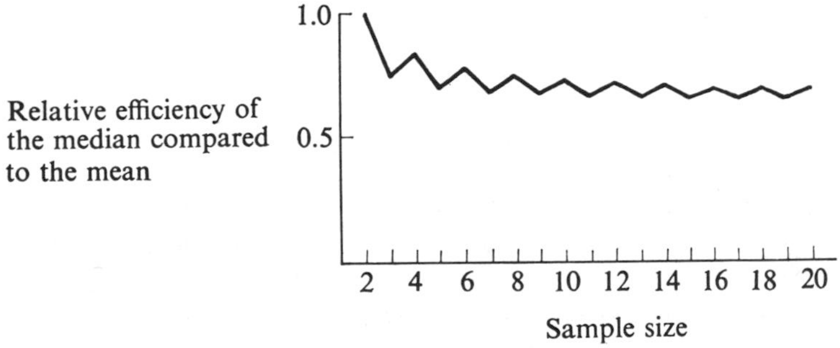

Figure XII.2

Here we see that the relative efficiency of M is larger for a given *even n* than it is for either adjacent odd value of n. In Appendix VIII, we find that for $n = 4$ the relative efficiency of M is 0.838, whereas for $n = 5$ it drops to 0.697. This reflects the difference in the way the median is calculated for odd and even sample sizes.

*XII.3.2. Short cut for estimating the population standard deviation

One very useful short cut for estimating the standard deviation has remarkably high relative efficiency when sampling from a normal population. The calculation of this estimator depends on a table found in Appendix IX.

For $n = 5$, the estimator is $0.4299(X_{[5]} - X_{[1]})$, where $X_{[1]}$ and $X_{[5]}$ are the smallest and the largest observations, respectively. For $n > 5$, the estimator includes more than just the two extreme observations. For example, if $n = 20$, the estimator is

$$0.09706(X_{[20]} + X_{[19]} + X_{[18]} + X_{[16]} - X_{[5]} - X_{[3]} - X_{[2]} - X_{[1]}).$$

Notice that it is *not* simply the highest four and lowest four observations that are included, since $X_{[17]}$ and $X_{[4]}$ are missing. The formulas for other values of n from 2 to 20 are found in Appendix IX.

This estimator is unbiased and for $2 \leq n \leq 20$ its relative efficiency ranges from 0.955 to 1.000 when sampling from a normal population. This is sufficient precision to warrant considerable confidence in such an estimate relative to the confidence one can place in S (which is biased).

The following random sample of IQ's was drawn from the approximately normal distribution of Figure X.13: (118, 100, 109, 107, 104, 108, 95, 99, 127, 113). It will be used to illustrate the calculation of this short-cut estimator for σ.

For $n = 10$, the table of Appendix IX gives the estimator

$$0.1968(X_{[10]} + X_{[9]} - X_{[2]} - X_{[1]}).$$

Ordering the observations, $X_{[10]} = 127$, $X_{[9]} = 118$, $X_{[2]} = 99$, and $X_{[1]} = 95$. Inserting these values,

$$\begin{aligned} 0.1968(X_{[10]} + X_{[9]} - X_{[2]} - X_{[1]}) &= 0.1968(127 + 118 - 99 - 95) \\ &= 10.04. \end{aligned}$$

This is not especially close to the population standard deviation of 16.4, but the estimate $S = 9.54$ is somewhat more in error for this particular random sample.

Notice that the figures cited here concerning the relative efficiency of this estimator and the preceding one are based on the assumption of a normally distributed observation variable. The effects of non-normality are difficult to assess.

XII.4
INTERVAL ESTIMATION

How well an *estimator* does its job is only one aspect of the problem. Another sort of question is how good is a particular *estimate.* In considering this distinction, it must be remembered that an estimator prescribes a procedure for estimating a parameter, whereas an estimate is based on a particular random sample.

An interval estimate specifies an interval and the confidence one has that it contains the parameter in question.

XII.4.1. Interval estimates for the population mean

The data of Table XII.1 are from a study of the auditory capacity of mental patients.[7] They represent the performance of a sample of 66 mentally ill, nonschizophrenic patients on an auditory word-recognition test. A standard list of phonetically balanced words was read at a constant

[7] Ludwig, A. M., D. W. Stilson, B. S. Wood, Jr., and M. P. Downs, "Further studies in audition in schizophrenia," *Amer. J. Psychiat.*, **120**, 70–71, 1963.

intensity 30 db above the subject's threshold for pure tones. A background of "speech noise" (a hissing sound) was increased by a small, fixed amount after the presentation of each word. The procedure continued until the subject was clearly unable to recognize additional words. The frequency function in Table XII.1 is for the lowest signal-to-noise ratio at which the subject was able to recognize words correctly. The

Table XII.1. Auditory word-recognition test data

Signal-to-noise ratio (X)	Frequency
4	1
6	4
8	11
10	22
12	17
14	9
16	2
	$n = 66$

problem is to estimate the mean of this variable in the population from which these subjects were drawn.

The sample mean of 10.58 does provide a suitable point estimate for the population mean, but it leaves a lot to be desired. Exactly what can be said about the accuracy of this estimate?

The frequency function of Table XII.1 suggests that the PD of the observation variable itself can be reasonably well approximated by a normal DF, so that it is reasonable to assume that the sampling distribution of the mean is normal (see Section XI.7.2). The sample variance is $S^2 = 2.05$. With this information we can construct an interval estimate for the population mean, μ.

This interval will be chosen in such a way that it has probability 0.9 of including the population mean. There is nothing magical about this choice; 0.9 was chosen simply because it seems to offer considerable

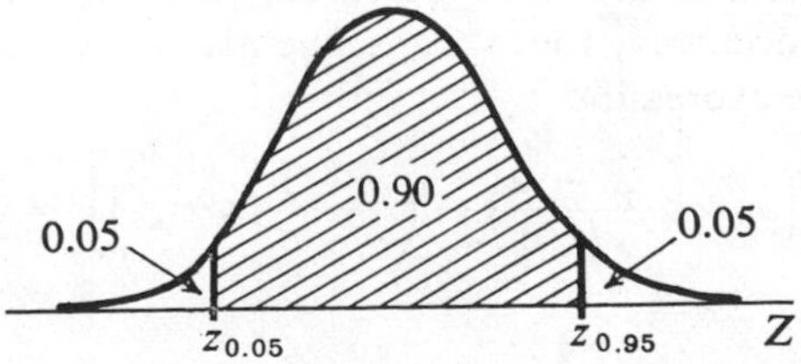

Figure XII.3

assurance that the interval defined will contain μ. Some other value might have been used, and in a moment some of the considerations connected with such a choice will be discussed. But first, the procedure for defining the interval estimate for the mean will be described.

If Z is a standardized normal deviate, then

$$\mathbf{P}(z_{.05} \leq Z \leq z_{.95}) = 0.9$$

gives the probability that a randomly selected value of Z will lie between the Z-value having a cumulative probability of 0.05 and the one having a cumulative probability of 0.95. This is illustrated in Figure XII.3. Now, if $\bar{X}$ has an approximately normal sampling distribution with standard error $\sigma/\sqrt{n}$, then

$$\mathbf{P}\left(z_{.05} \leq \frac{\bar{X} - \mu}{\sigma/\sqrt{n}} \leq z_{.95}\right) = 0.9,$$

which is identical to

$$\mathbf{P}\left[\left(z_{.05} \leq \frac{\bar{X} - \mu}{\sigma/\sqrt{n}}\right) \cap \left(\frac{\bar{X} - \mu}{\sigma/\sqrt{n}} \leq z_{.95}\right)\right] = 0.9.$$

Now, consider the event $z_{.05} \leq (\bar{X} - \mu)/(\sigma/\sqrt{n})$. This inequality can be solved for μ as follows:

$$z_{.05} \leq \frac{\bar{X} - \mu}{\sigma/\sqrt{n}}$$

$$z_{.05}\sigma/\sqrt{n} - \bar{X} \leq -\mu$$

$$\bar{X} - z_{.05}\frac{\sigma}{\sqrt{n}} \geq \mu.$$

(Notice that in order to eliminate the negative sign of μ, both sides of the inequality were multiplied by -1. This reversed the sense of the inequality.) Similarly, the event $(\bar{X} - \mu)/(\sigma/\sqrt{n}) \leq z_{.95}$ leads to

$$\bar{X} - z_{.95}\frac{\sigma}{\sqrt{n}} \leq \mu.$$

This shows that if the event $z_{.05} \leq (\bar{X} - \mu)/(\sigma/\sqrt{n})$ occurs, then the equivalent event $\bar{X} - z_{.05}(\sigma/\sqrt{n}) \geq \mu$ occurs also, and that if the event $(\bar{X} - \mu)/(\sigma/\sqrt{n}) \leq z_{.95}$ has been observed, then $\bar{X} - z_{.95}(\sigma/\sqrt{n}) \leq \mu$ is known to have occurred, too. Consequently, these equivalents can be substituted in the expression

$$\mathbf{P}\left[\left(z_{.05} \leq \frac{\bar{X} - \mu}{\sigma/\sqrt{n}}\right) \cap \left(\frac{\bar{X} - \mu}{\sigma/\sqrt{n}} \leq z_{.95}\right)\right] = 0.9.$$

This yields

$$\mathbf{P}[(\bar{X} - z_{.05}\sigma/\sqrt{n} \geq \mu) \cap (\bar{X} - z_{.95}\sigma/\sqrt{n} \leq \mu)] = 0.9.$$

This last expression is identical to

$$\mathbf{P}[\overline{X} - z_{.95}\sigma/\sqrt{n} \le \mu \le \overline{X} - z_{.05}\sigma/\sqrt{n}] = 0.9, \qquad \text{[XII.4]}$$

and it is this statement that defines the interval estimate for μ. This interval was defined so that the probability is 0.9 that it will include μ between its upper limit ($\overline{X} - z_{.05}\sigma/\sqrt{n}$) and its lower limit ($\overline{X} - z_{.95}\sigma/\sqrt{n}$).

For the example, $\overline{X} = 10.58$, $n = 66$, and from the table of cumulative normal probabilities of Appendix V, $z_{.05} = -1.65$ and $z_{.95} = +1.65$. If σ were known, these values could be inserted in the above equation to obtain an explicit interval estimate. However, since n is not too small, perhaps S can be substituted for σ. This will introduce some error, but for a sample of 66 observations, S is unlikely to differ too much from σ. Substituting $S = \sqrt{2.05} = 1.43$ for σ in Formula [XII.4], the interval estimate for the population mean is

$$\mathbf{P}\left(10.58 - 1.65\frac{1.43}{\sqrt{66}} \le \mu \le 10.58 - (-1.65)\frac{1.43}{\sqrt{66}}\right) = 0.9$$

$$\mathbf{P}(10.29 \le \mu \le 10.87) = 0.9.$$

How this result is to be interpreted is the topic of the next section.

XII.4.2. Interpreting an interval estimate

The expression $\mathbf{P}(10.29 \le \mu \le 10.87) = 0.9$ clearly is not an ordinary probability statement. It says that the probability that the parameter, μ, will lie within certain limits is 0.9. But μ is *not* a random variable. Instead, it is a parameter, a fixed characteristic of the population, and one cannot speak meaningfully of "the probability that a *constant* will take on a value within an interval." Either the parameter is in the interval or it is not. Then, exactly what is meant by the statement $\mathbf{P}(10.29 \le \mu \le 10.87)$? Two interpretations have been proposed.

The first was offered by Fisher. It is the idea of a *fiducial probability*, and it is similar to the notion of *likelihood* that Fisher introduced in connection with maximum-likelihood estimators (see Section XII.1.2). Fisher referred to statements like $\mathbf{P}(10.29 \le \mu \le 10.87) = 0.9$ as statements of fiducial probability. The term *fiducial* (which means "founded on faith or trust") is to remind us that such a statement is not to be interpreted as a proper probability. Its exact meaning is to be inferred from the way in which it was obtained.

The second interpretation, the one preferred here, was proposed by E. B. Wilson. In this formulation, it is the *limits of the interval* that vary from one random sample to another and to which the probability refers. One can think of intervals being tossed randomly at the parameter. Some of these random intervals will "cover" the parameter, whereas others will not. The 0.9 is the probability that an interval defined in this way for a given random sample will include the parameter between its limits.

But one cannot say, "the probability that the interval bounded by 10.29 and 10.87 covers the population mean is 0.9" *after* the random sample has been drawn. Once the limits of the interval have been calculated, either the parameter lies between them or it does not. However, following the procedure for defining the limits will generate an interval that contains the parameter in 90 percent of random samples. With this in mind, we can say, "the probability is 0.9 that an interval determined in this way for random samples of size 66 will contain the mean of this population." In this interpretation, the 0.9 is referred to as the *confidence coefficient*.

XII.4.3. Relationship between confidence coefficient and interval width

The width of an interval estimate and the confidence coefficient are positively related; they increase or decrease together. If a confidence coefficient of 0.99 had been used in the example of Section XII.4.1, then the interval estimate would be defined by

$$\mathbf{P}(\bar{X} - z_{.995}\sigma/\sqrt{n} \leq \mu \leq \bar{X} - z_{.005}\sigma/\sqrt{n}) = 0.99,$$

and its explicit limits are 10.12 and 11.03. The width of this interval is $11.03 - 10.12 = 0.91$, which is considerably larger than the width of $10.87 - 10.29 = 0.58$ obtained for a 0.9 confidence interval.

However, there are two ways of narrowing the interval and simultaneously increasing the confidence coefficient: increasing the sample size, or reducing the variability of the observation procedure. The latter can be achieved by eliminating irrelevant influences that affect the observations and by using procedures that keep the variability of the measurement process itself as low as possible. Both of these were discussed in Section I.5.

In any estimation problem, the investigator must arrive at some subjective balance of precision (interval width), degree of certainty that the parameter is included in the interval (confidence coefficient), and the time and cost he is willing to expend to achieve these (number of observations, degree of experimental precision, and reliability of measurements). Beyond this general statement, little guidance can be given for the rational choice of confidence coefficient and sample size.

There is one kind of situation in which the approach that has been illustrated may be incomplete. In order to deal with it, the idea of a parameter space will be introduced.

The parameter space is the set of all possible values of a parameter. Of course, the parameter has a particular value, but it is unknown to the researcher. Consequently, there exists a set of possible values as far as the investigator is concerned. For example, if a proportion is estimated, the parameter space consists of all real numbers between 0 and 1. If mean height, a mean length, or a variance is estimated, then the parameter space excludes negative numbers.

When a confidence interval is defined, it divides the parameter space into two subsets: the values included in the interval and those excluded from it. It can be seen that a confidence interval estimate is not very sensible if one of its limits lies outside the parameter space. For instance, the statement $\mathbf{P}(-0.15 \leq P \leq 0.35) = 0.99$ is questionable, at best, since the lower limit, -0.15, is well below the minimum possible value for a proportion. Perhaps it would be better if the confidence coefficient were reduced so that both limits of the interval are within the parameter space. Thus, with a confidence coefficient of 0.7, the statement $\mathbf{P}(0 < P \leq 0.20) = 0.7$ might be made.

Of course, another way to deal with the same problem is to increase the sample size, thus cutting down sampling variability and narrowing the interval without reducing the confidence coefficient.

A third way to handle this kind of difficulty is to define a confidence interval that is *asymmetric in probability*. The way this is done for the sample mean is described in Appendix XII.1.

XII.4.4. Definition of a confidence interval for a mean

If $\bar{X} = \sum X/n$ *is used as a point estimator for* μ, *if* $\bar{X}$ *has a normal sampling distribution, if* σ^2 *is the variance of the observation variable,* X, *if* $\mathbf{P}(Z \leqq z_{1-\alpha/2}) = 1 - \alpha/2$ *and* $\mathbf{P}(Z \leqq z_{\alpha/2}) = \alpha/2$, *and if*

$$\mathbf{P}(\bar{X} - z_{1-\alpha/2}\sigma/\sqrt{n} \leq \mu \leq \bar{X} - z_{\alpha/2}\sigma/\sqrt{n}) = 1 - \alpha, \qquad \text{[XII.5]}$$

then the interval from $\bar{X} - z_{1-\alpha/2}\sigma/\sqrt{n}$ *to* $\bar{X} - z_{\alpha/2}\sigma/\sqrt{n}$ *constitutes a* $1 - \alpha$ *confidence interval estimator for* μ. The example of Section XII.4.1 follows this definition.

XII.4.5. Interval estimates for a population proportion

Although there are more precise methods for obtaining interval estimates for proportions available,[8] only one approximate procedure will be described here.

According to the CLT, the sampling distribution of the random sample proportion will be approximately normal for large samples. Consequently, the method used to determine a confidence interval for a mean

[8] Crow, E. L., "Confidence intervals for a proportion." *Biometrika* **43**, 423–435, 1956.

can be applied to proportions. To begin with, if $\mathbf{P}(Z \le z_{\alpha/2}) = \alpha/2$ and $\mathbf{P}(Z \le z_{1-\alpha/2}) = 1 - \alpha/2$, then

$$\mathbf{P}(z_{\alpha/2} \le Z \le z_{1-\alpha/2}) = 1 - \alpha$$

$$\mathbf{P}\left(z_{\alpha/2} \le \frac{p - P}{\sigma_p} \le z_{1-\alpha/2}\right) = 1 - \alpha.$$

By a derivation exactly analogous to the one used in Section XII.4.1 for the mean, it can be shown that the above equation implies that

$$\mathbf{P}[p - z_{1-\alpha/2}\sigma_p \le P \le p - z_{\alpha/2}\sigma_p] = 1 - \alpha.$$

This expression defines a $1 - \alpha$ confidence interval estimator for P.

However, the upper and lower limits of this interval both include σ_p, and P must be known to calculate σ_p (e.g., see Formula [X.4]). Since it is P that is to be estimated, it cannot be known. The usual procedure is to replace P with p in the formula for σ_p.

If sampling is without replacement from a finite binomial population of size N, then

$$\mathbf{P}\left\{p - z_{1-\alpha/2}\sqrt{\left[\left(\frac{N-n}{N-1}\right)\frac{p(1-p)}{n}\right]} \le P \le p - z_{\alpha/2}\sqrt{\left[\left(\frac{N-n}{N-1}\right)\frac{p(1-p)}{n}\right]}\right\} \cong 1 - \alpha \quad \text{[XII.6a]}$$

defines an approximate $1 - \alpha$ confidence interval estimate for the population proportion P. For sampling with replacement or from an infinite binomial population, an exactly similar confidence interval for P is defined by

$$\mathbf{P}\left\{p - z_{1-\alpha/2}\sqrt{\left[\frac{p(1-p)}{n}\right]} \le P \le p - z_{\alpha/2}\sqrt{\left[\frac{p(1-p)}{n}\right]}\right\} \cong 1 - \alpha. \quad \text{[XII.6b]}$$

Note that formulas [XII.6a] and [XII.6b] are approximate in two respects.[9] First, they are based on the CLT. Second, the upper and lower limits of the interval are calculated by substituting p for P.

Data from a psychiatric follow-up study by Astrup, Fossum, and Holmboe[10] will be used to illustrate the application of Formula [XII.6b].

These investigators followed up all first admissions (from 1938 to 1950) to the Gaustad Hospital in Oslo, Norway, who were assigned a primary diagnosis of schizophrenia and who had been ill no more than 6 months prior to admission. Of the 664 who were followed for at least 5 years, 416 were described by the investigators as "deteriorated" at the end of

[9] See Crow, *op. cit.*, for a more precise procedure.

[10] *Prognosis in Functional Psychoses.* Springfield, Illinois, Charles C. Thomas, 1962, pp. 3–5.

the follow-up period. The problem is to construct a confidence interval estimate for the incidence of "deterioration."

Since the sample proportion described as "deteriorated" is $p = 416/664 = 0.627$, Formula [XII.6b] can be applied to find a $1 - \alpha = 1 - 0.01 = 0.99$ confidence interval estimate for P. This is done as follows:

$$\mathbf{P}\left\{p - z_{1-\alpha/2}\sqrt{\left[\frac{p(1-p)}{n}\right]} \leq P \leq p - z_{\alpha/2}\sqrt{\left[\frac{p(1-p)}{n}\right]}\right\} \cong 1 - \alpha$$

$$\mathbf{P}\left\{0.627 - (+2.58)\sqrt{\left[\frac{0.627(1-0.627)}{664}\right]} \leq P \leq 0.627 - (-2.58)\sqrt{\left[\frac{0.627(1-0.627)}{664}\right]}\right\} \cong 1 - 0.01$$

$$\mathbf{P}\{0.579 \leq P \leq 0.675\} \cong 0.99.$$

Thus, the interval from 0.579 to 0.675 would be expected to include the population proportion of "deteriorated" patients for 99 percent of random samples for which the interval is defined in this way.

XII.4.6. Interval estimates for the population variance

In this section, confidence interval estimates for the population variance will be obtained. In doing so, it will be assumed that the observation variable has a normal DF.

Suppose that $\chi^2_{\alpha/2}$ is a value of chi-square such that $\mathbf{P}(\chi^2 \leq \chi^2_{\alpha/2}) = \alpha/2$ and that $\chi^2_{1-\alpha/2}$ is chosen so that $\mathbf{P}(\chi^2 \leq \chi^2_{1-\alpha/2}) = 1 - \alpha/2$. Then,

$$\mathbf{P}[(\chi^2_{\alpha/2} \leq \chi^2) \cap (\chi^2 \leq \chi^2_{1-\alpha/2})] = 1 - \alpha.$$

This is illustrated graphically in Figure XII.4. Notice that the area under $f(\chi^2)$ between $\chi^2_{\alpha/2}$ and $\chi^2_{1-\alpha/2}$ is $1 - \alpha$.

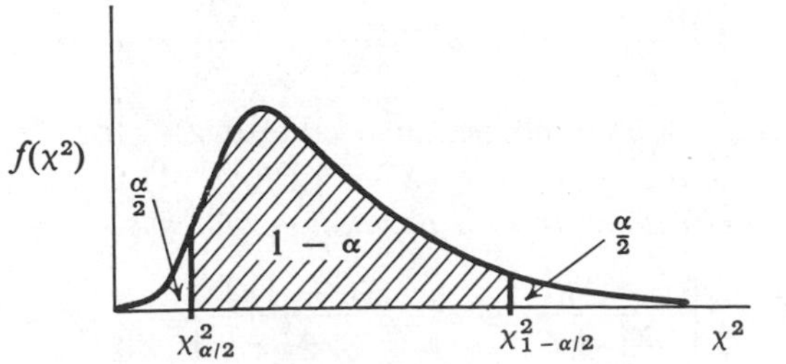

Figure XII.4

In Section XI.8 it was stated that if the observation variable has a normal distribution, then $\chi^2 = (n-1)S^2/\sigma^2$ has a chi-square distribution. Therefore, the equation above is identical to the statement

$$\mathbf{P}\left[\left(\chi^2_{\alpha/2} \leq \frac{(n-1)S^2}{\sigma^2}\right) \cap \left(\frac{(n-1)S^2}{\sigma^2} \leq \chi^2_{1-\alpha/2}\right)\right] = 1 - \alpha.$$

Beginning with the event to the left of the intersection,

$$\chi^2_{\alpha/2} \leq \frac{(n-1)S^2}{\sigma^2}$$

$$\frac{\chi^2_{\alpha/2}}{(n-1)S^2} \leq \frac{1}{\sigma^2}$$

$$\frac{(n-1)S^2}{\chi^2_{\alpha/2}} \geq \sigma^2.$$

(Notice that taking the reciprocal of both sides of the inequality reverses its sense, e.g., if $1/4 \leq 1/2$, then $4/1 \geq 2/1$.) Similarly, the event to the right of the intersection is the equivalent of

$$\sigma^2 \geq \frac{(n-1)S^2}{\chi^2_{1-\alpha/2}}.$$

These relationships show that if the event $\chi^2_{\alpha/2} \leq (n-1)S^2/\sigma^2$ has occurred, then the event $(n-1)S^2/\chi^2_{\alpha/2} \geq \sigma^2$ must have occurred also, and if $(n-1)S^2/\sigma^2 \leq \chi^2_{1-\alpha/2}$ has been observed, then $\sigma^2 \geq (n-1)S^2/\chi^2_{1-\alpha/2}$ is known to have occurred, too. Consequently,

$$\mathbf{P}\left[\left(\chi^2_{\alpha/2} \leq \frac{(n-1)S^2}{\sigma^2}\right) \cap \left(\frac{(n-1)S^2}{\sigma^2} \leq \chi^2_{1-\alpha/2}\right)\right] = 1 - \alpha$$

is identical to

$$\mathbf{P}\left[\left(\frac{(n-1)S^2}{\chi^2_{\alpha/2}} \geq \sigma^2\right) \cap \left(\sigma^2 \geq \frac{(n-1)S^2}{\chi^2_{1-\alpha/2}}\right)\right] = 1 - \alpha.$$

This last expression is equal to

$$\mathbf{P}\left[\frac{(n-1)S^2}{\chi^2_{1-\alpha/2}} \leq \sigma^2 \leq \frac{(n-1)S^2}{\chi^2_{\alpha/2}}\right] = 1 - \alpha,$$

which defines a $1 - \alpha$ confidence interval estimator for σ^2.

If the point estimator $S^2 = \sum (X - \bar{X})^2/(n-1)$ is based on a random sample of n observations from a population that has a normal DF, and if

$$\mathbf{P}\left[\frac{(n-1)S^2}{\chi^2_{1-\alpha/2}} \leq \sigma^2 \leq \frac{(n-1)S^2}{\chi^2_{\alpha/2}}\right] = 1 - \alpha, \qquad \text{[XII.7]}$$

then the interval from $(n-1)S^2/\chi^2_{1-\alpha/2}$ to $(n-1)S^2/\chi^2_{\alpha/2}$ is a $1-\alpha$ confidence interval estimate for σ^2.

The sample variance for the data of Table XII.1 is 2.05, and the frequency function for these data suggests that they were drawn from a PD that can be approximated reasonably well by a normal DF. Consequently, Formula [XII.7] can be used to obtain a confidence interval estimate for σ^2.

A $1 - \alpha = 0.95$ confidence coefficient will be employed, and, since $n = 66$, the expected value of the appropriate chi-square distribution is $D = n - 1 = 66 - 1 = 65$. From Appendix VII,

$$\mathbf{P}(\chi^2 \leq \chi^2_{\alpha/2}) = P(\chi^2 \leq \chi^2_{.025}) = P(\chi^2 \leq 44.62) = 0.025,$$

since $\alpha/2 = 0.05/2 = 0.025$. Similarly,

$$\mathbf{P}(\chi^2 \leq \chi^2_{1-\alpha/2}) = P(\chi^2 \leq \chi^2_{.975}) = P(\chi^2 \leq 89.16) = 0.975,$$

since $1 - \alpha/2 = 1 - 0.05/2 = 0.975$. Now, $\chi^2_{\alpha/2} = \chi^2_{.025} = 44.62$ and $\chi^2_{1-\alpha/2} = \chi^2_{.975} = 89.16$, $S^2 = 2.05$, $n = 66$, and $1 - \alpha = 0.95$ can be entered in Formula [XII.7] in the following manner:

$$\mathbf{P}\left[\frac{(n-1)S^2}{\chi^2_{1-\alpha/2}} \leq \sigma^2 \leq \frac{(n-1)S^2}{\chi^2_{\alpha/2}}\right] = 1 - \alpha$$

$$\mathbf{P}\left[\frac{(66-1)(2.05)}{89.16} \leq \sigma^2 \leq \frac{(66-1)(2.05)}{44.62}\right] = 0.95$$

$$\mathbf{P}[1.50 \leq \sigma^2 \leq 2.99] = 0.95.$$

Consequently, the interval from 1.50 to 2.99 is a 0.95 confidence interval estimate for σ^2. That is, 95 percent of random samples of size 66 from this population would include the parameter σ^2 within an interval defined in this way.

XII.5
PROBLEMS ON ESTIMATION

1. Using concise verbal statements, distinguish between consistency and maximum likelihood.
2. Distinguish among the meanings of probability, fiducial probability, and likelihood. In what ways are the terms *fiducial probability* and *likelihood* similar in meaning?
3. Define estimators not appearing in the text for each of three parameters defined in Chapter IX. Do not be entirely implausible.
4. The following questions are based on the data of Table XII.1.
   a. Construct a 0.7 confidence interval estimate for the mean. What is your estimate? Interpret it precisely.
   b. Compare this estimate with the 0.9 confidence interval constructed in Section XII.4.1.
   c. What assumptions were made in constructing your estimate?
   d. Construct a 0.7 confidence interval estimate for the variance. What is your interval estimate? Interpret this estimate precisely.
   e. Compare this estimate with the 0.95 confidence interval obtained in Section XII.4.6.

f. What assumptions were made in constructing this last estimate? What assumptions are different from those made to obtain an interval estimate for the mean?

5. The observations (1, 0, 0, 0, 1, 2, 1, 2, 0, 2, 1, 1, 1, 1, 1, 1, 2, 0, 0, 3) constitute a random sample from a Poisson population. Construct a 0.99 confidence interval estimate for the population variance.
   a. What is your interval estimate?
   b. What assumptions were required to obtain the estimate?
   c. If your estimate required the assumption that the observation variable is normally distributed, construct another 0.99 confidence interval that does not require this assumption.
   d. In the Poisson population from which these observations were drawn, the mean is 1. Does your confidence interval estimate include the variance of this population?

6. For Problem 4 of Section XI.6, construct a 0.95 confidence interval for the population mean.
   a. What is your estimate?
   b. Compare the estimated interval with the actual mean.
   c. What assumptions have you made?
   d. Are the assumptions reasonable for this application? Why?

*7. Find the sample median for the data of Table XII.1 and use it as a point estimate of the population mean.
   a. What is your estimate?
   b. What is its standard error?
   c. How does the variability of this estimator compare with that of the sample mean?
   d. Use the sample median to construct a confidence interval for the population *median*. Use a confidence coefficient of 0.90. What is your estimate?

*8. For the data of Problem 5, use the short cut of Section *XII.3.2 to determine a point estimate of the population standard deviation.
   a. What is your estimate?
   b. How does it compare with the estimate $S^2 = \sum (X - \bar{X})^2/n$?
   c. How does the estimate of *8a compare with the estimate you obtained for Problem 5c?
   d. On the basis of the appropriateness of the assumptions, do you prefer the method of Problem 5c or that of Problem *8a? Why?

APPENDIX XII.1

Definition of a confidence interval for the mean that is asymmetric in probability

If z_α is chosen so that $P(Z \leq z_\alpha) = \alpha$ and $z_{1-\beta}$ is chosen so that $P(Z \leq z_{1-\beta}) = 1 - \beta$, and if $P(\bar{X} - z_{1-\beta}\sigma/\sqrt{n} \leq \mu \leq \bar{X} - z_\alpha\sigma/\sqrt{n}) = 1 - \alpha - \beta$, then the interval from $\bar{X} - z_{1-\beta}\sigma/\sqrt{n}$ to $\bar{X} - z_\alpha\sigma/\sqrt{n}$ is a

$1 - \alpha - \beta$ confidence interval for μ. If $\alpha \neq \beta$, then the interval is said to be asymmetric in probability. An analogous definition can be applied to the proportion and the variance.

If the symmetric confidence interval (such as defined for the mean in Section XII.4.4) includes values not in the parameter space, then, by a suitable choice of α and β, it is usually possible to construct an interval that is asymmetric in probability and entirely within the parameter space.

SUGGESTED READING

1. Wallis, W. A., and H. V. Roberts, *Statistics: A New Approach.* New York, Free Press of Glencoe, 1957, Chap. 14.
   This provides a nonmathematical discussion of some of the ways to define estimators. It also describes methods for estimating means, proportions, and other statistics.
2. Chernoff, H., and L. E. Moses, *Elementary Decision Theory.* New York, John Wiley, 1959, Chap. 10.
   Standard methods of estimation are discussed from the point of view of modern decision theory. Free use is made of mathematical notation, but most of the derivations require no mathematics beyond algebra.
3. Most of the references given at the end of Chapter X deal with methods for estimation.

XIII

INTRODUCTION TO HYPOTHESIS TESTING

An unknown parameter is usually estimated when we have little information about it and no theory that permits us to predict its value. On the other hand, many research questions can be stated as hypotheses about the specific values of particular parameters. If the investigator applies hypothesis-testing methods to his data, the methods provide a basis for deciding whether his hypotheses are tenable. In the next section, the basic concepts of hypothesis testing are introduced in conjunction with an example that illustrates the application of these ideas.

XIII.1

BASIC CONCEPTS OF HYPOTHESIS TESTING

In Section X.1.2, it was argued that in the absence of ethnic cleavage, the distribution of the number of Anglos chosen[1] by an Anglo would follow a hypergeometric distribution. The five choices were viewed as a sample taken without replacement from a binomial population containing $R = 45$ Anglos and $N - R = 77$ non-Anglos. Consequently, according to Formula [X.6], the expected number of Anglos chosen by an Anglo is[2] $\mu = C(R/N) = 5(45/122) = 1.84$ if there is no ethnic cleavage. In this section, a statistical procedure for deciding whether this hypothesis is tenable will be described.

[1] The choices were given in response to "Who are the five kids *in this school* you would choose to mess around with?"

[2] The symbol C is used instead of n for the total number of choices made by each pupil. This will avoid confusion later.

Specifying the theoretical mean of 1.84 amounts to dividing the parameter space into two parts. The part specified by the theoretical prediction of μ contains only the value 1.84. The second part consists of all other values between 0 and 5, inclusive. If $\mu = 1.84$, then the theoretical prediction is correct, and for any other value of μ it is false.

In order to evaluate the theoretical prediction, the choices made by a random sample of 9 Anglos will be examined.[3] The frequency function

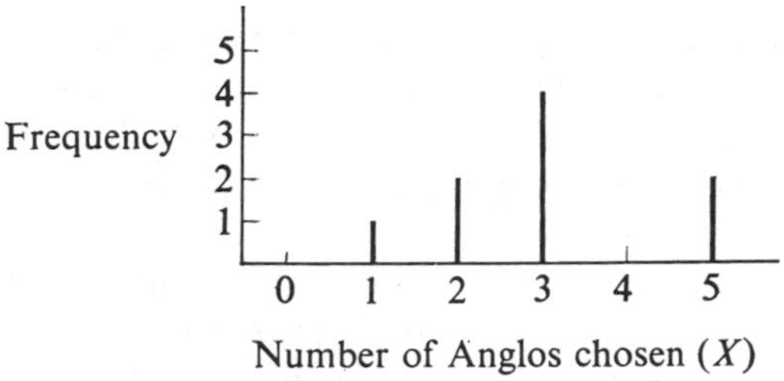

Figure XIII.1

for this sample is shown in Figure XIII.1. The mean of these data is $\bar{X} = 3$. The crucial question now becomes "What is the probability that a sample mean as discrepant as 3 would arise if $\mu = 1.84$ (i.e., if there is no ethnic cleavage)?" Notice that this is a conditional probability statement. It says, "What is $\mathbf{P}[(|\bar{X} - 1.84| \geq 3 - 1.84)|\mu = 1.84]$?" If this probability were small, we would be inclined to doubt that $\mu = 1.84$. If it were large, 1.84 would remain a plausible value for μ.

With this statement of the problem we turn to the definition of some terms that will prove helpful in constructing the statistical test.

XIII.1.1. Simple and composite statistical hypotheses

Notice that one of the two parts of the parameter space specifies a single value for the parameter ($\mu = 1.84$), whereas the other part specifies many values ($\mu \neq 1.84$). *Whenever a statistical hypothesis specifies a single value of a parameter, that hypothesis is referred to as a simple hypothesis. If a statistical hypothesis specifies more than one value of a parameter, then it is called a composite hypothesis.*

The statistical hypotheses for the example can be summarized as follows:

$$\text{H: } \mu = 1.84$$
$$\text{A: } \mu \neq 1.84,$$

where H stands for hypothesis and A for alternative.

[3] Thanks are due to Dr. Richard Jessor and the Tri-Ethnic Project (supported by NIMH Grant No. 3M-9156) for permission to use these data.

The simple hypothesis $\mu = 1.84$ is often called the *null hypothesis*. Here, it will be true if there is no ethnic cleavage. The composite hypothesis $\mu \neq 1.84$ is called the *alternative hypothesis*. Ethnic cleavage implies that the alternative hypothesis is true.

XIII.1.2. Connection between statistical hypotheses and research hypotheses

Notice the asymmetry of H and A. If it is decided that H is true, then we will act as if μ is exactly equal to 1.84, whereas, if it is concluded that A is true, action is not based on any specific value of the population mean. The first of these conclusions is compatible with the hypothesis that there is no ethnic cleavage, the second is compatible with the hypothesis that there is ethnic cleavage.

The art of formulating research questions as statistical hypotheses is a subtle one. It is altogether too easy to compromise or lose the original intent of the research in the process of forming hypotheses that are suitable for a statistical test. There is no sure way to prevent such distortion, but there is at least one crude indication of whether it has occurred. This is to ask whether one will *act* differently if it is concluded that H is true than if it is concluded that A is true. If not, it is likely that the research hypothesis has been distorted in the process of statistical formulation. This is true simply because research that is intended to test specific hypotheses is not usually undertaken unless the results have a definite bearing on subsequent experimentation or subsequent theoretical thinking.

XIII.1.3. Two ways to make a wrong decision

In the example, there are two ways to be right and two ways to be wrong in the statistical decision. These are summarized in Table XIII.1.

Table XIII.1. Two types of errors in a statistical decision

		True status of the parameter	
		H True ($\mu = 1.84$)	A True ($\mu \neq 1.84$)
Investigator's decision	Act as if H true	Correct decision	Error of type II
	Act as if A true	Error of type I	Correct decision

If $\mu = 1.84$ in the population, then deciding that A is true is an incorrect decision. Similarly, deciding that μ equals 1.84 would be erroneous if in fact the population mean were not 1.84. In general, *rejection of the null hypothesis when it is true is referred to as a Type I error. If the null hypothesis is accepted when it is false, this constitutes a Type II error.*

The use of numerals to designate the two kinds of errors is quite arbitrary. However, this usage is as close to universal as any notation in statistics, so it is important to know what each signifies.

XIII.1.4. The decision rule

When research data are gathered for statistical analysis, the observations must form a probability sample. For example, the nine observations summarized in Figure XIII.1 constitute a random sample from among the pupils of a particular high school. The sample space for such a data-gathering procedure will be referred to as a *data space.* Figure XIII.1 represents an event in the data space for the example. In general, outcomes in the data space provide information that is pertinent to the statistical hypothesis. If all of the observations in the example had been 5's, then it would appear doubtful that $\mu = 1.84$. In short, for some outcomes in the data space we are inclined to reject H, whereas for others H remains tenable.

The decision rule for a statistical test specifies whether or not the null hypothesis is to be rejected for every outcome in the data space. If the observed data constitute an outcome for which the decision rule specifies rejection of the null hypothesis, then the decision is that it is false. If the data constitute an outcome for which acceptance of the null hypothesis is specified, then the null hypothesis is considered tenable. For this reason, the set of outcomes for which rejection of the null hypothesis is specified is called the *rejection region* or *critical region*, and the set for which the null hypothesis is to be accepted is called the *acceptance region.*

In principle, it is always possible to define the decision rule in terms of the data space, but it is usually easier to designate regions of rejection and acceptance by specifying whether the null hypothesis is to be accepted or not for every value in the range of the relevant estimator. Defining the decision rule in terms of a relevant estimator is equivalent to defining it in terms of the data space, since the estimator assigns a value to every outcome in the data space.

In the ethnic cleavage example, the sample mean is clearly relevant to the statistical hypothesis. Therefore, its range must be divided into regions of acceptance and rejection. Since the null hypothesis ($\mu = 1.84$) could be false either because μ was too high or because it was too low, it seems reasonable to include in the rejection region values of $\bar{X}$ that are either high or low. Therefore, the decision rule will have the following form:

"Reject the hypothesis that $\mu = 1.84$ if $\bar{X} > \bar{x}_U$ ('high') or if $\bar{X} < \bar{x}_L$ ('low'). Accept the hypothesis that $\mu = 1.84$ if $\bar{x}_L \leq \bar{X} \leq \bar{x}_U$."

In order to make an explicit division of the range of $\bar{X}$ into rejection and acceptance regions, $\bar{x}_L$ and $\bar{x}_U$ must be found, and to do this, it is necessary to determine what is an acceptable probability for a Type I error. Postponing discussion of the rationale for this, **P**(Type I error) will be set equal to 0.1. Then if H is true and $\mu = 1.84$, the probability that $\bar{X} > \bar{x}_U$ or $\bar{X} < \bar{x}_L$ must equal 0.1. That is, **P**(Type I error) = $\mathbf{P}[(\bar{X} < \bar{x}_L) \cup (\bar{X} > \bar{x}_U) \mid \mu = 1.84] = 0.1$. This is identical to $\mathbf{P}(\bar{X} < \bar{x}_L \mid \mu = 1.84) + \mathbf{P}(\bar{X} > \bar{x}_U \mid \mu = 1.84) = 0.1$, since $(\bar{X} < \bar{x}_L)$ and $(\bar{X} > \bar{x}_U)$ are mutually exclusive events (an observed mean cannot be both too high and too low). The usual procedure is to set the two conditional probabilities equal to one another, so that

$$\mathbf{P}[\bar{X} < \bar{x}_L \mid \mu = 1.84] = \mathbf{P}[\bar{X} > \bar{x}_U \mid \mu = 1.84] = 0.05.$$

Then, the sum of these two probabilities equals the designated probability of a Type I error, as shown in Figure XIII.2.

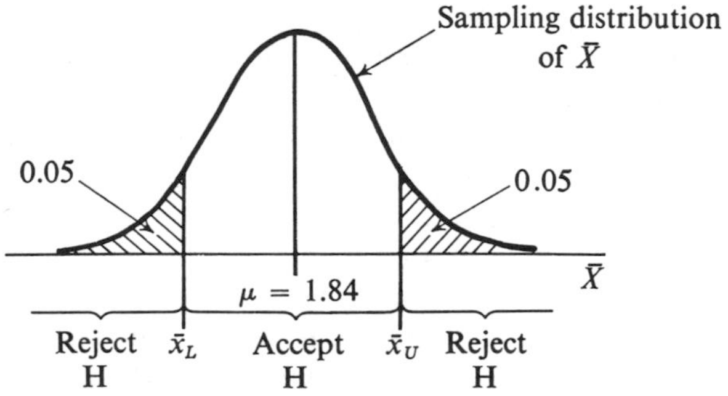

Figure XIII.2

If there is no ethnic cleavage, the observation variable (number of Anglos chosen) has a hypergeometric distribution with mean 1.84 and theoretical variance 1.125 (see Section X.1.2), and, according to the CLT, the sampling distribution of the mean will be approximately normal with standard error $\sigma/\sqrt{n} = \sqrt{1.125}/\sqrt{9} = 0.35$. Consequently,

$$Z = \frac{\bar{X} - \mu}{\sigma/\sqrt{n}} = \frac{\bar{X} - 1.84}{0.35}$$

can be considered a standardized normal deviate. Then, there exists z_U corresponding to $\bar{x}_U$ such that

$$\mathbf{P}[\bar{X} > \bar{x}_U \mid \mu = 1.84] = 0.05 = \mathbf{P}\left[Z > z_U = \frac{\bar{x}_U - 1.84}{0.35}\right].$$

The Z-value exceeded with probability 0.05 is $z_U = +1.65$, so that

$$z_U = 1.65 = \frac{\bar{x}_U - 1.84}{0.35},$$

and solving for $\bar{x}_U$,

$$1.65 = \frac{\bar{x}_U - 1.84}{0.35}$$

$$\bar{x}_U = 2.42.$$

Similarly, z_L is chosen so that

$$\mathbf{P}[\bar{X} < \bar{x}_L \mid \mu = 1.84] = 0.05 = \mathbf{P}\left[Z < z_L = \frac{\bar{x}_L - 1.84}{0.35}\right],$$

so that the value of $\bar{x}_L$ is obtained from the relation

$$z_L = -1.65 = \frac{\bar{x}_L - 1.84}{0.35}.$$

The solution is $\bar{x}_L = 1.26$. Therefore, the explicit decision rule is: "Reject the hypothesis that $\mu = 1.84$ if the sample mean is less than $\bar{x}_L = 1.26$ or if it exceeds $\bar{x}_U = 2.42$. Otherwise, accept the hypothesis that $\mu = 1.84$." This explicit decision rule is illustrated in Figure XIII.3.

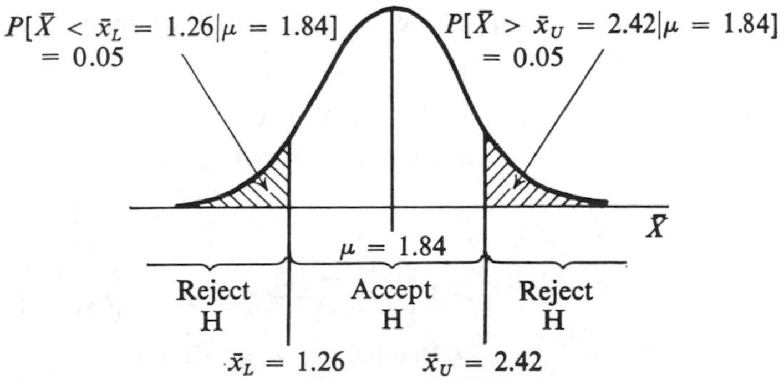

Figure XIII.3

The sample mean reported at the beginning of Section XIII.1 is $\bar{X} = 3$, and since this is greater than $\bar{x}_U = 2.42$, the null hypothesis must be rejected. The conclusion is that $\mu \neq 1.84$ and that the data are compatible with the hypothesis that ethnic cleavage exists in the high school.

XIII.2
PROPERTIES OF STATISTICAL TESTS

Like estimators, tests of statistical hypotheses can be appraised and compared according to certain characteristics. The applied statistician must often choose among statistical test procedures, and some of the considerations that enter such a choice are discussed in this section.

One of the most obvious ways to appraise a test is to examine the error probabilities it generates. Other things equal, the test with lowest error probabilities is preferable.

XIII.2.1. Type II error probabilities

When the null hypothesis is simple, there is only one Type I error probability to be considered. Furthermore, it is arbitrarily assigned by the investigator. On the other hand, a Type II error may occur for any value of the parameter specified by a composite alternative hypothesis. What is needed is a function that gives **P**(Type II error) for each value in the parameter space specified by the alternative hypothesis. Such a function is called a Type II error curve.

The decision rule for the ethnic cleavage example requires that H be accepted if the observed sample mean is between $\bar{x}_L = 1.26$ and $\bar{x}_U = 2.42$. Therefore, the probability of a Type II error is $\mathbf{P}[1.26 \leq \bar{X} \leq 2.42 \mid \mu = \mu_A]$, where μ_A is a value specified by the alternative hypothesis. To illustrate this calculation, the probability of a Type II error given $\mu = 1.5$ will be calculated.

If $\mu = 1.5$, then the mean of the sampling distribution of $\bar{X}$ must be 1.5 (since $E(\bar{X}) = \mu$), and[4]

$$\begin{aligned}
\mathbf{P}[\text{accept H} \mid \mu = 1.5] &= \mathbf{P}[\bar{x}_L \leq \bar{X} \leq \bar{x}_U \mid \mu = 1.5] \\
&= \mathbf{P}[1.26 \leq \bar{X} \leq 2.42 \mid \mu = 1.5] \\
&= \mathbf{P}\left[\frac{\bar{x}_L - \mu_A}{\sigma_{\bar{X}}} \leq Z \leq \frac{\bar{x}_U - \mu_A}{\sigma_{\bar{X}}}\right] \\
&= \mathbf{P}\left[\frac{1.26 - 1.5}{0.35} \leq Z \leq \frac{2.42 - 1.5}{0.35}\right] \\
&= \mathbf{P}[-0.69 \leq Z \leq +2.63] \\
&= 0.75.
\end{aligned}$$

Thus, if $\mu = 1.5$, the probability of a Type II error is 0.75. This calculation is shown graphically in Figure XIII.4.

By following analogous calculations for each of several values of μ, the Type II error curve shown in Figure XIII.5 can be plotted. Notice that if H is false but μ is close to 1.84, then there is a rather high probability of making a Type II error. For example, if $\mu = 2$, then the probability

[4] This calculation is based on the assumption that the standard error remains unchanged when μ changes. This may not be correct, but it is necessary to introduce additional assumptions in order to adjust for changes in the standard error that may occur, and it is not obvious just what assumptions are most appropriate. In any case, the effect of such adjustments is slight for this example.

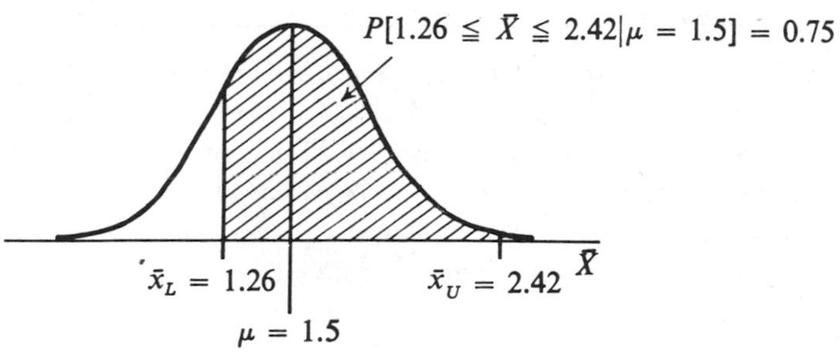

Figure XIII.4

of a Type II error is 0.868. However, if μ is as high as 3 or as low as 0.68, then the probability that the sample mean will fall in the acceptance region is less than 0.05.

Since a Type II error cannot occur if μ is 1.84, the curve in Figure XIII.5 should have a point deleted from it. However, deletion of a single point from a continuous function is not detectable on a graph.

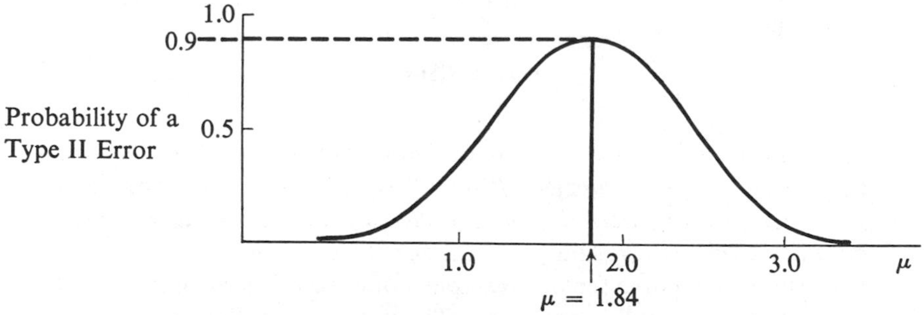

Figure XIII.5

Specification of a Type II error curve describes a statistical test. A desirable Type II error curve for the example is one that spreads out as little as possible about 1.84. That is, we want the probability of accepting H to be as small as possible for any value of μ other than 1.84.

XIII.2.2. Operating characteristic

The operating characteristic of a statistical test is a function that gives the probability of accepting the null hypothesis for each value in the parameter space.

Examination of Figure XIII.5 reveals that the operating characteristic (OC) is identical to the Type II error probability curve, except that the former includes the point for $\mu = 1.84$. For the example, the OC curve reaches maximum height at $\mu = 1.84$, and this maximum is

$$\mathbf{P}(\text{accept H} \mid \mu = 1.84) = 1 - \mathbf{P}(\text{Type I error}) = 1 - 0.1 = 0.9.$$

XIII.2.3. Power function

The power function for a statistical test is a function that gives the probability of rejecting the null hypothesis for each value in the parameter space.

Since the OC curve gives the probability of accepting H for each value of the parameter space, *one minus the height of the OC curve for each value in the parameter space determines the power function.* The power function for the example is shown in Figure XIII.6. Notice that it reaches

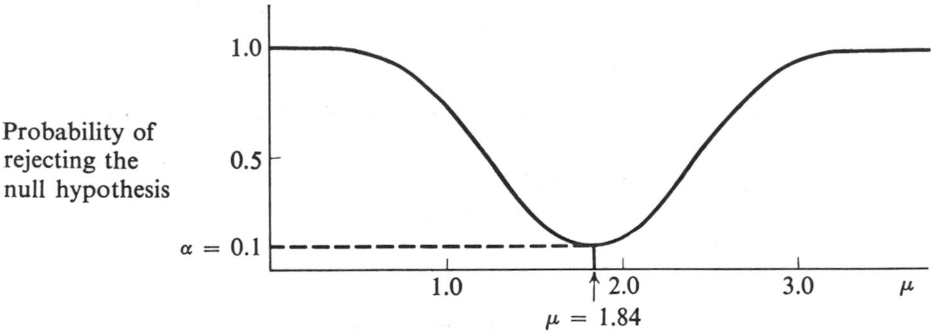

Figure XIII.6

a minimum at $\mu = 1.84$, and that this minimum is the probability of a Type I error. *When a simple null hypothesis is involved, the probability of a Type I error is referred to as the significance level of a test and is frequently designated* α. Thus, $\alpha = 0.1$ for the example.

The ideal power curve for the example would be one that rises abruptly on either side of the null hypothesis. The more abrupt the rise, the more powerful the test. Furthermore, if the minimum point is very low and the rise is abrupt, this means that errors of any kind are unlikely. However, the price for decreasing the Type I error probability is an increase in Type II error probabilities. This connection is discussed in the following section.

XIII.2.4. Relationship between Type I and Type II error probabilities

We are going to construct, for the example of Section XIII.1, a test in which the probability of a Type I error is 0.01 instead of 0.1. Then we can compare the OC curves for this test and the previous one.

For the new test, the decision rule is defined by

$$\mathbf{P}[(\bar{X} < \bar{x}_L) \cup (\bar{X} > \bar{x}_U) \mid \mu = 1.84)] = \alpha = 0.01$$

$$\mathbf{P}[\bar{X} < \bar{x}_L \mid \mu = 1.84] + \mathbf{P}[\bar{X} > \bar{x}_U \mid \mu = 1.84] = 0.01.$$

Assigning half of the significance level to the upper tail of the sampling distribution and half to the lower gives

$$\mathbf{P}[\bar{X} < \bar{x}_L \mid \mu = 1.84] = \alpha/2 = \mathbf{P}[\bar{X} > \bar{x}_U \mid \mu = 1.84]$$

$$\mathbf{P}\left[Z < z_L = \frac{\bar{x}_L - 1.84}{0.35}\right] = 0.005 = \mathbf{P}\left[Z > z_U = \frac{\bar{x}_U - 1.84}{0.35}\right]$$

$$\mathbf{P}\left[Z < -2.58 = \frac{\bar{x}_L - 1.84}{0.35}\right] = 0.005 = \mathbf{P}\left[Z > +2.58 = \frac{\bar{x}_U - 1.84}{0.35}\right].$$

The values of $\bar{X}$ corresponding to $Z = -2.58$ and $Z = +2.58$ are found by solving the equations

$$-2.58 = \frac{\bar{x}_L - 1.84}{0.35}, \quad \text{and} \quad +2.58 = \frac{\bar{x}_U - 1.84}{0.35},$$

so that

$$\bar{x}_L = 0.94, \quad \text{and} \quad \bar{x}_U = 2.74.$$

Therefore, the decision rule is "Reject the hypothesis that $\mu = 1.84$ if $\bar{X} < \bar{x}_L = 0.94$ or if $\bar{X} > \bar{x}_U = 2.74$. Otherwise accept the hypothesis that $\mu = 1.84$."

Using this decision rule, an OC curve can be constructed in the same way as for the previous test with $\alpha = 0.1$. The OC curves for both tests appear in Figure XIII.7.

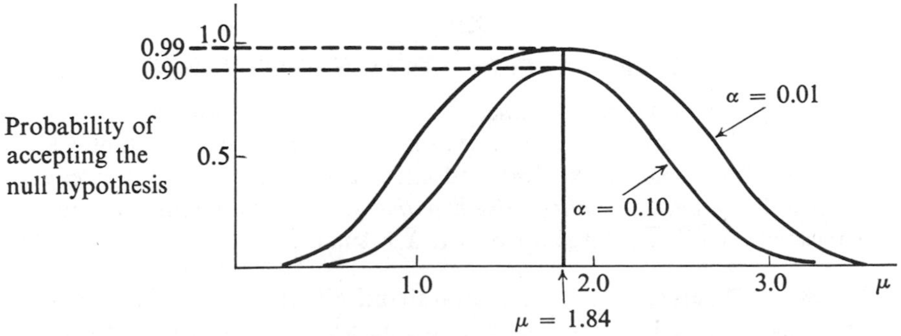

Figure XIII.7

Notice that for the test with a Type I error probability of 0.01 the probability of accepting the null hypothesis is greater for every value of μ. In general, *when the decision rule is chosen so that probabilities are reduced for one kind of error, then the probabilities for errors of the other kind are increased.*

But suppose that the sample size were 36 instead of 9 for the $\alpha = 0.01$ test. Then, the standard error of the sample mean would be $\sigma/\sqrt{n} = \sqrt{1.125}/\sqrt{36} = 0.175$, half the standard error for $n = 9$. The decision rule for this test is "Reject H if $\bar{X} < \bar{x}_L = 1.38$ or if $\bar{X} > \bar{x}_U = 2.30$. Otherwise, accept H." Using this decision rule, we can compare the OC curve for the test with $\alpha = 0.01$ and $n = 36$ with that for $\alpha = 0.1$ and

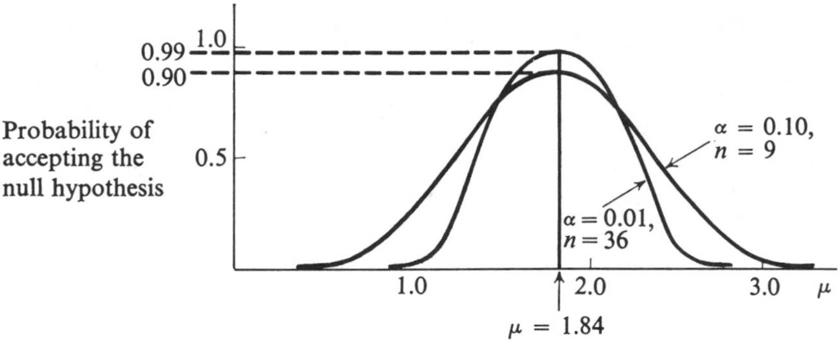

Figure XIII.8

$n = 9$. These curves are shown in Figure XIII.8. Except for values of μ near 1.84, the Type II error probabilities are smaller for the test with the smaller Type I error probability and the larger sample size. In general, increasing n permits one to decrease both Type I and Type II error probabilities for all but a limited range of values of the parameter.

XIII.3

ONE-SIDED ALTERNATIVE HYPOTHESES

In the ethnic cleavage example, the alternative hypothesis was that $\mu \neq 1.84$. In this case, a *two-sided alternative hypothesis* was employed. However, for reasons to be discussed later, it is sometimes advantageous to formulate a *one-sided alternative hypothesis*. Then, the null hypothesis is rejected only if $\bar{X}$ is large (or only if $\bar{X}$ is small).

XIII.3.1. Decision rule for a one-sided alternative hypothesis

The general procedure for constructing a decision rule for a test of a one-sided alternative is the same as that for a two-sided alternative. For the ethnic cleavage example, the hypotheses

$$\text{H: } \mu \leq 1.84$$
$$\text{A: } \mu > 1.84$$

might have been investigated. If a significance level of 0.1 were adopted, then the decision rule would be determined by finding $\bar{x}_C$ such that

$$\mathbf{P}(\bar{X} > \bar{x}_C \mid \text{H true}) = 0.1.$$

The general form of such a test is shown in Figure XIII.9.

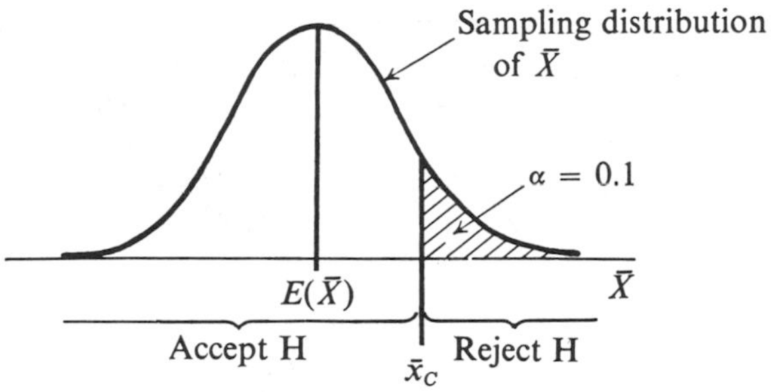

Figure XIII.9

But now we encounter a difficulty. The composite null hypothesis, $\mu \leq 1.84$, is true for any value of μ from 0 through 1.84, inclusive, so that a Type I error could occur for any one of this infinite set of values. Which one should be treated as the expected value of the sampling distribution (see Fig. XIII.9) when we set out to find $\bar{x}_C$ such that

$$\mathbf{P}(\bar{X} > \bar{x}_C \mid \text{H true}) = 0.1\,?$$

If a statistical test of hypotheses concerning the parameter π is to be constructed, then the maximum probability of a Type I error is called α, the significance level of the test. The decision rule is determined by assuming that the parameter has the value for which the probability of a Type I error is α. This value of the parameter is labeled π_0.

When the null hypothesis is simple, then π_0 equals the one value specified by the null hypothesis. For most tests in which the null hypothesis is composite, π_0 is the value of the parameter that is included in the null hypothesis but "least favorable" to it. In the null hypothesis $\mu \leq 1.84$, $\mu_0 = 1.84$ is "least favorable" in the sense that it lies on the boundary of the null hypothesis. For any larger value of μ, H is false. Later, we will show that the probability of a Type I error is greater for $\mu_0 = 1.84$ than for any other value of μ. But first, we must construct the decision rule for the test.

Since $\alpha = 0.1$ and $\mu_0 = 1.84$, we must find $\bar{x}_C$ such that

$$\mathbf{P}(\bar{X} > \bar{x}_C \mid \mu = 1.84) = \alpha = 0.1 = \mathbf{P}\left(Z > z_C = \frac{x_C - \mu_0}{\sigma/\sqrt{n}}\right)$$

From Appendix V, $\mathbf{P}(Z > +1.28) = 0.1$. Now, for $n = 9$ and $\sigma/\sqrt{n} = 0.35$,

$$z_C = \frac{\bar{x}_C - \mu_0}{\sigma/\sqrt{n}}$$

$$1.28 = \frac{\bar{x}_C - 1.84}{0.35},$$

and solving for $\bar{x}_C$, $\bar{x}_C = 2.29$. Therefore, the decision rule is "Reject the hypothesis that $\mu \leq 1.84$ if $\bar{X} > 2.29$. Otherwise, accept the hypothesis that $\mu \leq 1.84$, as illustrated in Figure XIII.10."

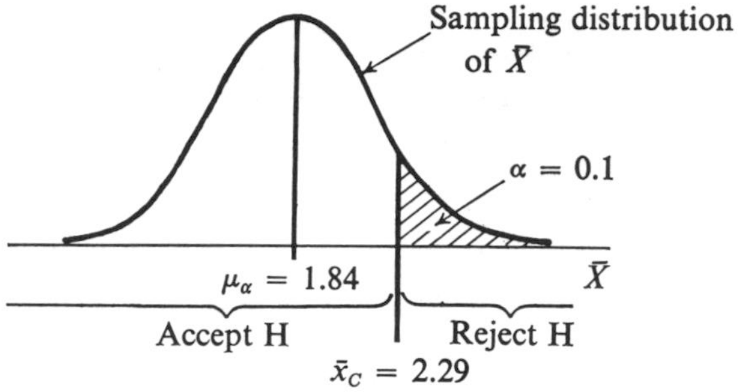

Figure XIII.10

Since the mean of the observed sample (Fig. XIII.1) is 3, we must reject the null hypothesis that $\mu \leq 1.84$. This test also indicates that there is ethnic cleavage in the high school.

XIII.3.2. Applicability of a one-sided alternative hypothesis

The investigator is free to choose between one-sided and two-sided alternative hypotheses. But how is the choice to be made? There are at least two circumstances in which a one-sided alternative may be preferred.

In the example, we might be interested in knowing whether $\mu \leq 1.84$ or $\mu > 1.84$, but it could be unimportant whether $\mu = 1.84$ or $\mu < 1.84$. In other words, subsequent action would be the same regardless of whether μ equalled 1.84 or were less than 1.84. This would mean that ethnic cleavage is of primary interest, and whether there was no cleavage or what might be called negative cleavage ($\mu < 1.84$, Anglos most often choose non-Anglos) is considered immaterial. If this were the case, then perhaps a one-sided alternative would be most appropriate.

Another possibility is that we can rule out $\mu < 1.84$ on the basis of previous research and limit ourselves to the question of whether $\mu = 1.84$ or $\mu > 1.84$. Here the simple null hypothesis $\mu = 1.84$ could be tested against the alternative $\mu > 1.84$. However, this amounts to excluding the values between 0 and 1.84 from the parameter space, which logically excludes them from further consideration of any kind. Because such confidence is rarely possible, the composite null hypothesis, $\mu \leq 1.84$, is probably preferable.

There is another way of stating the question: why not always use a two-sided alternative? The answer is that for a given significance level and a given sample size, Type II error probabilities are smaller for the one-sided alternative. This is illustrated in the following section.

XIII.3.3. Power function and operating characteristic for one-sided alternative hypotheses

The power function for the test of a one-sided alternative constructed in Section XIII.3.1 can be found by plotting $\mathbf{P}(\bar{X} > \bar{x}_C = 2.29 \mid \mu)$ for several values of μ. For example, the probability of rejecting H given $\mu = 1.25$ is

$$\begin{aligned}\mathbf{P}(\bar{X} > \bar{x}_C = 2.29 \mid \mu = 1.25) &= \mathbf{P}\left(Z > \frac{2.29 - 1.25}{0.35}\right) \\ &= \mathbf{P}(Z > 2.98) \\ &= 0.0014.\end{aligned}$$

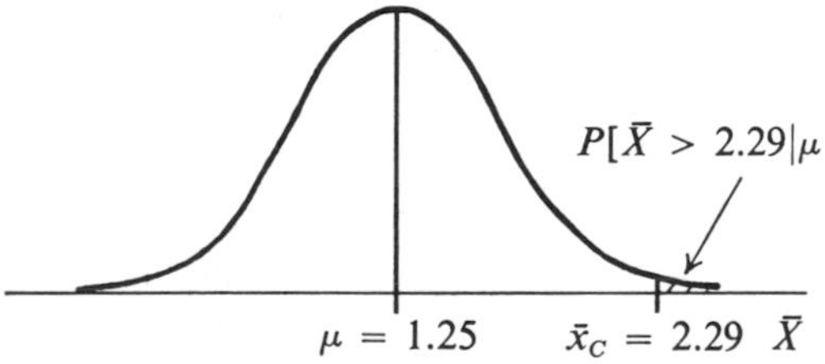

Figure XIII.11

This probability corresponds to the crosshatched area of Figure XIII.11. Analogous calculations have been carried out for several values of μ, and these have been used to plot the lazy-S curve of Figure XIII.12. This curve is the power function for the one-sided alternative test.

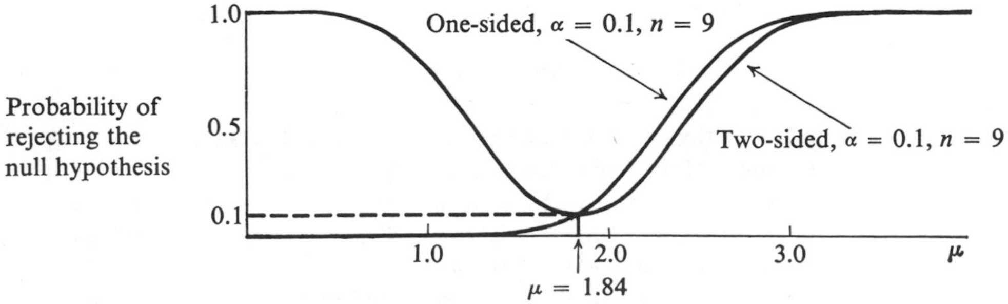

Figure XIII.12

From this power function, it can be seen that the probability of a Type I error is largest for $\mu = 1.84$. Furthermore, if the decision rule had been determined using as μ_0 any value less than 1.84, then the maximum Type I error probability would have been greater than 0.1. For example, suppose $\mu = 1.80$ had been used to determine the decision rule. Then it would have been "reject H if $\bar{X} > 2.25$ and otherwise accept H," and the Type I error probability associated with $\mu = 1.84$ would be

$$\mathbf{P}(\bar{X} > 2.25 \mid \mu = 1.84) = \mathbf{P}(Z > +1.17) = 0.121.$$

Consequently, the significance level (the maximum probability of a Type I error) would have been 0.121 rather than the 0.1 intended.

The power function for the two-sided alternative test of Section XIII.1.4 also appears in Figure XIII.12. Notice that for any value of μ greater than 1.84, the power of the one-sided alternative exceeds that of the two-sided test. Since one minus the power equals the probability of a Type II error, the test with the one-sided alternative also has smaller Type II error probabilities for all values of μ above 1.84. This is why a one-sided alternative may be preferred to the two-sided alternative.

The best test for the one-sided alternative in the example is one with a power curve that rises steeply to the right of $\mu = 1.84$ and drops to zero immediately to the left of $\mu = 1.84$.

One way to increase power is to increase the Type I error probabilities. In Figure XIII.13, the power curve for the one-sided test with $\alpha = 0.1$

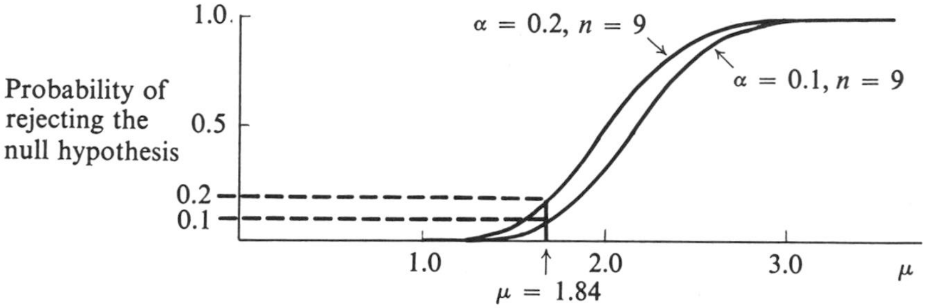

Figure XIII.13

is compared with that of a test for which $\alpha = 0.2$. The sample size is 9 for both tests. Notice that for the $\alpha = 0.2$ test the probabilities of Type II errors are less than those for the $\alpha = 0.1$ test. Just as with tests of two-sided alternatives, when n is fixed, Type II error probabilities decrease with increases in Type I error probabilities.

The OC curve for a one-sided test can be found by plotting one less the power as a function of the parameter.

Notice that a one-sided alternative hypothesis may be either an upper (e.g., $\mu > 1.84$) or a lower alternative (e.g., $\mu < 1.84$). Although it would not have been reasonable for the ethnic cleavage example, it would be possible to test

$$\text{H: } \mu \geq 1.84$$
$$\text{A: } \mu < 1.84.$$

XIII.4

THE BALANCE OF TYPE I AND TYPE II ERROR PROBABILITIES

So far, little has been said about the choice of significance level, but significance levels of 0.01 or 0.05 are almost universal among scientific investigators. This seems to be attributable to a combination of methodological ossification and a tendency to place the subjective value of a "small" probability in the neighborhood of 0.01 to 0.05. (See the discussion of Bilodeau's study in Section X.1.1.)

Usually, the research hypothesis entertained by an investigator corresponds to the alternative hypothesis rather than the null hypothesis.[5] In such cases, a small significance level is adopted in the name of scientific conservatism. That is, the investigator tries to minimize the probability of *incorrectly* finding that the data support his expectations. But, occasionally, the investigator's expectation is that the null hypothesis is true. If so, the same scientific conservatism seems to require a *large* significance level and, consequently, relatively small probabilities of Type II errors. Nonetheless, there are many instances in the literature in which acceptance of the null hypothesis supports the researcher's theory and where Type II probabilities are extremely high due to the choice of a small significance level.

Sometimes there are very clear reasons for guarding with special care against one kind of error. For example, if a Type II error means a deadly substance is to be distributed as medicine, whereas a Type I error simply means that money is lost by discarding the substance unnecessarily, it is apparent that Type II error probabilities must be kept low. Just such problems occur in connection with the manufacture of some drugs and vaccines. Under circumstances of this kind, a nonzero probability of distributing a deadly poison must be faced, and the question "How small is a small probability?" takes on a grave hue.

For most scientists, however, reasons for exerting more effort to avoid one type of error are unlikely to appear in such bold relief. Perhaps the best the scientist can do is to consider the relative amounts of wasted time and effort that would accrue to each of the two kinds of error and make a frankly subjective choice of a significance level with these considerations in mind.

[5] This would probably be true in the ethnic cleavage examples. The investigators would most likely expect to observe evidence for ethnic cleavage, and ethnic cleavage corresponds to the alternative hypothesis.

XIII.5

SUMMARY OF HYPOTHESIS TESTING PROCEDURES FOR POPULATION MEANS

This section is devoted to a brief summary of the procedures for constructing CLT tests of hypotheses regarding a single population mean.

1. *Assumptions:* Sampling must be random.

2. *Parameters required:* The population variance must be known, although, if n is large enough, perhaps σ^2 can be replaced by the sample variance, S^2.

3. *Sampling distribution:* The CLT provides the basis for assuming that $\bar{X}$ has an approximately normal DF for large n. Of course, if X is normal, then $\bar{X}$ has a normal sampling distribution for *any n*.

4. *Two-sided alternatives:* For a test of the hypotheses

$$\begin{aligned} \text{H:}\ & \mu = \mu_0 \\ \text{A:}\ & \mu \neq \mu_0, \end{aligned}$$

the decision rule has the form "Reject H if $\bar{X} < \bar{x}_L$ or if $\bar{X} > \bar{x}_U$. Otherwise, accept H." If α is the significance level of the test, then

$$\bar{x}_L = \mu_0 + z_{\alpha/2} \frac{\sigma}{\sqrt{n}}$$

and

$$\bar{x}_U = \mu_0 + z_{1-\alpha/2} \frac{\sigma}{\sqrt{n}},$$

where $z_{\alpha/2}$ is chosen so that $\mathbf{P}(Z < z_{\alpha/2}) = \alpha/2$ and $z_{1-\alpha/2}$ is chosen so that $\mathbf{P}(Z < z_{1-\alpha/2}) = 1 - \alpha/2$.

a. *Type I error probability:* The probability of a Type I error equals the significance level, α.

b. *Type II error probabilities:* If μ_A is a value of μ specified by the alternative, then the probability of accepting H given $\mu = \mu_A$ is

$$\mathbf{P}\left(\frac{\bar{x}_L - \mu_A}{\sigma/\sqrt{n}} \leq Z \leq \frac{\bar{x}_U - \mu_A}{\sigma/\sqrt{n}}\right).$$

5. *One-sided upper alternative:* For a test of the hypotheses

$$\begin{aligned} \text{H:}\ & \mu \leq \mu_0 \\ \text{A:}\ & \mu > \mu_0, \end{aligned}$$

the decision rule has the form "Reject H if $\bar{X} > \bar{x}_C$. Otherwise, accept H." If α is the significance level, then

$$\bar{x}_C = \mu_0 + z_{1-\alpha} \frac{\sigma}{\sqrt{n}},$$

where $z_{1-\alpha}$ is chosen so that $\mathbf{P}(Z \leq z_{1-\alpha}) = 1 - \alpha$.

a. *Type I error probabilities:* If μ_H is a value of μ specified by H, then the probability of rejecting H given $\mu = \mu_H$ is

$$\mathbf{P}\left(Z > \frac{\bar{x}_C - \mu_H}{\sigma/\sqrt{n}}\right).$$

The significance level is the largest probability of a Type I error.

b. *Type II error probabilities:* If μ_A is any value of μ specified by A, then the probability of accepting H given $\mu = \mu_A$ is

$$\mathbf{P}\left(Z \leq \frac{\bar{x}_C - \mu_A}{\sigma/\sqrt{n}}\right).$$

6. *One-sided lower alternative hypotheses:* For a test of the statistical hypotheses

$$\begin{aligned} \text{H}&: \ \mu \geq \mu_0 \\ \text{A}&: \ \mu < \mu_0, \end{aligned}$$

the decision rule is "Reject *H* if $\bar{X} < \bar{x}_C$. Otherwise, accept H." If α is the significance level, then

$$\bar{x}_C = \mu_0 + z_\alpha \frac{\sigma}{\sqrt{n}}$$

where z_α is chosen so that $\mathbf{P}(Z < z_\alpha) = \alpha$.

a. *Type I error probabilities:* If μ_H is any value of μ specified by H, then the probability that H will be rejected given $\mu = \mu_H$ is

$$\mathbf{P}\left(Z < \frac{\bar{x}_C - \mu_H}{\sigma/\sqrt{n}}\right).$$

The significance level, α, equals the maximum probability of a Type I error.

b. *Type II error probabilities:* If μ_A is any value of μ specified by A, then the probability of accepting H given $\mu = \mu_A$ is

$$\mathbf{P}\left(Z \geq \frac{\bar{x}_C - \mu_A}{\sigma/\sqrt{n}}\right).$$

XIII.6
TESTING HYPOTHESES ABOUT A PROPORTION

Since a proportion is simply the mean of a random variable with range (0, 1), it is reasonable to expect that methods for testing hypotheses regarding a population proportion will be similar to those for testing hypotheses about other means. In this section, such procedures are described. They are introduced with an example.

On each trial of a "guessing" experiment, a light either goes on (L) or not. The experimenter arranges things so that the sequence of light and no-light trials is random. At the sound of a signal indicating the beginning of each trial, the subject guesses that the light will go on (O) or that it will not. If $\mathbf{P}(L)$ is the experimenter-controlled light-on probability and $\mathbf{P}(O)$ is the probability that the subject will guess "light on," then, according to the Estes-Burke statistical learning theory (see Sections *III.2.3, *V.3.6, and *VIII.9), $\mathbf{P}(O)$ should approach $\mathbf{P}(L)$ as the number of trials becomes large.

Now, suppose that 16 subjects have received prolonged training in such a task and that $\mathbf{P}(L) = 0.6$. Then, if the Estes-Burke theory holds, $\mathbf{P}(O)$ should be equal to $\mathbf{P}(L) = 0.6$. The problem is to test the hypothesis that on a predetermined test trial, $\mathbf{P}(O) = \mathbf{P}(L) = 0.6$. If the theory holds for each of the 16 subjects, then their responses on a given trial constitute a random sample of size 16 from a binomial population in which $\mathbf{P}(O) = 0.6$.

XIII.6.1. Test for a two-sided alternative using exact probabilities

If X is the number of subjects who guess "light on" on the test trial, then $X/n = X/16$ is the corresponding sample proportion. Furthermore, the corresponding binomial probabilities,

$$\mathbf{P}(X = x) = \mathbf{P}\left(\frac{X}{n} = \frac{x}{n}\right) = \mathbf{P}\left(\frac{X}{16} = \frac{x}{16}\right),$$

can be found in the table of Appendix II for $n = 16$. These probabilities form the sampling distribution of X or of $X/16$.

First, we will construct a test of the two-sided alternative

$$\text{H: } P = 0.6$$
$$\text{A: } P \neq 0.6,$$

where P refers to the probability of the "light-on" response on a specified trial. Since accepting H must be considered as theoretical support, we will guard rather carefully against Type II errors (see Section XIII.4). Consequently, a relatively large significance level of 0.3 will be used.

The decision rule is to be constructed so that $\mathbf{P}(\text{rejecting H} \mid P = 0.6) = 0.3$. This can be done by examining the binomial distribution of $X/n = X/16$ for $P = 0.6$, which is shown in Figure XIII.14 (values for this plot were obtained from Appendix II).

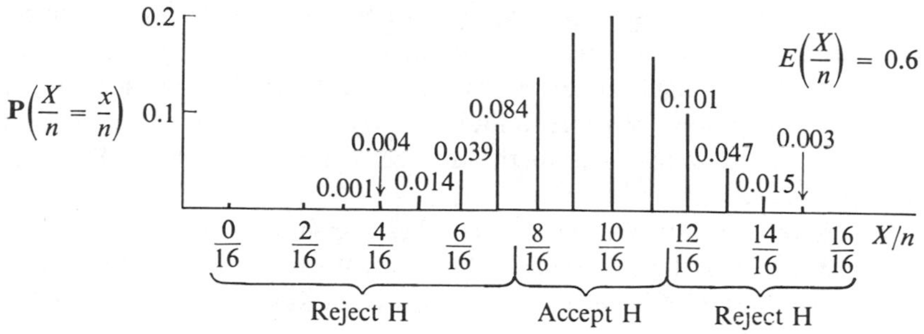

Figure XIII.14

Now, X/16 > 11/16 could be chosen for the upper portion of the rejection region so that

$$\begin{aligned}\mathbf{P}\left(\frac{X}{16} > \frac{11}{16}\,\middle|\, P = 0.6\right) &= \mathbf{P}\left(\frac{X}{16} = \frac{12}{16}\right) + \mathbf{P}\left(\frac{X}{16} = \frac{13}{16}\right) + \mathbf{P}\left(\frac{X}{16} = \frac{14}{16}\right)\\ &\quad + \mathbf{P}\left(\frac{X}{16} = \frac{15}{16}\right) + \mathbf{P}\left(\frac{X}{16} = \frac{16}{16}\right)\\ &= 0.101 + 0.047 + 0.015 + 0.003 + 0.000\\ &= 0.166,\end{aligned}$$

and $X/16 < 8/16$ could serve as the lower portion of the rejection region so that

$$\begin{aligned}\mathbf{P}\left(\frac{X}{16} < \frac{8}{16}\,\middle|\, P = 0.6\right) &= \mathbf{P}\left(\frac{X}{16} = \frac{7}{16}\right) + \mathbf{P}\left(\frac{X}{16} = \frac{6}{16}\right) + \mathbf{P}\left(\frac{X}{16} = \frac{5}{16}\right)\\ &\quad + \mathbf{P}\left(\frac{X}{16} = \frac{4}{16}\right) + \mathbf{P}\left(\frac{X}{16} = \frac{3}{16}\right) + \mathbf{P}\left(\frac{X}{16} = \frac{2}{16}\right)\\ &\quad + \mathbf{P}\left(\frac{X}{16} = \frac{1}{16}\right) + \mathbf{P}\left(\frac{X}{16} = \frac{0}{16}\right)\\ &= 0.084 + 0.039 + 0.014 + 0.004 + 0.001\\ &\quad + 0.000 + 0.000 + 0.000\\ &= 0.142.\end{aligned}$$

Then, the decision rule would be "Reject H if $X/16 < 8/16$ or if $X/16 >$ 11/16. Otherwise, accept H." However, the significance level for this decision rule is

$$\begin{aligned}\mathbf{P}\left[\left(\frac{X}{16} < \frac{8}{16}\right) \cup \left(\frac{X}{16} > \frac{11}{16}\right)\,\middle|\, P = 0.6\right] &= \mathbf{P}\left(\frac{X}{16} < \frac{8}{16}\,\middle|\, P = 0.6\right)\\ &\quad + \mathbf{P}\left(\frac{X}{16} > \frac{11}{16}\,\middle|\, P = 0.6\right)\\ &= 0.142 + 0.166\\ &= 0.308\end{aligned}$$

rather than the 0.3 chosen initially, and the rejection region is asymmetric in probability. Such discrepancies often arise when tests are based on small samples and use estimators that have but few values in their range. However, it is usually possible to find a nearly symmetrical critical region that comes reasonably close to the desired significance level. This has been done here.

The power function for this test can be determined by using the table of Appendix II to find $\mathbf{P}[(X/16 < 8/16) \cup (X/16 > 11/16) \mid P]$ for each of several values of P. Thus, the value of the power function for $P = 0.8$ is

$$\begin{aligned}\mathbf{P}\left[\left(\frac{X}{16} < \frac{8}{16}\right) \cup \left(\frac{X}{16} > \frac{11}{16}\right) \middle| P = 0.8\right] &= \mathbf{P}\left(\frac{X}{16} < \frac{8}{16} \middle| P = 0.8\right) \\ &\quad + \mathbf{P}\left(\frac{X}{16} > \frac{11}{16} \middle| P = 0.8\right) \\ &= [7(0.000) + 0.001] + (0.200 \\ &\quad + 0.246 + 0.211 + 0.113 \\ &\quad + 0.028) \\ &= 0.799.\end{aligned}$$

Of course, this probability was calculated with the aid of Appendix II. The power function for this test is the solid curve in Figure XIII.15. The broken line in this figure is discussed in Section XIII.6.3.

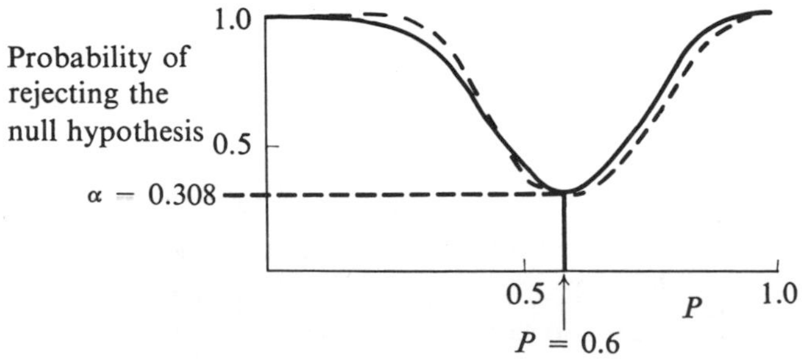

Figure XIII.15

XIII.6.2. Test for a one-sided alternative using exact probabilities

Instead of approaching the experimenter-controlled light-on probability, some subjects may adopt the strategy of always guessing "light on" if $\mathbf{P}(L) > 1/2$, or of always guessing that the light will not come on if $\mathbf{P}(L) < 1/2$. As illustrated at the end of Section *VIII.9, this strategy maximizes the expected proportion of correct guesses. For the example, $\mathbf{P}(L) = 0.6 > 1/2$, so that if a subject adopted this strategy, he would guess "light on" on every trial. If he did this, he could expect 60 percent of his guesses to be correct.

Now, suppose that the data for a given trial following prolonged training are to be examined to see whether some subjects adopt this strategy. The appropriate statistical hypotheses are:

$$\text{H: } P \leq 0.6$$
$$\text{A: } P > 0.6.$$

Rejection of the null hypothesis would be compatible with the hypothesis that some subjects guess the more probable event (light on, in this case) in excess of its objective probability. But since rejection of H for this test is consistent with the experimental hypothesis, a smaller significance level, 0.05, will be employed. Perhaps one should be more careful about Type I errors here, since a number of reports in the literature describe data for which mean response probabilities are close to experimenter-controlled event probabilities after prolonged training.

The decision rule for this test is defined by the relation

$$\mathbf{P}\left(\frac{X}{16} > \frac{x_C}{16} \,\middle|\, P = 0.6\right) = 0.05,$$

where $P = 0.6$ was selected in the way suggested in Section XIII.3.1. It is the value of P specified by H but least favorable to H.

From Appendix II,

$$\begin{aligned}\mathbf{P}\left(\frac{X}{16} > \frac{13}{16} \,\middle|\, P = 0.6\right) &= \mathbf{P}\left(\frac{X}{16} = \frac{14}{16}\right) + \mathbf{P}\left(\frac{X}{16} = \frac{15}{16}\right) + \mathbf{P}\left(\frac{X}{16} = \frac{16}{16}\right)\\ &= 0.015 + 0.003 + 0.000\\ &= 0.018,\end{aligned}$$

and

$$\begin{aligned}\mathbf{P}\left(\frac{X}{16} > \frac{12}{16} \,\middle|\, P = 0.6\right) &= \mathbf{P}\left(\frac{X}{16} = \frac{13}{16}\right) + \mathbf{P}\left(\frac{X}{16} = \frac{14}{16}\right)\\ &\qquad + \mathbf{P}\left(\frac{X}{16} = \frac{15}{16}\right) + \mathbf{P}\left(\frac{X}{16} = \frac{16}{16}\right)\\ &= 0.047 + 0.015 + 0.003 + 0.000\\ &= 0.065.\end{aligned}$$

Thus, Appendix II does not permit a decision rule that comes closer to the significance level of 0.05 than 0.065. However, since it was stated that Type I errors were to be carefully avoided, we will use the decision rule leading to a significance level of 0.018. That is, "Reject H if $X/16 > 13/16$. Otherwise, accept H."

The power function for this test is represented by the solid line in Figure XIII.16.

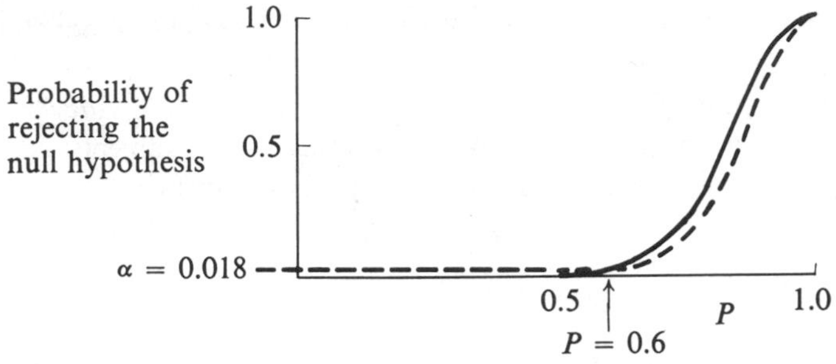

Figure XIII.16

If sampling *without* replacement from a finite binomial population, then procedures analogous to those just described in Sections XIII.6.1 and XIII.6.2 can be used to test hypotheses about a population proportion. However, such tests must be based on the hypergeometric rather than the binomial PD (see Section X.1.2).

XIII.6.3. Test for a two-sided alternative using a normal approximation

In this section, a test will be devised using the CLT to deal with the statistical hypotheses, experimental procedure, and sample size set forth in Section XIII.6.1. The statistical hypotheses are

$$\text{H: } P = 0.6$$
$$\text{A: } P \neq 0.6.$$

A significance level of 0.308 will be used to permit direct comparisons with the exact probability test.

According to the CLT, $p = X/n$ will have an approximately normal distribution for sufficiently large n. If H is true, $E(X/n) = P = 0.6$ and the variance of X/n is $\sqrt{[P(1-P)/n]} = \sqrt{[0.6(1-0.6)/16]} = 0.123$. Then, the decision rule is determined by

$$\mathbf{P}\left[\left(\frac{X}{16} < p_L\right) \cup \left(\frac{X}{16} > p_U\right) \middle| P = 0.6\right] = 0.308$$

$$\mathbf{P}\left(\frac{X}{16} < p_L \middle| P = 0.6\right) + \mathbf{P}\left(\frac{X}{16} > p_U \middle| P = 0.6\right) = 0.154 + 0.154 = 0.308.$$

The upper boundary of the lower portion of the rejection region is found by setting

$$\mathbf{P}\left(\frac{X}{16} < p_L \middle| P = 0.6\right) = 0.154.$$

Then,

$$\mathbf{P}\left(Z < z_L = \frac{p_L - 0.6}{\sqrt{[0.6(1-0.6)/16]}}\right) = 0.154,$$

and since $z_L = -1.02$, $p_L = 0.47$. This value bounds the lower portion of the rejection region. The boundary of the upper portion is determined by

$$\mathbf{P}\left(\frac{X}{16} > p_U \,\middle|\, P = 0.6\right) = 0.154.$$

Solving for p_U in a manner analogous to the solution for p_L, $p_U = 0.73$. Then the decision rule is "Reject H if $X/16 < 0.47$ or if $X/16 > 0.73$. Otherwise, accept H."

The power function for this test is represented by the broken line of Figure XIII.15. Values of this power function were computed by finding the probability of rejecting H for each of several values of P.

Notice that this power function is symmetrical, whereas the power curve for the exact test introduced in Section XIII.6.1 is asymmetrical. The difference arises because the normal DF is symmetrical, whereas the binomial PD for $P = 0.6$ is skewed.

XIII.6.4. Test for a one-sided alternative using a normal approximation

Next, the normal approximation will be used to construct a test for the hypotheses

$$\text{H: } P \leq 0.6$$
$$\text{A: } P > 0.6.$$

This test has the same context as the one in Section XIII.6.2, and the same significance level, 0.018, will be adopted here, too.

A test of these hypotheses requires that the null hypothesis be rejected for large values of the sample proportion. The critical region is defined by

$$\mathbf{P}\left(\frac{X}{16} > p_C \,\middle|\, P = 0.6\right) = 0.018.$$

Since the PD of $p = X/16$ can be approximated by a normal DF,

$$\mathbf{P}\left(\frac{X}{16} > p_C \,\middle|\, P = 0.6\right) = \mathbf{P}\left(Z > z_C = \frac{p_C - 0.6}{\sqrt{[0.6(1 - 0.6)/16]}}\right) = 0.018.$$

Since $\mathbf{P}(Z > +2.1) = 0.018$, $p_C = 0.858$. Consequently, the decision rule is "Reject H if $X/16 > 0.858$. Otherwise, accept H."

The broken line of Figure XIII.16 represents the power function for this test.

XIII.6.5. Summary of hypothesis testing procedures for proportions

This summary includes only the normal approximation procedures for testing hypotheses about proportions. Tests utilizing exact probabilities are difficult to summarize without the aid of an example.

1. *Assumptions:* Sampling must be random and from a binomial population. All of the formulas given in this section use the standard error of p for sampling from an infinite binomial population, or *with* replacement from a finite binomial population. This is from Formula [XI.2a]. If sampling without replacement from a finite binomial population, then $p = X/n$ has a hypergeometric distribution, and the standard error of p is

$$\sqrt{\left[\frac{N-n}{N-1}\frac{P(1-P)}{n}\right]}.$$

This is Formula [XI.2b] (Section XI.2.1), and it should replace $\sqrt{[P(1-P)/n]}$ throughout this section if sampling is without replacement from a finite binomial population.

2. *Parameters required:* No parameters need be known.

3. *Sampling distribution:* The CLT provides the basis for these tests. Consequently, their precision increases with the sample size.

4. *Two-sided alternative hypotheses:* For a test of the statistical hypotheses

$$\text{H}: P = P_0$$
$$\text{A}: P \neq P_0,$$

the decision rule is of the form "Reject H if $X/n < p_L$ or if $X/n > p_U$. Otherwise, accept H." If α is the significance level of the test, then p_L is defined by

$$p_L = P_0 + z_{\alpha/2}\sqrt{\left[\frac{P_0(1-P_0)}{n}\right]}$$

and p_U is defined by

$$p_U = P_0 + z_{1-\alpha/2}\sqrt{\left[\frac{P_0(1-P_0)}{n}\right]},$$

where $z_{\alpha/2}$ is chosen so that $\mathbf{P}(Z < z_{\alpha/2}) = \alpha/2$ and $z_{1-\alpha/2}$ is chosen so that $\mathbf{P}(Z < z_{1-\alpha/2}) = 1 - \alpha/2$.

a. *Type I error probability:* The probability of a Type I error equals the significance level, α.

b. *Type II error probabilities:* If P_A is any value of P specified by A, then the probability of accepting H given $P = P_A$ is

$$\mathbf{P}\left(\frac{p_L - P_A}{\sqrt{[P_A(1-P_A)/n]}} \leq Z \leq \frac{p_U - P_A}{\sqrt{[P_A(1-P_A)/n]}}\right).$$

5. *One-sided upper alternative hypotheses:* For a test of the statistical hypotheses

$$\text{H}: P \leq P_0$$
$$\text{A}: P > P_0,$$

the decision rule is "Reject H if $X/n > p_C$. Otherwise, accept H." If α is the significance level, then

$$p_C = P_0 + z_{1-\alpha}\sqrt{\left[\frac{P_0(1 - P_0)}{n}\right]},$$

where $z_{1-\alpha}$ is chosen so that $\mathbf{P}(Z < z_{1-\alpha}) = 1 - \alpha$.

a. *Type I error probabilities:* If P_{H} is any value of P specified by H, then the probability of rejecting H given $P = P_{\text{H}}$ is

$$\mathbf{P}\left(Z > \frac{p_C - P_{\text{H}}}{\sqrt{[P_{\text{H}}(1 - P_{\text{H}})/n]}}\right).$$

The maximum probability of a Type I error equals α.

b. *Type II error probabilities:* If P_{A} is any value of P specified by A, then the probability of accepting H given $P = P_{\text{A}}$ is

$$\mathbf{P}\left(Z \leq \frac{p_C - P_{\text{A}}}{\sqrt{[P_{\text{A}}(1 - P_{\text{A}})/n]}}\right).$$

6. *One-sided lower alternative hypotheses:* For a test of the statistical hypotheses

$$\text{H}: P \geq P_0$$
$$\text{A}: P < P_0,$$

the decision rule is "Reject H if $X/n < p_C$. Otherwise, accept H." If α is the significance level, then

$$p_C = P_0 + z_{\alpha}\sqrt{\left[\frac{P_0(1 - P_0)}{n}\right]},$$

where z_α is chosen so that $\mathbf{P}(Z < z_\alpha) = \alpha$.

a. *Type I error probabilities:* If P_{H} is any value of P specified by H, then the probability that H will be rejected given $P = P_{\text{H}}$ is

$$\mathbf{P}\left(Z < \frac{p_C - P_{\text{H}}}{\sqrt{[P_{\text{H}}(1 - P_{\text{H}})/n]}}\right).$$

The maximum probability of a Type I error equals α.

b. *Type II error probabilities:* If P_{A} is any value of P specified by A, then the probability that H will be accepted given $P = P_{\text{A}}$ is

$$\mathbf{P}\left(Z \geq \frac{p_C - P_{\text{A}}}{\sqrt{[P_{\text{A}}(1 - P_{\text{A}})/n]}}\right).$$

XIII.7

TESTING HYPOTHESES ABOUT A VARIANCE

Hypotheses about a population variance can be dealt with in a way similar to the treatment of means and proportions. In this section, one of the methods for constructing and evaluating tests regarding a population variance is described.

XIII.7.1. Test for a two-sided alternative

In the ethnic cleavage example, if sociometric choices are independent of ethnic group membership, then the variance of the number of Anglos among the $C = 5$ children chosen by an Anglo is

$$\sigma^2 = C\left(\frac{R}{N}\right)\left(1 - \frac{R}{N}\right)\left(\frac{N - C}{N - 1}\right) = 5\left(\frac{45}{122}\right)\left(1 - \frac{45}{122}\right)\left(\frac{122 - 5}{122 - 1}\right)$$
$$= 1.125.$$

A procedure will be developed that permits a test of the statistical hypotheses

$$\text{H: } \sigma^2 = 1.125$$
$$\text{A: } \sigma^2 \neq 1.125.$$

In Section XI.8, it was stated that if the observation variable has a normal DF, then $(n - 1)S^2/\sigma^2$ has a chi-square DF with expected value $D = n - 1$. It is this result that provides the basis for the test.[6] If S^2 is much larger or much smaller than the value specified by the null hypothesis, ${\sigma_0}^2$, then the null hypothesis will be rejected. Since $n - 1$ and ${\sigma_0}^2$ are fixed for a given problem, $\chi^2 = (n - 1)S^2/{\sigma_0}^2$ will be small if S^2 is small and large if S^2 is large. These considerations suggest that

$$\mathbf{P}\left[\left(\chi^2 = \frac{(n - 1)S^2}{{\sigma_0}^2} < \chi^2_{\alpha/2}\right) \cup \left(\chi^2 = \frac{(n - 1)S^2}{{\sigma_0}^2} > \chi^2_{1-\alpha/2}\right)\right] = \alpha$$

provides a basis for defining a decision rule. In this statement, α is the significance level chosen, $\chi^2_{\alpha/2}$ is the value of chi-square for which $\mathbf{P}(\chi^2 < \chi^2_{\alpha/2}) = \alpha/2$, and $\chi^2_{1-\alpha/2}$ is the value for which $\mathbf{P}(\chi^2 \leq \chi^2_{1-\alpha/2}) = 1 - \alpha/2$.

Now, examine each of the events in the union stated above. The one on the left is

$$\chi^2 = \frac{(n - 1)S^2}{{\sigma_0}^2} < \chi^2_{\alpha/2},$$

and multiplying both sides of the inequality by ${\sigma_0}^2/(n - 1)$,

$$S^2 < \frac{{\sigma_0}^2\chi^2_{\alpha/2}}{n - 1}.$$

This means that the event $(n - 1)S^2/{\sigma_0}^2 < \chi^2_{\alpha/2}$ occurs if and only if the event $S^2 < {\sigma_0}^2\chi^2_{\alpha/2}/(n - 1)$ occurs. Similarly, if $(n - 1)S^2/{\sigma_0}^2 > \chi^2_{1-\alpha/2}$

[6] A CLT test for the population variance is described by Hald, A., *Statistical Theory with Engineering Applications*. New York, John Wiley, 1952. However, the population fourth central moment is required if this method is applied.

is observed, then $S^2 > \sigma_0{}^2\chi^2_{1-\alpha/2}/(n-1)$ must have occurred. Therefore, the statement

$$\mathbf{P}\left[\left(\chi^2 = \frac{(n-1)S^2}{\sigma_0{}^2} < \chi^2_{\alpha/2}\right) \cup \left(\chi^2 = \frac{(n-1)S^2}{\sigma_0{}^2} > \chi^2_{1-\alpha/2}\right)\right] = \alpha$$

is identical to

$$\mathbf{P}\left[\left(S^2 < s_L{}^2 = \frac{\sigma_0{}^2\chi^2_{\alpha/2}}{n-1}\right) \cup \left(S^2 > s_U{}^2 = \frac{\sigma_0{}^2\chi^2_{1-\alpha/2}}{n-1}\right)\right] = \alpha,$$

and the decision rule is "Reject the null hypothesis if $S^2 < s_L{}^2 = \sigma_0{}^2\chi^2_{\alpha/2}/(n-1)$ or if $S^2 > s_U{}^2 = \sigma_0{}^2\chi^2_{1-\alpha/2}/(n-1)$. Otherwise, accept the hypothesis that $\sigma^2 = \sigma_0{}^2$." The significance level of this test is α.

Now this test can be applied to the ethnic cleavage example. The statistical hypotheses are

$$\text{H: } \sigma^2 = 1.125$$
$$\text{A: } \sigma^2 \neq 1.125.$$

The significance level to be used is 0.1, and the random sample of 9 observations of Figure XIII.1 provides the data.

To find the explicit decision rule, $\chi^2_{\alpha/2} = \chi^2_{.1/2} = \chi^2_{.05}$ must be found. From Appendix VII, for $D = n - 1 = 9 - 1 = 8$, $\mathbf{P}(\chi^2 \leq \chi^2_{.05}) = \mathbf{P}(\chi^2 \leq 2.733) = 0.05$. Similarly, $\chi^2_{1-\alpha/2} = \chi^2_{1-.1/2} = \chi^2_{.95}$, and

$$\mathbf{P}(\chi^2 \leq \chi^2_{.95}) = \mathbf{P}(\chi^2 \leq 15.507) = 0.95.$$

Then,

$$s_L{}^2 = \frac{\sigma_0{}^2\chi^2_{\alpha/2}}{n-1} = \frac{1.125(2.733)}{9-1}$$
$$= 0.38$$

bounds the lower portion of the rejection region, and

$$s_U{}^2 = \frac{\sigma_0{}^2\chi^2_{1-\alpha/2}}{n-1} = \frac{1.125(15.507)}{9-1}$$
$$= 2.18$$

bounds the upper portion. Consequently, the explicit decision rule is "Reject H if $S^2 < s_L{}^2 = 0.38$ or if $S^2 > s_U{}^2 = 2.18$. Otherwise, accept the hypothesis that $\sigma^2 = 1.125$." The significance level of this test is 0.1.

For the data of Figure XIII.1, the sample variance is $S^2 = 1.75$. Therefore, the decision is to accept the null hypothesis.

This test is based on the assumption that the observation variable has a normal DF in the population. Since the theoretical argument leading to the null nypothesis that $\sigma^2 = 1.125$ was based on the assumption that the observation variable has a hypergeometric distribution, this assumption is clearly wrong. However, as discussed in Section XIII.9.2, the assumptions of a statistical analysis are almost never satisfied. The choice of a statistical procedure usually reduces to finding the least objectionable method. Since the hypergeometric PD for the example is near symmetrical and has the general shape of a normal DF, the error introduced by failure to satisfy the normal DF assumption is probably not great.

*POWER FUNCTION FOR A TWO-SIDED ALTERNATIVE. The power function for a two-sided test for the population variance is constructed in a manner analogous to that for a mean.

Suppose that the height of the power function is to be found for a particular value of σ^2, call it σ_1^2. Then, it is necessary to calculate $\mathbf{P}(\text{Rejecting H} \mid \sigma^2 = \sigma_1^2)$, which is equal to

$$\begin{aligned}
&\mathbf{P}[(S^2 < s_L^2) \cup (S^2 > s_U^2) \mid \sigma^2 = \sigma_1^2] \\
&\quad = \mathbf{P}[(S^2 < s_L^2) \mid \sigma^2 = \sigma_1^2] + \mathbf{P}[(S^2 > s_U^2) \mid \sigma^2 = \sigma_1^2] \\
&\quad = \mathbf{P}\left[\left(S^2 < \frac{\sigma_0^2\chi^2_{\alpha/2}}{n-1}\right) \middle| \sigma^2 = \sigma_1^2\right] + \mathbf{P}\left[\left(S^2 > \frac{\sigma_0^2\chi^2_{1-\alpha/2}}{n-1}\right) \middle| \sigma^2 = \sigma_1^2\right].
\end{aligned}$$

Now, in general, $\chi^2 = (n-1)S^2/\sigma^2$, so that solving for S^2, $S^2 = \sigma^2\chi^2/(n-1)$. If the variance of the population is σ_1^2, then the variance of random samples of size n from this population is $S^2 = \sigma_1^2\chi^2/(n-1)$. Substituting $\sigma_1^2\chi^2/(n-1)$ for S^2 in

$$\mathbf{P}\left[\left(S^2 < \frac{\sigma_0^2\chi^2_{\alpha/2}}{n-1}\right) \middle| \sigma^2 = \sigma_1^2\right] + \mathbf{P}\left[\left(S^2 > \frac{\sigma_0^2\chi^2_{1-\alpha/2}}{n-1}\right) \middle| \sigma^2 = \sigma_1^2\right]$$

leads to

$$\mathbf{P}\left(\frac{\sigma_1^2\chi^2}{n-1} < \frac{\sigma_0^2\chi^2_{\alpha/2}}{n-1}\right) + \mathbf{P}\left(\frac{\sigma_1^2\chi^2}{n-1} > \frac{\sigma_0^2\chi^2_{1-\alpha/2}}{n-1}\right).$$

Multiplying both sides of the left-hand inequality by $(n-1)/\sigma_1^2$, the event

$$\frac{\sigma_1^2\chi^2}{n-1} < \frac{\sigma_0^2\chi^2_{\alpha/2}}{n-1}$$

becomes

$$\chi^2 < \frac{\sigma_0^2\chi^2_{\alpha/2}}{\sigma_1^2}.$$

Therefore, the event $\sigma_1^2\chi^2/(n-1) < \sigma_0^2\chi^2_{\alpha/2}/(n-1)$ can be replaced by $\chi^2 < \sigma_0^2\chi^2_{\alpha/2}/\sigma_1^2$. Similarly, the event $\chi^2 > \sigma_0^2\chi^2_{1-\alpha/2}/\sigma_1^2$ can be substituted for $\sigma_1^2\chi^2/(n-1) > \sigma_0^2\chi^2_{1-\alpha/2}/(n-1)$. Then,

$$\mathbf{P}(\text{Rejecting H} \mid \sigma^2 = \sigma_1^2) = \mathbf{P}\left(\chi^2 < \frac{\sigma_0^2\chi^2_{\alpha/2}}{\sigma_1^2}\right) + \mathbf{P}\left(\chi^2 > \frac{\sigma_0^2\chi^2_{1-\alpha/2}}{\sigma_1^2}\right).$$

Using this expression, it is a simple matter to compute the power function. In the example, $\sigma_0^2 = 1.125$, $\chi^2_{\alpha/2} = 2.733$, $\chi^2_{1-\alpha/2} = 15.507$, and for $\sigma_1^2 = 2$, the power is

$$\mathbf{P}\left(\chi^2 < \frac{\sigma_0^2\chi^2_{\alpha/2}}{\sigma_1^2}\right) + \mathbf{P}\left(\chi^2 > \frac{\sigma_0^2\chi^2_{1-\alpha/2}}{\sigma_1^2}\right)$$

$$= \mathbf{P}\left(\chi^2 < \frac{1.125(2.733)}{2}\right) + \mathbf{P}\left(\chi^2 > \frac{1.125(15.507)}{2}\right)$$

$$= \mathbf{P}(\chi^2 < 1.54) + \mathbf{P}(\chi^2 > 8.73) = 0.008 + 0.380$$

$$= 0.388.$$

This probability[7] is the height of the power function at $\sigma^2 = 2$. It gives the probability of rejecting the null hypothesis if the population variance is equal to 2. The entire power function for this test is shown in Figure XIII.17.

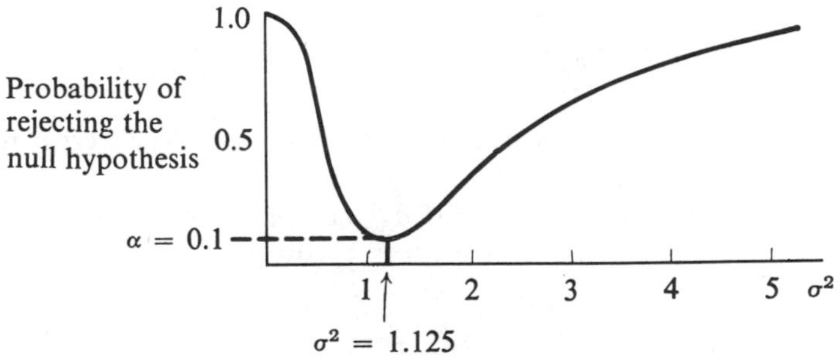

Figure XIII.17

Note the sharp asymmetry of this curve. The probability of rejecting H rises abruptly for values of σ^2 below the null hypothesis, but for values above 1.125 power increases slowly.

The operating characteristic and error curve for this test can be derived directly from the power function.

XIII.7.2. Summary of hypothesis testing procedures for a variance

Tests of one-sided alternative hypotheses regarding the variance have not been described, but they are summarized in Items 5 and 6 below. Two-sided tests are summarized in Item 4.

1. *Assumptions:* The observations are assumed to be drawn randomly from a population that has a normal DF.

2. *Parameters required:* No population parameters need be known.

[7] Linear interpolation in Appendix VII was used to obtain this probability.

3. *Sampling distribution:* If the assumptions are met, then $\chi^2 = (n - 1)S^2/\sigma^2$ has a chi-square distribution with expected value $D = n - 1$. This distribution provides the basis for these tests.

4. *Two-sided alternative hypotheses:* For a test of the statistical hypotheses

$$\text{H: } \sigma^2 = {\sigma_0}^2$$
$$\text{A: } \sigma^2 \neq {\sigma_0}^2,$$

the decision rule is of the form "Reject H if $S^2 < {s_L}^2$ or if $S^2 > {s_U}^2$. Otherwise, accept H." If α is the significance level of the test, then ${s_L}^2$ is determined by

$${s_L}^2 = \frac{{\sigma_0}^2\chi^2_{\alpha/2}}{n - 1}$$

and ${s_U}^2$ is determined by

$${s_U}^2 = \frac{{\sigma_0}^2\chi^2_{1-\alpha/2}}{n - 1},$$

where $\chi^2_{\alpha/2}$ is chosen so that $\mathbf{P}(\chi^2 < \chi^2_{\alpha/2}) = \alpha/2$ and $\chi^2_{1-\alpha/2}$ is chosen so that $\mathbf{P}(\chi^2 < \chi^2_{1-\alpha/2}) = 1 - \alpha/2$.

a. *Type I error probability:* The probability of a Type I error for this test equals α.

b. *Type II error probabilities:* If ${\sigma_A}^2$ is a value of σ^2 specified by A, then the probability of accepting H given $\sigma^2 = {\sigma_A}^2$ is

$$\mathbf{P}\left(\frac{{\sigma_0}^2\chi^2_{\alpha/2}}{{\sigma_A}^2} \leq \chi^2 \leq \frac{{\sigma_0}^2\chi^2_{1-\alpha/2}}{{\sigma_A}^2}\right).$$

5. *One-sided upper alternative hypotheses:* For a test of the statistical hypotheses

$$\text{H: } \sigma^2 \leq {\sigma_0}^2$$
$$\text{A: } \sigma^2 > {\sigma_0}^2,$$

the decision rule is "Reject H if $S^2 > {s_C}^2$. Otherwise, accept H." If α is the significance level, then

$${s_C}^2 = \frac{{\sigma_0}^2\chi^2_{1-\alpha}}{n - 1},$$

where $\chi^2_{1-\alpha}$ is chosen so that $\mathbf{P}(\chi^2 \leq \chi^2_{1-\alpha}) = 1 - \alpha$.

a. *Type I error probabilities:* If ${\sigma_H}^2$ is any value of σ^2 specified by the null hypothesis, then the probability of rejecting H given $\sigma^2 = {\sigma_H}^2$ is

$$\mathbf{P}\left(\chi^2 > \frac{{\sigma_0}^2\chi^2_{1-\alpha}}{{\sigma_H}^2}\right).$$

The maximum probability of a Type I error equals α. This maximum occurs for $\sigma^2 = {\sigma_0}^2$.

b. *Type II error probabilities:* If σ_A^2 is a value of σ^2 specified by A, then the probability that H will be accepted given $\sigma^2 = \sigma_A^2$ is

$$\mathbf{P}\left(\chi^2 \leq \frac{\sigma_0^2\chi_{1-\alpha}^2}{\sigma_A^2}\right).$$

6. *One-sided lower alternative hypotheses:* For a test of the statistical hypotheses

$$\text{H: } \sigma^2 \geq \sigma_0^2$$
$$\text{A: } \sigma^2 < \sigma_0^2,$$

the decision rule is "Reject H if $S^2 < s_C^2$. Otherwise, accept H." If α is the significance level of the test, then

$$s_C^2 = \frac{\sigma_0^2\chi_\alpha^2}{n-1},$$

where χ_α^2 is chosen so that $\mathbf{P}(\chi^2 \leq \chi_\alpha^2) = \alpha$.

a. *Type I error probabilities:* If σ_H^2 is any value of σ^2 specified by the null hypothesis, then the probability of rejecting H given $\sigma^2 = \sigma_H^2$ is

$$\mathbf{P}\left(\chi^2 < \frac{\sigma_0^2\chi_\alpha^2}{\sigma_H^2}\right).$$

The maximum probability of a Type I error equals α. This maximum occurs for $\sigma^2 = \sigma_0^2$.

b. *Type II error probabilities:* If σ_A^2 is any value of σ^2 specified by A, then the probability of accepting H given $\sigma^2 = \sigma_A^2$ is

$$\mathbf{P}\left(\chi^2 \geq \frac{\sigma_0^2\chi_\alpha^2}{\sigma_A^2}\right).$$

XIII.8

TESTING THE HYPOTHESIS THAT A POPULATION HAS A SPECIFIED DISTRIBUTION

In this section, methods for testing the hypothesis that a population has a specified PD or DF are described. The key to these tests is the multinomial distribution (Section X.1.3).

XIII.8.1. An exact multinomial test

Suppose that the variables $U, V, \ldots, Z$ have a multinomial PD with parameters $P_1, P_2, \ldots, P_i, \ldots, P_r$, and suppose we wish to test the hypothesis that P_1 has specific value P_{10}, and P_2 has the value $P_{20}, \ldots,$ and P_r has the value P_{r0}. Then the statistical hypotheses can be stated as

$$\text{H: } P_1 = P_{10}, P_2 = P_{20}, \ldots, P_r = P_{r0}$$
$$\text{A: } P_i \neq P_{i0} \text{ for at least one value of } i.$$

Here, $P_{10}, P_{20}, \ldots, P_{r0}$ are particular values of the parameters that are hypothesized on some theoretical basis.

If H is true, then certain combinations of values of $U, V, \ldots, Z$ are likely whereas others are not. To say that $u, v, \ldots, z$ is one of the unlikely combinations means that the multinomial probability

$$\mathbf{P}[(U = u) \cap (V = v) \cap \cdots \cap (Z = z) \mid P_1 = P_{10}, P_2 = P_{20}, \ldots, P_r = P_{r0}] = \frac{n!}{u!\, v! \cdots z!} P_{10}^u P_{20}^v \cdots P_{r0}^z$$

is small. If one of these unlikely combinations is observed for a given random sample, then we will be inclined to reject the null hypothesis, H. This provides the basis for defining the rejection region for such a test.

If α is the Type I error probability chosen, then the rejection region, R, consists of the combinations of values of $U, V, \ldots, Z$ that are least probable if H is true, and such that

$$\alpha = \sum_R \mathbf{P}[(U = u) \cap (V = v) \cap \cdots \cap (Z = z) \mid P_1 = P_{10}, P_2 = P_{20}, \ldots, P_r = P_{r0}] = \sum_R \frac{n!}{u!\, v! \cdots z!} P_{10}^u P_{20}^v \cdots P_{r0}^z.$$

The symbol $\sum_R$ indicates that the sum is over the least probable combinations of values of $U, V, \ldots, Z$. If one of the combinations of values of $U, V, \ldots, Z$ in R is observed, then H is rejected; otherwise, H is accepted. The application of this test is described below.

In Section X.1.3, preference for 5 percent, 7 percent, and 9 percent glucose solutions was examined in a sample of 12 rats. If the animals could not discriminate after familiarization with the preference testing situation, then **P**(choose 5 percent) $= P_1 = 1/3$, **P**(choose 7 percent) $= P_2 = 1/3$, and **P**(choose 9 percent) $= P_3 = 1/3$. Thus, the statistical hypothesis for this experiment can be stated as follows:

$$\text{H: } P_1 = \frac{1}{3}, P_2 = \frac{1}{3}, P_3 = \frac{1}{3}$$

$$\text{A: } P_i \neq \frac{1}{3} \text{ for at least one value of } i.$$

Now, let the number of animals choosing the 5 percent solution be U, the number choosing 7 percent be V, and the number choosing 9 percent be Z.

In order to determine a rejection region, the multinomial probability must be calculated for every combination of values of U, V, and Z. The results of these calculations are summarized in Table XIII.2. To see how they were obtained, consider the first row of the table. The multinomial probability is

$$\mathbf{P}\left[(U = 12) \cap (V = 0) \cap (Z = 0) \mid P_1 = P_2 = P_3 = \frac{1}{3}\right]$$
$$= \frac{n!}{u!\, v!\, z!} P_1{}^u P_2{}^v P_3{}^z$$
$$= \frac{12!}{12!\, 0!\, 0!} \left(\frac{1}{3}\right)^{12} \left(\frac{1}{3}\right)^{0} \left(\frac{1}{3}\right)^{0}$$
$$= 0.000001882.$$

However, since $P_1 = P_2 = P_3$, this is also the probability that $V = 12$ and $U = Z = 0$ as well as the probability that $Z = 12$ and $U = V = 0$. Therefore, the probability that one of these three mutually exclusive and equiprobable events will occur is $3(0.000001882) \cong 0.000006$, which appears under the fourth heading in Row 1 of Table XIII.2. In this way, the table was completed.

Table XIII.2. Determining the rejection region for an exact multinomial test

Values of 3 random variables			Multinomial probability given H is true	Number of ways to assign 3 values to 3 variables	Probability that 1 of the assignments will occur	Decision
12	0	0	.000002	3	.000006	Reject H
11	1	0	.000023	6	.0001	” ”
10	2	0	.00012	6	.0007	” ”
10	1	1	.00025	3	.0007	” ”
9	3	0	.00041	6	.002	” ”
8	4	0	.00093	6	.006	” ”
9	2	1	.0012	6	.007	” ”
7	5	0	.0015	6	.009	” ”
6	6	0	.0017	3	.005	” ”
8	3	1	.0037	6	.022	” ”
8	2	2	.0056	3	.017	” ”
7	1	4	.0075	6	.045	Accept H
6	5	1	.010	6	.063	” ”
7	2	3	.015	6	.089	” ”
6	4	2	.026	6	.156	” ”
5	2	5	.031	3	.092	” ”
6	3	3	.035	3	.104	” ”
5	3	4	.052	6	.313	” ”
4	4	4	.065	1	.065	” ”
					.997	

Now, notice that the rows of the table appear in the same order as the size of the *multinomial* probabilities. Since each probability was calculated on the assumption that H is true, it is those combinations of values of U, V, and Z that are least likely given H is true that appear in the upper rows. The rejection region includes the least likely combinations of values of U, V, and Z whose probabilities sum to α. If we choose $\alpha = 0.1$, then

$$\sum_R \mathbf{P}\left[(U = u) \cap (V = v) \cap (Z = z) \mid P_1 = P_2 = P_3 = \frac{1}{3}\right]$$

$$= \underbrace{0.000006 + 0.0001 + 0.0007 + \cdots + 0.017}_{11 \text{ terms}}$$

$$= 0.07.$$

This sum includes the first 11 rows of Table XIII.2, but it falls short of 0.1, the designated value of α. However, since adding one more combination would increase the probability of a Type I error to above 0.1, we revise α to 0.07.

In the right-most column of Table XIII.2, a decision is designated for each combination of values of the variables. Notice that the order of values of the variables under the first heading in the table has no significance. If *any* of the three variables equals 1, another equals 2, and a third equals 9, then H is rejected, since all of these combinations (Row 7) fall in the rejection region.

As shown in Table X.2, $U = 4$, $V = 2$, and $Z = 6$ for the observed sample. Since the values 6, 4, and 2 appear in the acceptance region (Row 15), the null hypothesis must be accepted. This indicates that rats are unable to discriminate 5 percent, 7 percent, and 9 percent glucose solutions.

In this example, the calculations were greatly simplified by the fact that H specified that the three parameters were equal. This is because each assignment of a given combination of values to the three variables has the same multinomial probability when $P_1 = P_2 = P_3$. If the three values of the parameters specified by H had all been different, then Table XIII.2 would have required 91 rows. From this it can be seen that even for moderate sample sizes and r more than 3 or 4, the exact multinomial test becomes burdensome to calculate.[8] A useful approximation is described in the next section.

X.8.2. An approximate test based on chi-square

The basis for the approximate test will be described first, and then its application will be illustrated.

[8] The use of the exact multinomial test is discussed in detail by Chapanis, A., "An exact multinomial one-sample test of significance." *Psychol. Bull.* **59**, 306–310, 1962; errors occurring in this paper are corrected in the *Psychol. Bull.* **59**, 532, 1962.

If $P_1, P_2, \ldots, P_r$ are the parameters of a multinomial population ($P_1 + P_2 + \cdots + P_r = 1$) and if $U, V, \ldots, Z$ are random variables with a multinomial PD ($U + V + \cdots + Z = n$), then the sampling distribution of

$$\mathscr{X} = \frac{(U - nP_1)^2}{nP_1} + \frac{(V - nP_2)^2}{nP_2} + \cdots + \frac{(Z - nP_r)^2}{nP_r}$$

can be approximated by a chi-square DF with $E(\mathscr{X}) = D = r - 1 - c$, where c is the number of parameters estimated in calculating the P_i. The quantity $r - 1 - c$ is the number of degrees of freedom associated with chi-square for this application. This approximation is generally considered adequate if all of the nP_i exceed 5.

In this application, the multinomial proportions $P_1, P_2, \ldots, P_r$ are called *expected proportions.* Each one represents the probability of an observation from one subclass of the multinomial population. They are determined on the basis of some theoretical formulation that is intended to describe the population. Similarly, since the sample contains n observations, each of the numbers $nP_1, nP_2, \ldots, nP_r$ is the *expected frequency* of observations from one subclass of the population. The variables $U, V, \ldots, Z$ are the *observed frequencies* of observations from each subclass of the multinomial population, so that nP_1 is the expected value of U, nP_2 is the expected value of V, and so on. The variables $(U - nP_1)^2/(nP_1)$, $(V - nP_2)^2/(nP_2), \ldots, (Z - nP_r)^2/(nP_r)$ measure the discrepancy between observed and expected frequencies.

Even though a derivation of this approximation is beyond the scope of this book,[9] a rough sketch of the rationale can be given. The marginal PD of U is a binomial distribution with expected value nP_1 and variance $nP_1(1 - P_1)$. Therefore, if nP_1 and $n(1 - P_1)$ are both large, the distribution of U is approximately normal (Section X.5.1), and the distribution of $(U - nP_1)^2/[nP_1(1 - P_1)]$ can be approximated by a chi-square DF (Section X.3.3). An analogous statement applies to each of the other variables, $V, \ldots, Z$. Therefore, if $U, V, \ldots, Z$ were statistically independent, the expression $(U - nP_1)^2/[nP_1(1 - P_1)] + (U - nP_2)^2/[nP_2(1 - P_2)] + \cdots + (Z - nP_r)^2/[nP_r(1 - P_r)]$ would have a chi-square DF. However, they are *not* independent, since $U + V + \cdots + Z$ must always equal n. This means that if the values of all but one of the variables are given, then the value of the remaining one is determined, too.[10] It turns out that replacing

[9] A derivation can be found in Hogg, R. V., and A. T. Craig, *Introduction to Mathematical Statistics.* New York, Macmillan, 1958, pp. 228–233.

[10] If $V, \ldots, Z$ are known, then since $U = n - V - \cdots - Z$,

$$\mathbf{P}[U = n - v - \cdots - z \mid (V = v) \cap \cdots \cap (Z = z)] = 1.$$

Since the marginal probability that $U = n - v - \cdots - z$ will not generally equal 1, this demonstrates that the restriction $U + V + \cdots + Z = n$ makes the variables statistically dependent.

the variances, $nP_i(1 - P_i)$, with the expected values, nP_i, provides an appropriate adjustment ensuring the applicability of the chi-square DF.

In using this approximation to test the statistical hypotheses

$$\begin{aligned} &\text{H: } P_1 = P_{10}, P_2 = P_{20}, \ldots, P_r = P_{r0} \\ &\text{A: } P_i \neq P_{i0} \text{ for at least one value of } i, \end{aligned}$$

the rejection region is determined by finding from Appendix VII the value of the chi-square, $\chi^2_{1-\alpha}$, such that

$$\mathbf{P}(\chi^2 > \chi^2_{1-\alpha}) = \alpha.$$

If the observed value of

$$\mathscr{X} = \frac{(U - nP_{10})^2}{nP_{10}} + \frac{(V - nP_{20})^2}{nP_{20}} + \cdots + \frac{(Z - nP_{r0})^2}{nP_{r0}}$$

is large, then this shows that the discrepancies between observed and expected frequencies are large. Consequently, the decision rule is "Reject H if $\mathscr{X} > \chi^2_{1-\alpha}$. Otherwise, accept H." The significance level of this test equals α, the probability of a Type I error.

This test will be illustrated for data reported by Mednick and described in Section X.1.5. The question is whether or not the relative frequency function of generalization responses found by Mednick for 60 patients suffering from cortical brain damage came from a population with a Poisson PD. The data appear in column two of Table XIII.3.

Table XIII.3. Summary of data reported by Mednick*

Number of generalization responses (X)	Observed frequency	Expected proportions based on Poisson PD, $\mathbf{P}(X = x) = P_i$	Expected frequencies, $n\mathbf{P}(X = x) = nP_i$
0	15	.212	12.72
1	18	.329	19.74
2	15	.255	15.30
3	7	.132	7.92
4	2	.051	3.06
5	2	.016	0.96
6	1	.004	0.24
7 or more	0	.001	0.06
	60	1.000	60.00

* Mednick, S. A., "Distortions of the gradient of stimulus generalization related to cortical brain damage and schizophrenia." *J. Ab. Soc. Psychol.* **51**, 536–542, 1955.

Using the sample mean of 1.55 instead of μ, the Poisson probabilities in the third column were calculated from

$$\mathbf{P}(X = x) = \frac{(\bar{x})^x e^{-\bar{x}}}{x!} = \frac{(1.55)^x e^{-1.55}}{x!}.$$

Now, the statistical hypothesis can be stated explicitly:

H: $P_1 = 0.212$, $P_2 = 0.329, \ldots, P_8 = 0.001$
A: Not all of the above qualities hold.

Although the range of X is infinite in theory, $P_8 \doteq \mathbf{P}(X \geq 7) = 0.001$ has been treated as one category.

Multiplying each of these theoretical probabilities by $n = 60$ yields the expected frequencies of Column 4 in Table XIII.3.

Since one parameter was estimated ($\bar{X} = 1.55$) in calculating the expected frequencies, $E(\mathscr{X}) = D = r - 1 - c = 8 - 1 - 1 = 6$. If we choose 0.25 as the probability of a Type I error, then

$$\mathbf{P}(\mathscr{X} > \chi^2_{1-\alpha} \mid \text{H true}) = \mathbf{P}(\mathscr{X} > \chi^2_{.75} \mid \text{H true}) = 0.25,$$

and $\chi^2_{.75} = 7.84$ for $D = 6$. The explicit decision rule is "Reject H if $\mathscr{X} > 7.84$. Otherwise accept H."

The observed value of $\mathscr{X}$ can be computed from Table XIII.3 as follows:

$$\begin{aligned}\mathscr{X} &= \frac{(U - nP_1)^2}{nP_1} + \frac{(V - nP_2)^2}{nP_2} + \cdots + \frac{(Z - nP_r)^2}{nP_r} \\ &= \frac{(15 - 12.72)^2}{12.72} + \frac{(18 - 19.74)^2}{19.74} + \cdots + \frac{(0 - 0.06)^2}{0.06} \\ &= 4.64.\end{aligned}$$

Therefore, H is accepted, and the hypothesis that the population has a Poisson PD is considered tenable.

The meaning of the term *degrees of freedom* for this application of chi-square is exactly similar to that of the estimators described in Section IX.10. Here, the number of degrees of freedom associated with chi-square equals $r - 1$ less the number of parameters estimated in the calculation of the theoretical frequencies. If each combination of values of the r observed frequencies, $U, V, \ldots, Z$, is represented by a point in an r-dimensional space, then since $U + V + \cdots + Z = n$, these r variables are "free" to vary as a function of random variability in only $r - 1$ dimensions. This is true since the value of any $r - 1$ of them determines the value of the remaining one. Thus, if values of $V, \ldots, Z$ are known, then U cannot vary at all as a function of sampling variability, since $U = n - V - \cdots - Z$. Since sampling variability in the value of $\mathscr{X}$ depends only on the random variables $U, V, \ldots, Z$, $\mathscr{X}$ can reflect random variability in no more than $r - 1$ dimensions.

In the example, $\bar{X}$ was used to estimate μ, and this further restricts the extent to which $\mathscr{X}$ is "free" to reflect sampling variability. In the notation of this section, $\bar{X}$ can be written as $\frac{1}{n}(Ux_1 + Vx_2 + \cdots + Zx_r)$, since U is the frequency of x_1 in the sample, V is the frequency of $x_2, \ldots,$ and Z is the frequency of x_r. Then, the restriction $\sum (X - \bar{X}) = 0$ is

$$U(x_1 - \bar{X}) + V(x_2 - \bar{X}) + \cdots + Z(x_r - \bar{X}) = 0.$$

As illustrated in Section IX.10, this also reduces the number of dimensions of random sampling variability by one, so that the number of degrees of freedom is $r - 1 - c = 8 - 1 - 1$ for the example.

In the example, expected values of less than 5 were used, and the chi-square approximation is likely to be poor under these conditions. One way to avoid such low expected frequencies is to treat $X \geq 3$ as a single category. Then, $r = 4$ and $D = r - 1 - c = 2$, and the rejection region is $\mathscr{X} > 2.77$ for $\alpha = 0.25$. Since the observed value of $\mathscr{X}$ is only 0.68 when $X \geq 3$ is treated as a single category, the decision is to accept H. The hypothesis that the population has a Poisson PD is supported by this procedure, too.

Although combining categories in this way does provide a means of avoiding low expected frequencies, it is not recommended. By combining categories, it is clearly possible to "hide" variations in the data that are relevant to the statistical hypothesis under test. The decision here is the same for the example whether or not one combines categories, but this will not always be true. Consequently, when expected frequencies are small, it is usually best to enlist the aid of a digital computer and apply the exact multinomial test described in the preceding section.

Methods described in Sections VII.2 and X.5.1 can be used to determine theoretical probabilities on the basis of a particular density function. Then the hypothesis that the population has this DF can be tested using either the exact multinomial test or the chi-square approximation.

Since power functions and Type II error probabilities for these tests are rarely used, they will not be described. However, they can be calculated using the principles described earlier in this chapter.

XIII.8.3. Summary of a test of the hypothesis that a population has a specified distribution

In this section, only the approximate test will be summarized.

1. *Assumptions:* The observations are assumed to be drawn randomly from a population that can be conceived of as a multinomial population.

2. *Parameters required:* The pertinent parameters of the population may be determined on the basis of some theoretical formulation, or they may be estimated from the data (see Item 3).

3. *Sampling distribution:* If n is the sample size and $U, V, \cdots, Z$ are random variables with a multinomial PD and with parameters $P_1, P_2, \ldots, P_i, \ldots, P_r$, then the distribution of

$$\mathscr{X} = \frac{(U - nP_1)^2}{nP_1} + \frac{(V - nP_2)^2}{nP_2} + \cdots + \frac{(Z - nP_r)^2}{nP_r}$$

can be approximated by a chi-square distribution with $D = r - 1 - c$ degrees of freedom, where c is the number of parameters that are estimated in order to calculate the expected frequencies $nP_1, nP_2, \ldots, nP_r$.

4. *The test:* For a test of the hypotheses

$$\text{H: } P_1 = P_{10}, P_2 = P_{20}, \ldots, P_i = P_{i0}, \ldots, P_r = P_{r0},$$
$$\text{A: } P_i \neq P_{i0} \text{ for at least one value of } i,$$

the decision rule has the form "Reject H if $\mathscr{X} > \chi^2_{1-\alpha}$. Otherwise, accept H."

In this statement, α is the significance level of the test, $\chi^2_{1-\alpha}$ is determined so that $\mathbf{P}(\chi^2 > \chi^2_{1-\alpha}) = \alpha$, and the observed value of

$$\mathscr{X} = \frac{(U - nP_{10})^2}{nP_{10}} + \frac{(V - nP_{20})^2}{nP_{20}} + \cdots + \frac{(Z - nP_{r0})^2}{nP_{r0}}.$$

a. *Type I error probability:* The probability of a Type I error equals the significance level, α.
b. *Type II error probabilities:* Type II error probability calculations will not be described for this test. However, see Problem 10 in Section XIII.10.

XIII.9
SOME GENERAL CONSIDERATIONS

In the first part of this section, a controversy regarding the proper formulation and interpretation of statistical hypotheses is discussed. In the second part, the connection between the mathematical conceptualization of a statistical procedure and its application is examined.

XIII.9.1. Research strategy and the formulation of statistical hypotheses

According to Grant,[11] formulating statistical hypotheses so that *rejection* of a simple null hypothesis supports the investigator's theory is preferable to a formulation in which *acceptance* provides theoretical support. If a simple null hypothesis, H, corresponds to the theoretical prediction, then

[11] Grant, D. A., "Testing the null hypothesis and the strategy and tactics of investigating theoretical models." *Psychol. Rev.* **69**, 54–61, 1962.

acceptance of H supports the theory. Unfortunately, says Grant, one can never "prove" H. Furthermore, since the power of a statistical test is less for small samples and for highly variable observations, a small, error-laden experiment is more likely to find support for the theory when the connection between statistical and theoretical hypotheses is of this kind. On the other hand, if rejection of a simple null hypothesis supports the theory, then a more precise experiment based on a large sample leads to greater power and, therefore, greater likelihood of theoretical support. It is this approach, says Grant, that is to be preferred.

Among the examples of this chapter, those of Sections XIII.1.4, XIII.6.2, and XIII.7.1 appear to follow the procedure preferred by Grant. Those of Sections XIII.6.1, XIII.8.1, and XIII.8.2. do not.

Binder[12] rejects Grant's views. First, he states that *neither* the null nor the alternative hypothesis is amenable to positive proof. One can only defend a choice of H or of A with statements of error probabilities. In addition, he bases another criticism on Grant's acknowledgement[13] that an experiment can be "too precise." Here, Grant's position is that, with a sufficiently large sample of well-controlled and relatively error-free observations, it is likely that virtually any precise theoretical prediction in psychology could be falsified. However, Grant considers it strategically unwise to perform such experiments, since in some cases the actual magnitude of the error in the rejected theory would be small, and a psychological theory that "comes close" should not be dismissed unless there is a clearly superior alternative. Binder points out that there is some risk that large precise experiments with high power will lead the investigator to unwise decisions if he follows Grant's advice and equates rejection of a simple null hypothesis with theoretical support. Therefore, says Binder, one should design experiments in which statistical power is at some optimum value, neither too large nor too small. In an experiment in which rejection of a simple H leads to theoretical support, power should not be so great that there is a high probability of rejecting the theory if the discrepancy between data and theory is negligible. On the other hand, if accepting H implies theoretical support, then the experiment should not be so small and imprecise that the statistical test is unlikely to lead to rejection of H even when the theory is grossly in error. Thus Binder concludes that designing experiments of appropriate sensitivity (or power) is a necessary step regardless of which type of connection between theory and statistical hypothesis one adopts. "Appropriate sensitivity" depends on the adequacy of theory in the area under investigation. If competing

[12] Binder, A., "Further considerations on testing the null hypothesis and the strategy and tactics of investigating theoretical models." *Psychol. Rev.* **70**, 107–115, 1963.

[13] Grant, *op. cit.*

theories are precise and detailed, then experiments of high sensitivity are required. If knowledge is sketchy and theories imprecise, then high sensitivity will be of little value.

Grant makes a second point that should be mentioned. He suggests that in a number of psychological investigations an interval estimate of the theoretical parameters might be more appropriate than any sort of hypothesis testing procedure. Then, if the estimated interval is reasonably narrow, has a large confidence coefficient, and includes the value of a parameter predicted by theory, this is to be interpreted as theoretical support.

Three observations regarding this controversy seem appropriate. The first is that, though Grant's argument is appealing, it often seems difficult to avoid equating acceptance of a simple null hypothesis with support of a theoretical prediction. For example, the tests of goodness of fit described in Section XIII.8 seem useful but difficult to formulate in other terms. Second, when accepting H provides theoretical support, Type II error probabilities can be varied as a function of the significance level chosen. Thus, in the tests of Section XIII.6.1 and XIII.8.2, Type II error probabilities were considerably reduced by permitting rather large Type I error probabilities. Finally, as the neo-Bayesian statistician is quick to point out, problems of this kind do not occur in the Bayesian approach (see Section V.3.5), in which a posterior probability is assigned to each hypothesis (i.e., to each value in the parameter space).

XIII.9.2. Mathematical models for estimation and hypothesis testing

Every statistical procedure has its price. Certain assumptions must be made when applying any method of statistical inference, and if they are not satisfied then the error probabilities or confidence coefficient thought to characterize the procedure may be wrong.

The reason for this is simple enough. Error probabilities and confidence coefficients are calculated on the basis of mathematical logic, and such logic must begin with assumptions. If the assumptions do not fit the empirical situation, then the subsequent mathematical argument cannot be expected to apply.

The assumptions one makes in a statistical analysis are of two kinds. First, assumptions are made about the population, and second, assumptions are made about the sampling process. For example, in order to estimate the population variance in Section XIII.1, it was assumed that there was no ethnic cleavage and that an individual's sociometric choices can be regarded as a random sample taken without replacement from a binomial population. Then, the central limit theorem was invoked in order to determine the sampling distribution of the sample mean. This required the additional assumption that nine observations was a sufficiently large random sample for the application of the central limit theorem.

The assumptions one makes in applying statistical induction procedures constitute a mathematical model. The mathematical model specifies certain characteristics of the population and of the sampling process.

In real life, the assumptions required by the methods of statistical induction are *never* satisfied. It is easy and trivial to criticize the research of others simply because they have failed to satisfy the assumptions of their statistical analysis. For example, it would not be difficult to find cogent reasons for doubting every assumption made in the tests of Sections XIII.1 to XIII.8.[14] But the task of the user of statistics is to choose the method for which failure to satisfy assumptions has the least serious consequences. This is the art of statistics. And while it is trivial to point out that a mathematical model does not fit the problem, not all models are equally poor. The skillful applied statistician is one who can make the best choice among bad alternatives.

Another aspect of the art is to plan research in such a way that the statistical methods available to analyze the data depend on mathematical models that fit the population and the sampling processes reasonably well. Of course, in searching for a method of analysis that fits as well as possible, one must not lose sight of the original problem. Occasionally, the desire to satisfy assumptions leads to the choice of a statistical analysis that is not relevant to the purposes of the research. This is an unfortunate case of the tail wagging the dog.

XIII.10

PROBLEMS ON HYPOTHESIS TESTING

1. In the high school studied by the Tri-Ethnic Project,[15] the question of ethnic cleavage can be examined for Indians in the same way it was investigated for Anglos. Table XIII.4 contains the number of Indians chosen by each of a random sample of 8 Indians in response to the sociometric question, "Who are the five kids *in this school* you would choose to mess around with?" Of the 122 pupils in the school, 36 are Indians.
   a. Find the expected number of Indians chosen by an Indian under the assumption that no ethnic cleavage exists.

[14] For example, a given Anglo pupil probably does not know the names of some pupils in his school. He couldn't name any of these unknown youngsters as his sociometric choices. Therefore, his choices should not be viewed as a random sample from the designated population. Also, the sample mean for this problem has a finite set of possible values. It is not a continuous variable, as the normal distribution requires, and so on.

[15] These data are used with the permission of the Tri-Ethnic Research Project, which is supported under NIMH Grant No. 3M-9156. My thanks to Dr. Richard Jessor for making them available.

Table XIII.4. Data from ethnic cleavage study

Indian chooser	Number of Indians chosen
1	5
2	5
3	4
4	5
5	4
6	1
7	4
8	4

b. What mathematical model did you employ in answering a?
c. What is the theoretical variance of the number of Indians chosen by an Indian under the assumption that there is no ethnic cleavage?
d. What is the sample variance of the number of Indians chosen by an Indian?
e. Compare the results of c and d and comment on the similarity or dissimilarity you find.
f. Set up an appropriate statistical hypothesis for investigating ethnic cleavage using these data. You may use a one-sided or two-sided alternative, as you choose, but defend your choice.
g. Using a significance level of 0.01, what is your decision rule? What is your decision? What does your decision imply about ethnic cleavage?
h. Given $\mu = 1$, what is the probability of a Type II error?
i. Construct a Type II error curve for your test.
j. Construct a power curve for your test.
k. Sketch the power curve you would obtain if you set up a test for $\alpha = 0.25$. Comment on the error probabilities associated with $\alpha = 0.01$ as compared to those for $\alpha = 0.25$.
l. Suppose that you are interested in constructing a 0.95 confidence interval for μ from these data. There are two ways in which you can obtain a measure of the variance of the number of Indians chosen; one is based on the data, the other on theory. Construct two 95 percent confidence intervals, one using each of the two variance measures. Compare the results.
m. Construct a 90 percent confidence interval for μ using the sample variance.
n. Both for the statistical test and for the interval estimates, you have used the CLT to specify the sampling distribution of $\bar{X}$. Comment on the reasonableness of the assumptions you have made in doing this.
o. What considerations might—or perhaps should—enter into your choice of significance level?

p. Now that you have completed a statistical test and an interval estimate, which do you think is most appropriate for this research? Explain your answer concisely.

2. Describe the "three levels of statistical analysis" as they apply to Problem 1.
   a. Construct a table summarizing your analysis.
   b. Are three levels adequate for this problem? If not, how would you modify the classification scheme?

3. Formulate Problems 7a and 7c of Section X.2 as tests of statistical hypotheses.
   a. Construct the test for Problem 7a using exact probabilities.
      i. What are the statistical hypotheses?
      ii. What is the significance level you chose?
      iii. What is your decision rule?
      iv. What is your decision?
   b. Construct the test for Problem 7c using an approximation.
      i. What are the statistical hypotheses?
      ii. What is the significance level you chose?
      iii. What is the decision rule?
      iv. What is your decision?
      v. Plot the probabilities of both kinds of errors as a function of P.

4. Formulate Problem 10a of Section X.2 as a test of a statistical hypothesis. Use exact probabilities.
   a. What are the statistical hypotheses?
   b. What is the significance level?
   c. Is sampling with or without replacement?
   d. What is the decision rule?
   e. What is your decision?
   f. What mathematical model have you used in constructing this test?

5. Formulate Problem 11b of Section X.2 as a test of a statistical hypothesis. Use $\alpha = 0.1$. Use an approximation procedure to construct the test.
   a. What are the statistical hypotheses?
   b. What is your decision rule?
   c. What is your decision?
   d. What is the probability of a Type I error for your test if $P = 1/2$?
   e. Comment on the appropriateness of treating this situation as a sequence of Bernoulli trials.
   f. Plot the Type II error curve for this test.
   g. What is $\mathbf{P}(\text{accept H} \mid P = 0.9)$?

6. Suppose you purchased four loaves of raisin bread from the baker described in Problem 16, Section X.2. The baker claims it *is* raisin bread, since he allowed for one raisin per loaf. He says he "can't help it" if chance has cheated you and there is not a single raisin in the four loaves you purchased. However, using your four loaves as "data," you decide

to test the baker's claim that he *did* allow for a raisin per loaf. Use a significance level of about 0.03.

a. List all the assumptions you must make in order to construct this test.
b. What mathematical model have you employed?
c. State your statistical hypotheses.
d. If the null hypothesis is true, what is the variance of the observation variable?
e. If the null hypothesis is wrong and $\mu = 2$, what is the variance of the observation variable?
f. Construct a decision rule for your test. (The CLT is probably inappropriate for such a small sample. Try to construct a test without using it. It will help to examine the data space itself and find the probabilities of certain of its outcomes.)
g. Interpret your decision in terms of the original problem. What should you tell the baker? What should his defense be?

7. In Figure XIII.7 and XIII.8, the relationship between Type I and Type II errors is described. Discuss the effects of varying n and α on the *power* of a test. Be concise.

8. For the data of Table XII.1, test the hypothesis that $\sigma^2 = 2.5$ using a two-sided alternative and $\alpha = 0.05$.
   a. What is your decision rule?
   b. What is your decision?
   c. What is the probability of a Type I error?
   d. What is the probability of a Type II error if $\sigma^2 = 2$?
   e. What is the power of this test for $\sigma^2 = 2$?
   f. Plot the power function for this test.
   g. Now construct a one-sided test for the same situation using as an alternative hypothesis $\sigma^2 < 2.5$. Use $\alpha = 0.1$. The remaining questions refer to this test.
   h. What is the decision rule for the one-sided test?
   i. What is the decision?
   j. Find $\mathbf{P}(\text{accept H} \mid \sigma^2 = 2)$.
   k. Find $\mathbf{P}(\text{reject H} \mid \sigma^2 = 3)$. Is this an error probability? If so, what kind?
   l. Plot the power function for the one-sided test.

9. Test the hypothesis that the frequency function of Table XIII.3 is from a population that has a normal DF. Use the sample to estimate both μ and σ^2. Use an approximation for the sampling distribution and a significance level of 0.1. It may be helpful to examine the procedures of Section VII.2 for approximating a relative frequency function with a DF and the procedure for approximating a binomial PD with a normal DF in Section X.5.1.
   a. What is the number of degrees of freedom associated with the relevant sampling distribution for this test?
   b. What is your explicit decision rule?

c. What are your estimates of μ and σ^2?
d. What are the values of the expected frequencies?
e. What is the value of $\mathscr{X}$ for the observed sample?
f. What is your decision?
g. What do you conclude from this test?

10. Using the same procedure and assuming the experimental set-up referred to in Section XIII.8.1, construct an exact test of the hypothesis

$$\text{H: } P_1 = P_2 = P_3 = 1/3$$
$$\text{A: Not all of the above equalities hold,}$$

for a random sample of size 10.

a. Find $\mathbf{P}[(U = 5) \cap (V = 3) \cap (Z = 2) \mid P_1 = P_2 = P_3 = 1/3]$, where U is the number of rats choosing the 5 percent solution, V is the number choosing 7 percent, and Z is the number choosing 9 percent.
b. Describe the rejection region for the test precisely if the significance level is to be as close to 0.05 as possible.
c. Suppose that in fact $P_1 = 0.1$, $P_2 = 0.3$, and $P_3 = 0.6$. What is the probability of a Type II error for the decision rule of b?
d. If $U = 1$, $V = 3$, and $Z = 6$, what is your decision?
e. What do you conclude?

XIII.11

CLASSIFICATION PROCEDURES

When empirical data are used to assign an individual to one of several predesignated subpopulations, this is a form of hypothesis testing. The classes constitute the hypotheses, the rule used to make the assignments is the decision rule, and the assignment made constitutes the decision. For example, the population might be divided into two diagnostic groups. Then, a previously undiagnosed patient is to be assigned to one group on the basis of his performance on a test.

This problem will be attacked with the aid of Bayes's theorem. Although it is unnecessary to depend on subjective estimates of the prior probabilities in this application, the logic is the same as that of the modern Bayesian statistician who incorporates subjective probabilities in his analysis (see Section V.3.5).

Two approaches will be distinguished. In the first, the distributions of the observation variable (e.g., the "test") in the subpopulations are unknown. This method is described and applied in Section XIII.11.1. The second approach requires that the distributions of the observation variable in the subpopulations be specified. This method is discussed and illustrated in Section *XIII.11.2. In Section *XIII.11.3, the same formulation is used to describe the perceptual behavior of human subjects.

XIII.11.1. Classification with unknown distributions in the subpopulations

The elementary ideas of this method were introduced in Sections IV.6.3 and V.3.5, but now the procedure will be developed in more general terms.[16]

Data reported by Price and Deabler[17] will be used as illustrative material. These investigators administered the Archimedes-spiral test to 40 functionally ill mental patients (F) and 120 patients suffering from brain damage (B) from a VA hospital population. The rotating spiral was presented four times to each patient, and the number of occasions on which the aftereffect was reported constituted the observation variable. We shall call this variable X and note that its range is (0, 1, 2, 3, 4). The relative frequency functions obtained by Price and Deabler are shown in Table XIII.5. Since it has been estimated[18] that

Table XIII.5. Aftereffect in Archimedes-spiral test

Sample	Sample size	X				
		0	1	2	3	4
Functionally ill (F)	40	0	0	.025	.025	.950
Brain damaged (B)	120	.600	.100	.200	.080	.020

the proportion of functionally ill patients in the VA mental hospital population is about 0.84 and the proportion of brain-damaged patients is about 0.16, we shall use as estimates of the base rates $\mathbf{P}'(F) = 0.84$ and $\mathbf{P}'(B) = 0.16$. The primes on these probabilities are to remind us that they are estimates and that they may be in error.

The relative frequency functions of Table XIII.5 can be used as estimates of the probability distributions of X in the two subpopulations, F and B. For example, the probability that X equals 3 in the brain-damaged

[16] This method and others related to it have been described by Lubin, A., in "Linear and non-linear discriminating functions." *Br. J. Psychol., Statistical Section* **3**, 90–104, 1950. Meehl and Rosen also discuss certain aspects of this type of problem in "Antecedent probability and the efficiency of psychometric signs, patterns, and cutting scores." *Psychol. Bull.* **52**, 194–216, 1955.

[17] "Diagnosis of organicity by means of the spiral aftereffect." *J. Consult. Psychol.* **19**, 299–302, 1955.

[18] Stilson, D. W., M. D. Gynther, and B. Gertz, "Base rates and the Archimedes spiral illusion." *J. Consult. Psychol.* **21**, 435–437, 1957.

subpopulation is estimated to be 0.08. These estimates of the two PD's will be denoted $\mathbf{P}'(X = x \mid F)$ for the functionally ill subpopulation and $P'(X = x \mid B)$ for the brain-damaged subpopulation.

CLASSIFICATION RULE. Now it is possible to apply Bayes's theorem to find which of the two diagnoses is most likely for a given number of reports of the illusion. Applying Formula [V.10b] for Bayes's theorem, the probability that a randomly selected individual from the composite population is one of the functionally ill given that he reports the aftereffect twice out of four trials is estimated by

$$\begin{aligned}\mathbf{P}'(F \mid X = 2) &= \frac{\mathbf{P}'(F)\mathbf{P}'(X = 2 \mid F)}{\mathbf{P}'(F)\mathbf{P}'(X = 2 \mid F) + \mathbf{P}'(B)\mathbf{P}'(X = 2 \mid B)} \\ &= \frac{0.84(0.025)}{0.84(0.025) + 0.16(0.200)} \\ &= 0.396.\end{aligned}$$

Similarly, the probability that he is from the brain-damaged subpopulation given $X = 2$ is estimated by

$$\begin{aligned}\mathbf{P}'(B \mid X = 2) &= \frac{\mathbf{P}'(B)\mathbf{P}'(X = 2 \mid B)}{\mathbf{P}'(F)\mathbf{P}'(X = 2 \mid F) + \mathbf{P}'(B)\mathbf{P}'(X = 2 \mid B)} \\ &= \frac{0.16(0.200)}{0.84(0.025) + 0.16(0.200)} \\ &= 0.604.\end{aligned}$$

These estimates indicate that the hypothesis "brain damage" is more likely than "functional illness" when an individual reports the aftereffect on two out of four presentations of the rotating spiral. Therefore, if $X = 2$ for an individual selected randomly from the composite population, the "best bet" is that he suffers from brain damage.

By applying this procedure, we can find whether the estimate of $\mathbf{P}(F \mid X = x)$ or of $\mathbf{P}(B \mid X = x)$ is larger for each value of the observation variable. This permits a diagnosis of any patient selected randomly from the population. If the patient reports the aftereffect on x out of four trials, we should diagnose "functional illness" if $\mathbf{P}'(F \mid X = x) > \mathbf{P}'(B \mid X = x)$. Otherwise, the diagnosis should be "brain damage."

Requiring that $\mathbf{P}'(F \mid X = x) > \mathbf{P}'(B \mid X = x)$ in order to make a diagnosis of "functional illness" is identical to requiring that

$$\frac{\mathbf{P}'(F \mid X = x)}{\mathbf{P}'(B \mid X = x)} > 1.$$

Then, $\mathbf{P}'(F \mid X = x)$ and $\mathbf{P}'(B \mid X = x)$ can be replaced by the expression of Formula [V.10a] for Bayes's theorem. This leads to

$$\frac{\mathbf{P}'(F \mid X = x)}{\mathbf{P}'(B \mid X = x)} = \frac{\mathbf{P}'(F)\mathbf{P}'(X = x \mid F)/\mathbf{P}'(X = x)}{\mathbf{P}'(B)\mathbf{P}'(X = x \mid B)/\mathbf{P}'(X = x)} > 1$$

$$= \frac{\mathbf{P}'(F)\mathbf{P}'(X = x \mid F)}{\mathbf{P}'(B)\mathbf{P}'(X = x \mid B)} > 1.$$

If both sides of the inequality in the last line are multiplied by $\mathbf{P}'(B)/\mathbf{P}'(F)$, then the condition becomes

$$\frac{\mathbf{P}'(X = x \mid F)}{\mathbf{P}'(X = x \mid B)} > \frac{\mathbf{P}'(B)}{\mathbf{P}'(F)}.$$

These results are summarized below.

Suppose that the discrete random variable X is to be used to assign individuals to one of two mutually exclusive and exhaustive subpopulations, F and B. Then, if the observed datum for a randomly selected individual from the composite population is $X = x$, he should be assigned to F if

$$L(X = x) = \frac{\mathbf{P}(X = x \mid F)}{\mathbf{P}(X = x \mid B)} > \frac{\mathbf{P}(B)}{\mathbf{P}(F)} \qquad \text{[XIII.1]}$$

where $\mathbf{P}(F)$ and $\mathbf{P}(B)$ are the base rates for subpopulations F and B, respectively. Otherwise, he should be assigned to B. $L(X = x)$ is called the likelihood ratio. If this procedure is followed, then the expected proportion of correct assignments, C, will be as large as possible.

Before discussing C, the method will be applied to the diagnostic example. For each value of X, an estimate of the likelihood ratio,

$$L'(X = x) = \frac{\mathbf{P}'(X = x \mid F)}{\mathbf{P}'(X = x \mid B)},$$

must be calculated. If this ratio exceeds $\mathbf{P}'(B)/\mathbf{P}'(F) = 0.16/0.84 = 0.19$ for a particular value of X, then any individual who obtains that value

Table XIII.6. Decision rules for diagnostic classification problem

	X				
	0	1	2	3	4
$\mathbf{P}'(X = x \mid F)$	0	0	.025	.025	.950
$\mathbf{P}'(X = x \mid B)$	.600	.100	.200	.080	.020
$L'(X = x) = \dfrac{\mathbf{P}'(X = x \mid F)}{\mathbf{P}'(X = x \mid B)}$	0	0	.0125	.3125	4.7500
$\dfrac{\mathbf{P}'(B)}{\mathbf{P}'(F)} = \dfrac{0.16}{0.84} = 0.19$	.19	.19	.19	.19	.19
Diagnosis	*B*	*B*	*B*	*F*	*F*

should be diagnosed "functionally ill" (i.e., he should be assigned to F). On the other hand, if $L'(X = x) \leq 0.19$, then the individual should be diagnosed "brain-damaged" (i.e., he should be assigned to B).[19] The application of this decision rule is summarized in Table XIII.6.

ASSESSMENT OF THE CLASSIFICATION RULE. The next question is when will such a procedure prove useful? One way of answering this question is to examine the expected proportion of correct classifications resulting from its use.

In the example, suppose that for a particular value of X, $L'(X = x) > 0.19$, so that the classification rule requires a diagnosis of functional illness. The joint probability that this value of X will be observed and a correct diagnosis will be made is $\mathbf{P}'[(X = x) \cap F] = \mathbf{P}'(F)\mathbf{P}'(X = x \mid F)$. For $X = 3$, this probability can be estimated by $\mathbf{P}'(F)\mathbf{P}'(X = 3 \mid F) = 0.84(0.025) = 0.021$. Now, if $\sum_{L' > .19}$ indicates a sum over all values of X for which the likelihood ratio exceeds $\mathbf{P}'(B)/\mathbf{P}'(F) = 0.19$, then the probability of a correct diagnosis of functional illness is estimated by

$$\begin{aligned}\sum_{L' > .19} \mathbf{P}'[(X = x) \cap F] &= \sum_{L' > .19} \mathbf{P}'(F)\mathbf{P}'(X = x \mid F) \\ &= \mathbf{P}'(F)\mathbf{P}'(X = 3 \mid F) + \mathbf{P}'(F)\mathbf{P}'(X = 4 \mid F) \\ &= 0.84(0.025) + 0.84(0.950) \\ &= 0.819.\end{aligned}$$

Similarly, the estimate of the probability of a correct diagnosis of brain damage is

$$\begin{aligned}\sum_{L' \leq .19} \mathbf{P}'[(X = x) \cap B] &= \sum_{L' \leq .19} \mathbf{P}'(B)\mathbf{P}'(X = x \mid B) \\ &= \mathbf{P}'(B)\mathbf{P}'(X = 0 \mid B) + \mathbf{P}'(B)\mathbf{P}'(X = 1 \mid B) \\ &\qquad + \mathbf{P}'(B)\mathbf{P}'(X = 2 \mid B) \\ &= 0.16(0.600) + 0.16(0.100) + 0.16(0.200) \\ &= 0.144.\end{aligned}$$

Therefore, the expected proportion of correct diagnoses using the classification rule[20] in the last row of Table XIII.3 is estimated by

$$\begin{aligned}C' &= \sum_{L' > .19} \mathbf{P}'(F)\mathbf{P}'(X = x \mid F) + \sum_{L' \leq .19} \mathbf{P}'(B)\mathbf{P}'(X = x \mid B) \\ &= 0.819 + 0.144 \\ &= 0.963.\end{aligned}$$

[19] If $L'(X = x) = 0.19$, it would be equally reasonable to assign the patient to F. Assigning him to the brain-damaged subpopulation is quite arbitrary.

[20] The classification rule suggested by Stilson, Gynther, and Gertz in "Base rates and the Archimedes spiral illusion." *J. Consult. Psychol.* **21**, 435–437, 1957, does *not* maximize the proportion of correct classifications for the Price and Deabler data.

Thus, *the expected proportion of correct classifications is*

$$C = \sum_{L > \mathbf{P}_B/\mathbf{P}_F} \mathbf{P}(F)\mathbf{P}(X = x \mid F) + \sum_{L \leq \mathbf{P}_B/\mathbf{P}_F} \mathbf{P}(B)\mathbf{P}(X = x \mid B) \qquad \text{[XIII.2]}$$

where $L > \mathbf{P}_B/\mathbf{P}_F$ *indicates that the first sum is over all values of X for which* $L(X = x) > \mathbf{P}(B)/\mathbf{P}(F)$, $L \leq \mathbf{P}_B/\mathbf{P}_F$ *indicates that the second sum is over all values of X for which* $L(X = x) \leq \mathbf{P}(B)/\mathbf{P}(F)$, *and other notation is as defined before.*

Earlier, it was stated that the decision rule employed here will ensure that C is as large as possible. A demonstration showing that this procedure maximizes the estimate of the expected proportion of correct diagnoses for the example is given in Appendix XIII.1.

Perhaps the simplest way to appraise this procedure is to compare the expected proportion of correct classifications with the higher population base rate. *If P is the base rate for the larger subpopulation, then*

$$\frac{C - P}{1 - P} \qquad \text{[XIII.3]}$$

provides an index for this comparison. By assigning every individual to the larger subpopulation, one can achieve an expected proportion P of correct classifications. The proportion of incorrect classifications is then $1 - P$, and the proportion of errors one expects to eliminate using the classification rule is $(C - P)/(1 - P)$.

For the example, this proportion is estimated by $(C' - P')/(1 - P') = (0.963 - 0.84)/(1 - 0.84) = 0.77$. This indicates that 77 percent of the errors that result when base rates provide the only basis for classification can be eliminated by using the spiral aftereffect and the classification rule of Table XIII.6.

If the PD's and the base rates of the two subpopulations were known, then the interpretation of C and $(C - P)/(1 - P)$ would be straightforward. However, in most applications, both must be estimated, so that C' and $(C' - P')/(1 - P')$ are themselves estimates that are subject to sampling variability. Furthermore, the sampling error is most likely to be in the direction of *overestimation* of C. Since the classification rule was calculated for a particular sample, we can be sure that it maximizes the proportion of correct diagnoses *for that sample.* But if the classification rule has been influenced by any atypical characteristic of the observed sample, then it will not produce the largest expected proportion of correct classifications for the population as a whole.

One way to deal with this is to define the decision rule for one sample and then obtain a direct empirical estimate of the expected proportion of correct classifications by applying it to a second, independent, random sample. Such an estimate is also susceptible to the effects of sampling variability, but it does provide an unbiased estimate of the expected proportion of correct classifications in the population. Such procedures are often referred to as *cross-validation.*

The cross-validation approach is quite attractive, but notice that since each subsample is smaller than the total sample, a classification rule based on one of them will be more affected by sampling variability than a rule based on the combined samples. Perhaps the best procedure is to construct three classification rules, one for each subsample and one for the combined sample. Then the classification rule for each subsample can be cross-validated using the other subsample. This will provide a basis for assessing the usefulness of the procedure. The most stable classification rule, the one based on the combined samples, can be used for classifying new observations.

The method described in this section can be generalized to any number of subpopulations and to any number of variables.[21] The basic procedures are the same as for the simpler case. Furthermore, they can be formulated so that they weight the different types of errors or the different types of correct decisions unequally. For example, a misdiagnosis of functional illness when a patient is suffering from a fast-growing, operative brain tumor is more serious than the converse error. If different "costs" could be assigned to the two kinds of errors, or different "values" assigned to the two kinds of correct diagnoses, then the analysis could follow the maximum expected gain or minimax regret procedures described in Sections II.4.1 and II.4.2.[22]

*XIII.11.2. Classification with known distributions in the subpopulations

When the PD's or DF's of the two subpopulations to be discriminated are known, a classification procedure described by Lubin[23] can be employed. This procedure is less sensitive to atypical sample characteristics than the method of Section XIII.11.1. It is introduced and illustrated below.

Suppose that the capacity of the "Personality Actualization Test" (PAT)[24] to discriminate schizophrenics from other functionally ill mental patients is to be assessed. The test has been administered to 143 functionally ill patients who are not schizophrenic (N) and to 73 schizophrenics (S). The frequency function, mean, and variance for each of these samples are shown in Table XIII.7.

[21] Rao formulates these procedures in general terms. See Reference 5 at the end of this chapter. For an introduction to the case of more than one observation variable, see Reference 4.

[22] Rao, *op. cit.*

[23] Lubin, *op. cit.*

[24] This test does not exist, and the data for it are artificial.

Table XIII.7. Data for hypothetical PAT test

X	Frequency function of the nonschizophrenics (N)	Frequency function of the schizophrenics (S)
1	0	2
2	0	3
3	14	14
4	17	15
5	33	15
6	28	9
7	24	8
8	16	5
9	11	2
	$n_N = 143$	$n_S = 73$
	$\bar{X}_N = 5.86$	$\bar{X}_S = 4.84$
	$S_N^2 = 2.90$	$S_S^2 = 3.42$

Using a suitable statistical test,[25] the hypothesis that the mean of the schizophrenic population equals the mean of the nonschizophrenic population can be rejected at the 0.01 level of significance. This indicates that the PAT has some concurrent validity (Section VI.2.3), but it says *nothing* about the diagnostic usefulness of the test. A procedure for investigating its usefulness is developed below.

Assume that the base rate for schizophrenia is $\mathbf{P}(S) = 1/3$ and that for the nonschizophrenic subpopulation it is $\mathbf{P}(N) = 2/3$.

An examination of the relative frequency functions of Table XIII.7 suggests that these two samples come from subpopulations in which the PD's of the PAT can be approximated by normal DF's. It will be assumed that this is correct.[26] In addition, since the two sample variances are quite similar ($S_S^2 = 3.42$ and $S_N^2 = 2.90$), it seems reasonable to assume that the two populations have the same variance. This common variance will be called σ^2. In order to obtain a single estimate of σ^2 based on both samples, the estimator

$$S_K^2 = \frac{(n_S - 1)S_S^2 + (n_N - 1)S_N^2}{n_S + n_N - 2} \qquad \text{[XIII.4]}$$

will be used. In Appendix XIII.2 it is shown that this estimator is unbiased. Furthermore, since S_K^2 is based on $n_S + n_N = 143 + 73 = 216$ observations, it is less susceptible to sampling variability than either S_S^2 or S_N^2 alone.

[25] Not described here.

[26] This can be tested using the method of Section XIII.8.2.

For the example, then,

$$S_K^2 = \frac{(n_S - 1)S_S^2 + (n_N - 1)S_N^2}{n_S + n_N - 2}$$
$$= \frac{(73 - 1)3.42 + (143 - 1)2.90}{73 + 143 - 2}$$
$$= 3.08,$$

and $S_K = 1.75$.

To summarize the mathematical model, it has been assumed that the DF in the schizophrenic subpopulation is

$$f(X \mid S) = \frac{1}{\sigma\sqrt{(2\pi)}} e^{-1/(2\sigma^2)(X - \mu_S)^2},$$

and that the DF in the nonschizophrenic subpopulation is

$$f(X \mid N) = \frac{1}{\sigma\sqrt{(2\pi)}} e^{-1/(2\sigma^2)(X - \mu_N)^2},$$

where μ_N and μ_S are the two subpopulation means. By replacing the parameters σ, μ_S, and μ_N by S_K, $\bar{X}_S$, and $\bar{X}_N$, respectively, probabilities associated with these two densities can be approximated.

*CLASSIFICATION RULE. Having formulated a mathematical model, we are ready to call on Bayes's theorem and develop a classification rule. The rationale for this rule is analogous to the one developed in Section XIII.11.1.

If a patient is drawn randomly from the schizophrenic subpopulation, then the probability that his PAT score lies between x_1 and x_2 ($x_2 > x_1$) is $\mathbf{P}[(x_1 < X < x_2) \mid S]$. This probability corresponds to the area under $f(X \mid S)$ between x_1 and x_2. Similarly, $\mathbf{P}[(x_1 < X < x_2) \mid N]$ corresponds to the area under $f(X \mid N)$ between x_1 and x_2.

If an undiagnosed patient is selected randomly from the composite population and his PAT score lies between x_1 and x_2, is he to be diagnosed nonschizophrenic? A reasonable basis for deciding is to assign him to N (i.e., diagnose nonschizophrenic) if it is more likely that he is from N than from S. In other words, if

$$\mathbf{P}[N \mid (x_1 < X < x_2)] > \mathbf{P}[S \mid (x_1 < X < x_2)],$$

then the diagnosis should be nonschizophrenic. Otherwise, a diagnosis of schizophrenia should be made. However, this is identical to making a diagnosis of "nonschizophrenia" whenever

$$\frac{\mathbf{P}[N \mid (x_1 < X < x_2)]}{\mathbf{P}[S \mid (x_1 < X < x_2)]} > 1,$$

and otherwise diagnosing "schizophrenia." Both numerator and denominator of this ratio can be replaced by the equivalent expression given by Formula [V.10a] for Bayes's theorem. Then, the criterion becomes

$$\frac{\mathbf{P}[N \mid (x_1 < X < x_2)]}{\mathbf{P}[S \mid (x_1 < X < x_2)]} = \frac{\mathbf{P}(N)\mathbf{P}[(x_1 < X < x_2) \mid N]/\mathbf{P}(x_1 < X < x_2)}{\mathbf{P}(S)\mathbf{P}[(x_1 < X < x_2) \mid S]/\mathbf{P}(x_1 < X < x_2)} > 1$$

$$= \frac{\mathbf{P}(N)\mathbf{P}[(x_1 < X < x_2) \mid N]}{\mathbf{P}(S)\mathbf{P}[(x_1 < X < x_2) \mid S]} > 1.$$

On the basis of this result, the decision rule can be stated: "If a patient's PAT score falls between x_1 and x_2, diagnose nonschizophrenia if

$$\frac{\mathbf{P}(N)\mathbf{P}[(x_1 < X < x_2) \mid N]}{\mathbf{P}(S)\mathbf{P}[(x_1 < X < x_2) \mid S]} > 1.$$

Otherwise, make a diagnosis of schizophrenia."

Since the mathematical model assumes that X is a continuous random variable, and since the classification rule must specify a decision for every value of X, it would be more precise to express the rule in terms of single values of the observation variable than in terms of intervals. To make this possible, begin by letting x be the midpoint of the interval from x_1 to x_2. Then, there is a positive number, a, such that $x_1 = x - a$ and $x_2 = x + a$ (so that $2a = x_2 - x_1$). But since $\mathbf{P}[(x_1 < X < x_2) \mid N] = \mathbf{P}[(x - a < X < x + a) \mid N]$, $\mathbf{P}[(x_1 < X < x_2) \mid N]$ can be approximated by $2af(x \mid N)$, where $f(x \mid N)$ is the height of the DF of X in the nonschizophrenic subpopulation for $X = x$. The nature of this approximation is illustrated in Figure XIII.18. The crosshatched area in this figure is an approximation of

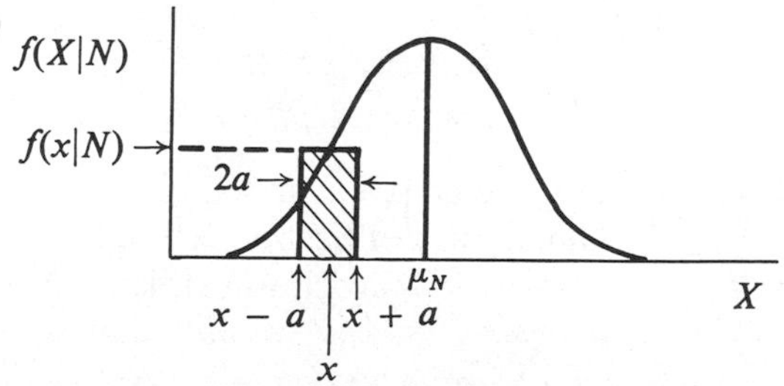

Figure XIII.18

$$\mathbf{P}[(x_1 < X < x_2) \mid N] = \mathbf{P}[(x - a < X < x + a) \mid N].$$

Of course, an exactly analogous approximation of $\mathbf{P}[(x_1 < X < x_2) \mid S]$ can be devised.

Now, the criterion for the classification rule can be expressed in terms of the approximation:

$$\frac{\mathbf{P}(N)\mathbf{P}[(x_1 < X < x_2) \mid N]}{\mathbf{P}(S)\mathbf{P}[(x_1 < X < x_2) \mid S]} = \frac{\mathbf{P}(N)\mathbf{P}[(x - a < X < x + a) \mid N]}{\mathbf{P}(S)\mathbf{P}[(x - a < X < x + a) \mid S]} > 1$$

$$\cong \frac{\mathbf{P}(N)2af(x \mid N)}{\mathbf{P}(S)2af(x \mid S)} > 1.$$

As indicated in Section VII.1.4, the precision of this approximation will increase as a decreases. In fact, if we let a approach zero as a limit, then the ratio $2a/(2a)$ remains equal to 1, and

$$\lim_{a \to 0} \left(\frac{\mathbf{P}(N)2af(x \mid N)}{\mathbf{P}(S)2af(x \mid S)} \right) = \frac{\mathbf{P}(N)f(x \mid N)}{\mathbf{P}(S)f(x \mid S)}.$$

Since a has disappeared, the ratio can be applied to single values of X.

With this result, the classification rule becomes "If the PAT score of a randomly selected, undiagnosed patient is $X = x$, then the diagnosis should be nonschizophrenic if

$$\frac{\mathbf{P}(N)f(x \mid N)}{\mathbf{P}(S)f(x \mid S)} > 1.$$

Otherwise, a diagnosis of schizophrenia should be made." This will be referred to as Form I of the classification rule.

Even though Form I is perfectly acceptable, such decision rules are usually expressed in terms of the likelihood ratio. By multiplying both sides of

$$\frac{\mathbf{P}(N)f(x \mid N)}{\mathbf{P}(S)f(x \mid S)} > 1$$

by $\mathbf{P}(S)/\mathbf{P}(N)$, we obtain

$$L(x) = \frac{f(x \mid N)}{f(x \mid S)} > \frac{\mathbf{P}(S)}{\mathbf{P}(N)}.$$

The ratio $f(x \mid N)/f(x \mid S)$ is called a likelihood ratio. It is analogous in its function to the likelihood ratio of Section XIII.11.1. This form of the classification rule, which will be called Form II, is summarized below.

Suppose that X is a continuous random variable that is to be used to classify individuals into one of two subpopulations, N and S. If the observed datum for an individual selected randomly from the composite population is $X = x$, then he should be assigned to N if

$$L(x) = \frac{f(x \mid N)}{f(x \mid S)} > \frac{\mathbf{P}(S)}{\mathbf{P}(N)}, \qquad \text{[XIII.5]}$$

where $\mathbf{P}(S)$ and $\mathbf{P}(N)$ are the population base rates and $f(X \mid S)$ and $f(X \mid N)$ are the DF's for the subpopulations S and N, respectively. Otherwise, he *should be assigned to S. This procedure will lead to as large an expected proportion of correct classifications, C, as any other classification rule.*

Forms I and II are equivalent in the sense that they both lead to exactly the same classification for any value of X. This follows from the way in which Form II was derived from Form I.

Before applying these rules to the example or discussing C, a third form will be derived from Form I. It will be clear in the derivation that this form is equivalent to Form I. Therefore, all three forms are equivalent.

The third form has the special advantage of permitting a geometric representation of the way the procedure operates. Furthermore, it is essential for calculating C.

According to Form I, the diagnosis should be nonschizophrenic if $\mathbf{P}(N)f(x \mid N)/[\mathbf{P}(S)f(x \mid S)] > 1$. If the ratio is less than or equal to 1, then the diagnosis should be schizophrenia. Consequently, if $\mathbf{P}(N)f(X \mid N)$ and $\mathbf{P}(S)f(X \mid S)$ are both plotted on a single graph, the point at which the two curves intersect, call it x_C, will separate values of X for which the ratio exceeds 1 from those for which it is less than 1. This can be seen in Figure XIII.19.

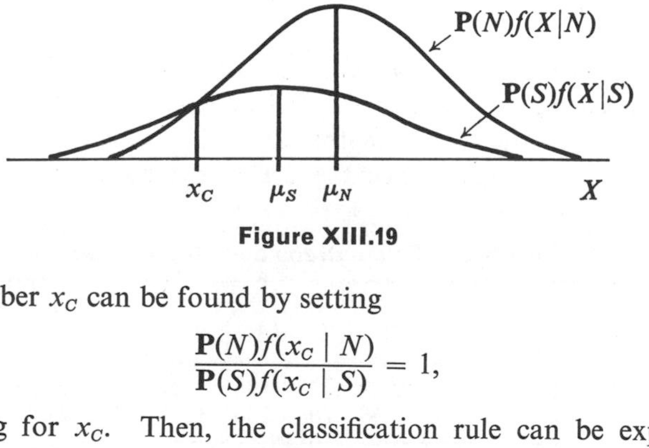

Figure XIII.19

The number x_C can be found by setting

$$\frac{\mathbf{P}(N)f(x_C \mid N)}{\mathbf{P}(S)f(x_C \mid S)} = 1,$$

and solving for x_C. Then, the classification rule can be expressed in terms of X as follows: "If the PAT score for a randomly selected individual

Table XIII.8. Three forms of classification rule

Form I	Form II	Form III
Diagnose N if $\frac{\mathbf{P}(N)f(x \mid N)}{\mathbf{P}(S)f(x \mid S)} > 1$	Diagnose N if $\frac{f(x \mid N)}{f(x \mid S)} > \frac{\mathbf{P}(S)}{\mathbf{P}(N)}$	Diagnose N if $X > x_C$
Diagnose S if $\frac{\mathbf{P}(N)f(x \mid N)}{\mathbf{P}(S)f(x \mid S)} \leq 1$	Diagnose S if $\frac{f(x \mid N)}{f(x \mid S)} \leq \frac{\mathbf{P}(S)}{\mathbf{P}(N)}$	Diagnose S if $X \leq x_C$

is $X = x$, then diagnose nonschizophrenic if $x > x_C$. Otherwise, diagnose schizophrenia." This is Form III of this classification rule. All three forms are summarized in Table XIII.8.

Next, each of the three forms will be applied to the example, and the results will be summarized. Form II will be applied first.

The first step is to estimate the likelihood ratio,

$$L(X) = f(X \mid N)/f(X \mid S),$$

for each value of X. This ratio is to be compared with $\mathbf{P}(S)/\mathbf{P}(N) = (1/3)/(2/3) = 0.5$ in each case. The estimate of the likelihood ratio is

$$L'(X) = \frac{f'(X \mid N)}{f'(X \mid S)} = \frac{\dfrac{1}{S_K\sqrt{(2\pi)}} e^{-1/(2S_K{}^2)(X-\bar{X}_N)^2}}{\dfrac{1}{S_K\sqrt{(2\pi)}} e^{-1/(2S_K{}^2)(X-\bar{X}_S)^2}},$$

so $L(3)$ is estimated from

$$L'(3) = \frac{f'(3 \mid N)}{f'(3 \mid S)} = \frac{\dfrac{1}{1.75\sqrt{(2\pi)}} e^{-1/[2(3.08)](3-5.86)^2}}{\dfrac{1}{1.75\sqrt{(2\pi)}} e^{-1/[2(3.08)](3-4.84)^2}}.$$

This ratio can be evaluated most conveniently with the aid of the table of heights of the standardized normal DF in Appendix VI. The Z-value corresponding to the denominator of $L'(3)$ is $Z = (X - \bar{X}_S)/S_K = (3 - 4.84)/1.75 = -1.05$. Since the DF is symmetrical, the height at

Table XIII.9. Calculations and classification rules

			PAT Score (X)								
		Row	1	2	3	4	5	6	7	8	9
Densities	$f'(X \mid N)$	(1)	.009	.035	.106	.228	.353	.397	.323	.190	.080
	$f'(X \mid S)$	(2)	.036	.108	.230	.355	.397	.321	.187	.079	.023
Form I	$\mathbf{P}(N)f'(X \mid N)$	(3)	.006	.024	.071	.152	.235	.265	.215	.127	.053
	$\mathbf{P}(S)f'(X \mid S)$	(4)	.012	.036	.077	.118	.132	.107	.062	.026	.008
	$\dfrac{\mathbf{P}(N)f'(X \mid N)}{\mathbf{P}(S)f'(X \mid S)}$	(5)	.5	.7	.9	1.3	1.8	2.5	3.5	4.9	6.6
	1	(6)	1	1	1	1	1	1	1	1	1
	Diagnosis	(7)	*S*	*S*	*S*	*N*	*N*	*N*	*N*	*N*	*N*
Form II	$L'(X) = \dfrac{f'(X \mid N)}{f'(X \mid S)}$	(8)	.25	.32	.46	.64	.89	1.2	1.7	2.4	3.5
	$\mathbf{P}(S)/\mathbf{P}(N)$	(9)	.5	.5	.5	.5	.5	.5	.5	.5	.5
	Diagnosis	(10)	*S*	*S*	*S*	*N*	*N*	*N*	*N*	*N*	*N*
Form III	x'_C	(11)	3.26	3.26	3.26	3.26	3.26	3.26	3.26	3.26	3.26
	Diagnosis	(12)	*S*	*S*	*S*	*N*	*N*	*N*	*N*	*N*	*N*

$Z = -1.05$ is the same as the height at $Z = +1.05$. From Appendix VI, this height is 0.230. Similarly, the height for the numerator is determined by $Z = (X - \bar{X}_N)/S_K = (3 - 5.86)/1.75 = -1.63$. By linear interpolation in Appendix VI, it is 0.106. Now, returning to the estimate of the likelihood ratio,

$$L'(3) = \frac{f'(3 \mid N)}{f'(3 \mid S)} = \frac{0.106}{0.23} = 0.46.$$

Since this is less than $\mathbf{P}(S)/\mathbf{P}(N) = 0.5$, an individual whose PAT score is $X = 3$ should be diagnosed as schizophrenic. Proceeding in the same way for each value of X, the explcit classification rule for Form II is given in Row (10) of Table XIII.9.

To apply Form I, $\mathbf{P}(N)f'(X \mid N)/[\mathbf{P}(S)f'(X \mid S)]$ must be found for each value of X. If this ratio exceeds 1, a diagnosis of nonschizophrenia should be made. Otherwise, the diagnosis should be schizophrenia. The preliminary calculations and explicit classification rule for this form appear in Rows (3) through (7) of Table XIII.9.

The application of Form III requires the calculation of x_C. Since x_C is defined by the equation

$$\frac{\mathbf{P}(N)f(x_C \mid N)}{\mathbf{P}(S)f(x_C \mid S)} = 1,$$

it can be estimated by solving

$$\frac{\mathbf{P}(N)f'(x'_C \mid N)}{\mathbf{P}(S)f'(x'_C \mid S)} = 1$$

for x'_C. Multiplying both sides by $\mathbf{P}(S)/\mathbf{P}(N)$ and substituting explicit normal DF's for $f'(x'_C \mid N)$ and $f'(x'_C \mid S)$,

$$\frac{\dfrac{1}{S_K\sqrt{(2\pi)}}\, e^{-1/(2S_K{}^2)(x'_C - \bar{X}_N)^2}}{\dfrac{1}{S_K\sqrt{(2\pi)}}\, e^{-1/(2S_K{}^2)(x'_C - \bar{X}_S)^2}} = \frac{\mathbf{P}(S)}{\mathbf{P}(N)}.$$

In Appendix XIII.3, this equation is solved for x'_C. The result[27] is

$$x'_C = \frac{S_K{}^2(2.3026)\log_{10}\left(\dfrac{\mathbf{P}(S)}{\mathbf{P}(N)}\right)}{\bar{X}_N - \bar{X}_S} + \frac{\bar{X}_N + \bar{X}_S}{2} \qquad \text{[XIII.6]}$$

$$= \frac{(3.08)(2.3026)\log_{10}\left(\dfrac{1/3}{2/3}\right)}{5.86 - 4.84} + \frac{5.86 + 4.84}{2}$$

$$= 3.26.$$

[27] If the two population variances are not assumed to be equal, then there are two values for the solution of x'_C. Though Forms I and II of the classification rule are stated in the same way when this is true, Form III becomes somewhat more complicated.

With this result, the third form of the classification rule can be stated explicitly. "Whenever $X > 3.26$, diagnose nonschizophrenia. Whenever $X \leq 3.26$, diagnose schizophrenia." This form of the rule is applied in Rows (11) and (12) of Table XIII.9.

Notice that the explicit classification procedures in Rows (7), (10), and (12) of Table XIII.9 are identical for all three forms. Thus, the earlier statement of equivalence is verified for the example.

The relative frequencies used to establish classification rules like the one of Section XIII.11.1 are less stable than the means and variance used to formulate rules such as those of this section. Nonetheless, this second method is affected by sampling variability, and additional error is introduced by the normal distribution assumption.

*EXPECTED PROPORTION OF CORRECT CLASSIFICATIONS. In order to evaluate this method, we shall begin with the expected proportion of correct classifications. To calculate C, one must find the probability that a patient will be schizophrenic and be diagnosed schizophrenic, or be nonschizophrenic and diagnosed as such. In terms of Form III of the decision rule, this probability is

$$\begin{aligned}\mathbf{P}[S \cap (\text{diagnose } S)] + \mathbf{P}[N \cap (\text{diagnose } N)]&\\ &= \mathbf{P}[S \cap (X \leq x_C)] + \mathbf{P}[N \cap (X > x_C)]\\ &= \mathbf{P}(S)\mathbf{P}[X \leq x_C \mid S] + \mathbf{P}(N)\mathbf{P}[X > x_C \mid N].\end{aligned}$$

Since $f(X \mid N)$ and $f(X \mid S)$ were assumed to be normal DF's, $\mathbf{P}[X \leq x_C \mid S]$ can be estimated from

$$\mathbf{P}\left(Z \leq \frac{x'_C - \bar{X}_S}{S_K}\right) = \mathbf{P}\left(Z \leq \frac{3.26 - 4.84}{1.75}\right) = \mathbf{P}(Z \leq -0.90)$$
$$= 0.18.$$

Similarly, $\mathbf{P}[X > x_C \mid N]$ can be estimated from

$$\mathbf{P}\left(Z > \frac{x'_C - \bar{X}_N}{S_K}\right) = \mathbf{P}\left(Z > \frac{3.26 - 5.86}{1.75}\right) = \mathbf{P}(Z > -1.49)$$
$$= 0.93.$$

Then, the estimate of C is

$$\begin{aligned}C' &= \mathbf{P}'[S \cap (\text{diagnose } S)] + \mathbf{P}'[N \cap (\text{diagnose } N)]\\ &= \mathbf{P}(S)\mathbf{P}'[X \leq x_C \mid S] + \mathbf{P}(N)\mathbf{P}'[X > x_C \mid N] = \tfrac{1}{3}(0.18) + \tfrac{2}{3}(0.93)\\ &= 0.68.\end{aligned}$$

The estimated proportion of correct decisions is 0.68.

If the two populations had exactly normal DF's, and if the parameters

P(S), **P**(N), μ_S, μ_N, and σ^2 had all been known, then the classification rules of Table XIII.9 would maximize the expected proportion of correct classifications. To see this, suppose that the rule were changed to "classify N if $X > x''_C$ and classify S if $X \leq x''_C$," where $x''_C > x_C$. This situation is illustrated in Figure XIII.20. The doubly crosshatched area under

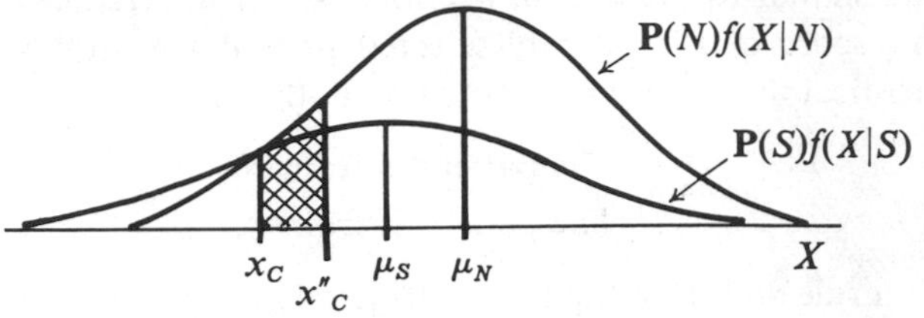

Figure XIII.20

P(S)f(X | S) represents the resulting increase in the proportion of correct classifications, and the entire crosshatched area under **P**(N)f(X | N) represents the decrease. Since the latter exceeds the former, the change from x_C to x''_C will decrease the expected proportion of correct diagnoses. An exactly similar decrease will result for *any* value of $x''_C > x_C$. Furthermore, if $x''_C < x_C$, a similar effect reduces C. Consequently, x_C is the value of X that maximizes C.

Using the PAT, the estimate of C is 0.68. However, by ignoring the test and diagnosing every patient nonschizophrenic, the expected proportion of correct diagnoses is 2/3. Of the errors remaining, the estimate

$$\frac{C' - P}{1 - P} = \frac{0.68 - (2/3)}{1 - (2/3)} = 0.04$$

indicates that 4 percent of them can be eliminated using the test and the classification rule. In spite of the concurrent validity of the PAT reported at the beginning of Section *XIII.11.2, it is doubtful that this 4 percent reduction in diagnostic errors would be worth the cost of administering the test. Furthermore, since the 4 percent figure is itself an estimate, it must be viewed with some suspicion. This figure is correct for the particular estimates of μ_S, μ_N, and σ^2 used here, but one cannot be sure that it will be correct for the population as a whole. It is possible that 4 percent is too low, but since it is based on a classification rule that maximizes the proportion of correct diagnoses for the sample, it is more likely that it is too high. Consequently, when appraising the usefulness of this method we encounter the same difficulties described in Section XIII.11.1, and it is probably wise to use a cross-validation procedure like the one suggested there.

On the other hand, for this particular application, the estimate $(C' - P)/(1 - P) = 0.04$ is so low that it is probably safe to conclude that

the test has little diagnostic usefulness in this population in spite of its concurrent validity.

If "schizophrenia" is thought of as a null hypothesis, then the values of X such that $X > x'_C$ constitute a rejection region and $X \leq x'_C$ an acceptance region. Now the classification procedure can be dealt with in a manner similar to the tests of Sections XIII.1 to XIII.8.

The PAT score of a randomly selected patient constitutes the datum for the statistical test, and the statistical hypotheses are[28]

H: The patient is from S

A: The patient is from N.

The decision rule will have the form "Reject H if the patient's PAT score exceeds x'_C. Otherwise, accept H."

Notice that H and A are both simple hypotheses. As a result of the mathematical model employed, H really states that the individual is selected randomly from a population that has a normal DF with mean μ_S and variance σ^2, and A states that he is from a normal DF with mean μ_N and variance σ^2. Each hypothesis specifies all parameters and the DF exactly. Consequently, each is a simple hypothesis.[29]

Notice, however, that the values of the parameters of the DF's were not specified a priori. That is, samples provided estimates ($\bar{X}_S$, $\bar{X}_N$, $S_K{}^2$) of these parameters, and *these estimates provided the hypotheses.* When all parameters are specified a priori, then procedures of the kind described in this section can properly be viewed as hypothesis testing, but when some of the parameters must be estimated (as in the example), then it is preferable to conceptualize such procedures as estimation. Of course, the estimate of the expected proportion of correct classifications is of central importance in assessing the usefulness of a classification procedure, and though it would be desirable to have confidence interval estimates of C, only point estimates are usually obtained.

*OPERATING CHARACTERISTIC. When a classification procedure such as this is thought of as a test, it is possible to appraise it in a way that is quite different from those discussed so far. If the hypotheses

H: The patient is from S ("schizophrenic")

A: The patient is from N ("nonschizophrenic")

were to be tested, but the merits of choosing x'_C as a lower boundary for the rejection region were not known, then we might try, for example,

[28] N could equally well have been designated as the null hypothesis.

[29] Here, the parameter space can be thought of as two-dimensional. The dimensions are μ and σ^2. Since each hypothesis specifies a single point in this space, each is simple.

$x''_C = 5$ as a lower boundary. If this were done, then the probability of a Type I error would be

$$\begin{aligned}\mathbf{P}[\text{reject H} \mid \text{H true}] &= \mathbf{P}(X > x''_C \mid S) \\ &\cong \mathbf{P}\left(Z > \frac{x''_C - \bar{X}_S}{S_K}\right) = \mathbf{P}\left(Z > \frac{5 - 4.84}{1.75}\right) \\ &\cong \mathbf{P}(Z > +0.09) \\ &\cong 0.464.\end{aligned}$$

Similarly, the probability of a correct rejection of H can be estimated for $x''_C = 5$. This is obtained from

$$\begin{aligned}\mathbf{P}[\text{reject H} \mid \text{H false}] &= \mathbf{P}(X > x''_C \mid N) \\ &\cong \mathbf{P}\left(Z > \frac{x''_C - \bar{X}_N}{S_K}\right) = \mathbf{P}\left(Z > \frac{5 - 5.86}{1.75}\right) \\ &\cong \mathbf{P}(Z > -0.49) \\ &\cong 0.688.\end{aligned}$$

By repeating such calculations for several trial values of x_C, we can construct a plot of **P**[reject H | H false] = **P**[diagnose $N \mid N$] against **P**[reject H | H true] = **P**[diagnose $N \mid S$]. This function is represented by the solid line in Figure XIII.21 for the example. It is called the *operating characteristic* of the statistical test.

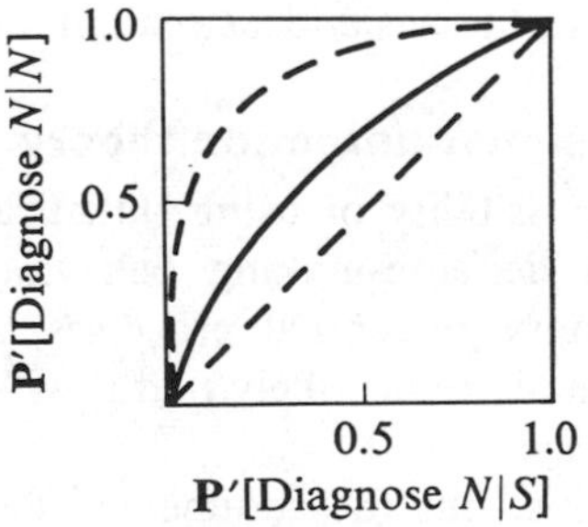

Figure XIII.21

The term *operating characteristic* is applied both to plots like the ones of Figure XIII.21 *and* to the OC-curves of Section XIII.2.2, but the meanings are not the same. However, this multiple usage is widespread, and one must be aware of it.

In the example, if the means of the two subpopulations differed more, then the operating characteristic might look like the broken curve in the upper left-hand portion of Figure XIII.21. As the means move further apart, the operating characteristic becomes an inverted L that squeezes into the upper left-hand corner of the graph. In order for this to happen, the probability of a correct rejection of the null hypothesis must increase for a given Type I error probability.

Of course, reducing the two variances without altering the means would have a similar effect on the operating characteristic. The smaller variances would reduce the overlap of $f(X \mid S)$ and $f(X \mid N)$ and reduce the likelihood of errors.

On the other hand, if the PAT were absolutely invalid, then the straight, broken line of Figure XIII.21 would represent the operating characteristic. Under this condition, the probability of correctly diagnosing "non-schizophrenia" equals the probability of incorrectly diagnosing a schizophrenic for any classification rule.

It should be noted that the operating characteristic does *not* take base rates into account, and, as stated in Section V.3.5, the usefulness of a classification test cannot be fully assessed without considering the base rates in the population.

Analyses like the one of this section can be carried out for any DF or PD. It is not necessary to assume that the distributions in the subpopulations are normal or even that both subpopulations have the same distribution. If other distributions are assumed, then the details of the calculations change, but the rationale remains the same.

Just as with the method of Section XIII.11.1, the "costs" of errors or the "values" of correct decisions can be differently weighted in formulations of the kind presented in this section. Although this complicates the procedure somewhat, the basic ideas remain the same.[30]

*XIII.11.3. Human signal-detection theory

In Section II.4.3, the possibility of using statistical decision theory as a description of human decision-making behavior was mentioned. In applications to elementary perceptual processes, this approach has met considerable success, and it seems likely that it will prove just as useful in other areas of psychology.

It may seem surprising, but the rudiments of signal-detection theory have been introduced already in Section *XIII.11.2. Our task here is to see how they have been applied to human perception.[31]

According to human signal-detection theory it is proper to think of any perceptual process as taking place in the presence of a background of irrelevant sensory activity. This seems reasonable, since it is impossible

[30] See Reference 5 at the end of this chapter for a general formulation. Also, Cronbach and Gleser, in *Psychological Tests and Personnel Decisions* (Urbana, University of Illinois Press, 1957), discuss such problems in connection with psychological applications.

[31] A summary of much of this work is given by Swets, J. A., W. P. Tanner, Jr., and T. G. Birdsall, "Decision processes in perception." *Psychol. Rev.* **68**, 301–340, 1961.

to eliminate all sources of irrelevant stimulation arising from outside the organism. Moreover, the effects that external, irrelevant stimulation may have on such psychological processes as detection, recognition, discrimination, and concept formation are of considerable interest. Since the important information received by human beings in their natural habitat is rarely free from such irrelevant stimulation, its effects are proper subject matter for psychological study. Even when irrelevant stimulation from outside the organism is virtually eliminated, the effects of specific stimuli are always superimposed on the spontaneous background of activity that characterizes the central nervous system itself.

It is convenient to think of background activity, whether it comes from inside or outside the organism, as random and to refer to it as "noise." When the psychologist presents "supraliminal" stimuli to his experimental subjects, responses sometimes indicate that the stimuli were not registered at all or that they have been distorted in some way. It appears that the stimuli have been lost or changed in much the same way that words sometimes become lost or garbled by noise when transmitted by radio or telephone. It is this sort of analogy that has led to the application of the term "noise" to human perception.

The communication engineer has found it extremely useful to conceive of noise as a random process. Similarly, the psychologist finds that even under laboratory conditions many forms of perceptual variation and distortion are unpredictable from moment to moment, and it is convenient to attribute this unpredictability to "random noise" in the perceptual system.

Thus, when a subject is attempting to detect a signal (tone, or light patch), the task always can be thought of as one of distinguishing signal plus noise (*SN*) from noise alone (*N*). During a specified observation period, either noise alone is present or else both signal and noise occur. The subject's task is to decide which of these is correct.

*Application of the signal-detection theory model. Assume that the psychologically significant characteristic (e.g., loudness, brightness) differentiating signal plus noise from noise alone can be represented by a single sensory continuum.[32] Due to the random character of the noise, the value on the sensory continuum representing the effect of noise alone varies from moment to moment. Therefore, there must be some probability that the sensory process corresponding to noise only will lie within a specified interval on the continuum at a given moment. Furthermore, since a background of noise is always combined with the signal, the

[32] As Swets, Tanner, and Birdsall (*op. cit.*) state, the restriction to one dimension is unnecessary.

sensory process corresponding to signal plus noise must also exhibit random variability. The DF of the sensory process resulting from noise alone will be denoted $f(X \mid N)$ and that of signal plus noise by $f(X \mid SN)$. The random variable, X, represents the value of the sensory continuum. This model is illustrated graphically in Figure XIII.22, where d is the

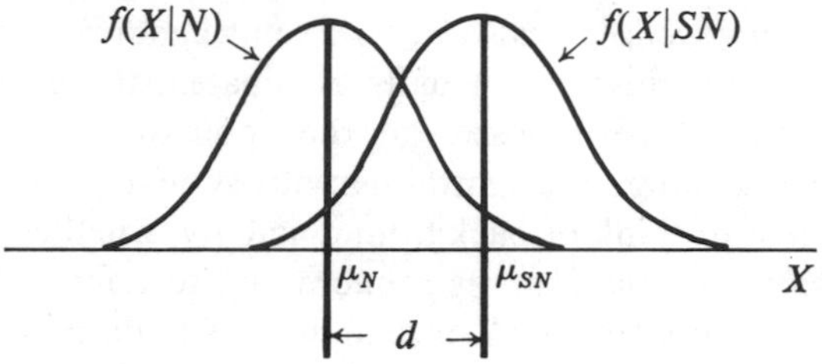

Figure XIII.22

distance between the means of the two DF's. If the "noise-alone" distribution represents the absence of a specifiable external source of stimulation, then d is a measure of the absolute sensitivity of the subject. If d is the distance between the means of two DF's, each of which is associated with a particular signal, then it is a measure of differential sensitivity. The distance d is usually measured using the standard deviation of the noise distribution as a unit;

$$d = \frac{\mu_{SN} - \mu_N}{\sigma_N}. \qquad \text{[XIII.8]}$$

*SUBJECT'S DECISION-MAKING. Now, suppose that the model applies to a particular subject who functions like a well-behaved statistician. For a given observation period, how would he decide whether to respond "yes" (signal present) or "no" (noise only)? The only datum at the subject's disposal is a value on the sensory continuum, $X = x$. The question is then whether x was generated by the process with DF $f(X \mid N)$ or the process with DF $f(X \mid SN)$. The proper statistical answer is that the subject should respond "yes" if

$$L(x) = \frac{f(x \mid SN)}{f(x \mid N)} > \frac{\mathbf{P}(N)}{\mathbf{P}(SN)}, \qquad \text{[XIII.9]}$$

where $\mathbf{P}(N)$ is the probability of noise only and $\mathbf{P}(SN)$ is the probability of signal plus noise. He should respond "no" if $L(x) \leq \mathbf{P}(N)/\mathbf{P}(SN)$. The rationale for this result is based on Bayes's theorem in exactly the same way as Form II of the decision rule of Section *XIII.11.2.

If the subject follows this procedure, then the expected proportion of correct responses,

$$C = \mathbf{P}(N)\mathbf{P}\{[L(X) \leq \mathbf{P}(N)/\mathbf{P}(SN)] \mid N\} + \mathbf{P}(SN)\mathbf{P}\{[L(X) > \mathbf{P}(N)/\mathbf{P}(SN)] \mid SN\},$$

will be as large as possible.

Of course, it is asking too much to expect all subjects to perform as optimum statisticians. It is probably more reasonable to assume that while all subjects utilize the likelihood ratio, many of them base their decisions on criteria other than the optimum one, $\mathbf{P}(N)/\mathbf{P}(SN)$. Furthermore, it seems plausible to expect that not all subjects will adopt the same criterion in a given situation. With this in mind, the decision rule for a subject can be formulated in the following way: "If the sensory process is x, respond 'yes' if

$$L(x) = \frac{f(x \mid SN)}{f(x \mid N)} > \beta. \qquad \text{[XIII.10]}$$

Otherwise, respond 'no.'" In this formulation, β may or may not be equal to the optimum value, $\mathbf{P}(N)/\mathbf{P}(SN)$. Furthermore, even for a well-controlled experimental situation, β can be expected to differ from one subject to another.

This does not imply that subjects make a conscious calculation of $L(x)$ and compare it with β. It is only intended that this formulation describe their decision-making *behavior*.

Notice that β is a kind of "cautiousness" parameter. The subject who operates with a large value of β is reluctant to respond "yes" unless he is quite certain that the signal was present. On the other hand, if β is small, this indicates less caution on the part of the subject and a willingness to respond "yes" even when it is quite possible that the sensory process arose as a result of noise only. For some subjects, β may be near $\mathbf{P}(N)/\mathbf{P}(SN)$, so that their performance is near the optimum of statistical decision theory.[33] For others, β may be very different from the optimum value.

*RECEIVER OPERATING CHARACTERISTIC. If the value of β were known for a given subject, then we could set

$$L(x_\beta) = \frac{f(x_\beta \mid SN)}{f(x_\beta \mid N)} = \beta$$

and solve for x_β in a manner analogous to that followed in Section *XIII.11.2 to define Form III of the classification rule. Then, the decision rule for

[33] One wonders if this would be true of the subject (described in Section *IX.8.5) whose subjective probability estimates seem to conform well to the rules of the mathematical theory of probability.

the subject would be described as "Respond 'yes' whenever $X > x_\beta$ and 'no' whenever $X \le x_\beta$." This rule is equivalent to the one stated in terms of $L(X)$, since x_β has been defined in such a way that $X > x_\beta$ if and only if $L(X) > \beta$.

If a subject behaves as an optimum statistician, then his value of β will equal $\mathbf{P}(N)/\mathbf{P}(SN)$. If $\mathbf{P}(SN)$ is changed, then β will change accordingly. However, even if β is not optimal, it seems likely that if $\mathbf{P}(SN)$ is near 1 the subject will be more inclined to respond "yes" than "no" if he has doubts about whether or not the signal is present on a given trial. If this were true, it would mean that his value of β became small when $\mathbf{P}(SN)$ was large. Thus, even if $\beta \neq \mathbf{P}(N)/\mathbf{P}(SN)$, it probably changes as a function of the value of $\mathbf{P}(SN)$. If β changes, then x_β must change, too, since it is determined by β. Furthermore, the *hit rate*,

$$\mathbf{P}(\text{“yes”} \mid SN) = \mathbf{P}[L(X) > \beta \mid SN] = \mathbf{P}(X > x_\beta \mid SN),$$

and the *false alarm rate*,

$$\mathbf{P}(\text{“yes”} \mid N) = \mathbf{P}[L(X) > \beta \mid N] = \mathbf{P}(X > x_\beta \mid N)$$

both depend on β. Consequently, according to the theory, these two probabilities vary with changes in $\mathbf{P}(SN)$.

Now, if hit rate is plotted against false alarm rate for several values of $\mathbf{P}(SN)$, this amounts to plotting the operating characteristic of a statistical test in which the hypotheses are

H: Noise only (N)

A: Signal plus noise (SN),

and the decision rule is "Reject H if $X > x_\beta$; otherwise accept H." Then, if the theory is correct, varying $\mathbf{P}(SN)$ experimentally should produce shifts in the plot of hit rate against false alarm rate *that follow the theoretical operating characteristic.*

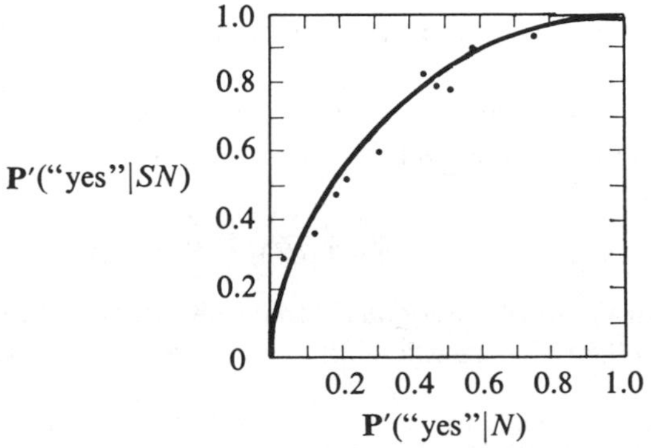

Figure XIII.23

By collecting data from a subject for each of several values of **P**(SN), an *empirical estimate* of the operating characteristic can be obtained. To do this, the experimenter first chooses a value of **P**(SN). Then, the proportion of the signal-present trials on which the subject responds "yes" is an estimate of **P**($X > x_\beta \mid SN$). Similarly, the proportion of noise-only trials on which the subject responds "yes" is an estimate of **P**($X > x_\beta \mid N$). By repeating this procedure for each of several values of **P**(SN), an empirical plot of the operating characteristic can be obtained. The dots in Figure XIII.23 represent such data points. The solid curve is a theoretical operating characteristic that was fitted to these data by Tanner, Swets, and Green.[34]

In this study, the subject's task was to press one button whenever he believed he had heard a tone burst ("yes") and a second button when he believed the tone burst had been absent ("no") during an observation period. A hiss ("white noise") was present throughout the experiment. Each dot in Figure XIII.23 represents the plot of an empirical estimate of **P**("yes" | SN) against an estimate of **P**("yes" | N) based on 300 observations. The single subject provided two estimates of each of these probabilities at each of 5 values of **P**(SN) (0.1, 0.3, 0.5, 0.7, 0.9). For example, the two data points nearest the upper right-hand corner were both obtained for **P**(SN) = 0.9. Thus, there are 10 data points in all.

In signal-detection theory, a curve like the one in Figure XIII.23 is called the *receiver operating characteristic* (ROC). Numerous studies have indicated that empirical points like those of the figure follow a theoretical ROC curve fairly well.

Though there are several ways of fitting a theoretical ROC curve, the method described here requires estimates of x_β and d, where $d = (\mu_{SN} - \mu_N)/\sigma_N$. In all of the following calculations, it is assumed that the noise and the signal-plus-noise DF's are normal and that they have the same variance. Though neither assumption is necessary, they simplify matters considerably. Furthermore, a number of studies suggest that the normal DF assumption is reasonable, and the equal variance assumption seems to work quite well for some kinds of data (e.g., detection of pure tones).

We will begin by arbitrarily fixing the mean of the noise DF at $\mu_N = 0$. Any other value would serve equally well, but the use of zero simplifies the calculations. Next, the standard deviation of the two DF's will be fixed at 1. This is an arbitrary choice, too, but since σ will be used as the unit for measuring distance along the sensory continuum, 1 is the most

[34] "Some general properties of the hearing mechanism." Electronic Defense Group, Univ. of Michigan, *Tech. Rept.* 30, 1956. Figure XIII.23 is based on this report. These data have been used with the kind permission of Wilson P. Tanner, Jr., John A. Swets, and David M. Green.

reasonable choice. The only other item required for an estimate of x_β is an empirical estimate of **P**("yes" | N). Theoretically, this probability is based on the relation

$$\begin{aligned}\mathbf{P}(\text{"yes"} \mid N) &= \mathbf{P}(X > x_\beta \mid N)\\ &= \mathbf{P}\left(Z > \frac{x_\beta - \mu_N}{\sigma}\right) = \mathbf{P}\left(Z > \frac{x_\beta - 0}{1}\right)\\ &= \mathbf{P}(Z > x_\beta).\end{aligned}$$

The second point from the upper right-hand corner of Figure XIII.23 will be used to estimate x_β. Since this point is at **P**′("yes" | N) = 0.59,

$$\begin{aligned}\mathbf{P}'(\text{"yes"} \mid N) &= \mathbf{P}(X > x'_\beta \mid N) = 0.59\\ &= \mathbf{P}(Z > x'_\beta) = 0.59.\end{aligned}$$

From the table of Appendix V, $\mathbf{P}(Z > -0.23) = 0.59$, so that $x'_\beta = -0.23$ is the estimate of x_β.

With this estimate in hand and with an empirical estimate of **P**("yes" | SN) it is possible to obtain an estimate of d. Since d is the difference between μ_{SN} and μ_N measured with $\sigma_N = 1$ as the unit,

$$d = \frac{\mu_{SN} - \mu_N}{\sigma_N} = \frac{\mu_{SN} - 0}{1} = \mu_{SN}.$$

Then, the relation

$$\begin{aligned}\mathbf{P}(\text{"yes"} \mid SN) &= \mathbf{P}(X > x_\beta \mid SN)\\ &= \mathbf{P}\left(Z > z_\beta = \frac{x_\beta - \mu_{SN}}{\sigma}\right) = \mathbf{P}\left(Z > z_\beta = \frac{x_\beta - \mu_{SN}}{1}\right)\\ &= \mathbf{P}(Z > z_\beta = x_\beta - \mu_{SN})\end{aligned}$$

can be used to solve for $\mu_{SN} = d$.

The empirical estimate of **P**("yes" | SN) (for the second point from the upper right-hand corner of Figure XIII.23) is 0.88. Using this estimate and the estimate $x'_\beta = -0.23$ obtained above,

$$\begin{aligned}\mathbf{P}'(\text{"yes"} \mid SN) &= \mathbf{P}(Z > z_\beta = x'_\beta - \mu'_{SN})\\ 0.88 &= \mathbf{P}(Z > z_\beta = -0.23 - \mu'_{SN}).\end{aligned}$$

From Appendix V, $\mathbf{P}(Z > z_\beta) = 0.88$ for $z_\beta = -1.18$. Therefore,

$$\begin{aligned}z_\beta &= x'_\beta - \mu'_{SN}\\ -1.18 &= -0.23 - \mu'_{SN}\\ \mu'_{SN} &= 0.95,\end{aligned}$$

so that the estimate of d is 0.95. This estimate differs little from the value of 0.92 obtained by Tanner, Swets, and Green[35] using all of the data points of Figure XIII.23.

[35] *Op. cit.*

Using the procedure just illustrated, such an estimate of d can be obtained for each data point. Then, the mean of these can be used as a final estimate of the difference between the means of the noise only and the signal-plus-noise distributions. This figure is an estimate of the perceptual sensitivity of the subject, large values being associated with greater sensitivity. The distance d can also be thought of as a scale value representing the psychological distance separating the stimulus conditions SN and N.

Once a final estimate of d has been obtained, the theoretical ROC curve can be generated. Using the estimate of d reported by Tanner, Swets, and Green,[36] this will be illustrated using Figure XIII.24 as a guide. For

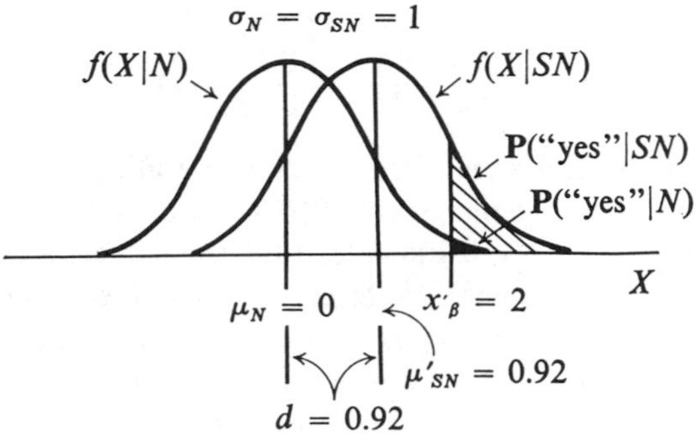

Figure XIII.24

example, the theoretical value of **P**("yes" | N) for $x'_\beta = 2$ is represented by the darkened area in Figure XIII.24. This probability is

$$\begin{aligned}\mathbf{P}'(\text{“yes”} \mid N) &= \mathbf{P}(X > x'_\beta \mid N)\\ &= \mathbf{P}\left(Z > \frac{x'_\beta - \mu_N}{\sigma}\right) = \mathbf{P}\left(Z > \frac{2-0}{1}\right)\\ &= \mathbf{P}(Z > 2)\\ &= 0.023.\end{aligned}$$

For the same value, $x'_\beta = 2$,

$$\begin{aligned}\mathbf{P}'(\text{“yes”} \mid SN) &= \mathbf{P}(X > x'_\beta \mid SN)\\ &= \mathbf{P}\left(Z > \frac{x'_\beta - \mu_{SN}}{\sigma}\right) = \mathbf{P}\left(Z > \frac{2-0.92}{1}\right)\\ &= \mathbf{P}(Z > +1.08)\\ &= 0.140.\end{aligned}$$

This probability is represented by the crosshatched area in Figure XIII.24. By repeating these two calculations for a few well-chosen criterion values, x'_β, the theoretical ROC curve of Figure XIII.23 was constructed.

[36] *Op. cit.*

It is also possible to estimate β for each data point on the graph of Figure XIII.23. This can be done by substituting the estimate of x_β for a given data point in the relation

$$\frac{f(x_\beta \mid SN)}{f(x_\beta \mid N)} = \beta.$$

The height of $f(x'_\beta \mid SN)$ can be found by entering Appendix VI with the Z-value corresponding to x'_β. Thus, for the second data point from the right in Figure XIII.23, the height corresponding to $(x'_\beta - \mu'_{SN})/\sigma = (-0.23 - 0.95)/1 = -1.18$ is 0.199. Similarly, the height corresponding to $(x'_\beta - \mu_N)/\sigma = (-0.23 - 0)/1 = -0.23$ is 0.388. Then, the estimate of β is

$$\beta' = \frac{f(x'_\beta \mid SN)}{f(x'_\beta \mid N)} = \frac{0.199}{0.388} = 0.51.$$

This estimate of β suggests that the subject is operating some distance from the statistical optimum value, $\mathbf{P}(N)/\mathbf{P}(SN) = 0.1/0.9$. In general, if β is larger than $\mathbf{P}(N)/\mathbf{P}(SN)$, it indicates that the subject is careful to avoid responding "yes" unless he is quite certain that the signal was present. When β is less than $\mathbf{P}(N)/\mathbf{P}(SN)$, it indicates that he often responds "yes" even when he is in considerable doubt about the presence of the signal.

When β is larger than $\mathbf{P}(N)/\mathbf{P}(SN)$, the subject's reluctance to respond "yes" is reducing the proportion of his responses that are correct. (Remember, the expected proportion of correct responses is largest when $\beta = \mathbf{P}(N)/\mathbf{P}(SN)$.) On the other hand, when $\beta < \mathbf{P}(N)/\mathbf{P}(SN)$, the subject has increased his hit rate at the expense of increasing the false-alarm rate beyond the optimum value.

Notice that the sensitivity of the subject (d) is measured independently of his propensity to respond "yes" (β). In many other psychophysical methods, it is impossible to separate response tendencies and sensitivity in this way, so that measures of "sensitivity" may be contaminated by the degree of cautiousness with which the subject makes his judgments. Moreover, the traditional idea of a threshold is entirely lacking in signal-detection theory. In classical psychophysics, it is often assumed that if a stimulus magnitude exceeds some critical value, then the subject can detect the stimulus and respond accordingly. Such an idea is not used in signal-detection theory, and Swets[37] has raised serious questions about the appropriateness of the classical threshold concept.

Signal-detection theory can be formulated so that the effects of differential costs and payoffs on the subject's detection behavior are included. For example, the effects of paying a subject for his correct responses and charging him for his errors can be investigated both theoretically and

[37] "Is there a sensory threshold?" *Science* **134**, 168–177, 1961.

empirically. The theory becomes only a little more complicated with this elaboration, and there have been several investigations of the effects of differential payoffs.[38] However, they will not be discussed here.

XIII.12
PROBLEMS ON CLASSIFICATION PROCEDURES

1. Solve the classification problem summarized in Table XIII.7 of Section *XIII.11.2 using the methods of Section XIII.11.1. Use **P**(S) = 1/3 and **P**(N) = 2/3.
   a. State your explicit decision rule in terms of a likelihood ratio.
   b. State your explicit decision rule in terms of values of the PAT.
   c. What is your estimate of the expected proportion of correct predictions?
   d. What is the expected proportion of incorrect predictions?
   e. Discuss briefly the practical merits of the PAT as a diagnostic procedure for this population.
   f. Compare the results of this procedure with those of the procedure developed in Section *XIII.11.2.
2. Is there any connection between the meaning of the term "likelihood" when it is used in connection with likelihood ratios and its meaning when it is used in connection with maximum-likelihood estimators? If so, what is it? If not, why not?

*3. Suppose that **P**(S) = **P**(N) = 0.5. Solve the classification problem of Section *XIII.11.2 using the data and methods described in that section.
   a. State your explicit classification rule in at least two equivalent forms.
   b. What is your estimate of the expected proportion of wrong decisions?
   c. Plot the operating characteristic of this classification procedure. Compare it with the one described in Section *XIII.11.2.
   d. Discuss briefly the effects of the change in the base rates on the practical merits of the PAT. Refer to the example of Section *XIII.11.2, where **P**(S) = 1/3 and **P**(N) = 2/3.

*4. For a given subject in a signal-detection experiment, the empirical estimate of **P**("yes" | N) is 0.3 and the empirical estimate of **P**("yes" | SN) is 0.8. Assume that $\mu_N = 0$, $\sigma_N = \sigma_{SN} = 1$, and that $f(X \mid N)$ and $f(X \mid SN)$ are normal DF's.
   a. Estimate x_β for this subject.
   b. Estimate d for this subject.
   c. Estimate β for this subject.
   d. Plot an estimate of the ROC curve for this subject.
   e. Is this subject more or less sensitive than the one on whom the plot of Figure XIII.23 is based? Assume the same detection task for both.
   f. What is the effect of increasing sensitivity on the ROC curve (assuming other factors are unchanged)?
   g. Interpret each of the parameters x_β, d, and β in a concise statement.

[38] Swets, Tanner, and Birdsall, *op. cit.*

*5. Suppose you are told that for one subject, $\mu_N = x_\beta = 0$, $\beta = 0.61$, and $d = 1$. Assume $f(X \mid N)$ and $f(X \mid SN)$ are normal and that $\sigma_N = \sigma_{SN} = 1$.
   a. Construct a diagram of the theoretical interpretation of this situation in terms of signal-detection theory.
   b. Calculate **P**("yes" | N) and **P**("no" | N) for this subject.
   c. If **P**(N) = 0.75 and **P**(SN) = 0.25, what is the probability of a correct response for this subject?
   d. Are the figures cited for x_β, β, and d consistent?

*6. Suppose that for a given subject $x_\beta = 0.5$, $d = 1.5$, $\mu_N = 0$, and $\beta = 0.69$. Assume that $f(X \mid N)$ and $f(X \mid SN)$ are normal DF's and that $\sigma_N = \sigma_{SN} = 1$.
   a. What is μ_{SN}?
   b. Compare this subject with the one described in Problem *4. Be specific, but interpret the differences in psychological terms.
   c. Suppose that $x_\beta = 1$ instead of 0.5. What other parameters describing the subject must change when x_β is changed?

APPENDIX XIII.1

Proof that the classification rule of Section XIII.11.1 maximizes the estimated expected proportion of correct diagnoses for the example

The demonstration will be complete if it can be shown that (1) substituting an F for a B or (2) substituting a B for an F in the last row of Table XIII.6 cannot increase the estimated expected proportion of correct diagnoses.

First, part (1) will be dealt with. Suppose that x is a value of X to which the classification rule assigns F. Then,

$$L'(X = x) = \frac{\mathbf{P}'(X = x \mid F)}{\mathbf{P}'(X = x \mid B)} > \frac{\mathbf{P}'(B)}{\mathbf{P}'(F)}.$$

It follows that

$$\frac{\mathbf{P}'(F)\mathbf{P}'(X = x \mid F)}{\mathbf{P}'(B)\mathbf{P}'(X = x \mid B)} > 1,$$

and $\mathbf{P}'(F)\mathbf{P}'(X = x \mid F) > \mathbf{P}'(B)\mathbf{P}'(X = x \mid B)$. If the F assigned to x were replaced by a B, then the term $\mathbf{P}'(F)\mathbf{P}'(X = x \mid F)$ would be subtracted from C' and the term $\mathbf{P}'(B)\mathbf{P}'(X = x \mid B)$ would be added. Since the latter is smaller than the former, the resulting estimate of the expected proportion of correct classifications would be reduced.

On the other hand, suppose that x is a value of X to which the classification rule assigns a B. Then,

$$L'(X = x) = \frac{\mathbf{P}'(X = x \mid F)}{\mathbf{P}'(X = x \mid B)} \leq \frac{\mathbf{P}'(B)}{\mathbf{P}'(F)},$$

and

$$\frac{\mathbf{P}'(F)\mathbf{P}'(X = x \mid F)}{\mathbf{P}'(B)\mathbf{P}'(X = x \mid B)} \leq 1,$$

so that $\mathbf{P}'(F)\mathbf{P}'(X = x \mid F) \leq \mathbf{P}'(B)\mathbf{P}'(X = x \mid B)$. Now, if the B assigned to x is replaced by an F, then $\mathbf{P}'(B)\mathbf{P}'(X = x \mid B)$ must be subtracted from C', and $\mathbf{P}'(F)\mathbf{P}'(X = x \mid F)$ must be added. Since the latter cannot exceed the former, the estimate of the expected proportion of correct classifications cannot increase. This completes the proof of part (2).

Notice that interchanging an F and a B amounts to performing both part (1) and part (2), so that this must decrease the estimate of the expected proportion correct. Furthermore, changing any number of B's or F's is simply repeating (1) or (2) several times, so that this cannot increase the estimated expected proportion correct. Consequently, the proof is complete.

APPENDIX XIII.2

Suppose S_1^2 is the variance of a random sample of size n_1 drawn from a population that has variance σ^2, and S_2^2 is the variance of an independent random sample of size n_2 drawn from a second population that also has variance σ^2. Then,

$$S_K^2 = \frac{(n_1 - 1)S_1^2 + (n_2 - 1)S_2^2}{n_1 + n_2 - 2}$$

is an unbiased estimator for σ^2.

The proposition is correct if $E(S_K^2) = \sigma^2$. Beginning with the expected value of S_K^2,

$$\begin{aligned} E(S_K^2) &= E\left[\frac{(n_1 - 1)S_1^2 + (n_2 - 1)S_2^2}{n_1 + n_2 - 2}\right] \\ &= E\left[\frac{(n_1 - 1)S_1^2}{n_1 + n_2 - 2} + \frac{(n_2 - 1)S_2^2}{n_1 + n_2 - 2}\right] \\ &= E\left[\frac{(n_1 - 1)S_1^2}{n_1 + n_2 - 2}\right] + E\left[\frac{(n_2 - 1)S_2^2}{n_1 + n_2 - 2}\right] \\ &= \frac{n_1 - 1}{n_1 + n_2 - 2} E(S_1^2) + \frac{n_2 - 1}{n_1 + n_2 - 2} E(S_2^2). \end{aligned}$$

Since S_1^2 is an unbiased estimator for σ^2 and S_2^2 is an unbiased estimator for σ^2, the last line can be written as

$$\begin{aligned} E(S_K^2) &= \frac{n_1 - 1}{n_1 + n_2 - 2}\sigma^2 + \frac{n_2 - 1}{n_1 + n_2 - 2}\sigma^2 \\ &= \sigma^2\left(\frac{n_1 - 1 + n_2 - 1}{n_1 + n_2 - 2}\right) \\ &= \sigma^2. \end{aligned}$$

This completes the proof.

APPENDIX XIII.3

In this appendix, *the equation*

$$\frac{f'(x'_C \mid N)}{f'(x'_C \mid S)} = \frac{\mathbf{P}(S)}{\mathbf{P}(N)}$$

is solved for x'_C *under the assumption that* $f'(x'_C \mid S)$ *and* $f'(x'_C \mid N)$ *are normal DF's with estimated means* $\bar{X}_S$ *and* $\bar{X}_N$ *and a common variance estimate,* $S_K{}^2$.

To begin with,

$$\frac{f'(x'_C \mid N)}{f'(x'_C \mid S)} = \frac{\dfrac{1}{S_K\sqrt{(2\pi)}}\, e^{-1/(2S_K{}^2)(x'_C - \bar{X}_N)^2}}{\dfrac{1}{S_K\sqrt{(2\pi)}}\, e^{-1/(2S_K{}^2)(x'_C - \bar{X}_S)^2}} = \frac{\mathbf{P}(S)}{\mathbf{P}(N)}$$

$$= \frac{e^{-1/(2S_K{}^2)(x'_C - \bar{X}_N)^2}}{e^{-1/(2S_K{}^2)(x'_C - \bar{X}_S)^2}} = \frac{\mathbf{P}(S)}{\mathbf{P}(N)}.$$

Taking the logarithm to the base e of both sides,

$$-\frac{1}{2S_K{}^2}(x'_C - \bar{X}_N)^2 + \frac{1}{2S_K{}^2}(x'_C - \bar{X}_S)^2 = \log_e\left(\frac{\mathbf{P}(S)}{\mathbf{P}(N)}\right).$$

Multiplying both sides of the equation by $2S_K{}^2$ and expanding the two squares,

$$-x'_C{}^2 + 2\bar{X}_N x'_C - \bar{X}_N{}^2 + x'_C{}^2 - 2\bar{X}_S x'_C + \bar{X}_S{}^2 = 2S_K{}^2 \log_e\left(\frac{\mathbf{P}(S)}{\mathbf{P}(N)}\right)$$

$$2x'_C(\bar{X}_N - \bar{X}_S) + \bar{X}_S{}^2 - \bar{X}_N{}^2 = 2S_K{}^2 \log_e\left(\frac{\mathbf{P}(S)}{\mathbf{P}(N)}\right)$$

$$x'_C = \frac{2S_K{}^2 \log_e\left(\dfrac{\mathbf{P}(S)}{\mathbf{P}(N)}\right) + \bar{X}_N{}^2 - \bar{X}_S{}^2}{2(\bar{X}_N - \bar{X}_S)}$$

$$x'_C = \frac{2S_K{}^2 \log_e\left(\dfrac{\mathbf{P}(S)}{\mathbf{P}(N)}\right) + (\bar{X}_N - \bar{X}_S)(\bar{X}_N + \bar{X}_S)}{2(\bar{X}_N - \bar{X}_S)}$$

$$x'_C = \frac{S_K{}^2 \log_e\left(\dfrac{\mathbf{P}(S)}{\mathbf{P}(N)}\right)}{\bar{X}_N - \bar{X}_S} + \frac{\bar{X}_N + \bar{X}_S}{2}.$$

Instead of stating the solution in terms of natural logarithms, common logarithms can be used. Then,

$$x'_C = \frac{S_K{}^2(2.3026)\log_{10}\left(\dfrac{\mathbf{P}(S)}{\mathbf{P}(N)}\right)}{\bar{X}_N - \bar{X}_S} + \frac{\bar{X}_N + \bar{X}_S}{2}.$$

This is the form of the solution employed in Section *XIII.11.2.

SUGGESTED READING

1. Wallis, W. A., and H. V. Roberts, *Statistics: A New Approach.* New York, Free Press of Glencoe, 1957, Chap. 12.
This is a well-organized, clear introduction to hypothesis testing. It includes an extended example that is relevant to clinical psychology. The discussion of error curves is excellent.

2. Chernoff, H., and L. E. Moses, *Elementary Decision Theory.* New York, John Wiley, 1959, Chap. 9.
An excellent introduction to orthodox methods of hypothesis testing presented within the framework of modern decision theory. Although mathematical notation is used freely, there are few mathematical proofs that require special skills beyond elementary algebra. For a broad view of modern statistics (i.e., statistical decision theory), the entire book is excellent. It provides a comprehensive picture of the field with minimal demands on mathematical skill.

3. Mood, A. M., *Introduction to the Theory of Statistics.* New York, McGraw-Hill, 1950, Chap. 12.
This provides an elementary mathematical introduction to standard methods of hypothesis testing.

4. Maxwell, A. E., *Analyzing Qualitative Data.* New York, John Wiley, 1961, Chaps. 10 and 11.
This contains an elementary discussion of the application of the method of Section XIII.11.1 when classification is based on more than one observation variable.

5. Rao, C. R., *Advanced Statistical Methods in Biometric Research.* New York, John Wiley, 1952, pp. 286–290.
A mathematically sophisticated discussion of the methods described in Section XIII.11.1. It describes generalizations of these procedures to more than one observation variable and more than two subpopulations and it includes differential costs and payoffs in the formulation.

SUGGESTED READINGS

Appendix I

VALUES OF *n*! AND log *n*!

The values of $n!$ are given to five significant figures; for $n \geq 9$ these values must be multiplied by a power of ten. This power is the raised number to the right of the five significant figures. For example, $15! \cong 13,077 \times 10^8$.

n	$n!$	$\log n!$	n	$n!$	$\log n!$	n	$n!$	$\log n!$
1	1	.00000	26	$40,329^{22}$	26.60562	51	$15,511^{62}$	66.19065
2	2	.30103	27	$10,889^{24}$	28.03698	52	$80,658^{63}$	67.90665
3	6	.77815	28	$30,489^{25}$	29.48414	53	$42,749^{65}$	69.63092
4	24	1.38021	29	$88,418^{26}$	30.94654	54	$23,084^{67}$	71.36332
5	120	2.07918	30	$26,525^{28}$	32.42366	55	$12,696^{69}$	73.10368
6	720	2.85733	31	$82,228^{29}$	33.91502	56	$71,100^{70}$	74.85187
7	5,040	3.70243	32	$26,313^{31}$	35.42017	57	$40,527^{72}$	76.60774
8	40,320	4.60552	33	$86,833^{32}$	36.93869	58	$23,506^{74}$	78.37117
9	$36,288^{1}$	5.55976	34	$29,523^{34}$	38.47016	59	$13,868^{76}$	80.14202
10	$36,288^{2}$	6.55976	35	$10,333^{36}$	40.01423	60	$83,210^{77}$	81.92017
11	$39,917^{3}$	7.60116	36	$37,199^{37}$	41.57054	61	$50,758^{79}$	83.70550
12	$47,900^{4}$	8.68034	37	$13,764^{39}$	43.13874	62	$31,470^{81}$	85.49790
13	$62,270^{5}$	9.79428	38	$52,302^{40}$	44.71852	63	$19,826^{83}$	87.29724
14	$87,178^{6}$	10.94041	39	$20,398^{42}$	46.30959	64	$12,689^{85}$	89.10342
15	$13,077^{8}$	12.11650	40	$81,592^{43}$	47.91165	65	$82,477^{86}$	90.91633
16	$20,923^{9}$	13.32062	41	$33,453^{45}$	49.52443	66	$54,434^{88}$	92.73587
17	$35,569^{10}$	14.55107	42	$14,050^{47}$	51.14768	67	$36,471^{90}$	94.56195
18	$64,024^{11}$	15.80634	43	$60,415^{48}$	52.78115	68	$24,800^{92}$	96.39446
19	$12,165^{13}$	17.08509	44	$26,583^{50}$	54.42460	69	$17,112^{94}$	98.23331
20	$24,329^{14}$	18.38612	45	$11,962^{52}$	56.07781	70	$11,979^{96}$	100.07841
21	$51,091^{15}$	19.70834	46	$55,026^{53}$	57.74057	71	$85,048^{97}$	101.92966
22	$11,240^{17}$	21.05077	47	$25,862^{55}$	59.41267	72	$61,234^{99}$	103.78700
23	$25,852^{18}$	22.41249	48	$12,414^{57}$	61.09391	73	$44,701^{101}$	105.65032
24	$62,045^{19}$	23.79271	49	$60,828^{58}$	62.78410	74	$33,079^{103}$	107.51955
25	$15,511^{21}$	25.19065	50	$30,414^{60}$	64.48307	75	$24,809^{105}$	109.39461

Reprinted by permission of the publisher, Addison-Wesley Publishing Co., Inc., Reading, Mass., from F. Mosteller, R. E. K. Rourke, and G. B. Thomas, Jr., *Probability and Statistics.* Reading, Mass., Addison-Wesley, 1961.

Appendix II

THE BINOMIAL DISTRIBUTION

								P							
n	X	.01	.05	.10	.20	.30	.40	.50	.60	.70	.80	.90	.95	.99	X
2	0	980	902	810	640	490	360	250	160	090	040	010	002	0+	0
	1	020	095	180	320	420	480	500	480	420	320	180	095	020	1
	2	0+	002	010	040	090	160	250	360	490	640	810	902	980	2
3	0	970	857	729	512	343	216	125	064	027	008	001	0+	0+	0
	1	029	135	243	384	441	432	375	288	189	096	027	007	0+	1
	2	0+	007	027	096	189	288	375	432	441	384	243	135	029	2
	3	0+	0+	001	008	027	064	125	216	343	512	729	857	970	3
4	0	961	815	656	410	240	130	062	026	008	002	0+	0+	0+	0
	1	039	171	292	410	412	346	250	154	076	026	004	0+	0+	1
	2	001	014	049	154	265	346	375	346	265	154	049	014	001	2
	3	0+	0+	004	026	076	154	250	346	412	410	292	171	039	3
	4	0+	0+	0+	002	008	026	062	130	240	410	656	815	961	4
5	0	951	774	590	328	168	078	031	010	002	0+	0+	0+	0+	0
	1	048	204	328	410	360	259	156	077	028	006	0+	0+	0+	1
	2	001	021	073	205	309	346	312	230	132	051	008	001	0+	2
	3	0+	001	008	051	132	230	312	346	309	205	073	021	001	3
	4	0+	0+	0+	006	028	077	156	259	360	410	328	204	048	4
	5	0+	0+	0+	0+	002	010	031	078	168	328	590	774	951	5
6	0	941	735	531	262	118	047	016	004	001	0+	0+	0+	0+	0
	1	057	232	354	393	303	187	094	037	010	002	0+	0+	0+	1
	2	001	031	098	246	324	311	234	138	060	015	001	0+	0+	2
	3	0+	002	015	082	185	276	312	276	185	082	015	002	0+	3
	4	0+	0+	001	015	060	138	234	311	324	246	098	031	001	4
	5	0+	0+	0+	002	010	037	094	187	303	393	354	232	057	5
	6	0+	0+	0+	0+	001	004	016	047	118	262	531	735	941	6
7	0	932	698	478	210	082	028	008	002	0+	0+	0+	0+	0+	0
	1	066	257	372	367	247	131	055	017	004	0+	0+	0+	0+	1
	2	002	041	124	275	318	261	164	077	025	004	0+	0+	0+	2
	3	0+	004	023	115	227	290	273	194	097	029	003	0+	0+	3
	4	0+	0+	003	029	097	194	273	290	227	115	023	004	0+	4
	5	0+	0+	0+	004	025	077	164	261	318	275	124	041	002	5
	6	0+	0+	0+	0+	004	017	055	131	247	367	372	257	066	6
	7	0+	0+	0+	0+	0+	002	008	028	082	210	478	698	932	7
8	0	923	663	430	168	058	017	004	001	0+	0+	0+	0+	0+	0
	1	075	279	383	336	198	090	031	008	001	0+	0+	0+	0+	1
	2	003	051	149	294	296	209	109	041	010	001	0+	0+	0+	2
	3	0+	005	033	147	254	279	219	124	047	009	0+	0+	0+	3
	4	0+	0+	005	046	136	232	273	232	136	046	005	0+	0+	4
	5	0+	0+	0+	009	047	124	219	279	254	147	033	005	0+	5
	6	0+	0+	0+	001	010	041	109	209	296	294	149	051	003	6
	7	0+	0+	0+	0+	001	008	031	090	198	336	383	279	075	7
	8	0+	0+	0+	0+	0+	001	004	017	058	168	430	663	923	8

Appendix II reprinted by permission of the publisher, Addison-Wesley Publishing Co., Inc., Reading, Mass., from F. Mosteller, R. E. K. Rourke, and G. B. Thomas, Jr., *Probability and Statistics.* Reading, Mass., Addison-Wesley, 1961.

Appendix II

THE BINOMIAL DISTRIBUTION (CONTINUED)

n	X	.01	.05	.10	.20	.30	.40	P .50	.60	.70	.80	.90	.95	.99	X
9	0	914	630	387	134	040	010	002	0+	0+	0+	0+	0+	0+	0
	1	083	299	387	302	156	060	018	004	0+	0+	0+	0+	0+	1
	2	003	063	172	302	267	161	070	021	004	0+	0+	0+	0+	2
	3	0+	008	045	176	267	251	164	074	021	003	0+	0+	0+	3
	4	0+	001	007	066	172	251	246	167	074	017	001	0+	0+	4
	5	0+	0+	001	017	074	167	246	251	172	066	007	001	0+	5
	6	0+	0+	0+	003	021	074	164	251	267	176	045	008	0+	6
	7	0+	0+	0+	0+	004	021	070	161	267	302	172	063	003	7
	8	0+	0+	0+	0+	0+	004	018	060	156	302	387	299	083	8
	9	0+	0+	0+	0+	0+	0+	002	010	040	134	387	630	914	9
10	0	904	599	349	107	028	006	001	0+	0+	0+	0+	0+	0+	0
	1	091	315	387	268	121	040	010	002	0+	0+	0+	0+	0+	1
	2	004	075	194	302	233	121	044	011	001	0+	0+	0+	0+	2
	3	0+	010	057	201	267	215	117	042	009	001	0+	0+	0+	3
	4	0+	001	011	088	200	251	205	111	037	006	0+	0+	0+	4
	5	0+	0+	001	026	103	201	246	201	103	026	001	0+	0+	5
	6	0+	0+	0+	006	037	111	205	251	200	088	011	001	0+	6
	7	0+	0+	0+	001	009	042	117	215	267	201	057	010	0+	7
	8	0+	0+	0+	0+	001	011	044	121	233	302	194	075	004	8
	9	0+	0+	0+	0+	0+	002	010	040	121	268	387	315	091	9
	10	0+	0+	0+	0+	0+	0+	001	006	028	107	349	599	904	10
11	0	895	569	314	086	020	004	0+	0+	0+	0+	0+	0+	0+	0
	1	099	329	384	236	093	027	005	001	0+	0+	0+	0+	0+	1
	2	005	087	213	295	200	089	027	005	001	0+	0+	0+	0+	2
	3	0+	014	071	221	257	177	081	023	004	0+	0+	0+	0+	3
	4	0+	001	016	111	220	236	161	070	017	002	0+	0+	0+	4
	5	0+	0+	002	039	132	221	226	147	057	010	0+	0+	0+	5
	6	0+	0+	0+	010	057	147	226	221	132	039	002	0+	0+	6
	7	0+	0+	0+	002	017	070	161	236	220	111	016	001	0+	7
	8	0+	0+	0+	0+	004	023	081	177	257	221	071	014	0+	8
	9	0+	0+	0+	0+	001	005	027	089	200	295	213	087	005	9
	10	0+	0+	0+	0+	0+	001	005	027	093	236	384	329	099	10
	11	0+	0+	0+	0+	0+	0+	0+	004	020	086	314	569	895	11
12	0	886	540	282	069	014	002	0+	0+	0+	0+	0+	0+	0+	0
	1	107	341	377	206	071	017	003	0+	0+	0+	0+	0+	0+	1
	2	006	099	230	283	168	064	016	002	0+	0+	0+	0+	0+	2
	3	0+	017	085	236	240	142	054	012	001	0+	0+	0+	0+	3
	4	0+	002	021	133	231	213	121	042	008	001	0+	0+	0+	4
	5	0+	0+	004	053	158	227	193	101	029	003	0+	0+	0+	5
	6	0+	0+	0+	016	079	177	226	177	079	016	0+	0+	0+	6
	7	0+	0+	0+	003	029	101	193	227	158	053	004	0+	0+	7
	8	0+	0+	0+	001	008	042	121	213	231	133	021	002	0+	8
	9	0+	0+	0+	0+	001	012	054	142	240	236	085	017	0+	9

Appendix II

THE BINOMIAL DISTRIBUTION (CONTINUED)

n	X	.01	.05	.10	.20	.30	.40	.50	.60	.70	.80	.90	.95	.99	X
								P							
12	10	0+	0+	0+	0+	0+	002	016	064	168	283	230	099	006	10
	11	0+	0+	0+	0+	0+	0+	003	017	071	206	377	341	107	11
	12	0+	0+	0+	0+	0+	0+	0+	002	014	069	282	540	886	12
13	0	878	513	254	055	010	001	0+	0+	0+	0+	0+	0+	0+	0
	1	115	351	367	179	054	011	002	0+	0+	0+	0+	0+	0+	1
	2	007	111	245	268	139	045	010	001	0+	0+	0+	0+	0+	2
	3	0+	021	100	246	218	111	035	006	001	0+	0+	0+	0+	3
	4	0+	003	028	154	234	184	087	024	003	0+	0+	0+	0+	4
	5	0+	0+	006	069	180	221	157	066	014	001	0+	0+	0+	5
	6	0+	0+	001	023	103	197	209	131	044	006	0+	0+	0+	6
	7	0+	0+	0+	006	044	131	209	197	103	023	001	0+	0+	7
	8	0+	0+	0+	001	014	066	157	221	180	069	006	0+	0+	8
	9	0+	0+	0+	0+	003	024	087	184	234	154	028	003	0+	9
	10	0+	0+	0+	0+	001	006	035	111	218	246	100	021	0+	10
	11	0+	0+	0+	0+	0+	001	010	045	139	268	245	111	007	11
	12	0+	0+	0+	0+	0+	0+	002	011	054	179	367	351	115	12
	13	0+	0+	0+	0+	0+	0+	0+	001	010	055	254	513	878	13
14	0	869	488	229	044	007	001	0+	0+	0+	0+	0+	0+	0+	0
	1	123	359	356	154	041	007	001	0+	0+	0+	0+	0+	0+	1
	2	008	123	257	250	113	032	006	001	0+	0+	0+	0+	0+	2
	3	0+	026	114	250	194	085	022	003	0+	0+	0+	0+	0+	3
	4	0+	004	035	172	229	155	061	014	001	0+	0+	0+	0+	4
	5	0+	0+	008	086	196	207	122	041	007	0+	0+	0+	0+	5
	6	0+	0+	001	032	126	207	183	092	023	002	0+	0+	0+	6
	7	0+	0+	0+	009	062	157	209	157	062	009	0+	0+	0+	7
	8	0+	0+	0+	002	023	092	183	207	126	032	001	0+	0+	8
	9	0+	0+	0+	0+	007	041	122	207	196	086	008	0+	0+	9
	10	0+	0+	0+	0+	001	014	061	155	229	172	035	004	0+	10
	11	0+	0+	0+	0+	0+	003	022	085	194	250	114	026	0+	11
	12	0+	0+	0+	0+	0+	001	006	032	113	250	257	123	008	12
	13	0+	0+	0+	0+	0+	0+	001	007	041	154	356	359	123	13
	14	0+	0+	0+	0+	0+	0+	0+	001	007	044	229	488	869	14
15	0	860	463	206	035	005	0+	0+	0+	0+	0+	0+	0+	0+	0
	1	130	366	343	132	031	005	0+	0+	0+	0+	0+	0+	0+	1
	2	009	135	267	231	092	022	003	0+	0+	0+	0+	0+	0+	2
	3	0+	031	129	250	170	063	014	002	0+	0+	0+	0+	0+	3
	4	0+	005	043	188	219	127	042	007	001	0+	0+	0+	0+	4
	5	0+	001	010	103	206	186	092	024	003	0+	0+	0+	0+	5
	6	0+	0+	002	043	147	207	153	061	012	001	0+	0+	0+	6
	7	0+	0+	0+	014	081	177	196	118	035	003	0+	0+	0+	7
	8	0+	0+	0+	003	035	118	196	177	081	014	0+	0+	0+	8
	9	0+	0+	0+	001	012	061	153	207	147	043	002	0+	0+	9

Appendix II

THE BINOMIAL DISTRIBUTION (CONTINUED)

n	X	.01	.05	.10	.20	.30	.40	.50	.60	.70	.80	.90	.95	.99	X
15	10	0+	0+	0+	0+	003	024	092	186	206	103	010	001	0+	10
	11	0+	0+	0+	0+	001	007	042	127	219	188	043	005	0+	11
	12	0+	0+	0+	0+	0+	002	014	063	170	250	129	031	0+	12
	13	0+	0+	0+	0+	0+	0+	003	022	092	231	267	135	009	13
	14	0+	0+	0+	0+	0+	0+	0+	005	031	132	343	366	130	14
	15	0+	0+	0+	0+	0+	0+	0+	0+	005	035	206	463	860	15
16	0	851	440	185	028	003	0+	0+	0+	0+	0+	0+	0+	0+	0
	1	138	371	329	113	023	003	0+	0+	0+	0+	0+	0+	0+	1
	2	010	146	275	211	073	015	002	0+	0+	0+	0+	0+	0+	2
	3	0+	036	142	246	146	047	009	001	0+	0+	0+	0+	0+	3
	4	0+	006	051	200	204	101	028	004	0+	0+	0+	0+	0+	4
	5	0+	001	014	120	210	162	067	014	001	0+	0+	0+	0+	5
	6	0+	0+	003	055	165	198	122	039	006	0+	0+	0+	0+	6
	7	0+	0+	0+	020	101	189	175	084	019	001	0+	0+	0+	7
	8	0+	0+	0+	006	049	142	196	142	049	006	0+	0+	0+	8
	9	0+	0+	0+	001	019	084	175	189	101	020	0+	0+	0+	9
	10	0+	0+	0+	0+	006	039	122	198	165	055	003	0+	0+	10
	11	0+	0+	0+	0+	001	014	067	162	210	120	014	001	0+	11
	12	0+	0+	0+	0+	0+	004	028	101	204	200	051	006	0+	12
	13	0+	0+	0+	0+	0+	001	009	047	146	246	142	036	0+	13
	14	0+	0+	0+	0+	0+	0+	002	015	073	211	275	146	010	14
	15	0+	0+	0+	0+	0+	0+	0+	003	023	113	329	371	138	15
	16	0+	0+	0+	0+	0+	0+	0+	0+	003	028	185	440	851	16
17	0	843	418	167	023	002	0+	0+	0+	0+	0+	0+	0+	0+	0
	1	145	374	315	096	017	002	0+	0+	0+	0+	0+	0+	0+	1
	2	012	158	280	191	058	010	001	0+	0+	0+	0+	0+	0+	2
	3	001	041	156	239	125	034	005	0+	0+	0+	0+	0+	0+	3
	4	0+	008	060	209	187	080	018	002	0+	0+	0+	0+	0+	4
	5	0+	001	017	136	208	138	047	008	001	0+	0+	0+	0+	5
	6	0+	0+	004	068	178	184	094	024	003	0+	0+	0+	0+	6
	7	0+	0+	001	027	120	193	148	057	009	0+	0+	0+	0+	7
	8	0+	0+	0+	008	064	161	185	107	028	002	0+	0+	0+	8
	9	0+	0+	0+	002	028	107	185	161	064	008	0+	0+	0+	9
	10	0+	0+	0+	0+	009	057	148	193	120	027	001	0+	0+	10
	11	0+	0+	0+	0+	003	024	094	184	178	068	004	0+	0+	11
	12	0+	0+	0+	0+	001	008	047	138	208	136	017	001	0+	12
	13	0+	0+	0+	0+	0+	002	018	080	187	209	060	008	0+	13
	14	0+	0+	0+	0+	0+	0+	005	034	125	239	156	041	001	14
	15	0+	0+	0+	0+	0+	0+	001	010	058	191	280	158	012	15
	16	0+	0+	0+	0+	0+	0+	0+	002	017	096	315	374	145	16
	17	0+	0+	0+	0+	0+	0+	0+	0+	002	023	167	418	843	17

Appendix II

THE BINOMIAL DISTRIBUTION (CONTINUED)

n	*X*	*P* .01	.05	.10	.20	.30	.40	.50	.60	.70	.80	.90	.95	.99	*X*
18	0	835	397	150	018	002	0+	0+	0+	0+	0+	0+	0+	0+	0
	1	152	376	300	081	013	001	0+	0+	0+	0+	0+	0+	0+	1
	2	013	168	284	172	046	007	001	0+	0+	0+	0+	0+	0+	2
	3	001	047	168	230	105	025	003	0+	0+	0+	0+	0+	0+	3
	4	0+	009	070	215	168	061	012	001	0+	0+	0+	0+	0+	4
	5	0+	001	022	151	202	115	033	004	0+	0+	0+	0+	0+	5
	6	0+	0+	005	082	187	166	071	015	001	0+	0+	0+	0+	6
	7	0+	0+	001	035	138	189	121	037	005	0+	0+	0+	0+	7
	8	0+	0+	0+	012	081	173	167	077	015	001	0+	0+	0+	8
	9	0+	0+	0+	003	039	128	185	128	039	003	0+	0+	0+	9
	10	0+	0+	0+	001	015	077	167	173	081	012	0+	0+	0+	10
	11	0+	0+	0+	0+	005	037	121	189	138	035	001	0+	0+	11
	12	0+	0+	0+	0+	001	015	071	166	187	082	005	0+	0+	12
	13	0+	0+	0+	0+	0+	004	033	115	202	151	022	001	0+	13
	14	0+	0+	0+	0+	0+	001	012	061	168	215	070	009	0+	14
	15	0+	0+	0+	0+	0+	0+	003	025	105	230	168	047	001	15
	16	0+	0+	0+	0+	0+	0+	001	007	046	172	284	168	013	16
	17	0+	0+	0+	0+	0+	0+	0+	001	013	081	300	376	152	17
	18	0+	0+	0+	0+	0+	0+	0+	0+	002	018	150	397	835	18
19	0	826	377	135	014	001	0+	0+	0+	0+	0+	0+	0+	0+	0
	1	159	377	285	068	009	001	0+	0+	0+	0+	0+	0+	0+	1
	2	014	179	285	154	036	005	0+	0+	0+	0+	0+	0+	0+	2
	3	001	053	180	218	087	017	002	0+	0+	0+	0+	0+	0+	3
	4	0+	011	080	218	149	047	007	001	0+	0+	0+	0+	0+	4
	5	0+	002	027	164	192	093	022	002	0+	0+	0+	0+	0+	5
	6	0+	0+	007	095	192	145	052	008	001	0+	0+	0+	0+	6
	7	0+	0+	001	044	153	180	096	024	002	0+	0+	0+	0+	7
	8	0+	0+	0+	017	098	180	144	053	008	0+	0+	0+	0+	8
	9	0+	0+	0+	005	051	146	176	098	022	001	0+	0+	0+	9
	10	0+	0+	0+	001	022	098	176	146	051	005	0+	0+	0+	10
	11	0+	0+	0+	0+	008	053	144	180	098	017	0+	0+	0+	11
	12	0+	0+	0+	0+	002	024	096	180	153	044	001	0+	0+	12
	13	0+	0+	0+	0+	001	008	052	145	192	095	007	0+	0+	13
	14	0+	0+	0+	0+	0+	002	022	093	192	164	027	002	0+	14
	15	0+	0+	0+	0+	0+	001	007	047	149	218	080	011	0+	15
	16	0+	0+	0+	0+	0+	0+	002	017	087	218	180	053	001	16
	17	0+	0+	0+	0+	0+	0+	0+	005	036	154	285	179	014	17
	18	0+	0+	0+	0+	0+	0+	0+	001	009	068	285	377	159	18
	19	0+	0+	0+	0+	0+	0+	0+	0+	001	014	135	377	826	19
20	0	818	358	122	012	001	0+	0+	0+	0+	0+	0+	0+	0+	0
	1	165	377	270	058	007	0+	0+	0+	0+	0+	0+	0+	0+	1
	2	016	189	285	137	028	003	0+	0+	0+	0+	0+	0+	0+	2
	3	001	060	190	205	072	012	001	0+	0+	0+	0+	0+	0+	3
	4	0+	013	090	218	130	035	005	0+	0+	0+	0+	0+	0+	4

Appendix II

THE BINOMIAL DISTRIBUTION (CONTINUED)

n	*X*	.01	.05	.10	.20	.30	.40	.50	.60	.70	.80	.90	.95	.99	*X*
								P							
20	5	0+	002	032	175	179	075	015	001	0+	0+	0+	0+	0+	5
	6	0+	0+	009	109	192	124	037	005	0+	0+	0+	0+	0+	6
	7	0+	0+	002	055	164	166	074	015	001	0+	0+	0+	0+	7
	8	0+	0+	0+	022	114	180	120	035	004	0+	0+	0+	0+	8
	9	0+	0+	0+	007	065	160	160	071	012	0+	0+	0+	0+	9
	10	0+	0+	0+	002	031	117	176	117	031	002	0+	0+	0+	10
	11	0+	0+	0+	0+	012	071	160	160	065	007	0+	0+	0+	11
	12	0+	0+	0+	0+	004	035	120	180	114	022	0+	0+	0+	12
	13	0+	0+	0+	0+	001	015	074	166	164	055	002	0+	0+	13
	14	0+	0+	0+	0+	0+	005	037	124	192	109	009	0+	0+	14
	15	0+	0+	0+	0+	0+	001	015	075	179	175	032	002	0+	15
	16	0+	0+	0+	0+	0+	0+	005	035	130	218	090	013	0+	16
	17	0+	0+	0+	0+	0+	0+	001	012	072	205	190	060	001	17
	18	0+	0+	0+	0+	0+	0+	0+	003	028	137	285	189	016	18
	19	0+	0+	0+	0+	0+	0+	0+	0+	007	058	270	377	165	19
	20	0+	0+	0+	0+	0+	0+	0+	0+	001	012	122	358	818	20
21	0	810	341	109	009	001	0+	0+	0+	0+	0+	0+	0+	0+	0
	1	172	376	255	048	005	0+	0+	0+	0+	0+	0+	0+	0+	1
	2	017	198	284	121	022	002	0+	0+	0+	0+	0+	0+	0+	2
	3	001	066	200	192	058	009	001	0+	0+	0+	0+	0+	0+	3
	4	0+	016	100	216	113	026	003	0+	0+	0+	0+	0+	0+	4
	5	0+	003	038	183	164	059	010	001	0+	0+	0+	0+	0+	5
	6	0+	0+	011	122	188	105	026	003	0+	0+	0+	0+	0+	6
	7	0+	0+	003	065	172	149	055	009	0+	0+	0+	0+	0+	7
	8	0+	0+	001	029	129	174	097	023	002	0+	0+	0+	0+	8
	9	0+	0+	0+	010	080	168	140	050	006	0+	0+	0+	0+	9
	10	0+	0+	0+	003	041	134	168	089	018	001	0+	0+	0+	10
	11	0+	0+	0+	001	018	089	168	134	041	003	0+	0+	0+	11
	12	0+	0+	0+	0+	006	050	140	168	080	010	0+	0+	0+	12
	13	0+	0+	0+	0+	002	023	097	174	129	029	001	0+	0+	13
	14	0+	0+	0+	0+	0+	009	055	149	172	065	003	0+	0+	14
	15	0+	0+	0+	0+	0+	003	026	105	188	122	011	0+	0+	15
	16	0+	0+	0+	0+	0+	001	010	059	164	183	038	003	0+	16
	17	0+	0+	0+	0+	0+	0+	003	026	113	216	100	016	0+	17
	18	0+	0+	0+	0+	0+	0+	001	009	058	192	200	066	001	18
	19	0+	0+	0+	0+	0+	0+	0+	002	022	121	284	198	017	19
	20	0+	0+	0+	0+	0+	0+	0+	0+	005	048	255	376	172	20
	21	0+	0+	0+	0+	0+	0+	0+	0+	001	009	109	341	810	21
22	0	802	324	098	007	0+	0+	0+	0+	0+	0+	0+	0+	0+	0
	1	178	375	241	041	004	0+	0+	0+	0+	0+	0+	0+	0+	1
	2	019	207	281	107	017	001	0+	0+	0+	0+	0+	0+	0+	2
	3	001	073	208	178	047	006	0+	0+	0+	0+	0+	0+	0+	3
	4	0+	018	110	211	096	019	002	0+	0+	0+	0+	0+	0+	4

Appendix II

THE BINOMIAL DISTRIBUTION (CONTINUED)

n	X	.01	.05	.10	.20	.30	.40	.50	.60	.70	.80	.90	.95	.99	X
22	5	0+	003	044	190	149	046	006	0+	0+	0+	0+	0+	0+	5
	6	0+	001	014	134	181	086	018	001	0+	0+	0+	0+	0+	6
	7	0+	0+	004	077	177	131	041	005	0+	0+	0+	0+	0+	7
	8	0+	0+	001	036	142	164	076	014	001	0+	0+	0+	0+	8
	9	0+	0+	0+	014	095	170	119	034	003	0+	0+	0+	0+	9
	10	0+	0+	0+	005	053	148	154	066	010	0+	0+	0+	0+	10
	11	0+	0+	0+	001	025	107	168	107	025	001	0+	0+	0+	11
	12	0+	0+	0+	0+	010	066	154	148	053	005	0+	0+	0+	12
	13	0+	0+	0+	0+	003	034	119	170	095	014	0+	0+	0+	13
	14	0+	0+	0+	0+	001	014	076	164	142	036	001	0+	0+	14
	15	0+	0+	0+	0+	0+	005	041	131	177	077	004	0+	0+	15
	16	0+	0+	0+	0+	0+	001	018	086	181	134	014	001	0+	16
	17	0+	0+	0+	0+	0+	0+	006	046	149	190	044	003	0+	17
	18	0+	0+	0+	0+	0+	0+	002	019	096	211	110	018	0+	18
	19	0+	0+	0+	0+	0+	0+	0+	006	047	178	208	073	001	19
	20	0+	0+	0+	0+	0+	0+	0+	001	017	107	281	207	019	20
	21	0+	0+	0+	0+	0+	0+	0+	0+	004	041	241	375	178	21
	22	0+	0+	0+	0+	0+	0+	0+	0+	0+	007	098	324	802	22
23	0	794	307	089	006	0+	0+	0+	0+	0+	0+	0+	0+	0+	0
	1	184	372	226	034	003	0+	0+	0+	0+	0+	0+	0+	0+	1
	2	020	215	277	093	013	001	0+	0+	0+	0+	0+	0+	0+	2
	3	001	079	215	163	038	004	0+	0+	0+	0+	0+	0+	0+	3
	4	0+	021	120	204	082	014	001	0+	0+	0+	0+	0+	0+	4
	5	0+	004	051	194	133	035	004	0+	0+	0+	0+	0+	0+	5
	6	0+	001	017	145	171	070	012	001	0+	0+	0+	0+	0+	6
	7	0+	0+	005	088	178	113	029	003	0+	0+	0+	0+	0+	7
	8	0+	0+	001	044	153	151	058	009	0+	0+	0+	0+	0+	8
	9	0+	0+	0+	018	109	168	097	022	002	0+	0+	0+	0+	9
	10	0+	0+	0+	006	065	157	136	046	005	0+	0+	0+	0+	10
	11	0+	0+	0+	002	033	123	161	082	014	0+	0+	0+	0+	11
	12	0+	0+	0+	0+	014	082	161	123	033	002	0+	0+	0+	12
	13	0+	0+	0+	0+	005	046	136	157	065	006	0+	0+	0+	13
	14	0+	0+	0+	0+	002	022	097	168	109	018	0+	0+	0+	14
	15	0+	0+	0+	0+	0+	009	058	151	153	044	001	0+	0+	15
	16	0+	0+	0+	0+	0+	003	029	113	178	088	005	0+	0+	16
	17	0+	0+	0+	0+	0+	001	012	070	171	145	017	001	0+	17
	18	0+	0+	0+	0+	0+	0+	004	035	133	194	051	004	0+	18
	19	0+	0+	0+	0+	0+	0+	001	014	082	204	120	021	0+	19
	20	0+	0+	0+	0+	0+	0+	0+	004	038	163	215	079	001	20
	21	0+	0+	0+	0+	0+	0+	0+	001	013	093	277	215	020	21
	22	0+	0+	0+	0+	0+	0+	0+	0+	003	034	226	372	184	22
	23	0+	0+	0+	0+	0+	0+	0+	0+	0+	006	089	307	794	23

Appendix II

THE BINOMIAL DISTRIBUTION (CONTINUED)

		P													
n	X	.01	.05	.10	.20	.30	.40	.50	.60	.70	.80	.90	.95	.99	X
24	0	786	292	080	005	0+	0+	0+	0+	0+	0+	0+	0+	0+	0
	1	190	369	213	028	002	0+	0+	0+	0+	0+	0+	0+	0+	1
	2	022	223	272	081	010	001	0+	0+	0+	0+	0+	0+	0+	2
	3	002	086	221	149	031	003	0+	0+	0+	0+	0+	0+	0+	3
	4	0+	024	129	196	069	010	001	0+	0+	0+	0+	0+	0+	4
	5	0+	005	057	196	118	027	003	0+	0+	0+	0+	0+	0+	5
	6	0+	001	020	155	160	056	008	0+	0+	0+	0+	0+	0+	6
	7	0+	0+	006	100	176	096	021	002	0+	0+	0+	0+	0+	7
	8	0+	0+	001	053	160	136	044	005	0+	0+	0+	0+	0+	8
	9	0+	0+	0+	024	122	161	078	014	001	0+	0+	0+	0+	9
	10	0+	0+	0+	009	079	161	117	032	003	0+	0+	0+	0+	10
	11	0+	0+	0+	003	043	137	149	061	008	0+	0+	0+	0+	11
	12	0+	0+	0+	001	020	099	161	099	020	001	0+	0+	0+	12
	13	0+	0+	0+	0+	008	061	149	137	043	003	0+	0+	0+	13
	14	0+	0+	0+	0+	003	032	117	161	079	009	0+	0+	0+	14
	15	0+	0+	0+	0+	001	014	078	161	122	024	0+	0+	0+	15
	16	0+	0+	0+	0+	0+	005	044	136	160	053	001	0+	0+	16
	17	0+	0+	0+	0+	0+	002	021	096	176	100	006	0+	0+	17
	18	0+	0+	0+	0+	0+	0+	008	056	160	155	020	001	0+	18
	19	0+	0+	0+	0+	0+	0+	003	027	118	196	057	005	0+	19
	20	0+	0+	0+	0+	0+	0+	001	010	069	196	129	024	0+	20
	21	0+	0+	0+	0+	0+	0+	0+	003	031	149	221	086	002	21
	22	0+	0+	0+	0+	0+	0+	0+	001	010	081	272	223	022	22
	23	0+	0+	0+	0+	0+	0+	0+	0+	002	028	213	369	190	23
	24	0+	0+	0+	0+	0+	0+	0+	0+	0+	005	080	292	786	24
25	0	778	277	072	004	0+	0+	0+	0+	0+	0+	0+	0+	0+	0
	1	196	365	199	024	001	0+	0+	0+	0+	0+	0+	0+	0+	1
	2	024	231	266	071	007	0+	0+	0+	0+	0+	0+	0+	0+	2
	3	002	093	226	136	024	002	0+	0+	0+	0+	0+	0+	0+	3
	4	0+	027	138	187	057	007	0+	0+	0+	0+	0+	0+	0+	4
	5	0+	006	065	196	103	020	002	0+	0+	0+	0+	0+	0+	5
	6	0+	001	024	163	147	044	005	0+	0+	0+	0+	0+	0+	6
	7	0+	0+	007	111	171	080	014	001	0+	0+	0+	0+	0+	7
	8	0+	0+	002	062	165	120	032	003	0+	0+	0+	0+	0+	8
	9	0+	0+	0+	029	134	151	061	009	0+	0+	0+	0+	0+	9
	10	0+	0+	0+	012	092	161	097	021	001	0+	0+	0+	0+	10
	11	0+	0+	0+	004	054	147	133	043	004	0+	0+	0+	0+	11
	12	0+	0+	0+	001	027	114	155	076	011	0+	0+	0+	0+	12
	13	0+	0+	0+	0+	011	076	155	114	027	001	0+	0+	0+	13
	14	0+	0+	0+	0+	004	043	133	147	054	004	0+	0+	0+	14
	15	0+	0+	0+	0+	001	021	097	161	092	012	0+	0+	0+	15
	16	0+	0+	0+	0+	0+	009	061	151	134	029	0+	0+	0+	16
	17	0+	0+	0+	0+	0+	003	032	120	165	062	002	0+	0+	17
	18	0+	0+	0+	0+	0+	001	014	080	171	111	007	0+	0+	18
	19	0+	0+	0+	0+	0+	0+	005	044	147	163	024	001	0+	19

Appendix II

THE BINOMIAL DISTRIBUTION (CONTINUED)

n	X	.01	.05	.10	.20	.30	.40	.50	.60	.70	.80	.90	.95	.99	X
25	20	0+	0+	0+	0+	0+	0+	002	020	103	196	065	006	0+	20
	21	0+	0+	0+	0+	0+	0+	0+	007	057	187	138	027	0+	21
	22	0+	0+	0+	0+	0+	0+	0+	002	024	136	226	093	002	22
	23	0+	0+	0+	0+	0+	0+	0+	0+	007	071	266	231	024	23
	24	0+	0+	0+	0+	0+	0+	0+	0+	001	024	199	365	196	24
	25	0+	0+	0+	0+	0+	0+	0+	0+	0+	004	072	277	778	25

Appendix III

2500 RANDOM DIGITS

00	49487	52802	28667	62058	87822	14704	18519	17889	45869	14454
01	29480	91539	46317	84803	86056	62812	33584	70391	77749	64906
02	25252	97738	23901	11106	86864	55808	22557	23214	15021	54268
03	02431	42193	96960	19620	29188	05863	92900	06836	13433	21709
04	69414	89353	70724	67893	23218	72452	03095	68333	13751	37260
05	77285	35179	92042	67581	67673	68374	71115	98166	43352	06414
06	52852	11444	71868	34534	69124	02760	06406	95234	87995	78560
07	98740	98054	30195	09891	18453	79464	01156	95522	06884	55073
08	85022	58736	12138	35146	62085	36170	25433	80787	96496	40579
09	17778	03840	21636	56269	08149	19001	67367	13138	02400	89515
10	81833	93449	57781	94621	90998	37561	59688	93299	27726	82167
11	63789	54958	33167	10909	40343	81023	61590	44474	39810	10305
12	61840	81740	60986	12498	71546	42249	13812	59902	27864	21809
13	42243	10153	20891	90883	15782	98167	86837	99166	92143	82441
14	45236	09129	53031	12260	01278	14404	40969	33419	14188	69557
15	40338	42477	78804	36272	72053	07958	67158	60979	79891	92409
16	54040	71253	88789	98203	54999	96564	00789	68879	47134	83941
17	49158	20908	44859	29089	76130	51442	34453	98590	37353	61137
18	80958	03808	83655	18415	96563	43582	82207	53322	30419	64435
19	07636	04876	61063	57571	69434	14965	20911	73162	33576	52839
20	37227	80750	08261	97048	60438	75053	05939	34414	16685	32103
21	99460	45915	45637	41353	35335	69087	57536	68418	10247	93253
22	60248	75845	37296	33783	42393	28185	31880	00241	31642	37526
23	95076	79089	87380	28982	97750	82221	35584	27444	85793	69755
24	20944	97852	26586	32796	51513	47475	48621	20067	88975	39506
25	30458	49207	62358	41532	30057	53017	10375	97204	98675	77634
26	38905	91282	79309	49022	17405	18830	09186	07629	01785	78317
27	96545	15638	90114	93730	13741	70177	49175	42113	21600	69625
28	21944	28328	00692	89164	96025	01383	50252	67044	70596	58266
29	36910	71928	63327	00980	32154	46006	62289	28079	03076	15619
30	48745	47626	28856	28382	60639	51370	70091	58261	70135	88259
31	32519	91993	59374	83994	59873	51217	62806	20028	26545	16820
32	75757	12965	29285	11481	31744	41754	24428	81819	02354	37895
33	07911	97756	89561	27464	25133	50026	16436	75846	83718	08533
34	89887	03328	76911	93168	56236	39056	67905	94933	05456	52347
35	30543	99488	75363	94187	32885	23887	10872	22793	26232	87356
36	68442	55201	33946	42495	28384	89889	50278	91985	58185	19124
37	22403	56698	88524	13692	55012	25343	76391	48029	72278	58586
38	70701	36907	51242	52083	43126	90379	60380	98513	85596	16528
39	69804	96122	42342	28467	79037	13218	63510	09071	52438	25840
40	65806	22398	19470	63653	27055	02606	43347	65384	02613	81668
41	43902	53070	54319	19347	59506	75440	90826	53652	92382	67623
42	49145	71587	14273	62440	15770	03281	58124	09533	43722	03856
43	47363	36295	62126	42358	20322	82000	52830	93540	13284	96496
44	26244	87033	90247	79131	38773	67687	45541	54976	17508	18367
45	72875	39496	06385	48458	30545	74383	22814	36752	10707	48774
46	09065	16283	61398	08288	00708	21816	39615	03102	02834	04116
47	68256	51225	92645	77747	33104	81206	00112	53445	04212	58476
48	38744	81018	41909	70458	72459	66136	97266	26490	10877	45022
49	44375	19619	35750	59924	82429	90288	61064	26489	87001	84273

Reprinted by permission of the publisher, Glencoe Free Press, Inc., a division of The Macmillan Company, from *A Million Random Digits with 100,000 Normal Deviates*, by The Rand Corporation.

Appendix IV

THE CUMULATIVE POISSON DISTRIBUTION FUNCTION

μ \ X	0	1	2	3	4	5	6	7	8	9	10	11	12
.05	.951	.999	1.000										
.10	.905	.995	1.000										
.15	.861	.990	.999	1.000									
.20	.819	.982	.999	1.000									
.25	.779	.974	.998	1.000									
.30	.741	.963	.996	1.000									
.35	.705	.951	.994	1.000									
.40	.670	.938	.992	.999	1.000								
.45	.638	.925	.989	.999	1.000								
.50	.607	.910	.986	.998	1.000								
.55	.577	.894	.982	.998	1.000								
.60	.549	.878	.977	.997	1.000								
.65	.522	.861	.972	.996	.999	1.000							
.70	.497	.844	.966	.994	.999	1.000							
.75	.472	.827	.959	.993	.999	1.000							
.80	.449	.809	.953	.991	.999	1.000							
.85	.427	.791	.945	.989	.998	1.000							
.90	.407	.772	.937	.987	.998	1.000							
.95	.387	.754	.929	.984	.997	1.000							
1.00	.368	.736	.920	.981	.996	.999	1.000						
1.1	.333	.699	.900	.974	.995	.999	1.000						
1.2	.301	.663	.879	.966	.992	.998	1.000						
1.3	.273	.627	.857	.957	.989	.998	1.000						
1.4	.247	.592	.833	.946	.986	.997	.999	1.000					
1.5	.223	.558	.809	.934	.981	.996	.999	1.000					
1.6	.202	.525	.783	.921	.976	.994	.999	1.000					
1.7	.183	.493	.757	.907	.970	.992	.998	1.000					
1.8	.165	.463	.731	.891	.964	.990	.997	.999	1.000				
1.9	.150	.434	.704	.875	.956	.987	.997	.999	1.000				
2.0	.135	.406	.677	.857	.947	.983	.995	.999	1.000				
2.2	.111	.355	.623	.819	.928	.975	.993	.998	1.000				
2.4	.091	.308	.570	.779	.904	.964	.988	.997	.999	1.000			
2.6	.074	.267	.518	.736	.877	.951	.983	.995	.999	1.000			
2.8	.061	.231	.469	.692	.848	.935	.976	.992	.998	.999	1.000		
3.0	.050	.199	.423	.647	.815	.916	.966	.988	.996	.999	1.000		
3.2	.041	.171	.380	.603	.781	.895	.955	.983	.994	.998	1.000		
3.4	.033	.147	.340	.558	.744	.871	.942	.977	.992	.997	.999	1.000	
3.6	.027	.126	.303	.515	.706	.844	.927	.969	.988	.996	.999	1.000	
3.8	.022	.107	.269	.473	.668	.816	.909	.960	.984	.994	.998	.999	1.000
4.0	.018	.092	.238	.433	.629	.785	.889	.949	.979	.992	.997	.999	1.000

This table is taken from Table A-15 of *Introduction to Statistical Analysis* by W. J. Dixon and F. J. Massey, Jr., and is reproduced here with the kind permission of Professor Dixon and the publishers, McGraw-Hill Book Company, Inc., New York.

Appendix V

THE CUMULATIVE NORMAL DISTRIBUTION FUNCTION

Z	.00	.01	.02	.03	.04	.05	.06	.07	.08	.09
.0	.5000	.5040	.5080	.5120	.5160	.5199	.5239	.5279	.5319	.5359
.1	.5398	.5438	.5478	.5517	.5557	.5596	.5636	.5675	.5714	.5753
.2	.5793	.5832	.5871	.5910	.5948	.5987	.6026	.6064	.6103	.6141
.3	.6179	.6217	.6255	.6293	.6331	.6368	.6406	.6443	.6480	.6517
.4	.6554	.6591	.6628	.6664	.6700	.6736	.6772	.6808	.6844	.6879
.5	.6915	.6950	.6985	.7019	.7054	.7088	.7123	.7157	.7190	.7224
.6	.7257	.7291	.7324	.7357	.7389	.7422	.7454	.7486	.7517	.7549
.7	.7580	.7611	.7642	.7673	.7704	.7734	.7764	.7794	.7823	.7852
.8	.7881	.7910	.7939	.7967	.7995	.8023	.8051	.8078	.8106	.8133
.9	.8159	.8186	.8212	.8238	.8264	.8289	.8315	.8340	.8365	.8389
1.0	.8413	.8438	.8461	.8485	.8508	.8531	.8554	.8577	.8599	.8621
1.1	.8643	.8665	.8686	.8708	.8729	.8749	.8770	.8790	.8810	.8830
1.2	.8849	.8869	.8888	.8907	.8925	.8944	.8962	.8980	.8997	.9015
1.3	.9032	.9049	.9066	.9082	.9099	.9115	.9131	.9147	.9162	.9177
1.4	.9192	.9207	.9222	.9236	.9251	.9265	.9279	.9292	.9306	.9319
1.5	.9332	.9345	.9357	.9370	.9382	.9394	.9406	.9418	.9429	.9441
1.6	.9452	.9463	.9474	.9484	.9495	.9505	.9515	.9525	.9535	.9545
1.7	.9554	.9564	.9573	.9582	.9591	.9599	.9608	.9616	.9625	.9633
1.8	.9641	.9649	.9656	.9664	.9671	.9678	.9686	.9693	.9699	.9706
1.9	.9713	.9719	.9726	.9732	.9738	.9744	.9750	.9756	.9761	.9767
2.0	.9772	.9778	.9783	.9788	.9793	.9798	.9803	.9808	.9812	.9817
2.1	.9821	.9826	.9830	.9834	.9838	.9842	.9846	.9850	.9854	.9857
2.2	.9861	.9864	.9868	.9871	.9875	.9878	.9881	.9884	.9887	.9890
2.3	.9893	.9896	.9898	.9901	.9904	.9906	.9909	.9911	.9913	.9916
2.4	.9918	.9920	.9922	.9925	.9927	.9929	.9931	.9932	.9934	.9936
2.5	.9938	.9940	.9941	.9943	.9945	.9946	.9948	.9949	.9951	.9952
2.6	.9953	.9955	.9956	.9957	.9959	.9960	.9961	.9962	.9963	.9964
2.7	.9965	.9966	.9967	.9968	.9969	.9970	.9971	.9972	.9973	.9974
2.8	.9974	.9975	.9976	.9977	.9977	.9978	.9979	.9979	.9980	.9981
2.9	.9981	.9982	.9982	.9983	.9984	.9984	.9985	.9985	.9986	.9986
3.0	.9987	.9987	.9987	.9988	.9988	.9989	.9989	.9989	.9990	.9990
3.1	.9990	.9991	.9991	.9991	.9992	.9992	.9992	.9992	.9993	.9993
3.2	.9993	.9993	.9994	.9994	.9994	.9994	.9994	.9995	.9995	.9995
3.3	.9995	.9995	.9995	.9996	.9996	.9996	.9996	.9996	.9996	.9997
3.4	.9997	.9997	.9997	.9997	.9997	.9997	.9997	.9997	.9997	.9998

This table is extracted from Table D.2 of *Introduction to the Theory of Statistics* by A. M. Mood, and is reproduced here with the kind permission of Professor Mood and the publishers, McGraw-Hill Book Company, Inc., New York.

Appendix VI

HEIGHTS OF THE STANDARDIZED NORMAL DENSITY FUNCTION

Z	Height	Z	Height
0	.399	1.50	.1295
.05	.398	1.55	.1200
.10	.397	1.60	.1109
.15	.394	1.65	.1023
.20	.391	1.70	.0940
.25	.387	1.75	.0863
.30	.381	1.80	.0790
.35	.375	1.85	.0721
.40	.368	1.90	.0656
.45	.361	1.95	.0596
.50	.352	2.00	.0540
.55	.343	2.05	.0488
.60	.333	2.10	.0440
.65	.323	2.15	.0396
.70	.312	2.20	.0355
.75	.301	2.25	.0317
.80	.290	2.30	.0283
.85	.278	2.35	.0252
.90	.266	2.40	.0224
.95	.254	2.45	.0198
1.00	.242	2.50	.0175
1.05	.230	2.55	.0154
1.10	.218	2.60	.0136
1.15	.206	2.65	.0119
1.20	.194	2.70	.0104
1.25	.183	2.75	.0091
1.30	.171	2.80	.0079
1.35	.160	2.85	.0069
1.40	.150	2.90	.0060
1.45	.139	2.95	.0051
1.50	.130	3.00	.0044

This table is extracted from Table III of *Statistical Tables* by R. A. Fisher and F. Yates, and is reproduced here with the kind permission of the publishers, Oliver and Boyd, Ltd., of London.

Appendix VII

THE CUMULATIVE CHI-SQUARE DISTRIBUTION FUNCTION

D	0.005	0.010	0.025	0.050	0.100	0.250	0.500
1	392704.10^{-10}	157088.10^{-9}	982069.10^{-9}	393214.10^{-8}	0.0157908	0.1015308	0.454937
2	0.0100251	0.0201007	0.0506356	0.102587	0.210720	0.575364	1.38629
3	0.0717212	0.114832	0.215795	0.351846	0.584375	1.212534	2.36597
4	0.206990	0.297110	0.484419	0.710721	1.063623	1.92255	3.35670
5	0.411740	0.554300	0.831211	1.145476	1.61031	2.67460	4.35146
6	0.675727	0.872085	1.237347	1.63539	2.20413	3.45460	5.34812
7	0.989265	1.239043	1.68987	2.16735	2.83311	4.25485	6.34581
8	1.344419	1.646482	2.17973	2.73264	3.48954	5.07064	7.34412
9	1.734926	2.087912	2.70039	3.32511	4.16816	5.89883	8.34283
10	2.15585	2.55821	3.24697	3.94030	4.86518	6.73720	9.34182
11	2.60321	3.05347	3.81575	4.57481	5.57779	7.58412	10.3410
12	3.07382	3.57056	4.40379	5.22603	6.30380	8.43842	11.3403
13	3.56503	4.10691	5.00874	5.89186	7.04150	9.29906	12.3398
14	4.07468	4.66043	5.62872	6.57063	7.78953	10.1653	13.3393
15	4.60094	5.22935	6.26214	7.26094	8.54675	11.0365	14.3389
16	5.14224	5.81221	6.90766	7.96164	9.31223	11.9122	15.3385
17	5.69724	6.40776	7.56418	8.67176	10.0852	12.7919	16.3381
18	6.26481	7.01491	8.23075	9.39046	10.8649	13.6753	17.3379
19	6.84398	7.63273	8.90655	10.1170	11.6509	14.5620	18.3376
20	7.43386	8.26040	9.59083	10.8508	12.4426	15.4518	19.3374
21	8.03366	8.89720	10.28293	11.5913	13.2396	16.3444	20.3372
22	8.64272	9.54249	10.9823	12.3380	14.0415	17.2396	21.3370
23	9.26042	10.19567	11.6885	13.0905	14.8479	18.1373	22.3369
24	9.88623	10.8564	12.4011	13.8484	15.6587	19.0372	23.3367
25	10.5197	11.5240	13.1197	14.6114	16.4734	19.9393	24.3366
26	11.1603	12.1981	13.8439	15.3791	17.2919	20.8434	25.3364
27	11.8076	12.8786	14.5733	16.1513	18.1138	21.7494	26.3363
28	12.4613	13.5648	15.3079	16.9279	18.9392	22.6572	27.3363
29	13.1211	14.2565	16.0471	17.7083	19.7677	23.5666	28.3362
30	13.7867	14.9535	16.7908	18.4926	20.5992	24.4776	29.3360
40	20.7065	22.1643	24.4331	26.5093	29.0505	33.6603	39.3354
50	27.9907	29.7067	32.3574	34.7642	37.6886	42.9421	49.3349
60	35.5346	37.4848	40.4817	43.1879	46.4589	52.2938	59.3347
70	43.2752	45.4418	48.7576	51.7393	55.3290	61.6983	69.3344
80	51.1720	53.5400	57.1532	60.3915	64.2778	71.1445	79.3343
90	59.1963	61.7541	65.6466	69.1260	73.2912	80.6247	89.3342
100	67.3276	70.0648	74.2219	77.9295	82.3581	90.1332	99.3341
∞	−2.5758	−2.3263	−1.9600	−1.6449	−1.2816	−0.6745	0.0000

This table is taken from Table 8 of the *Biometrika Tables for Statisticians*, Vol. I (first ed.), edited by E. S. Pearson and H. O. Hartley, and is reproduced here with the kind permission of the trustees of *Biometrika*.

Appendix VII

THE CUMULATIVE CHI-SQUARE DISTRIBUTION FUNCTION (CONTINUED)

D	0.750	0.900	0.950	0.975	0.990	0.995	0.999
1	1.32330	2.70554	3.84146	5.02389	6.63490	7.87944	10.828
2	2.77259	4.60517	5.99147	7.37776	9.21034	10.5966	13.816
3	4.10835	6.25139	7.81473	9.34840	11.3449	12.8381	16.266
4	5.38527	7.77944	9.48773	11.1433	13.2767	14.8602	18.467
5	6.62568	9.23635	11.0705	12.8325	15.0863	16.7496	20.515
6	7.84080	10.6446	12.5916	14.4494	16.8119	18.5476	22.458
7	9.03715	12.0170	14.0671	16.0128	18.4753	20.2777	24.322
8	10.2188	13.3616	15.5073	17.5346	20.0902	21.9550	26.125
9	11.3887	14.6837	16.9190	19.0228	21.6660	23.5893	27.877
10	12.5489	15.9871	18.3070	20.4831	23.2093	25.1882	29.588
11	13.7007	17.2750	19.6751	21.9200	24.7250	26.7569	31.264
12	14.8454	18.5494	21.0261	23.3367	26.2170	28.2995	32.909
13	15.9839	19.8119	22.3621	24.7356	27.6883	29.8194	34.528
14	17.1170	21.0642	23.6848	26.1190	29.1413	31.3193	36.123
15	18.2451	22.3072	24.9958	27.4884	30.5779	32.8013	37.697
16	19.3688	23.5418	26.2962	28.8454	31.9999	34.2672	39.252
17	20.4887	24.7690	27.5871	30.1910	33.4087	35.7185	40.790
18	21.6049	25.9894	28.8693	31.5264	34.8053	37.1564	42.312
19	22.7178	27.2036	30.1435	32.8523	36.1908	38.5822	43.820
20	23.8277	28.4120	31.4104	34.1696	37.5662	39.9968	45.315
21	24.9348	29.6151	32.6705	35.4789	38.9321	41.4010	46.797
22	26.0393	30.8133	33.9244	36.7807	40.2894	42.7956	48.268
23	27.1413	32.0069	35.1725	38.0757	41.6384	44.1813	49.728
24	28.2412	33.1963	36.4151	39.3641	42.9798	45.5585	51.179
25	29.3389	34.3816	37.6525	40.6465	44.3141	46.9278	52.620
26	30.4345	35.5631	38.8852	41.9232	45.6417	48.2899	54.052
27	31.5284	36.7412	40.1133	43.1944	46.9630	49.6449	55.476
28	32.6205	37.9159	41.3372	44.4607	48.2782	50.9933	56.892
29	33.7109	39.0875	42.5569	45.7222	49.5879	52.3356	58.302
30	34.7998	40.2560	43.7729	46.9792	50.8922	53.6720	59.703
40	45.6160	51.8050	55.7585	59.3417	63.6907	66.7659	73.402
50	56.3336	63.1671	67.5048	71.4202	76.1539	79.4900	86.661
60	66.9814	74.3970	79.0819	83.2976	88.3794	91.9517	99.607
70	77.5766	85.5271	90.5312	95.0231	100.425	104.215	112.317
80	88.1303	96.5782	101.879	106.629	112.329	116.321	124.839
90	98.6499	107.565	113.145	118.136	124.116	128.299	137.208
100	109.141	118.498	124.342	129.561	135.807	140.169	149.449
∞	+0.6745	+1.2816	+1.6449	+1.9600	+2.3263	+2.5758	+3.0902

Appendix VIII

CONSTANTS CONNECTED WITH THE USE OF THE SAMPLE MEDIAN AS AN ESTIMATOR

n	Multiplicative factor for variance of the median	Relative (to the mean) efficiency of the median
2	.500	1.000
3	.449	.743
4	.298	.838
5	.287	.697
6	.215	.776
7	.210	.679
8	.168	.743
9	.166	.669
10	.138	.723
11	.137	.663
12	.118	.709
13	.117	.659
14	.102	.699
15	.102	.656
16	.0904	.692
17	.0901	.653
18	.0810	.686
19	.0808	.651
20	.0734	.681
∞	$1.571/n$	.637

This table is adapted from Table A-8b(4) of *Introduction to Statistical Analysis* by W. J. Dixon and F. J. Massey, Jr., and is reproduced here with the kind permission of Professor Dixon and the publishers, McGraw-Hill Book Company, Inc., of New York.

Appendix IX

ESTIMATOR FOR THE POPULATION STANDARD DEVIATION AND ITS RELATIVE EFFICIENCY

n	Estimator	Relative efficiency
2	$.8862(X_{[2]} - X_{[1]})$	1.000
3	$.5908(X_{[3]} - X_{[1]})$	.992
4	$.4857(X_{[4]} - X_{[1]})$	.975
5	$.4299(X_{[5]} - X_{[1]})$	.955
6	$.2619(X_{[6]} + X_{[5]} - X_{[2]} - X_{[1]})$	.957
7	$.2370(X_{[7]} + X_{[6]} - X_{[2]} - X_{[1]})$	.967
8	$.2197(X_{[8]} + X_{[7]} - X_{[2]} - X_{[1]})$	.970
9	$.2068(X_{[9]} + X_{[8]} - X_{[2]} - X_{[1]})$	.968
10	$.1968(X_{[10]} + X_{[9]} - X_{[2]} - X_{[1]})$	.964
11	$.1608(X_{[11]} + X_{[10]} + X_{[8]} - X_{[4]} - X_{[2]} - X_{[1]})$	.967
12	$.1524(X_{[12]} + X_{[11]} + X_{[9]} - X_{[4]} - X_{[2]} - X_{[1]})$	.972
13	$.1456(X_{[13]} + X_{[12]} + X_{[10]} - X_{[4]} - X_{[2]} - X_{[1]})$	.975
14	$.1399(X_{[14]} + X_{[13]} + X_{[11]} - X_{[4]} - X_{[2]} - X_{[1]})$	.977
15	$.1352(X_{[15]} + X_{[14]} + X_{[12]} - X_{[4]} - X_{[2]} - X_{[1]})$	.977
16	$.1311(X_{[16]} + X_{[15]} + X_{[13]} - X_{[4]} - X_{[2]} - X_{[1]})$	.975
17	$.1050(X_{[17]} + X_{[16]} + X_{[15]} + X_{[13]} - X_{[5]} - X_{[3]} - X_{[2]} - X_{[1]})$	.978
18	$.1020(X_{[18]} + X_{[17]} + X_{[16]} + X_{[14]} - X_{[5]} - X_{[3]} - X_{[2]} - X_{[1]})$	.978
19	$.09939(X_{[19]} + X_{[18]} + X_{[17]} + X_{[15]} - X_{[5]} - X_{[3]} - X_{[2]} - X_{[1]})$	.979
20	$.09706(X_{[20]} + X_{[19]} + X_{[18]} + X_{[16]} - X_{[5]} - X_{[3]} - X_{[2]} - X_{[1]})$	.978

This table is taken from Table A-8b(3) of *Introduction to Statistical Analysis* by W. J. Dixon and F. J. Massey, Jr., and is reproduced here with the kind permission of Professor Dixon and the publishers, McGraw-Hill Book Company, Inc., of New York.

ANSWERS TO ODD-NUMBERED PROBLEMS

Section III.2.2

1. a. 9 samples. They are {(1, 1), (1, 2), (1, 3), (2, 1), (2, 2), (2, 3), (3, 1), (3, 2), (3, 3)}.
   b. 6 samples. They are {(1, 2), (1, 3), (2, 1), (2, 3), (3, 1), (3, 2)}.
   c. 27 samples. They are {(1, 1, 1), (1, 1, 2), (1, 1, 3), (1, 2, 1), (1, 2, 2), (1, 2, 3), (1, 3, 1), (1, 3, 2), (1, 3, 3), (2, 1, 1), (2, 1, 2), (2, 1, 3), (2, 2, 1), (2, 2, 2), (2, 2, 3), (2, 3, 1), (2, 3, 2), (2, 3, 3), (3, 1, 1), (3, 1, 2), (3, 1, 3), (3, 2, 1), (3, 2, 2), (3, 2, 3), (3, 3, 1), (3, 3, 2), (3, 3, 3)}.
   d. 6 samples. They are {(1, 2, 3), (1, 3, 2), (2, 1, 3), (2, 3, 1), (3, 1, 2), (3, 2, 1)}.
3. The one-to-one correspondence can be established as follows:

1	corresponds to	1
2	” ”	2
3	” ”	3
4	” ”	1
5	” ”	2
6	” ”	3,

   and so on.

   For samples of size $n = 2$, the answer to Problem 1a applies to this population whether sampling with or without replacement. For samples of size $n = 3$, the answer to Problem 1c applies to this population whether sampling with or without replacement.

Section IV.4

1. a. {(HHHH), (HHHT), (HHTH), (HTHH), (THHH), (HHTT), (HTHT), (THHT), (THTH), (TTHH), (HTTH), (TTTH), (TTHT), (THTT), (HTTT), (TTTT)}.
   b. 16.
   c. {(HHTT), (HTHT), (THHT), (THTH), (TTHH), (HTTH)}, **P**("exactly 2 heads") = 6/16.
   d. {(HHHH), (HHHT), (HHTH), (HTHH), (THHH), (HHTT), (HTHT), (THHT), (THTH), (TTHH), (HTTH)}, **P**("no more than 2 tails") = 11/16.
   e. **P**(impossible event) = 0, **P**(certain event) = 1.
3. a. **P**({(a, d), (b, d), (c, d), (d, d)}) = 0.7.
   b. **P**({(a, a), (a, b), (a, c), (a, d), (b, a), (b, b), (b, c), (c, a), (c, b), (c, c), (c, d), (d, a), (d, b), (d, c), (d, d)}) = 0.5.
   c. **P**({(b, d), (a, a), (a, b), (a, c), (c, a), (c, b), (c, c), (d, a), (d, b), (d, c)}) = 0.65.
   d. **P**("first item wrong and perfect paper") = 0.
   e. "Draw randomly the test performance of a student from among the 100 who took the test."
   f. The outcome probabilities are based on a sample of students and refer only to the performance of that group on a particular occasion.
5. a. {(R, R), (R, S), (R, P), (S, R), (S, S), (S, P), (P, R), (P, S), (P, P)}.
   b. 1/3. c. 1/3. d. 1/3.
   e. Always play paper. f. 1/2.
   g. No. The probability that you will win is reduced to 1/4.

Section IV.5.6

1. a. i. Φ; ii. $A \cap B = A = B$; iii. $A \cup B = A = B$.
   b. i. S; ii. Φ; iii. S; iv. S; v. A.
   c. In general, no. d. Yes.
   e. Yes. f. Yes.
   g. i. Φ; ii. A; iii. B.
   h. i. A; ii. A; iii. A; iv. C; v. C; vi. Φ; vii. $C \sim A$; viii. Φ.
   i. See Figure A.1. j. See Figure A.2.

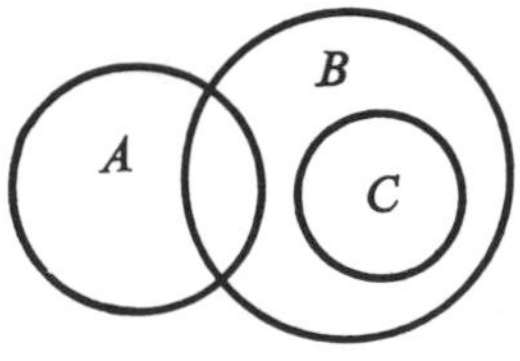

Figure A.1

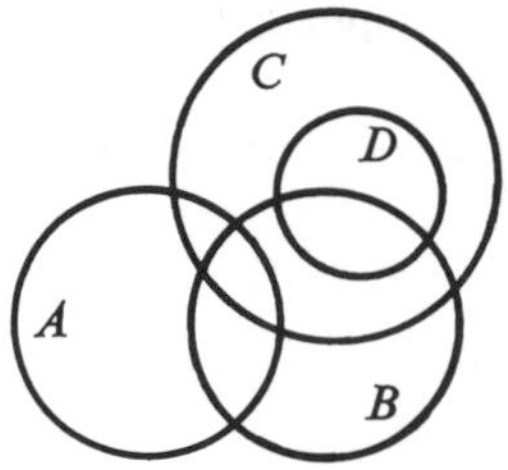

Figure A.2

k. The crosshatched area of Figure A.3 is $A \sim B$. In Figure A.4 the horizontal crosshatching represents $S \sim B$ and the vertical crosshatching is A, so that $A \cap (S \sim B)$ is represented by the doubly crosshatched area. This equals the crosshatched area of Figure A.3. A similar procedure can be followed for $A \cap B = \Phi$, $A \subset B$, $B \subset A$, and $A = B$.

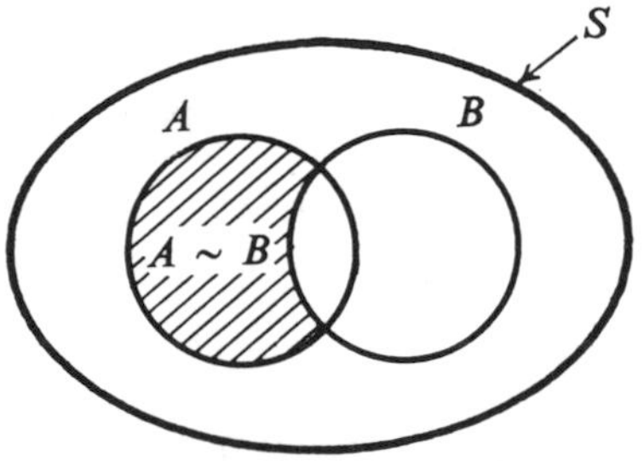

Figure A.3

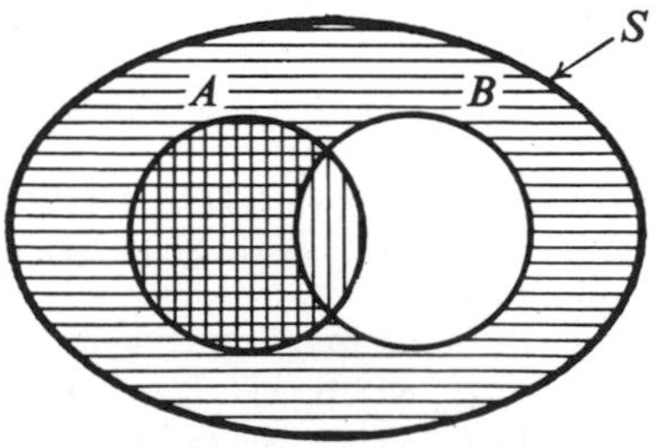

Figure A.4

3. a. **P**({(6, H), (6, T)}) = 1/6.
   b. **P**({(1, H), (2, H), (3, H), (4, H), (5, H), (6, H)}) = 1/2.
   c. **P**({(1, H), (1, T), (2, H), (2, T)}) = 1/3.
   d. **P**({(1, H), (1, T), (2, H), (2, T), (3, H), (4, H), (5, H), (6, H)}) = 2/3.
   e. **P**({(1, H), (2, H)}) = 1/6.
   f. **P**({(3, H), (4, H), (5, H), (6, H)}) = 1/3.
   g. **P**({(1, H), (1, T), (2, H), (2, T), (3, H), (4, H), (5, H), (6, H)}) = 2/3.
   h. The entire sample space.
   i. **P**({(6, H)}) = 1/12.
   j. **P**({(1, H)}) = **P**({(1, 1)}) = 1/12.

Section IV.6.2

1. a. 1/6. b. 1/2. c. 1/2.
3. 1/3.

Section IV.7.3

1. Independent, dependent, independent for 1a, 1b, and 1c, respectively.
3. Dependent, since

$$\mathbf{P}(\text{both boys}) = 1/4 \neq 1/3 = \mathbf{P}(\text{both boys} \mid \text{at least one boy}).$$

5. a.

	Grimacing	No grimacing	
History of rheumatic disease	35	82	117
No history of rheumatic disease	388	1437	1825
Totals	423	1519	1942

b. **P**("Grimacing") = 423/1942.
c. **P**("History of rheumatic disease") = 117/1942.
d. "Draw a patient at random from the sample of 1942."
e. **P**("Grimacing" | "History of rheumatic disease") = 35/117.
f. No; **P**("Grimacing" | "History of rheumatic disease") = 35/117 ≠ 423/1942 = **P**("Grimacing").
g. No; **P**("No grimacing" | "No history of rheumatic disease") = 1437/1825 ≠ 1519/1942 = **P**("No grimacing").
h. That, in this sample, a history of rheumatic disease and grimacing are associated.

Section IV.10

1. a. "Clinical psychology," since it is the most likely answer.
b. No, since "clinical psychology" is the most probable response for all specialties.
c. Each outcome consists of an answer to two questions: (1) "At the present time I consider myself primarily a:" and (2) "If I had my life to live over again, I would try to end up in:"
d. 102/166.
e. No, since **P**("Therapist") = 51/166 ≠ 31/102 = **P**("Therapist" | "Clinical psychology"), although the two probabilities are very close.
f. No, since **P**("Diagnostician") = 22/166 ≠ 7/23 = **P**("Diagnostician" | "Medicine: psychiatry"). However, these two sample probabilities differ little, and it is possible that the corresponding population probabilities are equal. A similar statement can be made about Problem 1e.
g. The events "Therapist," "Teacher," "Researcher," "Diagnostician," "Administrator-supervisor" are mutually exclusive, for example.
h. No, since **P**("Teacher") = 25/166 ≠ 0 = **P**("Teacher" | "Researcher").
i. 125/166.
3. a. 0.03. b. No. c. 0.05.

5. a. 24. b. 1/2. c. 1/2. d. Yes.
   e. **P**("*War and Peace* left of *Anna Karenina*" | "*Crime and Punishment* left of *The Brothers Karamazov*") = 1/2 = **P**("*War and Peace* left of *Anna Karenina*").

Section V.2

1. 1/20.
3. a. 1710. b. 1/1710.
5. a. 4/165. b. 8/165. c. 7/33.
7. a. 1/4. b. 1/64. c. 15/16. d. 1/64.
9. **P**("4 aces") = 1/54,145, **P**("Royal flush") = 1/649,740.
11. 3003, 756,756.
13. 1023.
15. 45.

Section V.3.2

1. a. 0. b. 1/24. c. 1/24. d. 23/24.
   e.

	a	*b*	*c*	*d*
Exact	0	1/24	1/24	23/24
Formula [V.9]	.061	.015	.076	.924

   The correspondence between exact probabilities (from Table V.3) and those based on Formula [V.9] is rather poor for $N = 4$.
3. Since the subject is permitted to use each symbol only once, there are 6 possibilities for the first card, 5 for the second, 4 for the third, and so on. The ESP investigator is closer to the correct figure.

Section V.3.4

1. Statements d and e are correct; the others are incorrect.

Section V.3.5

1. a. $\mathbf{P}(F \mid A) = 0.68, \mathbf{P}(B \mid A) = 0.32, \mathbf{P}(F \mid \sim A) = 0.20, \mathbf{P}(B \mid \sim A) = 0.80$.
   b. When the base rates, $\mathbf{P}(B)$ and $\mathbf{P}(F)$, both equal 0.5, the diagnostic procedure permits a $0.725 - 0.5 = 0.225$ improvement in the proportion of correct diagnoses (over the higher base rate). This amounts to an elimination of $0.225/0.5 = 0.45$ of the diagnostic errors. In a population in which $\mathbf{P}(B) = \mathbf{P}(F) = 0.5$, this might prove useful as a practical diagnostic procedure.
3. a. 0.60.
   b. Guess Urn I if a white ball is drawn; Urn II if a black ball.
   c. $\mathbf{P}(\text{I} \mid W) = 0.60 > 0.40 = \mathbf{P}(\text{II} \mid W)$ and $\mathbf{P}(\text{II} \mid B) = 0.57 > 0.43 = \mathbf{P}(\text{I} \mid B)$.
   d. 0.58.
   e. $\mathbf{P}(\text{I} \mid W) = 0.75$; always guess Urn I, since $\mathbf{P}(\text{I} \mid W) = 0.75 > 0.25 = \mathbf{P}(\text{II} \mid W)$ and $\mathbf{P}(\text{I} \mid B) = 0.60 > 0.40 = \mathbf{P}(\text{II} \mid B)$; $\mathbf{P}(\text{correct guess}) = 2/3$.

Section *V.3.7

*1. $p_t = 0.76$, $p_{t+1} = 0.83$, $p_{t+2} = 0.88$.

*3. See Figure A.5.

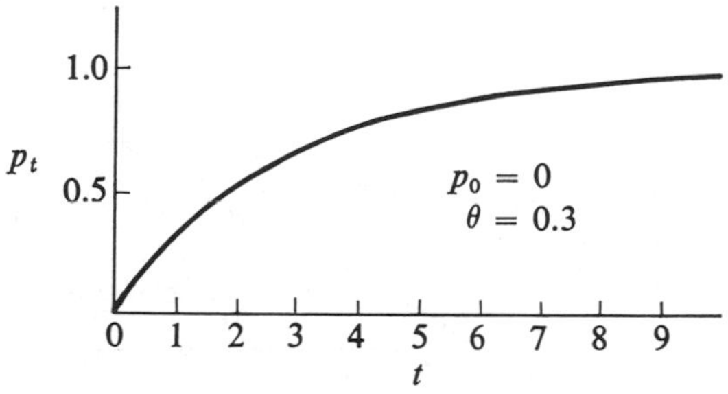

Figure A.5

Section VI.3

1.

Coin	0	0	0	0	0	0	1	1	1	1	1	1
Die	1	2	3	4	5	6	1	2	3	4	5	6
Sum	1	2	3	4	5	6	2	3	4	5	6	7

P(sum = 1) = 1/12,
P(sum = 2) = **P**(sum = 3) = **P**(sum = 4) = **P**(sum = 5) = **P**(sum = 6) = 1/6,
P(sum = 7) = 1/12.

3.

Sample space	RRR	LRR	RLR	RRL	LLR	LRL	RLL	LLL
Number correct	2	1	3	1	2	0	2	1

9. a. X, ordinal; Y, ordinal.
   b. X, ratio; Y, ratio.
   c. X, interval; Y, interval.
   d. X, ratio; Y, ratio.

11. If $S(x_2) - S(x_1) = S(x_4) - S(x_3)$, then $\log_{10} S(x_2) - \log_{10} S(x_1) \neq \log_{10} S(x_4) - \log_{10} S(x_3)$. For example, suppose that $S(x_1) = 1$, $S(x_2) = 2$, $S(x_3) = 9$, and $S(x_4) = 10$. Now compare the differences between the logs.

Section VII.1.3

1. a. $\mathbf{P}(Y = 2) = \mathbf{P}(Y = 12) = 1/36$, $\mathbf{P}(Y = 3) = \mathbf{P}(Y = 11) = 2/36$, $\mathbf{P}(Y = 4) = \mathbf{P}(Y = 10) = 3/36$, $\mathbf{P}(Y = 5) = \mathbf{P}(\mathbf{Y} = 9) = 4/36$, $\mathbf{P}(Y = 6) = \mathbf{P}(Y = 8) = 5/36$, $\mathbf{P}(Y = 7) = 6/36$.
   c. Yes, $\sum \mathbf{P}(Y = y) = 1.0$.
   d. $\mathbf{P}(Y \leq 2) = 1/36$, $\mathbf{P}(Y \leq 3) = 3/36$, $\mathbf{P}(Y \leq 4) = 6/36$, $\mathbf{P}(Y \leq 5) = 10/36$, $\mathbf{P}(Y \leq 6) = 15/36$, $\mathbf{P}(Y \leq 7) = 21/36$, $\mathbf{P}(Y \leq 8) = 26/36$, $\mathbf{P}(Y \leq 9) = 30/36$, $\mathbf{P}(Y \leq 10) = 33/36$, $\mathbf{P}(Y \leq 11) = 35/36$, $\mathbf{P}(Y \leq 12) = 1.0$.
   f. i. 1.0; ii. 21/36; iii. 15/36; iv. 9/36; v. 30/36; vi. 6/36; vii. 21/36; viii. 17/36.

3. a. 27/256.
   b. $S_1 = 1/4$; $S_2 = 7/16$; $S_3 = 37/64$; $S_4 = 175/256$; $S_5 = 781/1024$; $S_{100} \cong 1$; and $S_{1000} \cong 1$.
   c. 1.

Section VII.1.6

1. no no
   yes yes
   yes yes.

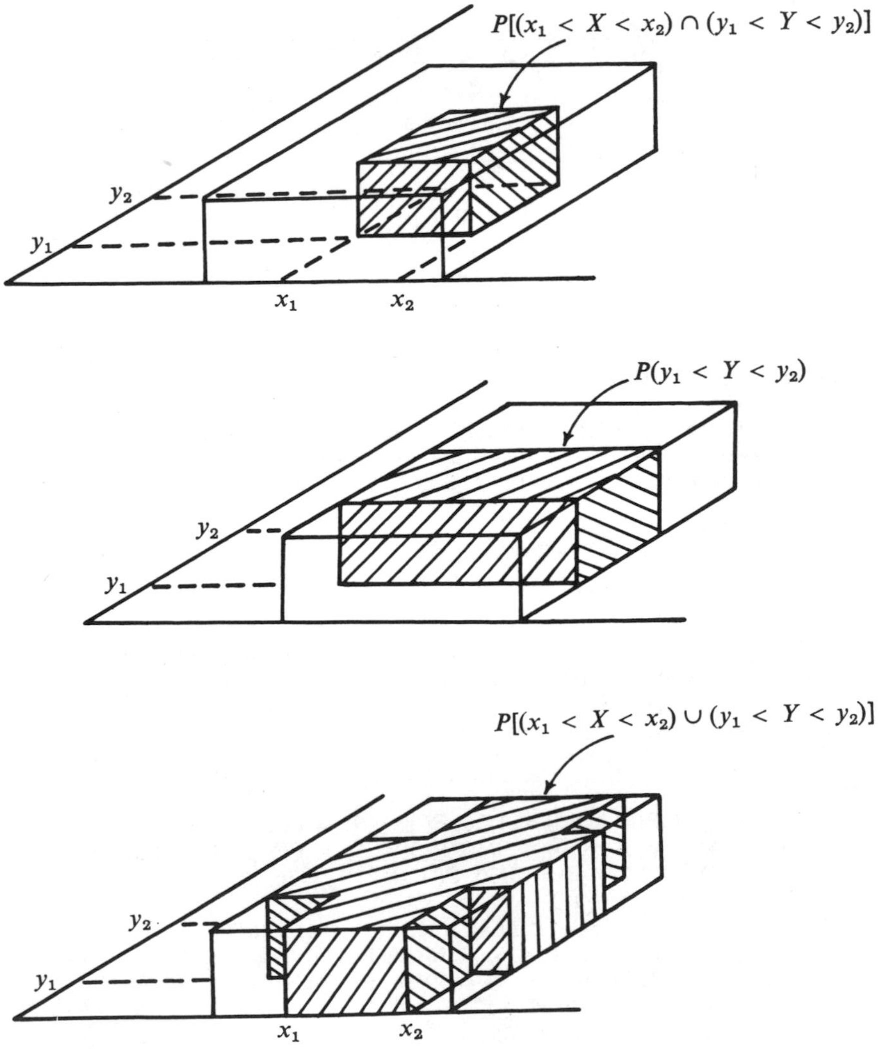

Figure A.6

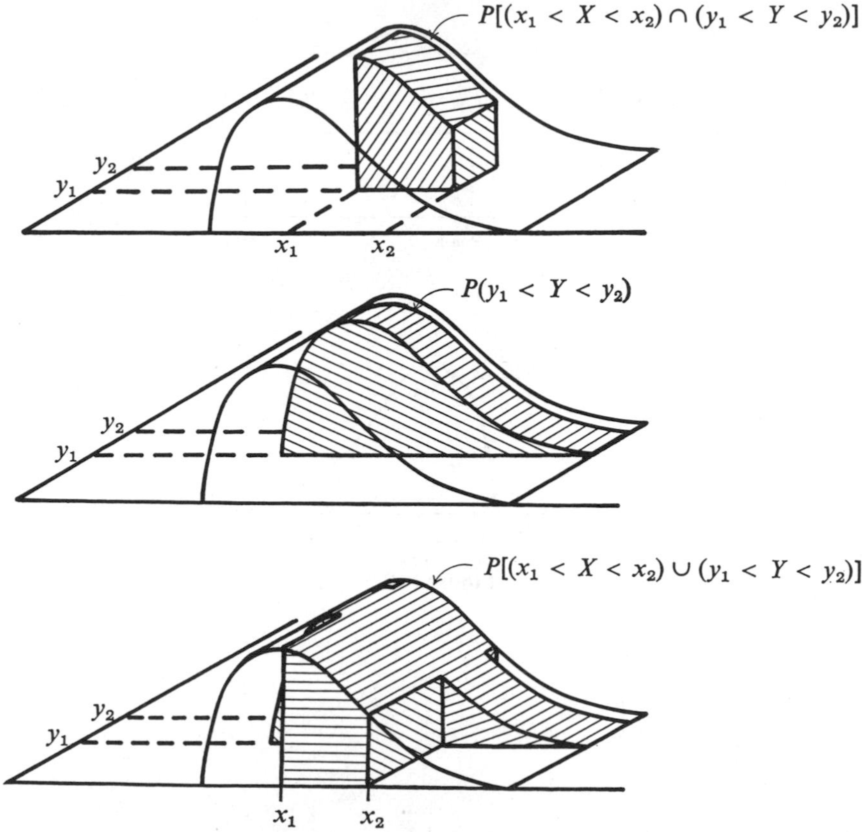

Figure A.7

Section VII.3.3

1. a. 39/216. b. 165/216. c. 36/216.
   d. 64/180. e. 36/216. f. 84/216.
3. a. No.
   b. That each historical variable is pairwise statistically independent of diagnosis.
   c. Yes. The two tables can be filled in as shown:

10	30	40	40	120	160
15	45	60	60	180	240
25	75	100	100	300	400

   d. i. Yes; **P**(None dead | Schiz.) = 75/100 = 375/500 = **P**(none dead).
   ii. Yes;
   P(Only child | Nonschiz.) = 160/400 = 200/500 = **P**(Only child).
   iii. No; **P**(Schiz. | Only child ∩ None dead) = 30/130 ≠ 100/500 = **P**(Schiz.).
   iv. **P**(Schiz.) = 1/5; **P**(Nonschiz.) = 4/5.
   v. **P**(At least 1 parent dead) = 125/500; **P**(None dead) = 375/500.

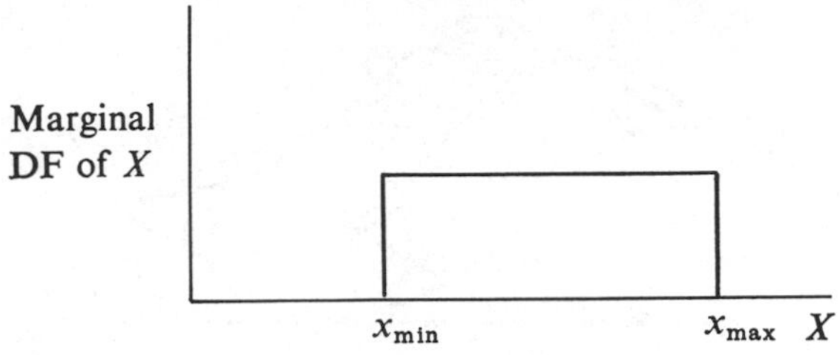

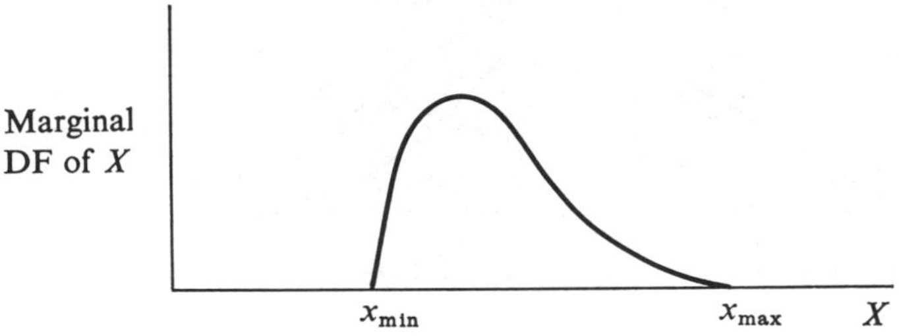

Figure A.8

Section *VII.3.5

*1. a. See Figure A.6.
   b. See Figure A.7.
*3. See Figure A.8.

Section VIII.1.1

1. $\bar{X} = 101.0$.
3. Yes.

Section VIII.2.6

1. a. $\overline{KX} = K\bar{X} = 1.5(101.0) = 151.5$.
   b. $\sum KX/n = [1.5(93) + 1.5(102) + 1.5(95) + 1.5(116) + 1.5(99)]/5$
   $= 151.5 = 1.5(101.0) = K\bar{X}$.
   c. $\overline{X+2} = \bar{X} + 2 = 101.0 + 2 = 103.0$.
   d. $\sum (X + 2)/n = [(93 + 2) + (102 + 2) + (95 + 2) + (116 + 2) + (99 + 2)]/5$
   $= 103.0 = 2 + 101.0 + 2 = \bar{X} + 2$.
   e. $\overline{1.5X + 2} = 1.5\bar{X} + 2 = 153.5$.
   f. $\sum [1.5(X) + 2]/5 = [1.5(93) + 2 + 1.5(102) + 2 + 1.5(95) + 2 + 1.5(116) + 2 + 1.5(99) + 2]/5 = 153.5 = 1.5(101.0) + 2$
   $= 1.5(\bar{X}) + 2$.
3. Yes. $\bar{X} = A + B_1X_1 + B_2X_2 + \cdots + B_nX_n$ where $A = 0$ and $B_1 = B_2 = \cdots = B_n = 1/n$.

Section VIII.3.3

1. a. $E(X) = 1.5.$
   b. $E(Y) = 7.0.$
   c. $E(X) = 1.0.$
3. Not a DF. Not a DF.
   $E(X) = 3.333$ $E(X) = 0.798$
   $E(X) = 2.50$ $E(X) = 2.667.$

Section VIII.6

1. a. $E(3) = 3.$
   b. $E(2R) = 2E(R) = 2(7.0) = 14.0.$
   c. $E(1 + 2R + 2.5B) = 1 + 2E(R) + 2.5E(B)$
   $= 1 + 2(7.0) + 2.5(7.0) = 32.5.$
   d. $E(R - B) = E(R) - E(B) = 7.0 - 7.0 = 0.$

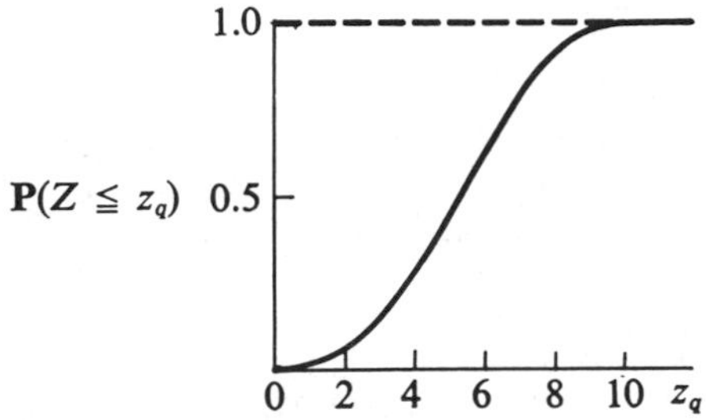

Figure A.9

3. No. Formula [VIII.7] assumes that the two random variables are statistically independent, but R and B are not.
5. a. Yes. b. See Figure A.9.
   c. See Figure A.10.

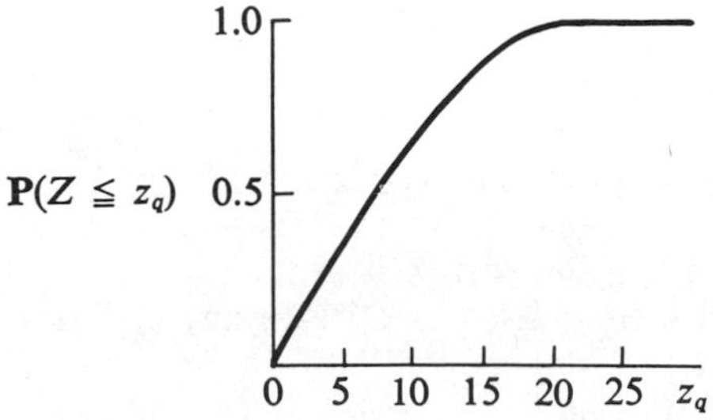

Figure A.10

Section *VIII.10

*1. The subject for whom $\theta = 0.3$ is a more rapid learner (in this task) than the one for whom $\theta = 0.1$.

*3. See Figure A.11.

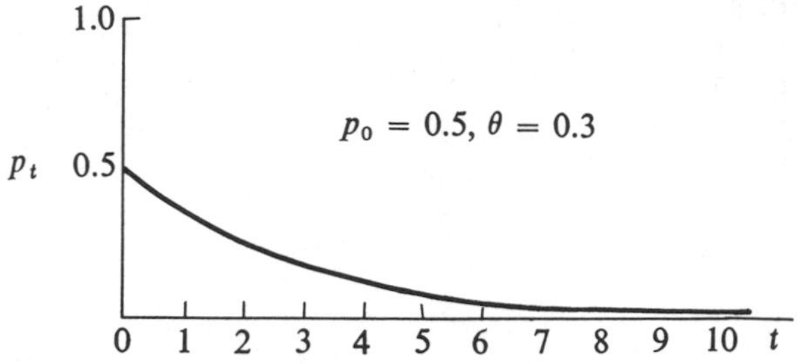

Figure A.11

*5. The greater $|\Pi - p_0|$, the greater the rate of change in p_t during acquisition. In effect, the greater the amount that must be learned ($|\Pi - p_0|$), the greater the rate of learning.

Section IX.3

1. a. $V = 1$.
   b. $\mu = E(X) = 0.808$.
   c. Yes; $E(|X - V|) = 0.626 \leq 0.661 = E(|X - \mu|)$.
   d. No. There are modes at $X = 0$ and $X = 1$.
   e. The geometric mean is undefined since one value of X is 0.
   f. Yours.
3. a. $\mathbf{P}(M = 0) = 20/27$, $\mathbf{P}(M = 1) = 7/27$.
   b. $\mathbf{P}(\bar{X} = 0) = 8/27$, $\mathbf{P}(\bar{X} = 1/3) = 12/27$,
   $\mathbf{P}(\bar{X} = 2/3) = 6/27$, $\mathbf{P}(\bar{X} = 1) = 1/27$.
   c. $E(\bar{X}) = 1/3$, $E(M) = 7/27$.
   d. M is biased. The magnitude of the bias is
   $$E(M) - V = 7/27 - 0 = +\,7/27.$$

Section IX.5

1. a. Range = 23.
   b. $MD = 6.4$.
   c. $S_X{}^2 = 82.5$.
   d. $S^2_{X+7.63} = 82.5$.
   e. $S^2_{1.6X} = (1.6)^2 S_X{}^2 = 211.2$.
3. $\sigma_X{}^2 = 11.0$.
5. Mean deviation = 15.92, variance = 411.24.
7. a. $E[(X - V)^2] = 0.698$.
   b. $E[(X - V)^2] = 0.698 > 0.66 = \sigma^2$.
   c. $E[(X - \mu)^2] = \sigma^2 < E[(X - C)^2]$ for any $C \neq \mu$.
9. a.

Outcome	S^2	Outcome	S^2
(1, 1)	0	(2, 3)	0.5
(1, 2)	0.5	(3, 2)	0.5
(2, 1)	0.5	(2, 4)	2.0
(1, 3)	2.0	(4, 2)	2.0
(3, 1)	2.0	(3, 3)	0
(1, 4)	4.5	(3, 4)	0.5
(4, 1)	4.5	(4, 3)	0.5
(2, 2)	0	(4, 4)	0

b. $\mathbf{P}(S^2 = 0) = 4/16$, $\mathbf{P}(S^2 = 0.5) = 6/16$, $\mathbf{P}(S^2 = 2.0) = 4/16$, $\mathbf{P}(S^2 = 4.5) = 2/16$.

c. $E(S^2) = \sum \mathbf{P}(S^2 = s^2)s^2 = 4/16(0) + 6/16(0.5) + 4/16(2.0) + 2/16(4.5) = 1.25,$

and

$\sigma_X{}^2 = E(X^2) - \mu^2 = 1/4(1)^2 + 1/4(2)^2 + 1/4(3)^2 + 1/4(4)^2 - (2.5)^2 = 1.25.$

Therefore, $E(S^2) = \sigma_X{}^2$, so that S^2 is an unbiased estimator for $\sigma_X{}^2$ in this example.

d. $\sigma^2_{S^2} = 2.0625$.

Section IX.7

1. $E[(X - \mu)^3] = +0.43$.
3. For the PD of Figure A.12, $(\mu - V)/\sigma = (1.75 - 2.0)/0.97 = -0.26$.

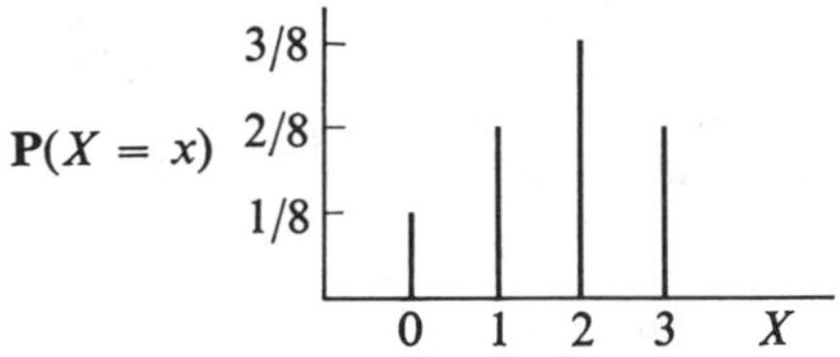

Figure A.12

Section IX.9

1. Notice the role of *growth* among the grade school children. As the children grow or develop, they become bigger *and* more intelligent. Growth plays almost no role in the adult population. The correlation among the children is due to the effect of growth more than to an intrinsic connection between size and mental age.
3. $r = -0.95$.
5. $S_X = 4.16$, $S_Y = 4.41$, $S_{XY} = 17.40$, $r_{XY} = -0.95$.

Section IX.10.1

1. a. 1. b. 9. c. 10.
3. (5, 9) or (9, 5).
5. a. 0/0. b. No.
   c. For a sample of size 2, the number of degrees of freedom is inadequate for an unbiased estimate of the third central moment of the population. At least three observations are required.

Section IX.12

1. a. $\sigma^2_{B+R} = \sigma_B{}^2 + \sigma_R{}^2 + 2\sigma_{BR} = 5.83 + 5.83 + 2(3.03) = 17.72.$
   b. $\sigma^2_{6(B+R)} = (6)^2\sigma_B{}^2 + (6)^2\sigma_R{}^2 + 2(6)(6)\sigma_{BR} = 36(5.83) + 36(5.83) + 72(3.03) = 637.92.$

c. $\sigma^2_{2-6B+3R} = (-6)^2\sigma_B{}^2 + (3)^2\sigma_R{}^2 + 2(-6)(3)\,\sigma_{BR}$
$= 36(5.83) + 9(5.83) - 36(3.03)$
$= 153.27.$

d. $\sigma^2_{-1000-6B+3R} = 153.27.$

e. $\sigma^2_{B+R} = 17.72 > 5.60 = \sigma^2_{B-R}$. Because of the positive correlation between B and R ($\rho_{BR} = +0.52$), large values of B and R are likely to occur together. Similarly, small values of B and R are likely to occur together. This means that the spread or variance of sums is larger than if there were no correlation. However, since B and R vary together, the variability of differences is small compared to the case of $\rho_{BR} = 0$.

3. $\sigma^2_{X+Y} = 3.167.$

Section X.2

1. a. 80/243. b. 130/243. c. 123/243. d. $1\frac{2}{3}$. e. $1\frac{1}{9}$.
   f. $\mathbf{P}(p = 0.4) = 80/243$, $\mathbf{P}(0.4 \leq p \leq 0.8) = 130/243$,
   $\mathbf{P}[(p \leq 0.2) \cup (p \geq 0.8)] = 123/243$, $\mu_p = 1/3$, $\sigma_p{}^2 = 2/9$.

3. $\sigma_X{}^2$ will be maximal for $P = 1/2$ when n is fixed. See Figure A.13.

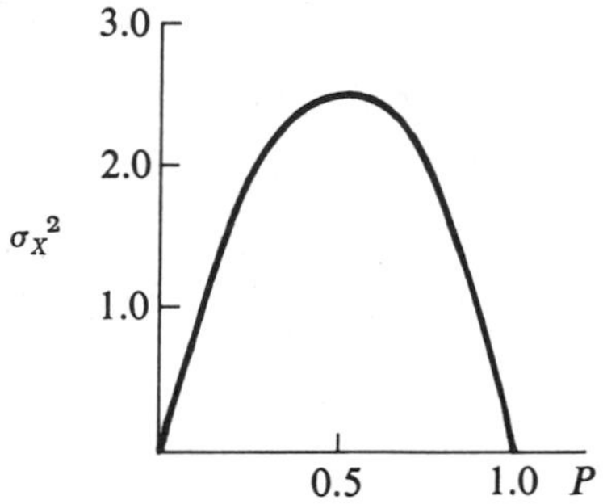

Figure A.13

5. The number of times a light is run is n; P is the probability of receiving a ticket on any occasion in which a light is run; X is the number of tickets received on n occasions in which a light is run. Although such a formulation might provide a workable first approximation, the conditions for Bernoulli trials are probably not satisfied. For example, P probably varies with the location of a stop light, the time of day, etc. Your friend seems to have adopted the gambler's fallacy.

7. a. 0.021. b. 10. c. 0.042.

9. a. Hypergeometric PD.
   b. i. 160/1827; ii. 1257/1827;
   iii. 570/1827; iv. $1\frac{1}{3}$; v. 0.80.

11. a. Refer him to a treatise on probability.
    b. 0.299.
    c. Binomial PD.

d. That the probability of recovery or improvement is the *same* for each *randomly selected* patient.

13. 9 items have been ranked; the variance of the ranks is 6.67.

Section X.4

1. a. 30.00. b. 33.33. c. 0.
   d. 0.50. e. 0.50. f. 0.50.
3. a. 0.50. b. 0.6826. c. 0.05.
   d. 0.0026. e. 100. f. 65.0.
   g. 124.675. h. 0. i. 24.675.
   j. 24.675. k. 19.230. l. 24.675.
   m. 19.230. n. 0.1146.
5. a. 0.900. b. 0.621. c. 0.721.
   d. 0.119. e. 0.251. f. 10.0.
   g. 20.0.

Section X.6

1. a. i. 0.932; ii. 0.836; iii. 0.860; iv. 0.164;
   v. 0.792; vi. 0.208; vii. 0.792.
   b. i. 0.932; ii. 0.836; iii. 0.860; iv. 0.164;
   v. 0.792; vi. 0.208; vii. 0.52.
3. The Poisson PD has variance 0.99; the variance of the binomial PD is 0.96.
5. a. The mean is 2.0 and the standard deviation is 0.816.
   b. $\mathbf{P}(X \le 0) = 1/42$, $\mathbf{P}(X \le 1) = 11/42$, $\mathbf{P}(X \le 2) = 31/42$, $\mathbf{P}(X \le 3) = 41/42$, $\mathbf{P}(X \le 4) = 1.0$, $\mathbf{P}(X \le 5) = 1.0$.
   c. See Figure A.14.

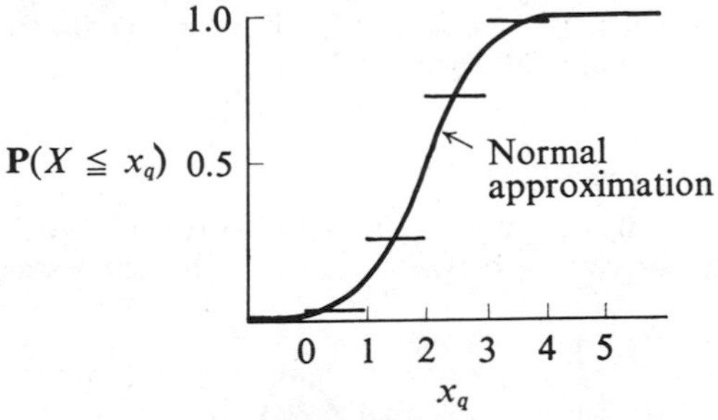

Figure A.14

d. i. 0.46; ii. 0.73; iii. 0.27; iv. 0.001.

e.

	Exact probability	Normal approximation
d. i	.476	.46
d. ii	.738	.73
d. iii	.262	.27
d. iv	0	.001

Section XI.3

1. A PD gives probabilities for a discrete random variable and a DF permits one to find probabilities associated with a continuous random variable. A sampling distribution may be a PD or DF. In either case, it describes the way an *estimator* varies from one probability sample to another.
3. a. 0.0918. b. 0.9082. c. 0.9544. d. 0.0456. e. 0.9772. f. 0.1146. g. 0.8854.
5. a. 0.095. b. 0.095^+. c. 0.029. d. 0.971. e. 0.029.
7. **P**(Range = 0) = 4/64, **P**(Range = 1) = 18/64, **P**(Range = 2) = 24/64, **P**(Range = 3) = 18/64; E(Range) = 1.875; $\sigma^2_{\text{Range}} = 0.80$.

Section XI.6

1. Both median and mean have zero bias for random samples from this symmetrical population.
3. Level III.

*5. $\mathbf{P}(|\bar{X} - 50| \geq 3.0) \leq 0.25$. This maximum probability is considerably larger than $\mathbf{P}(|\bar{X} - 50| \geq 3.0) = 0.0456$, the exact probability in the case of a normal sampling distribution of $\bar{X}$.

Section XI.10

1. 0.026.
3. Yes. On the basis of the central limit theorem, the mean of random samples of size 36 will be approximately normally distributed.
5. a. For most purposes this assumption would be reasonable.
   b. The normal DF can be used to approximate the binomial PD for nP and $n(1 - P)$ sufficiently large—say, larger than 5. The Poisson PD is the limiting PD for the binomial (see Appendix X.2). Consequently, for large values of $\mu = nP$, the normal DF can be used to approximate the Poisson. Then, $(n - 1)S^2/\sigma^2$ will have a PD that can be approximated by a chi-square DF (Section XI.8).
   c. 0.82.

*7. a. -1.5.
   b. See Figure A.15.
   c. For $n = 5$, -0.24; for $n = 10$, -0.135; for $n = 100$, -0.015. As n increases, the correlation between $\bar{X}$ and S^2 becomes small.

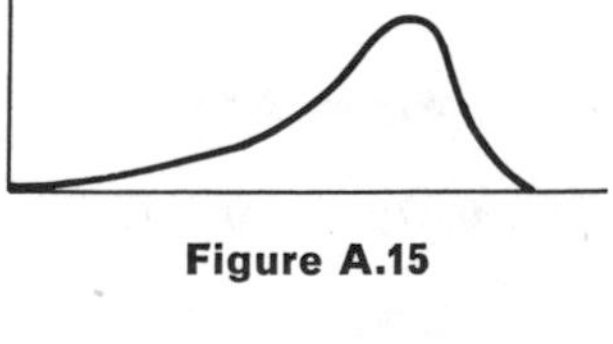

Figure A.15

Section XII.5

1. An estimator is *consistent* if the limit (as the sample size becomes infinite) of the expected value of the squared difference between it and the parameter it estimates is zero. If an estimator is defined as the value of the parameter for which the likelihood of the observed sample is a maximum, then it is a *maximum-likelihood estimator*.

5. a. Since the sample is from a Poisson population, $\bar{X}$ is an unbiased estimator for σ^2. Using this,

$$\mathbf{P}(\bar{X} - 2.575\sqrt{[\bar{X}/n]} \leq \sigma \leq \bar{X} + 2.575\sqrt{[\bar{X}/n]}) = \mathbf{P}(0.426 \leq \sigma \leq 1.574) \cong 0.99.$$

Since S^2 is an unbiased estimator for σ^2 also,

$$\mathbf{P}(\bar{X} - 2.575\sqrt{[S^2/n]} \leq \sigma \leq \bar{X} + 2.575\sqrt{[S^2/n]}) = \mathbf{P}(0.51 \leq \sigma \leq 1.49) \cong 0.99.$$

provides an interval estimate for σ.

b. Both of these estimates are based on the CLT. Both assume random sampling and a "large" n. The first assumes that $\sqrt{\bar{X}}$ can be substituted for σ, and the second assumes that S can be substituted for σ. The reasonableness of this also depends on the sample size.

c. See a. d. Yes.

*7. a. 10.0. b. 0.22.

c. Its relative efficiency is about 0.64.

d. $\mathbf{P}(9.64 \leq V \leq 10.36) = 0.90$.

Section XIII.10

1. a. 1.446.

b. The choices made by each chooser constitute a random sample from a finite binomial population.

c. 0.994. d. 1.714.

e. S^2 is larger than σ^2. This may be due to sampling variability or to the inappropriateness of the mathematical model used to calculate σ^2.

f. The statistical hypotheses one might entertain could be set up as follows:

$$\left.\begin{aligned} &\text{H: } \mu \leq 1.446 \\ &\text{A: } \mu > 1.446 \end{aligned}\right\}\text{one-sided alternative}$$

or,

$$\left.\begin{aligned} &\text{H: } \mu = 1.446 \\ &\text{A: } \mu \neq 1.446 \end{aligned}\right\}\text{two-sided alternative.}$$

g. One-sided: "Reject H if $\bar{X} > 2.27$. Otherwise, accept H." Two-sided: "Reject H if $\bar{X} < 0.54$ or if $\bar{X} > 2.35$. Otherwise, accept H." Since

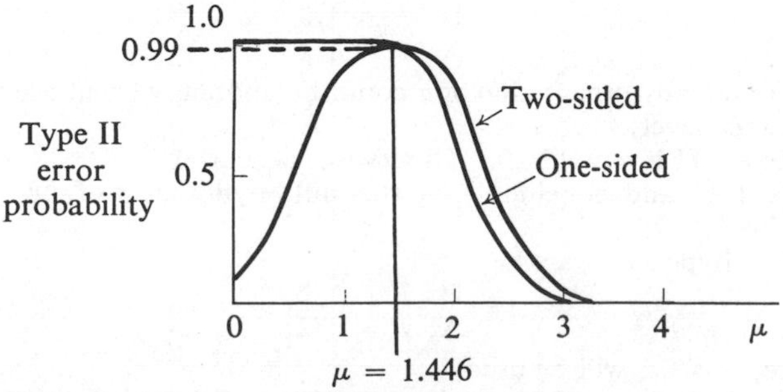

Figure A.16

$\bar{X} = 4.0$ for the sample, the decision is to reject H. This suggests that the hypothesis of no ethnic cleavage (H) is untenable.
h. One-sided: >0.9998; Two-sided: 0.905.
i. See Figure A.16. j. See Figure A.17.

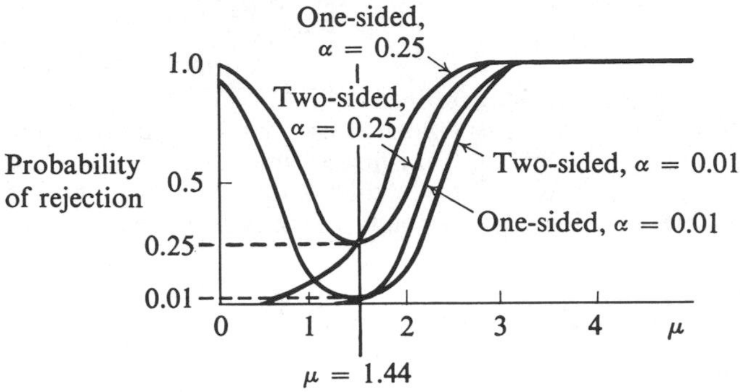

Figure A.17

k. See Figure A.17. Type II error probabilities are lower and Type I error probabilities are higher for the $\alpha = .25$ tests than for the $\alpha = 0.01$ tests.
l. One method is to employ the theoretical variance estimate, 0.994. Then, using the CLT, $\mathbf{P}(3.31 \leq \mu \leq 4.69) \cong 0.95$. This interval is narrower than the one based on the sample variance, 1.714, which gives $\mathbf{P}(3.09 \leq \mu \leq 4.91) \cong 0.95$. The latter procedure is probably preferable, since the theoretical variance was calculated on the basis of a hypothesis that appears to be untenable (see Problem 1g).
m. $\mathbf{P}(3.24 \leq \mu \leq 4.76) \cong 0.90$.
n. The CLT is a little shaky here, since the sample size is only 8 and the sample suggests that the PD of the observation variable is quite skewed.
p. If the ethnic cleavage question were central to the research, then the hypothesis-testing procedure would be most appropriate. If no such specific hypothesis were entertained, then a confidence interval estimate would probably be most suitable.

3. a. i. Let P = the probability of a correct response on trial 100. Then, the statistical hypotheses can be stated as

$$\text{H: } P \leq 1/2$$
$$\text{A: } P > 1/2;$$

ii. Although any other value of α could be chosen, we will use 0.132 for a significance level;
iii. "Reject H if $p > 12/20$. Otherwise, accept H";
iv. Reject H and conclude that the null hypothesis of no learning is untenable.
b. i. The hypotheses are

$$\text{H: } P = 1/2$$
$$\text{A: } P \neq 1/2;$$

ii. Here, $\alpha = 0.1$ will be used;
iii. "Reject H if $p < 0.316$ or if $p > 0.684$. Otherwise, accept H";

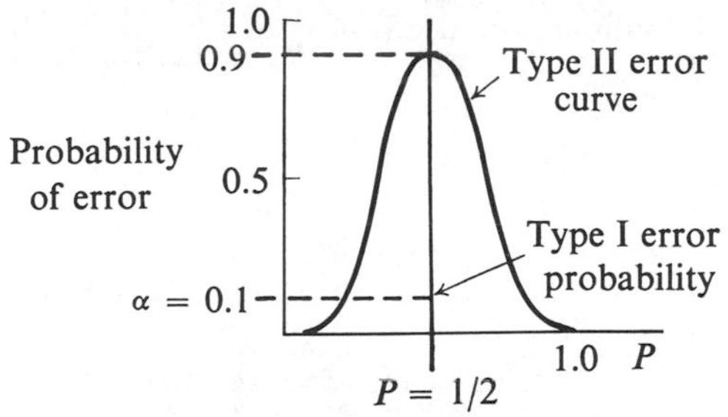

Figure A.18

iv. Reject H and conclude that the hypothesis of no learning is untenable;
v. See Figure A.18.

5. a. The statistical hypotheses are

$$\text{H: } P \leq 2/3$$
$$\text{A: } P > 2/3.$$

b. "Reject H if $p > 0.858$. Otherwise, accept H." However, since only the values 0, 0.1, 0.2, . . . , 0.9, 1.0 can occur as sample proportions, perhaps it is most reasonable to use the decision rule "Reject H if $p > 0.85$. Otherwise, accept H." For this second rule, $\alpha = 0.11$ instead of 0.10.

c. Since the observed proportion is 0.8, accept H and conclude that the data are most compatible with the hypothesis that the psychiatrist's treatment has accomplished nothing in excess of the spontaneous recovery rate.

d. Using the first decision rule in b, 0.012. Using the second, 0.014.

e. Sampling of patients is unlikely to be random.

f. See Figure A.19.

g. 0.33 for the first decision rule in b, 0.30 for the second.

7. Increasing n increases the power of a test for all values of the parameter other than the one specified by H (for a simple null hypothesis) or the one included in but "least favorable" to H (for a composite null hypothesis). Increasing α increases the power for all values in the parameter space.

9. a. If 8 values of the variable are distinguished (0, 1, 2, . . . , 6, $X \geq 7$), then $D = r - c - 1 = 8 - 2 - 1 = 5$, since two parameters, μ and σ^2, must be estimated. If $X \geq 4$ is treated as a single class, then $D = r - c - 1 = 5 - 2 - 1 = 2$.

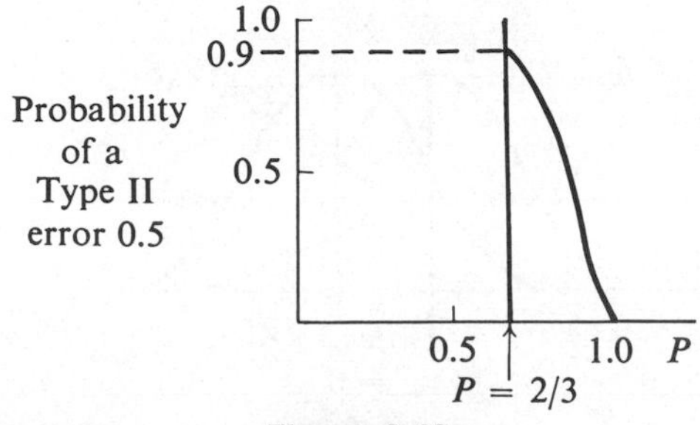

Figure A.19

b. If $D = 5$, "Reject H if $\mathscr{X} > \chi_C^2 = 9.24$. Otherwise, accept H." If $D = 2$, "Reject H if $\mathscr{X} > \chi_C^2 = 4.61$. Otherwise, accept H."
c. $\bar{X} = 1.55$, $S^2 = 1.95$.
d. If $D = 5$,
$nP_1 = nP(X \leq 0.5) = 13.60$, $nP_2 = nP(0.5 < X \leq 1.5) = 15.44$,
$nP_3 = nP(1.5 < X \leq 2.5) = 16.06$, $nP_4 = nP(2.5 < X \leq 3.5) = 10.05$,
$nP_5 = nP(3.5 < X \leq 4.5) = 3.83$, $nP_6 = nP(4.5 < X \leq 5.5) = 0.88$,
$nP_7 = nP(5.5 < X \leq 6.5) = 0.13$, $nP_8 = nP(X > 6.5) = 0.01$.
If $D = 2$,
nP_1, nP_2, nP_3, and nP_4 are the same, and $nP_5 = nP(X > 3.5) = 4.85$.
e. If $D = 5$, $\mathscr{X} = 9.88$. If $D = 2$, $\mathscr{X} = 1.57$.
f. If $D = 5$, reject H. If $D = 2$, accept H.
g. If one rejected H, conclude that the population does not have a normal distribution. If one accepted, conclude that it does. In this example, the approximation must be questioned, since the way one combines categories of the variable affects the decision.

Section XIII.12

1. a. "Diagnose N if $\mathbf{P}'(X = x \mid N)/\mathbf{P}'(X = x \mid S) > 1/2$. Otherwise, diagnose S." This is equivalent to "Diagnose S if $\mathbf{P}'(X = x \mid S)/\mathbf{P}'(X = x \mid N) > 2$. Otherwise, diagnose N."
b. Diagnose N if $X > 2$. Otherwise, diagnose S.
c. 0.69. d. 0.31.
e. Using the test leads to an estimated 2.3 percent more correct diagnoses than one could achieve by simply diagnosing every patient N. The test is probably of little practical use.
f. C' is nearly the same for both procedures (0.68 as opposed to 0.69) in spite of the fact that the diagnostic decision for $X = 3$ has been changed.

*3. a. "Diagnose N if $f'(X \mid N)/f'(X \mid S) > 1$. Otherwise, diagnose S." This is equivalent to "Diagnose S if $f'(X \mid S)/f'(X \mid N) > 1$. Otherwise, diagnose N." Note that for $\mathbf{P}(S) = \mathbf{P}(N) = 1/2$, forms I and II are identical. Form III can be stated "Diagnose N if $X > 5.35$. Otherwise, diagnose S."
b. 0.38.
c. This plot is exactly the same as the solid curve in Figure XIII.21. Changing the base rates does not alter the operating characteristic of a classification procedure.

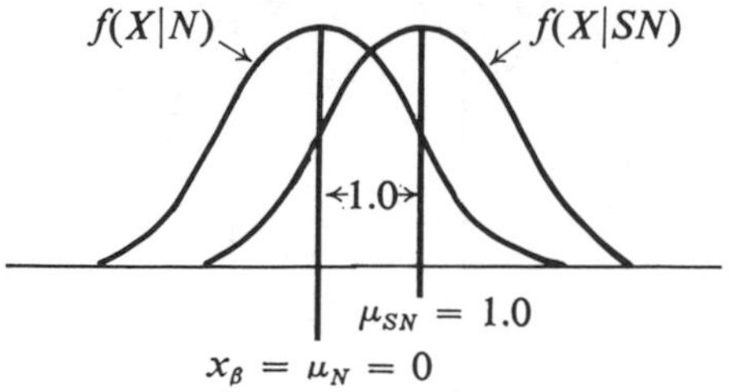

Figure A.20

d. The difference between the expected proportion correct using the classification rule and diagnosing every patient S (or every patient N) is $0.61 - 0.50 = 0.11$. This is a 22 percent reduction in the estimated proportion of incorrect classifications. The test might be useful. However, empirical testing of the decision rule on a cross-validation sample would be necessary before one could make an enlightened decision.

*5. a. See Figure A.20. b. $\mathbf{P}(\text{"yes"} \mid N) = 0.5$, $\mathbf{P}(\text{"no"} \mid N) = 0.5$. c. 0.585. d. Yes.

INDEX